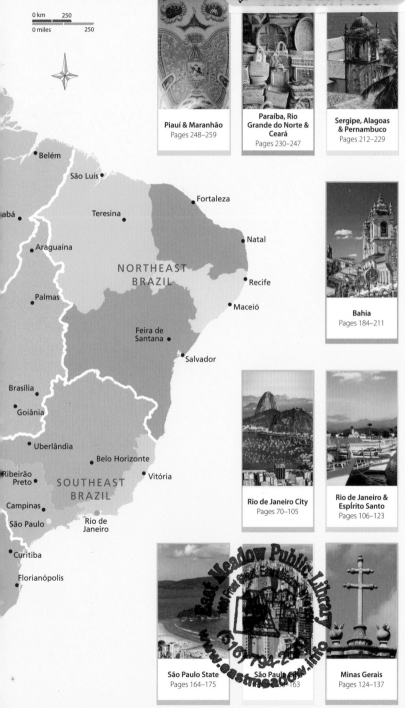

JAN 1 1 2018

P9-CDX-314

0 km 250
0 miles 250

Piauí & Maranhão
Pages 248–259

Paraíba, Rio Grande do Norte & Ceará
Pages 230–247

Sergipe, Alagoas & Pernambuco
Pages 212–229

• Belém

São Luís •

• Fortaleza

abá •

Teresina •

• Natal

• Araguaína

NORTHEAST BRAZIL

• Recife

• Palmas

• Maceió

Feira de Santana •

• Salvador

Bahia
Pages 184–211

• Brasília

• Goiânia

• Uberlândia

• Belo Horizonte

Ribeirão Preto •

SOUTHEAST BRAZIL

• Vitória

• Campinas

São Paulo •

Rio de Janeiro

• Curitiba

Florianópolis •

Rio de Janeiro City
Pages 70–105

Rio de Janeiro & Espírito Santo
Pages 106–123

São Paulo State
Pages 164–175

São Paulo City
Pages 138–163

Minas Gerais
Pages 124–137

EYEWITNESS TRAVEL

Brazil

EYEWITNESS TRAVEL

Brazil

Penguin
Random
House

Managing Editor Aruna Ghose
Editorial Manager Ankita Awasthi
Design Manager Priyanka Thakur
Project Editor Alka Thakur
Project Designer Mathew Kurien
Editors Arundhti Bhanot, Nandita
Jaishankar, Vandana Mohindra
Designers Rajnish Kashyap,
Baishakhee Sengupta
Cartography Manager Uma Bhattacharya
Senior Cartographer Suresh Kumar
Senior Picture Researcher Taiyaba
Khatoon
Picture Researcher Sumita Khatwani
Senior DTP Designer Vinod Harish

Contributors
Alex Bellos, Shawn Blore, Dilwyn Jenkins,
Oliver Marshall, Christopher Pickard,
Alex Robinson, Neiva Augusta Silva

Consultant
Alex Robinson

Photographers
Demetrio Carrasco, Nigel Hicks, Alex
Robinson, Linda Whitwam

Illustrators
Surat Kumar Mantoo, Arun Pottirayil, Gautam
Trivedi, Mark Warner

Printed and bound in China

First American Edition, 2007

18 19 20 21 10 9 8 7 6 5 4 3 2 1

Published in the United States by
DK Publishing, 345 Hudson Street, New York,
New York 10014

**Reprinted with revisions 2010, 2012,
2016, 2018**

Copyright © 2007, 2018 Dorling
Kindersley Limited, London
A Penguin Random House Company

Published in Great Britain by Dorling
Kindersley Limited.

A catalog record for this book is available
from the Library of Congress.

ISSN 1542-1554

ISBN 978-1-4654-6796-6

MIX
Paper from
responsible sources
FSC   FSC™ C018179
www.fsc.org

Brazil's most famous landmark, Christ the
Redeemer, Rio de Janeiro

Introducing Brazil

Discovering Brazil **10**

Putting Brazil on the
Map **16**

A Portrait of Brazil **20**

Brazil Through the Year **44**

The History of Brazil **50**

The beautiful coast at Tibaú do Sul, Rota do Sol

**The information in this
DK Eyewitness Travel Guide is checked regularly.**

Every effort has been made to ensure that this book is as up-to-date as possible
at the time of going to press. Some details, however, such as telephone numbers,
opening hours, prices, gallery hanging arrangements and travel information are
liable to change. The publishers cannot accept responsibility for any consequences
arising from the use of this book, nor for any material on third party websites, and
cannot guarantee that any website address in this book will be a suitable source of
travel information. We value the views and suggestions of our readers very highly.
Please write to: Publisher, DK Eyewitness Travel Guides, Dorling Kindersley,
80 Strand, London, WC2R 0RL, UK, or email: travelguides@dk.com.

◀ **Title page** Rio de Janeiro's spectacular coastline **Front cover image** Christ the Redeemer and Sugar Loaf Mountain, Rio de Janeiro
Back cover image The stunning Iguaçu Falls on the Brazil side

Contents

Brazil Area by Area

Southeast Brazil **64**

Northeast Brazil **176**

Northern Brazil **260**

Central West Brazil **294**

Southern Brazil **328**

Travelers' Needs

Where to Stay **366**

Where to Eat & Drink **382**

Shopping in Brazil **398**

Entertainment in Brazil **400**

Specialized Holidays & Outdoor Activities **402**

Survival Guide

Practical Information **408**

Travel Information **418**

General Index **428**

Acknowledgments **444**

Phrase Book **447**

Wooden mask from Northeast Brazil

Samba dancers in flamboyant costumes at a Carnaval parade in Rio de Janeiro

The Modernist Catedral Metropolitana Nossa Senhora Aparecida, Brasília

HOW TO USE THIS GUIDE

This guide helps you get the most from your visit to Brazil, providing expert recommendations and detailed practical information. *Introducing Brazil* maps the country and sets it in its historical and cultural context. The following sections are devoted to the country's capital and various regions, and include the major towns, sights and attractions. Information on accommodation, restaurants, shopping, entertainment, and activities can be found in the *Travelers' Needs* section, while the *Survival Guide* contains practical tips on everything you need to know, from money and language to getting around the country and seeking medical care.

Major Cities

In this guide, Brazil is described in 15 sections, two of which concentrate on the country's major cities – Rio de Janeiro and São Paulo. A section is devoted to each city. All the sights are numbered and plotted on an *Exploring Map*. Information on each sight is easy to locate within the chapter as it follows the numerical order on the map.

RIO DE JANEIRO CITY

1 Introduction
An overview of the history and characteristics of each city.

Each city can be quickly identified by its color-coding.

Country maps show the location of each of the cities.

Exploring São Paulo City

2 City Map
For easy reference, the sights are numbered and located on a map. The main streets, bus stations and railway stations, parking areas and tourist offices are also shown. Sights in the city centre are also shown on the Street Finders for Rio de Janerio City *(see pp100–105)* and for São Paulo City *(see pp158–63)*.

Sights at a Glance lists the chapter's sights by category: churches, cathedrals, monasteries, historic buildings, museums, parks, gardens, streets, and neighborhoods.

Avenida Paulista

Liberdade

Museu do Futebol

3 Detailed Information
All the sights in each city are described individually. Addresses, telephone numbers, opening hours, admission charges, and information on how to get there are given for each sight. The key to symbols is shown on the back flap.

Each area of Brazil is identified by color-coded thumb tabs.

Country maps show the location and area of each region of Brazil.

1 Introduction
An overview of the history and characteristics of each region.

Brazil Area by Area

In this book, the country is described in 15 chapters, two of which concentrate on Brazil's major cities and 13 on the country's main regions. The map on the inside front cover shows this regional division. The most interesting places to visit are given on the *Regional Map* at the beginning of each chapter.

2 Regional Map
This shows the main road network and gives an illustrated overview of the whole region. All interesting places to visit are numbered and there are useful tips on getting around.

Story boxes explore some of the region's historical and cultural subjects in detail.

3 Detailed Information
All the important towns and other places to visit are dealt with individually. They are listed in order, following the numbering given on the *Regional Map*. Each entry also contains practical information such as map references, addresses, telephone numbers, and opening times.

Practical information at the beginning of each entry gives helpful information about visiting the sight or attraction.

The Visitors' Checklist provides a summary of the practical information you need to plan your visit.

Stars indicate the best sights and important features.

4 Brazil's Top Sights
These are given two or more full pages. Buildings are dissected to show their interiors.

INTRODUCING BRAZIL

Discovering Brazil **10–15**

Putting Brazil on the Map **16–19**

A Portrait of Brazil **20–43**

Brazil Through the Year **44–49**

The History of Brazil **50–63**

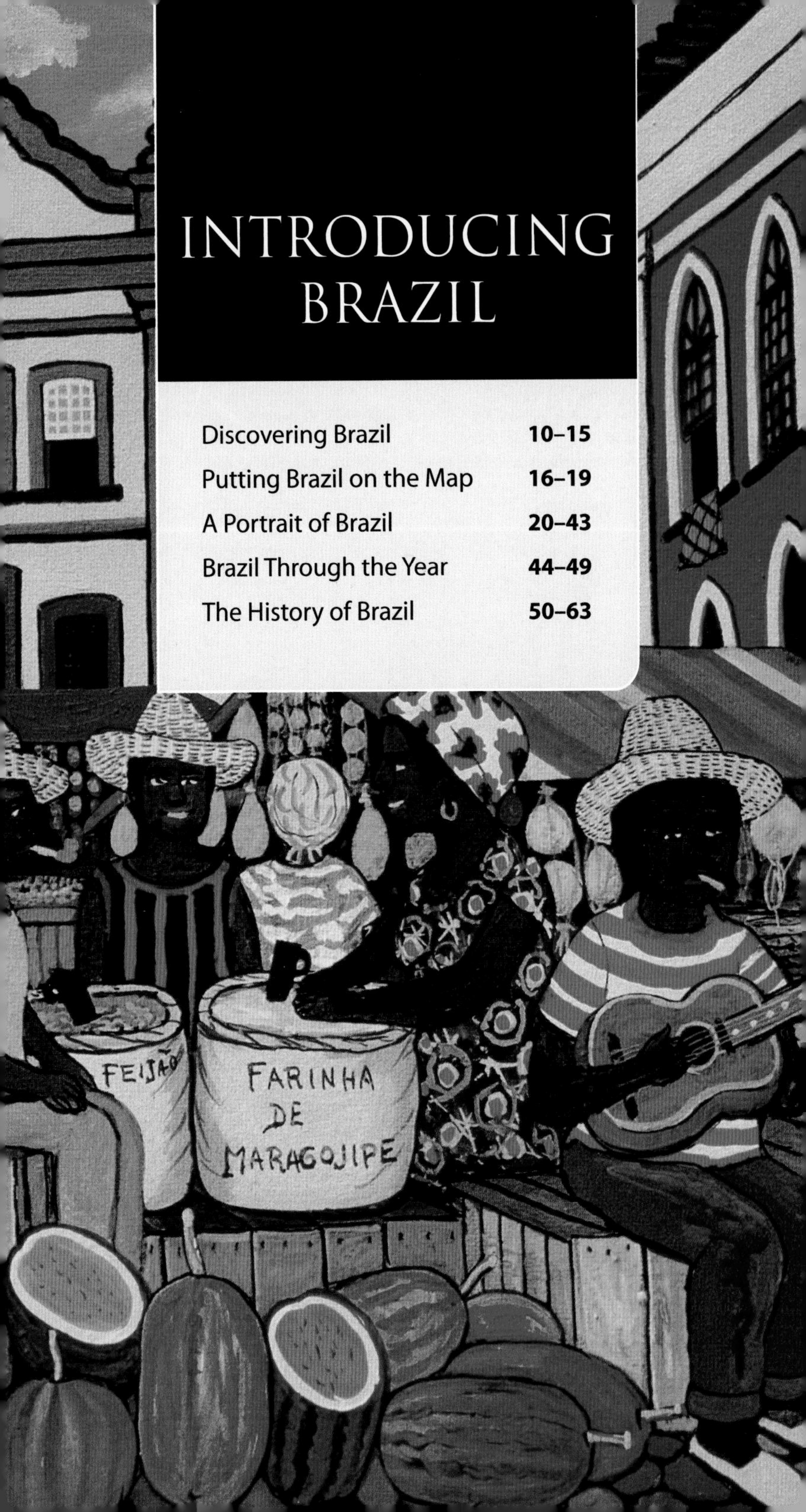

FEIJÃO

FARINHA DE MARAGOJIPE

DISCOVERING BRAZIL

No visitor to Brazil should ever underestimate the size of the country or its largest cities. Brazil is a place of continental dimensions that can comfortably house all of Europe – with room to spare. Therefore, when we suggest a two-week itinerary of popular Brazilian highlights, keep in mind that this is the same as trying to visit all of Europe over a two-week period, and that it will require air travel. Brazilian highlights include the falls at Foz do Iguaçu; the Modernist Brazilian capital, Brasília; the world's largest wetland, the Pantanal; the

Amazon rainforest; Salvador, one of the jewels of the country's northeast coast; and Rio de Janeiro itself. There is also the suggestion for a one-week coastal drive traveling from São Paulo, the country's business capital, to Rio de Janeiro, its leisure and culture hub. Finally, there are two-day itineraries for Rio de Janeiro and São Paulo, as well as Salvador. Time is tight on most of these itineraries, all of which are easy to extend and expand to the time available so that you can learn more about this gigantic and diverse country.

The large auditorium at the Teatro Amazonas in Manaus, in the northwest of the country, still features its original and impressive *belle époque* decor.

```
0 km        400
0 miles        400
```

Manaus

Amazon

AMAZONAS

RONDÔNIA

MATO GROSSO

Cuiabá

Pantanal

MATO GROSSO DO SUL

Foz do Iguaçu
Parque Nacional
Iguazú

Two Weeks around Brazil

- Explore the Brazilian and Argentinian sides of **Foz do Iguaçu**, where a river is divided by 275 spectacular waterfalls.

- Marvel at the Modernist architecture and innovative urban planning in the Brazilian capital, **Brasília**.

- Get up close and personal with the flora and fauna that make up the **Pantanal**, the planet's largest wetlands.

- Travel along the **Amazon river** and experience a night in the **Amazon rainforest**.

- Visit the famous opera house in **Manaus**, in the heart of the Amazon.

- Discover the African influences behind **Bahia**'s cuisine, religion, music, dance, dress, and arts and crafts.

- Admire one of greatest collections of colonial architecture and treasures in the world in **Pelourinho**, **Salvador**'s historic center.

- Stand at the feet of **Rio de Janeiro**'s iconic statue of **Christ the Redeemer**, on the summit of **Corcovado**.

- Walk on the sands of some of the world's most famous beaches, including **Copacabana** and **Ipanema**.

- Experience **São Paulo**'s superb restaurants and nightlife, and visit its great museums.

- Appreciate the diversity of this great country in terms of landscapes, cuisine, culture, and its people.

◀ A painting in naive style by Calixto Sales, depicting a market scene in Maragojipe, Bahia

The Museu de Arte de São Paulo (MASP) is one of the most distinctive architectural landmarks in Brazil. Built in the 1960s, it contains a prestigious collection of art from Europe and Brazil.

A Week on the Costa Verde (Green Coast)

- Experience one of the world's great coastal drives.

- Discover **Rio de Janeiro**'s most westerly suburb, **Barra da Tijuca**, home to the **Olympic Village**.

- Enjoy the contrast between the greenery of the **Atlantic rainforest** and pristine **sandy beaches**.

- Stop off and enjoy a wide variety of **beaches** along the way.

- Explore the enchanting islands of **Ilha Grande** and **Ilhabela**.

- Wander the colonial-era streets of **Paraty** and soak up the atmosphere of times gone by.

- Enjoy the hospitality of some of Brazil's most charming and atmospheric small hotels, bars, and restaurants.

Key

Two-week tour

Costa Verde (Green Coast) tour

Pará • Belém

PARÁ

MARANHÃO

• Fortaleza

CEARÁ

RIO GRANDE DO NORTE

PIAUÍ

PARAÍBA

São Francisco

PERNAMBUCO • Recife

ALAGOAS

TOCANTINS

SERGIPE

BAHIA

• Salvador

Tocantins

Atlantic Ocean

• Brasília

GOIÁS

MINAS GERAIS

Paraná

ESPÍRITO SANTO

SÃO PAULO

RIO DE JANEIRO

Rio de Janeiro

See Costa Verde inset map below

PARANÁ

SANTA CATARINA

RIO GRANDE DO SUL

Costa Verde

Rio de Janeiro

Angra dos Reis

Barra da Tijuca

Paraty

Ilha Grande

São Paulo

Ubatuba

São Bernardo do Campo

Camburi

São Sebastião

Atlantic Ocean

Maresias

Ilhabela

Guarujá

0 km 50

0 miles 50

This aerial view of Rio de Janeiro highlights some of the city's most appealing aspects: its verdant mountains and its sandy coastline, gently caressed by the ocean.

Two Days in Rio de Janeiro

Rio de Janeiro is one of the world's most beautiful and exciting cities, blessed by a backdrop of mountains, rainforest, beaches, and the sea.

- **Arriving** Tom Jobim International Airport is located 12 miles (20 km) from the city. If traveling from São Paulo, you may land at the Santos Dumont airfield. Both have bus and taxi links.

- **Moving on** Take a flight or a long-distance bus to explore Brazil. Alternatively, rent a car and follow the coast to São Paulo *(see p14)*.

Day 1

Morning Start at the summit of **Morro do Corcovado** *(pp86–7)*, atop which stands the statue of **Cristo Redentor** (Christ the Redeemer; *p86*). From here, much of Rio is laid out before you. Take the **cog train** *(p87)* from the station in Rua Cosme Velho to the top. On the 17-minute journey you will pass through parts of the **Tijuca Forest** *(p87)*. Spend at least an hour at the summit. Back at the Rua Cosme Velho station, drop in on the neighboring **Museu Internacional de Arte Naïf** (International Naïve Art Museum; *p87*) before taking a taxi across town to the **docks and waterfront** (Porto Maravilha) *(p76)* for a stroll along the pedestranized boulevard. Visit either the innovative science museum, **Museu de Amanhã**

(Museum of Tomorrow) or admire the art chronicling the city's history in **Museu de Arte do Rio**.

Afternoon Continue to explore the city's **historic center** *(pp74–9)*, an area that is packed with museums, galleries, cultural centers, and historic churches. The city center is fairly compact and easy to walk around, with plenty of options for a lunchtime break, such as the famous **Confeitaria Colombo** *(p76)*. In the evening, see a show at the **Theatro Municipal** *(p77)* or **Circo Voador** *(p78)*, or enjoy the nightlife and bohemian feel of **Lapa** *(p97)* and its great live music venues.

Day 2

Morning Take a leisurely walk along the beachfront of **Copacabana** *(p82)*, **Ipanema** *(p83)*, or **Leblon** *(p83)*, soaking up the scenery and vibe. Swap the sand for greenery, and head across to the **Botanical Garden** *(p84)*. Nearby is the **Lagoa Rodrigo de Freitas** *(p84)*, where for lunch you can choose a lakeside kiosk or the more sophisticated Lagoon center, with views across the Lagoa to Corcovado.

Afternoon Pass through Botafogo, home to a number of museums, most notably the **Museu do Índio** *(p85)*, or stop off at the **Rio Sul** mall *(pp94–5)* for some retail therapy. Mid-afternoon, explore **Sugar Loaf Mountain** *(pp80–81)*, one of the city's iconic sights. Leave plenty of time to enjoy both **Morro da Urca** *(p80)* and the

summit. If your timing is right, you will be able to enjoy the change in light as darkness envelops the city below. After dinner, enjoy some *bossa nova* or *samba (p97)*, or return to Lapa.

> **To extend your trip…**
> Visit the historic mountain town of **Petrópolis** *(pp116–19)*, or head to the Costa do Sol and its highlight, the town of **Búzios** *(pp120–21)*. Also within a comfortable drive are the historic towns of **Minas Gerais** *(pp125–37)*.

Two Days in São Paulo

São Paulo is the business capital of Brazil and South America. The city spreads over a vast area, but many of its attractions sit close together or in clusters.

- **Arriving** Guarulhos International Airport is located 17 miles (28 km) northeast of the city. If coming from Rio de Janeiro, you may land at the smaller, more central Congonhas in the southwest.

- **Moving on** To explore Brazil, take a flight or a long-distance bus. Alternatively, rent a car and follow the coast to Rio *(see p14)*.

Day 1

Morning São Paulo's historic center *(pp142–6)* is well worth a visit. After rush hour, head for Praça de Sé, a good location from which to visit many of the area's attractions, including the **Catedral Metropolitana** *(p142)* and the **Pátio do Colégio** *(p142)*, where São Paulo was founded. Arrive at the **Edifício Itália** *(p143)* for lunch. The view may be better than the food, but you won't regret it. **Edifício Altino Arantes** *(p143)*, a miniature version of the Empire State Building, is a famous landmark.

Afternoon Slightly north is another cluster of historic attractions, many located close to Praça da Luz. These include one of

Cog train traveling through the Tijuca Forest on its way to Morro do Corcovado, Rio de Janeiro

For practical information on traveling around Brazil's cities, see pp426–7

View across the Parque do Ibirapuera, which features many museums and is an important green lung in the city of São Paulo

South America's main museums, the **Pinacoteca de São Paulo** *(pp144–5)*, as well as the **Museu de Arte Sacra** *(p146)* and the Victorian-styled **Estação da Luz** *(p146)*. São Paulo's nightlife is highly rated, so in the evening catch a show or visit a club *(p156)*.

Day 2
Morning Head to the huge **Parque do Ibirapuera** *(pp150–51)*, which is home to a number of important museums and galleries, including the **Museu de Arte Moderna** *(p151)*, the Museu Afro Brasil, and the Bienal Building. Walk along **Avenida Paulista** *(p148)* to understand why São Paulo is the financial capital of South America, then go into the internationally acclaimed **Museu de Arte de São Paulo (MASP)** *(p147)*. Next, head to Rua Oscar Freire and Rua Bela Cintra, an area that offers plenty of charming options for lunch. Browse the distinctive, top-end boutiques around here.

Afternoon After lunch, go north to Praça Charles Miller, named for the Englishman who brought soccer to Brazil. Here is the Estádio do Pacaembu, built in 1940 and used for the 1950 World Cup, and also the highly celebrated **Museu do Futebol** *(pp148–9)*. Options for the rest of the afternoon include a visit to the **Instituto Butantã** *(p152)*, one of the world's most important research centers for venomous animals, or to **Liberdade** *(p149)*, the hub for the city's massive Japanese community. In the evening, experience the city's restaurants and nightlife.

Two Days in Salvador

Salvador, the first capital of Brazil, was also at the center of the slave trade, which makes it the most "African" of all Brazilian cities. The continent's influences can be found in everything from cuisine and arts to religion.

- **Arriving** The Deputado Luíz E. Magalhães International Airport is located 17 miles (28 km) to the north of the city. There are bus and taxi links.

- **Moving on** To explore Brazil, take a flight from the airport.

Day 1
Morning The crown jewel of Salvador is the restored historic center, **Pelourinho** *(pp190–93)*, a UNESCO World Heritage Site with colonial houses, Baroque churches, and museums. Don't miss the church and convent of **São Francisco** *(pp194–5)*. Spend the entire morning walking in and around Pelourinho, which offers many charming and atmospheric places for lunch.

Afternoon Take the **Elevador Lacerda** *(p193)*, built in 1873, down to the lower city to visit the **Mercado Modelo** *(p196)*, which houses a wide selection of northeastern arts and crafts. Since the market is popular with visitors, you can expect to see a demonstration of *capoeira* *(p203)*. Bahia is famous for its cuisine, so find a restaurant for dinner and experience the local dishes and delicacies.

Day 2
Morning Start the day in Nazaré, at the Arena Fonte Nova, one of the most admired stadiums of the 2014 World Cup. The tours start at 9am and take 1 hour and 15 minutes. Close by are the **Museu de Arte Sacra** *(p196)*, the **Museu de Arte Moderna** *(p196)*, and the **Solar do Unhão** *(p196)*, a 17th-century colonial sugar mill. The complex's atmospheric restaurant, with its wonderful views, is a great choice for lunch.

Afternoon Visit and enjoy the beaches of Salvador, which stretch west along the **Atlantic coast** *(pp198–9)*. Start at the most famous, Praia do Farol da Barra, which features a lighthouse and the **Forte de Santo Antônio** *(p197)*, a city landmark in its own right. Nearby, Porto da Barra is a popular beach from which to watch the sunset. Try Praia de Amaralina if you are interested in surfing or sailboarding.

> **To extend your trip...**
> Spend time exploring the coast of Bahia. To the south are **Ilha de Itaparica** *(p200)* and **Morro de São Paulo** *(p202)*. The coast to the north is known as the **Linha Verde**, or Green Line *(p211)*, and includes Praia do Forte and Costa do Sauípe. Or head inland to visit **Lençóis** *(p208)* and the spectacular **Parque Nacional de Chapada Diamantina** *(pp208–9)*.

Christian cross in front of the church and convent of São Francisco in Salvador

A Week on the Costa Verde (Green Coast)

Travel along a spectacular coastline and explore historic towns, beautiful beaches, and pretty islands.

- **Airports** Arrive and depart from São Paulo and Rio de Janeiro's international (Guarulhos/Tom Jobim) or domestic (Congonhas/Santos Dumont) airports.

- **Transport** This itinerary is best done by rental car. It is also possible to do most of the route by using the bus services that link the towns.

- **Booking ahead** It is best to have all accommodation booked in advance, particularly on weekends. If you are sure of your timings, you can also pre-book the ferries to Ilhabela and Ilha Grande.

- **Tips** You can start this itinerary in Rio de Janeiro and work back to São Paulo.

Day 1: São Paulo
Pick a day from the city itinerary on pp12–13.

Day 2: São Paulo to Ilhabela
Plan to leave mid-morning, after the worst of the city's rush hour is over. Head for the 050 (SP-150), which will take you south, to the coast, via São Bernardo do Campo. As you leave the city, the scenery changes to a series of lakes surrounded by hills. You will wind your way through them before dropping down to **Guarujá** *(p169)* – this descent to the coast is spectacular. Guarujá offers excellent options for lunch on the beachfront. Continue east along the coastal road toward **São Sebastião** *(p168)*. You will pass many beautiful beaches, such as Camburi, Camburizinho, and **Maresias** *(p169)*. From São Sebastião, take the 15-minute ferry to **Ilhabela** *(p169)*, an island and yachting center offering mountain scenery, beaches, and waterfalls. Enjoy

the landscape and nightlife, and spend the night at one of the numerous *pousadas*. The island is especially lively at the weekend.

Day 3: Ilhabela to Paraty
Spend the morning exploring Ilhabela, before taking the ferry back to the mainland and following the coast east to **Ubatuba** *(p168)*, a small beach resort with a colonial center. This part of the coast offers nearly 60 miles (100 km) of beaches for you to discover, all wrapped up in Atlantic rainforest. Praia Grande, close to Ubatuba, is a popular location for lunch. Continue to the historic colonial town of **Paraty** *(pp110–11)*, much of which dates from the 18th century. En route, you will cross the state border between São Paulo and Rio de Janeiro, shortly after which the road will no longer hug the coast. Paraty's picturesque historic center is where the majority of the charming *pousadas*, bars, and restaurants are located.

Day 4: Paraty
Wander around Paraty's cobbled, pedestrian, sea-washed streets, popping into the beautifully restored colonial houses, museums, churches, and art galleries, or take a relaxing schooner ride around the many **islands** *(p112)* close by.

> **To extend your trip…**
> Consider staying two nights in Paraty to fully soak up the colonial atmosphere.

Days 5 and 6: Ilha Grande
It is quite possible to drive straight from Paraty to Rio de Janeiro. However, if you have time, stop at **Angra dos Reis** *(p114)*, leave the car, and take the ferry over to **Ilha Grande** *(p114)*, one of the largest of the 365 islands to be found in the bay. Spend at least two nights on this beautiful, unspoilt island, and explore it on foot or by boat. You will need to take cash, since there are no banks or ATMs there, and no cars. Most of the main *pousadas* are a short distance from the ferry dock, at Vila do Abraão. There are nearly 100 miles (160 km) of trails that cover the entire island, so enjoy a hike and visit ruins, waterfalls, mountains, and beaches, including Lopes Mendes, one of the island's – and Brazil's – most beautiful. (You will need to take a boat taxi.)

Day 7: Rio de Janeiro
From the ferry terminal in Angra dos Reis, take the coastal road, following the signs to **Rio de Janeiro** *(pp70–105)* via **Barra da Tijuca** *(pp90–91)*. This is one of Rio's most affluent suburbs. If you have time, it is worth visiting a number of attractions as you pass through Barra, such as **Sitio Roberto Burle Marx** *(p91)* and **Casa do Pontal** *(p91)*. Alternatively, head to **Barra Shopping Center** *(p90)* for some retail therapy.

> **To extend your trip…**
> Spend a couple of days exploring Rio de Janeiro. See the city itinerary on p12.

A beach in the small town of Trindade, near Paraty, on the Costa Verde

For practical information on traveling around Brazil's cities, see pp426–7

Two Weeks around Brazil

This itinerary offers a tour of many iconic Brazilian sights, experiences, and highlights.

- **Airports** Because of the distances involved, you will need to fly between the main cities and gateways to be visited. Consider purchasing a Brazil Air Pass before arriving in Brazil. For more information about domestic air travel, see pp420–21.

- **Transport** Taxis and public transport are available. In most of the cities and locations, you will have the option to join an organized tour.

- **Booking ahead** It is best to book all city accommodations, Amazon lodges, and the trips to the Pantanal in advance.

Day 1: Iguaçu Falls (Brazilian side)
Start the tour in **Foz do Iguaçu** *(pp344–6)*. Visit the Brazilian side of the falls first – there are more than 275 spreading over 2 miles (3 km). If you have time, take an exhilarating inflatable-boat trip to the mouth of the falls (be prepared to get wet). There are many places to stay in Foz. If your budget allows, stay at the **Hotel das Cataratas Belmond** *(p381)*, the only hotel that lies in the national park next to the falls. It allows you to visit and view the falls when the park is closed to everyone else.

Day 2: Iguaçu Falls (Argentinian side)
Take an organized tour to the Argentinian **Parque Nacional Iguazú** *(p347)*; check in advance if you need a visa. The park offers many more walkways through and along the falls than are to be found on the Brazilian side. The popular Devil's Throat is the most impressive fall, so avoid the crowds by walking there first, then working your way back to the park entrance. In the evening, visit the falls on the Brazilian side again. Have dinner

at the Hotel das Cataratas, so you have access to the park. If you can time your visit with a full moon, you may get the chance to see a moonbow, or lunar rainbow – truly a memorable experience. If you have spare time on the second day, visit nearby **Itaipu Binacional** *(p346)*, one of the world's largest hydroelectric dams. Other options include **Parque das Aves** *(p346)*, an impressive aviary full of exotic birds, or a helicopter flight over the falls.

Day 3: Brasília
Take an early flight from Foz to the Brazilian capital, **Brasília** *(pp306–9)*. This relatively small and compact city has an array of attractions and can easily be explored on foot or as part of an organized tour. Visit the **TV Tower** *(p306)* for a bird's-eye view of the city and to appreciate its Modernist architecture and innovative urban planning. Brasília was one of the host cities of the 2014 World Cup, and the National Stadium (Estádio Nacional de Brasília Mané Garrincha) was built for the tournament.

Days 4 & 5: Pantanal
Head to the **Pantanal** *(pp324–5)*, the planet's largest wetland, which covers an area of 89,000 sq miles (230,000 sq km). To reach the Pantanal, take a short flight from Brasília to **Cuiabá** *(p322)*, credited with being the warmest city in Brazil. There is not a lot to see in Cuiabá, so you will be met at the airport and taken straight out to a lodge or farm. All accommodations in the Pantanal offer guided excursions to see the area's unique and rich ecosystem, with special tours for birders, visitors keen on tracking the Brazilian jaguar, horse riders, and those interested in the region's abundant fish life. It is much easier to spot Brazil's fauna and prolific birdlife in the Pantanal than in the more dense vegetation of the Amazon.

Day 6: Manaus
Return to Cuiabá for the flight to Manaus, in the heart of

Visitors at Foz do Iguaçu, the largest waterfalls in the world

the Amazon. On arrival in **Manaus** *(pp284–5)*, use the rest of the day to explore the city, the **Teatro Amazonas** *(pp286–7)*, the **Museu do Índio** *(p285)*, the waterfront, and the **market** *(p284)*.

Days 7 & 8: The Amazon
Spend two days out in a remote Amazon lodge. Take a cruise on a traditional Amazon riverboat to explore parts of the world's biggest rainforest *(pp288–9)*.

Days 9 & 10: Salvador
Return to Manaus for the flight to **Salvador** *(pp188–99)*. Follow the city itinerary on p13.

Days 11–14: Rio de Janeiro
Fly to **Rio de Janeiro** *(pp70–105)*. You will need at least two or three full days to do any justice to Brazil's most famous city. See the city itinerary on p12.

To extend your trip…
This itinerary could comfortably be extended to three weeks or more if you have the time, since virtually all the cities included offer the option to explore other areas of Brazil in more detail, be it the **south** *(pp328–63)* from Foz do Iguaçu; the **central west** *(pp294–327)* from Brasília; the **northeast** coast *(pp176–259)* from Salvador; or the historic towns of **Minas Gerais** *(pp124–137)* from Rio de Janeiro.

Putting Brazil on the Map

The largest country in South America, Brazil borders most other South American countries and covers over 3.3 million sq miles (8.5 million sq km), from the vast tropical Amazon region in the north to the cooler, more European-style South. It is divided into 26 states and one federal district – its political and administrative capital, Brasília. Brazil's population, now reaching almost 200 million, is mostly concentrated in the Southeast (*see pp18–19*).

VENEZUELA   GUYAN

RORAIMA   ✈ Boa Vista

Caracaraí

Nora Para

Uaupés   Catrimani

Equator   Negro

COLOMBIA   Maraã

Itacoatiara

ECUADOR   Tefé   Amazon   Manaus ✈

Guayaquil

AMAZONAS   Purus

Novo Aripuar

Iquitos   Tabatinga

Loja   Lábrea   Barra d São Manu

Piura   Boco do Acre   Humaitá   Conceiçã

Tarapoto   Feijó   Porto Velho ✈   B R

Trujillo   Cruzeiro do Sul   364   Ariquemes

Pucallpa   ACRE   Ji-Paraná

PERU   Rio Branco   RONDÔNIA

Costa Marques   Vilhen

PACIFIC OCEAN   Lima

Puno   BOLIVIA

Nuestra Señora de La Paz

Cochabamba   Santa Cruzde de La Sierra

PARAGUA

Tropic of Capricorn

Antofagasta

Asunc

CHILE

San Miguel de Tucuman

ARGENTINA

Cordoba

Rosario

Mendoza

Buenos Aire

Santiago

Greater Brasília

Parque Nacional de Brasília   Sobradinho

Represa Santa Maria   20

Paranoá

Taguatinga   Cruzeiro   BRASÍLIA   Lago Paranoa

Guará

Núcleo Bandeirante   60

Recanto das Emas   ✈ Aeroporto Int. Pres Juscelino Kubitschek   São Sebastião

0 km   10

0 miles   10

For keys to symbols *see back flap*

Central & South America

Atlantic Ocean

NICARAGUA
COSTA RICA
PANAMA
VENEZUELA
COLOMBIA
GUYANA
SURINAME
FRENCH GUIANA
ECUADOR
PERÚ
BRAZIL
BOLIVIA
PARAGUAY
CHILE
ARGENTINA
URUGUAY

Pacific Ocean

See pp18–19

SURINAME
FRENCH GUIANA
Asoenangka
AMAPÁ
Serra do Navio
Macapá
ATLANTIC OCEAN
Equator
Porteira
Óbidos
Monte Alegre
arintins
Santarém
Belém
São Luís
316
PARÁ
Itaituba
230
10
Araras
163
Marabá
Imperatriz
Timon
Teresina
Caxias
CEARÁ
Fortaleza
Ilha Fernando de Noronha
Mossoró
Natal
304
Araguaina
MARANHÃO
20
Juàzeiro do Norte
João Pessoa
PARAÍBA
226
PIAUÍ
232
Cachimbo
230
PERNAMBUCO
Recife
101
Alta resta
Peixoto de Azevedo
Palmas
Petrolina
Juàzeiro
Paulo Afonso
Maceió
20
nop
Jacaré
TOCANTINS
Barreiras
Aracaju
116
242
Feira de Santana
Alagoinhas
MATO GROSSO
GOIÁS
20
BAHIA
Salvador
Cuiabá
70
Ceilândia
Brasília
Jequié
Vitória da Conquista
Ilhéus
Várzea Grande
Rondonópolis
Anápolis
Gama
163
Goiânia
MINAS GERAIS
Montes Claros
101
ATO GROSSO DO SUL
364
Rio Verde
Uberlândia
135
Teófilo Otôni
Campo Grande
São José do Rio Preto
Uberaba
Belo Horizonte
Ipatinga
ESPÍRITO SANTO
ATLANTIC OCEAN
267
262
Ribeirão Preto
Vitória
Vila Velha
urados
Araçatuba
Juiz de Fora
ourados
Ponta Porã
SÃO PAULO
Campinas
Campos dos Goitacazes
Maringá
Londrina
São Gonçalo
Cascavel
PARANÁ
São Paulo
Santos
Rio de Janeiro
Tropic of Capricorn
277
Foz do Iguaçu
Guarapuava
Curitiba
Joinville
SANTA CATARINA
Passo Fundo
Lajes
Florianópolis
285
116
Criciúma
RIO GRANDE DO SUL
Caxias do Sul
Urugu-aiana
Porto Alegre
Bagé
Pelotas
Rio Grande
RUGUAY
471

Key

—— Highway
—— Major road
····· Minor road
- - - Railroad
▬▬ International border
—— State border

0 km   400
0 miles   400

Southeastern Brazil

The densely populated southeastern part of Brazil contains the country's two biggest cities. A dynamic, sprawling business center, São Paulo has more than 12 million inhabitants in the city proper. Beautiful Rio de Janeiro, with its legendary beaches, is home to around 5 million people. With a well-developed infrastructure and economy, this region has a stunning Atlantic coastline and a wealth of historic towns.

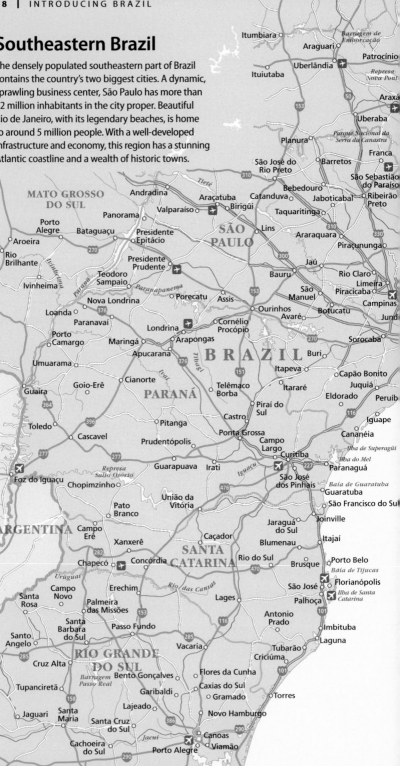

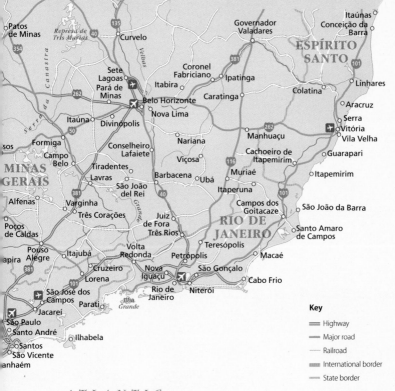

Key

▬▬▬ Highway
▬▬▬ Major road
▬▬▬ Railroad
▭▭▭ International border
▬▬▬ State border

ATLANTIC

OCEAN

Mileage chart

Rio de Janeiro													
326	Vitória												
525													
276	**327**	Belo Horizonte											
444	526												
720	**776**	**460**	Brasília										
1160	1250	741											
1307	**750**	**864**	**476**	Salvador									
1669	1207	1391	1542										
1464	**1174**	**1289**	**1381**	**523**	Recife								
2357	1890	2075	2223	842									
1537	**1247**	**1363**	**1452**	**586**	**78**	João Pessoa							
2474	2007	2195	2338	944	125								
1763	**1491**	**1590**	**1422**	**872**	**496**	**427**	Fortaleza						
2838	2400	2559	2290	1403	799	688							
1898	**1626**	**1724**	**1342**	**1006**	**995**	**1015**	**665**	São Luís					
3055	2618	2776	2161	1620	1601	1635	1070						
2016	**1904**	**1748**	**1326**	**1284**	**1270**	**1298**	**949**	**499**	Belém				
3246	3065	2814	2134	2068	2044	2090	1527	803					
2164	**2229**	**1906**	**1610**	**2568**	**2995**	**3068**	**3108**	**2692**	**2756**	Porto Velho			
3483	3588	3068	2592	4133	4821	4938	5002	4333	4436				
716	**1042**	**811**	**1048**	**1670**	**2098**	**2171**	**2422**	**2248**	**2274**	**2153**	Florianópolis		
1153	1678	1306	1687	2689	3377	3494	3858	3618	3661	3466			
533	**859**	**628**	**865**	**1487**	**1915**	**1987**	**2213**	**2051**	**2039**	**1964**	**192**	Curitiba	
858	1383	1011	1392	2394	3082	3199	3563	3302	3282	3161	310		
266	**595**	**364**	**630**	**1232**	**1642**	**1732**	**1953**	**1861**	**1843**	**1949**	**432**	**253**	São Paulo
429	958	586	1015	1983	2643	2788	3144	2996	2967	3137	695	408	

10 = Distance in miles
10 = Distance in kilometers

0 km ▬▬▬ 100
0 miles ▬▬▬ 100

A PORTRAIT OF BRAZIL

Brazil evokes iconic images of lively Carnaval celebrations, brilliant soccer teams, *bossa nova* and *samba* performances, sensual Brazilians swaying across the sands of Ipanema and Copacabana, and the beautiful city of Rio de Janeiro. Beyond these popular images, however, there remains a lot to discover about Brazil, with its wide variety of landscapes and peoples.

Covering over half of South America, Brazil is the world's fifth-largest nation. The sheer size of the country helps to explain the extraordinary diversity of environments and cultures. The larger cities are known for cosmopolitan sophistication and extensive technological development, while in the Amazon region there are indigenous populations who have their own traditions and cultures closely linked to the rainforests.

The Portuguese colonization that began in the 1500s, combined with an estimated 900,000 indigenous peoples, a large number of descendents of slaves from Africa, and the influx of immigrants from a wide geographical and ethnic spectrum, has lent an eclectic character to the social fabric of the country. Portuguese is spoken by the vast majority of the 190 million Brazilians, although there are many commonly used words derived from indigenous and African languages.

The country's striking diversity is reflected in the major cities, each of which has its own distinctive character. The impressive Modernist architecture of the nation's capital Brasília, the ravishing city-scape of Rio de Janeiro, embraced by the gigantic statue of Cristo Redentor (Christ the Redeemer), the colonial buildings and Baroque gems of Minas Gerais, the historic cities of the Northeast, and the picturesque European-influenced, wine-producing towns in Southern Brazil, are just a few examples of this remarkable heterogeneity.

An aerial view of high-rise concrete towers in the ultra-modern city of São Paulo

◄ Carnival parade of *samba* dancers at the Sambódromo, held in Rio de Janeiro

Caiman and butterflies in the splendid Amazonian greenery

The diverse character of Brazil is reflected in its five distinct ecosystems – the Amazon rainforest, the semi-arid *sertão*, the central *cerrado* (savanna), the wildlife-rich Pantanal wetlands, and the lush Mata Atlântica. The varied natural attractions of the country include the spectacular falls at Foz do Iguaçu, captivating Amazônia, the splendid beaches of Rio de Janeiro and the Northeast, the luxuriant grasslands of Rio Grande do Sul, the pristine-white sand dunes of Lençóis Maranhenses, and the abundant, breathtaking flora and fauna of the Pantanal.

The Economy

The Brazilian economy is counted among the world's 10 largest, though it is riddled with contradictions – *favelas* (shantytowns) coexist with skyscrapers in the cities. The foundations for modern economic prosperity were laid, ironically, during the years of the military dictatorship from 1964 to 1984, when Brazil's rulers borrowed heavily from international banks to fund various large projects. However, it was only during the administration of Fernando Henrique Cardoso (1995–2002) that Brazil's economy became more market-oriented, a trend that was carried forward by his successor, Luiz Inácio Lula da Silva – "Lula."

Today, Brazil's major exports feature mainly primary commodities, such as soya beans and coffee, as well as some manufactured goods, including machinery and automobiles. Since 2003, Brazil has emerged as an economic powerhouse and a strong advocate of opening up global trade to developing nations. Its vision of exploring new energy production methods is manifested by Petrobras, Brazil's largest oil-producing company. Run by the state, Petrobras is a pioneer in the development of advanced technology from deep-water oil production.

Alongside Brazil's growing global signifi-cance, there still remain deep economic

The verdant countryside near Bento Gonçalves, a wine-producing town in the Serra Gaúcha, Rio Grande do Sul

Petrobras (Petróleo Brasileiro), Brazil's state-run gas and oil refinery, near Rio de Janeiro

disparities and regional differences. It is common to see the super-rich and the urban poor in Brazil's major cities, mainly Rio de Janeiro and São Paulo, two of the largest metropolises in the world. Inequitous growth is also visible not only in the undeveloped interiors, but also in the agriculture-dominated regions where there is a rising number of landless peasants and indigenous peoples who have been driven out of the rainforests.

Political Life

Politicians have tremendous power in Brazil, and many start and make their way up through municipal and state politics. Some political positions outside of the capital are extremely powerful in their own right, especially that of mayor of one of the big cities, or governor of a state.

Since 1985, when the military dictatorship came to an end, Brazil has been one of the world's largest democracies. However, the country's political elite have immersed Brazil in a series of scandals, involving corruption, misuse of public funds, and abuse of power. When the leftist, ex-trade union leader Lula was elected president in 2002, Brazilians hoped for a democracy that favored the "majority of society," as promised in his Workers' Party (Partido dos Trabalhadores – PT) manifesto, but although a great many people were removed from extreme poverty, there were large corruption scandals, and much inequality still prevails. In 2011, Dilma Rousseff, also of the PT, was inaugurated as the country's first female president.

Brazilians, for the most part, are united in their distrust and lack of respect for

Supporters waving flags of Lula during his 2002 electoral campaign

The Congreso Nacional at dusk, Brasília

their politicians and political parties. The average educated Brazilian resents the perceived close alliance between the politicians and their ambitious business allies.

The People

Home to over half the population of South America, Brazil is the fifth most populous country in the world. The vast majority of people live in the coastal parts and major cities, and the population density grows progressively scantier toward the interior. Brazil has such a varied mix of races, nationalities, and ethnic groups that it is difficult to define a typical Brazilian. It is often argued that being Brazilian is more a state of mind than anything else.

The Portuguese, the first Europeans to explore Brazil, were followed by other colonial powers laying claim to areas along the Brazilian coast. However brief the influence of the French and the Dutch, and later the British, they all made their mark on Brazil, along with the dominant Portuguese. Their influence is still visible in its

culture and its people. The millions of slaves brought to Brazil from West Africa, between the 16th and 19th centuries, have also played an important role in the development of Brazil as a country and as a vibrant culture. Between the 18th and 19th centuries, the influx of immigrants from Europe, especially Italy and Germany, and also from Japan and Korea, have played their part in forming the multicultural and ethnically diverse population of Brazil.

Although Brazil has reputedly the world's largest Catholic population, its unique mix of people has given rise to many different religions and sects. The animistic beliefs of the indigenous Brazilians, ritualistic Afro-Brazilian cults, and spiritualist Kardecism, coexist with other faiths including Judaism, Islam, and Buddhism. Candomblé, a syncretic cult, which originated in Salvador in Bahia, is a unique amalgamation of Catholicism and African beliefs, practiced across Brazil.

Brazil upholds the ideal of racial harmony. However, though not blatant, racial discrimination does still exist, and indigenous populations are under constant risk of losing land to plantations and infrastructure projects. As well as having limited access to education and work opportunities, black people remain inadequately represented in the higher echelons of politics, academia, and business.

Baianas in front of the Convento de São Francisco, Salvador

Residents of Rio de Janeiro (Cariocas) playing soccer on Enseada de Botafogo

Sport & Culture

Brazil's sporting and cultural influence has made the "Brasil" brand known throughout the world. Brazil is the world's greatest soccer (*futebol*) nation, having won the

Ayrton Senna, winner of the Monaco Grand Prix in 1992

World Cup on five occasions and having been the only nation to play at every World Cup. Pelé *(see p172)*, hailed as a great national hero, is the most famous soccer player of all time.

Brazil's sporting prowess has not been restricted to soccer. In Ayrton Senna, Nelson Piquet, and Emerson Fittipaldi, it has had three Formula 1 World Champions, and in tennis it saw success in the 1950s and 1960s with Maria Esther Bueno and, more recently, with Gustavo Kuerten.

Culture has also played its part in establishing how the world views Brazil. The first musicians to make a mark internationally were composer Heitor Villa-Lobos and legendary performer Carmen Miranda. In literature too, writers as different in their subject matter as Jorge Amado and Paulo

Coelho, have helped spread the word about their homeland. The music of Brazil, be it *samba*, *bossa nova*, or one of the many other musical styles to be found across the country, has been a powerful calling card since the 1960s. More recently, talented filmmakers have gone on to produce critically acclaimed works, including Walter Salles with *Central do Brasil* (*Central Station*, 1998), Fernando Meirelles with *Cidade de Deus* (*City of God*, 2002), and Kleber Mendonça Filho with *Aquarius* (2016).

Brazilians celebrate life with their colorful festivals. Carnaval, the cultural event that helped put Brazil on the map, is perceived as the biggest and best in the world, and its revelry embraces the whole country.

A group of musicians rehearsing Brazil's country music *sertanejo*, in Cidade de Goiás

The Landscapes of Brazil

Larger than the US (excluding Alaska) and bordering 10 of the 12 other South American countries, Brazil is home to a wide variety of breathtaking landscapes, from vast swamps to desert, and thick rainforest to metropolitan cityscapes. Covering over 2 million sq miles (3.5 million sq km) and embracing over 40 percent of Brazilian territory, the Amazon rainforest is the most dominant landscape in Brazil and the best known. Although massive and spectacular, the Amazon Basin is only one biome out of several in Brazil, each with its own distinct scenery, fascinating wildlife, and climate.

Key

- The Amazon rainforest
- The Pantanal
- The *sertão*
- The *cerrado*
- Mata Atlântica
- International border
- △ Peak

The Northern Highlands in Amazônia are impressive mountains, strung along the frontier with Venezuela and Guyana.

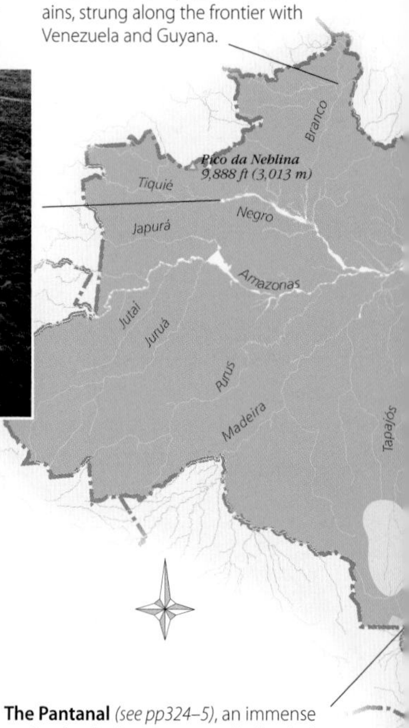

The Amazon rainforest *(see pp264–5)*, one of the most complex ecosystems in the world, is characterized by vast expanses of dense forest, with a wide range of vegetation. Large areas, such as the buriti palm-dominated *igapós*, are annually flooded by the waters of the Rio Negro.

Branco

Pico da Neblina
9,888 ft (3,013 m)

Tiquié

Negro

Japurá

Amazonas

Jutaí

Juruá

Purus

Madeira

Tapajós

The Pantanal *(see pp324–5)*, an immense wetland, is the largest seasonally flooded area on the planet, inundating as much as two-thirds of its total area for half the year, during the rainy season. Dotted with small, forested elevations, the southern Pantanal is used for cattle grazing during the dry season.

The Wet and the Dry Season

During the wet season, which lasts from December to March, the rising rivers inundate the flat land. This process creates *cordilhieras* (isolated islands) amid vast lakes and flowering shrubs. However, it is during the dry season (May to September), that wildlife is at its most spectacular in the Pantanal. During this time, the ponds teem with fish, and thousands of birds flock around the water holes.

The Pantanal in the wet season, near Porto Jofre

The Pantanal with tiny forests in the dry season

The *sertão* *(see p237)* is a semi-arid region in the interior of Brazil's northeast and parts of northern Minas Gerais. The essentially barren landscape, dominated by *caatinga*, is a uniquely Brazilian habitat. The *sertão* receives very little rainfall during the dry months, and is largely strewn with cacti and thorny shrubs. There are periods of intense drought, which makes it a harsh environment for wildlife and people alike. As a result, much of the flora and fauna have specially adapted themselves to the lack of water.

The cerrado *(see pp300–1)* features wide expanses of open, tropical grassland scattered with small, closed canopy forests. Brazil's central plateau is the world's most biologically rich savanna with over 10,000 plant species.

Mata Atlântica *(see p113)*, or the Atlantic rainforest, is a 4,600-mile (7,400-km) coastal band endowed with a stunning diversity of landscapes, from the granite peaks and sheer cliffs of the Great Escarpment to the beautiful white sands and surf of the Costa do Sol.

Brazil's Flora & Fauna

Home to over 55,000 plant species and three of the most diverse ecosystems on the planet, the wealth of flora and fauna in Brazil is unmatched. Some of the most valuable resources of the modern world, such as rubber, originate from the rainforests of the Amazon. As a result of the relative stability of the rainforest compared to temperate areas, the fauna here has had the freedom to evolve and to adapt to very specialized local conditions. With a few of the tributaries of the Amazon river still unexplored, there are numerous species yet to be discovered. Brazil has five principal ecosystems, each with its own distinct array of plant life. From forest and swamp to desert and savanna, these stark contrasts in climate and landscape have resulted in an immensely vibrant and diverse flora, much of which is unique to the country.

Aquatic plants, including the versatile water hyacinth, are commonly found in the Pantanal, which has the richest collection of these plants.

Amazônia

The Amazon rainforest *(see p264–5)* possesses a wealth of flora and fauna. It is characterized by vast expanses of dense forest, extensive savannas, and other ecosystems. Vegetation and wildlife vary because of the annual flooding of large areas.

Blue and gold macaws are brilliantly colored large birds that live on cliffs and high in trees in rainforests and swamps. They are considered an endangered species.

Aguapé is an invasive floating plant with medicinal properties. Found in the wetlands of the Pantanal and Amazônia, it acts as a natural water filter.

The Sertão

The arid *sertão (see p237)*, which comprises 75 percent of the land area in the northeast, has its own unique wildlife including lizards, snakes, and foxes. Birdlife manages to flourish in this minimalist, unfriendly landscape, and sheep and goats are also reared.

Juazeiro, a shrub-like tree indigenous to the *sertão*, is used in wine-making and medicine, as a hair tonic, and for timber.

Mandacaru cactus is a symbol of rebirth and resilience in the arid *sertão*. According to local legend, this tree-like cactus with fragrant blossoms originates on the site of a massacre.

The Cerrado

The *cerrado (see p300–1)* is a vast open savanna dotted with clusters of scattered woodlands. This is the world's most biologically rich grassland. There are over 4,000 endemic plant species, as well as wolves and giant anteaters, whose existence is theatened by the expansion of soya plantations.

The mutum, or crested currasow, is a large bird which is often seen in the forested areas of the *cerrado*.

Pequi, also known as souari nut, provides sweet berries with small thorns inside. It is eaten fresh, used in food, and made into a liqueur.

Giant anteaters are commonly spotted in the *cerrado*. These solitary animals have a long tail and tongue, a bristly brown coat, and five short, sharp claws on both their paws. They are sometimes hunted for their meat.

The Mata Atlântica

The Mata Atlântica *(see p113)*, or Atlantic rainforest, is formed by remnants of Brazil's coastal rainforest. The development of cities and intensive agriculture has severely reduced this habitat, but it remains home to monkeys and exotic birds.

The *piaçava* is a fibrous palm tree. Its fibers are extensively used to make brooms, thatch, mats, and cord.

Woolly spider monkeys are the largest primates in the Americas. This endangered species eats mainly fruits, leaves, and seeds.

The Pantanal

The largest inland wetland *(see pp324–5)* on the planet is constantly abuzz with bird- and wildlife. Hundreds of birds can be heard screeching overhead or fishing in the waters while caimans bask along the river banks. The best time to visit is the dry season.

The anaconda is a large water boa, which can grow to 32 ft (10 m) in length. It kills its prey, sometimes many times its size, by constriction as well as drowning.

The *gravatá* is a member of the *Bromeliaceae* family. *Gravatá* (also known as *karatas*) is a kind of fruit, similar to a pineapple, that grows on the ground.

Peoples of Brazil

When the Portuguese arrived in 1500, the Brazilian population consisted of over 5 million indigenous people divided into at least 1,000 communities. When their numbers began depleting due to the severity of slavery and foreign diseases, the Portuguese started shipping slaves from Africa in the mid-16th century. Many of these slaves assimilated with the white and local population. Over the centuries, Brazil's peoples were diversified further by several waves of immigration from the Middle East, Asia, and Europe. After over 500 years of immigration and integration, modern Brazil is a true ethnic mosaic, where diverse elements combine to create a vibrant nation renowned for its spirit.

Indigenous Brazilians also include the Ticuna community, who are a large group with their own language and written literature.

Some indigenous groups *(see pp266–7)* continue to live as they had done before the arrival of the Portuguese, particularly in the forested interior.

Multiracial Brazil

Brazil is unique in its assimilation of various races and ethnic groups. A white-and-indigenous Brazilian is called a mestiço, *an Afro-Brazilian is called a cafuzo, while a mulatto is born of white and African parentage.*

European immigrants *(see pp332–3)* started moving to Brazil after slavery ended in 1888. They tended to concentrate in various parts of Southern Brazil, where people of Azorean, German, Italian, Slav, Dutch, Austrian, and other descents still thrive.

The Portuguese, the dominant ethnic group in Brazil today, introduced Catholicism *(see p38)*, and have given the country its official language.

Mulattoes, born of black and white parentage, make up at least half the population. Prominent in music, sports, and the arts, famous Brazilian mulattoes include pop music icon Gilberto Gil *(see p36)* and professional soccer player Ronaldo.

Baianas are recognizable in their lace dresses with colorful beads that represent the various *orixás*, or Afro-Brazilian deities *(see p181)*. Baianas play an integral role in keeping alive the Afro-Brazilian traditions that came to Brazil, especially in the slave ships from Angola and Nigeria.

Japanese Brazilians *(see p173)* are mainly descended from immigrants who came to Brazil around 1908 as laborers. There are numerous Buddhist and Shinto shrines around Brazil, and the Japanese influence can be seen in the art scene and in the popularity of its cuisine. São Paulo City's Liberdade district is home to the largest Japanese community outside of Japan.

Cariocas & Paulistanos

Cariocas frolicking on Copacabana beach, Rio City

Residents of Brazil's two largest cities, Rio de Janeiro and São Paulo, have successfully stereotyped themselves and each other. The fun-loving Cariocas of Rio are seen as too easy-going by the Paulistanos of São Paulo, whom the Cariocas regard as workaholics with no zest for life. Paulistanos see their city as the economic force driving Brazil, while Rio is considered to be a playground for Carnaval *(see pp68–9)*. The self-image of Cariocas is that they have better music and more beautiful people. The Paulistanos, on the other hand, take pride in their diligent nature and the distinct cadence of their spoken Portuguese. The key difference really revolves around beach life. Rio's long stretch of trendy beaches forms a vital part of the city's daily life *(see pp42–3)*. The beaches around São Paulo, on the other hand, demand the weekend to enjoy, being at least 40 miles (65 km) away from the city.

Architecture

The first buildings in Brazil were made by the indigenous peoples. As these structures were made from perishable materials, little is known of them beyond early European descriptions. Colonial churches and other buildings were in spectacular form in the 18th century during the Baroque era. After independence, Brazil followed European trends until architects such as Lúcio Costa and Oscar Niemeyer developed Brazilian Modernism, most strikingly expressed in the new capital Brasília. Today, Brazil is dominated by high-rises punctuated by the occasional striking building by a contemporary architect such as Ruy Ohtake.

Avenida Atlântica at Copacabana beach, Rio de Janeiro

Indigenous

Francisco de Orellana (1511–46), the first European to navigate the Amazon, described large cities created by Curucirari people extending for as much as 6 miles (10 km) and cut by large roads. These large cities no longer exist. Today, traditional indigenous villages are smaller and focus on a large communal maloca. Less traditional ones are made up of wattle-and-daub houses.

Kayapó malocas, or *ocas,* are communal longhouses, usually measuring 92 ft (28 m) in length and 59 ft (18 m) in width. Their shape and design influenced many of Oscar Niemeyer's buildings.

Dyed tree bark
Open entrance
Sloping thatched roof

Baroque

Baroque architecture began in 17th-century Europe but reached its most exuberant in Latin America. Brazilian Baroque is characterized by elaborately carved, painted interiors and ornate, florid forms set in modest, whitewash-and-raw-stone façades. The style found its zenith in Salvador and Recife, and in the sculptures of Aleijadinho *(see p135)* in Minas Gerais.

Elaborately carved stone tablet

The monumental door, offset by the modest façade

São Francisco de Assis, in Salvador, is a display of wealth and splendor. The interior of the church is covered with almost 900 lb (450 kg) of gold. Silver, gold leaf, and solid gold are coupled with stunning *azulejos,* that is blue Portuguese tile work.

São Pedro dos Clérigos, in Recife, is rich in ornamental flourishes typical of the Baroque. Its second tower was left incomplete in order to avoid a tax on churches.

Neo-Classical

Neo-Classicism is associated with Imperial Brazil and came to the country with the Portuguese monarchy who fled Napoleon in 1807, bringing the most fashionable European architectural ideas with them. The first Neo-Classical buildings were civic edifices in Rio de Janeiro and palaces in Petrópolis. These quickly became the norm for buildings of state in the rest of the Empire.

Typical Palladian portico

Frieze in bas-relief style

Ionic column

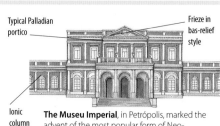

The Museu Imperial, in Petrópolis, marked the advent of the most popular form of Neo-Classicism. Its architect, Julius Köhler, was influenced by the English Palladian style.

Eclectic

Eclecticism is an architectural style associated with 19th-century Republican Brazil. Like the styles that preceded it, it was strongly influenced by European trends, particularly French and English. Eclecticism is characterized by a combination of forms, motifs, and styles from Neo-Classical and Baroque through to Manueline, a style that fuses together in one building Portuguese Late Gothic with ornamentation in portals, windows, and arcades, along with Oriental elements.

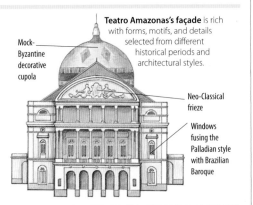

Teatro Amazonas's façade is rich with forms, motifs, and details selected from different historical periods and architectural styles.

Mock-Byzantine decorative cupola

Neo-Classical frieze

Windows fusing the Palladian style with Brazilian Baroque

Modernist

Modernism was shaped by architects such as Le Corbusier and Max Bill. Brazilian architects at first adhered to the strict precepts these Europeans laid down, but from the 1940s, architects such as Oscar Niemeyer developed a unique form of Brazilian Modernism, influenced by indigenous design and employing curved forms.

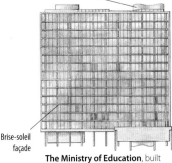

Le Corbusier canopy style

Brise-soleil façade

The Ministry of Education, built in Rio in 1943 with a striking glass *brise-soleil* façade, was the first Modernist building in the Americas to combine civic architecture with a contemporary medium.

Parliament buildings, in Brasília, are a harmony of simple lines and curves incorporating water and the landscape into the design.

Contemporary Brazil

Beyond Brasília and Oscar Niemeyer's structures in Rio and Curitiba, contemporary Brazilian architecture is largely functional and not particularly inspiring. Cities are seas of identical tower-block flats broken by snaking highways. The most daring designs tend to be private homes hidden away behind high walls or corporate buildings such as Ruy Ohtake's stunning Hotel Unique (see p373) and Hotel Unique Garden in São Paulo.

Open-air Skye Bar

Glass set windows

Concrete Pillars supporting the hotel

Landscaped Garden

Hotel Unique is a combination of bravado and functionalism. Built by Ruy Ohtake, a leading figure in contemporary Brazilian architecture, the inverted arc has 3-ft- (1-m-) wide windows overlooking a stunning garden. The open-air rooftop bar has a spectacular view over the city.

Brazilian Artists & Writers

Brazil's first colonial artists and writers were religious, and a tradition of uniquely Brazilian ecclesiastical art continued into the 20th century. Secular art in Brazil ceased to derive from Europe only in the 1920s after the emergence of the *antropofagismo* movement, which appropriated western themes into specifically Brazilian contexts. Brazil's leading 19th-century authors include Joaquim Maria Machado de Assis and Euclides da Cunha. The explosion of Modernism in the early 20th century left Brazil with a diverse literary output, while the 21st century has seen the emergence of writers from Brazil's diverse ethnic communities.

Ceiling painted by Dom Adelbert Gresnicht, Mosteiro São Bento, São Paulo

Church Art

Brazil's first great artists were European priests. Frei Domingos da Conceição (1643–1718) was responsible for the interiors of the São Bento monasteries in Rio and Olinda. Father Agostinho de Piedade (1580–1661) and 18th-century Francisco Xavier Brito, whose works can be found in Rio de Janeiro and Minas Gerais, introduced the Baroque style, developing it as uniquely Brazilian.

Brito almost certainly taught the great artist, Aleijadinho (*see p135*), whose statuary mocks the racist Portuguese colonists, most notably at the basilica in Congonhas and the Igreja São Francisco in Ouro Preto. The latter also preserves the finest paintings by another subtle satiricist, Mestre (Manuel da Costa) Athayde (1762–1830). Illusionism in religious art was developed by José Joaquim da Rocha (1737–1807) in Salvador, Mestre Valentim (1750–1813)

in Rio, and José Joaquim da Veiga Valle (1806–74) in Goiás. In the 19th and 20th centuries, illusionism was largely lost but for the work of Benedito Calixto (1853–1927) in Santos and São Paulo, and the Dutch artist Adelbert Gresnicht, who painted the Beuronese interior of São Paulo's Mosteiro São Bento.

Secular Art

Brazil's first secular art was European in theme and technique, best seen in the

Alfredo Volpi, painter known for his signature Brazilian palette

pastoral idylls of the Dutch artist Frans Post (1612–80) and the formal portraits of the Frenchman Jean-Baptiste Debret (1768–1848).

The first painting to make use of Brazil's rich tropical light was *Caipira Picando Fumo* by José Ferraz de Almeida Júnior (1850–99). However, a truly Brazilian style emerged only in the 1920s with *antropofagismo*, a movement propagating "cultural cannibalism," which adapts ideas from European art and literature and reworks them in Brazilian terms. Tarsila do Amaral (1886–1973) produced the movement's most representative paintings, and was followed by Lasar Segall (1891–1957) and Anita Malfatti (1896–1964).

Other artists pursued Modernism according to their own ideas. Emiliano Di Cavalcanti (1897–1976) turned to the masses for inspiration, producing impressionistic, erotic icons of black Brazilian women. Candido Portinari (1903–62), with a far more obvious social conscience, produced *O Mestiço* that showed the dignity of Brazilian workers, while his *Os Retirantes* portrayed their misery. The sculptor Victor Brecheret (1894–1955) offered a Brazilian take on Art Deco, while Alfredo Volpi (1896–1988) brought Brazilian colors to abstract impressionism. São Paulo's large ethnic Japanese community continues to produce artists, such as Tomie Ohtake (b.1913), who pay Brazilian homage to the styles and techniques of Japan.

Brazil's contemporary art scene is lively and diverse. Most prominently, the works of photographer Sebastião Salgado (b.1944) are rooted in the ideas of Liberation Theology (*see p38*). Artist Siron Franco (b.1947) uses naive, surreal forms to highlight social and environmental issues.

Colonial Literature

European Jesuits are credited with the earliest writing to come out of Brazil. José Anchieta (1534–97) chronicled his work and described the evangelization of the indigenous people. The sermons of Antônio Vieira (1608–97) are fine examples of Portuguese prose.

Gregório de Matos (1623–96), who was born in Bahia, is sometimes cited as Brazil's first celebrated homegrown literary figure. During the 18th century, poetry academies in Minas Gerais were producing writers such as Cláudio Manuel da Costa (1729–89), José Basílio da Gama (1740–95), and Tomás Antônio Gonzaga (1744–1810). They introduced revolutionary French ideas to Brazil and wrote lyric and epic poems on Brazilian themes, but in a lofty European classical style.

Legendary mulatto writer, Joaquim Maria Machado de Assis

The Empire & the Republic

Brazil began to find its own voice in the last days of the Empire with the great 19th-century novelist, Joaquim Maria Machado de Assis (1839–1908), who was of mixed black and Portuguese ancestry. Starting out with traditional sentimental romances, he later became celebrated for his darkly humorous novels with their subversive social criticism. *Dom Casmurro* is considered by some to be the greatest Latin American novel of the 19th century. After independence in 1889, Machado de Assis's social criticisms were taken a step further by a generation of Republican novelists, influenced by scientific and nascent socialist ideas from Europe. In *Triste fim de Policarpo Quaresma*, the black novelist, Afonso Lima Barreto (1881–1922), was openly critical of the corruption that characterized the Republic. Euclides da Cunha's *Os Sertões* chronicled a gory and disastrous military campaign against a messianic rebel, Antônio Conselheiro *(see p210)*, and his bandit followers in the harsh landscape of the Bahian *sertão*.

Modernism in Literature

Modernism proper began in Brazil with Mário and Oswald de Andrade, who sought to articulate contemporary and uniquely Brazilian styles and themes. Mário (1893–1945) traveled throughout the country, searching for a unifying traditional culture which he enunciated in his comic rhapsody *Macunaíma*. Oswald (1890–1953), together with his wife Tarsila do Amaral, formulated the ideas behind the *antropofagismo cultural* movement. The de Andrades cleared the way for the Modernist poets Carlos Drummond (1902–87) and Manuel Bandeira (1886–1968), and the greatest of all Brazilian writers, João Guimarães Rosa (1908–67), whose grand metaphysical novel, *Grande Sertão: Veredas*, invented a new syntax based on the isolated idioms of the interior of Minas Gerais.

A string of writers, including Gilberto Freyre (1900–87), Sérgio Buarque de Holanda (1902–82), and Darcy Ribeiro (1922–97), emerged from the social sciences. The 20th century also produced major popular novelists, including Jorge Amado (1902–2001), Carolina Maria de Jesus (1914–77), and Clarice Lispector (1920–77). Vinícius de Moraes

Grande Sertão exhibition, Museum of Portuguese Language, São Paulo

(1913–80), a seminal figure in the contemporary Brazilian music scene, was the first to plough the furrow between music and literature by writing the lyrics of many famous songs. He has since been followed by songwriter Chico Buarque (b.1944), who wrote the novel *Budapest*.

Since 2000, writers from Brazil's manifold ethnic communities have risen to prominence. In *Relato de um Certo Oriente*, Milton Hatoum (b.1952) probes the psyche of an Arab immigrant, while Moacyr Scliar (b.1937) explores the Jewish-Brazilian experience in his writings.

Today, Brazilian fiction accounts for about half the literary output of Latin America. Writers include Paulo Coelho (b.1947), feminist novelists such as Conceição Evaristo (b.1946) and Lygia Fagundes Telles (b.1923), and Amazonian poet Aníbal Beça (b.1946).

Leading 20th-century novelist, Clarice Lispector

The Music of Brazil

The vibrant music of Brazil reflects the diversity of the cultural and ethnic backgrounds that make up the country's resident population. The music mirrors the influences of both the native and immigrant population. The rhythms of Africa are more often than not the base on which the harmonies and melodies introduced from Europe are built. Brazil is not about one musical style, but a varied selection. Internationally, *samba* and *bossa nova* are the best known of the country's musical styles, but regional forms, such as *frevo (see p221)*, *axé*, *forró (see p240)*, and *sertanejo (see p237)*, are just as popular within Brazil.

Heitor Villa-Lobos, one of Brazil's greatest classical composers

Samba

Derived from Angolan religious rhythms, samba has permeated virtually every other Brazilian musical form that followed it. Historically strong in Rio, São Paulo, and Bahia, samba made a remarkable impact throughout the country in the 1930s. Samba comes in many forms, and most of these have a link to dance.

Zeca Pagodinho, who emerged in the late 1980s, is one of the most popular and best-selling *samba* stars.

Clara Nunes was one of the most prolific and popular *samba* singers of all time. Her career was tragically cut short when she died at the age of 39 in 1983.

Gilberto Gil went from Brazilian superstar to political exile before becoming Minister of Culture in 2003. He remains an active musical force.

Bossa nova

Bossa nova, a marriage of Brazilian rhythms and American jazz, has been the most exportable form of Brazilian music since international audiences first discovered it through an album, Getz/Gilberto, recorded by Stan Getz and João Gilberto in 1964. The album included a number of compositions from a young and unknown composer from Rio, Antônio Carlos ("Tom") Jobim. Gilberto, Jobim, and Jobim's lyricist, Vinícius de Moraes, were to become the "Holy Trinity" of bossa nova.

Antônio Carlos Jobim was responsible for many of the *bossa nova* classics including "The Girl From Ipanema," one of the most played and recorded songs in popular music history.

Sergio Mendes and his group, Brasil '66, helped launch *bossa nova* globally in the 1960s. They have recorded with acts such as Black Eyed Peas, Erykah Badu, and Justin Timberlake.

Céu's albums have garnered praise from both national and international critics since the late 2000s and have earned a series of awards, including two Latin Grammys.

Caetano Veloso helped launch the *tropicalismo* movement in 1967, and is considered a Brazilian musical treasure.

Chico Buarque is a composer, lyricist, performer, and author. He is as popular today as when he first performed in 1964.

Tropicalismo & Música Popular Brasileira

Tropicalismo *was a form of Brazilian music that arose in the late 1960s from a mix of* bossa nova, *rock and roll, Bahia folk, and African music. Many* tropicalismo *artists, led by Caetano Veloso and Gilberto Gil, were driven by political activism following the coup of 1964. Inspired in part by* tropicalismo, *música popular Brasileira (MPB), or popular Brazilian music, includes many Brazilian musical styles and is the most popular music played on the radio and in the clubs and bars of Brazil.*

Daniela Mercury burst on to Bahia's *axé* and reggae music scene in the 1990s. Her explosive live performances have won her a growing international following.

Regional Music

Although MPB covers a multitude of Brazilian musical genres, there are a number of distinctive regional styles that include axé, choro, forró, frevo, *and* pagode. *Bahia, one of the powerhouses of regional Brazilian music, has its own versions of jazz, reggae, hip-hop, soul, funk, rock and roll, heavy metal, electronica, and the popular homegrown country and western style known as* sertanejo.

Carlinhos Brown, a prolific performer, composer, drummer, and dancer, is equally popular as a solo artist or when collaborating with others.

The São Paulo Scene

São Paulo has produced some of Brazil's most creative and politically acute musicians. Since the late 2000s, several Paulistano singers and songwriters have been revolutionizing Brazilian music by blending afrobeat with other genres such as pop, hip-hop, jazz, techno, and punk. Metá Metá, Criolo, Liniker, and Tássia Reis are some of the most notable artists. Their creative influence has reached worldwide acclaim with Elza Soares, whose album *A Mulher do Fim do Mundo (The Woman at the End of the World)* made it to *The New York Times'* list of the ten best albums of 2016.

Elza Soares performing her contemporary style of Samba

Religions of Brazil

Few countries in the world can match Brazil for religious diversity. A typical São Paulo or Rio neighborhood will be home to Catholic and Evangelical Protestant churches, Buddhist temples, synagogues, mosques, Spiritist churches, Afro-Brazilian ceremonial centers, as well as a range of smaller religious institutions. Evangelical Protestantism is the fastest growing religion. The 21st century has seen an increase in secularism, though this remains very much in the minority; those who believe in nothing are still largely looked upon with a mixture of incredulity and pity.

Igreja Nossa Senhora do Rosário dos Pretos in São Paulo

Catholicism

Catholicism arrived with the Portuguese, and Catholics remain Brazil's dominant religious group. Brazil has the largest number of Catholics of any country in the world.

From its earliest days, the Church in Brazil, as in most colonies, was divided into an establishment linked to the Crown (and later to the Emperor and the Republican State) and factions who campaigned on behalf of the oppressed. One of these factions was the Jesuits who, while treating the indigenous people as objects of pro-selytization, nonetheless fought doggedly against their enslavement and murder by the *bandeirantes* and other settlers. The Jesuits began to be seen as a threat to the Portuguese Crown and were expelled from the colonies in 1757.

The Church establishment in Brazil did little to criticize the treatment of the indigenous people, or the slaves from Africa who replaced them. Churches were divided along strict social and racial lines. The poorest churches were reserved for Afro-Brazilian slaves and were often dedicated to the black Madonna, Nossa Senhora do Rosário dos Pretos.

Latin American churches were instrumental in influencing Pope John XXIII and Pope Paul VI's groundbreaking Church reforms of the mid-1960s, known as Vatican II, and promoting a more egalitarian Catholic Church throughout the world. Vatican II led to the most important movement in the Catholic Church in the 20th century, Liberation Theology.

Churches in Brazil today are largely apolitical and gregarious, and are increasingly influenced by Evangelical preaching and musical styles.

Evangelical Protestants at Igreja Universal do Reino, São Paulo

Evangelical Protestantism

The Evangelical movement emphasizes the Protestant beliefs in the authority of the Bible and of every person's right to interpret the Scriptures for themselves. Services are emotive, with pastors making use of fiery language, and often strongly encouraging their congregation to donate a *dízimo* (usually 10 percent of any monthly salary) to the Church. The movement has been widely criticized.

Leonardo Boff presiding over a service

Liberation Theology

In the 1970s, groups of Latin American Catholic thinkers preached what they called "a preferential option for the poor." In Brazil they were led by Leonardo Boff, Hélder Câmara, and Pedro Casaldáliga. They campaigned against the rich establishment and the dictatorships. Many of the priests involved were murdered or tortured and the movement was suppressed by the established Church.

Nonetheless, Evangelicalism is very popular in Brazil, so much so that in 2016, Rio elected Marcelo Crivella, a bishop of an international Evangelical church, as its mayor.

Spiritism

Developed by the Frenchman Allan Kardec, Spiritism is a systematization of divergent 19th-century occult practices dealing with communication with the spirits of the dead. Kardec called Spiritism "a science which deals with the nature, origin, and destiny of Spirits, as well as their relationship with the corporeal world." Brazil has the largest number of Kardecian Spiritists of any country in the world.

Chagdud Khadro Ling temple in Tres Coroàs, Rio Grande do Sul

Buddhism & Other Asian Religions

The largest population of ethnic Japanese in Latin America and immigrants from many other East Asian countries live in Brazil. Consequently, there are large communities of Nichiren Daishonin Mahayana Buddhists in the country. Their beliefs are based on the teachings of a 13th-century Japanese monk who stressed the need to elevate one's state of life from being trapped within the limits of desires and instincts. The method for achieving this is through strong ethical practice and the chanting of the Nam-Myoho-Renge-Kyo mantra. The movement has proved especially successful at bridging Brazil's trenchant class divide. Yoga and Krishna

Consciousness are also popular in Brazil, though often as alternative lifestyle options.

Afro-Brazilian Religions

West African religions came to Brazil with slaves and developed into religions, such as Candomblé *(see p181)*, Batuque, and Umbanda. Worship involves the invocation of *orixás* – spirits who intervene between humans and Olorun, the supreme creator. The Brazilian government legalized their practice in the mid-19th century, but followers of these religions are still sometimes discriminated against and persecuted by the Church.

Indigenous Religions

Brazil is home to hundreds of different indigenous belief systems. These can all be loosely banded together as shamanism, which is not so much a religion as a distinct way of understanding reality. Rather than believing that we are made of material, indigenous peoples believe that material, time, and space itself are mere manifestations of a far deeper reality. Spiritual life is organized in harmony with this inner state by a shaman. A number of popular religious movements have grown up in Brazil from indigenous roots. The most widely practiced is Santo Daime, which makes use of Amazonian psychotropic plants to achieve a state of super-consciousness.

Al Iman Ali Ibn Abi Taleb mosque in Curitiba

Islam

Brazil has the largest Islamic community in Latin America, but Islamic fundamentalism is almost unknown. The community is private, conservative, and is generally more concerned with preserving links to Lebanese and Syrian culture and the Arabic language than it is with proselytizing. The community has produced numerous prolific writers and politicians.

Judaism

Brazil's Jewish community has about 150,000 members, most of whom are concentrated in São Paulo (which has the largest Ashkenazi synagogue on the continent), Recife, and Rio de Janeiro. Many are descended from the Jews who fled Europe in the 1930s. The community is active in political and cultural life. The writer Moacyr Scliar is one of the country's successful literary exports.

Santo Daime followers in Visconde de Mauá, Rio de Janeiro

Soccer in Brazil

In the first half of the 20th century, soccer went from being the private sport of Brazil's white European elite to becoming the greatest symbol of nationhood. The game united all sections of the population and, after the national team's first World Cup victory in 1958, brought about unprecedented national pride. The Brazilian way of playing *futebol* – with more emphasis on attacking, dribbling, and acrobatic ball skills – has become a benchmark for excellence, and is also known as *jogo bonito*, or "the beautiful game."

In a favela, the main leisure activity for children is always soccer. Rough terrain helps them develop trademark ball skills such as the dribble.

Charles Miller is the father of Brazilian soccer. In 1894, returning to the country after attending boarding school in Southampton, UK, he brought two footballs, a pump, and a rule book. The first reported game took place a few months later.

The 1938 national soccer team received a joyous welcome on their return home from France. Brazil, which came third after defeating Czechoslovakia, had also won the hearts of the Europeans.

The 1950 World Cup was hosted in Brazil. In the final game, favorites Brazil only needed a draw against Uruguay to win the tournament. However, they lost 2–1 in front of a record 200,000 crowd, causing the greatest moment of collective sporting tragedy in the country's history. The 7–1 defeat to Germany in the 2014 semi-finals comes a close second.

The National Side

With their iconic yellow shirts, the Brazilian national team, known as the Seleção, or Selection, is the most glamorous soccer team in the world. It is the only team to have taken part in every World Cup and have won it more times than anyone – in 1958, 1962, 1970, 1994, and 2002.

Brazilian Greats

Brazil has produced more soccer legends than any other country and also the greatest player of all time: Pelé (see p172). The first great player was Artur Friedenreich in the 1910s. Each generation reveals new stars and the soccer factory shows no signs of stopping. Since the inauguration of FIFA's (Fédération Internationale de Football Association) World Player of the Year award in 1991, only Brazil has won it with more than one player: Romário (1994), Ronaldo (1996, 1997, 2002), Rivaldo (1999), and Ronaldinho (2004, 2005).

Leônidas da Silva, also called "Rubber Man" for his elasticity, was the highest scorer in the 1938 World Cup.

Garrincha, the "Little Bird," was born with bent legs and is considered to be the finest dribbler of all time.

The Dream Team of 1970 is considered the best soccer team of all time. Their 4–1 victory against Italy won them the World Cup for the third time.

The torcidas, or soccer fans, have adapted aspects of Carnaval to *futebol*, playing lively music at stadia, dressing up in team colors, and bringing noisemakers, colorful banners, and flags.

Major Teams & Stadia

There are several hundred professional clubs in Brazil. The number is impossible to calculate, since local leagues are constantly changing and teams shutting down and starting up. Brazil's best-known stadia are the Maracanã *(see p88)* in Rio, which was built for the 1950 World Cup, and the Morumbi in São Paulo.

Estádio do Maracanã in Rio de Janeiro, one of the largest soccer stadia in the world

Brazil's Biggest Clubs & Stadia

 Sociedade Esportiva Palmeiras (1914)
Stadium: Allianz Parque, São Paulo
Capacity: 48,000

 Cruzeiro Esporte Clube (1921)
Stadium: Mineirão, Belo Horizonte, Minas Gerais
Capacity: 61,846

 Clube de Regatas do Flamengo (1895)
Stadium: Gávea/Maracanã, Rio de Janeiro
Capacity: 15,000 (Gávea)/78,838 (Maracanã)

 Fluminense Football Club (1902)
Stadium: Maracanã, Rio de Janeiro
Capacity: 78,838

 Grêmio Foot-Ball Porto Alegrense (1903)
Stadium: Arena do Grêmio
Capacity: 60,540

 São Paulo Futebol Clube (1930)
Stadium: Morumbi, São Paulo
Capacity: 72,000

 Sport Club Corinthians Paulista (1910)
Stadium: Parque São Jorge/Pacaembu, São Paulo.
Capacity: 18,500 (P. São Jorge)/40,199 (Pacaembu)

 Club de Regatas Vasco da Gama (1898)
Stadium: São Januário, Rio de Janeiro.
Capacity: 21,880

Pelé was a World Cup champion at 17, and scored a record-breaking 1,283 goals in 1,367 games.

Sócrates, the 1982 and 1986 World Cup captain, was famous for his back heels and his political beliefs.

Romário, the "Baixinho" (Shorty), was the star player in the 1994 World Cup, won by Brazil.

Ronaldo, with two World Cup winner's medals, broke the competition's goal-scoring record in 2006.

Brazilian Beach Culture

The beach represents a big playground for Brazilians. People living near Brazil's extensive coastline go to the beach daily to socialize and to eat and drink, while vacationers can spend all day near the sand and warm water. Brazilian music plays nonstop at the local beach stalls and, as dusk falls, beachgoers party long into the night. It is a Brazilian tradition to play soccer, beach volleyball, and footvolley, or go for a walk or bike ride along the beach or promenades. At some resorts, visitors can rent a horse or a beach buggy, or practice surfing, kayaking, paragliding, and *skibunda* (sandboarding).

Surfer at Praia Joaquina, Ilha de Santa Catarina

Urban Beaches are popular for their promenades and cycle lanes, where people go to exercise before or after work. Some beaches offer good facilities with bathrooms, showers, and gym equipment, and are illuminated at night for playing sports such as soccer and footvolley.

Colorful Food Stalls selling *coalho* cheese, corn-on-the-cob, peanuts, and shrimp sticks line the beaches. Popular local drinks include fresh coconut water, cold beer, and *caipirinha*.

Brazil's Beaches can vary from calm bays to unspoiled, wild beaches accessed only by tracks through the forest. There are also exclusive resort beaches with aquatic parks and modern facilities.

Beach sports are very popular. Besides soccer and volleyball, people play *frescobol* (a kind of tennis). Some beaches also offer paragliding and delta-wings during holidays.

Umbrellas in bright colors are rented for a small amount or lent by the food stalls to their patrons.

The *canga*, a Brazilian sarong, is worn to and from the beach, and also used as a towel to lie on.

Watersports, such as surfing, windsurfing, kayaking, scuba diving, and snorkeling, are popular throughout the year. All equipment can be easily rented at the beach.

Beach safety is monitored by lifeguards on buggies during holidays and at weekends. Flags offer advice on currents and deep water. Asking locals may be useful if there is no patrol.

Locals on the Beach

Relaxed and spontaneous by nature, Brazilians carry only the bare essentials with them to be free to walk, swim, play, or just lie on a canga *to tan and watch the world go by.*

Beach fashion for women popularly features tiny bikinis that ensure the smallest tan line. The men, on the other hand, can be seen wearing swimming trunks under informal shorts.

Beach parties, or *luaus* (moon parties), are kept alive all night by typical Brazilian dance music such as *forró (see p240)* or *axé*. Electronic music and live concerts are also played at these parties.

BRAZIL THROUGH THE YEAR

Brazilians are a fun-loving people. In this unique land of diverse ethnic groups and races, there is a colorful and vibrant culture, which is celebrated in the numerous parties, carnivals, festivals, rallies, and parades held through the year, but particularly in summer. The most significant events include the spectacular Carnaval and a series of popular religious festivals related to Catholicism and a combination of syncretic traditions. The climate varies, but on average it stays warm, making it favorable to outdoor celebrations. The seasons are not so perceptible, except in Southern and Southeastern Brazil where temperatures are moderate in autumn and spring and dip sharply in winter.

Spring

As flowers begin to decorate the landscape, Brazil prepares to display its wealth of spring flowers and gears up for festivities that last through the season. The most remarkable spring celebrations are related to the Catholic religion, but the highly charged Brazilian Grand Prix also generates great excitement.

September

Expoflora (*Sep weekends*), Holambra (São Paulo state). More than 1,000 species of flora are for sale. Dutch folk dances, music, and Dutch and Brazilian food are also featured, emphasizing the town's Dutch character.

International Fishing Festival (*2nd fortnight, but sometimes held in June*), Cáceres (Mato Grosso). Listed by the *Guinness World Records* as the biggest fishing tournament in the world, the angling event attracts more than 1,500 competitors.

October

São Paulo International Film Festival (*2nd fortnight*), São Paulo. Lasting two weeks, the festival screens around 350 critically acclaimed films from more than 50 countries.

São Paulo Art Biennial (*Oct–Dec, even years*), São Paulo. The Parque do Ibirapuera is the site of an amazing display of modern visual art.

Círio de Nazaré (*2nd Sun*), Belém. Our Lady of Nazareth procession follows the Romaria fluvial pilgrimage a day earlier.

Oktoberfest (*mid-Oct*), Blumenau (Santa Catarina). A lively street party, second only to Munich's, celebrates German music, beer, and way of life.

Brazilian Formula 1 Grand Prix (*late Oct*), São Paulo. Organized at Interlagos Circuit, the race is usually the final round of the Formula 1 season.

Recifolia (*last week*), Recife. A lively carnival with crowds dancing the whole week to Bahian bands.

Paying homage at Padre Cícero's towering statue, Juazeiro do Norte

November

Padre Cícero Pilgrimage (*Nov 2*), Juazeiro do Norte (Paraíba). On Dia de Finados (All Souls' Day), thousands of pilgrims visit patron saint Padre Cícero's statue and the church where he is buried.

National Handicraft Fair (*late Nov/early Dec*), Belo Horizonte. A major exhibition and sale of handicrafts from all over Brazil. There are interactive workshops where many of the crafts can be learnt.

Smoke rising from the wheels of a Ferrari competing in the Brazilian Grand Prix, São Paulo

A spectacular display of Reveillon fireworks on Copacabana beach

Summer

Summer is the most important time of the year for Brazilians. It marks the beginning of the year and vacation time. It rains heavily in most parts, but the sun continues to shine through. Besides a number of outdoor events to mark the advent of summer, there are trade fairs and important religious festivals. The culmination of the summer is Carnaval.

December

Festa Santa Bárbara (*Dec 4*), Salvador. A popular three-day Candomblé ceremony at Fonte de Santa Bárbara. The image of Santa Bárbara, syncretized in Candomblé with Yansã or Oyá, is carried through the streets of the historic center.

Carnatal (*early Dec*), Natal. Out-of-season Carnaval, where famous bands test their repertoire for the next Carnaval, with throngs of people singing and dancing through the streets.

São Silvestre Race (*Dec 31*), São Paulo. Amateur and recreational runners join professional athletes for a 9-mile (15-km) race through the streets of São Paulo.

Reveillon at Copacabana (*Dec 31*), Rio de Janeiro. A New Year's Eve party along Copacabana beach with performances by leading pop stars and a lavish midnight fireworks display at Forte de Copacabana and Windsor Atlântica Hotel.

January

Processão dos Navegantes (*Jan 1*), Angra dos Reis. A *samba* school percussion group parade across the Baia de Ilha Grande in boats of different shapes and sizes.

Processão do Bom Jesus dos Navegantes (*Jan 1*), Salvador. Hundreds of fishing boats follow a galliot, a long ship, that carries the image of Our Lord of Navigators.

Lavagem do Bonfim (*2nd Thu*), Salvador. A colorful parade and ceremonial washing (*lavagem*) of the steps of the Igreja de Nossa Senhora do Bonfim.

Fest Verão Paraíba (*early–mid-Jan*), João Pessoa. Taking place over three weeks, this is one of the country's largest music festivals, with big Brazilian acts.

Festas dos Ticumbi & Alardo (*Jan 19 & 20*), Itaúnas. People in colorful clothes pay homage to São Bento and São Sebastião to the strains of traditional music.

Pré Cajú (*end Jan*), Aracaju. One of the dozens of *micaretas* (out-of-season Carnaval) before the real Carnaval in February/March.

Festa de São Lázaro (*last Sun*), Salvador. A festival in honor of Candomblé deity Omolu, the God of Plague.

February

Pescadores do Rio Vermelho (*Feb 2*), Salvador. A procession of boats carrying offerings to Yemanjá, the Goddess of the Sea, accompanied by Afro-Brazilian music.

Nossa Senhora dos Navegantes (*Feb 2*), Porto Alegre. A boat procession on the Rio Guaíba carrying the image of Yemanjá.

Carnaval (*Feb/Mar, about 40 days before Easter*). The most famous Carnaval takes place in the city of Rio de Janeiro. Salvador and Olinda also have fantastic celebrations.

Festa Nacional da Uva (*Feb/Mar, biennial, even years*), Caxias do Sul. Wine production is the highlight of this festival that keeps alive the customs and traditions of the early Italian immigrants.

Carnaval performers in striking costumes, Rio de Janeiro City

Hooded torchbearers at the Procissão do Fogaréu, Cidade de Goiás

Autumn

In Southern Brazil and the Southeast, the autumn season is marked by steady breezes and comfortable temperatures. Religious festivals, such as the Semana Santa and Festa do Divino Espírito Santo, are celebrated with great involvement. The Hot-Air Balloon Festival is an additional attraction.

March
International Book Biennial (*Mar/Apr*), São Paulo (even years) and Rio de Janeiro (odd years). A 10-day fair marked by book launches, interactive author sessions, lectures, and cultural performances.
Semana Santa (*Mar/Apr*), across Pernambuco & Minas Gerais. In Nova Jerusalém, the play *Paixão de Cristo* (Passion of Christ) is staged with over 500 professional actors; the audience also participates. In the historic towns of Minas Gerais, crowds accompany the religious processions.
São Paulo Fashion Week (*late Mar/early Apr*), São Paulo. Fashion shows featuring top Brazilian models and fashion designers are held *(see p149)*. It also takes place in January.

April
Procissão do Fogaréu (*Wed before Good Friday*), Cidade de Goiás. The city glows with lights and the streets blaze with torches during the solemn procession of the Semana Santa, when the burial of Christ and the Resurrection are re-enacted to the sound of tambours.

Festa Nacional da Maçã (*Apr/May*), São Joaquim (Santa Catarina). Exhibitions, musical shows, and German folk performances, as well as bestowing of the "best apple producer" title.
Hot-Air Balloon Festival (*Easter week*), Torres. A spectacular annual hot-air balloon event that ahs been held since 1989. Other attractions include a parachute display and rodeo competition.

May
Festa do Bembé do Mercado (*approx May 13*), Santo Amaro. The festival marks the abolition of slavery in 1889. Traditional Bahian music and dance performances also take place.
Festa do Divino Espírito Santo (*May/Jun, 45 days after Easter*), Pirenópolis & Alcântara. Mock battles between Moors and Christians are enacted. Forró and *sertanejo* parties are held.

Winter

With cooler climatic conditions, the southern and southeastern regions are attractive to visitors. Across Brazil, the festivities begin in June, paving the way for international music and art festivals that are a huge draw. The GLBT (Gay, Lesbian, Bisexual, and Transgender) Parade is also significant.

Women in traditional dresses performing *samba-da-roda* at the Festa do Bembé do Mercado, Santo Amaro

Elaborate headgears for the Festa do Bumba-meu-boi, São Luís

Public Holidays

New Year's Day (Jan 1)

Carnaval (Tue, 40 days before Easter)

Good Friday (Mar/Apr)

Easter Sunday (Mar/Apr)

Tiradentes Day (Apr 21)

Labor Day (May 1)

Corpus Christi (Jun)

Independence Day (Sept 7)

Our Lady of Aparecida Day (Oct 12)

All Souls' Day (Nov 2)

The Republic Proclamation Day (Nov 15)

Christmas Day (Dec 25)

June

Festas Juninas (*weekends through June*), across Southeast Brazil. Homage is offered to St. Antony (Jun 13), St. John (Jun 24), and St. Peter (Jun 29). The festivities that take place at the *arraiá* (imitations of old country villas) are marked by traditional feasting.

Festa do Pinhão (*early Jun*), Lages (Santa Catarina). Celebrating the edible *pinhão* (seed of the Paraná pine), the festival includes lively music performances.

LGBT Parade (*early Jun*), São Paulo. Organized since 1997, the parade is one of the biggest events of its kind in the world.

Festa do Bumba-meu-boi (*whole month*), São Luís. Improvised songs and dances by skilled performers tell the story of the death and resurrection of a bull.

Festa do Boi Bumbá (*Jun 28–30*), Parintins. In Amazonas, Bumba-meu-boi is known as Boi Bumbá. Two groups, Caprichoso (in blue) and Garantido (in red), compete inside a *bumbódromo* built to hold 35,000 spectators.

São João (*Jun/Jul*), Caruaru & Campina Grande. Forró is the predominant rhythm at the dance festival, which draws many leading performers.

International Puppet Theater Festival (*Jun/Oct*), Canela. Puppeteers perform in theaters, schools, and streets over four days.

Rally dos Sertões (*late Jun*), across Brazil. A 10-day event, when cars, truck pilots, and motorcycles drive 2,796 miles (4,500 km) through Brazil's rough interior.

July

Festival de Inverno (*Jul 1–30*), Campos do Jordão (São Paulo). Begun in 1990, this is the greatest festival of classical music in Latin America.

Festival Internacional da Dança (*2nd fortnight*), Joinville (Santa Catarina). Dance performances, workshops, and competitions take place at one of the world's largest dance festivals, featuring dance forms ranging from jazz and folk to classical ballet.

Ilhabela Sailing Week (*date varies*), Ilhabela. Known as the sailing capital, the island is famed for competitive races and regattas, organized by the Yacht Club de Ilhabela.

Fortal (*last week*), Fortaleza. The country's biggest *micareta*, held at Cidade Fortal, draws crowds with *axé* music and small schools of *samba*.

August

Festa da Nossa Senhora das Neves (*Aug 5*), João Pessoa. Street celebrations for 10 days to mark the day of the city's patroness, Our Lady of the Snow. The rhythm of *frevo* defines the mood.

Festival de Gramado (*2nd week*), Gramado. The most important film awards event in Brazil offers viewers the best in Brazilian and Latin American cinema.

Festa Literária Internacional de Paraty (FLIP) (*early Aug*), Paraty. An acclaimed literary gathering of Brazilian and international writers. Literary reunions, plays, lectures, and concerts feature on the versatile program list.

Festa do Peão de Boiadeiro (*beginning on the 3rd Thu*), Barretos (São Paulo state). The world's largest 10-day rodeo event receiving almost one million visitors every year. Concerts and food fairs.

Pinga Festival (*3rd weekend*), Paraty. Local *cachaça* samplings (*see p383*), also known as *pinga*, musical shows, and food stalls offering regional delicacies.

International Festival of Culture and Gastronomy (*date varies*), Tiradentes. A 10-day international gastronomic event with workshops and exhibitions in restaurants or at public squares all over the town.

Taking the bull by the horns, Festa do Peão de Boiadeiro, Barretos

The Climate of Brazil

Brazil's climate, divided into four broad zones, varies greatly from region to region. Amazônia is hot and humid all year round, though parts experience a distinct dry season from July to October. The central band of the country is also humid, with a marked dry season, while the coastal areas enjoy pleasant tropical breezes and short seasonal downpours. High temperatures and infrequent rainfall characterize the semi-arid desert in the Northeast. In Southern Brazil, cool, wet winters contrast with humid summers. Most of Brazil can be visited at any time of the year, with the exception of the wetlands of the Pantanal during the rainy season, and the extreme south of the country during winter, when it can get very cold.

Manaus and central Amazônia are constantly humid, but experience a distinct dry season from July to October.

Boa Vista

Novo Airão

Parintins • Sar

Manaus

• Tefé

Porto Velho

Rio Branco

Alta Floresta

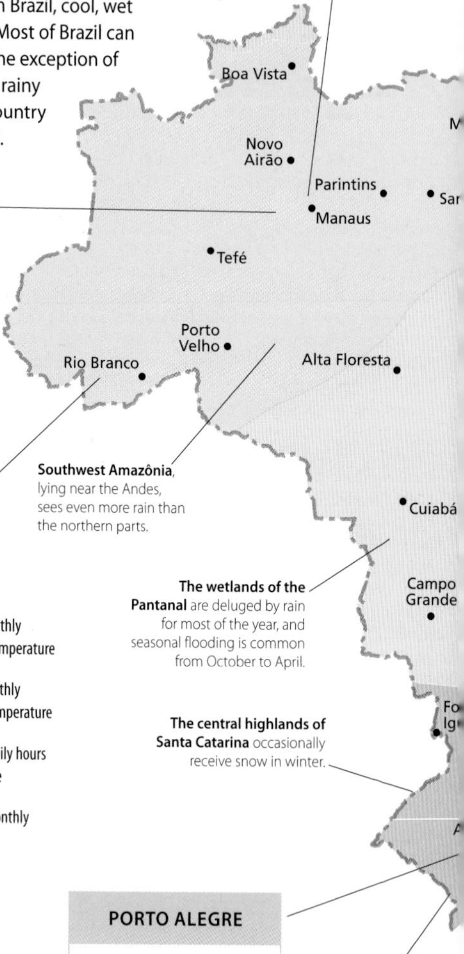

Southwest Amazônia, lying near the Andes, sees even more rain than the northern parts.

• Cuiabá

Campo Grande

The wetlands of the Pantanal are deluged by rain for most of the year, and seasonal flooding is common from October to April.

The central highlands of Santa Catarina occasionally receive snow in winter.

The lowest temperatures are in the far south of the country, where winters are cold, windy, and rainy.

MANAUS

°C/F			
30/85	**32**/89	**33**/91	**31**/88
23/73	**23**/73	**24**/75	**24**/75
4 hrs	8 hrs	7 hrs	4 hrs
8/203 in/mm	2/51 in/mm	4/102 in/mm	10/254 in/mm
month **Apr**	**Jul**	**Oct**	**Jan**

RIO BRANCO

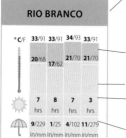

°C/F			
33/91	**33**/91	**34**/93	**33**/91
20/68	**17**/62	**21**/70	**21**/70
7 hrs	8 hrs	7 hrs	3 hrs
9/229 in/mm	1/25 in/mm	4/102 in/mm	11/279 in/mm
month **Apr**	**Jul**	**Oct**	**Jan**

Average monthly maximum temperature

Average monthly minimum temperature

Average daily hours of sunshine

Average monthly rainfall

Climate Zones

- Humid: Heavy rainfall, high humidity.
- Tropical: Distinct hot humid and cold dry seasons.
- Semi-arid: Hot weather conditions, scanty rainfall.
- Humid subtropical: Cold winter, year-round rainfall.

0 kilometers   500

0 miles   500

PORTO ALEGRE

°C/F			
	25/77	**24**/75	**31**/88
16/61	**20**/68	**21**/70	**21**/70
		15/59	
	10/50		
6 hrs	5 hrs	7 hrs	8 hrs
4/102 in/mm	4/102 in/mm	3/76 in/mm	11/279 in/mm
month **Apr**	**Jul**	**Oct**	**Jan**

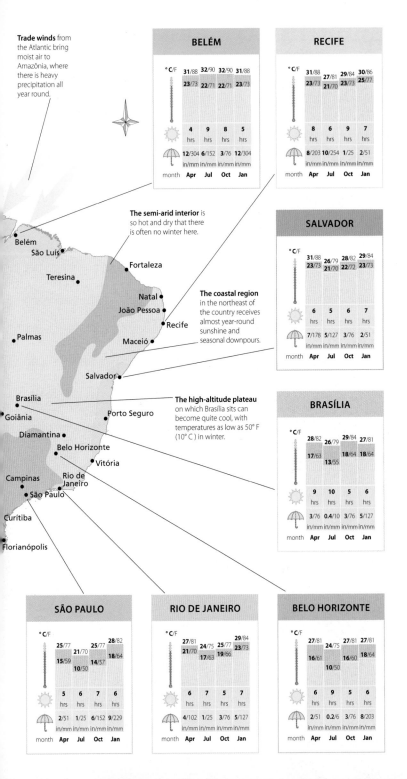

Trade winds from the Atlantic bring moist air to Amazônia, where there is heavy precipitation all year round.

BELÉM

°C/F				
	31/88	**32**/90	**32**/90	**31**/88
	23/73	**22**/71	**22**/71	**23**/73
	4 hrs	9 hrs	8 hrs	5 hrs
	12/304	**6**/152	**3**/76	**12**/304
	in/mm	in/mm	in/mm	in/mm
month	**Apr**	**Jul**	**Oct**	**Jan**

RECIFE

°C/F				
	31/88	**27**/81	**29**/84	**30**/86
	23/73	**21**/70	**23**/73	**25**/77
	8 hrs	6 hrs	9 hrs	7 hrs
	8/203	**10**/254	**1**/25	**2**/51
	in/mm	in/mm	in/mm	in/mm
month	**Apr**	**Jul**	**Oct**	**Jan**

The semi-arid interior is so hot and dry that there is often no winter here.

- Belém
- São Luís
- Fortaleza
- Teresina
- Natal
- João Pessoa
- Recife
- Palmas
- Maceió
- Salvador
- Brasília
- Porto Seguro
- Goiânia
- Diamantina
- Belo Horizonte
- Vitória
- Campinas
- Rio de Janeiro
- São Paulo
- Curitiba
- Florianópolis

The coastal region in the northeast of the country receives almost year-round sunshine and seasonal downpours.

SALVADOR

°C/F				
	31/88	**26**/79	**28**/82	**29**/84
	23/73	**21**/70	**22**/72	**23**/73
	6 hrs	5 hrs	6 hrs	7 hrs
	7/178	**5**/127	**3**/76	**2**/51
	in/mm	in/mm	in/mm	in/mm
month	**Apr**	**Jul**	**Oct**	**Jan**

The high-altitude plateau on which Brasília sits can become quite cool, with temperatures as low as 50° F (10° C) in winter.

BRASÍLIA

°C/F				
	28/82	**26**/79	**29**/84	**27**/81
	17/63	**13**/55	**18**/64	**18**/64
	9 hrs	10 hrs	5 hrs	6 hrs
	3/76	**0.4**/10	**3**/76	**5**/127
	in/mm	in/mm	in/mm	in/mm
month	**Apr**	**Jul**	**Oct**	**Jan**

SÃO PAULO

°C/F				
	25/77	**21**/70	**25**/77	**28**/82
	15/59	**10**/50	**14**/57	**18**/64
	5 hrs	6 hrs	7 hrs	6 hrs
	2/51	**1**/25	**6**/152	**9**/229
	in/mm	in/mm	in/mm	in/mm
month	**Apr**	**Jul**	**Oct**	**Jan**

RIO DE JANEIRO

°C/F				
	27/81	**24**/75	**25**/77	**29**/84
	21/70	**17**/63	**19**/66	**23**/73
	6 hrs	7 hrs	5 hrs	7 hrs
	4/102	**1**/25	**3**/76	**5**/127
	in/mm	in/mm	in/mm	in/mm
month	**Apr**	**Jul**	**Oct**	**Jan**

BELO HORIZONTE

°C/F				
	27/81	**24**/75	**27**/81	**27**/81
	16/61	**10**/50	**16**/60	**18**/64
	6 hrs	9 hrs	5 hrs	6 hrs
	2/51	**0.2**/6	**3**/76	**8**/203
	in/mm	in/mm	in/mm	in/mm
month	**Apr**	**Jul**	**Oct**	**Jan**

THE HISTORY OF BRAZIL

Very little is known about the history of Brazil before 1500, when Europeans first traveled there. Archaeological remains, which consist mainly of pottery, suggest a number of complex societies that were in existence long before the colonialists arrived. After more than 300 years of Portuguese colonization, Brazil became a republic in 1889. Long periods of totalitarian rule finally led to the return of democracy in 1989. Democracy, however, has always been hard to maintain, and Brazil's history has been pervaded by coups d'état and dictatorships.

For over a millennium, before the Europeans arrived in Brazil, Amazônia had a vast network of sophisticated societies with populations of up to 100,000. The abundance of fish in the Amazon river and its tributaries was almost certainly one of the main reasons for the wealth and rapid growth of cultures in Amazônia.

Up until the beginning of the 16th century, the middle Amazon region around Santarém was an important center for ceramic art and trading. It was home to thousands of semi-settled indigenous people who grew maize and cassava, and had access to plentiful fish. Living on higher land, up above the flood plain, as well as in longhouses along riverbanks, they left important ceramic remains. Archaeological evidence from the earth mounds near Santarém and also on the Ilha de Marajó (*see p274*) suggests that some of the shell mounds were part of these complex fishing societies. The most widespread of the 1,000 semi-nomadic indigenous peoples that inhabited the territory at the time of the European conquest were the Tupi-Guaraní Indians. While they lived off slash-and-burn farming, the Tupinambá, another large group, cultivated crops, primarily maize.

European Discovery

The coastline was widely inhabited when Spanish explorer Vicente Yáñez Pinzón disembarked on the northeastern shore in Pernambuco, on January 26, 1500. He could not claim the newfound land for Spain, as he was officially limited by the Tordesillas meridian. The Treaty of Tordesillas, signed in 1494 between Spain and Portugal, determined that all lands discovered west of a meridian located 3 miles (5 km) west of the Cape Verde Islands would belong to Spain, and those to the east of this line could be claimed by Portugal. On April 23, 1500, Pedro Álvares Cabral landed in southern Bahia, marking the Portuguese arrival in Brazil. Portugal, which already controlled the Indian Ocean and the spice trade, bolstered its position as a mercantile power rivaled only by Spain.

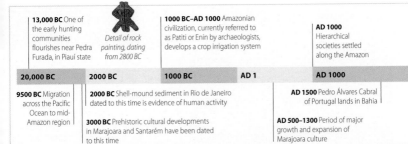

13,000 BC One of the early hunting communities flourishes near Pedra Furada, in Piauí state	*Detail of rock painting, dating from 2800 BC*	**1000 BC–AD 1000** Amazonian civilization, currently referred to as Patiti or Enin by archaeologists, develops a crop irrigation system		**AD 1000** Hierarchical societies settled along the Amazon
20,000 BC	**2000 BC**	**1000 BC**	**AD 1**	**AD 1000**
9500 BC Migration across the Pacific Ocean to mid-Amazon region	**2000 BC** Shell-mound sediment in Rio de Janeiro dated to this time is evidence of human activity			**AD 1500** Pedro Álvares Cabral of Portugal lands in Bahia
	3000 BC Prehistoric cultural developments in Marajoara and Santarém have been dated to this time			**AD 500–1300** Period of major growth and expansion of Marajoara culture

◀ Detail of a meeting of Portuguese sailors and natives of Brazil, a 1592 line engraving by Theodor de Bry

The Portuguese Conquest

When the Portuguese reached Brazil in 1500, their period of maritime expansion was at its peak. In 1501, Emperor Manuel I ordered Amerigo Vespucci to explore the new territory further, leading to the settlement of Guanabara Bay (Rio de Janeiro). In 1530, an expedition led by Martim Alfonso de Sousa resulted in the first colonial towns – São Vicente and São Paulo. Preoccupied with Africa and the Far East, Portugal neglected Brazil until 1532, when João III divided the land into 15 captaincies. The early settlers mainly comprised impoverished Portuguese peasants and nobles, who were expected to explore and govern these captaincies.

Armillary sphere, a globe used by early navigators

Manuel I (1469–1521)
An illuminated Portuguese manuscript features the royal coat of arms, as well as armillary spheres symbolizing Emperor Manuel's reign as a golden age of exploration.

Priests also joined the expedition, hoping to spread Christianity in the New World.

Cabral erected a cross and held a Catholic service to signify the ownership of Brazil.

Pedro Álvares Cabral

The commander of the fleet sent to India by Emperor Manuel I, Cabral landed at Porto Seguro in southern Bahia on April 23, 1500. The Portuguese navigator baptized the bay, where they anchored for 10 days, Terra de Vera Cruz, or "Land of the True Cross." His onward voyage to India was beset with calamities, and Cabral finally drowned in a shipwreck a few months later.

Indigenous People meeting the Portuguese
Initial Portuguese fleets were received by friendly indigenous people. Gradually, these confrontations and meetings became more hostile in nature.

The Naming of Brazil

Officially, the land was named for *pau-brasil* (*Paubrasilia echinata*), or brazil wood, a tree yielding a valuable red dye. However, the name "Brazil" appeared in the Irish legend of St. Brendan as Hy Brazil ("Blessed Land" in Gaelic). It became part of European maritime folklore, designating a hypothetical land located somewhere in the Atlantic. When Cabral found a new land in that general area, he may have identified it with Brendan's Brazil. The tree might have been named after the land, rather than the other way around.

Early Brazil map, showing a couple under brazil wood

Botocudos Man
Still surviving in some parts of Brazil, the Botocudos were hunter-gatherers.

Woodcut Showing Tupinambá People
Ritually practicing cannibalism, the Tupinambá were some of the first Brazilians to make contact with the Portuguese. They soon died from diseases carried by the Europeans, and from the conditions of their capture and enslavement.

João III (1502–57)
King João III ascended to the throne while the Portuguese Empire was at the height of its mercantile and colonial power. Unable to directly govern Brazil, King João III divided the land into 15 *capitanias*, or captaincies. Settlement was focused mainly on the long coastline. Only São Vicente and Pernambuco immediately prospered. In 1548, the king repossessed the captaincies and brought Brazil under his direct control.

A Jesuit Admonishing Indigenous People
The influence of the Jesuits accompanied this early period of colonization. The first missionaries had arrived in 1549 and acquired great power in Brazil through their influence on the Portuguese court. A zealous missionary movement began, aimed at converting the local people.

Skilled captains accompanied Cabral in his explorations to discover new territories.

Painting showing a group of indigenous Brazilian slaves at work in a sugar plantation

Colonization & Expansion

King João III conferred special colonial privileges to the *donatários*, the aristocrats and minor gentry, who were expected to develop and govern the *capitanias* on behalf of the Crown. The *donatários*, however, met with adverse climatic conditions and hostile indigenous people. Some of the *capitanias* were attacked by the indigenous Brazilians. In 1549, the Crown was forced to send Tomé de Sousa as the first governor, who was assigned the task of protecting the few remaining captaincies.

Sugar & the Slave Trade

Introduced to Brazil in 1532, sugar replaced the country's first major export, brazil wood, which was nearly wiped out as a result of over-exploitation. Setting up his capital in Salvador, Tomé de Sousa enlisted the support of the Jesuits. The indigenous people who did not convert to Christianity were enslaved and sent to work in sugar plantations. As a result of the high demand for sugar in Europe, sugar cane grown in

engenhos (plantations) along the northeastern coast soon became the base of the Brazilian economy. Salvador and Olinda emerged as key centers for the sugar trade.

The hunting-gathering indigenous people, however, were found to be unsuitable slaves for the plantations. They were better suited for the brazil wood trade, and were made to log and transport timber instead. From the 1550s, the landowners turned to Africa, importing millions of slaves.

Colonial Wars

While the Portuguese Crown was still struggling to consolidate its hold on Brazil, the Dutch and French forces continued to encroach on its territories. In 1555, the French had made inroads into the bay of Guanabara, establishing their own colony, French Antarctic. Portuguese forces seized the colony in 1565, and founded a new city, Rio de Janeiro.

Throughout the first half of the 17th century, French and Dutch privateers continued to plunder the coastal cities. With a powerful fleet, the Dutch offered

African slaves in a sugar mill, using an early form of grinder for refining sugar

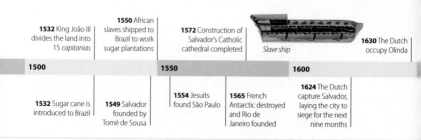

1532 King João III divides the land into 15 *capitanias*	**1550** African slaves shipped to Brazil to work sugar plantations	**1572** Construction of Salvador's Catholic cathedral completed	*Slave ship*	**1630** The Dutch occupy Olinda
1500		**1550**		**1600**
1532 Sugar cane is introduced to Brazil	**1549** Salvador founded by Tomé de Sousa	**1554** Jesuits found São Paulo	**1565** French Antarctic destroyed and Rio de Janeiro founded	**1624** The Dutch capture Salvador, laying the city to siege for the next nine months

An engraving depicting naval combat between French and Portuguese ships off the coast of Brazil

a greater challenge. In 1624, the Dutch captured Salvador and laid siege to the city, until the combined fleet of the Portuguese and Spanish expelled them. The Dutch occupied Olinda in 1630 and, by 1641, controlled a vast stretch of coastline, ending Portugal's monopoly of the sugar trade. During 1648 and 1649, two battles were fought at Guararapes, in Pernambuco, where the Dutch were routed and their territory reduced to an enclave around Recife. Following several years of open warfare, the Dutch formally withdrew in 1661.

The Discovery of Gold

The decline of the sugar industry coincided with the discovery of gold. In 1695, gold was first discovered in Sabara, Minas Gerais, by the *bandeirantes* (paramilitary adventurers), who faced grueling conditions as they pressed inland toward the Andean foothills. Gold was also found in Cuiabá, Mato Grosso, in 1719. Both events led to

further development and expansion of the country's interior. Traffic to São Paulo and Rio de Janeiro rapidly increased and new communities drew people away from the Northeast coast. The focus of power in Brazil moved from the Northeast to the Southeast, and Rio de Janeiro was made the new capital in 1763.

Struggle for Independence

The gold rush lasted not more than 70 years. The decline of gold in the 18th century led to high taxes, as Brazil was forced to meet the quota set by the Crown for the minimum annual gold production. This, coupled with the Brazilian resentment at their exclusion from administration and the Portuguese dominance of foreign trade, culminated in the 1789 Inconfidência Mineira rebellion. Led by Tiradentes (*see pp130–31*), who was eventually executed, the uprising was aimed at Brazilian independence from Portuguese rule.

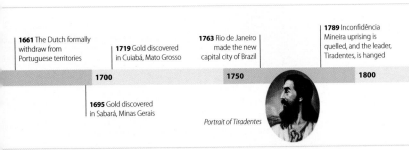

1661 The Dutch formally withdraw from Portuguese territories

1719 Gold discovered in Cuiabá, Mato Grosso

1763 Rio de Janeiro made the new capital city of Brazil

1789 Inconfidência Mineira uprising is quelled, and the leader, Tiradentes, is hanged

1700

1750

1800

1695 Gold discovered in Sabará, Minas Gerais

Portrait of Tiradentes

Dom Pedro proclaiming "Independéncia ou Morte!" at the Rio Ipiranga, on September 7, 1822

The First Emperor of Brazil

The advance of French Emperor Napoleon, in 1808, forced King Dom João VI, who was ruling from Lisbon, to relocate his government to Brazil. In 1821, the royal family were forced to return to deal with rebels back home. Dom João's son, the Prince Regent, who had stayed back in Brazil, proclaimed independence from Portugal on September 7, 1822. In a famous scene at the Rio Ipiranga, he tore the Portuguese insignia from his uniform, drew his sword, and declared, "Independéncia ou Morte!" (Independence or Death). Three months later, he crowned himself Emperor Dom Pedro I.

Although the assumption of independence had been easy, Dom Pedro soon realized that organizing the new government was riddled with challenges. His own autocratic nature proved to be the biggest hurdle in winning the confidence of his subjects. The new consitution he proposed based on his own unlimited power, was strongly opposed by the assembly. When Dom Pedro dismissed his assembly in 1831, demonstrators demanded its reinstatement.

Provincial Unrest

Dom Pedro I was forced to abdicate in favor of his five-year-old son, Dom Pedro II. From 1831 to 1840, three appointed regents ruled the country in the young Emperor's name, during a period of turmoil in which local factions struggled to gain control of their provinces and to keep the masses in line. The regency in Rio de Janeiro gave considerable power to the provinces in 1834, when Brazil became a federation of locally autonomous regional powers, with loose allegiance to the center. The rebellions, riots, and popular movements that marked these years did not spring from economic misery, but from attempts to share in the prosperity stemming from the North Atlantic demand for Brazil's exports.

The Coffee Industry

Coffee, which was introduced to Brazil in the early 1800s, filled the void left by the collapse of the sugar industry and the waning gold rush. An army officer, Francisco de Mello,

A formal portrait of Brazil's Emperor Dom Pedro II (1825–91), depicting him in full regalia

---

1808 Napoleon's advance forces Dom João to flee Portugal, and relocate to Brazil

Dom Pedro I

1825 Britain and Portugal sign a treaty recognizing Brazilian independence

1837–38 The Sabinada Rebellion in Salvador

1842 Rebellions in Minas Gerais and São Paulo

| 1810 | 1820 | 1830 | 1840 |

1822 The Prince Regent proclaims independence from Portugal, crowning himself Emperor Dom Pedro I

1831 Pedro dismisses the Constituent Assembly after a draft constitution is proposed

1834 Brazil becomes a federation of autonomous regional powers

1838–41 The Balaiada Rebellion in Maranhão

was believed to have brought the first coffee beans into Brazil, from his journey to French Guiana. The coffee industry began to flourish, mainly in Minas Gerais and São Paulo. Expanding coffee production in the 1850s and 1860s attracted British investment in railroads to speed transport of the beans to the coast. The coastal Santos–São Paulo railroad (1868) was followed by a series of railroads that linked the northeastern coast to the interior.

The Surrender of Uruguaiana, painted during the war

The War of the Triple Alliance

From 1864 to 1870, Paraguay and the allied countries of Argentina, Brazil, and Uruguay fought one of the bloodiest conflicts on the American continent. Also known as the Paraguayan War, it has been widely attributed to the expansionist ambitions of Paraguayan dictator Francisco Solano Lopez, and the Brazilian and Argentinian meddling in internal Uruguayan politics. The outcome of the war was the devastating defeat of Paraguay by the Triple Alliance, but at the cost of over 100,000 casualties.

Slavery Abolished

As coffee exports rose steadily, so did the numbers of imported slaves. In Rio de Janeiro alone, they soared from around 26,000 in 1825 to 44,000 in 1828. While slave owners argued that slavery was not demoralizing, others were in favor of replacing slavery with free European immigrant labor. Eventually, a contract system that was little better than slavery was established by the parliament. New laws and decrees, unacceptable to slave owners, were simply not enforced, such as the 1829 order forbidding slave ships to sail for Africa, which caused regional slave rebellions throughout the 19th century. In 1850, British and domestic pressure finally forced the Brazilian government to outlaw the African slave trade. Over the next five years, even

An 1857 portrayal of black slaves on a plantation

clandestine landings stopped, ending the transatlantic trade. In 1871, the cabinet in Rio Branco approved a law freeing newborn slaves and requiring masters to care for them until they were eight years old. By the 1880s, the slave population was reduced to half its size. In 1888, the Golden Law was passed, finally abolishing slavery. However, African-Brazilians still had no property or education and struggled to find work after a mass of European immigrants replaced their labor. The detrimental legacy of slavery is manifest to this day in racial inequality.

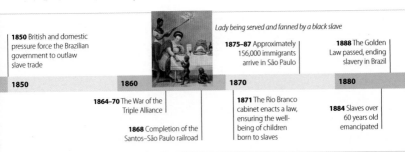

Lady being served and fanned by a black slave

1850 British and domestic pressure force the Brazilian government to outlaw slave trade

1875–87 Approximately 156,000 immigrants arrive in São Paulo

1888 The Golden Law passed, ending slavery in Brazil

1850   **1860**   **1870**   **1880**

1864–70 The War of the Triple Alliance

1868 Completion of the Santos–São Paulo railroad

1871 The Rio Branco cabinet enacts a law, ensuring the well-being of children born to slaves

1884 Slaves over 60 years old emancipated

The First Republic

In 1889, the monarchy was overthrown by a military coup, which was led by Marechal Deodoro da Fonseca and supported by Brazil's coffee barons. Dom Pedro II was exiled in Paris, where he died two years later. A republic was born, with Deodoro as the first president. The Constituent Assembly that drew up the 1891 constitution was a confrontation between the São Paulo coffee oligarchy that sought to limit executive power and the radical authoritarians who wanted to expand presidential authority. The growing opposition culminated in a navy revolt, forcing Deodoro to step down only a few months later. It was recognized that the central government could exercise control only through the local oligarchies, or *patrias*. The constitutional system was offset by the *coronelismo*, or the real system of unwritten agreements among these local white male bosses, by which local oligarchies chose the state governors, who in turn selected the president.

The informal distribution of power emerged as the result of armed struggles and bargaining. In order to check the nationalizing tendencies of the army, the oligarchic republic strengthened the navy and police, turning them into small armies in the larger states.

Le Petit Journal

The funeral of King Dom Pedro II in Paris, reported in a French journal

Scooping coffee beans for shipment after drying, on a São Paulo plantation

"Café Com Leite" Republic

The early years of the republic were called *café com leite* (coffee and milk) by its opponents. Brazilian politics was dominated by an oligarchy that comprised São Paulo coffee barons and Minas Gerais cattle ranchers. These groups controlled electoral politics, and the presidency alternated between the two wealthy states of coffee and milk.

The Struggle For Modernization

At the turn of the 19th century, Brazil lacked an integrated economy. Domestic consumption was largely neglected, and the middle class was not yet active in political life. The economy was organized around large agricultural estates, or *latifundia*. Brazil had lost its sugar market to Caribbean producers, while the rubber boom in Amazônia was beginning to lose its primacy to more efficient Southeast Asian plantations. The outbreak of World War I was the turning point for the dynamic urban sectors. Industrial production doubled, and agricultural diversity received an impetus, as the growing demand by the Allies for staple products sparked a new boom for goods other than sugar and coffee. The old order

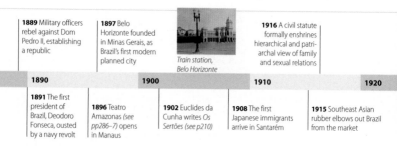

1889 Military officers rebel against Dom Pedro II, establishing a republic

1897 Belo Horizonte founded in Minas Gerais, as Brazil's first modern planned city

Train station, Belo Horizonte

1916 A civil statute formally enshrines hierarchical and patriarchal view of family and sexual relations

1890

1900

1910

1920

1891 The first president of Brazil, Deodoro Fonseca, ousted by a navy revolt

1896 Teatro Amazonas (see pp286–7) opens in Manaus

1902 Euclides da Cunha writes Os Sertões (see p210)

1908 The first Japanese immigrants arrive in Santarém

1915 Southeast Asian rubber elbows out Brazil from the market

gave way to the political aspirations of the new urban groups – government, white-collar workers, professionals, bankers, merchants, and industrialists. Increasing support for industrial protectionism marked Brazilian politics in the 1920s. Disparate social reform movements cropped up during this period. Between 1922 and 1926, junior military officers staged a revolt against the landed elite, demanding socio-economic modernization.

Brazilian army confronts rebels during the 1930 coup

The New State

A bloodless coup by the military installed Getúlio Vargas as provisional president in 1930. Between the World Wars, he built a corporatist, centralized state along fascist lines, although he did advocate some liberal reforms. The collapse of the old order had created a vacuum, which was filled by the fascist Integralistas and communists. The former had once enjoyed Vargas's support, but later turned against him when they realized that creating a strictly fascist state was not on his agenda. They were bidding to seize power in the 1938 election, which the Constitution barred Vargas from contesting. Months before the election, Vargas declared a state of emergency to avert an alleged communist plot. He dissolved the Constitution and established the Estado Novo (New State), which used repressive political tactics and rejected free-market liberal capitalism. Vargas's promise of a "postwar era of liberty" could not save the fall of the Estado Novo in 1945, when he was ousted by General Eurico Dutra. His return as elected president in 1951 was marred by inflation, corruption, and a political scandal involving an attack on a journalist by the president's bodyguard. Faced with the ultimatum to resign, Vargas ended his life in 1954 by shooting himself.

Citizens of Rio de Janeiro welcoming rebel troops upon the success of the 1930 coup

1932 Young army officers lead their units against the old order in Minas Gerais and Rio

1938 Vargas establishes the Estado Novo, or the "New State"

Poster, World Cup, 1950

1950 World Cup soccer held in Brazil

1954 Vargas commits suicide with a bullet to the heart

1930

1940

1950

1930 A military coup installs Getúlio Vargas as provisional president

1937 Vargas assumes dictatorial powers under a new constitution

1945 The Estado Novo collapses, Eurico Dutra comes to power

1950 Vargas re-elected president

The Vargas Era (1930–54)

Spanning the creation of Brazil as a modern nation-state, the long political career of Getúlio Vargas exemplifies the various contradictions at the heart of the Brazilian national character. His rise to power in 1930 marked the resurgence of a generation of young, dynamic administrators, but also the start of an authoritarian rule. During his first term, he assumed absolute power to overthrow the old order, founded the Estado Novo, and passed labor-protection laws to gain popular support. Forced to step down after World War II, he remained popular and was re-elected in 1950.

Getúlio Dornelles Vargas
A pro-industry nationalist and virulent anti-communist, Vargas possessed an authoritarian streak. The hero of the newly emerged urban working class, he favored capitalism and liberal reforms to some extent.

Crowd Cheering Vargas's Victory
A bloodless coup in 1930 ended the reign of President Washington Luis, and brought Vargas into power.

Nationalized Fascism

Exploiting communist paranoia, Vargas assumed dictatorship in 1937, abolishing opposition parties and imposing censorship. He tolerated anti-Semitism, initially encouraging the fascist Integralistas (see p59) until they decided to contest the elections against him in 1938.

Vargas, diminutive in stature, emulated Hitler and Mussolini in some ways.

Ties with Mussolini
In January 1931, 11 Italian aircraft, one of them piloted by Mussolini's son, were received in Brazil with great applause.

Integralistas in Rio de Janeiro, 1938
A group of Integralistas led a short-lived revolt against the corrupt Vargas regime. They attacked the Palácio Guanabara, and made a bid for Vargas's life, but government forces promptly suppressed the uprising.

**Carmen Miranda
(1909–55)**
During the Vargas era, the
Portuguese-Brazilian singer-
actress charmed post-World
War USA and the world.

1950 World Cup
Brazil was confident of winning the World Cup in the first tournament
to be held after World War II. The final was played on home ground
at Rio's Estádio Maracanã. However, in a surprise victory, Uruguay
defeated Brazil 2–1. With slighted pride, the humiliated nation
plunged into mourning.

New Ministry of Education
Vargas was responsible for the erection of a
sky-scraping new Ministry of Education, whose
cutting-edge design was emphasized by its
incongruous location behind a colonial church
in Rio de Janeiro.

Toward the Future
Vargas recognized that Brazil's strength lay in its
vast natural resources. He created Petrobras,
the state oil company, and invested in road and
air transport.

Daily Life
Under Vargas's rule, modern tramways were
constructed to carry white-collar employees
to their various offices in the capital city of
Rio de Janeiro.

President Juscelino Kubitschek on the cover of *Time* magazine dated January 13, 1970

Into Modernity

The reign of Juscelino Kubitschek, Vargas's successor, lasted from 1956 to 1961, ushering Brazil into modernity. Campaigning on a platform of "Fifty years of progress in five," Kubitschek tried to achieve this progress with generous incentives for foreign investors, such as low taxes, privileges for the importation of machinery, and donations of land. All this gave impetus to the economic growth rate, which paved the way for the economic boom in the next decade. The most notable

Trans-Amazon Highway construction near Altamira Brazil, July 1971

manifestation of Kubitschek's nationalistic aspirations was the creation of Brasília *(see pp298–9)* as the new capital of Brazil.

Despite instilling national confidence, Kubitschek's era was also beset with massive inflation. Also, the influx of foreign capital rapidly captured domestic industry, and the urban bourgeoisie found state control threatening rather than protective. Mild structural reforms took place under President João Goulart (1961–64), but corporate elites demonstrated their intolerance towards any form of social welfare and sponsored a military coup in 1964.

The Era of Military Rule

A period of right-wing military dictatorship followed. In a bid to appease the hard-liners, the new president, Marshal Humberto Castelo Branco, recessed and purged Congress, and decreed the expansion of the president's powers at the expense of the legislature and the judiciary. His gamble curbed the populist left, but gave his successor, Artur da Costa e Silva (1967–69), a basis for authoritarian rule. Despite their victory, the hard-liners were still unable to institutionalize their agenda politically. They did not give up their liberal constitutionalism as they feared damage to their alliance with the US, the citadel of anti-communism. In 1969, the democratic mask fell off when General Médici came to power and

1960 Brasília inaugurated as the new capital of Brazil

1970 Brazil wins the soccer World Cup in Mexico

1977 *Dona Flor and Her Two Husbands* brings international fame to Brazilian cinema

1979 General Figueiredo is sworn in as president

1985 Civilian Tancredo Nev is elected to presidency

1960	1965	1970	1975	1980	1985

1961 Janio Quadros elected president, replaced by João Goulart in the same year

Jules Rimet trophy

1974 Ernesto Geisel's rule begins, marking a slow return to democracy

1980 Film *Bye Bye Brasil* brings more recognition to Brazilian cinema

1984 Benedita da Silva becomes the first black woman in Congress

continued to rule an authoritarian regime without popular support. An extremely oppressive government apparatus hounded and tortured political opponents. Yet the Médici administration cloaked itself in the green and gold flag when Brazil won the Jules Rimet trophy for its third consecutive victory in the soccer World Cup in 1970. From 1968 to 1974, during the darkest days of dictatorship, the military-civil alliance took shape as the economy boomed, reaching annual GDP growth rates of 12 percent. During this period, the Trans-Amazon Highway was built, and the Rio Paraná was dammed.

Former President Dilma Roussef, who was removed fom office in 2016

Geisel's accession in 1974 signaled a move toward democratic rule. He attempted to restrain the growing strength of the opposition parties by creating an electoral college that would approve his selected replacement. He allowed the return of exiles, restored *habeas corpus*, and installed General João Figueiredo as his successor in 1979. A 1981 bombing incident at Rio City's RioCentro confirmed direct military involvement in terrorism. The Figueiredo regime's inaction in punishing the guilty strengthened the public's resolve to end military rule, as Brazil faced inflation and mounting foreign debt.

The Return to Democracy

In 1985, civilian Tancredo Neves was voted into office as president. However, he died before taking office. Brazil completed its transition to a popularly elected government in 1989, when Fernando Collor de Mello won 53 percent of the vote. The democratization of the government was visible in the impeachment of the corrupt de Mello regime, forcing him to resign in 1992. The 1994 elections brought to power Fernando Henrique Cardoso, who served two terms but failed to match the growth of the country's wealth and power with better living conditions. Socio-economic contradictions helped usher in Lula da Silva in 2002 as Brazil's first elected left-wing president. His Workers' Party (Partido dos Trabalhadores – PT) government managed to raise 40 million Brazilians out of poverty while appeasing the wealthy with investments in housing and infrastructure, a trend followed by his successor, Dilma Rousseff, elected in 2011 and 2015. Her second term was troubled by an economic crisis, and she was controversially impeached in 2016 for manipulating the budget in order to preserve social investments. Vice-president Michel Temer took over office against a backdrop of economic recession that began in 2014.

Brazilians protesting against the Dilma Rousseff government in March 2016, in the largest demonstration of its kind in the country

Brazilian President Fernando Collor de Mello		**2001** Congress approves a civil code, giving equal rights to men and women		**2008** Brazil appointed as host country for the 2014 World Cup		**2016** Rio de Janeiro hosts the Olympics. Dilma Rousseff impeached in August; Michel Temer replaces her as president
	1995 Fernando Cardoso takes office as president			**2009** Rio announced as host city for the 2016 Olympics		
1995	**2000**		**2005**	**2010**	**2015**	**2020**
994 Brazil ats Italy to the World Cup title	**2000** UNESCO declares the Atlantic rainforest a World Heritage Site	**2002** Brazil wins its fifth World Cup title defeating Germany	**2006** Lula da Silva is re-elected in a landslide victory, returning as Brazil's president	**2011** Dilma Rousseff elected first female president	**2015** Dilma Rousseff begins second term as president	
					2014 Brazil hosted the 2014 FIFA World Cup	

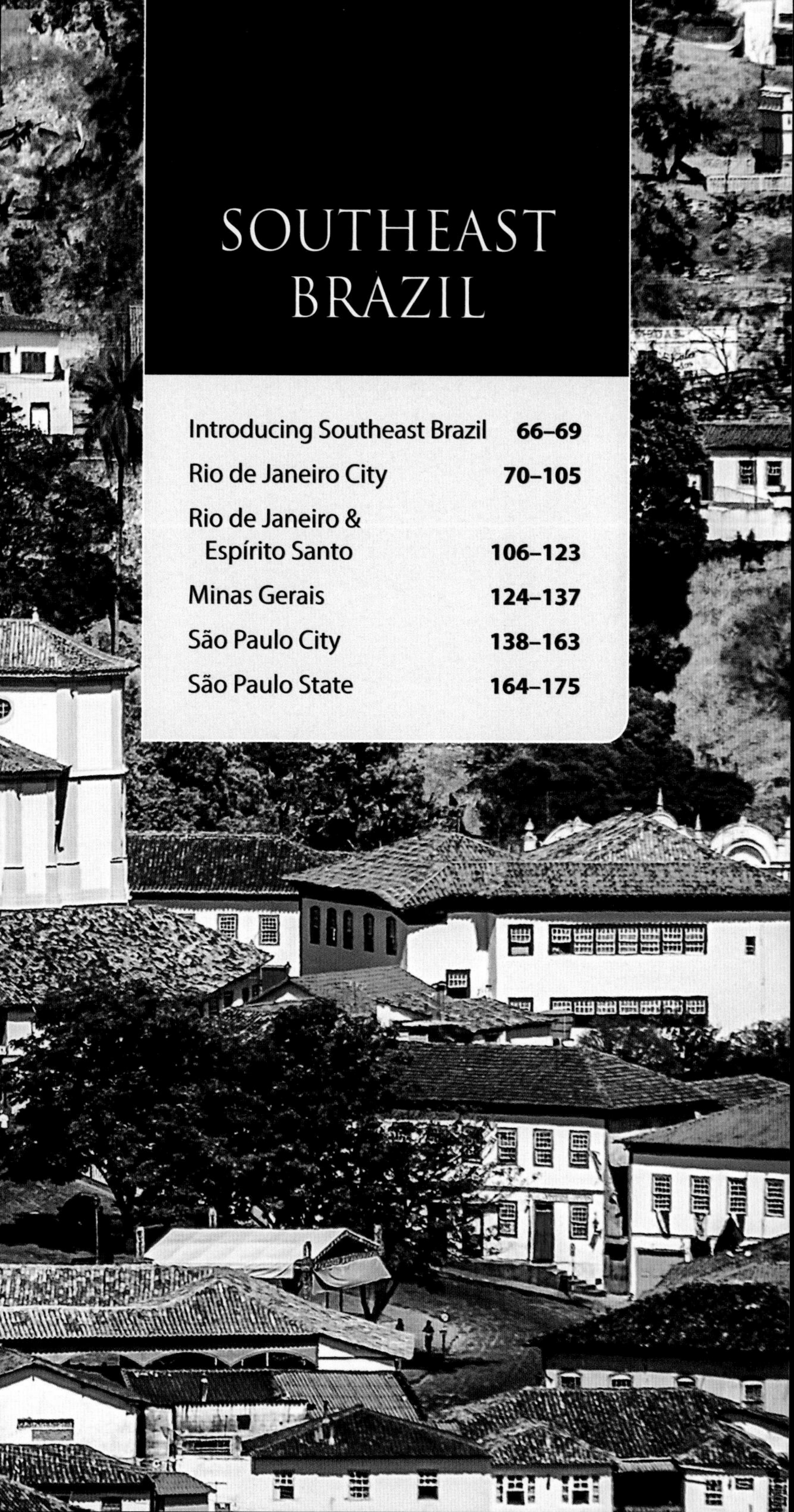

SOUTHEAST BRAZIL

Introducing Southeast Brazil   66–69

Rio de Janeiro City   70–105

Rio de Janeiro &
  Espírito Santo   106–123

Minas Gerais   124–137

São Paulo City   138–163

São Paulo State   164–175

Introducing Southeast Brazil

The four states of Rio de Janeiro, Espírito Santo, Minas Gerais, and São Paulo constitute Brazil's economic heartland. The giant metropolises – Rio de Janeiro, Belo Horizonte, and São Paulo – burst with energetic cultural life. Rio de Janeiro holds the greatest attractions, with its Carnaval and breathtaking mountains and beaches. Beyond the urban hubs, nature and rural life exist undisturbed. Wild islands lie a short boat ride away. Inland, in the folds of the rugged Minas hills, are colonial towns whose cobbled streets, colorful Portuguese town houses, and ornate Baroque churches remain little changed since colonial times.

BRAZIL

SOUTHEAST BRAZIL

Parque Nacional Serra da Canastra *(see p137)*, one of the protected areas dotting the region, preserves pristine rainforest and *cerrado*, as well as rich fauna.

Uberlândia

Uberaba

São José de Rio Preto

Ribeirão Preto

SÃO PAULO STATE
(See pp164–75)

Presidente Prudente

São Paulo City *(see pp138–63)*, the capital of São Paulo state, is relentlessly urban and frenetic, but has Brazil's best restaurants, shops, and nightlife.

Campinas

Jacare

SÃO PAULO CITY
(See pp138–63)

São Paulo's coast *(see pp168–75)*, stretching across 250 miles (400 km), features beaches and islands that serve as the weekend playground for the city.

◀ The pretty colonial city of Diamantina, Minas Gerais

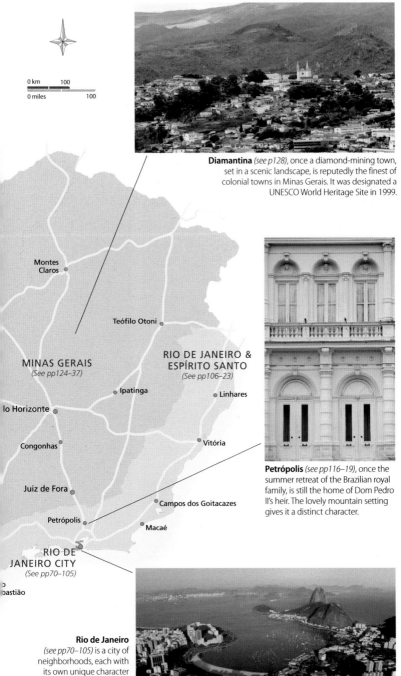

0 km 100
0 miles 100

Diamantina *(see p128)*, once a diamond-mining town, set in a scenic landscape, is reputedly the finest of colonial towns in Minas Gerais. It was designated a UNESCO World Heritage Site in 1999.

Montes Claros

Teófilo Otoni

MINAS GERAIS
(See pp124–37)

Ipatinga

lo Horizonte

Congonhas

Juiz de Fora

Petrópolis

**RIO DE JANEIRO &
ESPÍRITO SANTO**
(See pp106–23)

Linhares

Vitória

Campos dos Goitacazes

Macaé

**RIO DE
JANEIRO CITY**
(See pp70–105)

astião

Petrópolis *(see pp116–19)*, once the summer retreat of the Brazilian royal family, is still the home of Dom Pedro II's heir. The lovely mountain setting gives it a distinct character.

Rio de Janeiro
(see pp70–105) is a city of neighborhoods, each with its own unique character and most endowed with a great view. The panorama of Sugar Loaf and Botafogo from Mirante Dona Marta is simply unparalleled.

Carnaval in Rio

One of the world's most spectacular festivals, Carnaval is celebrated all over Brazil, but the celebrations in Rio are justly famous. They remain unmatched for their sheer scale and splendor. Falling in February or early March, Carnaval is linked to the calendar of the Catholic Church. Traditionally, Carnaval is the last celebration of excess and joy before the austerity and fasting of the Lenten period. Its key elements include street celebrations, carnival balls, and the world-famous parade of top *samba* schools, which traditionally takes place at the Sambódromo in downtown Rio.

Carnaval Dates

2018 Feb 9–14
2019 Mar 1–6
2020 Feb 21–26
2021 Feb 12–17
2022 Feb 25–Mar 2
2023 Feb 17–22
2024 Feb 9–14
2025 Feb 28–Mar 5

Samba Schools are large social clubs found in Rio's poorer communities and neighborhoods, often linked to the local *favelas*. Mangueira, one of the most prominent schools, was founded in 1928, and Portela, which began in 1923, has won the most Carnaval titles. Many top schools date from the 1940s and 1950s, while Grande Rio formed as late as 1988.

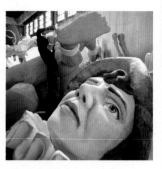

Giant Puppets are put together to decorate the floats and fascinating costumes are created for the participants. Craftspeople work throughout the year, as Carnaval is a year-round industry. Much of the work can now be seen at close quarters in the Cidade de Samba in downtown Rio.

Porta bandeira is the school's standard bearer, dressed in lavish 18th-century formal wear, regardless of the school's theme.

Street Carnivals take place wherever there is a band that can strike up a *samba* and move around the streets. Bands attract a large following who dance and sing through the neighborhoods.

Party-loving Cariocas consider Carnaval more important than any other event in the calendar, and that includes both Christmas and New Year. It is a week-long holiday for partying around the clock and a sign that summer is finally coming to a close.

Tips for Visitors

Transport: Take the metro. Use Central Station if your ticket is for an uneven-numbered sector and Praça Onze for an even one.

Winner's Parade: Those who missed the event can see part of the parade by winning schools on the Saturday after Carnaval.

Tickets: Book your tickets in advance from the League of Samba Schools (LIESA), (21) 3032 0001.

A different theme is chosen by every school, and conceptualized by the *carnavalesco* (director). The history of Espírito Santo, represented by the state colors, pink, blue, and white, was the theme of the Caprichosos de Pilares school in 2006. This float shows *antropofagismo*, the concept of "cultural cannibalism," putting foreign art, music, and literature in a Brazilian context.

The central display is the focal point of the float, and is often the most elaborately designed aspect, with the most creative costumes on display.

Passistas, or participants, numbering a minimum of 2,500, join each float with at least 200 in the *bateria* (percussion section).

The Parade

Each of the 12 main samba schools will have around 4,000 participants who must cover the Passarela do Samba in not less than 65 minutes and not more than 80 minutes. In that time, they will put on a performance every bit as complex and visually exciting as any musical showing on Broadway or in London's West End. Six schools parade each night.

Mestre sala is the school's dance master who, along with the *porta bandeira*, performs a complex series of dance steps as they move along the route.

Sambódromo, or Passarela do Samba, was inaugurated in 1984. Designed by Oscar Niemeyer, it can accommodate over 60,000 spectators at any one time. The end square is used for Carnaval, outdoor concerts, and festivals.

RIO DE JANEIRO CITY

Rio de Janeiro is quite simply one of the world's most beautiful and vibrant cities, and is the number-one destination for visitors coming to Brazil. Its unique setting, with dramatic mountains and beaches at its very center, sets it apart from the other great cities of the world. In addition, Rio's flamboyant Carnaval, *samba*, and *bossa nova* make for a heady mix that is impossible to ignore.

Rio de Janeiro was first discovered by European explorers on January 1, 1502. They mistook the huge Guanabara Bay for the mouth of a river (*rio*) and called the site "River of January," thus giving the city its name. Evidence of the city's colonial past can still be seen in downtown Rio, with buildings and artifacts dating from the 16th to the 19th centuries. In 1763, the city became the capital of Brazil's Vice-Royalty and in 1808, the Portuguese royal family and court abandoned Lisbon for Rio, making it the capital of both Brazil and the Portuguese Empire. It remained home to the Brazilian monarchy until 1889 and the capital of the Brazilian Republic until 1960, when the title was awarded to the newly built Bauhaus-style Brasília.

Today, Rio is an international metropolis and a spectacular tropical resort. Iconic sights include the enormous statue of Christ that looms protectively over the city from Corcovado mountain and the easily recognizable Sugar Loaf Mountain at one end of Urca Bay. The landscape is interspersed with *favelas*, areas of poor housing (*see p89*), which form a large part of the city.

Rio's residents, affectionately called "Cariocas," are a laid-back, friendly people who love to go out. Visitors will be spoiled for choice in this hedonistic city, and can visit Lapa for its extravagant clubs, Gávea for its bars, and Ipanema and Leblon for their boutiques and restaurants. Rio's beaches provide ample opportunity for all manner of water sports and are a great meeting place for the city's residents, both rich and poor. Infrastructure and building developments for the 2014 World Cup and the 2016 Olympic games have further enhanced the city's attractions.

The colorful Copacabana beach, lined with palm trees

◄ Sunset over Botofogo Bay and the Sugar Loaf Mountain, Rio de Janeiro

Exploring Rio de Janeiro City

Rio de Janeiro covers a vast area of 473 sq miles (1,225 sq km) and is home to 6.5 million people, making it Brazil's second-largest and second most populous city after São Paulo. It has two main zones – Zona Norte (North Zone), encompassing working class neighborhoods and most *favelas*; and Zona Sul (South Zone), with plush areas and famous beaches such as Ipanema and Copacabana. Centro is Rio's main business district, and has a concentration of historic buildings, museums, and churches.

Sights at a Glance

Historic Buildings, Streets, Neighborhoods & Townships

1. Praça XV & Centro pp74–5
3. Docks & Waterfront
6. Confeitaria Colombo
8. Theatro Municipal & Cinelândia
10. Santa Teresa
11. Lapa
28. Morro do Corcovado & Cristo Redentor pp86–7
30. Quinta da Boa Vista
31. Sambódromo & Cidade do Samba
32. Centro Cultural do Banco do Brasil
33. Barra pp90–91
36. Niterói

13. Museu Histórico Nacional
14. Museu de Arte Moderna
16. Museu da República
17. Oi Futuro Ipanema
25. Museu do Índio
26. Museu Villa-Lobos
27. Museu Casa de Rui Barbosa

National Parks

34. Parque Nacional da Tijuca

Soccer Clubs & Stadiums

23. Jóquei Clube Brasileiro
29. Estádio do Maracanã

Areas of Natural Beauty

18. Sugar Loaf Mountain pp80–81

Churches & Monasteries

2. Mosteiro de São Bento
7. Igreja de São Francisco da Penitência
9. Catedral Metropolitana
15. Igreja Nossa Senhora da Glória do Outeiro

Parks & Gardens

24. Jardim Botânico

Beaches & Lagoons

19. Copacabana p82
20. Ipanema p83
21. Leblon p83
22. Lagoa Rodrigo de Freitas
35. Baía de Guanabara

Museums

4. Museu do Amanhã
5. Museu de Arte do Rio (MAR)
12. Museu Nacional de Belas Artes

0 meters	1000
0 yards	1000

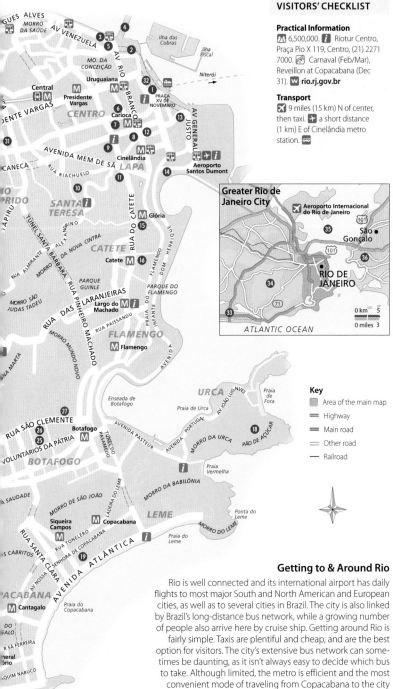

Greater Rio de Janeiro City

Aeroporto Internacional do Rio de Janeiro

São Gonçalo

RIO DE JANEIRO

ATLANTIC OCEAN

0 km 5
0 miles 3

Key

- Area of the main map
- Highway
- Main road
- Other road
- Railroad

Getting to & Around Rio

Rio is well connected and its international airport has daily flights to most major South and North American and European cities, as well as to several cities in Brazil. The city is also linked by Brazil's long-distance bus network, while a growing number of people also arrive here by cruise ship. Getting around Rio is fairly simple. Taxis are plentiful and cheap, and are the best option for visitors. The city's extensive bus network can some-times be daunting, as it isn't always easy to decide which bus to take. Although limited, the metro is efficient and the most convenient mode of traveling from Copacabana to the city center. A small light-rail network, launched in 2016 and still expanding, links the port area to Centro. It is possible to rent a car, but first-time visitors may find driving here a little difficult.

For keys to symbols *see back flap*

❶ Street-by-Street: Praça XV de Novembro & Centro

Originally called the Largo do Paço, Praça XV de Novembro is the historic heart of Rio, even if it was only so named after the declaration of the republic on November 15, 1889. The Praça witnessed the arrival of Dom João VI of Portugal in 1808 as he fled with his court from Napoleon. The House of the Viceroy became the Paço Imperial, and for a time the square was the center of Brazil's political and commercial power. Today, Praça XV and the surrounding area is packed with historic buildings and streets. Restoration of the palace in the 1980s and renovation of the square in 2016, opening it up to views of the sea, have acted as catalysts in bringing culture and life back to the city center.

Statue of General Osório
General Manuel Luís Osório defended the Empire in the War of the Triple Alliance between 1864 and 1870 *(see p57)*.

Nossa Senhora do Monte do Carmo once served as the royal chapel.

★ Arco do Telles
Today a pedestrian exit, Arco de Telles dates from 1757 and is all that remains of the old Senate House that was destroyed by a fire in 1790. It is Rio's only surviving colonial arch.

AVENIDA RIO BRANCO

PRAÇA XV DE NOVEMBRO

Statue of General Osório

★ Paço Imperial
The Paço Imperial has been the backdrop for many key events in Brazilian history, including the signing of the Lei Aurea in 1888, abolishing slavery in Brazil.

0 meters	25
0 yards	25

Chafariz da Pirâmide
was built in 1789 to distribute fresh water to the city and to visiting ships.

Locator Map
See Street Finder, map 5

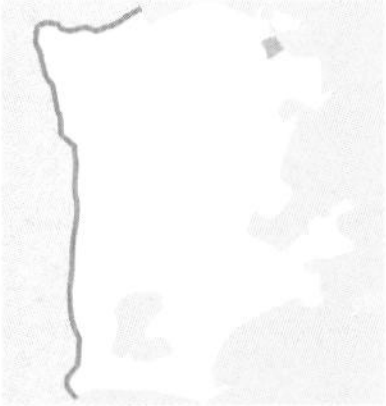

Key

— Suggested route

VISITORS' CHECKLIST

Practical Information
Rio de Janeiro.
Paço Imperial: Praça XV de Novembro 48. **Map** 5 E3.
Tel (21) 2215 2431.
Open noon–6pm Tue–Sun.
Nossa Senhora da Candelária: Praça Pio X, Centro. **Map** 5 D2.
Open 7:30am–4pm Mon–Fri, 8am–noon Sat, 9am–1pm Sun.
Espaço Cultural da Marinha: Av Alfred Agache, Centro. **Map** 5 E2.
Tel (21) 2532 5992. **Open** noon–5pm Tue–Sun.

Transport
Ⓜ Uruguaiana.
⛴ Estação de Barcas.

AV PRES VARGAS
DO ROSARIO
I DE MARÇO
VIDOR
MERCADO
AV PRES KUBITSCHEK

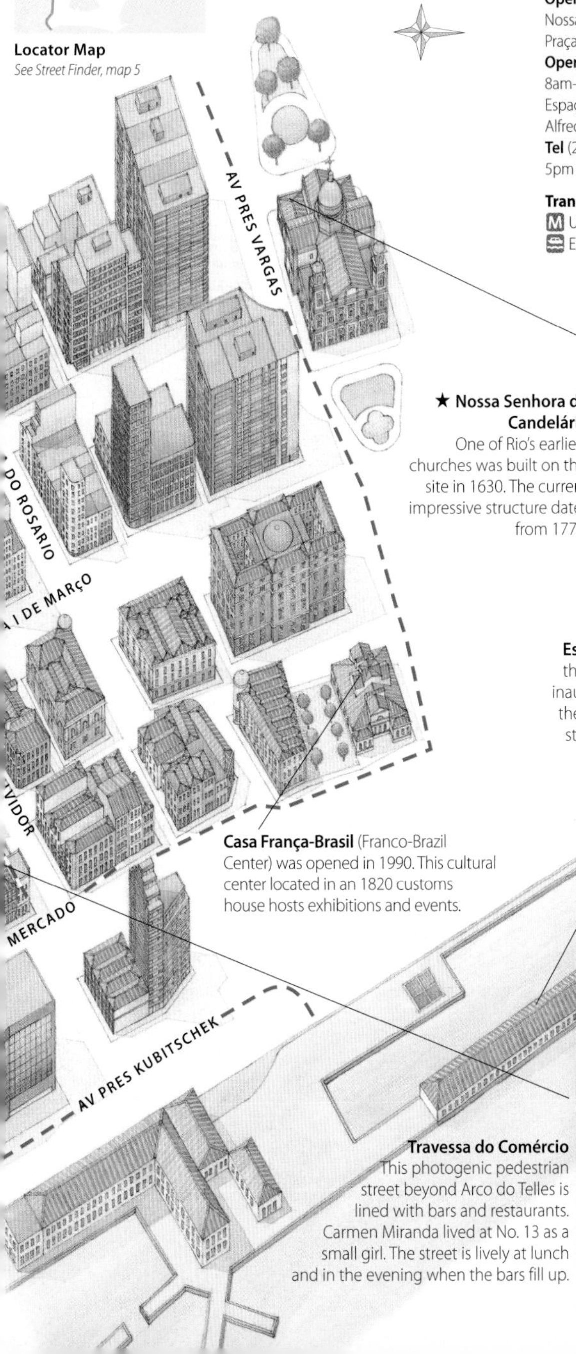

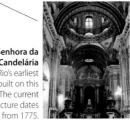

★ Nossa Senhora da Candelária
One of Rio's earliest churches was built on this site in 1630. The current impressive structure dates from 1775.

Espaço Cultural da Marinha, the Navy's cultural center, was inaugurated in 1996. Located in the old docks, the center is the starting point for tours of Baía de Guanabara.

Casa França-Brasil (Franco-Brazil Center) was opened in 1990. This cultural center located in an 1820 customs house hosts exhibitions and events.

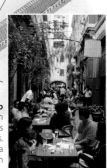

Travessa do Comércio
This photogenic pedestrian street beyond Arco do Telles is lined with bars and restaurants. Carmen Miranda lived at No. 13 as a small girl. The street is lively at lunch and in the evening when the bars fill up.

Detail of the gilded Baroque interior of Mosteiro de São Bento

❷ Mosteiro de São Bento

Rua Dom Gerardo 68 (entrance by elevator at No. 40), Centro. **Map** 5 D2. **Tel** (21) 2206 8100. Ⓜ Uruguaiana. **Open** 7am–6pm daily. 🖼 ♿ ✝ 7:30am Mon–Fri, 8am Sat, 10am Sun. Ⓦ osb.org.br

Benedictine monks from Bahia founded the São Bento Monastery in 1590 and much of the historic building, located on the hills of São Bento, has been structurally untouched since it was built between 1617 and 1641. The exterior of the main building reflects the simplicity of the time of its construction and gives no hint of the opulence of the gilded Baroque interior.

A number of the works on display were carved by one of the monks, Frei Domingos da Conceição (1643–1718). They include the main altar of the monastery's church. The painting displayed on it, which was created around 1676, is dedicated to Nossa Senhora de Montserrat (Black Virgin).

São Bento is still very much a working monastery. The Benedictine monks are protective of the monastery and their work and have tried hard to keep the church from becoming simply a tourist attraction. Many areas, such as the beautiful cloisters, remain out-of-bounds except on special occasions. Mass for the public is said daily, with a full Gregorian chant at 10am on Sundays. Visitors should remember to dress appropriately if they wish to view the interior of the monastery.

❸ Docks & Waterfront

Praça Mauá, Centro. **Map** 5 D2. Ⓜ Carioca, Uruguaiana. ♿ Instituto Pretos Novos: Rua Pedro Ernesto 32/34, Gamboa. 🎨 free Sat. **Tel** (21) 2516 7089. **Open** 1–7pm Tue–Fri, 11am–2pm Sat (call for local tours). Ⓦ **pretosnovos.com.br** AquaRio: Praça Muhammad Ali, Gambôa. 🎨 🖼 💻 📷 **Tel** (21) 3613 0700. **Open** 10am–6pm daily. Ⓦ **aquario.rio**

As part of the preparations for the 2016 Olympics, Rio revamped its docks, now called Porto Maravilha (Port of Wonder), into a 2.1-mile (3.5-km) pedestrian boulevard named Orla Conde.

The dock area used to be a slave-trade port during the colonial period. Its regeneration unveiled numerous artefacts and ruins related to African heritage. These are now exhibited at Instituto Pretos Novos, which also offers tours about the area's history, including the remains of a large slave cemetery and the port and market where slaves were traded upon arrival.

Lovers of marine life will enjoy AquaRio, South America's largest aquarium, where visitors walk in underwater tunnels to view over 300 species of marine fauna.

❹ Museu do Amanhã

Praça Mauá 1, Centro. **Map** 5 D2. Ⓜ Uruguaiana. **Tel** (21) 3812 1812. **Open** 10am–5pm Tue–Sun. 🎨 free Tue. 🖼 ♿ 📷 🎨 💻 Ⓦ **museudoamanha.org.br**

Inaugurated in late 2015, the Museum of Tomorrow is dedicated to science and technological advancements in building sustainable cities. There are interactive displays about the impact that human beings have on the environment and on what the future holds. The impressive, eco-efficient building designed by Neo-Futurist Spanish architect Santiago Calatrava is an attraction in itself, with its lights visible from across the bay at night.

❺ Museu de Arte do Rio

Praça Mauá 5, Centro. **Map** 5 D2 Ⓜ Uruguaiana. **Tel** (21) 3031 2741 **Open** 10am–5pm Tue–Sun. 🎨 free Tue and last Sun of month. 🖼 ♿ 📷 🖼 💻 Ⓦ **museudeartedorio.org.br**

The Rio Museum of Art displays works illustrating the history, life, and social fabric of the city of Rio de Janeiro. Housed in a heritage-listed palace, formerly known as Dom João VI, fused with a modern former bus station, the museum's exhibits are arranged by theme over four floors, and feature art ranging from the Baroque period through to 20th-century Modernists. It also hosts temporary exhibitions.

❻ Confeitaria Colombo

Rua Gonçalves Dias 32, Centro. **Map** 5 D3. **Tel** (21) 2505 1500. Ⓜ Carioca. **Open** 9am–7pm Mon–Fri, 9am–5pm Sat. ♿ limited. Ⓦ **confeitariacolombo.com.br**

The Colombo Tearoom dates from 1894 and remains a wonderful mix of Art Nouveau and *belle époque*. Located in what was then the very heart of Rio, it was

The striking Museu do Amanhã

Opulent façade of the Theatro Municipal

a meeting point for intellectuals, artists, and politicians. Regulars included politician Ruy Barbosa, President Getúlio Vargas, and composer Heitor Villa-Lobos.

The mirrors were shipped in from Belgium and the marble from Italy, while much of the original furniture is made of Brazilian jacaranda wood. Visitors can savor the atmosphere of Rio's past by eating a snack in the Bar Jardim, or a meal at the restaurant.

❼ Igreja de São Francisco da Penitência

Largo de Carioca 5, Centro. **Map** 5 D4. Ⓜ Carioca. **Tel** (21) 2262 0197. **Open** 9am–noon, 1–4pm Tue–Fri. 📷 🎥
Ⓦ museusacrofranciscano.org.br

Restored to its former glory, the church of São Francisco da Penitência is considered one of the richest and most beautiful examples of Baroque art in Brazil. Built between 1657 and 1772, the church exhibits various works of the Portuguese artist Francisco Xavier de Brito. His art heavily influenced the Brazilian artist Aleijadinho (see p135), whose own work spectacularly adorns many of the Baroque churches of Minas Gerais. One of the church's highlights is the 1738 painting of the glorification of St. Francis by Caetano da Costa Coelho, the first Brazilian painting to be done in perspective.

❽ Theatro Municipal & Cinelândia

Av Rio Branco, Centro. **Map** 5 D4. **Tel** (21) 2332 9191. Ⓜ Cinelândia. 🕐 11:30am–4pm Tue–Fri, 11am–1pm Sat & Sun. 🎥
Ⓦ theatromunicipal.rj.gov.br

Rio's Municipal Theater, built between 1905 and 1909 and inspired by Paris's Opéra Garnier, is the main venue for the city's ballet, opera, and orchestra (including the Municipal Symphony Orchestra of São Paulo), and continues to attract the best talent from both Brazil and abroad. After renovation in the early 2010s, the guided tours now include the picturesque inner stairway, a basement restaurant with Persian-style decor, and a snippet of rehearsals.

Stained-glass window at the Catedral Metropolitana

Farther south along Avenida Rio Branco is the heart of Cinelândia or "cinema land," the area around which the city's movie houses sprang up in the 1920s. Many are still in operation, most notably the Cine Odeon BR which opened in 1926 and closed in 1999 to be renovated. It reopened a year later as the headquarters of the Rio Film Festival. Other buildings in the area include the Museu Nacional de Belas Artes (see p78), Biblioteca Nacional, and Palácio Pedro Ernesto.

❾ Catedral Metropolitana

Av República do Chile 245, Centro. **Map** 5 D4. **Tel** (21) 2240 2669. Ⓜ Cinelândia. **Open** 7am–5pm daily. ♿ 🎵 noon Mon–Sat, 10am Sun. Museu Arquidiocesano de Arte Sacra: **Open** 9am–4pm Wed & Fri, 9am–noon Sat & Sun. ♿
Ⓦ catedral.com.br

Rio's striking Metropolitan Cathedral, with its truncated conical shape, was conceptualized by Ivo Calliari (1918–2005), a Catholic priest.

The cathedral's first stone was laid on January 20, 1964, and the inauguration of the still unfinished building was held 12 years later, in 1976, marking the 300th anniversary of the Diocese of Rio. Standing 248 ft (75 m) high with no interior columns, this huge cathedral has a seating capacity of 5,000 and can accommodate up to 20,000 people standing. The interior is dominated by four magnificent stained-glass windows that stretch 197 ft (60 m) to the ceiling. They represent the apostolic (yellow), Catholic (blue), ecclesiastical (green), and saintly (red) traditions.

The **Museu Arquidiocesano de Arte Sacra** (Sacred Art Museum) in the basement includes historical items in its collection, such as the baptismal fonts used for christening the Brazilian royal family, the golden rose gifted to Princess Isabel by Pope Leo XIII to celebrate her signing the abolition of slavery, and the throne of Dom Pedro II.

The Bondinho de Santa Teresa streetcar in Santa Teresa

⓾ Santa Teresa

Santa Teresa, Centro.
Ⓜ Carioca.

At the top of the Santa Teresa hill, the neigborhood of Santa Teresa offers a magnificent view of the city, particularly from Parque das Ruínas. Its colonial charm has been retained through a resistance to development, and it is famed for its winding cobbled streets, old mansions, and for being an artistic hot spot. The construction of the Santa Teresa convent in the 18th century marked the beginning of the development of this area, and it is a popular tourist site, with restaurants, live music, cultural centers, and other attractions. A ride on the distinctive yellow streetcar, the Bondinho de Santa Teresa, is an experience not to be missed. This is the last of the many streetcars that used to crisscross the city, and it connects the neighborhood with downtown Rio.

⓫ Lapa

Lapa, Centro. Ⓜ Carioca.

The most famous image of the area known as Lapa is the **Arcos da Lapa**, an aqueduct built in 1724 to bring water down from the Santa Teresa forest to the public fountain in Largo da Carioca. In 1896, it became the base for the viaduct that carries streetcars to Santa Teresa.

Lapa has always had a slightly bohemian feel and during the first half of the 1900s was the center of Rio's alternative nightlife. The area still boasts a vibrant nightlife, attracting people from all over the city who come looking for the best of Brazilian music. Key hot spots include Rio Scenarium, Carioca da Gema, and Dama da Noite. In 2004, the area saw the return of the **Circo Voador** (Flying Circus), now held in a purpose-built music venue that replaced the earlier tent of the 1980s and early 1990s. Many of the leading names in contemporary Brazilian music – including Seu Jorge – got their first break at the Circo Voador (see pp96–9).

⓬ Museu Nacional de Belas Artes

Av Rio Branco 199, Centro. **Map** 5 E4.
Tel (21) 3299 0600. Ⓜ Cinelândia.
Open 10am–6pm Tue–Fri, 1–6pm Sat, Sun & public hols. 🖼 free on Sun.
by appt. 🧎 🔗 **mnba.gov.br**

The National Museum of ine Arts is one of the most important permanent art collections in Latin America. The building in which it is housed dates from 1908.

The collection, which has over 16,000 pieces in its archive, features Brazilian artists from the colonial period as well as from the 19th and 20th centuries. Artists include Frans Post, who painted Brazilian landscapes in classical Dutch style, the Frenchman Jean Baptiste Debret, who painted the immortal *Battle of Guararapes* (1879), Vitor Meireles, and Pedro

Américo, whose *A Batalha do Avaí* (1877) is one of the largest paintings in the world painted on an easel. There is also a gallery for contemporary exhibits.

The gallery has an extensive collection of non-Brazilian works and a particularly fine selection of Baroque Italian art dating from the 17th and 18th centuries. The museum was created on the basis of a prized art collection, brought to Brazil from Europe by Portugal's King Dom João VI and his court when they fled Napoleon in 1808 (see p56).

⓭ Museu Histórico Nacional

Praça Marechal Âncora.
Map 5 F4. **Tel** (21) 2550 9224.
Ⓜ Cinelândia. **Open** 10am–5:30pm Tue–Fri, 1–5pm Sat, Sun & public hols. 🖼 🧎 restricted.
🔗 **museuhistoriconacional.com.br**

Founded in 1922, the country's leading history museum recounts the history of Brazil up to 1889. Its collection of 287,000 pieces and 80% of Brazil's museological heritage includes everything from paintings and coins to carriages and rarities such as the pen used by Princess Isabel to sign the decree abolishing slavery. Apart from displaying period furniture, 19th-century firearms, and locomotives, the museum also traces Brazil's colonial past in its charts and written declarations. The building is one of the oldest in Rio, with a portion belonging to Santiago Fort, dating from 1603.

A Batalha do Avaí (1877) by Pedro Américo, Museu Nacional de Belas Artes

⑭ Museu de Arte Moderna

Av Infante Dom Henrique 85, Centro.
Map 5 F5. **Tel** (21) 3883 5600.
Ⓜ Cinelândia. **Open** noon–6pm
Tue–Fri, 11am–6pm Sat, Sun & public
hols (last adm half hour before closing).
🅿 💷 🅱 🆆 **mamrio.org.br**

Rio's Modern Art Museum (MAM) has one of the best collections of 20th-century art in Brazil, surpassed only by MASP in São Paulo *(see p147)*. The museum also houses one of the largest archives of Brazilian films.

The strikingly modern building that houses the MAM was far ahead of its time in its design and architecture when it was built in 1958. In 1978, a major fire destroyed many of its irreplaceable exhibits, including the works of Miró, Picasso, Salvador Dalí, Max Ernst, and René Magritte. It has taken time and the generosity of collectors in Brazil and abroad to rebuild the collection. Today, the MAM is once more a highly regarded institution, not only for its own archive but also for the visiting exhibitions from around the world that it stages frequently.

Located close to its gardens is a monument to the victims of World War II. In 1980, Pope John Paul II said mass from the steps of the monument to a crowd of more than 2 million people. Below the monument is a museum describing Brazil's participation in the Allied operations, known as the Italian Campaign, in and around Italy between 1944 and 1945.

⑮ Igreja Nossa Senhora da Glória do Outeiro

Praça Nossa Senhora da Glória 135, Glória. **Tel** (21) 2557 4600. Ⓜ Glória.
Open 9am–4pm Tue–Fri, 8am–noon
Sat & Sun. 🕆 9am, 11am & 6:30pm
Sun. 🆆 **outeirodagloria.org.br**

Most visitors to downtown Rio cannot help but notice the beautiful octagonal church of Our Lady of Gloria, as it sits

Igreja Nossa Senhora da Glória do Outeiro rising above tree tops

majestically on top of a hill beside the freeways cutting through Flamengo Park.

The spot where the church was built, in 1714, was first used as a place of worship in 1608, when the image of Our Lady of Gloria was placed in a grotto.

The church, which was completed in 1739, became the favorite place of worship for Dom Pedro VI and his family after their arrival from Portugal in 1808. Known for its hand-painted tiles dating from the 1730s, it was declared a national monument by President Vargas in 1937.

The church can be reached by car, or by foot up the steps known as Ladeira de Nossa Senhora. It is also possible to take a small cable car from Rua do Russel 312. There are views across the bay, as well as a small sacred art museum that also includes objects from the royal family.

⑯ Museu da República

Rua do Catete 153, Catete.
Tel (21) 2127 0324. Ⓜ Catete.
Open 10am–4:30pm Tue–Fri,
11am–5:30pm Sat & Sun. 🅿 🅲
🆆 **museudarepublica.gov.br**

The story of Brazil's history, as told by the Museum of the Republic, picks up where the Museu Histórico Nacional left off. It begins with the

Proclamation of the Republic in 1889, and covers events until 1960, when the capital and the then president, Kubitschek, moved from Rio de Janeiro to Brasília. What makes the museum particularly special is that its building, constructed between 1858 and 1866, was the presidential residence from 1897 until 1954. In that year, President Getúlio Vargas *(see pp60–61)*, Brazil's most influential statesman who was president for 24 years, committed suicide in his bedroom, which has been preserved exactly as it used to be when he lived here. In total, the palace was home to 18 Brazilian presidents, all of whom feature in the museum's various exhibits.

Apart from the museum and palace, there is also an attractive garden on the grounds.

Attractive garden outside the Museu da República

⑰ Oi Futuro Ipanema

Rua Visconde de Piraja 54.
Tel (21) 3131 9333. Ⓜ General
Osório **Open** 1–9pm Tue–Sun.
🆆 **oifuturo.org.br**

A renovated 1918 building near Ipanema beach houses Oi Futuro, a hypermodern cultural center for art and technology. It hosts innovative exhibitions of avant-garde visual arts with multimedia installations that blend art forms such as painting, photography, film, music, and poetry. There are also film screenings, dance performances, and concerts of experimental musical styles from all over the world.

⑱ Sugar Loaf Mountain

Guarding the entrance to Guanabara Bay, the monolithic granite and quartz Sugar Loaf rises 1,300 ft (396 m) above the waters of the southern Atlantic Ocean. From the summit, it is easy to understand why the early explorers believed that they had sailed into the mouth of a great river they christened Rio de Janeiro. The Sugar Loaf experience takes in two mountains, Morro do Urca and Pão de Açúcar (Sugar Loaf). It is possible to scale both these mountains via organized climbs on most weekends. Demanding less effort, the cable car, originally opened in 1912, stops at the 705-ft- (224-m-) high Morro da Urca before ascending to the summit.

The original 1912 cable car, a remarkable feat of its times

Pão de Açúcar
The name of Sugar Loaf, adopted in the 19th century, is assumed to have been derived from the mountain's shape, which resembles conical clay molds used earlier to refine sugar. The Tupi Indians, however, called it "Pau-nh-Açuquã" (high, pointed, or isolated hill).

KEY

① **The summit** provides unforgettable views out over Copacabana, Ipanema, and the scenic Corcovado and Tijuca.

② **Helisight**, with a heliport base at Morro da Urca, offers flights around Sugar Loaf and Corcovado (see pp86–7).

③ **Morro da Urca** The flat summit of Morro da Urca has a small museum, restaurants, bars, and a theater that hosts popular shows, concerts, and even Carnaval balls.

④ **Wooded Trails** A series of trails that lead to a number of good climbing locations wind their way up to the summit. The trails are also an ideal place to spot marmosets.

⑤ **Cable car station at Praia Vermelha**

⑥ **Boats** can be hired at many key locations for an enjoyable ride in the calm waters to the base of Sugar Loaf.

Rock Climbing
Since British nanny Henrietta Carstairs made the first recorded solo ascent in 1817, climbing the smooth Sugar Loaf has become a popular sport, with over 60 known routes to the towering summit.

Cable Car Ride
The current Italian cable system carries as many as 1,360 passengers every hour. The glass walls of the cable car allow sweeping views of the city.

Rio City at Night
The city of Rio de Janeiro boasts a stunning nightscape. The magnificent Sugar Loaf remains illuminated, even in the dead of the night, by powerful 1,000-watt projectors.

James Bond's Moonraker
In 1979, Sugar Loaf and the cable car formed the backdrop for a main action sequence in *Moonraker*, with Roger Moore playing James Bond. In real life, the Great Train Robber, Ronald Biggs, was kidnapped in 1981 by a group of British mercenaries from a restaurant, which was then located next to the cable car station. Ironically, during a first kidnap bid in 1979, the kidnappers had claimed to be part of the *Moonraker* crew.

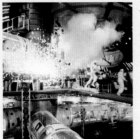

A scene from the film *Moonraker*

Bustling Copacabana beach, popular with locals and vacationers

⑲ Copacabana

Ⓜ Siqueira Campos. ℹ Av Princesa Isabel 183, (21) 2541 7522.

One of the world's most celebrated beaches, the iconic Copacabana is the center of Rio's tourist trade. On New Year's eve, the neighborhood becomes Rio's spiritual and festive heart, as millions of Cariocas and visitors take to the beach to party, and honor Yemanjá, Goddess of the Sea.

The name Copacabana, or "Copa Caguana" (Luminous Place) in Quechua, an ancient language spoken in Peru, was given by the Incas to a lovely site by the Lagoa Titicaca, where they built a temple. In the 17th century, the captain of a Spanish galleon erected a chapel in honor of Our Lady of Copacabana, who came to his aid during a shipwreck. Built in 1914, on the promontory of the chapel as Rio's defense against attack, the **Forte de Copacabana** offers scenic views of the entire sweep of Copacabana.

The main attraction of Copacabana is the beach which, along with Leme, constitutes a magnificent 3-mile (5-km) stretch from Le Meridien hotel in the north on the corner of Avenida Princesa Isabel, to the Forte de Copacabana and Sofitel Rio in the south. Until 1892, it had been a leading trek for those from the city to reach Copacabana. In that year, a tunnel was cut through from Botafogo to Copacabana, followed by a second tunnel in 1904 that allowed the trams to reach the beach. The real turning point, however, was the creation of the Neo-Classical **Copacabana Palace** hotel (see p370), a part of the fabric of Rio life since its opening in 1923. It has hosted both authentic royalty and the royalty of the entertainment world, including Queen Elizabeth II and Marlene Dietrich. The hotel continues to draw the rich and famous.

The **Museu da Imagem e do Som** (Museum of Image and Sound) places an emphasis on the history of Brazilian music and film. The striking modern building opens in 2018 and will incorporate the collection previously housed in Museu Carmen Miranda, including the costumes that belonged to the starlet, her records, and films.

The beachfront kiosk bars lining Avenue Atlântica – the road that runs the length of the beach – are popular. The entire length of Copacabana is divided into stations (postos). Postos 5 and 6 attract older residents and favela youngsters. The fresh catch of the day can be bought at Posto 7 – at the southern end – known as the posto de pescadores (fisherman's post).

🏰 **Forte de Copacabana**
Av Atlântica Posto 6. **Tel** (21) 2521 1032. **Open** 10am–6pm Tue–Sun. 🆆 forte decopacabana.com 🅿 📷 ♿

🏛 **Museu da Imagem e do Som**
Av Atlântica 3432. **Tel** (21) 2332 9521. **Open** see website for times.
🆆 mis.rj.gov.br 🅿 📷 ♿

Map of Copacabana, Ipanema & Leblon

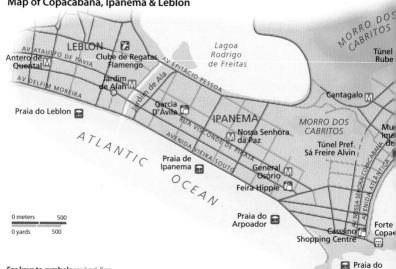

Exterior of an upmarket jewelry store in Ipanema

⑳ Ipanema

Ⓜ General Osório, Nossa Senhora da Paz. ⓘ Rua Visconde de Pirajá/Rua Joana Angélica. **Open** 9am–6pm daily.

Almost as famous as Copacabana, Ipanema shot into the limelight in the 1960s with the globally famous song written by Antônio Jobim and Vinícius de Moraes, "The Girl from Ipanema" *(see p36)*.

The actual name of this fashionable area is credited to the native Tupi-Guaraní who called the area Y-panema, or "rough water." The first non-native residents moved into the area around 1884, and today Ipanema and neighboring

The Girl from Ipanema

One of the most played and recorded songs in popular music history, "The Girl from Ipanema," or "A Garota de Ipanema," was written in 1962 by Antônio Carlos Jobim and Vinícius de Moraes. The duo are said to have been inspired by a sensual girl from Ipanema, Helô Pinheiro. A year later, the recording of the song's most famous version took place in New York's A&R Studio, featuring João and Astrud Gilberto, in the Portuguese and English versions, respectively. In 1964, Stan Getz, Jobim, and the Gilbertos took *bossa nova* to a global audience with the release of *Getz/Gilberto*. With "The Girl from Ipanema" as the opening track, the album stayed in the US charts for 96 weeks and won four Grammys.

Astrud Gilberto

Leblon are considered the most desirable places to live in Rio. More residential than Copacabana, Ipanema is also more stylish, its back streets dotted with chic boutiques, bars, restaurants, and nightclubs.

The most prestigious address in Rio is Avenida Vieira Souto, while running parallel, two streets back, is Rua Visconde de Pirajá, the backbone to the Ipanema shopping experience. At the Copacabana end is Praça General Osório, the public square that plays host to Rio's popular **Feira Hippie de Ipanema** (Hippie Fair), every Sunday. The fair has been a part of life in Ipanema and Rio since opening in 1968.

The mile-long stretch of Ipanema beach runs from Leblon in the west, up to Arpoador in the east. Arpoador extends the beach by another half-mile, and is popular with the surf set, while the rock next to it is a great spot to watch the sunset.

㉑ Leblon

Ⓜ Jardim de Alah, Antero de Quental. ⓘ Rua Antero de Quental/Av Ataulfo Paiva. **Open** 9am–6pm.

For many years, Leblon sat in the shadow of Ipanema. But today it is considered as fashionable and desirable as its neighbor, with perhaps an even greater density

and mix of bars, clubs, and restaurants. Rua Dias Ferreira, at the most westerly point, boasts a particularly eclectic mix. Like Ipanema, there are only a few hotels along the beachfront Avenida Delfim Moreira.

While the beaches of Copacabana and Leme flow seamlessly into each other, Leblon and Ipanema are separated by Jardim de Alah and the canal that links the Lagoa Rodrigo de Freitas with the sea. The 1-mile- (2-km-) long Leblon is said to have been given its name in honor of a blond foreigner, one of the first residents in the area. The nationality of "Le Blond" is debatable. Some scholars say that he was French, while others surmise he was Dutch.

Leblon is the headquarters of Clube de Regatas Flamengo, of which the most famous is the Flamengo Football Club, the World Club Champions in 1981.

The exclusive Leblon neighborhood and its fashionable beach

MORRO DE SÃO JOÃO

Siqueira Campos

Ⓜ Arcoverde

COPACABANA

Copacabana Palace Hotel ★

Praia de Copacabana

For hotels and restaurants in this region see pp370–71 and pp386–8

View of Lagoa Rodrigo de Freitas and Jóquei Clube Brasileiro from Corcovado

㉒ Lagoa Rodrigo de Freitas

Lagoa. **Map** 2 A3. Ⓜ Jardim de Alah ♿

The picturesque Lagoa Rodrigo de Freitas, or Lagoa (lagoon) as it is often called, sits at the foot of Corcovado peak and separates the Serra da Carioca from Ipanema and Leblon. A full circuit of the lagoon is about 5 miles (8 km) and is popular with joggers, cyclists, and parents with children in prams. There are plenty of halts en route, with kiosks selling everything from coconut water to full meals. Some kiosks even offer live music in the evenings.

The Lagoa is also bordered by more conventional restaurants and bars, especially along the Ipanema stretch. One of Rio's most traditional places, **Bar Lagoa** *(see p387)* opened here in 1934. Along the northern shore, highlights include Claude Troisgros' **Olympe** *(see p388)*, which, despite a change in name since it opened in 1983, is still one of Rio's best restaurants.

Several sports clubs are also located here. Among the most famous are the Jockey Club Brasileiro, the **Sociedade Hípica Brasileira**, the city's main equestrian center, and the headquarters of the Clube Regatas do Flamengo. Flamengo, along with Vasco da Gama, Fluminense, and Botafogo, is one of Brazil's top soccer teams and has won the National and South American titles on many occasions. All clubs have rowing divisions as the Lagoa is Brazil's main rowing

center. Several international regattas have been held here.

Visitors can go boating, as *pedallos* and other craft are available for rent. It is also possible to rent bicycles.

The **Fundação Eva Klabin** is one of Rio's prolific cultural centers and museums. Its exhibits are part of the private collection of Eva Klabin, whose family made a fortune in paper in the mid-20th century.

The scenic **Parque da Catacumba** around Lagoa is interspersed with sculptures by artists Roberto Moriconi, Bruno Giorgi, and Caribé. Monkeys roam the park, which offers views over the Lagoa and toward Ipanema.

🏛 **Fundação Eva Klabin**
Av Epitácio Pessoa 2480.
Tel (21) 3202 8550. **Open** 2–4pm Tue–Sun. 🎟 free Sun.

🌳 **Parque da Catacumba**
Av Epitácio Pessoa 3000. **Tel** (21) 2247 9949. **Open** 8am–5pm daily (to 6pm summer).

🏛 **Sociedade Hípica Brasileira**
Av Borges de Medeiros 2448. **Tel** (21) 2156 0156. **Open** only for events. 🎟 ♿

㉓ Jóquei Clube Brasileiro

Rua Jardim Botânico 1003, Gávea.
Map 1 A2. **Tel** (21) 3534 9061.
Ⓜ Botafogo. 🚌 **Open** from 6pm Mon, from 5:30pm Fri, from 3:15pm Sat & Sun. 🎟 ♿ 🌐 jcb.com.br

With a great view of the Lagoa and the Corcovado mountain, the Jockey Club has one of the most spectacular settings of any racecourse in the world. Races are held four days a week, all

year round, so it is easy to catch the action. The club will allow even non-members and visitors into the members' stand to enjoy the race.

The track first opened in 1926, with the main stand designed in a Louis XV style. In total, there are five stands, a paddock, a turf track, two sand tracks, and an equestrian village. The biggest race of the year – and one of South America's most important – is the Grande Prêmio Brasil do Turfe, that was first run in 1933. It traditionally takes place every June.

㉔ Jardim Botânico

Rua Jardim Botânico 920 & 1008, Gávea. **Map** 1 A1. **Tel** (21) 3874 1808. 🚌 **Open** 8am–5pm daily (Mon: from noon). **Closed** Jan 1 & Dec 25. 🎟 📷 ♿ restricted. 🌐 jbrj.gov.br

Rio's fascinating Jardim Botânico was founded in 1808 by the Prince Regent, Dom João VI. Originally meant to acclimatize plants and spices coming from the Orient and the East Indies, it later became the Royal Garden and opened to the public in 1822. Among its many illustrious visitors were Charles Darwin in 1832 and Albert Einstein in 1925.

Today, Jardim Botânico includes an area of natural rainforest, and is home to many species of plants, as well as innumerable types of birds and animals. However, the

A track lined with palm trees in Jardim Botânico

garden's signature are the 200 imperial palms that line its main avenues.

Jardim Botânico has other attractions within its grounds. These include Rio's original gunpowder factory dating from 1808, the old gates of the Fine Arts Academy, and the Empress's Mansion, which became the headquarters of the National School of Tropical Botany in 2001.

㉕ Museu do Índio

Rua das Palmeiras 55, Botafogo.
Tel (21) 3214 8702. **M** Botafogo.
Open 9am–5:30pm Tue–Fri, 1–5pm Sat, Sun & public hols.
W museudoindio.gov.br

Founded in 1953, the Museum of the Indian is run by the National Indian Foundation (Funai) with the aim of giving an insight into the lives of Brazil's Indian and indigenous groups. Housed in a 19th-century mansion, this dynamic institution has more than 14,000 indigenous artifacts, 50,000 photographs, and over 200 films. With 16,000 books and magazines, it also has one of the most complete libraries covering topics related to indigenous peoples.

There are several permanent exhibits in the gardens, including a Guaraní house, inside which is a well-stocked store that sells genuine indigenous artifacts.

㉖ Museu Villa-Lobos

Rua Sorocaba 200, Botafogo.
Tel (21) 2226 9818. **M** Botafogo.
Open 9am–5pm Mon–Fri.
W museuvillalobos.org.br

With over 1,000 compositions to his credit, Heitor Villa-Lobos (1897–1959) is considered one of the greatest composers in Latin America (see p36). It is believed that it was through his work that Brazilian music first became popular abroad, eventually gaining universal appeal with the advent of *bossa nova*.

The Villa-Lobos Museum, which moved to a stately 19th-century mansion in Botafogo in 1986, helps organize the Villa-Lobos Festival that begins on the anniversary of his death, November 17, each year. His second wife, Arminda Neves d'Almeida, set up the museum in 1960, one year after his death. Its aim is to preserve the composer's personal collection of artifacts and keep his work alive. Exhibits include his books, music scores, photographs, and instruments.

Villa-Lobos's best-known work is his cycle of the nine *Bachianas Brasileiras*, which pays homage to both Bach and Brazilian folk music. Such was his versatility that he wrote a variety of music from *choros* (an upbeat waltz or polka), concertos, symphonies, and orchestral works, to chamber music, operas, and ballets, as well as guitar and solo piano pieces.

Stately building housing the Museu Casa de Rui Barbosa

㉗ Museu Casa de Rui Barbosa

Rua São Clemente 134, Botafogo.
Tel (21) 3289 8686. **M** Botafogo.
Open 10am–5:30pm Tue–Fri, 2–6pm Sat & Sun.
W casaruibarbosa.gov.br

A renowned politician, diplomat, and jurist, Rui Barbosa de Oliveira (1849–1923) helped shape several important Brazilian policies, including those pertaining to direct elections and the abolition of slavery. He made his mark internationally during the 1907 Peace Conference at the Hague, where he argued that all countries should be treated equally. Barbosa contested twice for the Brazilian presidency – in 1910 and 1919 – but lost on both occasions.

Barbosa was also a great essayist and was one of the founders (and later president) of the Brazilian Academy of Letters. He was eventually elected as a judge to the International Court of Justice at the Hague.

The 1850 building that houses the Rui Barbosa Museum was the statesman's home from 1895 until his death in 1923. When it opened to the public in 1930, it was the first private residence in Brazil to be turned into a museum. The museum showcases a collection of Barbosa's personal possessions, such as furniture and art, and a library containing 200 of his own works.

Indigenous roundhouse on the grounds of Museu do Índio

㉘ Morro do Corcovado & Cristo Redentor

The 2,316-ft (706-m) Corcovado mountain derives its name from *corcova* (hunchback), which describes the physical appearance of the mountain itself. On the summit, the iconic Cristo Redentor statue towers over Rio, and is Brazil's most recognizable landmark. It was officially inaugurated in 1931 to mark the centenary of Brazil's independence. The enormous statue sits in the center of the gorgeous tropical jungle of Parque Nacional da Tijuca.

Making the Head
Work on the statue began in Paris in 1926, with French sculptor Paul Landowski working on the head and hands. The head alone weighs 30 tons.

The Statue
Having been shipped from France to Brazil, the 98-ft (30-m) statue was faced in limestone and hauled up the mountain by rail to be assembled and attached to supporting pillars.

Wide Open Arms
The entire Rio City is embraced by Christ, and the statue's open arms are seen as a testament to the warmth of the Brazilians.

Famous Visitors
Pope John Paul II, Pope Pius XII, and Albert Einstein are some of the famous people to have visited Corcovado.

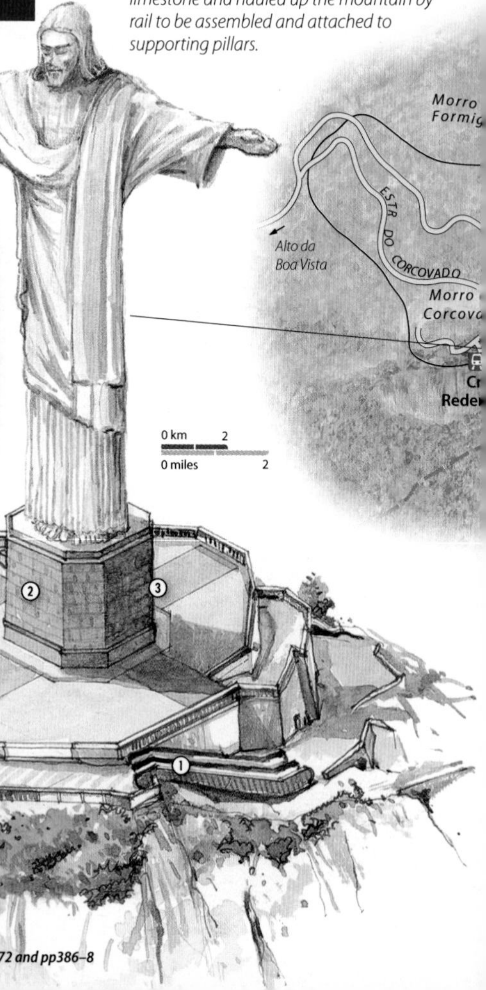

Morro
Formig

Alto da
Boa Vista

E. STR. DO CORCOVADO

Morro
Corcova

Cr
Rede

0 km   2

0 miles   2

②   ③

①

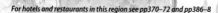

★ **Museu Internacional de Arte Naïf**
The museum has one of the largest collections of naive art in the world, featuring more than 6,000 works, dating from the 15th century to the present.

VISITORS' CHECKLIST

Practical Information
Morro do Corcovado.
🛈 Corcovado, (21) 2492 2252.
Open 8:30am–6:30pm daily.
(entrance at Parque Nacional
da Tijuca). 🆆 **corcovado.com.br**

Transport
🚇 Cosme Velho station, Rua
Cosme Velho 513, 8:30am–7pm
daily. 🚌 180, 184, 583 & 584.
Shuttle van: 🆆 **paineiras**
corcovado.com.br

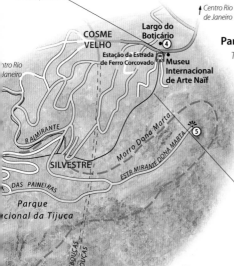

↑ *Centro Rio de Janeiro*

COSME VELHO

Largo do Boticário ④

Estação da Estrada de Ferro Corcovado

Museu Internacional de Arte Naïf

ntro Rio Janeiro

R. ALMIRANTE

Morro Dona Marta

ESTR. MIRANTE DONA MARTA

⑤

SILVESTRE

DAS PAINEIRAS

Parque cional da Tijuca

TÚNEL ANTONIO REBOUÇAS
TÚNEL ANDRE REBOUÇAS

Key

▬ Major road
▭ Other road
▭ Minor road
— Cog train route
= = Tunnels
▬ ▬ Park boundary

Parque Nacional Da Tijuca

The statue of Christ sits in this scenic national park, which contains the world's largest urban forest – Floresta da Tijuca. Dotted with natural springs, the park is home to more than 200 species of birds and several small mammals. It draws regular crowds of resident Cariocas, especially on the weekend (see p92).

Cog Train
Passing through the dense Atlantic rainforest, the train ride up the summit is a plus. The line was originally built in 1882 by Dom Pedro II; the current Swiss train dates from 1979.

KEY

① **Escalators** link the base to the train station and car park.

② **The pedestal**, on which the statue stands, is 26 ft (8 m) high.

③ **The chapel** at the base of the statue can accommodate 150 people.

④ **Largo do Boticário** is a lovely square surrounded by seven private houses. Colonial in appearance, the houses date from around 1920.

⑤ **Mirante Dona Marta** offers splendid views of Rio City.

★ **Stunning Views**
Corcovado is located right in the center of Rio and can be seen from most areas of the city. The views over and across Rio from the summit offer a sweeping aerial panorama.

For keys to symbols *see back flap*

㉙ Estádio do Maracanã

Rua Prof. Eurico Rabelo (gate 18), Maracanã. **Closed** until further notice ♿

Rio's Maracanã Stadium is one of the most famous soccer grounds in the world. It is also the largest, having hosted crowds of up to 200,000 people.

The stadium, which was refurbished for the 2007 Pan-American Games, was built for the 1950 World Cup and inaugurated on June 16 the same year, with a game between Rio and São Paulo.

The first game played by the Brazilian team took place on June 24, 1950, with Brazil beating Mexico 4–0. A month later, a crowd of almost 200,000 tested the stadium's capacity to see Brazil play Uruguay in the final game. Brazil lost 2–1, and thus began its eternal rivalry with Uruguay.

It is not only soccer that has set stadium records. Big artists have attracted massive crowds to the Maracanã, including Frank Sinatra, Paul McCartney, Kiss, Madonna, the Rolling Stones, Sting, Tina Turner, and the second "Rock in Rio" Festival. Pope John Paul II's public appearances in 1980 and 1997 were also attended by thousands.

Since the conclusion of the 2016 Olympic Games, however, the stadium has fallen into a state of disrepair. A political imbroglio between the stadium's owner and the operator has prevented it from re-opening for matches and tours until further notice.

Rio Zoo's main gate, gifted to Dom Pedro I by an English aristocrat

㉚ Quinta da Boa Vista

Av Pedro II (between Rua Almirante Baltazar & Rua Dom Meinrdo, São Cristóvão). Ⓜ São Cristóvão. Museu Nacional: **Tel** (21) 3938 1123. **Open** noon–4pm Mon (5pm summer), 10am–4pm Tue–Sun (5pm summer). **Closed** Jan 1, Dec 25, Carnaval & Good Friday. 🏛 Jardim Zoológico: **Tel** (21) 3461 4616. **Open** 9am–5pm Tue–Sun. 🌐 riozoo.com.br

The Quinta da Boa Vista, the landscaped grounds of a former royal estate, includes the **Museu Nacional** and the **Jardim Zoológico** (Rio Zoo). Founded by Dom João VI in 1818, the Museu Nacional is the country's oldest scientific institution, which started out as the House of Birds before becoming the Royal Museum, the Imperial Museum, and, finally, the National Museum.

Its permanent exhibits cover a variety of fields from archaeology, biodiversity, and botany to ethnology, geology, and palaeontology. A part of the collection belonged to Emperor Pedro II, a botanist, and his wife, the Empress Teresa Cristina,

who was an archaeologist. The museum's gardens and the former royal palace are an attraction in their own right, and their lakes and grottos are a big draw on the weekends. They were landscaped by the French architect Auguste Glaziou in 1869.

The Jardim Zoológico is considered one of the best in the world and is Brazil's oldest zoo, having been founded in 1888. It is home to approximately 350 species and more than 2,100 animals, including one of the most complete collections of Brazilian mammals and butterflies. Particular highlights include the Brazilian monkeys and birds. The zoo boasts an excellent aviary and an aquarium that houses a variety of fascinating Brazilian river species.

The zoo's beautiful main entrance was a wedding gift, presented to Dom Pedro I and the Empress Leopoldina by an English aristocrat in the early 19th century.

㉛ Sambódromo & Cidade do Samba

Sambódromo: Av Marquês de Sapucaí, Centro. **Map** 4 A4. **Tel** (21) 2563 9000. Ⓜ Praça XI. **Open** 9am–4pm Mon–Fri (partially closed Dec–Carnaval). ♿ Cidade do Samba: Rua Rivadávia Correa 60, Gamboa. **Tel** (21) 2213 2503. ♿ 🌐 cidadedosambarj.com.br 🌐 liesa.com.br

The Sambódromo, or Passarela do Samba, is where Rio's famous *samba* schools parade each February during Carnaval *(see pp68–9)*.

Before Carnaval was as popular as it is today, the schools simply paraded on the streets and people stood on the sidewalk, and later, on specially built stands. As the crowds got bigger, the disruption caused by the building of the stands each year meant another solution was needed.

The renowned Brazilian architect, Oscar Niemeyer *(see p299)*, came up with a permanent solution. He built what is today the Sambódromo, which

Aerial view of the Estádio do Maracanã

The Sambódromo, venue of parades by Rio's samba schools during annual Carnaval

was inaugurated in time for the 1984 Carnaval. In order to complement the Sambódromo, a large complex, known as the **Cidade do Samba** (City of Samba), was established in 2005. This space is used by the main *samba* schools to build their floats and make their vibrant costumes. Throughout the year, visitors are allowed in to watch the preparations and see how a *samba* school puts on its parade, but the schedules vary and visitors should call ahead and check with each school.

❷ Centro Cultural do Banco do Brasil

Rua Primeiro de Março 66, Centro. **Map** 5 E3. **Tel** (21) 3808 2020. Ⓜ Carioca. **Open** 9am–9pm Wed–Sun. 🔗 🖥 🗔 **bb.com.br/cultura**

Located in what used to be the financial quarter of Rio de Janeiro's Centro district in an impressive building dating from 1880, the Centro Cultural do Banco do Brasil (CCBB) was originally the headquarters for the Trade Association and the Bank of Brazil. In 1989 the building was converted into a major cultural center with three theaters, four exhibition rooms, a cinema, a large public library, and a bookstore.

The gallery spaces offer a wide selection of changing exhibitions, from paintings and sculpture to photography. There is one permanent exhibition on the evolution of Brazil's currency. The cinema screens art films and hosts experimental film festivals, while the theaters stage dance performances and lunchtime and evening concerts of both classical and modern music, as well as plays. Many of the cultural center's events are free of charge *(see also pp98–9)*.

The building itself is worth a visit; it consists of imposing columns and a rotunda (the old trading floor stock exchange), a marbled lobby, and grand staircases.

Rio's Favelas

As much a part of the city's landscape as Corcovado and Sugar Loaf, Rio's *favelas* are famous, largely due to their prominence in Fernando Meirelles' 2002 film, *Cidade de Deus* (City of God). Rio has about 8,000 *favelas* – areas of informal, often precarious urbanization, most of which lack basic services such as water and electricity. What started as one or two shacks on a hillside has slowly grown into cities in their own right. Estimates suggest that about 20 percent of the city's population may now live in these areas. Some *favelas* have grown into giant communities, such as Rocinha in São Conrado, with over 150,000 residents. Others, such as Pavão, Cantagalo, Vidigal, and Chapéu Mangueira, are strategically located in hilly Zona Sul areas offering breathtaking views.

Favelas are complex and vibrant communities, whose inhabitants mostly have low-wage jobs in wealthier neighborhoods, while some make a living from small local businesses. Many *favelas* still have drug lords who run *bocas de fumo*, where narcotics are sold. This practice has been reduced with the introduction of pacifying police units in some *favelas* since the mid-2000s, although cases of police brutality are not uncommon. It is still advisable only to visit these areas as part of a guided tour. There are several good tours on offer. Favela Tour is run by Marcelo Armstrong, who was brought up in an apartment block adjoining the Vila Canoas *favela*. He and his team have been guiding visitors around Vila Canoas and Rocinha since 1992. The tours offer valuable insights into the lives of thousands of Rio's less privileged citizens and into the corporate responsibility projects developed by Favela Tour in two of Rocinha's schools. Brazilidade in *favela* Santa Marta is run by Sheila Souza, who was born and raised in this *favela* where Michael Jackson recorded the video for "They Don't Care About Us". Revenue from her tours is reinvested in the community. For more information and to book, visit www.favelatour.com.br and www.brazilidade.com.br).

Rocinha, located in São Conrado, one of Rio's largest and most complex *favelas*

㉝ Barra

The fastest growing suburb of Rio, Barra da Tijuca houses the Riocentro, Latin America's largest convention and exhibition center, and the Sítio Roberto Burle Marx, a superb collection of tropical plants from around the world. Besides Barra Shopping Center, one of the largest shopping malls in South America, Barra boasts many other modern malls and supermarkets. There are also Rio City's most modern multiplex cinemas and an ever-growing number of restaurants, bars, clubs, and hotels. Barra is bordered by the city's longest beach, Praia da Barra da Tijuca.

Barra Shopping Center, one of the largest shopping malls in Latin America

Map of Barra da Tijuca

① 🏖 **Praia da Barra da Tijuca**
Av Sernambetiba.
Stretching for over 11 miles (18 km), Praia da Barra da Tijuca is Rio's longest beach. The first 4 miles (6 km) are the most built-up, a modern-day Copacabana, with large condominiums.

There are different hot spots along the length of the beach, the most famous of which is Barraca do Pepê, a tremendously busy food outlet that has been a favorite with the surfing and hang-gliding crowd, with a kiosk that served organic food long before people had heard of it.

Crowds from all over Rio are drawn to this beach at weekends, but farther along it becomes less crowded and unspoilt. During the week, when schools are in session, it is even possible to find large isolated stretches.

② 🏬 **Barra Shopping Center**
Av das Américas 4666.
Tel (21) 4003 4131.
This large and popular shopping center has an impressive range of shops. There are also eight movie theaters, a medical center, a bowling alley, and many coffee shops.

③ 🏛 **Cidade das Artes**
Trevo das Palmeiras. **Tel** (21) 3325 0102.
📷 🌐 cidadedasartes.org
This cultural center houses one of the largest concert halls in Latin America and is home to the Brazilian Symphony Orchestra.

With the main building suspended 33 ft (10 m) above the ground, the center has a 1,800-seater main hall, smaller halls, four movie theaters, and shops, bars, and restaurants.

④ 🏛 **Museu Seleção Brasileira**
Av Luís Carlos Prestes 130. **Tel** (21) 3572 1963. **Open** 10am–5:30pm daily. 🌐 museuselecaobrasileira.com.br 📷
Soccer arrived in Brazil in 1894. Twenty years later, the

The long stretch of Praia da Barra da Tijuca

For keys to symbols *see back flap*

Fascinating collection of tropical plants at Sítio Roberto Burle Marx

VISITORS' CHECKLIST

Practical Information
Rio de Janeiro.
🏠 30,000.
🛈 Praça Pio X 119,
(21) 2088 0070.
🆆 visit.rio

Transport
Ⓜ Jardim Oceânico

Brazil squad played its first official match and won its first trophy, the Copa Roca. So began a legend. Trophies, photos, and more are on display at this shrine to the national team.

⑤ Parque dos Atletas

Av Salvador Allende, Portão 9.
Open 6am–10pm Tue–Sun.
Also known as Parque do Olympíco Cidade do Rock, the Althletes' Park was built in preparation for the 2016 Olympic Games to provide sports facilites and a venue for large events. The large park's leisure facilities are now open to the public, and include tennis courts, an ice skating rink, a climbling wall, a children's playground, and tracks for running and biking. The biennial Rock in Rio Festival is held here.

⑥ 🏛 Centro de Conveções Riocentro

Av Salvador Allende 6555.
Tel (21) 2441 9100. 🅿 ♿
🆆 riocentro.com.br
Latin America's largest exhibition and convention center, Riocentro received tremendous global attention when it hosted the 1992 United Nations Conference on Environment and Development, the Earth Summit, which was unprecedented for its magnitude and the scope of its concerns.
The large complex has five pavilions, and includes a heliport, lawns, gardens, a natural lake, and parking facilities.

⑦ Projac-TV Globo

Estrada dos Bandeirantes 6700,
Jacarepaguá. **Tel** (21) 2540 2000.
Globo is one of the world's largest television networks and produces most of its own prime-time programming, including its famous soap operas, called the *novelas*, three of which are screened daily. A complete entertainment factory, Projac includes four studios, two auditoriums, scenery and costume workshops, a restaurant, and the production offices.

⑧ 🌳 Sítio Roberto Burle Marx

Estrada Burle Marx 2019. **Tel** (21) 2410 1412. **Open** 9:30am and 1:30pm Tue–Sat by appointment only. 🅿
This private garden belonged to Roberto Burle Marx (*see p299*), one of the most important landscape architects of the 20th century. In 1949, Burle Marx bought a plantation and started to organize his private collection of amazing plants. He moved here in 1973 and stayed until his death. In 1985, he donated the entire estate to the National Institute for Cultural Heritage (IPHAN).
With around 3,500 plant species, the garden is considered one of the most important collections of tropical and semi-tropical plants in the world. This horticultural paradise also displays the works of Burle Marx, from the designs for his landscape projects to his paintings and sculptures. The garden also has a small Benedictine chapel dating from the 17th century, dedicated to St. Anthony.

⑨ 🏛 Casa do Pontal

Estrada do Pontal 3295. **Tel** (21) 2490 2429. **Open** 9:30am–5pm Tue–Sun.
🅿 ♿ 🆆 museucasadopontal. com.br
Almost the entire collection in this charming museum is based on the private collection by the Frenchman, Jacques Van de Beuque. Around 200 artists from every region of Brazil have had their works represented here.
The superb collection at the Casa do Pontal consists of more than 8,000 works of Brazilian folk art including sculptures, wood carvings, models, and mechanized sets. These are made from a variety of materials including clay, wood, cloth, sand, iron, aluminium, straw, wire, and even bread dough.

⑩ 🏖 Praia Prainha & Grumari

Av Estado da Guanabara.
Prainha and Grumari are the city's most unspoilt beaches, and are deserted during the week as they are only accessible by car. Prainha, just 164 yards (150 m) long, is particularly popular with the surf crowd, while Grumari is larger and attracts couples and families. Some scenes from the 1984 Hollywood comedy *Blame It on Rio* were filmed along the road to Grumari.
The restaurant and bar, Point de Grumari, on the top of the hill to the west, offers spectacular views along the coast to the west.

A surfer at the picturesque and secluded Prainha beach

The lush setting of the Mayrink Chapel, Parque Nacional da Tijuca

❸ Parque Nacional da Tijuca

Tel (21) 2492 2253. 🚌 345 from Ⓜ Uruguai. **Open** 8am–6pm daily. ♿
🛈 Estrada da Cascatinha 850, Terra Brasil, (21) 2492 2252.

Covering 15 sq miles (39 sq km), the Tijuca National Park encompasses the last remaining tracts of Atlantic rainforest that once surrounded Rio de Janeiro. It includes the Floresta da Tijuca (Tijuca Forest), Serra da Carioca (Carioca Mountains), and the monoliths of Pedra da Gávea and Pedra Bonita. The park's most famous landmark is the towering statue of Cristo Redentor atop Corcovado peak (see pp86–7). Other well-known viewpoints are the Dona Marta, the Vista Chinesa (with a Chinese-style pavilion), and the Mesa do Imperador (Emperor's Table), all of which offer spectacular city views.

Sights within the Floresta da Tijuca include **Cascatinha do Taunay**, a waterfall near the main gate named after the French painter Nicolau Taunay

Cascatinha do Taunay, one of Parque Nacional da Tijuca's many waterfalls

(1755–1830); the 19th-century **Mayrink Chapel**, featuring the work of Candido Portinari (1903–62), one of the most important Brazilian painters; the lovely Os Esquilos restaurant; and the hundreds of species of plants, birds, and mammals that live here.

Many of the park's 150-odd trails, originally made by Brazil's indigenous people and African slaves, exist even today. One of them, dating from the 19th century, takes walkers up from Largo do Bom Retiro, a picnic spot in the Floresta da Tijuca, to the 3,940-ft-

Tiled map of park routes in Alto da Boa Vista

(1,201-m-) high Tijuca Peak. It is easy to get lost in the dense foliage, so stick to the main trails and do not go without a guide if planning on trekking. Book in advance if a guide is required.

Another attraction near the Floresta da Tijuca is the **Museu do Açude**, a museum housed in the Neo-Colonial building that once served as the residence of the successful businessman, Raymundo Ottoni de Castro Maya (1894–1968). The museum is known for its French, Dutch, Spanish, and Portuguese tiles from the 17th and 18th centuries, and for Castro Maya's personal collection of Oriental art.

🏛 Museu do Açude

Estrada do Açude 764, Alto da Boa Vista. **Tel** (21) 3433 4990. **Open** 11am–4:30pm Wed–Mon. 📷 free on Thu. 📷 ♿

❸ Baía de Guanabara

Without Baía de Guanabara, Rio de Janeiro would probably have been known by a different name. On January 1, 1502, the navigators Andre Gonçalves and Amerigo Vespucci became the first Europeans ever to sail into the bay. Assuming it was the mouth of a great river, they called it Rio de Janeiro or "River of January." Guanabara, meaning "Lagoon of the Sea," was the name given to the dominant bay by indigenous Brazilians and is rather more accurate.

The bay is flanked by Rio to its west and Niterói to its east, and encompasses countless islands. As well as the ferry services that begin at Praça XV, boats can be hired from the **Marina da Glória** in Flamengo Park, the center of all nautical activities in Rio. One of the more pleasant ways to enjoy the bay is by taking the special cruise that starts from the **Espaço Cultural da Marinha** (Navy Cultural Center) in Centro. Centro has a number of fine nautical exhibits, including an Imperial Barge built in Salvador in 1808, and also offers a cruise on the historic tugboat, Laurindo Pitta, which was built in England in 1910 and took part in World War I. The cruise lasts an hour and a half and passes several interesting sights along the way.

The Tom Jobim International Airport is located on the largest of the islands in the bay, **Ilha do Governador**, while the tiny **Ilha Fiscal** houses a palace built in 1889 at the request of Emperor Dom Pedro II in the style of a 14th-century French castle. The castle's highlights include its exceptional carved stonework and cast-iron work, and the turret's mosaic floor, which is made from different species of

Museu de Art Contemporârnea (MAC-Niterói), hovering like a flying saucer above Boa Viagem

hardwood. Also noteworthy are the wall paintings by 19th-century Dutch artist Frederico Steckel, and the tower clock and stained-glass windows, which were imported from England.

Ilha Paquetá, north of the bay, is an oasis of calm where no cars are allowed. Ferries and hydrofoils cruise up the bay to the island from the Estação das Barcas in front of the historic Praça XV. Crossing the bay is the Rio-Niterói Bridge (officially the Presidente Costa e Silva Bridge), which is one of the longest in the world at 9 miles (13 km). The project was financed by Britain, and construction began in 1968 in the presence of Queen Elizabeth II.

🏛 Espaço Cultural da Marinha
Av Alfred Agache, Centro. **Tel** (21) 2532 5992. **Open** noon–5pm Tue–Sun. 🎫 🚻 📷 🏛

🚢 Ilha Fiscal
Baía de Guanabara. **Tel** (21) 2233 9165. **Open** only for tours at 12:30pm, 2pm & 3:30pm Thu–Sun. 📷 🎫

⚓ Marina da Glória
Av Infante Dom Henrique, Glória. **Tel** (21) 2555 2200. 🚻

🟤 Niterói

🏙 475,000. 🚢 Ipanema, Copacabana: 740D; Botafogo, Flamengo: 750D, 775D; Lapa: 775D, 565D 🚌
🌐 niteroiturismo.com.br

Cariocas like to joke that the best thing about Niterói is its view across the bay to Rio de Janeiro. Whereas the view is indeed stunning, Niteroi, or the "Smiling City" as locals call it, has its own charm. The city used to be the state's capital, but lost the title to Rio after both were connected by the Rio-Niterói bridge and Brasilia took over as the nation's capital from Rio.

The British preferred Niterói to Rio, and in 1872, founded the Rio Cricket and Athletic Club that is still active there today. Praia de São Francisco in Guanabara Bay is the city's answer to Copacabana beach, but for the most part is not ideal for swimming. Niterói's better beaches – **Camboinhas**, **Itaipu**, and **Itacoatiara** – lie on the Atlantic coast, and are very popular on weekends.

The two most popular sights in the city are the imposing **Fortaleza de Santa Cruz** and the **Museu de Arte Contemporârnea** (MAC-Niterói). The Fortaleza de Santa Cruz (Santa Cruz Fort) sits on a rocky outcrop just outside the city and guards the entrance to Guanabara Bay. Parts of the fort date from the 16th century, when the French built an improvised fortification to protect the city. The structure grew until it became the most important fortress in Brazil. It helped protect Niterói from two invasions, the first of which came from the Dutch in 1599, and the second from the French in 1710.

The stunning Museu de Arte Contemporârnea (Contemporary Art Museum) appears to hover above the neighborhood of Boa Viagem. The illusion comes from its slender base pillar, which is only 30 ft (9 m) in diameter. Inaugurated in 1996, it was the brainchild of the acclaimed Brazilian architect, Oscar Niemeyer (see p299), and is one of a series of his buildings scattered along Niterói's coast-line on Caminho Niemeyer. Its exhibits consist of 1,000 pieces of Brazilian art donated by the eminent art collector, João Sattamini. The view from inside the museum at dusk, when Rio's lights twinkle from across the bay, is particularly enchanting.

🚢 Fortaleza de Santa Cruz
Estrada Gaspar Dutra, Jurujuba. **Open** 10am–5pm Tue–Sun. 📷 🎫

🏛 Museu de Arte Contemporârnea
Mirante da Boa Viagem, Niterói. **Tel** (21) 2620 2400. **Open** 10am–6pm Tue–Sun. 📷 🎫 book in advance. 🚻
🌐 culturaniteroi.com.br/macniteroi

A panoramic view of the Marina da Glória, Baía de Guanabara

SHOPPING IN RIO

Resident Cariocas have turned shopping into something of an art form and use it as an alternative form of entertainment when they are bored with the beach. Visitors will be pleased to find out just how far their money goes in Rio's stores, especially when it comes to buying items that have been manufactured in Brazil. This includes top fashion clothing, beach and sportswear, leather goods, jewelry, and numerous other items. Until the 1980s, the best place to shop was along Visconde de Pirajá in Ipanema. Although the area is still considered to have the hippest boutiques, Rio's residents have fallen in love with the experience of shopping in the larger malls, such as Rio Sul and Barra Shopping Center, one of the largest shopping and entertainment complexes in Latin America. The historic districts of Centro and Copacabana (mainly the area along Avenida Nossa Senhora de Copacabana) cannot be overlooked, as it is here that most of Rio's quirky, special interest shops are found. The Hippie Fair is the best place to buy arts and crafts items, trinkets, curios, and souvenirs to take home as gifts.

Rio Sul, one of the two giant malls dominating Rio's shopping scene

Opening Hours

Most stores in Rio open from 9 or 10am in the morning until 6 or 7pm in the evening Monday to Friday, and between 9 or 10am until 1pm on Saturday. The big shopping malls, such as Barra Shopping and Rio Sul, stay open from 10am to 10pm Monday through Saturday and from 3 to 9pm on Sunday.

Most supermarkets are open from 8am to 10pm Monday to Saturday, with a limited selection remaining open on Sunday. There are also several 24-hour supermarkets scattered throughout the city.

Shopping Malls

Two giant malls have dominated Rio's shopping scene since the 1980s and offer just about anything people could want under one roof. The closest and most convenient for visitors staying in Copacabana and Ipanema is the **Rio Sul** mall, which is located on the main artery linking the Sugar Loaf end of Copacabana to Botafogo and the city. Rio Sul has more than 400 stores, plus restaurants and cinemas. It also runs a free bus service that picks up shoppers from all the main hotels along the beachfront and drops them back with their purchases. Of course, there are always plenty of taxis at Rio Sul.

Barra Shopping Center (see p90) can almost be treated as a tourist attraction in its own right. It has about 600 stores, as well as a good selection of bars and restaurants, and entertainment that includes a modern bowling alley, an 18-screen multiplex cinema, and a gaming area known as Hot Zone. Both Rio Sul and Barra Shopping Center have branches of virtually all the top Brazilian retailers as well as some familiar international names. The two giant malls are not the only shows in town, and malls in every shape and size can be found all over Rio, including the popular **Fashion Mall** in São Conrado.

Jewelry

Brazil has huge deposits of precious and semi-precious gemstones, and, in some cases, holds more than 90 percent of the world's total supply. This has turned Brazil into one of the most important manufacturers of jewelry, both traditional and modern, and has made Rio de Janeiro into one of the jewel capitals of the world.

The two market leaders, **H. Stern** and **Amsterdam Sauer**, have stores in most of the city's major hotels, and at the airport. They also organize special jewelry tours at the Ipanema headquarters.

H. Stern, offering a wide range of traditional and modern jewelry

The famous Blue Man line of beachwear

Bikinis & Beachwear

The girls from Ipanema, Copacabana, and Barra have helped make the bikini a symbol of the city's lifestyle. Shops specializing in bikinis, swim, surf, and beachwear can be found all over Rio, especially in Copacabana, Ipanema, and all the big malls. Famous chains in bikiniwear include **Blue Man**, **Bum-Bum**, and for beachgoers on a budget, **Santa Clara 33.**

What you wear to the beach is a fashion statement in Rio, so designs, shapes, and colors change with every season. Many stores offer a special line for visitors who find Brazilian fashions a bit daring.

Fashion Wear

Brazil features prominently in the international fashion scene, and Brazilians like to keep up with the latest trends. Walk around Ipanema or any of the large malls to get an idea of what is available. Items on display are usually of high quality and are also well priced.

Shoes

Brazil is one of the largest manufacturers of shoes and footwear in the world. Even the local supermarket is likely to stock fashionable flip-flops, and the two most famous brands are Havaianas and Grendha. The most popular chains, that sell well-made and reasonably priced leather shoes, are **Mr. Cat**, **Andarella** and Datelli.

Music

While no one music chain dominates in Rio, some music stores are better than others. **FNAC** megastore in Barra Shopping Center has a very good selection. **Arlequim** is a charming music shop and bookstore with a cozy café, a wide selection of CDs, and knowledgeable staff. Another top name is **Saraiva**, which has a large store in Rio Sul. Leading supermarkets, especially Lojas Americanas, sell cheap CDs.

Arts & Crafts Markets

The best and most famous arts and crafts market in Rio is the **Hippie Fair**, taking place every Sunday in and around Praça General Osório in Ipanema. The fair, which first began in 1968, runs from 10am to 6pm and is the perfect place to pick up souvenir paintings or Brazilian arts and craft works. Those looking for authentic, traditional items should also visit **Feira de São Cristóvão** (known also as Centro Luiz Gonzaga de Tradições Nordestinas), a popular market and fair, with arts, crafts, music, and food from the inner regions of Brazil.

Flip-flops

There are a number of specialized arts and crafts stores throughout the city, including those in malls and on Avenida Nossa Senhora de Copacabana.

Ipanema's Hippie Fair, a great place for souvenir shopping

DIRECTORY

Shopping Malls

Barra Shopping Center
Av das Américas 4666, Barra da Tijuca.
Tel (21) 4003 4131.
🆆 barrashopping. com.br

Fashion Mall
Estrada da Gávea 899, São Conrado.
Tel (21) 2111 4444.
🆆 fashionmall. com.br

Rio Sul
Rua Lauro Müller 116, Botafogo.
Tel (21) 2122 8070.
🆆 riosul.com.br

Jewelry

Amsterdam Sauer
Rua Garcia d'Ávila 105, Ipanema. **Map** 2 A4.
Tel (21) 2512 9878.

H. Stern
Rua Garcia d'Ávila 113, Ipanema. **Map** 2 A4.
Tel (21) 2106 0000.

Bikinis & Beachwear

Blue Man
Rio Sul, Botafogo.
Tel (21) 2541 6896.

Bum-Bum
Rua Visconde Pirája 351, Ipanema. **Map** 2 B4. **Tel** (21) 2287 9951.

Santa Clara 33
Rua Santa Clara 33, Copacabana. **Map** 3 D2.
Tel (21) 2549 4820.

Shoes

Andarella
Rio Sul, Botafogo.
Tel (21) 2543 2744.
🆆 andarella.com.br

Mr. Cat
Rua Visconde de Pirajá 414, Ipanema. **Map** 2 B4.
Tel (21) 2227 6521.

Music

Arlequim
Praça XV de Novembro 48, Centro. **Map** 5 E3.
Tel (21) 2220 8471.

FNAC
Barra Shopping Center.
Tel (21) 2109 2000.

Saraiva
Rio Sul, Botafogo.
Tel (21) 2543 7002.

Arts & Crafts Markets

Feira de São Cristóvão
Campo de São Cristóvão.
Closed Mon.
Tel (21) 2580 5335.

Hippie Fair
Praça General Osório.
Map 2 B5.

ENTERTAINMENT IN RIO

As a major world city, Rio offers a wide variety of high-quality entertainment. However, these are targeted more toward local residents than casual tourists. The big local and international acts perform mainly for the Brazilians, and the same is true of what is presented at the theater, in the movie houses, clubs, and bars. Though some clubs offer a watered-down take on Brazilian culture, on the whole, visitors can enjoy a scintillating nightlife. The trendiest and most fashionable choices are found in Ipanema and Leblon, and around the Lagoa. Downtown Rio is also back in fashion, with Lapa being particularly popular when it comes to clubs and bars that play upbeat Brazilian music.

Information

For details of entertainment in Rio, check the daily newspapers or their websites, most notably **O Globo** and weekly news magazine *Veja* which includes the local supplement *Veja Rio*. The website **Catraca Livre** is also a popular source. These normally offer an accurate guide to the current scene. The concierge at any big hotel would also be of help.

Booking Tickets

Brazilians traditionally only buy their tickets at the very last moment. Even for the biggest events, tickets may go on sale only a few days ahead. In many cases, the tickets will be sold at the venue itself, or through an agency. Large ticket agencies, such as **Ingresso Rápido**, and **Ingresso**, operate country-wide, and offer tickets to both events and particular venues.

Major Venues

Rio is an important venue and tour stop not only for the top names in Brazilian music, but also for all the leading international acts. The major foreign acts tend to prefer to play in one of two big show houses in Rio, **Rio Arena** and the **Metropolitan** in Barra da Tijuca.

Vivo Rio, located in the Modern Art Museum in Flamengo, puts on various shows. The **Cidade das Artes** in Barra is one of South America's largest concert halls and is home to the Brazilian Symphony Orchestra.

Smaller bands, or big names looking for a more intimate setting, also use the **Circo Voador** in Lapa. Circo, as locals call it, was launched in 1982 and has launched nationally acclaimed bands like Barão Vermelho and Legião Urbana. A similar audience attends the neighboring **Fundição Progresso**. Other smaller venues include **Teatro João**

Caetano and **Rival** in Centro, the beautiful **Sala Baden Powell** in Copacabana, and even **Morro da Urca** on the halfway stage of Sugar Loaf *(see pp80–81)*.

The open-air venue of **Praça da Apoteose** stages large acts. Even the Copacabana and Flamengo beaches sometimes hold free concerts.

Rio also hosts a number of festivals during the year that cover all genres. The largest and most famous festival is Rock in Rio *(see p91)*, though this is not an annual event.

Over the years, Rio has offered a number of shows that primarily target the visitor who might want a quick, though somewhat over-simplified, version of the vast range of Brazilian culture. The glitziest show to outlast them all takes place daily at Leblon's **Plataforma 1**. The kitschy variety show features *samba*, *bossa nova*, and other Brazilian sounds.

Colorfully costumed *samba* performers in the floor show at Plataforma 1

Samba, Bossa Nova & Gafieira

Most visitors to Rio will hope to catch a little live music and dance action when they are in town. While the big Brazilian acts will be found at Canecão and Claro Hall, there will also be a lot of artistes performing in smaller, more intimate venues, many of which are also bars and clubs.

Fans of *bossa nova* flock to **Vinícius** in Ipanema and **Bar do Tom** in Leblon. Celebrated for its outstanding music and a lively bar, the tiny **Bip Bip** in Copacabana is a well-frequented haven for MPB. **Arab** is a restaurant and bar in Lagoa that often hosts live music, including jazz, instrumental, and MBP.

Since the end of the 1990s, the reinvigorated nightlife in the city center has given a special boost to *samba* and *choro* (an upbeat waltz or polka). Lapa remains the main hub, with places such as **Carioca da Gema**, **Bar da Ladeira**, and **Rio Scenarium**. **Clube dos Democráticos** is a spacious club in Lapa particularly renowned for its *samba* and popular with a young crowd. Close by, **Rivalzinho** is a small bar that has a crowd of music lovers occupying its pavement at weekends. Praça Mauá is also establishing itself on the nightlife scene. Head to **Pedra do Sal**, a small outdoor square where live *samba* and *choro* music are played on Friday, Saturday, and Monday evenings. Drinks and food are sold from street stalls around the square.

Even when the center of Rio was not in fashion, two clubs prospered there and still hold sway as the city's authentic ballrooms, or *gafieiras*. **Estudantina**, in Praça Tiradentes, dates from 1928, while the 1918 **Cordão da Bola Preta** in Lapa is the oldest carnival *bloco*. For those who wish to learn the basics of dance there are a number of schools in Rio. The Centro Cultural Carioca offers beginner classes for individuals or groups for *samba*, *forró*, and *gafieira*.

The Pé de Moleque group playing at the Carioca da Gema bar in Lapa

Samba Schools

The number of shows and opportunities increase the closer it gets to Carnaval (*see pp68–9*), with the "high season" for *samba* running from December through February. However, those who are not visiting the city during this time can watch the *samba* schools in their own headquarters. For instance, **Mangueira**, one of the most traditional and popular samba schools in Rio de Janeiro, organizes weekly sessions of samba and *feijoada* throughout the year at its main venue.

The *samba* schools are also known to host programs featuring performances and other events at the **Cidade do Samba**, which opened in Centro in early 2006. Any good hotel will be able to organize a visit to the technical rehearsals or a guided tour of the Cidade do Samba.

People dancing to a live *gafieira* show in Rio Scenarium

Bars & Clubs

Rio enchants visitors with its unique range of bars and clubs. Bars go through every degree of sophistication, from periodically changing hot spots to those specializing in *cachaça* and *caipirinhas*, such as the popular **Academia da Cachaça** in Leblon and Barra. Enhancing the variety are several pub-like venues, the most famous of which is **Lord Jim** in Ipanema, while sophisticated bars in the top hotels offer a more formal elegance. Then there are the traditional *botequins*, or the corner bars, with plenty to eat and drink, well into the early hours. **Bar Luiz** in Centro, **Lamas** in Flamengo, **Cervantes** in Copacabana, **Hipódromo** in Gavea, and **Bar Lagoa** on the Lagoa, have been drawing a steady clientele. Favored by visitors, **Garota de Ipanema** was where Tom Jobim and Vinícius de Moraes are said to have seen the girl who inspired them to write the song "A Garota de Ipanema."

The line between bars, DJ bars, and clubs can get blurred in Rio, with a surfeit of bars offering dancing and music as the night goes on. The "in" venues change extremely quickly in terms of popularity and name. Therefore, it is always a good idea to ask a resident or the concierge at the hotel about the places that may be currently in vogue.

Gay & Lesbian

Rio has a very active gay and lesbian scene, much of which simply blends into the everyday life of the city. While the cozy **Fosfobox** is popular with young clubbers, **La Cueva** has a diverse clientele. **The Week** is a larger venue that is popular with techno music lovers.

A good starting point is Ipanema beach. The block running back from the beach, especially around Posto 9 and Rua Farme de Amoedo, has a number of gay and lesbian bars.

Eating Out

For many Cariocas, eating out *(see p382–3)* is an entertainment in its own right. Foreign visitors get the best value from dining at the *churrascaria rodizios*, the large barbecue houses with a fixed-price menu.

In Rio, trying traditional Brazilian cuisine normally means a *feijoada (see p384)*, a sumptuous feast usually served for lunch on Wednesday or Saturday.

Theater

Theater in Rio de Janeiro is of a high quality, but a majority of the productions will be in Portuguese. The main theaters, generally small and intimate, are found in Copacabana, Ipanema, and Leblon. In Centro, the **Centro Cultural Banco do Brasil** is a major venue. For listings, check *O Globo* and *Jornal do Brasil*.

Cinema

Brazil is one of the world's biggest cinema-going markets.

A soccer game in progress at the Estádio do Maracanã

However, the latest multiplex operations all tend to be in Barra, such as the 18-screen **UCI**. Smaller and older theaters can be found in Copacabana and Ipanema.

International films quickly make their way into Brazil, and, unless they are aimed at children, will be left in their original language with subtitles added. At least one new Brazilian film is released each week, a few of which will go on to international acclaim.

Independent world cinema takes over the city each September and October, when the city's main film festival, Festival do Rio, holds public screenings.

Classical Music, Opera & Dance

Rio de Janeiro has a healthy and vibrant music, opera, and dance scene that is focused in the **Theatro Municipal** and the **Cidade das Artes** in Barra. Small concerts and recitals also use the **Sala Cecília Meireles** in Lapa.

Rio has its own music, opera, and dance companies, but also attracts the very best from the rest of Brazil and the world.

Helicopter Tours

One of the most popular tours with visitors to Rio, a helicopter ride takes people over the city and beaches, or around Sugar Loaf and Corcovado mountains.

Since 1991, **Helisight** has been offering seven different tours that vary from eight minutes to an hour. The most popular tours are those that circle Corcovado and the statue of Christ the Redeemer.

Helisight has modern heliports at Morro da Urca and the Lagoa. Prices range from US$90 to US$400.

Soccer

The mecca of soccer lovers, Rio is world-renowned for its abiding passion for the game. Matches take place all through the year, and are usually held on Wednesday evenings or Sunday afternoons. The city's four big clubs are Flamengo, Fluminense, Vasco da Gama, and Botafogo.

Estádio Olímpico Nilton Santos hosts some of the best football matches. Almost synonymous with Brazil's legendary sport is the **Estádio do Maracanã**, which is undergoing renovation.

Horse Racing

Unusual as it may seem to list it among the entertainment options, horse racing at the **Jóquei Club Brasileiro** on the Lagoa takes place four times a week. On Monday and Friday evenings, one can enjoy drinks or dinner in the members' stand, and watch the racing go on under the floodlights.

An aerial view of the Helisight heliport at Morro da Urca

DIRECTORY

Information

Catraca Livre
W catracalivre.com.br/rio

O Globo
W oglobo.globo.com

Booking Tickets

Ingresso
W ingresso.com.br

Ingresso Rápido
W ingressorapido.com.br

Major Venues

Cidade das Artes
Trevo das Palmeiras, Barra.
Tel (21) 3325 0102.

Circo Voador
Rua dos Arcos, Lapa.
Map 5 D5.
Tel (21) 2533 0354.

Fundiçao Progresso
Rua dos Arcos 24, Centro.
Map 5 D5.
Tel (21) 3212 0800.

Metropolitan
Av Ayrton Senna 3000,
Barra da Tijuca.

Morro da Urca
Av Pasteur 520, Praia
Vermelha, Urca.
Tel (21) 2546 8400.

Plataforma 1
Rua Adalberto Ferreira 32,
Leblon. **Tel** (21) 2274 4022.

Praça da Apoteose
Rua Marquês de Sapucaí,
Cidade Nova. **Map** 4 A5.
Tel (21) 2563 9000.

Rio Arena
Av Embaixador Abelardo
Bueno 3401, Barra da
Tijuca. **Tel** (21) 2430 1753.

Rival
Rua Álvaro Alvim 33,
Centro. **Map** 5 D5.
Tel (21) 2240 4469.

Sala Baden Powell
Av Nossa Senhora de
Copacabana 360,
Copacabana. **Map** 3 D3.
Tel (21) 2255 1067/1366.

Teatro João Caetano
Praça Tiradentes, Centro.
Map 4 C4.
Tel (21) 2332 9257.

Vivo Rio
Av Infante Dom Henrique
85, Flamengo.
Tel (21) 2272 2901.

Samba, Bossa Nova & Gafieira

Arab
Av Borges de Medeiros,
Parque dos Patins, Kiosk 7.
Map 1 B2.
Tel (21) 2540 0747.

Bar da Ladeira
Rua Evaristo da Veiga 149,
Lapa.
Map 5 D5.
Tel (21) 2226 9691.

Bar do Tom
Rua Adalberto Ferreira 32,
Leblon. **Map** 1 A4.
Tel (21) 2274 4022.

Bip Bip
Rua Almirante Gonçalves
50, Copacabana.
Map 2 C4.
Tel (21) 2267 9696.

Carioca da Gema
Av Mem de Sá 79, Lapa.
Map 5 D5.
Tel (21) 2221 0043.

Clube dos Democráticos
Rua Riachuelo 91, Lapa.
Map 4 C5.
Tel (21) 2252 4611.

Cordão da Bola Preta
Rua da Relação 3, Lapa.
Map 4 C4.
Tel (21) 2240 8049.

Estudantina
Praça Tiradentes 79,
Centro.
Map 4 C4.
Tel (21) 2232 1149.

Pedra do Sal
Largo João da Baiana,
Rua Argemiro Bulcão,
Saúde (Centro).
Map 4 C2.

Rio Scenarium
Rua do Lavradio 20, Lapa.
Map 4 C4.
Tel (21) 3147 9000.

Rivalzinho
Rua Álvaro Alvim 34,
Centro. **Map** 5 D5.
Tel (21) 2240 4469.

Vinícius
Rua Vinícius de Moraes
39, Ipanema.
Map 2 B4.
Tel (21) 2287 1497.

Samba Schools

Cidade do Samba
Rua Rivadávia Correa 60,
Gamboa.
Tel (21) 2213 2503.

Mangueira
Rua Visconde de Niterói
1072, Mangueira.
Tel (21) 2567 3419.

Bars & Clubs

Academia da Cachaça
Rua Conde Bernadotte 26,
Leblon.
Tel (21) 2239 1542.
Av Armando Lombardi
800, Barra.
Tel (21) 2492 1159.

Bar Lagoa
Av Epitácio Pessoa 1674,
Lagoa. **Map** 2 A4.
Tel (21) 2523 1135.

Bar Luiz
Rua da Carioca 39, Centro.
Map 5 D4.
Tel (21) 2262 6900.

Cervantes
Av Prado Júnior 335,
Copacabana. **Map** 3 F1.
Tel (21) 2275 6147.

Garota de Ipanema
Rua Vinícius de Moraes
49, Ipanema. **Map** 2 A5.
Tel (21) 2523 3787.

Hipódromo
Praça Santos Dumont
108, Gávea.
Tel (21) 2274 9720.

Lamas
Rua Marquês de Abrantes
18, Flamengo.
Tel (21) 2556-0799.

Lord Jim
Rua Paul Redfern 44,
Ipanema. **Map** 1 C4.
Tel (21) 2249 4881.

Gay & Lesbian

Fosfobox
Rua Siqueira Campos 143,
Copacabana. **Map** 2 D1.
Tel (21) 2548 7498.

La Cueva
Rua Miguel Lemos 51,
Copacabana. **Map** 2 C3.
Tel (21) 2267 1364.

The Week
Rua Sacadura Cabral 135,
Saúde (Centro). **Map** 4 C2.
Tel (21) 2253 1020.

Theater

Centro Cultural Banco do Brasil
Rua Primeiro de Março 66,
Centro. **Map** 5 E3.
Tel (21) 3808 2020.

Cinema

UCI
Barra Shopping Av das
Américas 4666, Barra da
Tijuca. **Tel** (21) 4003 4131.

Classical Music, Opera & Dance

Sala Cecília Meireles
Largo da Lapa 47.
Map 5 D5.
Tel (21) 2332 9223.

Theatro Municipal
Av Rio Branco. **Map** 5 E4.
Tel (21) 2332 9195.

Helicopter tours

Helisight
Lagoa: Av Borges de
Medeiros, Heliponto da
Prefeitura. **Map** 1 B2.
Tel (21) 2259 6995.
Morro da Urca: Av Pasteur
520, 1st cable car stop.
Tel (21) 2542 7935.

Soccer

Estádio do Maracanã
Rua Eurico Rabelo,
São Cristóvão.
Tel (21) 2334 1705.

Estádio Olimpico Nilton Santos
Rua José dos Reis 425,
Engenho do Dentro.
Tel (21) 2546 1994.

Horse Racing

Jóquei Clube Brasileiro
Rua Jardim Botânico 1003.
Map 1 A2, A3, B2, B3.
Tel (21) 3534 9000.

RIO DE JANEIRO CITY STREET FINDER

Map references given in this guide for entertainment venues and other attractions in Rio City refer to the Street Finder maps on the following pages. Map references are also provided for Rio City restaurants *(see pp386–8)* and hotels *(see pp370–71)*. The first figure in the map reference indicates which Street Finder map to turn to, and the letter and number

which follow refer to the grid reference on that map. The map below shows the different areas of Rio City – Leblon, Copacabana, Ipanema, and Centro – covered by the five Street Finder maps. Symbols used for sights and useful information are displayed in the key below. A list of important places of interest marked on the maps can be found on page 72.

Key

- ▨ Place of interest
- ▨ Other building
- 🚉 Train station
- ⛴ Ferry terminal
- Ⓜ Metro station
- 🚊 Light rail
- 𝒊 Visitor information
- ➕ Hospital
- 🏢 Police station
- ✚ Church
- ═══ Railroad
- ▬▬ Pedestrian street

Scale of Maps 1 & 2–3

0 meters — 400
0 yards — 400

Scale of Map 4–5

0 meters — 200
0 yards — 200

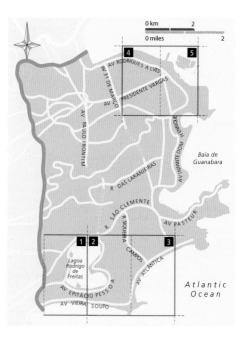

Streetwise in Rio

Though street crime is prevalent in Rio, a few precautions could help to prevent it from happening.

Contrary to general belief, it is probably best to avoid taking a stroll on the deserted streets of Centro on Sundays. Praça Mauá, just to the north of Centro, is best avoided after nightfall. Lapa, a popular nightspot in Rio, must be explored with great caution.

It is advisable not to wander unaccompanied around the darker corners of the Parque do Flamengo, or to walk between Cosmo Velho and Corcovado late at night. Robbery and assault in these areas are common.

Passengers taking a bus are easy targets for thieves, and need to be vigilant. Taxis are plentiful and inexpensive, so avoid walking along empty and unfamiliar streets.

Make sure the driver turns on the meter and ask for an estimate of the average fare to your destination.

Various instances of bag-snatching are common on the crowded beaches of Copacabana and Ipanema, especially during the weekends, so visitors must keep a keen eye on their belongings. Again, do not go down to the water after dark. Stay on the well-lit, busy sidewalks.

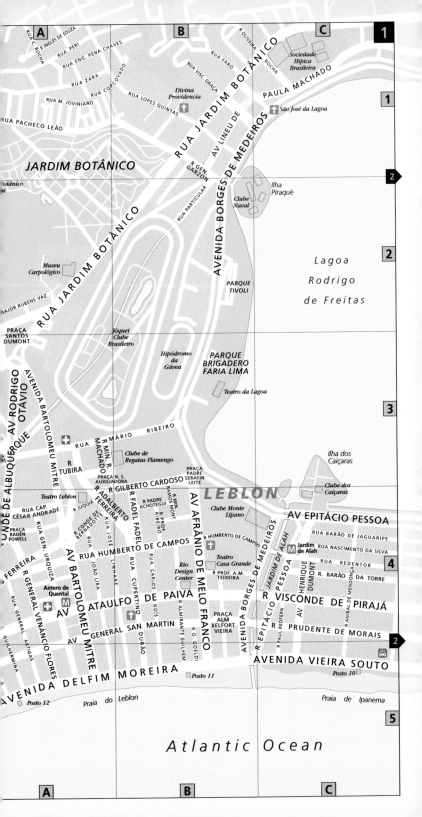

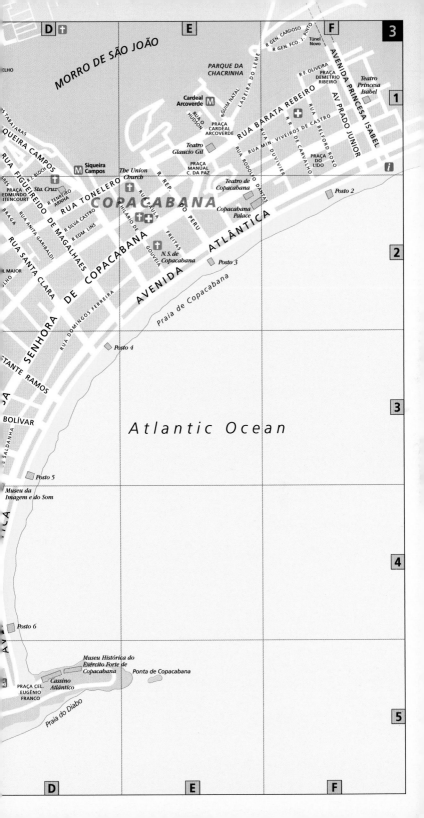

D 🏛 **E** **F** **3**

MORRO DE SÃO JOÃO

PARQUE DA
CHACRINHA

R GEN. CARDOSO
R GEN. FCO. J. PINTO
Túnel
Novo

AVENIDA PRINCESA ISABEL

R F. OLIVEIRA
PRAÇA
DEMETRIO
RIBEIRO

Teatro
Princesa
Isabel

1

Cardeal
Arcoverde Ⓜ

R GIM NATAL

LADEIRA DO LEME

RUA BARATA REBEIRO

AV PRADO JUNIOR

ELHO

S TARAJARAS

QUEIRA CAMPOS

RUA FIGUEIREDO DE MAGALHÃES

R. T. BLOCH

Teatro
Glaucio Gil

RUA
HUDSON

PRAÇA
CARDEAL
ARCOVERDE

✚

RUA RODOLFO DANTAS

RUA MIN. VIVEIROS DE CASTRO

R R

RUA DUVIVIER

R R

RUA BELFORD ROXO

PRAÇA
DO
LIDO

ℹ

Ⓜ Siqueira
Campos

The Union
Church

PRAÇA
MANUAL
C. DA PAZ

Teatro de
Copacabana

Posto 2

ARES
EDMUNDO
ITENCOURT

🏛 Sta. Cruz

R. TENREIRO
ARNHA

🏛

RUA PAULA

R. REP.

COPACABANA

Copacabana
Palace

2

BRAGA

RUA ANITA GARIBALDI

R SILVA CASTRO

🏛✚

HILARIO DE

DO PERU

ATLÂNTICA

RUA SANTA CLARA

R. EDM. LINS

FREITAS

GOUVEIA

N.S. de
Copacabana

Posto 3

IL MAJOR

LHO

SENHORA DE COPACABANA

RUA DOMINGOS FERREIRA

AVENIDA

Praia de Copacabana

Posto 4

TANTE RAMOS

3

BOLÍVAR

SALDANHA

Atlantic Ocean

Posto 5

Museu da
Imagem e do Som

4

Posto 6

5

Museu Histórica do
Exército Forte de
Copacabana

Ponta de Copacabana

Cassino
Atlântico

PRAÇA CEL.
EUGÊNIO
FRANCO

Praia do Diabo

D **E** **F**

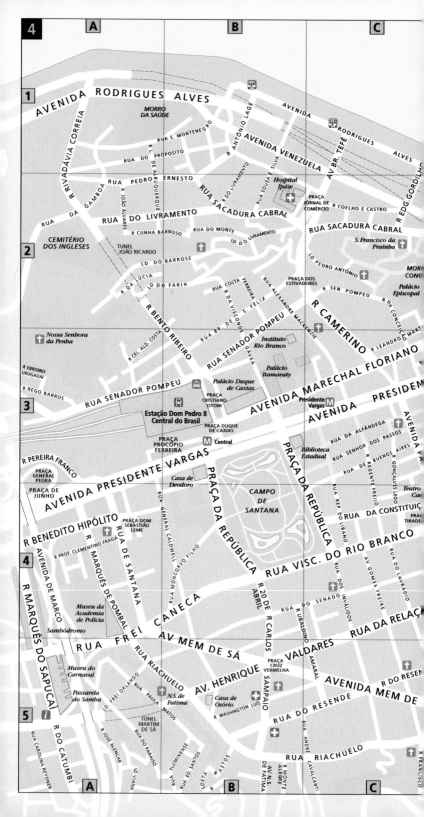

RIO DE JANEIRO & ESPÍRITO SANTO

Beyond the capital cities of Rio and Vitória, the magnificent scenery dominating the areas continues unchecked by rapid modernization. Along the coast are giant boulder-strewn mountains, while farther inland are the steep, lushly forested ridges of the Mata Atlântica. Spectacular beaches, picturesque islands, and several resort towns are among the area's other attractions.

Stretching north and south of Rio City are long strands of beaches and half-moon coves lapped or pounded by a bottle-green Atlantic and visited by troops of sea turtles. Some surround the popular resort towns of Búzios, "discovered" by Brigitte Bardot in the 1960s, and Cabo Frio, while others lie close to the colonial port of Paraty, which once lay at the end of the mule route from the gold mines of Minas Gerais. Its cobbled streets are better preserved than others on the southeastern coast.

Inland, the steep ridges of the Mata Atlântica begin to rise vertiginously towards Minas Gerais and São Paulo, protecting a string of national and state parks, including Itatiaia and the Serra dos Órgãos, in their folds. This area, considered one of the world's biodiversity hot spots, has an astounding 950 species of birds and 40 percent of the plants here are unique, including the cattleya orchid, referred to as the "Queen of Flowers." The largest among the islands, Ilha Grande has no roads. Steep walking trails leave its only town Abraão, to cut through the forest to still more beaches deserted but for surfboards and fishing shacks.

The Espírito Santo coast is equally beautiful with its mountains, beaches, and small towns. One of them, Itaúnas, is backed by sand dunes large enough to swallow it. A stunning sight here is Pedra Azul, a granite monolith which changes from slate gray to fiery orange with the passage of the sun.

Pedra Azul, a spectacular granite monolith in Espírito Santo

◀ Colorful fishing boats lined up along the coast of Paraty, Rio de Janeiro state

Exploring Rio de Janeiro & Espírito Santo

Several towns pepper the coast of Rio de Janeiro state. Among these, Búzios draws the most visitors and has the best hotels and restaurants, while the colonial town of Paraty, nestled between the coastal mountains and an island-strewn sea, emerged in the 2000s as a center for the arts. North of Rio is the imperial city of Petrópolis. Brazil's oldest national park, Itatiaia, lies just off the interstate between Rio and São Paulo. Ilha Grande, off the coast of Rio, and the resorts of northern Espírito Santo are relatively untouched. Vitória, the state's capital, dates to the 1550s. To its south is the beach town of Guarapari, while inland is the dramatic peak of Pedra Azul.

Statue of King Dom Pedro II, the founder of the magnificent city of Petrópolis

Typical colonial buildings in Paraty

Sights at a Glance

Towns & Cities

① Paraty pp110–12
② Angra dos Reis
⑤ Petrópolis pp116–19
⑥ Teresópolis
⑨ Guarapari
⑩ Vitória
⑫ Itaúnas

National Parks & Areas of Natural Beauty

③ Ilha Grande
④ Parque Nacional do Itatiaia
⑦ Parque Nacional da Serra dos Órgãos
⑧ Búzios pp120–21
⑪ Pedra Azul

Getting Around

The Rio and Espírito Santo coasts are served by the well signposted BR-101 interstate highway. Rio de Janeiro state has a good interstate bus service to all the beach towns. The Mata Atlântica, however, is best visited on a tour or with a hired car, as are the national parks of Itatiaia and Serra dos Órgãos. To visit northern and central Espírito Santo, visitors will need their own transport. Ilha Grande can be reached by passenger ferry twice a day.

Key

▬▬ Highway
▬▬ Major road
╍╍╍ Minor road
╼╼ Railroad
▬▬ State border
△ Peak

Lush Mata Atlântica in Parque Nacional do Itatiaia, Rio de Janeiro

For keys to symbols *see back flap*

❶ Paraty

One of the most photographed colonial towns on the Brazilian coast, Paraty has been a UNESCO World Heritage Site since 1958. Though settled by the Portuguese in the 16th century, it was developed a century later as an important port from where gold was shipped to Europe. Extremely charming, the whitewashed churches and terra-cotta roofs offset the lush green of the rainforest-clad mountains, and the placid bay whose emerald waters lap at the town's quay. Paraty has an impressive literary tradition; the annual Festa Literária Internacional de Paraty (FLIP) is a big draw. It is also an ideal base for exploring the dazzling Brazilian coastline, and boasts lovely *pousadas* (exclusive hotels).

Statue of St. Benedict, Nossa Senhora do Rosário e São Benedito

Sturdy iron bars of the Casa de Cadeia, a former prison

🏛 Casa de Cadeia

Rua Travessa Santa Rita. **Tel** (24) 3371 1056. **Open** 9am–5pm daily.

The 18th-century Casa de Cadeia served as the town's prison until 1890. Retaining its original iron prison bars, this building now serves as the public library, besides housing the Casa do Artesão (Artisan's House).

🏛 Santa Rita dos Pardos Libertos

Largo da Santa Rita. **Tel** (24) 3371 8751; (24) 3371 8328. **Open** 9am–5pm Tue–Sun.

The façade of Paraty's oldest church now graces travel brochures of the city. It was built in 1722 by, and for, all those considered not white enough to attend the church of the ruling elite. These would have included the illegitimate offspring of the aristocracy, their children, indigenous people, and freed slaves. In design the church is typically Jesuit, with three windows in the upper chancel and a curvilinear door. Except for the beautifully worked altarpiece in the sanctuary and fine woodwork on the doorways its interior is plain. Deconsecrated in the 20th century, the church now serves as the sparse Museu de Arte Sacra. Displayed religious artifacts include gold and silver remonstrations.

🏛 Nossa Senhora do Rosário e São Benedito

Rua Tenente Francisco Antônio. 🕐 7:30pm daily (8pm during daylight saving time).

Slaves worshipped at Nossa Senhora do Rosário e São Benedito, which was built in 1725. The interior of this church is almost entirely free of embellishment, except for heavy gilt on the altarpiece. However, it retains a simple dignity and a sacred atmosphere. Its design resembles the Minas Gerais chapels of the same period. Every November, locals celebrate A Festa dos Santos (Feast of All Saints) here, where they remember some of the building's historical past. Mass is followed by a procession where churchgoers carry figures of a king and queen, recalling the Maracatú monarchs of Pernambuco, and icons of the various saints.

Paraty's whitewashed buildings reflected in the placid waters at the quay

For hotels and restaurants in this region see pp372–3 and p388

🏛 Matriz Nossa Senhora dos Remédios

Praça Monsenhor Helio Pires.
🕐 7:30pm daily (8pm during daylight saving). 🎥 🖂

Originally meant for the white elite, this stately church took 100 years to build. When it was near completion in 1873, architects discovered that the soil was too muddy to support it. It was left in its current squat state, slowly subsiding to the left. Today, it serves as a parish church.

🏛 Nossa Senhora das Dores

Rua Fresca. 🕐 7:30pm daily (8pm during DST). 🖂

The colonial aristocracy also attended the graceful chapel of Nossa Senhora das Dores. Built in 1800, it was renovated in 1901. There are some fine carvings on the balustrades in the upper chancel. A catacomb-like cemetery adjoins the chapel.

🏰 Forte Defensor Perpétuo

Morro do Forte. **Open** 9am–noon, 2–5pm Wed–Sun. 🎥 Centro de Artes e Tradições Populares: **Open** 10am–5pm Tue–Sun. 🖂

Located on the northern headland, just outside town, this 19th-century fort looks more like an elongated squat town house. Rusted cannons and remnants of a wall sit in front of it. The Centro de Artes e Tradições Populares (Center for Popular Art) occupies its principal room, displaying local handicrafts and items related to the traditional way of life of the local people.

Cannons resting outside Forte Defensor Perpétuo

VISITORS' CHECKLIST

Practical Information
Rio de Janeiro. 🚉 37,000. ℹ️ Av Roberto Silveira 36, (24) 3371 1222. 🎭 Carnaval (Feb), Festa de Divino Espírito Santo (May), Festas Juninas (Jun), Festa Literária Internacional de Paraty (Jul), Festival da Pinga (Aug), Festa da Nossa Senhora dos Remédios (Sep). 🌐 visiteparaty.tur.br

Transport
✈ 🚌 Rua Jango Pádua.

Quilombo do Campinho da Independência

BR 101, km 584. **Tel** (24) 999 316 875; (24) 998 441 385.

Founded at the end of the 19th century by three slave women who escaped captivity, Quilombo do Campinho da Independência is a remnant of a rebel slave community. Today, it consists of about 120 families, who have retained much of their cultural heritage. Visitors can book a tour to learn about their traditions, handicrafts, and cuisine, and enjoy an unforgettable lunch in the restaurant.

Paraty

① Casa de Cadeia
② Santa Rita dos Pardos Libertos
③ Nossa Senhora do Rosário e São Benedito
④ Matriz Nossa Senhora dos Remédios
⑤ Nossa Senhora das Dores
⑥ Forte Defensor Perpétuo
⑦ Quilombo do Campinho da Independência

0 meters 150
0 yards 150

Beaches Around Paraty

Paraty, with its forest-swathed spurs of the coastal mountains, lies at the heart of a beautiful stretch of coastline. A short way offshore are a string of islands. Until only a few decades ago, this area was little-known even to Brazilian holiday makers. Much of the area, surrounded by a wealth of exotic flora and fauna, is protected by national and state parks. The islands can be reached by boat from Paraty town, or the nearby Paraty-Mirim.

Beaches & Islands Around Paraty

| 0 km | | 6 |
| 0 miles | | 4 |

Ilha do Breu
Praia do Araújo
Ilha do Araújo
Ilha Rapada
Ilha Comprida
Ilha do Mantimento
Ilha dos Meros
Praia do Jabaquara
Praia das Lulas
Ilha dos Cocos
Paraty
Praia do Pontal
Praia Vermelha
Ilha do Algodão
Poço das Andorinhas
Praia Boa Vista
Paraty-Mirim
Ponta de Cajaiba
Praia da Venda
SACO DE MAMANGUÁ
Praia Deserta
Rio dos Meros
Rio Para Mirim
Patrimônio
Praia de Sá
Praia Laranjeiras
Praia do Sono
Trindade
Praia do Meio
Praia de Fora
Praia do Cepilho
Praia da Ponta Negra
ATLANTIC OCEAN

The small town of **Trindade**, 13 miles (21 km) south of Paraty, is popular with surfers from São Paulo. It offers a choice of simply appointed *pousadas* and some pretty beaches connected by footpaths. The scenic beach running south of Trindade, **Praia de Fora**, is backed by forest-covered hills. **Praia do Meio** is a long stretch of fine sand, washed by waves perfect for bodysurfing. **Laranjeiras**, a small distance downhill, is the hideaway for Rio's super-rich who flock to its private condo-miniums. Trails lead from here through the forest to a string of pristine beaches to the south. **Praia do Cepilho** is one of the best surfing spots along this stretch of coast.

Located 21 miles (34 km) from Paraty, **Ilha do Breu** is a tiny private island dominated by a single *pousada*. The owner breeds rare golden lion tamarins, which he lets run free on his island. He also maintains a small aviary, and has planted trees to attract Atlantic rainforest birds. **Poço das Andorinhas**, one of the many waterfalls in the region, is a popular spot for bathing.

Exploring Around Paraty

The bays and islands off Paraty are a favorite playground for Brazil's rich elite, who moor their expensive yachts in the Paraty Marina and fly in to the adjacent airport in their private jets for a weekend cruise.

Paraty's city beach, close to the historic center, is **Praia do Pontal** and it lies across the Rio Perequê-Açu. The water is not very clean, but the *barracas* (restaurants) are pleasant. A shallow and spacious beach, **Praia do Jabaquara**, is within walking distance of Paraty town. A glorious long beach, **Paraty-Mirim**, lies 17 miles (27 km) east of town, and can be reached by a bumpy dirt road. Just south, **Saco de Mamanguá** is lined with old fishing villages and secluded beaches against a backdrop of the lush Mata Atlântica. A deep sleeve of water, it is good for snorkeling. **Ilha dos Meros**, 9 miles (14 km) northeast of Paraty, is another snorkeling spot, though marine life is limited to large shoals of sheepshead bream and the occasional turtle.

Secluded scenic Praia de Fora near Trindade

Mata Atlântica

The Atlantic coastal forest, or Mata Atlântica, is one of the best bird-watching sites in the world, with 950 resident species, almost 200 of which are endemic. It once covered the lowlands and coastal mountains from Rio Grande do Norte to Rio Grande do Sul. Today, less than 5 percent remains, concentrated mainly in Rio de Janeiro, Minas Gerais, São Paulo, and Paraná. Its proximity to the Atlantic blesses it with heavy rainfall. The vegetation is thick with epiphytic plants, and the forest is particularly rich in breathtaking orchid species. There are many rare mammals too, including the most endangered primate in the world, the woolly spider monkey, as well as several striking species of uniquely colored marmosets and tamarins.

Epiphytes are plants encrusting every available nook and cranny of the larger trees, drawing moisture directly from air.

Clearwater streams cut across the thick forest, which receives heavy rainfall, especially in the Southeast.

Vegetation at the water's edge tends to consist of fast-growing species that quickly replenish their numbers after floods.

BRAZIL

Locator Map
⬛ Mata Atlântica

Biodiversity
Mata Atlântica is one of the world's most biodiverse regions, with some 20,000 plant species, 40 percent of which are endemic, and one of the highest numbers of threatened or endangered vertebrates in the world.

The seven-colored tanager is one of the local species listed as endangered or threatened by CITES.

The cattleya orchid, the world's most famous orchid genus, was discovered by Englishman William Cattley in 1818.

The woolly monkey, among South America's largest primates, can weigh more than 13 lb (6 kg).

The golden lion tamarin, one of the three lion tamarin species, lives on a few islands and in the Atlantic forest.

Ocelots, the third-largest of Brazil's eight indigenous big cats, are most abundant in southern São Paulo.

The Costa Verde

The Costa Verde (Green Coast) stretching south of Rio, past Paraty and Trindade *(see pp110–12)*, deserves its name. Rainforests swathe the coastal mountains, which reach almost 9,143 ft (2,787 m) in the alpine meadows and the forests of Parque Nacional do Itatiaia. From here, they plunge down into steep ridges to meet an emerald ocean, tinged with turquoise at numerous long sandy beaches. Beyond are a scattering of breathtaking islands set in aquamarine and sitting in the deep, bottle-green Atlantic. The largest, Ilha Grande, is particularly lush, with trees covering its rocky mountains and sheltering its spectacular strands of fine white sand. The island is also the playground for the rich, who host extravagant parties in the summer.

❷ Angra dos Reis

Rio de Janeiro. 🏘 192,000. 🚢 from Rio or São Paulo. 🛈 Av Ayrton Senna 580, (24) 3367 7826.
🌐 visiteangradosreis.com.br

This unprepossessing port is today mainly a jumping-off point for the islands of Ilha Grande and Ilha da Gipóia. It was once a charming colonial town and vestiges of its once dignified past are hidden among the ever-expanding *favelas*. Angra dos Reis was once as pretty a town as Paraty. The main church, **Nossa Senhora da Conceição**, was built in 1626 in front of the docks, while the nearby **Nossa Senhora do Carmo** dates from 1593. The colonial naval complex lies some 2 miles (3 km) north of the town center towards the Praia do Bonfim.

Environs

Ilha da Gipóia, an hour's boat ride off the port of Angra dos Reis, is the second-largest island in the bay after Ilha Grande, and is known for its stunning white-sand beaches such as Jurubaíba, Praia do Dentista, and Norte. Most of the beaches here are bustling with bars floating offshore, which can be reached by the yachts and boats that ply the waters of the bay.

The forested **Serra do Mar** lies 25 miles (40 km) inland from Angra. On weekends and holidays, visitors can take a picturesque train journey there. Train tickets should be booked a day in advance from the tourist office.

Town church in Vila do Abraão, Ilha Grande, against a lush backdrop

❸ Ilha Grande

Rio de Janeiro. 🏘 5,000. 🚢 from Angra dos Reis, Mangaratiba or Conceição do Jacareí. 🛈 Parque Estadual Peig, Av Nacib Monteiro de Queiroz s/n, (24) 3361 5540/5800. 🚢 Vila do Abraão. 🌐 ilhagrande.com.br

The most romantic and pretty of southeastern Brazil's many islands, Ilha Grande remains unspoilt by development and heavy tourism. The island's pristine state is owed in great part to its long isolation. From the earliest colonial days it was a notorious pirate lair, it then became a landing port for slaves destined for Rio and in the late 20th century it was the site of an infamous prison for political prisoners. Nowadays Ilha Grande is populated mostly by fishermen and small tourist businesses.

Some sixty percent of the 75-sq-mile- (193-sq-km-) island is protected and forms part of the Parque Estadual da Ilha Grande. Its virgin Atlantic rainforest, mangrove swamps, and coastal vegetation is home to abundant wildlife, including brown howler monkeys, sloths, small mammals, and macaws.

The village of **Vila do Abraão** is the main settlement. Tour operators and hotels in Abraão offer trips around the island, many of them on pretty, wooden fishing boats. The most popular trip is to the sheltered cove at **Palmas**, from where a trail leads to **Lopes Mendes**, one of Ilha Grande's longest beaches, washed by powerful surf. Other trips include snorkeling at **Saco do Céu** or a visit to the 18th-century **Igreja de Santana**.

Self-guided trails from Abraão, lead throughout the island. Many of them are steep and rocky, but offer wonderful views out over the Atlantic. The most challenging is to the 3,248-ft- (990-m-) high peak of **Pico do Papagaio**.

Pristine beach alcove surrounded by lush green forest, Ilha Grande

Steep mountain ridges in Parque Nacional do Itatiaia, Brazil's oldest national park

❹ Parque Nacional do Itatiaia

Estrada Parque Nacional, Km 8,5 Rio de Janeiro. 🚌 from Itatiaia.
ℹ️ (24) 3352 1292/2288/6894.
🌐 **cmbio.gov.br/parnaitatiaia** 🏨
🏨 Hotel Donati, Estrada do Parque Nacional, Km 9,5. (24) 3352 6496.
🌐 hoteldonati.com.br

Brazil's oldest national park, Parque Nacional do Itatiaia was founded in 1937. It was established to protect the high alpine meadows and the gradations of thick Atlantic rainforests that cover its steep mountain ridges. It is the only part of Rio de Janeiro State ever to see snow, albeit rarely.

The scenery here is magnificent. The highest regions of the park are capped with giant boulders, eroded into strange organic shapes by millions of years of rain and wind. They sit on expansive grassland coursed by babbling brooks, which become fast-flowing, clear-water rivers once they reach the warmer forested areas below. Here they tumble, roar, and fall over waterfalls and rapids.

The trees around them are busy with primates. Curious brown capuchin monkeys are a common sight on the numerous trails. Scarcer are the beautiful and shy muriqui monkeys, a threatened species.

Birdlife, too, is prolific in the park, which is home to 350 species, many of which are endangered. The park plays a crucial role in their conservation. Dusky-legged guans wander along the park's few paved roads, brilliant seven-colored and black and gold cotingas flit about with toucans, and the early morning air buzzes with the sound of dozens of different hummingbirds.

The park can be crowded on weekends when families romp in the numerous waterfalls and wildlife makes itself scarce. But during the week the various trails are deserted and quiet. The ranger station provides rather poor walking maps but the trails are fairly clear. Hotel Donati, which is the best hotel in the park, can organize walking tours and, with advance notice, wildlife guides.

Trail through the verdant rainforests of Parque Nacional do Itatiaia

❺ Petrópolis

Located in the mountains near Rio, Petrópolis owes its creation to the Brazilian royal family. Dom Pedro I's dream of building a summer residence here was fulfilled by his son, Dom Pedro II, who was equally taken by the charms of the region. In 1843, before construction of the palace began, he decreed the creation of Petrópolis as the summer seat of his government. The city soon rose in importance, as trappings of royalty made their mark. Today, Petrópolis is popular for its royal attractions, as well as for its mountain scenery and the national park of Serra dos Órgãos (see p119).

🏛 Palácio Imperial
See pp118–19.

🏛 Palácio Rio Negro
Av Koeller 255, Centro. **Tel** (24) 2246 2423. **Open** 10am–5pm Tue–Sat.

Built in 1889 by Barão do Rio Negro, a wealthy coffee baron, the palace acted as the seat of the state government between 1894 and 1902, when Petrópolis was the capital of Rio de Janeiro state.

Between 1903 and 1960, the palace served as the summer residence of the presidents of the Republic. While Vargas converted a wine cellar into a Roman-style bathhouse, Kubitschek added built-in closets. All the original rooms are in excellent condition.

Detail on the façade of Palácio Rio Negro

Exterior of French-Gothic Catedral de São Pedro de Alcântara

🏛 Catedral de São Pedro de Alcântara
Rua São Pedro de Alcântara 60, Centro. **Tel** (24) 2242 4300. **Open** 8am–6pm daily. 8am Mon–Sat; 9:30am, 11:30am & 6:30pm Sun.

Though the cathedral's first stone was laid in 1884 by Dom Pedro II, much of its current structure dates from 1925. Built in French-Gothic style with a beautiful rose window, it has a striking interior decorated in Carrara marble. The walls here depict detailed scenes from the Crucifixion.

The Imperial Chapel, to the right of the main entrance, contains the mortal remains of King Dom Pedro II, Princess Regent Dona Teresa Cristina, their daughter Isabel, her husband Count d'Eu, and several other members of the royal family. Statues of the royal family are also featured inside the chapel. The 1848 baptismal font is the original.

🏛 Palácio de Cristal
Rua Alfredo Pachá, Centro. **Tel** (24) 2247 3721. **Open** 9am–6pm Tue–Sun.

The metal structure and glass enclosure of the Palácio de Cristal (Crystal Palace) were made in France in 1879 and shipped to Brazil. Inaugurated on February 2, 1884, the palace is a fine example of the architectural style that emerged during the French industrial revolution.

Although it was originally planned as a greenhouse for growing orchids, the Palácio de Cristal was later meant to be an exhibition hall for hosting regular displays of local products. However, it ended up as the imperial ballroom, and has been the sight of many spectacular

parties. Most momentous were the extravagant balls hosted by Princess Isabel and Count d'Eu, who is believed to have conceived the palace's basic design. It was during one such event in 1888 that Isabel signed an order liberating 103 slaves. On May 13 of the same year, Isabel went on to sign the Lei Aurea (Golden Law), the decree that, in theory, abolished slavery in Brazil.

The metal-and-glass exhibition hall at the Palácio de Cristal

Although most of its former glory is lost, the palace today serves as an exhibition hall. It occasionally hosts art shows and cultural events.

🚇 Casa de Santos Dumont
Rua do Encanto 22, Centro.
Tel (24) 2247 5222. **Open** 9am–5pm Tue–Sun. 🎫

In 1918, the great Brazilian aviator and inventor of the wristwatch, Alberto Santos Dumont (1873–1932), designed and built his summerhouse in the style of a French alpine chalet and named it "A Encantada," or enchanted. The three floors contain a workroom, a lounge-cum-dining room, a bedroom, and an office. The alcohol-heated shower in the bathroom was the first of its kind in Brazil. There is no kitchen because Dumont had all his meals sent in by the then Palace Hotel.

The fascinating personal collection of this delightful inventor includes everyday objects, such as furniture, photographs, and various artifacts, including beautiful vases and lamps.

🚇 Quitandinha
Av Joaquim Rolla 2. **Tel** (24) 2245 2020. **Open** 10am–5pm Tue–Sat, 10am–4pm Sun & public hols. 🎫 ♿

An imposing palace built in Norman style, Quitandinha is located southwest of the town center. Entrepreneur Joaquim Rolla built it in 1944 to be the largest casino complex in South America. For the exterior, Rolla copied the large casinos that were popular at the time along the Normandy coast, while the interior was by Dorothy Drape, a famous Hollywood set designer.

Quitandinha's glory ended in 1946, when President Dutra banned gambling. Remarkably well preserved, today it is mainly used for drama and music performances. The guided tour takes visitors back in time to the 1940s, when Quitandinha's guests were global celebrities.

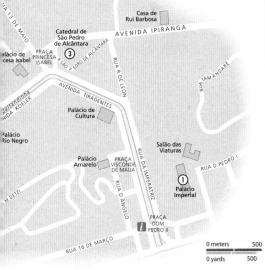

Petrópolis

1. Palácio Imperial
2. Palácio Rio Negro
3. Catedral de São Pedro de Alcântara
4. Palácio de Cristal
5. Casa de Santos Dumont
6. Quitandinha

The Norman-style architecture of the Quitandinha palace complex

For keys to symbols *see back flap*

Petrópolis: Palácio Imperial

Built by Dom Pedro II between 1845 and 1864, the Neo-Classical Imperial Palace was used by the Emperor as his summer residence every year from 1848 until the end of the monarchy and declaration of independence in 1889. In that year, the palace was leased out as a college, and continued to function as such until President Vargas passed a decree in 1943 creating the Imperial Museum. Among the highlights of the museum, which faithfully reflect the daily life of the Brazilian royal family, are the Imperial Crown Jewels, as well as other artifacts, paintings, and furniture that belonged to the Emperor and his family.

★ **Crown Jewels**
The Imperial Crown of Dom Pedro II is the most valuable piece in the collection and was made for his coronation on July 18, 1841, when he was just 15 years old.

Sala do Primeiro Reinado
This room features the last painting of Dom Pedro I in Brazil prior to his abdication on April 7, 1831.

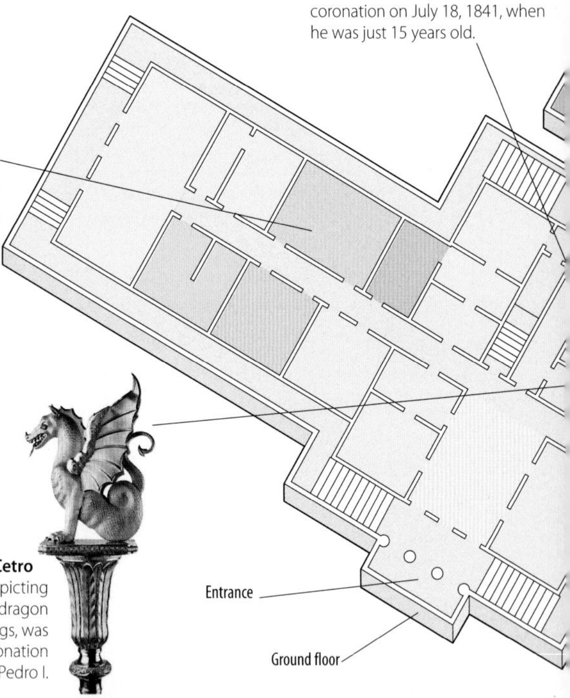

★ **Cetro**
The Imperial Scepter, depicting an open-mouthed dragon with outstretched wings, was made in 1822 for the coronation of Dom Pedro I.

Entrance

Ground floor

Museum Guide
The ground floor displays royal exhibits, and prominently features the Crown Jewels. The first floor houses the State Room, as well as the royal bedrooms. The museum is set in a pretty garden designed by Jean Baptiste Binot, a French landscape artist.

Elegant Neo-Classical façade of the Palácio Imperial

For hotels and restaurants in this region see pp372–3 and p388

Gabinete
The study features Brazil's first telephone, presented to Dom Pedro II in 1876 by Alexander Graham Bell.

First floor

Sala de Música
Besides a rare triangular spinet built by Mathias Bosten in 1788, the music room also has a beautiful harp.

Sala do Senado features the 1872 *Fala do Trono* (Speech from the Throne), a portrait of Dom Pedro II in full regalia.

VISITORS' CHECKLIST

Practical Information
Rua da Imperatriz 220, Petrópolis.
Tel (24) 2233 0300.
Open museum: 11am–6pm Tue–Sun; sound & light show: 8pm Thu, Fri & Sat. free entry to the garden from 8am–5pm on Sun.
w museuimperial.gov.br

★ **Sala de Estado**
The throne on show in the State Room came from the palace in São Cristovão.

Key

▨ The Dining Room
▨ The Music Room
▨ The Royal Costumes & Scepter
☐ The Imperial Throne
▨ Dom Pedro II's Study
▨ The Princesses' Room
▨ Imperial Brazilian Jewelry
▨ Dom Pedro I's Room

▨ Room of His Majesty
▨ Princesa Isabel's Room
☐ Lobby
▨ The Empress's Sewing Room
▨ The Empress's Piano Room
☐ Saleta
☐ Senate Room
☐ Other Exhibition Space
☐ Non-Exhibition Space

❻ Teresópolis

Rio de Janeiro. 🚉 160,000. 🚌 from Rio de Janeiro City. 🛈 Av Rotariana s/n, Soberbo, (21) 3642 3471; Av J. J. de Araujo Regadas, Praça Luis de Camões, (21) 2742 5561.

Set amid pretty countryside, Teresópolis is known for its artisan fair in Praça Higino da Silveira, which is lined with more than 700 stands at weekends. Just 3 miles (5 km) south of the town center is **AraBotânica**, one of Brazil's largest orchid farms.

🌱 AraBotânica

Estrada Francisco Smolka 601, Quebra-Frascos. **Tel** (21) 3641 2985. 🎫 ♿ 📧
Open 9am–4:30pm Wed–Sun.

❼ Parque Nacional da Serra dos Órgãos

Rio de Janeiro. 🚌 from Rio de Janeiro & São Paulo. 🛈 (21) 2152 1108, (21) 2152 1100. **Open** 8am–5pm daily.
🎫 🎫 ♿ 🅿 w icmbio.gov.br/parnaserradosorgaos

Created in 1939, this national park covers an area of approximately 100 sq miles (200 sq km) that stretches from Teresópolis across to Petrópolis. The park offers good climbing and treks, including a spectacular 20-mile-(32-km-) long trek between both cities. Among the park's most notable peaks are the 7,475-ft (2,263-m) Pedra do Sino, the highest in the mountain range, and the more famous Dedo de Deus (God's Finger), which stands 5,512 ft (1,680 m) high.

Of the many entrance points to the park, the most popular and best equipped is 3 miles (5 km) south of Teresópolis.

Dedo de Deus (God's Finger), Parque Nacional da Serra dos Órgãos

⑧ Búzios

Rio de Janeiro. 🚌 from Cabo Frio.
ℹ Praça Santos Dumont; Av José
Bento Ribeiro Dantas 100; (22) 2623
4254. 🚢 🅦 **buziosturismo.com**

Since Brigitte Bardot's visit to
Búzios in 1964 with her then
boyfriend, Brazilian actor Bob
Zagury, this peninsula has
developed from a quiet
string of isolated fishing
villages lost in semitropical
maquis, into one of the
country's most stylish low-
key resorts. Private
homes, designer
boutiques, and little
pousadas cling to its
hills or watch over the
numerous beaches.
Beach buggies driven
by vacationers buzz

**Statue of Brigitte
Bardot on the Orla
Bardot**

along the scruffy roads. Yachts
bob in the bay in front of Búzios
town, which is little more than a
cluster of cobblestoned streets
lined with smart boutiques
and restaurants. During high
season, the resort buzzes with
cruiseship passengers and
middle-class Brazilian tourists
who shop by day on **Rua das
Pedras**, the town's main
thoroughfare, sip cocktails in
the evening at one of the
oceanfront *pousadas*, and
then dance the night away
in the Ibiza-style clubs
and beachside bars.
Búzios's *raison d'être*
is its beaches, which
range from half-
moon bays to long
stretches of fine
white sand. The best

One of the souvenir shops lining Rua das
Pedras in Búzios

way to see them is to rent a
beach buggy and explore,
armed with one of the
ubiquitous free maps of the
peninsula available from every

Beaches of Costa do Sol

The stretch of coast extending between Niterói and Búzios,
is best known for its landscape, outstanding beaches, and
upmarket resorts. Attractive beaches and sparkling waters
make it ideal for a lazy stretch on the sand, or a dip in the
clean waters. With its crashing waves and a steady breeze,
this stretch is popular for windsurfing. It is easy to find
accommodation here, both in busy resorts and isolated
fishing villages.

SOUTHEAST
BRAZIL

RIO DE
JANEIRO
&
ESPÍRITO
SANTO

Rio de
Janeiro

Locator Map
░ Costa do Sul

Maricá, a quiet resort town, sits at the foot of
forest-covered hills and looks over its own lagoon.
Of its many beaches, the best is 11-mile (17-km)
Praia de Itaipuaçu, which is watched over by the
Pedra do Elefante, a miniature Sugar Loaf.

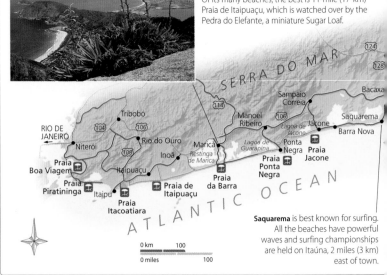

Saquarema is best known for surfing.
All the beaches have powerful
waves and surfing championships
are held on Itaúna, 2 miles (3 km)
east of town.

0 km   100
0 miles   100

For hotels and restaurants in this region see pp372–3 and p388

other hotel reception. The peninsula is extremely well signposted, and since it is only 4 miles (6 km) long and 2 miles (4 km) wide, it is difficult to get lost here.

Many of the beaches, including the two sets of twin sheltered coves – at **Praia João Fernandes**, **Praia João Fernandinho**, **Praia Azeda**, and **Praia Azedinha** – are within half an hour's walk of town. Others are a beach buggy ride away. **Praia da Ferradura**, on the opposite side from Búzios, is one of the most beautiful beaches near town, and one of the least spoilt by hotel development. Fishermen still work from here at dawn and dusk. **Praia Brava**, at the peninsula's eastern extreme, is washed by

the fiercest waves and is a popular surf beach. **Olho de Boi**, which can be reached only via a rocky trail that runs from Brava's southern end, is surrounded by rocky hills on

all sides, and is an unofficial nudist beach. **Ferradurinha**, at the peninsula's southern extreme, has clear, calm waters and natural swimming pools, good for a dip.

The small, isolated Praia Azeda, known for its tranquil waters

Cabo Frio is a triumph of concrete over natural beauty. The region's busiest resort, it overflows with locals at weekends. There is good surf on the numerous beaches and dune-boarding at Praia do Peró, 5 miles (8 km) north.

VISITORS' CHECKLIST

Practical Information
Rio de Janeiro. Cabo Frio:
🛈 Av Américo Vespúcio 200, (22) 2645 2505. Arraial do Cabo:
🛈 R. General Bruno Martins, s/n, (22) 2622 1949. Araruama:
🛈 Av Brasil 655 (22) 2665 5700. Saquarema: 🛈 Secretaria de Turismo, Rua Coronel Madureira 77, (22) 2651 2123. Maricá:
🛈 Praça Conselheiro Macedo Soares, (21) 3731 5094.

Transport
🚌 from Rio.

Praia da Tartaruga — Armação dos Búzios

Praia de Tucuns

(106)

(178)

(104)

Praia do Peró

Iguaba Grande — São Pedro da Aldeia

(138)

Iguaba Pequena — Porto do Carro

Praia das Conchas

Cabo Frio

Araruama — *Lagoa de Araruama*

Praia Seca — Figueira — (132)

Praia Grande — Arraial do Cabo

Praia Massambaba — Praia do Cabo Frio — ILHA DO CABO FRIO

Araruama, one of the largest lakes in Brazil, is ringed by myriad long white-sand beaches. A constant breeze makes for good windsurfing. It is also famous for its medicinal mud and high salinity.

Arraial do Cabo town itself is uninspiring but the confluence of currents around the cape provides the best diving in southeastern Brazil and a wealth of magnificent beaches.

Terceira Ponte Bridge connecting Vila Velha to Vitória

❾ Guarapari

Espírito Santo. �· 122,000. 🚌 from Vitória. 🔢 Rua Alencar Moraes de Rezende 100, Jardim Boa Vista, (27) 3262 8759.

Espírito Santo's busiest beach resort is fringed by dozens of long, white beaches. People from Minas Gerais rush down on weekends to the sandy beaches of Guarapari, said to have mildly radioactive healing properties. The best beach, **Praia do Morro**, lies to the north of the city and has a nature reserve. **Praia do Meio**, also to the north, has rock pools filled with clear water, and is good for snorkeling.

Guarapari offers light adventure activities, such as rappeling, rafting, and some of the best diving in the Southeast. The town also has a lively nightlife scene.

Located about 20 km (12 miles) north of Guarapari is the nature reserve, **Parque Estadual Paulo César Vinha**, with its dunes,

mangroves, and reddish lagoon, the Lagoa de Caraís.

🏕 **Parque Estadual Paulo César Vinha**
Rodovia do Sol, Km 38. **Tel** (27) 3242 3665. ♿

❿ Vitória

Espírito Santo. �· 360,000. ✈️ 🚌 🚆 from Rio. 🔢 Secretaria Municipal de Turismo, Av Marechal Mascarenhas de Morais 1927, Bento Ferreira. **Tel** (27) 3235 2237. 🎭 Carnaval (Feb/Mar).

The capital city of Espírito Santo is dominated by a lovely bay with sheltered crescent coves, and surrounded by open ocean. Vitória was originally made up of 36 distinct islands, but landfills have reduced these to just a handful, connected by a series of bridges. **Praia do Camburí**, the main beach south of the city is a 4-mile (6-km) stretch, dotted with restaurants and hotels.

Across the bay lies **Vila Velha** (Old Town), the most interesting part of the metropolitan area, reached by the majestic bridge, **Terceira Ponte**. Although few colonial buildings remain, it is home to the architectural symbol of the city, **Convento da Nossa Senhora da Penha**. Sitting high on a palm-covered hill overlooking Vitória Bay, its thick fortified walls reflect both the sunrise and sunset. The monastery was founded in 1558 and preserves fine 16th-century wood carvings and one of Brazil's first paintings, *Nossa Senhora das Alegrias*, by an unknown early 16th-century Iberian artist. At the base of the hill is the 1551 Igreja Nossa Senhora do Rosário, the oldest church in the state.

South of Vilha Velha, **Praia da Costa** is not as busy a beach as Camburí, but is a good place to go bodysurfing.

Manguezal de Vitória, northwest of Vitória, is the largest stretch of urban mangroves in South America. The mangroves are an important nursery for marine life and can be visited by boat alongside some of the bay's wilder islands.

🏛 **Convento da Nossa Senhora da Penha**
Rua Vasco Coutinho, Prainha, Vila Velha, Vitória. **Tel** (27) 3329 0420. **Open** 5:15am–5pm Mon–Sat, 4:15am–5pm Sun.

🏕 **Manguezal de Vitória**
Santuário de Santo Antônio. 🚤 boat tours by Cores do Mar: Praia de Camburi, Pier de Iemanjá, (27) 999 895 107. 🌐 escunacoresdomar.com.br

Sunbathers on Praia do Morro in Guarapari

For hotels and restaurants in this region see pp372–3 and p388

⓫ Pedra Azul

Espírito Santo. 🚌 from Vitória.
ℹ️ Parque Estadual da Pedra Azul,
(27) 3248 1156, (27) 997 398 005.
Open 8am–5pm Tue–Sun.
🌐 **pedraazul.com.br**

Sitting in a tiny island of remnant Mata Atlântica forest, the 500-m- (1,640-ft-) high Pedra Azul (Blue Stone) rises in the middle of the Parque Estadual da Pedra Azul, forming a stunning centerpiece. Its natural color is an almost polished blue-grey, but shifts in hue and shade depending on the light: coal-black and brooding under a dark cloud, burning orange with the setting sun, or silvery white under a full moon.

The small visitors' center at the foot of the stone is a good place to collect a detailed map of the park. The easiest trekking circuit, around the stone's base, is 0.8 miles (1.3 km). The one leading through the natural pools of the park is 1 mile (1.6 km) long, and tougher, so it is advisable to hire a guide. Equipment and booking are required for climbing the stone, and camping is forbidden.

The forest surrounding Pedra Azul is small but it is the nesting ground for a diverse variety of wildlife. Hummingbirds, tanagers, and tiny tufted-eared marmosets are a common sight.

Dramatic Pedra Azul, a granite monolith

⓬ Itaúnas

Espírito Santo. 🏠 2,500. 🚌 from Vitória. ℹ️ (27) 3762 5196. 🎭 Festa de Forró (Jul).

This sleepy little fishing town lies tucked away in the far north of Espírito Santo on the border with Bahia. Long strands of beaches stretch to the north and south of the town. These have drifted into dunes so large that the first settlement here lies submerged, the remains of the original church tower occasionally appearing from the sand after a strong wind. The town lies next to the Rio Itaúnas which spreads into broad marshy meadows behind the sea. Ocelots, caimans, and capybaras live here, along with an impressive variety of rare waterbirds and small mammals.

The smattering of hotels in town offer dune buggy tours, during which you cross dozens of towering dunes and empty turtle-nesting beaches, eventually reaching the sandy cliffs on the state border with Bahia.

Itaúnas itself is surprisingly lively for a town so small. It is famous, particularly among students, for its exuberant *samba* and *axé* parties, which continue from December to March, and its exciting *forró* dance festival in July.

Sand dunes flanking the sleepy fishing town of Itaúnas along the Rio Itaúnas

MINAS GERAIS

The state of Minas Gerais is dotted with pretty colonial towns, set in a stunning landscape of rugged hills. Of these, Ouro Preto, Congonhas, and Diamantina are UNESCO World Heritage Sites. Beyond the towns is pastoral country broken by wilderness, much of which has been protected by a series of national and state parks, where several rare species of animals, birds, and plants can be seen.

Minas's old mining towns are laid out along the Estrada Real, once Brazil's first great wagon trail and now one of its major tourist routes. The most famous is Ouro Preto, named after the black gold that was discovered here in the late 17th century by an itinerant adventurer (*bandeirante*), who came through the vast interior in search of slaves. Gold brought a rush of speculators and new discoveries and by the mid-18th century ramshackle mining camps had grown into prosperous towns. Today, Ouro Preto, Tiradentes, Mariana, São João del Rei, Congonhas, and Diamantina preserve some of the finest ecclesiastical buildings and Baroque carvings in the Americas.

The state's spectacular parks are home to the maned wolf, as well as a plethora of endemic birds and plants. The Serra do Cipó and the Serra da Canastra lie on the tablelands of the Brazilian shield. Their *cerrado* forests are cut by several rivers that plunge dramatically over the edges of the *mesetas* (tabletop mountains), forming some of the world's highest waterfalls. The mountains of the Serra do Caparaó protect a swathe of the Mata Atlântica, dripping with orchids and the habitat of one of the few remaining populations of woolly spider monkey – the Americas' largest and rarest primate.

The state capital, Belo Horizonte, is a modern industrial city with a lively café life. President Juscelino Kubitschek's favorite architect, Oscar Niemeyer, adorned the city's Pampulha neighborhood with several structures before building the nation's capital, Brasília. Minas is also well known for its distinct cuisine and its rich literary and musical heritage.

A breathtaking view of mauve *ipê* flowers in full bloom outside Diamantina

◀ The cross at the top of the Igreja de São Francisco de Assis, Ouro Preto

Exploring Minas Gerais

Belo Horizonte, the capital of Minas Gerais, is the focus of life here. Most colonial mining towns, including Ouro Preto and Congonhas, lie immediately to its south. Mariana, another colonial city south of Belo Horizonte, is still a working mining center. Farther south, and a day's drive from the capital, is the hilly Serra da Canastra National Park. Northern Minas is much wilder, with large tracts of *cerrado* forest in the Serra do Cipó and around Diamantina. The extreme north is arid, dominated by the *sertão*, a region of scrub and grassland, whose distinct culture and language was mythologized in the most famous of all Brazilian novels, *Grande Sertão: Veredas*, by João Guimarães Rosa *(see p35)*.

Painting inside Igreja Nossa Senhora do Carmo, Diamantina

Sights at a Glance

Towns & Cities

1 Diamantina
3 Belo Horizonte
4 Ouro Preto *pp130–32*
5 Mariana
7 Tiradentes
8 São João del Rei

National Parks & Areas of Natural Beauty

2 Parque Nacional Serra do Cipó
9 Parque Nacional Serra da Canastra

Historic Buildings

6 Basílica do Senhor Bom Jesus de Matosinhos, Congonhas *pp134–5*

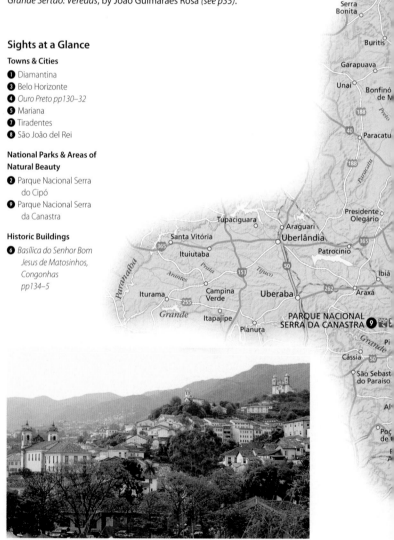

Ouro Preto, the architecturally stunning colonial city in Minas Gerais

For hotels and restaurants in this region see p373 and pp388–9

Sunset in the *cerrado* landscape of Serra da Canastra

0 kilometers 100

0 miles 100

Key

▬ Highway

▬ Major road

┄ Minor road

⌐ Railroad

▬ State border

△ Peak

Getting Around

Belo Horizonte has two airports and is connected several times a day with all the Brazilian state capitals. There are few other airports in the state and transport beyond the capital is limited to buses, which are generally comfortable and frequent. Another option is to rent a car. Driving is possible during the day, even though many of the smaller roads are blighted with enormous potholes.

For keys to symbols *see back flap*

Old *fazenda* in the beautiful village of Biribiri near Diamantina

❶ Diamantina

🗺 48,000. 🚌 Largo Dom João 134,
(38) 3531 1471. 🛈 Praça Antonio
Eulálio 53, (38) 3531 9532.
🌐 diamantina.mg.gov.br/turismo

Nestled in rugged hills and shrouded with *cerrado* forest, Diamantina is the prettiest and best preserved of all the colonial cities in the state, and also a UNESCO World Heritage Site. Diamonds were discovered here in 1728, when the city was a small settlement called Arraial do Tijuco. Within a few decades the mud huts and encampments transformed into one of the wealthiest towns in Brazil.

The city is tiny and most of its historic buildings and churches lie within easy walking distance of the main square, Praça Guerra. This is an obvious point of orientation as it is dominated by the twin towers of the largest building in the city – the Catedral Metropolitana de Santo Antônio, built in the 1930s. Just south of this in the adjacent Praça Juscelino Kubitschek is a small **Museu Casa do Diamante**, which houses a handful of the stones, together with iron collars once fitted onto slaves.

South again is the **Museu de Juscelino Kubitschek**, the modest former home of the Brazilian president, Juscelino Kubitschek (1902–76), who built Brasília (*see pp306–7*). Two blocks west is the city's most beautiful landmark, the Casa da Gloria, consisting of two houses

on opposite sides connected by an enclosed, brilliant blue, second-story passageway. The building is not open to the public.

There are several churches in Diamantina. The oldest is the **Nossa Senhora do Rosário**, in the square of the same name, a short distance to the northeast of the Praça Guerra. It was built and used by the enslaved black community and the city's poor. Next to it is an original 18th-century fountain whose waterspouts are bas-reliefs of African heads.

A block south is the spectacular **Nossa Senhora do Carmo**. Built between 1760 and 1784, it was the town's richest church and attended by the elite white community. It is remarkable chiefly for the interior paintings by José Soares de Araujo, from Braga, Portugal. Araujo's works lie in many of the town's churches but those here are his finest. The ceiling paintings are very striking. Near the back of the church is a portrait of the Prophet Elijah ascending to heaven in a chariot of fire.

The **Casa de Chica da Silva**, a smart town house one block south of the Nossa Senhora do Carmo, is famous more for its former owner than it is for its small collection of period furniture. During the 18th century, Francisca (Chica) da

Silva was a mulatta slave who became one of the few black people to become accepted by high colonial society through sheer force of personality.

Environs
A string of stunning natural locations lies within easy reach of Diamantina, the most impressive of which is **Biribiri**, located 7 miles (12 km) north of town. A historical village, Biribiri is home to many *fazendas* and is surrounded by waterfalls and mountains. Next to Biribiri is a winding blackwater river and the Parque Rio Preto, a good location for bird-watching.

🏛 **Casa de Chica da Silva**
Praça Lobo Mesquita 266.
Tel (38) 3531 2491. **Open** noon–
5pm Tue–Sat, 9am–noon Sun.

🏛 **Museu Casa do Diamante**
Rua Direita 14. **Tel** (38) 3531 1382.
Open 10am–5pm Tue–Sat,
9am–1pm Sun. 🗺

🏛 **Museu de Juscelino Kubitschek**
Rua São Francisco 241. **Tel** (38) 3531
3607. **Open** 8am–5pm Tue–Sat,
8am–1pm Sun. 🗺

⛪ **Nossa Senhora do Carmo**
Rua do Carmo. **Tel** (38) 3531 1667.
Open 2–5pm Tue, Thu & Fri,
9am–4pm Sat.

⛪ **Nossa Senhora do Rosário**
Largo do Rosário. **Tel** (38) 3531 1667.
Open 8–11am & 1–5pm Tue–Sat,
9am–1pm Sun.

Nave, Igreja de Nossa Senhora do Carmo

Magnificent waterfall at Parque Nacional Serra do Cipó

❷ Parque Nacional Serra do Cipó

🚌 from Belo Horizonte to Jaboticatubas, or Santana do Riacho.
Tel (31) 3718 7484, (31) 3718 7469.
W icmbio.gov.br/parnaserradocipo
Open 8am–4pm daily. 🛏 Cipó Veraneio Hotel, Rodovia MG-10, Serra do Cipó, (31) 3718 7000.
W cipoveraneiohotel.com.br

Just northeast of Belo Horizonte, the state capital, this 131-sq-mile (338-sq-km) national park lies in high rugged country in the Serra do Espinhaço mountains, which run through the middle of northern Minas Gerais. Cipó protects some pristine areas of *cerrado* as well as the watersheds of many of the tributaries of the São Francisco and the Doce rivers. Waterfalls, plants, rare animals, and birds are abundant, making this one of the most beautiful national parks in Minas Gerais.

It is particularly lovely in May and June when the skies are invariably blue, the rivers full, and many of the numerous wildflowers in bloom. This is also a good time to go on a guided tour, at dawn or dusk, to spot pumas, giant anteaters, ocelots, maned wolves, and howling monkeys on the quieter trails.

The park itself does not offer accomodation, but the area has plenty of lodging options.

❸ Belo Horizonte

🏠 2,514,000. ✈ 🚢 🚌 🚃
ℹ Mercado das Flores: Av Afonso Pena 1055, (31) 3277 7666. Rodoviária: Praça Rio Branco s/n, (31) 3277 6907.
🎭 Carnaval (Feb/Mar).
W belohorizonte.mg

The capital city of Minas Gerais was laid out in the 1890s and resembles a mini São Paulo. Clusters of seemingly endless skyscraper apartment blocks sit in a broad valley under lush hills. Belo Horizonte is known worldwide for its visionary architecture. Its architectural highlights lie in the suburb of Pampulha, often regarded as the blueprint for Brasília. The buildings are set in expansive gardens designed by Roberto Burle Marx (1909–94), gathered around a large, beautiful artificial lake. All were commissioned by the then mayor of Belo Horizonte, Juscelino Kubitschek, and designed by the renowned architect Oscar Niemeyer in the 1940s.

The most impressive of all the buildings is the **Igreja de São Francisco de Assis**, which was built in 1943 as a series of parabolic arches in concrete, and has a wonderful sense of light and space. On the outside walls are a series of *azulejos*, or Portuguese blue tiles, depicting scenes from the life of St. Francis and painted by Brazil's foremost Modernist artist, Candido Portinari (1903–62). Other important buildings in the Pampulha complex include

Azulejos on the outside walls of São Francisco de Assis

the dance hall **Casa do Baile**, with its sweeping curved walkway that functioned as a ballroom till 1946, and the twin sports stadia, which are a clear precursor to the gymnasium Niemeyer designed for Brasília.

In the inner city, the **Museu Mineiro** preserves some fine colonial-era religious art, including a number of paintings attributed to Mestre Athayde (1762–1830). Beyond this, Belo Horizonte's main attractions are the lively restaurant and nightlife scene around the inner-city neighbor- hoods of Lourdes and Savassi. These areas have many chic restaurants, which often have live music playing during the weekends (*see pp388–9*). The Lourdes and Savassi neighborhoods are easily explored on foot and make a pleasant walk.

Environs
The colonial towns of Sabará, Caeté, and Santa Luiza, to the east of Belo Horizonte, lie less than half an hour's drive away. All preserve fine Baroque churches and streets of 18th-century town houses.

🏛 **Igreja de São Francisco de Assis**
Av Otacilio Negrão de Lima 3000, Pampulha. **Tel** (31) 3427 1644. **Open** 8am–5pm Mon–Sat & hols, noon–5pm Sun. ⛪ 10am Sun, 8pm Tue 🅿 ♿ ✉

🏛 **Museu Mineiro**
Av João Pinheiro 342. **Tel** (31) 3269 1168. **Open** 10am–7pm Tue, Wed & Fri, noon–9pm Thu, noon–7pm Sat & Sun. 🅿

Igreja de São Francisco de Assis in Pampulha, Belo Horizonte

❹ Street-by-Street: Ouro Preto

Ouro Preto, or "Black Gold," earned its name shortly after its founding in 1698 from tarnished gold nuggets mined in the surrounding areas. It still resembled a boom town when it was given city status in 1711. By the mid-18th century, however, the gold rush had turned Ouro Preto into a wealthy town with fine buildings. It nurtured a generation of some of Latin America's finest artists and craftsmen, including the ecclesiastical painter Mestre Athayde and the great sculptor Aleijadinho among others. Ouro Preto became the base of the Inconfidência rebellion led by Tiradentes against Portuguese colonists.

Casa dos Contos
Once the gold exchange, then a prison, the building is now a small museum dedicated to money and finance.

A cluster of colonial buildings in hilly Ouro Preto

★ **Matriz de Nossa Senhora do Pilar**
Exquisite artwork is showcased in this opulent Brazilian Baroque church, resplendent in gold. The carvings in the chancel are breathtaking.

PRAÇA REINALDO ALVES DE BRITO

CONDE DE BOBADELA

RUA PARANÁ

RUA XAVIER D

RUA DO PILAR

0 meters 100
0 yards 100

Key

— Suggested route

★ Matriz de Nossa Senhora da Conceição
Manuel Francisco Libsoa transformed this once-rustic church into one of the city's most magnificently decorated cathedrals.

Statue of Tiradentes
The leader of the Inconfidentes was the only rebel against the Portuguese colonizers to be executed. He is a cult figure in Brazil, mainly for the poor.

Museu do Oratório

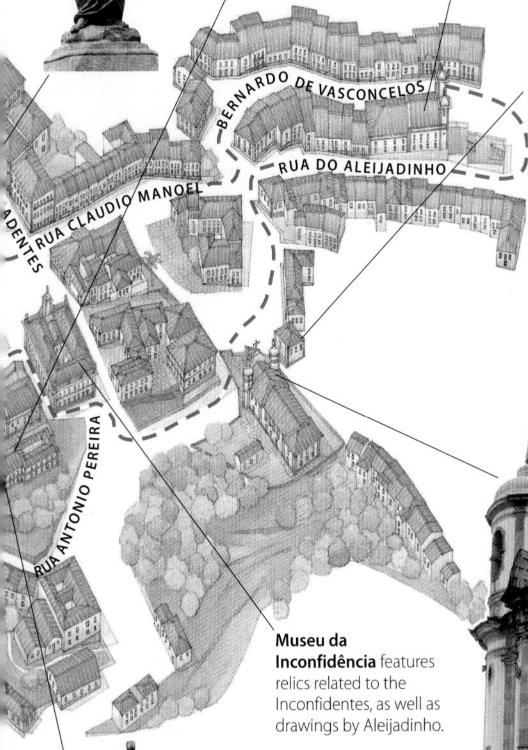

BERNARDO DE VASCONCELOS

RUA DO ALEIJADINHO

RUA CLAUDIO MANOEL

ADENTES

RUA ANTONIO PEREIRA

VISITORS' CHECKLIST

Practical Information
Minas Gerais. 🚉 74,000.
ℹ️ Praça Tiradentes 4, (31) 3559 3269. 🌐 **ouropreto.org.br**
🎭 Carnaval (Feb/Mar). Casa dos Contos: Rua São José 12. **Tel** (31) 3551 1444. Igreja de Nossa Senhora de Carmo: Rua B. Musqueira. **Tel** (31) 3551 2601.

Transport
🚌 from Belo Horizonte.

Portrait of Aleijadinho
This likeness, which was painted long after the sculptor's death, is housed in the Museu Aleijadinho. The museum preserves a small collection of Aleijadinho's works.

Museu da Inconfidência features relics related to the Inconfidentes, as well as drawings by Aleijadinho.

Igreja de Nossa Senhora do Carmo
The Rococo font (in the sacristy), door-case, the altars, and the statue of Santa Helena in this church are all attributed to Aleijadinho.

★ Igreja de São Francisco de Assis
One of Latin America's most important Rococo buildings, the church combines the finest work of Aleijadinho and Mestre Athayde.

Exploring Ouro Preto

One of the first gold towns in Minas Gerais and a former state capital, Ouro Preto is built on a series of hills. Steep, curving streets lined with 18th-century residences, many of which have now been converted into restaurants, bars, and shops, link the hills. Within the town, the streets lead to pretty little squares dominated by Baroque churches and stately town houses. These include the churches of São Francisco de Assis and Nossa Senhora do Pilar, whose interiors bear the stamp of some of Latin America's finest artists and craftsmen.

⊞ Igreja de São Francisco de Assis

Largo de Coimbra. **Tel** (31) 3551 4661.
Open 8:30am–noon, 1:30–5pm Tue–Sun. 🚫

This understated, elegant little church was constructed between 1766 and 1802 and seems modest next to many of Latin America's grand Baroque churches. It is characterized by gentle curves, from the elegant S-shaped balustrades of its façade to the exquisitely unified, undulating lines of its interior. The quality of the church's beauty lies in the mastery of its art, created by two of Brazil's greatest artists, Aleijadinho *(see p135)* and his long-term partner Manuel da Costa Athayde (1762–1830). The tablet on the church's façade showing St. Francis receiving the stigmata

is believed to have been Aleijadinho's first great carving. It was followed by others, including the ornately carved door-case and the front of the sacristy at the rear of the church.

⊞ Matriz de Nossa Senhora do Pilar

Praça Mons Castilho Barbosa. **Tel** (31) 3551 4736. **Open** 9am–5pm daily.
✝ 7am daily. 🚫 📷

Commissioned by two of the wealthiest ecclesiastical orders in Ouro Preto, this church was intended as a showpiece of their influence. Pomp and circumstance surrounded its inauguration in 1731, which witnessed grand processions of clergy in opulent vestments and horses in velvet mantles mounted by knights in diamond-studded robes.

Nearly half a ton each of gold and silver were used to gild its interior, which is largely the work of 18th-century sculptor Francisco Xavier de Brito, an expatriate Portuguese. The gilt carving of Christ on the Cross on the door-case to the *capela-mor* (apsidal chapel) and the Resurrection scene on the tabernacle are regarded as de Brito's finest work.

Façade of Matriz de Nossa Senhora da Conceição

⊞ Matriz de Nossa Senhora da Conceição

Praça Antônio Dias. **Tel** (31) 3551 3282
Built by Manuel Francisco Lisboa between 1727 and 1770, this church is most celebrated for its harmonious proportions – the unity of curves and straight lines on the façade, and the sense of space generated by what is in reality a modest nave and chancel. Manuel Francisco only added the finishing touches to the interior and the sculptors remain largely unknown.

⊞ Mina do Chico Rei

Rua Dom Silvério 108. **Tel** (31) 3552 2866. 🚫
This former gold mine offers guided tours, which take visitors on a journey through the lives of miners, many of whom were African slaves. It gives an insight into their technical skills, resilience, and importance in the golden days of Ouro Preto. Chico Rei was said to be an enslaved African king who bought his freedom in the 1740s by hiding the gold he found in his hair.

Ceiling painting by Athayde in Igreja de São Francisco de Assis

For hotels and restaurants in this region see p373 and pp388–9

Praça Gomes Freire in Mariana, lined by fine 18th-century houses

⑤ Mariana

🚗 58,000. 🚌 ℹ️ Rua Direita 91, (31) 3558 1062, (31) 3558 2315.
🌐 mariana.mg.gov.br/turismo

The oldest colonial town in Minas Gerais, Mariana, which was also a significant mining town, was the capital of the state in the first half of the 18th century and far more important than its immediate neighbor, Ouro Preto.

The simple 18th-century **Basílica de São Pedro dos Clérigos** stands on top of the San Pedro hill. From here, there are spectacular views of Mariana's small colonial center.

An important attraction in the old town is the **Praça Gomes Freire**, a lovely garden square surrounded by 18th-century town houses. A short distance west of Praça Gomes Freire are the twin churches of **São Francisco de Assis** and **Nossa**

Unique window in Mariana

Senhora do Carmo. Both date from the late 18th century and sit next to each other in front of the colonial building, the Casa de Camara.

The church of São Francisco de Assis is decorated with ceiling paintings by Manuel da Costa Athayde, who was buried in the church. Visitors should not miss the evocative scenes of the death of St. Francis, as well as the relief on the door of St. Francis receiving the stigmata.

Nossa Senhora do Carmo, although damaged by fire in 1999, is still remarkable for its delicately balanced and very Portuguese exterior. Known for its gentle curves and round towers, it also has exquisite lozenge-shaped key windows.

The city's other famous church is the **Basílica de Nossa Senhora da Assunção**, which dates from 1760 and is also

referred to as the Basílica da Sé. Its exterior is modest, but the interior has some of the finest ceiling paintings by the 16th-century Portuguese artist, Manuel Rabello de Sousa. It also contains an exquisite 18th-century German organ and altarpieces by Francisco Xavier de Brito, and a portal and *lavebo* attributed to Aleijadinho. The organ was a gift from king João V of Portugal to the diocese when Mariana officially became a city and earned its current name. Restored in 1984, it can be heard during regular weekend organ recitals.

Just around the corner to the south of the basilica is the most interesting of the civic buildings, the **Museu Arquidiocesano de Arte Sacra**. This preserves paintings by Athayde, *objets d'art* by Aleijadinho, and antique liturgical objects. Its façade is crowned with a medal by Aleijadinho.

🏛 **Basílica de Nossa Senhora da Assunção**
Rua Padre Gonçalves Lopes. **Tel** (31) 3557 1216. **Open** 8am–5pm Tue–Sun.

🏛 **Museu Arquidiocesano de Arte Sacra**
Rua Frei Durão. **Tel** (31) 3557 2581. **Open** 8:30am–noon, 1:30–5pm Tue–Sat, 8:30am–2pm Sun & public hols. ⚲

🏛 **Nossa Senhora do Carmo**
Praça Minas Gerais.
Open 9am–4pm daily.

🏛 **São Francisco de Assis**
Praça Minas Gerais.
Open 9am–5pm daily.

View of Mariana and the twin churches from Basílica de São Pedro dos Clérigos

◐ Basílica do Senhor Bom Jesus de Matosinhos, Congonhas

Completed in 1771, the Baroque church of Bom Jesus de Matosinhos was built by the diamond miner Feliciano Mendes, who, after recovering from the brink of death, vowed to build a church in homage to "Bom Jesus." At the entrance of the church, 12 soapstone statues of prophets from the Old Testament overlook a garden, where six chapels containing life-size figures commemorate the Passion of Christ. The church is famous for preserving the most impressive ensemble of statues in Latin America, carved by Aleijadinho between 1780 and 1814. Next door is Museu de Congonhas, a museum devoted to the church and Baroque art.

Painted Ceiling
Painted by Bernardo Pires da Silva in 1776, the artwork on the ceiling is regarded as the finest Rococo church painting in Brazil.

Carved Altar
Designed by sculptor Aleijadinho, the altar was beautifully carved by his disciple, João Antunes de Carvalho.

KEY

① **The Crucifixion** is particularly grisly, depicting smiling soldiers hammering nails into a spread-eagled Christ, his face contorted in agony.

② Amos

③ Jonah

④ Obadiah

⑤ Baruch

⑥ Daniel

⑦ Hosea

⑧ Ezekiel

⑨ Jeremiah

⑩ Joel

⑪ Nahum

⑫ **Christ carrying the cross**, a sculpture portraying one of the stations in the Passion of Christ.

⑬ **The Flagellation of Christ and the Coronation with Thorns** depicts a prelude to the Crucifixion.

Isaiah
The sculpture of Isaiah has narrow shoulders and disproportionately short arms, and is thought to have been carved by Aleijadinho's students.

★ **The Prophet Habakukk**
Aleijadinho's sculptures are celebrated for having an air of theatricality and accentuated characteristics, both striking in his statue of Habakukk.

Façade of the church inspired by and modeled on the Santuário do Bom Jesus in Braga, Portugal, with the prophets at the entrance

★ The Capture of Christ
Jesus is captured by Herod's soldiers, led to him by his disciple, Judas Iscariot, in the Garden of Gethsemane.

Aleijadinho

Aleijadinho (1738–1815) meaning "Little Cripple," was nicknamed due to the disfigurement he suffered from leprosy. When he carved the statues at Bom Jesus de Matosinhos, he could no longer walk and had completely lost the use of his hands. His students carried him up the hill each day and strapped hammers and chisels to his arms. The figure watching the Crucifixion and hiding his hands is reputed to be a self-portrait by Aleijadinho. The statues are, without doubt, his masterpieces, and his final works of art.

Statue of Aleijadinho (standing, right) witnessing the Crucifixion

The Angel
The figure of an angel carrying a cup filled with Faith for Christ is in the chapel of the Mount of Olives.

★ The Last Supper
The figures are so life-like that when they were completed, some pilgrims are said to have greeted them as if they were real people.

Colonial Portuguese buildings in Tiradentes

❼ Tiradentes

🏛 6,000. 🚌 ℹ Largo dos Forros, Rua Resende Costa 71, (32) 3355 1212. 🎭 Festival de Cinema (Jan), Carnaval Mardi Gras (Feb/Mar).

Like Ouro Preto and Mariana, Tiradentes became rich on gold, producing some of the most lavish Baroque church interiors and façades in all of Brazil. The town takes its name from the nickname "Tiradentes" (Tooth-puller) of José da Silva Xavier (1746–92), an erstwhile resident who became a martyr of the Inconfidência Mineria, the first movement in Brazil towards independence from Portugal.

Tiradentes is a delightful colonial town. Its multicolored Portuguese cottages and miniature Baroque churches flank the cobbled roads on the steep, low São José hills around the Rio Santo Antônio. There is a craft shop, an arty little café, or a gourmet restaurant on every other corner. Pretty horse-drawn carriages gather in Largo das Forras, the town's main plaza, and a narrow gauge steam train, Maria Fumaça *(see p424)*, with wooden Pullman coaches, puffs and heaves its way to and from neighboring São João del Rei on weekends and public holidays.

The center of Tiradentes is tiny and best seen on foot. Rua da Praia runs west from Largo das Forras following the course of the Rio das Mortes. Rua Direita runs parallel to it and a series of

smaller streets cross the two. The most important of these is Rua da Câmara, whose steep cobbles rise to the town's most imposing church, the **Matriz de Santo Antônio**, built between 1710 and 1752. This is one of the finest Baroque churches in Brazil, with wonderful wood carvings and gilt interiors. It hosts concerts and sound-and-light shows on weekends. Parts of the façade are attributed to the architect and sculptor Aleijadinho *(see p135)*.

There are various other small churches scattered throughout the town and these are all worth a visit. The best of these churches is **Igreja Nossa Senhora do Rosário dos Prestos**, on Rua Direita, which features some elegant statues and painted panels.

Also on Rua Direita is a cultural center, **Centro Cultural Yves Alves**, which hosts concerts, theatrical performances, films, and art exhibitions.

Gilt altar and interior of Matriz de Santo Antônio, Tiradentes

A highlight of Tiradentes is the magnificent blue soapstone public fountain dating from the 18th century, the **Chafariz de São José**, just across from Rua da Camara. It features an oratory with an image of São Jose de Botas and three faces representing love, good fortune, and health. The water comes from a spring in the São José hills overlooking the town, an area that offers excellent hiking.

🏛 **Centro Cultural Yves Alves**
Rua Direita 168. **Tel** (32) 3355 1604.

⛪ **Matriz de Santo Antônio**
Rua da Camara. **Open** 9:30am–5pm daily. 🎭 📷 ⛪ 7pm Sat.

Chafariz de São José, an 18th-century fountain in Tiradentes

❾ São João del Rei

🏛 85,000. 🚂 Maria Fumaça from Tiradentes, Fri–Sun & public hols, (32) 3371 8485. 🚌 from Tiradentes, Belo Horizonte, Rio de Janeiro, São Paulo. ℹ Praça Frei Orlando 90, (32) 3372 7338. 🎭 Carnaval Mardi Gras (Feb), Semana de Inconfidência (Apr), Holy Week. 🌐 saojoaodelrei.mg.gov.br

The largest of the historic towns of Minas Gerais, Sao João del Rei is a bustling place with well-preserved colonial buildings, situated 7 miles (12 km) from Tiradentes. It boasts a number of Baroque and Rococo churches, including Carmo, Rosário, and Pilar, whose bells can often be heard ringing.

The principal reason for visiting São João is to see the **Igreja de São Francisco de Assis**, whose unusual curved façade, turtle-back roof and

Façade, Igreja de São Francisco de Assis, São João del Rei

intricately carved medal overlook a square lined with towering palms. The square is in the shape of a lyre and at sundown the shadows of the palms form the instrument's strings. Together with the Santuário do Bom Jesus do Monte Sítio in Braga, Portugal, and the church of São Francisco in Ouro Preto *(see p130–32)*, this church is one of the jewels in the crown of Baroque architecture.

The town has a handful of other interesting sights. The **Museu Regional de São João del Rei**, a colonial mansion, full of antique furniture and sacred art, is one of the best in Minas Gerais. The **Museu Ferroviário**, at the Maria Fumaça railway station, is a tiny locomotive museum housing an old, Philadelphia-built, narrow gauge steam train. It sits alongside the Pullman carriages used by Emperor Dom Pedro II when he traveled to Minas Gerais from Rio in the 19th century.

🏛 Igreja de São Francisco de Assis
Praça Frei Orlando.
Open 8am– 5:30pm Sun-Fri.

🏛 Museu Ferroviário
Estacão Ferroviária, Av Hermílio Alves 366. **Tel** (32) 3371 8485. **Open** 9–11am & 1–4pm Wed, 9am–12:30pm & 2–4pm Thu–Sat, 9am–noon Sun.

🏛 Museu Regional de São João del Rei
Rua Marechal Deodoro 12. **Tel** (32) 3371 7663. **Open** 9:30am–5:30pm Tue–Fri, 9am–1pm Sat & Sun.

❾ Parque Nacional Serra da Canastra

🚌 from Belo Horizonte to Piuí, from Piuí to São Roque de Minas. **ℹ** Av Presidente Tancredo Neves 498, São Roque de Minas, (37) 3433 1326; (37) 3433 1324. **Open** 8am–6pm daily.
w serradacanastra.com.br

The extensive Parque Nacional Serra da Canastra, tucked away in the far southwest of Minas Gerais, protects the head waters of one of South America's largest rivers – the Rio São Francisco. This great waterway flows 1,963 miles (3,160 km) through the rippling hills of Minas, and the semi-arid regions of the northeastern interior. But in the Serra da Canastra it is little more than a large mountain stream cutting through rugged terrain. Bare granite peaks rise to

Giant anteater in the Parque Nacional Serra da Canastra

almost 4,920 ft (1,500 m). Sparse *cerrado* forest sprinkled with boulders gathers at their feet. Around the numerous waterfalls and along the wild rivers are stretches of lush, gallery forest. The most famed of the falls is the **Cachoeira d'Anta**. Here the river's ice-cold waters form a series of pools before plunging 186 m (610 ft) off an escarpment. The park's most famous trail, the **Trilha Casca d'Anta**, begins in front of the waterfall and offers a spectacular view out over the park to the denuded pasture land beyond.

There is plenty of wildlife in the Serra da Canastra, though it can be hard to see. Maned wolves and giant anteaters are relatively common here, as are the pig-sized giant armadillos. The park is especially rich in birdlife, and is one of the few places in the world where it is possible to see the endangered Brazilian Merganser duck.

Granite peaks looming over the *cerrado* and pasture land beyond, Parque Nacional Serra da Canastra

SÃO PAULO CITY

Bristling concrete towers extend interminably over São Paulo, an expansive, vibrant city located on a high plateau. The impressive number of immigrants settled in its many districts makes it one of the world's largest metropolises. Its immense cultural diversity has blessed it with the liveliest and most creative artistic, musical, and gastronomic scene in the country.

São Paulo was founded in 1554 by Manuel da Nóbrega and José de Anchieta, and established as a Jesuit missionary outpost. The 17th century saw the town become the headquarters for *bandeirantes*, or slave-trading pioneers. São Paulo became a major stopover point for explorers and pioneers, lured by the prospect of gold mines and slave trading in the interiors. The expansion of the sugar and coffee industries in the late 18th and 19th centuries attracted immigrants from the Middle East, Spanish America, the Russian republics, Central Asia, Europe – including Spain and Portugal – and Japan.

Internal migrants from every corner of the nation came to São Paulo in the mid-20th century. Among them was an impoverished metal-worker from Pernambuco, Luíz Inácio da Silva, who by a wave of public support went on to become Brazil's president in 2002, and again in 2006. Regional festivals from all over the country are celebrated with great enthusiasm in the city's enormous *favelas* (shantytowns).

São Paulo's vastness and complex character can be intimidating to an outsider. Many of the city's pleasures are to be found behind closed doors – in museums, galleries, concert halls, and in a wealth of restaurants and shops. A true haven for gourmets, São Paulo is known to serve the best food in South America. The city center offers a host of attractions, such as the 17th-century Igreja de São Francisco and the 20th-century Mosteiro São Bento. The city's finest museum, Museu de Arte de São Paulo (MASP), is one of the highlights of the famed Avenida Paulista.

Carnaval dancers participate in the final night of the São Paulo parade

◀ São Paulo skyline, including the Palace of Justice and Metropolitan Cathedral, seen from the top of Edifício Altino Arantes

Exploring São Paulo City

Brazil's largest city covers an area of 588 sq miles (1,520 sq km). The conurbation of São Paulo, which includes the cities of São Bernardo de Campo, Guarulhos, and São Caetano, is home to about 22 million people, making it the largest urban area in the world. The old city center preserves the few remaining historical buildings, including the Catedral Metropolitana. A short distance to the southwest is Avenida Paulista, home to the famous Museu de Arte Contemporânea (MAC). The commercial districts of Itaim and Brooklin lie south, on the banks of the Rio Tietê. The city's posh neighborhood, Jardins, is lined with South America's finest shops and restaurants. Another upscale area, Vila Mariana, is home to Parque do Ibirapuera, a green oasis among the relentless high-rises.

Sights at a Glance

Historic Buildings, Streets, Towns & Neighborhoods

❸ Pátio do Colégio
❺ Theatro Municipal
❼ Centro Cultural Banco do Brasil
❽ Edifício Itália
❾ Edifício Altino Arantes
⓬ Estação da Luz
⓮ Sala São Paulo
⓰ Avenida Paulista
⓲ Liberdade

❹ Mosteiro São Bento
❻ Igreja da Consolação

Museums

❿ Pinacoteca de São Paulo pp144–5
⓫ Museu Arte Sacra
⓭ Estação Pinacoteca
⓯ Museu de Arte de São Paulo (MASP) p147
⓱ Museu do Futebol
⓴ Parque da Independência
㉑ Museu de Arte Contemporânea (MAC)

Parks & Gardens

⓳ Parque do Ibirapuera pp150–51
㉒ Instituto Butantã
㉓ Jardim Botânico
㉔ Parque Burle Marx

Churches, Cathedrals & Monasteries

❶ Catedral Metropolitana
❷ Igreja de São Francisco de Assis

High-rise modern buildings dominating the skyline, central São Paulo

For hotels and restaurants in this region see pp373–4 and pp389–90

VISITORS' CHECKLIST

Practical Information
12,000,000. Congonhas Airport; Guarulhos Airport; Tietê bus station; Praça Antônio Prado 9, (11) 3104 6898. Festas Juninas (Jun), Bienal Internacional de São Paulo (Sep–Nov), Festa da Primavera (Sep).
w cidadedesaopaulo.com

Transport
19 miles (30 km) NE of center.
9 miles (4 km) S of center.

Key

Area of the main map

Major road

Minor road

Getting Around

São Paulo is well connected, with daily international flights to most major European, and North and South American cities. Most of these depart from Cumbica airport in Guarulhos, 19 miles (30 km) northeast of the city. Domestic flights leave from Congonhas Airport, just south of Ibirapuera Park in the main urban center. There are buses to every corner of Brazil and beyond to Bolivia, Argentina, Paraguay, and Uruguay. There is an extensive network of taxis and buses within the city. The metro and urban railway are clean, fast, and efficient. Cars can be rented at both the airports, although the city's numerous one-way systems and choking traffic make driving a little daunting.

For keys to symbols *see back flap*

❶ Catedral Metropolitana

Praça da Sé, Centro. **Map** 1 C3.
Tel (11) 3107 6832. Ⓜ Sé.
Open 8am–7pm Mon–Fri, (to 5pm
Sat and 1pm Sun). 🔲 ✝ 9am, noon,
6pm Mon & Fri; noon, 6pm Tue–Thu;
noon Sat; 9am, 11am, 5pm Sun.

At the heart of old downtown
São Paulo, the Catedral
Metropolitana (also known as
Catedral da Sé) watches over
the large pebbled **Praça da Sé**,
shaded by tropical fig and palm
trees. Built between 1912 and
1954, the cathedral finally
gained its full complement of
14 turrets in 2002.

Built by Maximiliano Hell,
the exterior is a fusion of Neo-
Gothic and Renaissance, with an
overly narrow nave squeezed
between two enormous
318-ft- (97-m-) high spires and
a bulbous copper cupola. The
cavernous interior, said to seat
up to 8,000 people, looks starkly
European. The only obvious
local influences are visible in the
capitals, delicately carved with
distinctly Brazilian flora and
fauna. The stained-glass
windows were designed in
Germany and Brazil.

The cathedral's façade has
watched over the country's
largest public protests, when
crowds gathered in the square
outside the cathedral in the late
1980s to demand the end of
military rule.

Exterior of São Paulo Catedral
Metropolitana, Praça da Sé

Carved altar in the interior of Igreja de São
Francisco de Assis

❷ Igreja de São Francisco de Assis

Largo de São Francisco 133.
Map 1 A3. **Tel** (11) 3291 2400. Ⓜ Sé.
Open 7am–6:30pm daily. 📷

Immediately to the west of
Catedral Metropolitana is
the Igreja de São Francisco
de Assis, one of the city's
oldest churches. Parts
of the modest Baroque
interior, featuring an
intricately carved altar
and ornaments, date
from the mid-1600s.
The church is often
referred to as O
Convento São
Francisco after
the exquisite Baroque
convent that stood
here until the 1930s,
when it was demolished
along with parts of the
colonial center.

❸ Pátio do Colégio

Praça Pátio do Colégio 2. **Map** 2 D3.
Ⓜ Sé. **Open** 9am–4:30pm Tue–Sun.
✝ noon Tue–Fri, 10am–noon Sun.
Museu Padre Anchieta: **Tel** (11) 3105
6899. 📷 📷

Located within easy walking
distance from the Praça da Sé,
the Pátio do Colégio has an
interesting history behind it.
On January 25, 1554, the Jesuits
inaugurated the Colégio de São
Paulo de Piratinga on a small
bluff overlooking an extensive
forest. The original wattle-and-

daub shack, built for them by
their Guaraní cohorts, eventually
became a school. That school
became a church, and around
the church arose the buildings
that formed the core of the
original city of São Paulo.

In 1760, the Jesuits were
expelled from the city, but
the college and chapel
they founded remained and
came to be known as the
Pátio do Colégio. In 1886, the
tower of the original church
collapsed and the whole
building was demolished.

Upon their return in 1954, the
Jesuits immediately set about
building an exact replica of their
original church and college,
which is what stands today as
Pátio do Colégio.

Most of the buildings are
occupied by the **Museu Padre
Anchieta**, named after the
Jesuit captain who led the first
mission. The collection features
a Modernist portrait of the
priest, by the Italian artist
Menghini, some of the priest's
remains, a 17th-
century font used to
baptize indigenous
people, as well as a
collection of Guaraní
artifacts from the
colonial era. A model
reproduction
of São Paulo in the
16th century is also
on display.

Visão de Anchieta by
Menghini

❹ Mosteiro São Bento

Largo de São Bento. **Map** 1 C2.
Tel (11) 3328 8799. Ⓜ São Bento.
Open 6am–6:40pm Mon–Fri, 6am–
noon & 4–6pm Sat & Sun. ✝ 7am,
1pm & 6pm Mon–Fri, 6am, 7am Sat,
8:30am, 10am & 6pm (masses in Latin)
Sun. 🌐 **mosteiro.org.br**

Brazil is the only South
American country where the
Benedictine order gained a
foothold, arriving in São Paulo
on this site in 1598. The current
building, however, dates from
the 1920s and was designed
by Munich-based architect
Richard Bernl.

The monastery has a
beautifully painted Beuronese

interior. This style is named after techniques developed in the late 19th and early 20th centuries by Benedictines in the monastery of Beuron in southwest Germany. It is characterized by a compressed perspective and vivid colors. The finest representation of Beuronese art in Latin America is visible inside this beautiful Blessed Sacrament chapel. Scenes from the life of St. Benedict are depicted on the stained-glass windows and the ceiling. The church has a large organ, which is the centerpiece of a festival held in November and December every year. There is also a shop selling sweets and cakes made by the monks.

The 1920s interior of Mosteiro São Bento, with its painted ceiling

❺ Theatro Municipal

Praça Ramos de Azevedo. **Map** 1 C2. **Tel** (11) 3053 2090. Ⓜ Anhangabaú. 🎫 English: 11am, 5pm Tue–Fri; noon Sat. Portuguese: 11am, 3pm, 5pm Tue–Fri; 11am, noon, 2pm, 3pm Sat & public hols. Ⓦ **theatromunicipal.org.br**

Located near the Parque Anhangabaú, São Paulo's largest central park with some pretty fountains, the Theatro Municipal overlooks the Praça Ramos. The theater is one of the continent's most important venues, hosting a program of events. Opera and theater were very popular among the elite in turn-of-the-19th-century São Paulo and Rio de

View of the exterior of Theatro Municipal

Janeiro. The theater was modeled on the Paris Opera and the city waited in fevered anticipation for its inaugural night. It opened on September 12, 1911, with a production of *Hamlet*, starring the Italian baritone Titta Ruffo. Nijinski, Caruso, and Toscanini have all performed here. Visits are limited, so book ahead.

❻ Igreja da Consolação

Rua da Consolação 585. **Map** 1 C3. **Tel** (11) 3256 5356. Ⓜ Anhangabaú. **Open** 8am–7pm. 🎫

Designed by Maximiliano Hell, the architect of the Catedral Metropolitana, the Igreja da Consolação is a similar fusion of European styles. Some of the 19th-century master Benedito Calixto's *(see p34)* best religious paintings adorn the Blessed Sacrament chapel.

❼ Centro Cultural Banco do Brasil

Rua Álvares Penteado 112. **Map** 1 C3. **Tel** (11) 3113 3649. Ⓜ São Bento/Sé. **Open** 9am–9pm Wed–Mon. 🎫 Ⓦ **bb.com.br/cultura**

This early 20th-century building with a lovely Art Deco glass ceiling was once the Bank of Brazil. It now houses the Centro Cultural Banco do Brasil. Inside, there are a series of spaces devoted to showing contemporary arts – from photography, installation works, and fine art to cinema and theater. The exhibition spaces are contained within the bank's original vaults, some of which retain their massive iron doors.

❽ Edifício Itália

Av Ipiranga 344. **Map** 1 B2 & B3. **Tel** (11) 2189 2929. **Open** noon–5pm daily. Ⓜ República. 🎫

The Edifíco Itália, one of São Paulo's tallest buildings, was built in 1965 to honor the thousands of Italian immigrants to the city. The famous postcard shot of Oscar Niemeyer's Edifíco Copan with the vast environs of São Paulo behind was taken from the **Terraço Itália** restaurant *(see p389)* and viewing deck on the 45th floor of the building. People do not usually come for the food – most come for the unbeatable view of this incredible city, a view that is second only to that from the Edifíco Altino Arantes. Tickets include a glass of sparkling wine.

❾ Edifício Altino Arantes

Rua João Bricola 24. **Map** 1 C3. Ⓜ São Bento. **Closed** for renovation.

Also known as Edifício Banespa due to its original function as the headquarters of São Paulo's State Bank, this 161-m- (527-ft-) high edifice was built in 1939 and inaugurated in 1947, resembling a miniature version of New York's Empire State Building. It was for a long time Brazil's largest concrete building and the tallest skyscraper in Latin America until 1968. It is now occupied by Santander bank. The building and observation deck are currently closed to the public for renovations.

⑩ Pinacoteca de São Paulo

The Pinacoteca is a significant repository of Brazilian art, with an archive of over 10,000 paintings and sculptures representing all major Brazilian artists and artistic movements. The galleries trace the evolution of Brazilian styles from the 19th-century colonial period to Modern and contemporary art, including the 1960s Avant Garde. In the mid-1990s, the Pinacoteca was magnificently renovated by the noted architect Paulo Mendes de Rocha, who filled the original Neo-Classical building with carefully positioned partitions and capped it with a translucent roof. The magical sense of space and light perfectly complements the intensity of color and tone which characterizes Brazilian art.

★ Composição
This Brazilian Constructivist composition by Alfredo Volpi (1896–1988) fuses European style with tropical colors.

Serie Bahia Musa da Paz
Belonging to an infuential group of Paulista artists, José Pancetti (1902–58) rejected a European academic approach to art and strove to return to a more naive style.

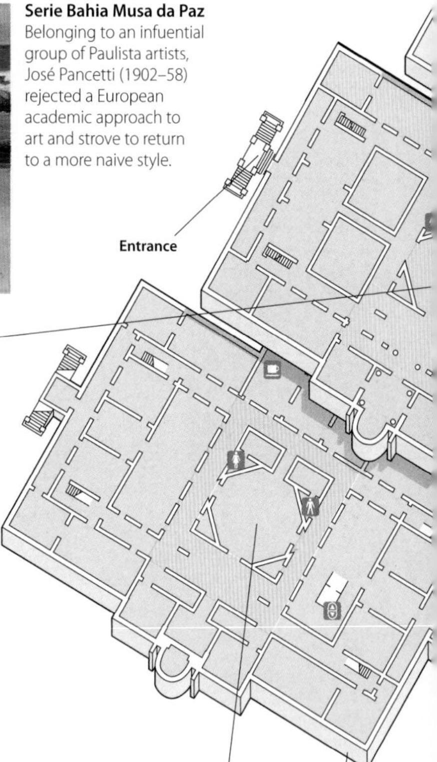

Entrance

Octagonal Exhibition Hall

Façade
The Pinacoteca was tastefully refurbished in the 1990s, leaving only the shell of the original building.

Auditorium

First floor

Gallery Guide

The Pinacoteca's permanent collection forms long-term displays, which change periodically. The third-floor galleries cover the history of Brazilian art since the colonial period. The second floor is devoted to temporary exhibitions and Modern Brazilian art. The first floor features an educational area, which provides activities for families, and a café.

For hotels and restaurants in this region see pp373–4 and pp389–90

★ Tropical
Portraying a *caboclo* woman in a tropical setting, this painting by Anita Malfatti (1889–1964) is a fine example of Brazilian Modernism.

VISITORS' CHECKLIST

Practical Information
Praça da Luz 2, Jardim da Luz.
Map 1 C1.
Tel (11) 3324 1000.
Open 10am–5:30pm Wed–Mon.
♿ 📷
🌐 pinacoteca.org.br

Transport
Ⓜ Luz. 🚌

Third floor

Formal portraits of Portuguese colonial dignitaries are the most European of the Brazilian paintings.

★ Caipira Picando Fumo
Almeida Júnior (1850–99) was one of the first to paint Brazil's rich tropical light and everyday Brazilians.

Génio do Repouso Eterno
This statue is regarded by many to be one of the most beautiful works of legendary French sculptor, Auguste Rodin (1840–1917).

Second floor

Pintura (1969)
Brazilian artist Tomie Ohtake (1913–2015), mother of the famous architect Ruy Ohtake, introduced Japanese elements into Brazilian art.

Second floor, with a temporary exhibition area

Key
- 19th-Century Brazilian Art
- Landscapes (1850–1930)
- Sculpture Yard
- Brazilian Contemporary Art
- Brazilian 1960s Avant-Garde
- Brazilian Sculpture
- Brazilian Modern Art
- Temporary Exhibition Gallery
- Educational area
- Non-Exhibition Space

Elegant façade of the Mosteiro da Luz, housing the Museu Arte Sacra

⑪ Museu Arte Sacra

Av Tiradentes 676. **Tel** (11) 3326 3336. Ⓜ Tiradentes. 🚌 Circular Turista. **Open** 9am–5pm Tue–Sun. 🎟 free Sat 🌐 **museuartesacra.org.br**

Often overlooked by visitors, this small museum boasts one of the finest collections of religious artifacts in the Americas. The exhibits are housed in a large wing of a distinguished colonial building, the early 19th-century Mosteiro da Luz. Restful and serene, the entire complex is a peaceful haven from the frenetic chaos of São Paulo.

The museum's priceless objects and artifacts include lavish monstrances (ceremonial vessels), ecclesiastical jewelry, and church altarpieces. Of particular note is the statuary, with pieces by many of the most important Brazilian Baroque masters such as Aleijadinho, Mestre Valentim, and Frei Agostinho da Piedade. One of the gems is the 18th-century *Mary Magdalene* by Francisco Xavier de Brito, which displays an effortless unity of motion and melancholy contemplation. Among the sculptures, mostly by anonymous Brazilian indigenous artists, two pieces stand out – a majestic African-Brazilian São Bento (with blue eyes) and an exquisitely detailed 18th-century Neapolitan nativity crib comprising around 2,000 pieces, which is the most important of its kind outside Naples. The collection also

features works by 18th-century masters such as Benedito Calixto and Mestre Athayde. Of special significance is the one that depicts Padre Anchieta taming a wild ocelot with the cross, a symbol of the Jesuit founder of São Paulo's mission to the indigenous Brazilians.

⑫ Estação da Luz

Praça da Luz 1. **Map** 1 C1. **Tel** 0800 550 121. Ⓜ Luz. 🚌 🌐 **estacaodaluz. org.br**

One of modern Brazil's prominent symbols of industrial progress, São Paulo's railway station was built in 1901. The design of the Estação da Luz is a homage to the English railroad, and imitates the Victorian eclectic style.

Just like all of São Paulo's railways, Estação da Luz was the creation of Brazil's first industrialist, the Visconde de Mauá. After a visit to London in the 1840s, Mauá was convinced that Brazil's future lay in rapid industrialization. He founded an ironworks, employing some 300 workers from England and Scotland. In 1854, Mauá opened his first railway, which was designed and run by the British. It linked Jundiaí, in the heart of São Paulo's coffee region, with Santos on the coast. Today, the Estação da Luz serves only the São Paulo city area. Romanesque red-brick arches and stately cast-iron pillars support a single vault that covers four tracks and platforms.

São Bento with baby, Museu Arte Sacra

⑬ Estação Pinacoteca

Largo General Osório 66. **Map** 1 C1. **Tel** (11) 3335 4990. Ⓜ Luz. 🚌 **Open** 10am–5:30pm Wed–Mon. 🌐 **pinacoteca.org.br**

Located in an attractive early 20th-century Neo-Classical building, the annex of the Pinacoteca do Estado (*see pp144–5*) is one of the city's best contemporary exhibition spaces. Some of Brazil's finest Modernist paintings, taken from the archive of the Fundação José e Paulina Nemirovsky, are displayed here.

An important milestone in Brazilian Modernism is *Antropofagia* by Tarsila do Amaral (1886–1973), the founder of the vital *antropofagismo* movement (*see pp34–5*). There are also key pieces by Candido Portinari, Anita Malfatti, and Lasar Segall. International art is represented by Marc Chagall, Pablo Picasso, and Georges Braque, among others.

⑭ Sala São Paulo

Praça Júlio Prestes 16. **Map** 1 B1. **Tel** (11) 3223 3966. Ⓜ Luz. 🚌 **Open** 10am–6pm Mon–Fri. 📷 by appointment a day in advance, 1pm & 4:30pm Mon–Fri, 1:30pm Sat, 1pm Sun. 🌐 **salasaopaulo.art.br**

Known for the finest acoustics in Latin America, this concert hall was inaugurated in 1997. It is the city's premier classical music venue for symphonic and chamber music and the home of Brazil's top orchestra, the Orquestra Sinfônica do Estado de São Paulo (OSESP).

The orchestra's artistic director Arthur Nestrovski is a composer and classical guitarist specializing in Brazilian music.

The grand railway building, the Estação Júlio Prestes, in which the hall is housed, was designed in 1938 by Brazilian architect Cristiano Stockler. Largely inspired by New York, it contrasts strongly with the English Estação da Luz.

⓯ Museu de Arte de São Paulo (MASP)

Entrepreneur Assis Chateaubriand founded MASP in 1947 as Brazil's first modern museum, and invited renowned Italian critic and collector Pietro Maria Bardi to manage it. Bardi's first acquisitions included the now priceless works by Degas, Van Gogh, Velázquez, Rembrandt, Turner, Titian, Bellini, and Raphael. Bought at absurdly low prices at the time, these compose the Southern hemisphere's most significant collection of European art, along with works from Africa, Asia, and the Americas. The extensive collection is constantly rotating, as works are taken in and out of the archive. The museum also includes a cultural center that hosts courses, seminars, and talks.

The Schoolboy by van Gogh (1888), Northern European Collection

Resurrection of Christ (1501/1502) by Raphael, Italian collection

The Building

Inaugurated in 1968, the current home of the museum is actually its second address. Italian-Brazilian architect Lina Bo Bardi's striking building focuses on the use of glass and concrete in the creation of a Brutalist structure with a light interior *(see p11)*.

The plaza below the museum, popularly known as *Vão Livre* ("free span"), is intended as a public square. This covered space is often full of street artists, crafts for sale, and young crowds having fun and watching passers-by.

The Collections

There are more than 8,000 works in the collections, including paintings, photographs, sculptures, and installations. The oldest item is the statue of the goddess Hygieia (c. 400 BC). Among recent artworks is Paulistano Marcelo Cidade's *Tempo Suspenso de um Estado Provisório* (2011).

The museum has a number of important pieces by Northern European and Spanish artists such as Bosch, Rembrandt, Velázquez, El Greco, and Goya. There are also works by prominent Brazilian Modernists such as Brecheret, Tomie Ohtake, and Candido Portinari.

Italian artists in the collections include a range of Renaissance names, such as Mantegna, Raphael, and Tintoretto. Modern French art is represented by works by Millet, Seurat, Manet, Cezanne, Toulouse-Lautrec, Van Gogh, Chagall and Picasso.

Exhibition Design

Instead of being hung on walls, the artworks in the permanent collection are mounted on panels of glass fixed into concrete plinths designed by Lina Bo Bardi, and scattered around the entire second floor. There are no divisions of rooms or rigid timelines. The art seems to float in air, providing visitors with a unique experience of walking among different artistic ages and cultures, freed from the weight of chronological linearity. Captions are displayed on the backs of the works.

The museum's three other floors have been assigned to temporary exhibitions.

Works of art displayed on iconic glass easels designed by Lina Bo Bardi at MASP

Aerial view of the exclusive Avenida Paulista

⑯ Avenida Paulista

Map 4 E2, F2 & F3. Ⓜ Brigadeiro/ Trianon-Masp/Consolação. 🏳️‍🌈 Gay Pride (Jun).

Modern São Paulo's first symbol of prosperity, Avenida Paulista and its crowded skyscrapers continue to attest to Brazil's status as South America's major economic power. Though often compared to New York's Fifth Avenue, it is a corporate valley, business-like and functional.

In the 19th century, when a Uruguayan named Joaquin Eugenio de Lima first set up house here, Paulista was a hill on the outskirts of a small colonial town surrounded by pastoral land and forest. Around this time, São Paulo was growing rich on trains and coffee. Others followed de Lima and began to build large houses here.

By the turn of the 19th century, the avenue had become São Paulo's most desirable address, and was lined with large, opulent mansions owned by extremely wealthy Brazilian moguls, or the coffee barons. Each mansion reflected the architectural predilections of the owner, be it Neo-Classical, Rhineland, or even mock-Tudor. Having suffered large-scale demolition after World War II, the avenue had lost its splendid character by the

1960s. Today, only one mansion remains, the French-style **Casa das Rosas**, which is now a cultural center managed and run by São Paulo state. Interesting art shows are often held here, but the 1935 mansion itself is well worth visiting for its pretty rose garden and Art Nouveau stained-glass window.

A stroll along Paulista is an attraction in its own right, especially on Sundays, when it becomes a pedestrian park for families, skaters, and tourists. There's also a range of museums, large book shops, and cultural centers. The **Instituto Itaú Cultural**, near Brigadeiro metro station, hosts a range of concerts and exhibitions, all of which are free of charge. It also houses the largest currency museum in the country, the Itaú Numismática. The **Centro Cultural FIESP**, at Trianon-Masp, is a business headquarters with a small Centro Cultural that presents free live theater and art shows.

Immediately to its north and opposite MASP is the **Parque Trianon**, the only green respite from the concrete. It was named in homage to the gardens of the Palace of Versailles, to which it bears no resemblance. However, in the quiet of the early morning, small mammals, including agouti and marmosets, can be seen foraging here, and in the heat of the day, the trees provide welcome shade. There are plenty of

cinemas in and around Paulista, along the avenue itself, in the Shopping Paulista Mall, near Brigadeiro metro, and dotted along Rua da Consolação, near Paulista's northern end.

Together with the Praça da Sé *(see p142)*, Paulista is one of the city's most important venues for protests and celebrations.

For a taste of Avenida Paulista as it once was, head a few blocks south, across the chic shopping streets of the Jardins and into Jardim Europa. Here, along Avenida Brasil and Avenida Groenlandia, the stately homes of the city's current rich can be seen.

🔳 Casa das Rosas
Av Paulista 37. **Tel** (11) 3285 6986.
Open 10am–10pm Tue–Sat, 10am–6pm Sun & public hols.

🏛 Centro Cultural FIESP
Av Paulista 1313. **Tel** (11) 3146 7406.
Open 1–9pm Wed–Sat, 10am–7:30pm Sun.

🏛 Instituto Itaú Cultural
Av Paulista 149. **Tel** (11) 2168 1777.
Open 9am–8pm Tue–Fri, 11am–8pm Sat & Sun.

🌳 Parque Trianon
Rua Peixoto Gomide 949.
Open 6am–6pm daily.

⑰ Museu do Futebol

Estádio do Pacaembu, Praça Charles Miller s/n. Ⓜ Clínicas. 🚌 177C-10, 917M-10, 6232-10. **Open** 9am–5pm Tue–Sun (hours may change on match days). Ⓦ **museudofutebol.org.br**

The Museum of Football is not to be missed by any fan of "the beautiful game." Explore the history of soccer in Brazil and its

Parque Trianon, with its lush greenery, on Avenida Paulista

impact on both local society and the global community. The focus here is as much on Brazilian people as it is on the sport itself, allowing visitors to get a sense of how habits and behaviors changed in this country throughout the 20th century.

The temporary exhibits at the museum are complemented by a 16-stage "fan path," which visitors may walk through. Each room along the route offers a mixture of some of the history and excitement of soccer.

⑱ Liberdade

Praça da Sé, via Av da Liberdade.
Ⓜ Praça de Sé/Liberdade.
🚌 Liberdade Rodoviária.

São Paulo is home to more ethnic Japanese people than any other city outside Japan. Liberdade, located just south of the city center, is the hub of the Japanese community, and recently for Koreans and Chinese. The neighborhood, small and easily manageable on foot, is best explored during the afternoon. Streets are lined with shops and restaurants selling everything, from woks and manga comics to sushi and sashimi. On Sundays, there is a lively market in the **Praça de Liberdade**, where stalls serve up steaming lacquer bowls of miso soup and yakisoba noodles.

Liberdade's main thoroughfare, Rua Galvão Bueno, runs south from this square, lined with the bulk of the shops and decorated with red Japanese arches, or *torii*. Many of Liberdade's most traditional Japanese restaurants are located on, and around, Rua Tomaz Gonzaga, which cuts across Galvão Bueno, south of the square.

At the corner of Galvão Bueno and Rua São Joaquim, an undistinguished block houses the **Museu da Imigração Japonesa** (Japanese Immigration Museum). The museum was opened in 1978 by the erstwhile prince, now Emperor Akihito of Japan. It has two floors of artifacts and displays devoted to telling the story of the Japanese immigrant

Shrine Gate at Oriental Quarter Japanese Town, Liberdade

community, their origins, and their lives in early 20th-century Brazil. These include a replica of the *Kasato-Maru* – the ship which brought the first immigrants in 1908 *(see p173)* and a complete early Japanese-Brazilian agricultural cottage. The building also features a lovely rooftop garden.

One of São Paulo's many Buddhist temples, built in 1995, the **Templo Busshinji** lies west of the Museu da Imigração Japonesa on the same street. Its traditional Japanese-style architecture comprising wood is topped with a pyramid-shaped roof. Visitors are welcome to attend the various ceremonies, the most impressive of which is the Cerimônia de Kannon, which takes place each month. The rituals, paying homage to the Buddha's compassionate nature, are accompanied by traditional Japanese instruments.

🏛 **Museu da Imigração Japonesa**
Rua São Joaquim 381. **Tel** (11) 3209 5465. **Open** 1–5pm Tue–Sun. ♿

🔳 **Templo Busshinji**
Rua São Joaquim 285. **Tel** (11) 3208 4515. **Open** 8am–5pm daily.
🗓 by prior appointment. ♿
🌐 sotozen.org.br

São Paulo Fashion Week

Established in 1996, São Paulo's fashion week is Latin America's most important fashion event. All of the top Brazilian names and faces, including Amir Slama and Havaianas, are showcased here, together with supermodels from around the world. The fashion fraternity can be seen in hip bars and boutiques in the wealthy corners of the city. Over 100,000 people visit the show itself, which takes place twice a year – usually in January and March or April – in Oscar Niemeyer's Bienal building in Parque do Ibirapuera *(see pp150–51)*. More column inches are devoted to the event than to any other activity in Brazil, except for soccer and political scandals. The event generates an estimated $45 million through the media alone, with more than 2,500 newspaper and magazine pages and almost 200 hours of television coverage.

A fashion show in full swing, with models displaying a collection

⓳ Parque do Ibirapuera

Parque do Ibirapuera is the largest green space in central São Paulo, and its native Brazilian woodlands and lakes are a welcome respite from the city's urban sprawl. Opened in 1954, it houses several museums and exhibition spaces, as well as a complex of buildings by the country's celebrated architect, Oscar Niemeyer (1907–2012). These stage major exhibitions, which have included the Terracotta Warrior exhibition from China and the Rodin retrospective.

Monumento às Bandeiras
Completed in 1950, this tribute to explorers or *bandeirantes,* who opened up Brazil's interior, is one of the more severe works by Brazil's foremost sculptor, Victor Brecheret.

★ Hotel Unique
Hotel Unique *(see p373),* the intriguing, half-melon structure on stilts, is the most famous work of Brazil's leading contemporary architect, Ruy Ohtake, son of the artist Tomie Ohtake.

KEY

① **The Bosque da Leitura** or "reading wood" is the place to head for on Sundays. Visitors can borrow a book and read in the shade of the trees.

② **The small vivarium** houses a few species of native subtropical trees.

③ **The restored, state-of-the-art planetarium Planetário Aristóteles Orsini**, is one of the most impressive in Latin America and is very popular with children. All shows are in Portuguese.

④ **A son et lumière** fountain show is held here on weekends.

⑤ **The Monumento do Pedro Álvares Cabral** honors the Portuguese explorer who first set foot on Brazilian soil in 1500.

⑥ **Museu Afro Brasil** is devoted to celebrating Afro-Brazilian culture. It hosts films, exhibitions, dance, music, and theater events.

⑦ **Auditório Ibirapuera**

⑧ **The Bienal Building**, also by Niemeyer, stages the city's flagship fashion, art, and other premier events – São Paulo fashion week and the Art Bienal, among others.

Pavilhão Japonês
This pavilion and its gardens were built in strict accordance with traditional Japanese design, using only Japanese materials. There is also an exhibition space and a Japanese tearoom.

The lush expanse of Lago do Ibirapuera (Ibirapuera Lake) in the park

VISITORS' CHECKLIST

Practical Information
Av Pedro Álvares Cabral. **Map** 4 E5.
Open 5am–midnight daily.
Museu de Arte Moderna, Gate 3:
Tel (11) 5085 1300. **Open** 10am–
6pm Tue–Sun. 🎟 free on Sun.
Museu Afro Brasil, Gate 10:
Tel (11) 3320 8900. **Open** 10am–
5pm Tue–Sun. Bosque da Leitura,
Gate 7: Av República do Líbano
1551. **Open** 9:30am–4pm Sun.
Planetário Aristóteles Orsino,
Gate 10: **Tel** (11) 5575 5206.
Open 10am, noon, 3pm, 5pm Sat
& Sun (daily Dec–Feb and Jul).

0 meters 300
0 yards 300

★ O Obelisco aos Heróis de 32
This giant Cleopatra's needle was
built to honor the Paulistano
rebels who died in 1932 when
President Vargas crushed
resistance to his Estado Novo
regime (see p59).

Oca do Ibirapuera
Designed by Oscar Niemeyer,
this dome pays homage to the
indigenous Brazilian
roundhouse. It hosts major
international art exhibitions and
cultural events.

★ Museu de Arte Moderna (MAM)
The best of Brazilian modern and
contemporary art is showcased in this
building designed by Lino Bo Bardi and
Oscar Niemeyer. The mural on part of its
facade is by graffiti artists OSGEMEOS .

The formal gardens in front of the Museu Paulista do Ipiranga, Parque da Independência, Ipiranga

⓴ Parque da Independência

Av Nazareth s/n, Ipiranga.
Tel (11) 2273 7250. ▥ 5108-10.
Open 5am–8pm daily. Ⓦ mp.usp.br

In 1822, Dom Pedro I declared the famous "Grito de Ipiranga," or call for independence from Portugal (Independência ou Morte, or Independence or Death), on the banks of the Rio Ipiranga *(see p56)*. The large formal park that now occupies this site was inaugurated in 1989 and includes an 1890 palace, one of the earliest monuments of independent Brazil.

The mock French Renaissance gardens in front of the palace include an enormous bronze sculpture to the nation's independence, *Monumento a Independência*, made by the Italian sculptor Ettore Ximenes in 1921. In the chapel at the base of the monument a tomb contains the remains of Dom Pedro I and Empress Leopoldina. Also in the grounds is the **Casa do Grito**, a replica of the simple adobe house depicted by Pedro Américo in his painting, *Independência ou Morte* (1888).

The Museu Paulista is housed in the palace at the top of extensive formal gardens. It is closed for restoration and will reopen in 2022. The museum is devoted to the nation's history, and contains a collection of exhibits which includes old maps, traditional colonial furniture, carriages, rare documents, old coins, clothing, and paintings. The artist Pedro Américo's monumental canvas *Independência ou Morte* (1888), depicting the young prince shouting his *grito* (cry), sits in the building's most handsome room, the Salão Nobre.

㉑ Museu de Arte Contemporânea

Av Pedro Alvares Cabral 130,
Ibirapuera. **Tel** (11) 2648 0254. ▥
Open 10am–9pm Tue, 10am–6pm
Wed–Sun. 🄲 by appointment. ♿
Ⓦ mac.usp.br

A treasure trove of modern and Post-Modern European and Brazilian art lies tucked away in the campus of São Paulo's most distinguished university. The collection at the Museu de Arte Contemporânea (MAC) is an amalgamation of donations given by wealthy individuals since the early 20th century and prizes from São Paulo's Art Biennials. The collection comprises some 8,000 works of art. Prominent among is a

Estrada de Ferro Central do Brasil by Tarsila de Amaral at MAC

notable collection of early 20th-century Italian paintings, important, little-seen works by Pablo Picasso, Max Ernst, and Henri Matisse, and Amedeo Modigliani, which sit alongside the cream of Brazil's artists. Brazilian Modernists, such as Anita Malfatti, Vitor Brecheret, and Candido Portanari, are well represented. MAC also holds three of the most celebrated works by one of the most significant Latin American Modernists, Tarsila do Amaral – *A Negra*, *Estrada de Ferro Central do Brasil*, and *A Floresta*. Tarsila was the founder of *antropofagismo (see pp34–5)* – a movement that paved the way for many important artistic trends within postwar Brazil.

㉒ Instituto Butantã

Av Vital Brazil 1500, Cidade
Universitária. **Tel** (11) 3726 7222.
▥ **Open** 9am–4:45pm Tue–Sun.
🄲 🄲 by appointment.
Ⓦ butantan.gov.br

The Instituto Butantã is a biomedical research center affiliated to the Cidade Universitária, the University of São Paulo. Founded in 1901 by Vital Brasil to conduct research into venomous animals, the institute is now one of the leading producers of anti-venoms and sera in the world. It is also one of the city's principal tourist attractions, as it is located in a pretty forested garden full of hummingbirds.

Pits alongside the center and an adjacent museum house many of South America's more exotic snakes and arachnids. Smaller but even deadlier creatures can be seen through microscopes in the institute's **Museu de Microbiologia**. This bright, modern space also includes excellent interactive displays which are particularly popular with children.

❷❸ Jardim Botânico

Av Miguel Stéfano 3031. **Tel** (11) 5067 6000. 🚌 **Open** 9am–5pm Tue–Sun. 🐾 ⚘

Other than the Serra da Cantareira mountains on the city's western fringe, the Jardim Botânico is the largest area of green in São Paulo's metropolitan area. It combines formal gardens, laid out around a series of lakes with areas of forest large enough to support several resident troops of red howler monkeys. Their guttural calls can be heard here at dawn and dusk and sometimes the monkeys themselves can be seen in the trees. There is plenty of other wildlife too, including agoutis, pacas, and tufted-eared marmosets. The latter often loiter about in the trees around the lawns of the sculpture garden hoping to grab a fruity morsel.

The entrance to the park is through an avenue of magnificent royal palms, surrounded by tropical and subtropical trees. Most are labeled with their common and scientific names (the former in Portuguese only). The avenue leads to the **Jardim Lineu**, inspired by the gardens in Uppsala, Sweden, and, like them, are laid out in homage to 18th-century biologist Carl Linnaeus. Glass houses here contain a number of Atlantic rainforest plants and a botanical museum preserves a bank of Brazilian seeds from flowering plants and important fruit species.

Beyond the Jardim Lineu are areas of ponds and lawns popular with picnickers on the weekends. These are fringed

Pond with a tropical forest glade at the Jardim Botânico

with tropical forest cut by short trails and little running streams. Walkers should be wary of snakes.

❷❹ Parque Burle Marx

Av Dona Helena Pereira de Morais 200. **Tel** (11) 3746 7631; (11) 3776 7497. 🚌 6291-10, 5119-23. **Open** 7am–7pm daily. 🐾 🌐 parqueburlemarx.com.br

Roberto Burle Marx (1909–94) was South America's greatest landscape architect and one of the three core designers of Brasília (see pp298–9). His designs were strongly influenced by Modernist ideas inspired by his

studies in Germany, and his early work with the architect Lucio Costa who had worked with Le Corbusier. Burle Marx was one of the first architects to combine sculptural and painting techniques with landscape design.

His gardens in the Parque Burle Marx have been compared to abstract paintings, utilizing simple shapes, and some curvilinear and rectilinear patterns to create blocks of color and texture, broken by paths and areas of woodland. Marx was a keen ecologist and promoted the use of Brazilian native species, and the park is surrounded by a small area of forest, comprising various Mata Atlântica species.

Although Marx contributed to Parque do Ibirapuera (see pp150–51), this park is the only exclusive example of his work in his home city. The gardens were originally private, commissioned for the millionaire industrialist "Baby" Pignatari in the 1940s.

As well as landscaping, Burle Marx was allowed to experiment and place abstract structures in the gardens. These include mirrors of water and rectangular blocks reminiscent of the low Mixtec buildings in Mitla, Mexico. The constructions near the avenue of palms at the park's entrance are by Oscar Niemeyer.

Abstract rectangular structures, Parque Burle Marx

SHOPPING IN SÃO PAULO

Shopping in São Paulo is like shopping in a large North American city. It is largely mall- and boutique-based and geared toward high-end luxury goods. However, more interesting are markets and fairs that take place around town on weekends, selling traditional goods. Handicrafts and traditional artisan wares can be found at some markets, and there are a few arts and crafts specialist shops. The city is Latin America's fashion capital and the districts of Jardins, Pacaembu, and Vila Madalena are bursting with smart boutiques. The numerous opulent malls, which are are large, elegant, and air-conditioned, also contain many boutiques and shops selling international brands and leading Brazilian designers, as well as restaurants and entertainment areas. São Paulo's other good buys, such as coffee and *cachaça*, can also be bought in malls, while CDs and books are best sought in mega-bookstores. Rua Gabriel Monteiro Silva in Jardins is the place for high-quality household items.

Designer shops lining Rua Oscar Freire

Shopping hours

Shops in São Paulo are open from 8am to 6pm. Street shops tend to open from 8 or 10am to 6pm. They are closed on Brazilian public holidays. Most shopping centers and malls are open from 10am to 10pm and on weekends (including Sunday) from 10am to 8pm. They often do not close on public holidays.

Fashion

The domestic fashion market in Brazil is flourishing, with almost all Brazilian labels coming from São Paulo. The market is strongest for women's clothing and the best place to begin a browse is in Jardins. Here, hundreds of tasteful little shops sell colorful, beautifully cut clothes. Many of the latest generation of young Paulistana designers, such as **Adriana Barra** and **Cris Barros**, have their showrooms in Jardins. These labels are particularly strong on dresses and evening wear. More established names can be found too. **Amir Slama** opened his own store here and now stocks the world's sexiest and most fashionable bikinis.

Other designers, such as the eco-friendly **Flavia Aranha**, who is popular with those looking for elegant simplicity, can be found around the leafy streets of Vila Madalena.

Music & Film

Bossa nova, *samba*, *frevo*, *forró*, *axé*, *choro* – it is difficult to think of a country with as many homegrown musical genres as Brazil. São Paulo is the best place in the country either to begin an acquaintance with this diversity or to explore its variety.

Many of the larger stores give customers the chance to listen to CDs before buying. Such shops are to be found in many of the larger malls but the best in the city is probably **FNAC**, which also stocks an excellent selection of Brazilian DVDs. Its selections of Latin American art-house films are particularly strong.

Grandes Galerias, or the **Galeria do Rock**, has a large choice of rock CDs and DVDs. This arcade has around 100 different small shops selling every manner of CD and DVD. However, only a few stores offer the desirable option of listening before buying.

Beverages

The raw ingredient for the *caipirinha* cocktail, Brazilian *cachaça* or sugar-cane rum is sometimes difficult to find outside of Brazil. But in São Paulo, bottles are on sale in any corner shop at a reasonable price. The **Cachaçaria Paulista**, however, is a bar and shop for connoisseurs, selling more than 300 different *cachaças*, the best of which are said to be from Minas Gerais.

Fine coffee beans and grounds can be bought here. **Santo Grão** in Jardins and boutiques in the various malls have shops selling gourmet and quality blends. Some of the very best are to be found in the shop of the Museu do Café in Santos *(see p172)*.

Books & Magazines

Brazilian music CDs

Large bookshops can be found in the malls and are usually well-stocked with English-language novels. The greatest variety is to be found in FNAC, and **Livraria Cultura**. The bookshops attached to the **MASP** and **MAM** galleries are well worth a browse. Brazilian art books are of a very high international standard and much of the material, including reproductions of European art kept in Brazil, can only be found here. Particularly interesting are the gorgeous photographic books. Brazilian art and social photography is excellent and well represented in the gallery souvenir shops.

Overpriced international papers and magazines can also be bought at larger bookshops. There are no English-language publications in Brazil. Portuguese readers will find newsstands or *bancas* dotted throughout the city. Lovers of vintage books and those on a budget will enjoy **Sebo do Messias**, Brazil's largest used-book store.

Arts, Crafts & Design

Although arts and crafts are best bought regionally, particularly in centers such as Manaus, Palmas, or Caruaru, there are a few specialist shops in São Paulo. The **Casa das Culturas Indígenas**

Iguatemi shopping mall

sells indigenous jewelry and household goods. There is an arts and crafts market on **Praça da Republica** on Sundays, selling handicrafts mainly from North and Northeast Brazil. **Feira de Artes Benedito Calixto** is a traditional street market selling antiques, handicrafts, and art every Saturday.

Paulistanos adore decor. **Etel Interiores** has exquisite top-end home furnishings from furniture to small decorative items. The most interesting pieces are made from sustainable materials in Acre in the Brazilian Amazon. **Firma Casa** stocks the best of Brazil's furniture makers.

Shopping Malls

There are shopping malls throughout the city, many of which stock similar items and brands, making it difficult to choose between them. The best design names are to be found in South America's oldest mall, **Iguatemi**, which still looks as if it was built yesterday. **Shopping Ibirapuera** has the most shops and perhaps the greatest middle-brow choice.

High-end **Daslu** is internationally famous and attracts élite and wealthy clients. Many international and Brazilian big design names are sold here, together with Daslu's own label.

DIRECTORY

Fashion

Adriana Barra
Alameda Franca 1243.
Map 4 F3.
Tel (11) 2925 2300.
W adrianabarra.com.br

Amir Slama
Rua Oscar Freire 977.
Map 4 D2.
Tel (11) 3061 0450.
W amirslama.com.br

Cris Barros
Rua Vitório Fasano 85.
Map 4 D3.
Tel (11) 3082 3621.
W crisbarros.com.br

Flavia Aranha
Rua Aspicuelta 224,
Map 3 A1.
W flaviaaranha.com.

Music & Film

FNAC
Av Paulista 901.
Map 4 F3.
Tel (11) 2123 2000.

Galeria do Rock
Rua 24 de Maio 62 & Av
São João 439. **Map** 1 B2.

Beverages

Cachaçaria Paulista
Rua Mourato Coelho 593,
Pinheiro. **Map** 3 A3.
Tel (11) 3815 4756.

Santo Grão
Rua Oscar Freire 413.
Map 4 D3.
Tel (11) 3082 4892.
W santograo.com.br

Books & Magazines

Livraria Cultura
Av Paulista 2073.**Map** 4 E2.
Tel (11) 3170 4033.
W livrariacultura.com.br

MAM
Parque do Ibirapuera,
Portão 3. **Map** 4 E5.
Tel (11) 5085 1300.
W mam.org.br

MASP
Av Paulista 1578.
Map 4 F2.
Tel (11) 3251 5868.
W masp.art.br

Sebo do Messias
Praça Joao Mendes 140.
Map 1 C4.
Tel (11) 3104 7111.

Arts, Crafts & Design

Casa das Culturas Indígenas
Rua Augusta 1371, loja
107. **Map** 4 E1.
Tel (11) 3283 4924.
W casadasculturas
indigenas.com

Etel Interiores
Al Gabriel Monteiro da
Silva, 1834.
Map 3 A4.
Tel (11) 3064 1266.
W etelinteriores.
com.br

Feira de Artes Benedito Calixto
Praça Benedito Calixto.
Map 3 B2. **W** praca
beneditocalixto.com.br

Firma Casa
Al Gabriel Monteiro da
Silva 1487. **Map** 3 B4.
Tel (11) 3385 9595.
W firmacasa.com.br

Praça da Republica
Map 1 B2.

Shopping Malls

Daslu
Rua Haddock Lobo,
1583 Jardins. **Map** 4 D3.
Tel (11) 3078 1827.
W daslu.com.br

Iguatemi
Av Brig. Faria Lima 2232.
Map 3 A5.
Tel (11) 3048 7344.

Shopping Ibirapuera
Av Ibirapuera 3103.
Tel (11) 5095 2300.

ENTERTAINMENT IN SÃO PAULO

São Paulo has an incredible nightlife with a bewildering choice of activities on offer. Live music, in diverse styles, is performed every night by the most distinguished artists in the country. Brazil's finest orchestra, theater, and concert halls are also located in São Paulo. The city boasts myriad dance clubs offering *samba*, *forró*, and a dozen other traditional styles, alongside ubiquitous international club music, often with a Brazilian twist. A wide range of films can be viewed as well, with state-of-the-art multiplexes showing the latest blockbusters from Europe, Latin America, or Asia and art-house theaters offering popular national cinema. A progressive city, São Paulo has the largest Gay Pride parade in the world, which takes place in June. Children are welcome everywhere – even in bars and restaurants, and the largest theme park in South America, Playcenter, lies on the city's doorstep.

Guides & listings

The Friday edition of the *Folha de São Paulo* and *Estado do São Paulo* newspapers and *Veja* magazine's cultural insert, *Veijinha*, have comprehensive listings in Portuguese. The website **Catraca Livre**, popular with a young crowd, offers reviews of the latest events, including those that are free.

The main ticket-selling websites for São Paulo are **Ingresso Rápido** and **Ingresso.com**.

Live Music

A plethora of small venues in the *bairros* of Vila Madalena, Pinheiros, and Vila Olímpia play host to all manner of live acts. Almost all have a small restaurant area, a dance floor, and a sitting area. All have bars and serve beer and excellent cocktails. Musical performances may vary from week to week – from *samba* to Brazilian funk, *bossa nova*, or the latest post-*mangue* beat sounds from the state of Pernambuco. The best venues include **Akbar** and the **Bourbon Street Music Club**, featuring jazz and Dixieland.

More popular performers, such as João Bosco or Otto, play in the **SESC**s – cultural centers with excellent concert halls. The best are in Vila Mariana and Pompéia. Legendary singers such as Milton Nascimento and Caetano Veloso play in numerous concert halls such as the **Espaço das Américas** and **Citibank Hall**, which are some of the largest in the city.

Sergio Dias, Ceumar, and Rebecca Matta performing at SESC Pompéia

The most popular national and international groups, such as Ivete Sangalo and U2, play in the Pacaembu stadium.

Classical Music & Dance

Brazil's most reputable orchestra, the São Paulo State Symphony Orchestra, has its home in Latin America's best 1,500-seat concert hall, the **Sala São Paulo**. The acoustics here are almost perfect. The Sala São Paulo regularly advertises its upcoming programs on its website. The city's other key music venue for opera and classical concerts is the distinguished **Theatro Municipal**. The **Teatro Alfa** specializes in ballet.

Dance Bars & Clubs

Dance bars and clubs are largely concentrated in two areas of the city – Vila Madalena and Pinheiros, southwest of the center, and the contiguous *bairros* of Vila Olímpia, Itaim, and Moema in the south. The former is more lively, with live *forró* and *samba* bands playing to bars filled with university students. **Bambú Brasil** and the **Canto da Ema** are always packed at weekends. Vila Olímpia, Itaim, and Moema are generally livelier neighborhoods and are home to the bulk of clubs which play host to big-name DJs, such

Renowned trumpet player Shamarr Allen performing at the Bourbon Street Music Club

as Marky and Patiffe, and play techno and trance music. The Consolação area is very popular for nightlife and has numerous trendy venues, including **Z Carniceria** and **Club Yacht**, while an alternative crowd hangs out in the old city center in clubs such as **Cine Joia**, which also hosts concerts.

Cinema & Theater

The city has some 250 cinema houses and hosts several important film festivals. Almost all the shopping malls have large multiplexes showing not only the latest films from Hollywood but also national releases. There are more than 20 art-house cinemas, including the **Cine SESC** and the **Reserva Cultural** off Avenida Paulista. Non-Portuguese films are subtitled rather than dubbed.

São Paulo has more than 100 theaters with shows almost exclusively in Portuguese. Most of the theaters are found in Bela Vista and Bixiga. The **Cultura Inglesa** features English-language films and TV shows.

Fans cheering during a championship match at the Estádio Morumbi

Children

São Paulo's urban environment makes outdoor attractions for children relatviely few and far between, although there are some popular amusement and theme parks scattered across the city. One of the biggest theme parks in Brazil, **Hopi Hari**, is located 40 miles (70 km) north of downtown São Paulo. The city also boasts the large **Fundação Parque Zoológico de São Paulo** (São Paulo Zoo), which is set in a state preserve of coastal rainforest.

Soccer

Soccer is an obsession in São Paulo, as it is throughout the country, and the city has the most prestigious soccer teams in Brazil. There are three First Division teams based in São Paulo who play in the impressive Morumbi and Pacaembu stadiums. **Estádio Morumbi** is the home ground of São Paulo Futebol Clube. Matches are generally held on Wednesday and on weekends, and guided tours take place daily.

DIRECTORY

Guides & Listings

Catraca Livre
w catracalivre.com.br

Ingresso
w ingresso.com

Ingresso Rápido
w ingressorapido.com.br

Live Music

Akbar
Rua Inácio Pereira da Rocha 109, Vila Madalena. **Map** 3 A2.
Tel (11) 3816 0403.
w akbar.com.br

Bourbon Street Music Club
Rua dos Chanés 127, Moema. **Tel** (11) 5095 6100.

Citibank Hall
Av das Nações Unidas 17955, Vila Almeida.
Tel (11) 4003 5588.

Espaço das Américas
Rua Tagipuru 795 - Barra Funda. **Tel** (11) 3868 5860.
w casadasamericas.com.br

SESC

SESC Vila Mariana, Rua Pelotas 141.
Tel (11) 5080 3000.
w sescsp.org.br

Classical Music & Dance

Sala São Paulo
Praça Julio Prestes 16.
Map 1 B1.
Tel (11) 3223 3966.

Teatro Alfa
Rua Bento Branco de Andrade Filho 722, Santo Amaro. **Tel** (11) 5693 4000.

Theatro Municipal
Praça Ramos de Azevedo.
Map 1 C2 & C3.
Tel (11) 3053 2090.

Dance Bars & Clubs

Bambu Brasil
Rua Purpurina 272. **Map** 3 A1. **Tel** (11) 3031 2331.

Canto da Ema

Av Brig. Faria Lima 364, Pinheiros.
Tel (11) 3813 4708.

Cine Joia
Praça Carlos Gomes 82, Sé.
Map 1 C4
Tel (11) 3101 1305.
w cinejoia.tv

Club Yacht
Rua Treze de Maio 703, Bela Vista. **Map** 1 B5.
Tel (11) 3231 3705.

Z Carniceria
Rua Augusta 934.
Map 4 F1.
Tel (11) 2936 0934.

Cinema & Theater

Cine SESC
Rua Augusta 2075.
Map 4 E2.
Tel (11) 3087 0500.

Cultura Inglesa
Rua Deputado Lacerda Franco 333.
Tel (11) 3032 4888.
w cultrainglesasp.com.br

Reserva Cultural

Av Paulista 900, São Paulo. **Map** 4 E2.
Tel (11) 3287 3529.

Children

Fundação Parque Zoológico de São Paulo
Av Miguel Stéfano 4241.
Tel (11) 5073 0811.
w zoologico.com.br

Hopi Hari
Rodovia dos Bandeirantes, km 72 - Vinhedo.
Tel (11) 3270 3609.
w hopihari.com.br

Soccer

Estádio Morumbi
Praça Roberto Gomes Pedrosa 1, São Paulo.
Tel (11) 3749 8000;
(11) 3739 5222.

SÃO PAULO STREET FINDER

Map references given in this guide for entertainment venues, shopping areas, and other attractions in São Paulo City refer to the Street Finder maps on the following pages. Map references are also provided for São Paulo City restaurants *(see pp389–90)* and hotels *(see p373–4)*. The first figure in the map reference indicates which Street Finder map to turn to, and the letter and number that follow refer to the grid reference on that map. The map below shows the different areas of São Paulo City – Centro, Bela Vista, Jardins, and Jardim Paulista – covered by the five Street Finder maps. Symbols used for sights and useful information are displayed in the key below. A list of important places of interest marked on the maps can be found on page 140.

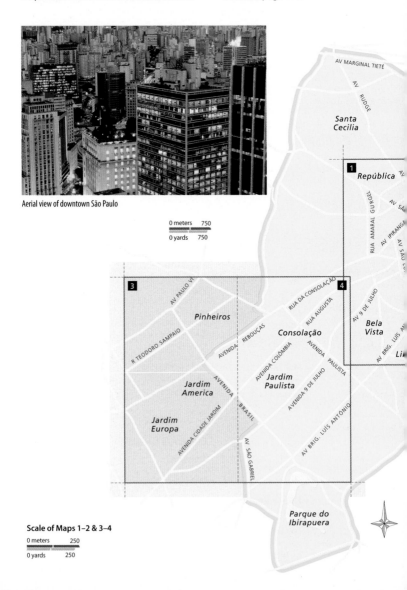

Aerial view of downtown São Paulo

0 meters 750
0 yards 750

Scale of Maps 1–2 & 3–4

0 meters 250
0 yards 250

Streetwise in São Paulo

São Paulo has one of the highest crime rates of any city in the world. However, most of the violence is restricted to the isolated areas dominated by the *favelas* (shantytowns), which lie on the periphery of the city far from the upmarket areas more frequented by visitors. Though you are unlikely to meet with serious trouble in São Paulo, it is important nonetheless to take all adequate precautions. Visitors are required to carry their identification documents at all times.

Visitors must exercise greater caution while traveling in certain parts of the city, including the district of Luz,

areas around the city's main train station, Praça da Sé, Praça da República, and Praça Roosevelt. Be careful in the city center late at night, as well as in the cheap accommodation area around Rua Santa Efigênia.

Cameras, credit cards, and cash should be kept out of sight, preferably in a money belt, with a few notes left in a pocket or handbag. It is wise to withdraw cash only during the day and use ATMs that are within the bank premises rather than in a crowded street.

The metro is safe for commuting during the day, but it is recommended to use taxis after dark. These can be booked through a hotel or rented at one of the many taxi stands.

Driving and navigation in São Paulo are difficult. Carjacking and red-light robberies are common after dark. As a result, the traffic law allows drivers to slow down at red lights and continue driving without stopping if there is little or no traffic on the roads.

Brigadeiro metro station entrance in Paulista Avenue, São Paulo

If held up or driven at gunpoint to an ATM machine, avoid any provocation that could prove fatal.

There have been many incidents of organized violence by the PCC (Primeiro Comando da Capital) against public servants and police. In the unlikely event of PCC activity, it is advisable to stay in your hotel.

Crowded shopping street lined with a selection of stores, São Paulo

Key

 Place of interest

Other building

🚆 Train station

Ⓜ Metro station

🚌 Bus station

ℹ️ Visitor information

➕ Hospital

Police station

Church

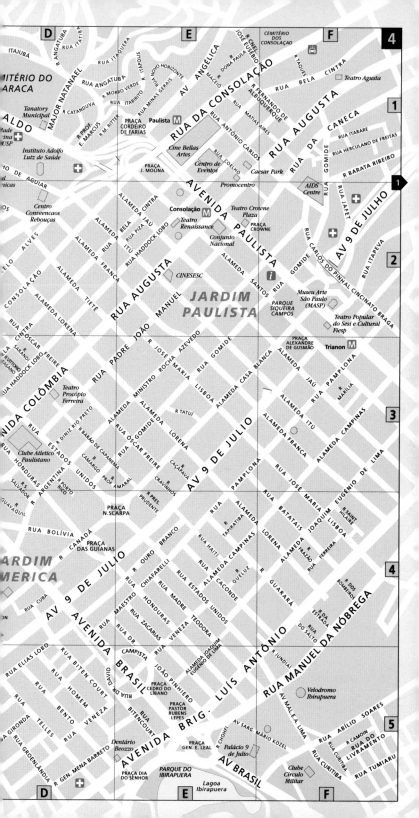

SÃO PAULO STATE

São Paulo is famous for its beaches, pristine island resorts, spectacular surf, and majestic rainforests. Divided into Litoral Norte and Litoral Sul, the state's coastline is one of the most incredible in the southern half of Brazil. São Paulo's agricultural hinterland is the main reason it is Brazil's economic powerhouse. It is also home to a diverse range of immigrant communities.

The colony of Brazil was officially established in São Vicente (present-day Santos) in 1532 by Martim Afonso de Souza. The handful of sailors that remained formally named the beach São Vicente, and, as pioneers, had to fend for themselves in a new land, coping with assaults launched by the local Tamoio Indians. Settlements followed shortly after in nearby Santos and in São Sebastião, opposite the island of Ilhabela, now a beautiful resort. All towns in the region preserve interesting sights and legacies dating from their early colonial days.

Most visitors, however, come to the São Paulo coast not for history but for sand, surf, and rainforest. Ilhabela, Brazil's largest tropical island, Ubatuba, whose 70 beaches stretch to the state's far north, and Guarujá, similar to Copacabana in

Rio City, with similar numbers of high-rise buildings facing the ocean, are the most popular destinations. All three have beaches that have consistently been rated among the nation's top ten by the country's tourist magazines. Puma and ocelot still hunt in the wild Atlantic mountain forests which lie only a short distance behind them.

The full majesty of the Atlantic coastal forest, the Mata Atlântica, unfolds around Mosaico Juréia-Itatins, and Cananéia in the Litoral Sul. Lush ridges, waterfalls, and abundant plant life are its main attractions. The forest is also home to a wide array of animals, birds, and brilliantly colored butterflies. One of the loveliest spots is Ilha do Cardoso, a boat ride from Cananéia, where caimans can be seen basking in the sun on the beaches.

Stream flowing through the lush Mata Atlântica near Ubatuba

◀ Ilha Urubuqueçaba, Santos, as seen from Morro Voturuá

Exploring São Paulo State

The São Paulo coast is divided into the Litoral Norte, which stretches towards Rio in the northeast from the port city of Santos, and the Litoral Sul, which stretches from Santos towards Paraná state. The Litoral Norte is one of the most heavily visited coastlines in southeastern Brazil. Beaches on the Ilhabela, Brazil's largest tropical island, and the resort of Ubatuba, are magnificently backed by towering spurs swathed in tropical rainforest. The sands of the Litoral Sul are darker and siltier than those of the Litoral Norte. Around Cananéia and Juréia, and stretching into Paraná, are the largest tracts of lowland coastal forest outside the Amazon. The beautiful beaches of the Ilha do Cardoso are just a boat ride away from Cananéia.

Key

⬜ Area illustrated

Sights at a Glance

Towns & Cities

① Ubatuba
② São Sebastião
⑤ Guarujá
⑥ Santos
⑦ São Vicente
⑨ Iguape
⑩ Cananéia

**State Parks & Areas
of Natural Beauty**

⑧ Mosaico Juréia-Itatins

Islands

③ Ilhabela
⑪ Ilha do Cardoso

Beaches

④ Maresias

Key

🝙 Highway
— Major road
···· Minor road
⊷⊷ Railroad
— State border
△ Peak

For hotels and restaurants in this region see p374 and pp390–91

The Praia das Toninhas in Ubatuba

Getting Around

There are two large airports –
international and domestic – in São
Paulo City. Regular bus services ply
between São Paulo City and the major
towns on the coast, but reaching the
best of the beaches requires a car. The
main routes to the coast are the
Anchieta and Imigrantes highways
between São Paulo City and Santos.
From Santos, the route north follows
the Rio–Santos (SP-055), which passes
through all the major beach towns
and heads into Rio de Janeiro state.
The Litoral Sul can be reached by
SP-055, which reaches only as far as
the northern part of Mosaico Juréia-
Itatins. Towns farther to the south can
be reached off highway BR-116.

A beautiful beach on the tropical island of Ilhabela

For keys to symbols see back flap

Picinguaba beach in Ubatuba with Serra do Mar mountains in the distance

❶ Ubatuba

🏠 65,000. ✈️ 🚌
ℹ️ Av Iperoig 214, (12) 3833 9123.
🌐 **vivaubatuba.com.br**

Lying at the northern extreme of São Paulo state and sitting at the feet of the Serra do Mar mountain range, Ubatuba is a little beach resort with a small colonial center lined with terraced houses. Glorious beaches surround the resort.

The most popular beaches, especially those south of the town center such as **Praia Grande**, have an excellent infrastructure, including play areas for children. Buses running along the coastal road pass other nearby beaches, such as **Enseada**, **Picinguaba**, and **Flamengo**. Even in high season it is easy to find a quiet stretch of sand or lonely cove tucked away along the coast to the south of Ubatuba.

The **Aquário de Ubatuba** in the center of the town contains some of the largest tanks and most diverse range of tropical marine life in all of Brazil. The office of the **Projeto Tamar**, a Brazil-wide organization that monitors and preserves turtle nesting beaches, is also located in town. Visitors are permitted to witness turtle hatchings under supervision.

The Serra do Mar rises in a vertiginous green wall only a short distance north of Ubatuba and an easy drive away from the town. Carpeted in thick primary forest, the Serra is home to many endangered endemic species. Birdlife, too, is prolific in this picturesque mountainous area.

🐟 **Aquário de Ubatuba**
Rua Guaraní 859. **Tel** (12) 3834 1382. **Open** 10am–8pm Sun–Thu, 10am–10pm Fri & Sat. 🈂️

🐢 **Projeto Tamar**
Rua A. Atanázio 273. **Tel** (12) 3832 6202. **Open** 10am–6pm Mon–Thu & Sun, 10am–8pm Fri–Sat (closed Wed in low season).

Environs
The twin beaches of **Domingas Dias** and **Lázaro**, whose white sands curve gently on either side of a forest-clad promontory, are located 11 miles (18 km) south of Ubatuba. The **Peninsula da Ponta da Fortaleza** lies just south of Domingas Dias and is fringed with many quiet beaches, including **Praia Vermelha do Sul**. Surfers head north of Ubatuba to **Praia Vermelha do Norte** for the best waves on the Litoral Norte.

❷ São Sebastião

🏠 83,000. 🚌 ℹ️ Av Doutor Altino Arantes 174, (12) 3892 2620.
🎉 Festas do 20 de Janeiro (Jan).
🌐 **turismosaosebastiao.com.br**

São Sebastião was founded in the early 17th century, when Brazil's coastline was cloaked in a forest larger than the Amazon. North of Guanabara Bay was Tamoio indigenous country, and São Sebastião became the northernmost Portuguese outpost for the indigenous slave trade. As it grew, the city became one of the country's first sugar-growing centers and the thirst for slave labor became unquenchable. The city was also among the first to receive Africans in the slave trade.

Although most people who come to São Sebastião do so merely to pass through on their way to Ilhabela, the town has a colonial center of historical importance which merits at least a couple of hours' leisurely stroll before departing.

São Sebastião's colonial streets lie in the few blocks between the shoreline and the Praça Major João Fernandes at the heart of the city, easily recognizable by the imposing 17th-century church, the **Igreja Matriz**, which watches over it. This is largely a 19th-century reconstruction devoid of much of its original church art. However, the refurbished **Museu de Arte Sacra**, housed in the 17th-century chapel of São Gonçalo, a block to the south of the church, preserves a number of beautiful, delicate images of Christ. Dating from the 16th century, these images were found within cavities in the wall of the Igreja Matriz during its restoration in 2003.

There are also a few streets lined with Portuguese houses and a number of civic buildings, the most impressive of which is the **Casa Esperança** on the waterfront. Built from stone

Façade of Igreja Matriz, São Sebastião

and wattle and daub congealed with whale oil, the exterior is whitewashed with lime made from thousands of crushed shells. The Casa contains some faded but original 17th-century ceiling paintings and statuary.

🏛 Casa Esperança
Av Altino Arantes 144. **Open** 9am–5pm Mon–Fri, 7–10am Sat & Sun.

⛪ Igreja Matriz
Praça Major João Fernandes. **Tel** (12) 3892 1110. **Open** 8am–6pm Mon–Fri. 🕐 7pm Mon, Tue & Thu–Sat; 3pm Wed; 7:30am, 9am & 7:30pm Sun.

🏛 Museu de Arte Sacra
Rua Sebastião Silvestre Neves 90. **Tel** (12) 3892 4286. **Open** 9am–noon, 2–6pm Tue–Sat. 🚻 📷

❸ Ilhabela

🏘 32,000. 🚢 from São Sebastião to Barra Velha. 🛈 Praça Vereador José Leite dos Passos 14, Barra Velha, (12) 3895 7220. 🎭 Festa do Camarão (Aug). 🌐 ilhabela.sp.gov.br

One of Brazil's largest islands, Ilhabela rises steeply out of the Atlantic, a short distance offshore from São Sebastião. With a coastline sculpted by dozens of bays and beaches, it is covered in rainforest, much of it cut by fast-flowing mountain streams. Visitors from São Paulo throng here during weekends, but during the week (outside of holiday season) the island is all but deserted. Much of the forest is protected as part of the **Parque Estadual de Ilhabela** and there is plenty of wildlife, including ocelots and several species of primates. The presence of biting flies, or *borrachudos*, on the island make insect repellent essential.

Ilhabela has just two roads. One is paved and runs the entire length of the western, leeward coast. Most of the numerous *pousadas* and guesthouses lie here, as do the villages of **Perequê** (where the ferry arrives), **Borrifos**, **São Pedro**, and **Vila Ilhabela**. The latter has a few colonial remains. Rusting 18th-century

Waterfront at Vila Ilhabela with 18th-century cannon

cannons adorn its waterfront and there is a little avenue of Portuguese buildings, including a 16th-century church, the Matriz de Nossa Senhora d'Ajuda.

The island's other road is a dirt track, usable only by four-wheel drives, which cuts across the interior from Perequê into the park and to the windward beaches. The most spectacular of these is the **Baía de Castelhanos**, a perfect half-moon of sand backed by rainforest-covered slopes. The island's longest beach, and the best for surfing, is **Bonete**, which is 9 miles (15 km) south from Borrifos village, along a rough forest trail.

Ilhabela's forests are dripping with waterfalls, but many are either completely inaccessible or reachable only by trail. A short distance inland from Perequê beach, **Cachoeira da Toca** waterfalls plunge in a series of little cascades into swimming pools, replete with waterslides. **Cachoeira da Água Branca** is larger, with more swimming pools. It is an hour's walk along a trail which begins at the entrance to the state park, a short distance beyond the turn-off to Cachoeira da Toca.

Numerous shipwrecks off Ilhabela also make it a popular scuba-diving destination, despite the murky water.

Blue dacnis, Ilhabela

🌊 Cachoeira da Toca
Estrada Baía de Castelhanos. **Open** 24 hrs daily. 📷

❹ Maresias

🏘 5,000. 🛈 Estrada do Cascalho 1470, Boiçucanga, 4 miles (7 km) W of Maresias, (12) 3865 4335.

South of São Sebastião lie a number of beautiful beach resorts. Maresias, the liveliest of the lot, is busy with young, hip Paulistanos at weekends and holidays. **Praia de Maresias** is famous for its powerful surf, which has been the site for many international surfing competitions. **Toque Toque Grande** and **Toque Toque Pequeno**, 6 miles (9 km) south-east, are smaller, quieter beaches, sheltered by rainforest-covered spurs. There are plenty of *pousadas* and restaurants on, or just off, the São Sebastião road, which runs along the coast.

❺ Guarujá

🏘 310,000. 🛈 Av Marechal Deodoro da Fonseca 723, (13) 3344 4600. 🌐 portal.guaruja.sp.gov.br

Situated close to São Paulo and on the way to Santos, this beachtown is a popular weekend and day-trip destination for São Paulo residents. It is known as the "Pearl of the Atlantic" and has about 14 miles (23 km) of white beaches that stretch along the coast. The longest of these, Enseada Beach, is popular with surfers, and its shores are lined with hotels and kiosks. For those who don't only want to soak up the sun, other activities include artisan fishing and looking at the town's historical buildings. The town also has an aquarium.

A fishing village on the coastal outskirts of the city of Santos, São Paulo State ▶

Stained-glass skylight, depicting a representation of Brazil, the *Mãe Douro*, Bolsa e Museu do Café, Santos

❻ Santos

🏠 418,000. 🚌 ℹ️ Praça das Bandeiras, 0800 173 887.
🌐 **turismosantos.com**

When Santos was founded in 1535, it was one of Portugal's first New World settlements. Since the mid-16th century, when neighboring São Vicente was established, Santos had been a port. First it dealt with sugar, and then with African slaves. However, it grew rich on coffee, which was brought out of the mountains on Brazil's first trains, built by the British in the late 19th century.

Scottish tram

Unlike São Vicente, Santos has preserved vestiges of its historical legacy, and, under recent enlightened municipal governance, is reinventing and refurbishing itself. Once decrepit, the city center is undergoing a spruce-up and is now very attractive. Scottish trams in British racing green run through its streets, taking visitors on a whistle-stop tour of the various attractions. The city center is also small enough to stroll around and have a closer look at these sights on foot.

The jewel in the city's crown is the Art Nouveau **Museu do Café**. Its modest Victorian exterior hides an opulent marble-floored turn-of-the-19th-century stock exchange and museum, together with a café shop serving excellent coffee and desserts. The Bolsa was once open only to wealthy (and exclusively male) coffee barons who traded here. When it was built, coffee was the most important and coveted commodity in Brazil.

The auction room is crowned by a magnificent stained-glass skylight, with an arresting representation of Brazil, the *Mãe Douro*; crowned with a star, she rises from flames in a landscape thick with tropical animals and startled-looking indigenous people. The skylight and the beautiful Neo-Renaissance painting of Santos that adorns the walls of the stock exchange are by Brazil's most celebrated mid-19th-century artist, Benedito Calixto *(see p34)*.

A number of Calixto's paintings are displayed in the **Pinacoteca Benedito Calixto**, which is housed in one of the few remaining coffee baron mansions. The landscapes shown here give an idea of the city's once breathtaking natural beauty.

Santos has a handful of interesting churches, but the only one open to the public is the **Santuário Santo Antônio do Valongo**. The church's mock-Baroque interior dates from the 1930s. The fine original 17th-century altarpiece remains preserved in the Franciscan chapel to the left of the main entrance; the statue of Christ is particularly striking. Next door to the church is the British-built terminus of the now defunct Santos–São Paulo railway. Built between 1860 and 1867, the station is vaguely reminiscent of London's Victoria.

The once-filthy city beaches are now much cleaner and are lively with bustling bazaars, and people playing volleyball and football, every evening and weekend.

A monument to the thousands of Japanese-Brazilians who

Pelé during Champions World Series 2003, New York

Football Legend Pelé

Regarded as the world's most famous sportsman, Pelé was born in Tres Corações, Minas Gerais. He started his career in Santos when, in 1956, the Santos Futebol Clube signed him. Soon, he was offered a place in the Brazilian national team, and went on to play in three of Brazil's five World Cup-winning teams. Since his retirement in 1977, Pelé has worked as a charity patron Goodwill Ambassador for UNICEF. In 1992, he became the UN Ambassador for Ecology and Environment. In 1995, he was appointed Minister of Sports, a post he resigned after becoming caught up in one of the rumored, or real, corruption scandals that blight Brazilian politics.

rrived in São Paulo state in he early 20th century sits here, ogether with the small but popular **Aquário de Santos**. n addition to a stunning range of tropical marine life, it displays hree of the five species of sea turtles found in Brazil. The beaches lying farther out n the Baía de Santos (Bay of All Saints) bustle with activity at the weekends.

For all its history, it is for football that Santos is most famous outside Brazil. Pelé played here for almost all his professional life. The Santos Football Club has an excellent museum, the **Memorial das Conquistas**, devoted to the club's illustrious history.

Aquário de Santos
Av Bartolomeu de Gusmão, Ponta da Praia. **Tel** (13) 3278 7830. **Open** 9am–6pm Tue–Fri, 9am–8pm Sat & Sun.

Museu do Café
Rua 15 de Novembro 95. **Tel** (13) 3213 1750. **Open** 9am–5pm Tue–Sat, 10am–5pm Sun.

Pinacoteca Benedito Calixto
Av Bartolomeu de Gusmão 15. **Tel** (13) 3288 2260. **Open** 9am–6pm Tue–Sun.

Memorial das Conquistas
Rua Princesa Isabel 77, Vila Belmiro. **Tel** (13) 3257 4099. **Open** 1–7pm Mon, 9am–7pm Tue–Sun. prior booking required.

Santuário Santo Antônio do Valongo
Largo Marquês de Monte Alegre 13. **Tel** (13) 3219 1481. **Open** 10am–7pm Tue–Sun.

Japanese Immigration

Brazil is home to the largest number of ethnic Japanese people outside Japan, and almost all their ancestors arrived at Santos. Immigration began in earnest after the Russo-Japanese War (1904–5). Although Japan emerged victorious, the penalty was high, leaving the poorer Japanese population with a bleak future. São Paulo seemed to offer hope, as the state was rich in coffee and workers were in short supply.

The first Japanese ship to land was the *Kasato Maru*, which brought 165 families to Santos on June 18, 1908. They left for the coffee plantations in the Mogiana region. By the beginning of World War II, almost 150,000 Japanese had arrived. After freeing themselves from their labor contracts, communities began to grow in metropolitan São Paulo *(see p149)* and other parts of Brazil.

Japanese Immigration Monument, Santos

❼ São Vicente

🅜 332,000. 🚌 🆆 saovicente. sp.gov.br

The pleasant, laid-back port town of São Vicente is known more for its historical significance than the usual tourist attractions.

In 1532, Martim Afonso de Sousa established a small settlement on the eastern shores of South America. Thus Brazil was born, in the words of Afonso's brother, with "each man as lord of his own property, and private injuries redressed, and all the other benefits of a secure and sociable life." São Vicente is the scene of that noble beginning, though only a handful of relics belonging to that distinguished past can be found today.

First capital of the Captaincy of São Vicente, as São Paulo

state was formerly known, São Vicente won the epithet of "Cellula Mater" (Mother Cell) for being Brazil's first organized town. The 18th-century Baroque parish church, the **Igreja Matriz de São Vicente Mártir**, is one of the very few historical buildings in the city to have survived the ravages of time. A tidal wave destroyed the first church, built close to this site by Martim Afonso shortly after his arrival. The second parish church was built inland on this present site. However, it fared no better, and was ransacked by pirates. The current building, standing on its ruins, is named in honor of the Spanish saint who is patron of the city.

Also in the city center are the remains of Martim Afonso's former home, and the first brick building in Brazil. These are housed inside the impressive late 19th-century **Casa Martim Afonso**, along with a few other interesting pieces of colonial bric-a-brac.

Casa Martim Afonso
Praça 22 de Janeiro 469, Centro. **Tel** (13) 3568 8948. **Open** 9am–5pm Tue–Sun & public hols.

Igreja Matriz de São Vicente Mártir
Praça João Pessoa s/n, Centro. **Tel** (13) 3468 2658. **Open** 8am–7:30pm daily. 8am, 7pm Mon & Wed–Fri; 8am Tue; 7pm Sat; 7:30am, 10am, 6pm Sun.

Proud display of trophies at the Memorial das Conquistas, Santos

Striking hills in the Mosaico Juréia-Itatins

❽ Mosaico Juréia-Itatins

🚌 to Iguape or Peruíbe, then taxi.
ℹ️ Peruíbe: Estrada do Guaraú 4,
164 Bairro Guaraú, (13) 3457 9243.
Iguape: Praça São Benedito 110,
Centro, (13) 3841 2193. 🔲

Brazil's coastal rainforest stretches in a series of rippling mountains and lowland forests cut by broad rivers, mangrove wetlands, and pristine beaches, as well as traditional fishing and farming communities, along São Paulo State's coast. The Mosaico Juréia-Itatins encompasses six protected areas of rainforest, four of which are open to visitors – Parque Estadual Itinguçu, Parque Estadual Prelado, Reserva de Desenvolvimento Sustentável da Barra do Una, and Reserva de Desenvolvimento Sustentável do Despraiado. Iguape is a good base for information on organized tours and walking trails in these rainforest areas.

This region protects Atlantic rainforest and its associated ecosystems. It is one of the most important breeding grounds for marine species in the southern Atlantic and the myriad forest types growing here protect one of the world's greatest diversities of vascular plant, vertebrate, and invertebrate species. There is a unique range of birds, butterflies, and mammals. Many larger animals, such as jaguars and tapirs, which have all but disappeared from coastal Brazil, live in healthy numbers here.

Juréia itself protects a wide variety of habitats; as a result the scenery is magnificent. Lush green forest swathes the high slopes of the Serra do Itatins in the eastern extremity of the park and continues all the way through to the lowland coastal areas, mixing with mangrove wetlands and perfuming the park's extensive beaches. These beautiful stretches of fine sand, many of which are cut by clear rivers or washed by waterfalls, are so deserted that caimans can occasionally be seen basking in the sun at dawn.

❾ Iguape

🏘️ 31,000. 🚌 ℹ️ Rua Claudino P.
Silva 248, (13) 3841 3012.
🌐 **iguape.sp.gov.br**

This pretty little colonial town sits in a pocket of the Brazilian coastal rainforest, the Complexo Estuarino Lagunar de Iguape-Cananéia biosphere reserve, a UNESCO world heritage site. The verdant Serra do Mar mountains rise up behind the town which is surrounded by pristine mangrove wetlands and lowland subtropical forest on all sides including the wilds of the two nature reserves – Juréia-Itatins and Chauás. The **Mirante do Morro do Espio** is a lookout point with a fabulous view of the port and surrounding area.

Iguape was founded in 1538 by the Portuguese. No buildings remain from that time but the city center preserves the largest and oldest heritage-listed collection of post-17th-century colonial architecture in the state. Most are civic buildings and town houses painted in thick primary colors and clustered around **Praça São Benedito**, a sleepy central square watched over by a towering 18th-century basilica.

There are also two small museums in the city center. The **Museu Histórico e Arqueológico** is housed in a 17th-century building which was once the first gold foundry in Brazil. It showcases a mixed bag of historical material, from pre-Columbian remains found

Rio Ribeira do Iguape estuary and Igreja do Rosário rising over Iguape town

nearby middens to artifacts from the slaving era, and early photographs. The **Museu de Arte Sacra** in the Basílica do Bom Jesus houses some 100 ecclesiastical objects, most of which date from the 18th and 19th centuries.

🏛 Museu de Arte Sacra
Basílica do Bom Jesus de Iguape, Praça da Basílica. **Open** 9–11:30am, 2–5:30pm daily.

🏛 Museu Histórico e Arqueológico
Rua das Neves 45. **Tel** (13) 3841 1012. **Open** 8:30am–11:30am, 2–5pm daily.

Environs
Just across the Rio Ribeira do Iguape estuary, east of the town center, are extensive stretches of fine white-sand beaches which make up the island of **Ilha Comprida**. They are accessible by road, or a 5-mile (8-km) walk across the estuary and sand flats via the pedestrian bridge.

Boqueirão Norte, located immediately across the town, and **Praia do Viareggio**, 6 miles (10 km) south, are popular in high season and lined with holiday homes. Farther south still and reachable by dune buggy or by car is the far quieter **Praia das Pedrinhas**.

⓾ Cananéia

🄰 14,000. 🚌 ℹ️ Praça Martin Afonso de Souza s/n, Centro, (13) 3851 1931. 🆆 **cananeia.sp.gov.br**

Cananéia is the farthest south of São Paulo's colonial seaside towns, and like the others it lies nestled at the feet of the Serra do Mar mountains overlooking stretches of mangrove dotted with forest-covered islands. Outside of the high season few visitors ever make it here and the town's crumbling colonial streets and central square often have a sleepy feel to them.

The most compelling reason to come to Cananéia is to take a boat trip out to the beaches and islands that are heritage-listed by UNESCO as part of the Lagamar estuary. Fishing boats and launches can be chartered

Stuffed great white shark, Museu Municipal, Cananéia

from the docks in Cananéia to **Ilha do Cardoso**, which is a a breeding ground for several marine species. Car and passenger rafts take 10 minutes to ferry across the estuary in front of the town to the southern reaches of the **Ilha Comprida**, east of Iguape, and do so several times per day. The beaches here lie a short distance beyond the island's ferry port along a sandy road, which is lined with several tumble-down *pousadas*.

While in Cananéia, it is worth visiting the tiny town museum, **Museu Municipal**, which preserves bits of nautical miscellany. Pride of place among the exhibits goes to what is reputed to be the second largest great white shark ever, weighing a hefty 7,716 lb (3,500 kg), now stuffed, painted, and hanging safely from the museum ceiling.

🏛 Museu Municipal
Rua Tristão Lobo 78. **Tel** (13) 3851 1753. **Open** 9am–6pm Tue–Sun.

⓫ Ilha do Cardoso

🚢 from Cananéia. ℹ️ Núcleo Perequê, Cananéia, (13) 3851 1163, (13) 3851 1108. 🆆 **cananela.net**

Just a 30-minute boat ride south of Cananéia, Ilha do Cardoso, a rugged 58 sq-mile- (150 sq-km-) island, rises dramatically out of the Atlantic Ocean. The island is primarily an ecological reserve which also has beautiful deserted beaches and walking trails. Together with Juréia-Itatins, this forms part of the longest stretch of preserved coastal rainforest in Brazil. Wetlands, mangroves, extensive beaches, coastal dunes, and all of the numerous forest types associated with the Mata Atlântica are found here. Several species of turtle nest on the island, caimans live in the rivers and estuaries, and jaguars and pumas still hunt in the forests that cover the upper reaches. The island is also rich in birdlife.

Pre-Columbian shell middens, or *sambaquis*, dot the park's beaches and seven traditional *caiçara* fishing communities live within the park, preserving a semi-indigenous way of life which has so far largely resisted the pressures of urbanization. *Caiçara* tidal fish traps can be seen in the shallows of the various little rivers and bays, attesting to the strong indigenous heritage the communities preserve to this day. Many of the *caiçaras* act as guides and boatmen.

Virgin beach on Ilha do Cardoso, near Cananéia

NORTHEAST
BRAZIL

Introducing Northeast Brazil **178–183**

Bahia **184–211**

Sergipe, Alagoas
  & Pernambuco **212–229**

Paraíba, Rio Grande
  do Norte & Ceará **230–247**

Piauí & Maranhão **248–259**

Northeast Brazil at a Glance

Comprising the nine states of Bahia, Sergipe, Alagoas, Pernambuco, Paraíba, Rio Grande do Norte, Ceará, Piauí, and Maranhão, the Northeast is truly a tropical paradise. Most of the states have three distinct areas – the fertile coastal strips with idyllic sand beaches giving way to the intermediate hilly areas with lush Atlantic rainforests, also home to a variety of fauna, and finally the vast semi-arid interiors. The beaches here range from the fascinating Canoa Quebrada beach in Ceará, to Genipabu and its sand dunes in Rio Grande do Norte, Porto de Galinhas in Pernambuco, and the Fernando de Noronha archipelago, among many others. The legacy of the Northeast's colonial history can still be seen in numerous, impressive historic monuments in Salvador, Olinda, and São Luís.

BRAZIL

Fernando de Noronha

NORTHEAST BRAZIL

São Luís

P

Santa Inês

Teresina

Imperatriz

PIAUÍ & MARANHÃO
(See pp248–59)

Flo

Balsas

São Luís *(see pp256–8)*, capital of Maranhão, was founded by the French. It is a town with a beautiful historic core, Centro Histórico, with cobbled streets and 5,600 pastel-colored colonial buildings, which have been renovated. A UNESCO World Heritage Site, it is one of Brazil's finest examples of Portuguese architecture.

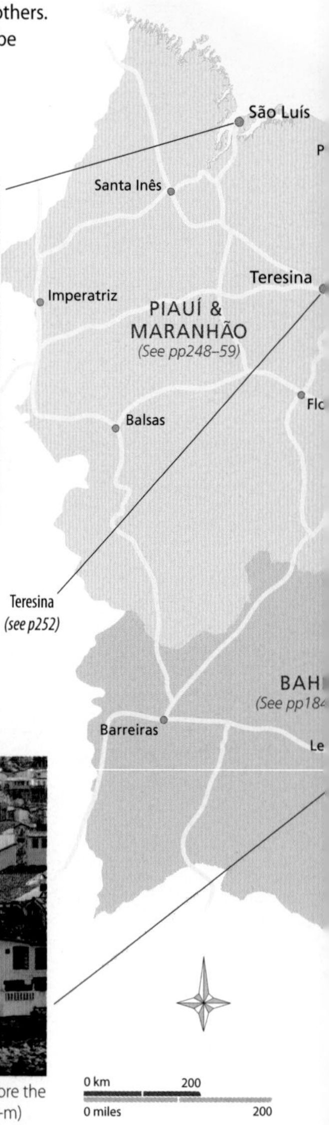

Teresina
(see p252)

BAH
(See pp184

Barreiras

Le

Lençóis *(see p208)*, in Bahia, is the perfect starting point to explore the Chapada's caves and waterfalls, or to hike up the 3,937-ft (1,200-m) surrounding peaks. Miners flocked to this area during the gold and diamond rush.

0 km | 200
0 miles | 200

◀ Dazzling white sand surrounds a lagoon at Parque Nacional dos Lençóis Maranhenses, Maranhão

Fernando de Noronha

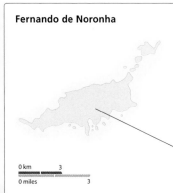

0 km   3

0 miles   3

Fernando de Noronha *(see pp228–9)*, part of Pernambuco, comprises 21 islands. The warm, clear waters here offer Brazil's best scuba diving and snorkeling experience.

- Sobral
- Fortaleza
- Mossoró

PARAÍBA, RIO GRANDE DO NORTE & CEARÁ *(See pp230–47)*

- Natal
- algueiro
- João Pessoa
- trolina
- Recife

SERGIPE, ALAGOAS & PERNAMBUCO *(See pp212–29)*

- Maceió
- Aracaju
- Recife *(see pp220–23)*
- íra de ntana
- Alagoinhas
- Salvador
- equié
- Itabuna
- ixera
- Freitas

Natal *(see p240)*, capital of Rio Grande do Norte, is a popular sunshine destination. The beaches around Natal, with their huge moving dunes shaped by the shifting wind, create fascinating landscapes of snowy white sand.

Salvador *(see pp188–99)*, capital of Bahia, has beautifully restored complexes of Baroque churches and palaces, built during the 18th-century sugar boom. Its historic center, a UNESCO World Heritage Site, offers a unique glimpse into Brazil's history and is the crown jewel of Portuguese architecture.

Afro-Brazilian Culture

A direct legacy of three centuries of slavery, there is a particularly strong presence of African culture in the Northeast of Brazil. Throughout the slavery period in colonial Brazil, there was little or no sanction on miscegenation. Over the years, masters, slaves, former slaves, and their descendants integrated into the new society of Brazil, creating an interesting blend of cultures and bloodlines with Portuguese, Dutch, West African, and Indian elements. This has uniquely resulted in what is now called Afro-Brazilian culture, visible in the people, clothing, food (see pp182–3), religion, and music.

Colorful ribbons, bringing luck if tied around the wrist

Music

Africans brought along their fine command of percussion. Bahia's characteristic brand of Afro-Brazilian music grew in many forms, with axé becoming the signature sound of Salvador's Carnaval. In Pernambuco, as many as 13 distinct rhythms developed, including Recife's signature beat, frevó (see p221). During the 20th century, African music became part of the mainstream. Samba won acceptance in the 1930s.

Pop star Carlinhos Brown is one of the traditional singers who have become world-famous with their percussion-heavy rhythms. This noted advocate of Afro-Brazilian culture hails from Bahia.

Capoeira

A rhythmic, dance-like form of martial arts, capoeira was once practised only by slaves and former slaves. Over the years, it came to put less emphasis on fighting and more on the cooperative elements of dance and display, with rhythmic, graceful moves (see p203).

Traditional instruments used in *capoeira* mainly constitute *berimbau*, a single-stringed percussion instrument featuring a steel string and a hollowed-out gourd; *atabaque*, a large drum, and the *pandeiro*, which resembles a tambourine.

Capoeira was a way for the slaves to continue practicing martial arts, with kicks disguised as fluid body movements. Increasingly popular, today it is taught and performed all over the region, and indeed the world.

Religion

Of West African origin, most of Brazil's original slave population believed in a pantheon of deities, or orixás (see p198). Each orixá was endowed with its own personality and unique powers, and was associated with a particular set of natural elements. The Portuguese, however, insisted that all new arrivals be forcibly converted to Catholicism. The struggle gave rise to Candomblé, a blending of Catholicism and the African beliefs (see p39).

Festive celebrations, such as the Lavagem do Bonfim *(see p199)*, can be experienced in and around Salvador. The day is meant to honor Yemanjá, the Goddess of the Sea. The ceremonies blend Catholic-style processions with African beats and music.

Arts & Crafts

Many of the Bahian arts and crafts are strongly influenced by Afro-Brazilian traditions. The Mercado Modelo (see p196) in Salvador is a good place for souvenirs. Look for berimbaus and percussion instruments, sometimes painted in bright colors, as well as masks and pottery.

Wooden Masks are intricately carved and decorated with stones, shells, and beads. The northeastern masks are allegoric representations of the *orixás*.

Colorful figurines are produced by local artisans as part of the rich pottery tradition in the Northeast. Drawn from popular folklore, these figurines are sold throughout the region.

Dress

The most striking sartorial examples of African influence are the Baianas, the women in turbans and long white dresses, often seen on the streets of Salvador selling acarajé (see p183). The ensemble is believed to be derived from the traditional dress of women in Nigeria. While their dresses are often similar, each Baiana wears a different set of jewelry to pay homage to her particular orixá (deity).

Colorful beads and trinkets can be bought from the Baianas. Every color is known to denote a specific *orixá*; the blue is for Oshun, while red represents Yansá.

A young Baiana in traditional dress of layers of starched lace skirts, a shoulder cloth, high turban, and yellow and white beads and accessories.

The Flavors of Northeast Brazil

Northeast Brazil has two distinct regional cuisines, a reflection of both culture and climate. The narrow, densely populated coast, rich in fresh fruit and sugar cane and bordered by a generous sea, is home to an African-descended population who flavor their food with coconut milk and red *dendê* (palm) oil. The interior, or *sertão*, is arid semi-desert, largely given over to cattle tended by the cowboy descendents of Portuguese immigrants. The interior cuisine consists of sober, simple dishes, whose staples include sun-dried meat, manioc (cassava) root, rice, and black beans.

Spicy cayenne pepper

Distinctive *caju* fruit of the cashew tree, showing the nut

Cozinha Nordestina

When Brazilians refer to *cozinha nordestina* (north-eastern food) they usually mean the dishes of the hot, dry hinterland. Fresh ingredients are few here, and refrigeration virtually nonexistent. Ingredients include the more resilient vegetables such as beans, corn and, especially, manioc. Meat – beef or, just

as often, goat – in the Northeast is usually either sun-dried *(carne de sol)* or air-dried and heavily salted *(carne seca)*. Both are served in small portions, often shredded, and mixed in with either beans, rice, or manioc. Manioc, indeed, is a centerpiece of northeastern cooking. Sliced into strips and fried, the sweeter version of this versatile

root is known as *macaxeira*. Plain ground manioc flour *(farinha)* is often served as a side dish; locals put it in their morning coffee. Pan-fried with a little oil, the manioc flour becomes another common side dish, *farofa*. Finally, the lighter parts of the manioc root are made into tapioca, the base ingredient of desserts and breakfast

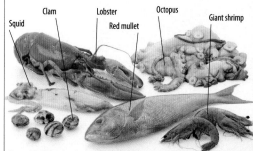

Squid — Clam — Lobster — Octopus — Red mullet — Giant shrimp

Some of the fish and seafood of Brazil's Atlantic coastline

Regional Dishes & Specialties

Bahian cuisine is the most popular and sophisticated in all of the Northeast. The cooking is characterized by the use of coconut milk, hot peppers, and, importantly, *dendê* oil, which gives the dishes their deep orange color. This oil is extracted from a palm tree that was brought to Brazil by African slaves.

Dendê oil

Signature Bahian dishes include *moqueca*, *vatapá*, and *bobó de camarão*. All are variations on a tasty seafood stew. Traditionally, a *moqueca* is cooked in a large clay pot and served with white rice and a serving of *pirão*, a manioc paste. Both *bobó de camarão* and *camarão na moranga* (see p385) feature large, juicy prawns cooked in coconut milk. The *camarão na moranga* comes served in a hollowed-out pumpkin shell, its broth thickened with the addition of fresh, sweet pumpkin, locally called *jerimum*.

Bolinho de bacalhau is a Portuguese snack made from mashed potatoes and shredded salt cod.

Baiana woman in traditional all-white costume, selling *acarajé*

Acarajé

Acarajé is one of the most popular snacks, especially in Bahia. Cooked only by Baianas, it was originally served as an offering to Yansã, the Goddess of Tempests. Balls of mashed black-eyed beans are fried in *dendê* oil, then cut open and served with dried shrimp, *vatapá* (shrimp paste), *caruru* (okra stew), and hot sauce. *Abará* is another kind of *acarajé*, steamed and served on a banana leaf with the same toppings.

pancakes. Desserts in the Northeast are usually simple mixtures of sugar and tapioca or cornflour, often covered in condensed milk. Also popular are small and intensely sweet portions of dried and concentrated fruits, such as *caju* (cashew), *jaca* (jackfruit), *goiaba* (guava), and banana, usually consumed together with a small, very sweet cup of coffee.

Fish & Seafood

The long Atlantic coastline from Bahia to Maranhão yields a wealth of fish, shellfish, and crustaceans. Everywhere on the coast, the *guaiamu*, a small, blue-shelled crab with tasty meat, is usually steamed and served up as an appetizer. Larger, soft-shelled crabs are also popular, served steamed and eaten whole, including the shell. Another crustacean

is the *cavaquinha*, a small lobster known for its sweet and tender meat, but the full-size south Atlantic lobster is also found to the north, around Ceará. Large and succulent shrimp are another regular menu item. However, the tastiest northeastern shrimp, the *pitu*, is a freshwater variety. Spicy *pitu moqueca* is among the best featured on any menu.

Grated manioc root ready to be processed into tapioca

ON THE MENU

Baião de dois Made with rice, beans, cheese, and garlic, this dish is often served with sun- or air-dried meat.

Caldo de sururu A rich broth made from tiny clams with coconut milk, *dendê* oil, coriander, and spices.

Carne de sol Goat meat or beef is sun-dried to seal in moisture. It may be served grilled or sautéed.

Casquinha de siri A savory appetizer of shredded crab-meat flavored with coriander, coconut milk, and spices.

Tapioca Small pancakes made with tapioca, served stuffed with sweet or savory fillings.

Xinxim de galinha Chicken sautéed in *dendê* oil with ginger, dried shrimp, and cashew nuts. Served with white rice and manioc flour.

Moqueca is a rich fish dish made with coconut milk, *dendê* oil, cayenne pepper, and coriander (cilantro).

Ensopado is a seafood and coconut milk stew made without *dendê* oil, making it lighter in flavor.

Cocada is a sweet made with sugar and coconut. The darker variety is sweetened with dried sugar-cane juice.

BAHIA

The largest state in the Northeast, Bahia is known for its endless stretches of stunning beach along the Atlantic coast. The idyllic white-sand coast is dotted with laid-back resorts along its length. Beyond the gorgeous beaches and plains, where most of Bahia's population lives today, lies the *sertão*, an arid semi-desert partially covered in *caatinga*, a dry scrub forrest rich in plant and bird life.

When the Portuguese first arrived in Bahia in 1500, the entire 621-mile (1,000-km) coastline was covered in a swathe of lush green Atlantic rainforest. Today, only a few pockets of the rainforest remain along the coast in isolated patches. Inland from the coast, the Portuguese successfully established the cultivation of sugar cane, and later cotton and cocoa in the Recôncavo, a narrow, flat, well-watered plain, which they called the *agreste*.

Bahia played a key role in the history of Brazil. Salvador, its capital, was founded in 1549, and served for over two centuries as the administrative and political center of colonial Brazil. The legacy of that period is on display in Salvador's colonial core, Pelourinho, a jewel of colonial Baroque churches, cathedrals, and palaces.

Bahia was also the key point of entry for the thousands of slaves brought to Brazil from ports in Africa. The legacy of that transatlantic trade can be seen in Bahia's cultural diversity. The state has Brazil's highest percentage of Afro-Brazilian residents. Bahia's percussion-driven music, the fast fight-dance known as *capoeira*, and the spiritualist Yoruban Candomblé religion all have their roots in Africa.

In addition to these legacies, visitors to Bahia can experience one of Brazil's longest and most beautiful coastlines. Fine beach resorts such as Praia do Forte and Costa do Sauípe lie to the north of Salvador. To the capital's south, there are small villages such as Morro de São Paulo and Itacaré. Inland, Bahia provides unique hiking amid the mesas and valleys of the Chapada Diamantina.

A view of the Parque Nacional Marinho dos Abrolhos, comprising an archipelago of five islands

◀ The bright colors of Pelourinho's Old Town

Exploring Bahia

Living up to its official motto, *Sorria, você está na Bahia* (Smile, you're in Bahia), Bahia offers a diverse range of sights. The extensive coastline varies from fine Linha Verde resorts to sleepy villages with stunning unspoilt beaches such as Trancoso. Salvador and the historic towns of the Recôncavo provide fascinating glimpses into Brazil's history. The Chapada Diamantina is a highland region that resembles the mesas of Arizona and New Mexico in Southwest USA. Lençóis, founded during the area's 19th-century gold and diamond rush, boasts caverns, waterfalls, and some of Brazil's best hiking.

Sights at a Glance

Towns & Cities

1 *Salvador pp188–99*
3 Santo Amaro
4 Cachoeira
5 São Félix
8 Itacaré
9 Ilhéus
10 Porto Seguro
11 Trancoso
13 Lençóis
15 Canudos

National Parks

12 Parque Nacional Marinho de Abrolhos
14 *Parque Nacional de Chapada Diamantina pp208–9*

Areas of Natural Beauty

2 Ilha de Itaparica
6 Morro de São Paulo
7 Península de Maraú

Beaches & Resorts

16 *Linha Verde p211*

0 kilometers   100
0 miles   100

A white-sand beach resort near Itacaré, with palm trees lining the shore

For hotels and restaurants in this region see pp374–5 and pp391–2

Key

▬▬ Highway
▬▬ Major road
▬▬ Minor road
--▬- Railroad
▬▬ State border
△ Peak

Key

Area illustrated

A Baiana under Mario Cravo's towering
A Cruz Caida

Getting Around

Bahia is large, and the roads are mostly precarious.
However, the Linha Verde (BA-099), which runs north
along the coast from Salvador to the border with
Sergipe, provides easy, quick access to the beach
towns. South from Salvador, the BR-101 runs parallel
to the coast, about 37 miles (60 km) inland. Access
to beach towns on the southern coast is via
secondary roads. The best way to get around
is to fly to one of the major destinations, such as
Salvador, Ilhéus, or Porto Seguro, and proceed by
bus to explore the surrounding regions. The main
destination inland, the Chapada Diamantina, is a
drive from Salvador on the BR-324, BR-116, and
BR-242 highways. Lençóis in the Chapada
Diamantina can be reached by road and plane.

For keys to symbols *see back flap*

❶ Salvador

Founded by the Portuguese in 1549 on the protective shores of the Baía de Todos os Santos (Bay of All Saints), Salvador is Brazil's fourth-largest city, after São Paulo, Rio de Janeiro, and Belo Horizonte. Modern Salvador offers a fascinating blend of old and new. In the colonial heart, Pelourinho, the cobblestoned streets are lined with the restored 17th- and 18th-century palaces and Baroque churches. The city's recent growth has been eastwards along the beaches that face the Atlantic. The city's vibrant community of musicians draws from the region's African and Portuguese heritage, blending these into a unique Bahian sound.

Azulejos in the cloisters of Igreja e Convento de São Francisco

Imposing buildings in Pelourinho, the heart of Salvador

Sights at a Glance

Historic Buildings, Streets, Towns & Neighborhoods
① Pelourinho pp190–91
② Fundação Casa de Jorge Amado
⑦ Praça da Sé
⑧ Palácio Rio Branco
⑨ Elevador Lacerda
⑩ Mercado Modelo
⑮ Forte de Santo Antônio

Churches, Cathedrals & Monasteries
⑤ Catedral Basílica
⑥ Igreja e Convento de São Francisco pp194–5
⑯ Nosso Senhor do Bonfim

Museums
③ Museu Tempostal
④ Museu Afro-Brasileiro
⑪ Museu de Arte Sacra
⑫ Solar do Unhão
⑬ Museu de Arte da Bahia
⑭ Museu Rodin-Bahia

For hotels and restaurants in this region see p375 and p391

RUA DA POLÔNIA
RUA COND
RUA DANTAS
RUA UNIDOS
RUA MIGUEL CALMON
SARAIVA
RUA F. GONÇALVES
R DA ARGENTINA
RUA CONS.
RUA CONS.
RUA OURIVES
AVENIDA DA FRANÇA
AVENIDA ESTADOS UNIDOS
RUA PINTO MARTINS
RUA ALGIBERES
AVENIDA
RUA MIGUEL CALMON
RUA PORTUGAL
CIDADE BAIXA
R FRED. REBELO
RUA SANTOS DUMONT
RUA LOPES CARDOSO
LADEIRA DA MONT
Terminal da França
RUA MIGUEL CALMON
R VISC. DO ROSARIO
PRAÇA DA BELGICA
⑩
Terminal Marítimo Turístico
PRAÇA DO MERCADO
⑨
Baía de Todos os Santos
LADEIRA DA PREGUIÇA
LAD DA CONCEIÇÃO
CIDAD ALTA
AVENIDA DAS NAUS
AVENIDA DE CONTORNO
AVENIDA DE CONTORNO
AD PAU DA BANDEIR
PRAÇA CASTR ALVE

Getting Around

Most of the attractions in Salvador are concentrated in Cidade Alta (Upper City), linked to the Cidade Baixa (Lower City) by a funicular railway and the Carlos Lacerda elevator. The historic neighborhood of Pelourinho is located downtown, on top of a bluff overlooking the harbor. The main sights outside Pelourinho are within walking distance of the bustling waterfront. Bus services easily connect to every part of the city. Travelers coming from the south can take BR-101 around the Baía de Todos os Santos and connect to the BR-324. Those arriving from the north can follow the BR-009, called the Linha Verde.

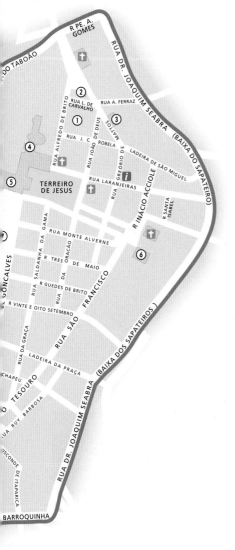

VISITORS' CHECKLIST

Practical Information

2,900,000. Corner of Rua João & Laranjeiras, Pelourinho, (71) 3321-2133.
daily market at Mercado Modelo, Praça Cayru, (71) 3241 2893. Lavagem do Bonfim (Jan), Carnaval (Feb/Mar).
bahiatursa.ba.gov.br

Transport

22 miles (35 km) from city center. Av Antônio Carlos Magalhães 4362, Pernambués, (71) 3616 8357/8358.
Av Oscar Pontes 1051, (71) 3254 1020.

0 meters	200
0 yards	200

Greater Salvador

Bonfim
São Caetano
Terminal da Estação Marítima
Quintas

0 km	1
0 miles	1

Barris
Rio Vermelho
Pituba
Barra
Ondina
Amaralina
ATLANTIC OCEAN

Key

Area of the main map
Highway
Major road
Minor road
Railroad

For keys to symbols *see back flap*

① Street-by-Street: Pelourinho

The crown jewel of Salvador is the restored historic center, Pelourinho, which means whipping post. This originally described only the small triangular plaza in the heart of the city where slaves were publicly flogged. Located on a high bluff overlooking the commercial city below, Pelourinho was built by the Portuguese in the boom years of the 18th and 19th centuries as a residential and administrative center. Abandoned for a greater part of the 20th century, Pelourinho was designated a UNESCO World Heritage Site in 1985. Today, visitors can explore its magnificent colonial houses, Baroque churches, and museums.

④ ★ **Museu Afro-Brasileiro**
The large wood carvings of the Candomblé deities by renowned artist Carybé are the highlights of this museum of Afro-Brazilian culture.

⑤ **Catedral Basílica**
Built in 1657, the renovated cathedral has a cedar-wood altar, and two smaller side altars, both covered in thin layers of gold

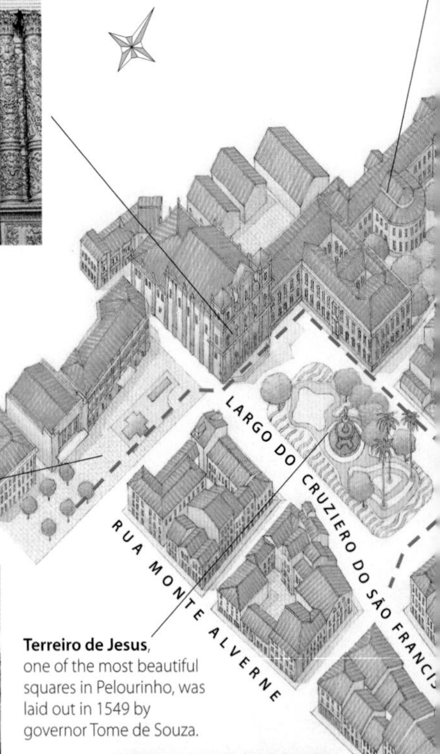

⑦ **Praça da Sé** offers views across the Baía de Todos os Santos

LARGO DO CRUZIERO DO SÃO FRANCI

RUA MONTE ALVERNE

Terreiro de Jesus, one of the most beautiful squares in Pelourinho, was laid out in 1549 by governor Tome de Souza.

Pastel-hued buildings along the slope of Pelourinho

Key

 Suggested route

⑥ ★ **Igreja e Convento de São Francisco**
A silver chandelier weighing 176 lb (80 kg) hangs over the ornate carvings of this richly embellished church

Locator Map
See Salvador map pp188–9

**Igreja Nossa Senhora
do Rosário dos Pretos**
Built by slaves in the
18th century, the church
remains the center of
Afro-Brazilian traditions
in Pelourinho.

VISITORS' CHECKLIST

Practical Information
Bahia. 🛈 Rua Laranjeiras 12, (71)
3321 2133. **Open** 8:30am–11pm
daily. 🎭 Terça da Benção (every
Tue). Igreja Nossa Senhora do
Rosário dos Pretos: Praça José de
Alencar s/n. **Open** 8am–5pm
daily (Sat & Sun: to noon). 🕆
6pm Tue, 10am Sun. Igreja da
Ordem Terceira de São Francisco:
Rua Inácio Accioli. **Tel** (71) 3321
6968. **Open** 8:30am–5pm daily.
🕆 8:30am Wed & Sun. 🎭

Transport
🚌 Barra from Praça da Sé.

② ★ **Fundação Casa de Jorge Amado**
The lovely café inside Foundation House, which is
dedicated to the life of one of Brazil's most famous
authors, is decorated with hundreds of book jackets
from Amado's novels published around the world.

0 meters	100
0 yards	100

**Museu Abelardo Rodrigues
Solar do Ferrão**
One of Brazil's largest private
collections of sacred art is
housed here.

**Igreja da Ordem Terceira
de São Francisco**
The fine 18th-century
sandstone façade of
this church was
rediscovered only in the
1930s. Craftsmen chipped
away at plaster for nine
years to reveal this
marvelous building.

② Fundação Casa de Jorge Amado

Largo do Pelourinho s/n. **Tel** (71) 3321 0070. **Open** 10am–6pm Mon–Fri, 10am–4pm Sat. **W** jorgeamado. org.br

Although Brazilian author Jorge Amado (1912–2001) never lived in Pelourinho, many of his beloved novels were set in this neighborhood *(see p204)*. Opened in 1987, the Casa de Jorge Amado is a small museum housed in a pretty blue colonial building located at the top end of Largo do Pelourinho. It is one of the main monuments dedicated to Bahia's most famous author. Its four floors comprise the entire archive of his work and include a research center.

The collection on display consists mostly of covers of his books and personal belongings that tell the story of his life. A mural on the ground floor shows the languages into which his works have been translated – over 49 in total.

Covers of Amado's books exhibited at Fundação Casa de Jorge Amado

③ Museu Tempostal

Rua Gregorio de Matos 33, Pelourinho. **Tel** (71) 3117 6383. **Open** noon–6pm Tue–Fri, noon–5pm Sat & Sun.

Housed in a beautiful colonial building in the heart of Pelourinho, this museum displays only a fraction of founder Antônio Marcelino's collection of 30,000 postcards and photographs. Most date from the 19th and 20th centuries. Antique postcards comprising the main display tell the history of Salvador as it

Antique postcard displayed at the Museu Tempostal

has developed and grown. Some cards are enlarged to give visitors a better view of the photographic details. A smaller exhibit of *belle époque* postcards showcases some elaborate samples of postcard "art," some adorned with embroidery, others painted like aquarelles.

④ Museu Afro-Brasileiro

Praça XV de Novembro, Terreiro de Jesus s/n. **Tel** (71) 3283 5540. **Open** 9am–5pm Mon–Fri.

This small museum in the former Faculty of Medicine building houses a collection of photographs, artwork, and artifacts all related to the African diaspora in Brazil. The main exhibit displays objects and crafts from the original African cultures of regions such as Angola and Nigeria where Brazil-bound slaves were captured. The highlight of the collection is the 27 life-sized wood carvings of the *orixás* *(see p181)* by Bahian artist Carybé (1911–97), depicting their weapons and regalia, together with the animals or domain over which they are thought to rule. Yemanjá, Goddess of the Sea, is shown with a fish and seashells and the mirrors and trinkets offered to her by supplicants; the warrior Ogun is shown with his sword and armor.

Yansã, Candomblé Goddess of Tempests, at Museu Afro-Brasileiro

⑤ Catedral Basílica

Praça XV de Novembro, Terreiro de Jesus s/n. **Tel** (71) 3321 4573. **Open** 9am–5pm Mon–Sat, 1–5pm Sun. 11th–noon Sun; Baroque concert held every Sun at 11am.

Salvador's main cathedral, built between 1657 and 1672, is considered to be one of the richest examples of Portuguese Baroque architecture. The cathedral's façade is made of Portuguese *lioz*, a type of limestone. The interior walls and tall pillars are also covered with the pale-colored stone, giving the church a bright and spacious feel.

The vaulted ceiling of the main nave is made from wood. The decorations are carved in relief and stand out from the ceiling with an almost three-dimensional effect. The main altar and two smaller side altars are also carved out of wood and covered in gold leaf.

Dedicated to St. Francis, the altar contains a silver-plated statue of Nossa Senhora das Maravilhas (Our Lady of Miracles), which is said to have inspired Father Antônio Vieira, a 17th-century Jesuit priest who fought against the enslavement of indigenous people. His fiery, anti-slavery sermons did not sit well with the Inquisition, who subsequently ordered his arrest. The former Jesuit library now holds a small museum of religious art. The collection includes silver and gold religious artifacts such as chalices and candle-holders. The most modern piece in the cathedral is the powerful German organ with more than 500 pipes, 18 registers, and two keyboards.

Altar of Catedral Basílica, the main cathedral of Salvador

⑥ Igreja e Convento de São Francisco

See pp194–5.

⑦ Praça da Sé

Pelourinho's Praça da Sé blends the modern with the historic. The square is a transition point between the Terreiro de Jesus and the Praça Tomé de Sousa. Extensive renovations have added fountains and benches,

so people can linger and enjoy the *capoeira* presentations or other cultural events often held in the square.

There is a lookout point, the Belvedere, on the north side of the square which provides a beautiful view of the Lower City and the Baía de Todos os Santos (Bay of All Saints).

⑧ Palácio Rio Branco

Praça Tomé de Sousa s/n. **Tel** (71) 3116 6928. **Open** 10am–6pm Tue–Fri, 9am–1pm Sat & Sun.

The original Palácio Rio Branco has nothing in common with the building that currently goes by that name. The first palace was built on this site in 1549 to house Bahia's first governor, Tomé de Sousa. The Portuguese queen and later the prince regent resided in this palace temporarily in 1808, when the entire Portuguese court relocated to Rio de Janeiro in order to escape Napoleon's invasion of Portugal *(see p56)*. The building survived until 1900, when the whole structure was leveled and then rebuilt from scratch in Renaissance style.

A fire in 1912 forced another major overhaul by the Italian architect Júlio Conti, giving the building the eclectic look it still has today. Used as an official government building until 1979,

the Palácio Rio Branco was rededicated in 1986 as a cultural foundation, the Centro Memoria da Bahia. The former reception hall on the ground floor now tells the history of Bahia's 40 governors through paintings, historic documents, and their personal belongings.

The fine interior is a blend of Rococo plasterwork and frescoes. Of particular note are the big dome and the magnificent views from the belvedere in the wing looking onto the sea, as well as the iron and crystal stairway and a sculpture representing Tomé de Souza.

Art Deco Elevador Lacerda with market stalls below

⑨ Elevador Lacerda

Praça Tomé de Sousa s/n (Upper City); Praça Visconde Cairu (Lower City). **Open** 6am–11pm. ♿

Built by merchant Antônio Francisco de Lacerda in 1873 from the original Jesuit-installed manual pulley, the famous Elevador Lacerda connects Salvador's Upper and Lower cities.

The Elevador Lacerda is a popular site in Salvador, used by more than 30,000 people daily. The elevator's current Art Deco look dates from a 1930s restoration. Four elevators make the 236-ft (72-m) trip up vertical shafts in just 30 seconds, where the view across the bay on a clear day is simply stunning.

Preparations for a cultural show outside Palácio Rio Branco

⑥ Igreja e Convento de São Francisco

The complex of the Church and Convent of St. Francis, which was constructed between 1708 and 1750, is one of Brazil's most impressive Baroque monuments. The convent's church stands out for its rich and opulent interior. The inner walls and the ceiling are largely covered in gold leaf. The main altar and the large side altars are magnificently carved out of wood and in typical Baroque style, ornately decorated with angels, birds, mermaids, fruits, and leaves. An enormous silver chandelier hangs above intricate wooden carvings, and hand-painted blue-and-white Portuguese tiles.

★ Franciscan Shield
Featuring the crossed forearms of Jesus and St. Francis, the shield represents the bond between the two.

São Pedro de Alcântara
The altar of São Pedro de Alcântara, carved by Brazilian artist Manuel Inácio da Costa, is a particularly fine example of Brazilian Baroque.

Façade
The church façade dominates the Largo de São Francisco with imposing twin bell towers.

KEY

① **Doors and windows** in bright tones adorn the outer walls of the church.

② **Detailing** of pure gold leaf decorates the church interior.

Oil Painting of St. Francis
The oil painting depicting an event in the life of St. Francis in the church entryway is one of the classic examples of Brazilian Baroque Illusionism.

★ Main Altar
A statue of Jesus on the cross with St. Francis by his side graces the main altar. The blue-and-white tiles behind the main altar tell the life story of the saint. The gold-and-white motif is offset by dark jacaranda wood hand railings.

Cloisters
These secluded interior arcades are where the monks of St. Francis would gather for prayer or quiet contemplation.

Black Saint, Saint Benedict
Two of the side altars are dedicated to black saints such as Santa Efigênia, an Ethiopian princess, and São Bento, the son of African slaves.

★ Azulejos
Brought over from Portugal in 1743, the decorative tiles are based on the etchings by Flemish painter Otto van Veen in his book of moral emblems.

Igreja Terceira Ordem de São Francisco

The ornately carved and detailed sandstone façade of the church of the Third Order of St. Francis next door is the only one of its kind in Brazil. The façade remained hidden for many years behind a layer of plaster, only to be uncovered accidentally when wiring was being installed in the 1930s. The church also has a museum and a room of Franciscan tombs.

Soapstone exterior of the church

Pretty lace hammocks displayed in the stalls outside the Mercado Modelo

⑩ Mercado Modelo

Praça Visconde de Cairu, Comércio, Cidade Baixa. **Tel** (71) 3241 2893. **Open** 9am–7pm Mon–Sat, 9am–2pm Sun.

The Mercado Modelo was built in 1861 as a customs building. The square behind the market, now used by *capoeiristas* (*see p203*), was where boats would dock to unload their merchandise for inspection. The building was transformed into an indoor craft market in 1971, and renovated after a major fire in 1984. Nowadays, the Mercado's two floors house 259 stalls that offer a variety of northeastern arts and crafts. Popular items include naive art paintings of Pelourinho, *berimbaus* (a stringed instrument), embroidered lace tablecloths, hammocks, colorful hats, spices, and sweets.

⑪ Museu de Arte Sacra

Rua do Sodré 276. Cidade Alta. **Tel** (71) 3283 5600. **Open** 11:30am–5:30pm Mon–Fri.

One of Brazil's best collections of religious art can be found in this museum, which is housed in a former Carmelite convent. The serene and beautiful structure was built between 1667 and 1697, and serves as the perfect backdrop for the varied exhibits, which include statues, icons, paintings, *oratorios* (portable altars), and numerous finely wrought silver crosses, candlesticks, chalices, censors, and other artifacts from the 16th to 19th centuries.

The Museu de Arte Sacra, housed in a 17th-century convent

⑫ Solar do Unhão

Av do Contorno s/n. **Tel** (71) 3117 6132. Museu de Arte Moderna: **Open** 1–7pm Tue–Fri, 2–7pm Sat & Sun. **Tel** (71) 3117 6132.

A renovated colonial sugar mill, the Solar do Unhão beautifully blends the old and the new. The original design is typical of the 17th century – a chapel, a big house with slave quarters on the lower floor, and a large mill where cane was transformed into sugar.

During the sugar boom of the 18th century, the owners added a courtyard fountain and a full-size church, Nossa Senhora da Coneição. After the sugar trade collapsed in the 19th century, the Solar was used variously as a factory, a warehouse, and naval barracks. Finally, in the 1940s it was designated a National Historic Monument and chosen as the site for the **Museu de Arte Moderna**. A series of renovations restored the buildings to their former glory, while upgrading the facilities to include eight exhibit rooms, a theater, and a library.

The complex also houses an excellent restaurant, besides displaying paintings, etchings, and sculptures by some of Brazil's best-known modern artists. In the evenings, it hosts a presentation of traditional Bahian dance and folklore, held in the former slave quarters.

Exterior of the Solar do Unhão, once a colonial sugar mill

For hotels and restaurants in this region see p375 and p391

⑬ Museu de Arte da Bahia

Av 7 de Setembro 2340, Vitória.
Tel (71) 3117 6903. **Open** 2–7pm Tue–Sun.

The Museu de Arte da Bahia offers a glimpse of the opulent lifestyle of Salvador's colonial elite. The collection includes paintings, *azulejos*, furniture, silverware, glass, china, and crystal used by the local ruling families during the 18th, 19th, and early 20th centuries.

The south wing holds landscape paintings by such artists as José Joaquim da Rocha.

⑭ Museu Rodin-Bahia

Rua Graca 284. **Tel** (71) 3117 6910. **Open** 1–7pm Tue–Fri, 2–7pm Sat & Sun.

This small museum, in a 19th-century mansion near Barra, holds four original Rodin sculptures and 62 models made by Rodin prior to construction of the final pieces. Among them are *The Kiss* and *The Thinker*.

The Forte de Santo Antônio, topped by the lighthouse

⑮ Forte de Santo Antônio

Praça Almirante Tamandaré, Largo do Farol s/n, Barra. **Tel** (71) 3264 3296. **Open** 8:30am–7pm Tue–Sun.

One of Salvador's best-known landmarks, the Forte Santo Antônio was erected in 1535. The fort was strengthened in the early 17th century, in response to Dutch attacks on the coast, and upgraded to its present star shape at the beginning of the 18th century. A lighthouse atop the fort was originally built in 1698, and is still used by boats navigating the entrance to the bay.

Inside the fort, the Museu Hidrográfico (Museum of Hydrography) shows historic navigation instruments and a variety of charts. There is also a notable collection of coins and China from a Portuguese galleon that foundered in 1668, off Rio Vermelho beach.

The fort also boasts a café with an outdoor terrace offering sweeping views of Salvador's skyline.

Carnaval in Salvador

Salvador's signature event, the Carnaval, is celebrated during February or March. The centerpiece is the *trio elétrico*, a giant flatbed truck carrying a massive array of speakers, topped by a rectangular stage. The tradition was started in the 1950s with Dodó and Osmar, two local musicians who took their music to the street on top of a 1929 Ford. Running out from behind the *trio elétrico* truck, a large roped-off area serves as a movable dance floor. Access to this area is restricted to those in an *abadá*, or uniform-style tank top. Revelers outside the roped-off area are called *pipoca*, or popcorn, as they pop up everywhere.

Blocos (neighborhood groups) parade along one of three routes – Pelourinho, mostly for smaller and more traditional groups; Campo Grande, which runs through the narrow streets of downtown Salvador; and Ondina, which goes through the beachside neighborhoods of Barra and Ondina. Performers at the Carnaval include major Brazilian artists such as Daniela Mercury, Caetano Veloso, Gilberto Gil, Carlinhos Brown, and popular groups such as Olodum, Ara Ketu, and Chiclete com Banana. In addition to these name-brand performers, there are Afro-Brazilian *blocos* such as Ilê Aye, which only allows people of black heritage in their parade. The queen of the Carnaval is Ivete Sangalo, a noted exponent of *axé*, Bahia's unique rhythm that combines pop with *samba* and Afro-Brazilian beats.

The grand finale occurs in the wee hours of Ash Wednesday. All the various *blocos* make their way to Praça Castro Alves for the Encontro dos Trios, a last late-night jam that marks the closure of the Carnaval.

Costumed dancers at the Salvador Carnaval

Exquisite Portuguese *azulejo* (tile work) at Nosso Senhor do Bonfim

⑯ Nosso Senhor do Bonfim

Largo do Bonfim s/n. **Tel** (71) 3316 2196. **Open** 7am–6pm daily (Mon: from 9am; Fri & Sun: from 6am).
✚ 7am, 8am, 5pm Tue–Sun.

Nosso Senhor do Bonfim (Our Lord of Good Success) stands atop a small hill on the Bonfim Peninsula, a strip of land jutting out into the Baía de Todos os Santos about 6 miles (10 km) north of Pelourinho. The church was built between 1746 and 1754 by Captain Rodrigues de Faria in fulfilment of a pledge he made in the midst of a fierce Atlantic storm. While the hilltop setting is picturesque, what sets the church apart is not its architecture but the role it plays in Bahia's Afro-Brazilian religion. The church is dedicated to God the Father, but it also honors Oxalá, the supreme deity in the Candomblé religion (*see p181*). On Fridays, worshippers dress in white and dedicate their prayers to Oxalá. On other days, in a small chapel just to the right of the main altar, one can visit the Sala dos Milagres (Chamber of Miracles). Believers come here to offer items made of wax, wood, or even gold. The item represents a miracle that has been bestowed upon them. The room is packed with replicas of hearts, lungs, livers, and breasts, as well as babies, houses, and even cars.

Outside, visitors are besieged with offers of *fitas*, little colored ribbons purchased as a good luck charm. The ribbon is meant to be tied around the wrist with three knots, and a wish is made for each knot. The ribbon is then worn until it falls off in order for the wishes to be granted.

The impressive 16th-century **Forte de São Felipe** is located

Salvador's Atlantic Coast

The tip of Porto da Barra is the beginning of a string of ocean beaches. The best beaches for swimming and sunbathing are close to the southern edge of the city. The best beach close to the city center is Porto do Barra. Farther out, Amaralina's *acarajé (see p183)* kiosks are popular on weekends. Itapoã is known for its calm waters and reefs that form natural pools at low tide.

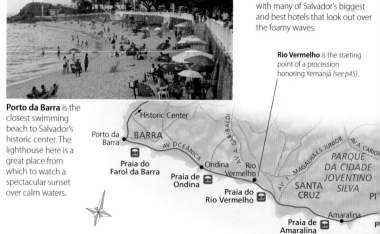

Ondina's beautiful beach is lined with many of Salvador's biggest and best hotels that look out over the foamy waves.

Rio Vermelho is the starting point of a procession honoring Yemanjá (*see p45*).

Porto da Barra is the closest swimming beach to Salvador's historic center. The lighthouse here is a great place from which to watch a spectacular sunset over calm waters.

close to the church, in the neighborhood of Boa Viagem. Just below the fort is the popular beach, **Praia de Boa Viagem**, which is usually bustling with locals and lined with busy stalls selling a variety of trinkets and snacks on weekends.

⊞ Forte de São Felipe
Rua Rita Durão s/n, Monte Serrat, Boa Viagem. **Tel** (71) 3313 7339.
Open 8am–noon daily.

Colorful ribbons on the railing outside Nosso Senhor do Bonfim

A group of colorfully dressed women during Lavagem do Bonfim

Lavagem do Bonfim

Salvador is home to some of the largest celebrations of the Candomblé religion. One event that occurs each year at the Nosso Senhor do Bonfim is the Lavagem do Bonfim (Washing Ceremony), which takes place on the third Thursday of January. A procession of thousands of devotees makes its way from Salvador city center to the church. Once the procession has reached the church, women in traditional white lace dresses wash the church steps with perfumed water in honor of Oxalá. The tradition is said to stem from the days when the slaves were not allowed inside the church and had to worship outside. The Catholic church does not entirely approve of the ceremony, and keeps its doors shut throughout the festival.

Amaralina, subject to large waves and strong winds, is an excellent beach for surfing and boardsailing. Baianas dressed in traditional garb sell *acarajé* at the numerous kiosks lining the shore.

0 km 1
0 miles 1

VISITORS' CHECKLIST

Practical Information
Bahia. 🛈 on the corner of Rua João de Deus & Laranjeiras, Pelourinho.
Tel (71) 3321 2133.
W bahiaturas.ba.gov.br
🎭 Festa de Yemanjá (Feb).

Transport
🚌 Barra from Praça da Sé.

PARQUE METROPOLITANO DE PITUAÇU

PITUAÇU

Itapuã

AV. DORIVAL CAYMMI

AV. PINTO DE AGUIAR

AVENIDA OTAVIO MANGABEIRA

BOCA DO RIO

Praia de Pituaçu

Praia de Piatã

Praia de Jaguaribe

Praia de Itapuã

ARMAÇÃO

M. NATU

Praia do Corsário

ATLANTIC OCEAN

Praia Boca do Rio

Jardim de Alá

Praia Jardim de Alá

Jardim de Alá, a seaside park with grassy slopes descending to the sea, has a coconut tree plantation.

Itapuã features turquoise waters and reefs teeming with marine life. Poet and lyricist Vinícius de Moraes *(see p35)* immortalized the place in a popular song.

Ilha de Itaparica, one of the tropical islands in the Baía de Todos os Santos

❷ Ilha de Itaparica

📍 18,000. 🚢 from Salvador. 🏠 Zimbo Tropical, (71) 3638 1148.

The largest island in the Baía de Todos os Santos (Bay of All Saints), with summerhouses lining its shore, Itaparica is a popular weekend refuge for the residents of Salvador.

Located on the northern tip of the island, the main city is guarded by the Forte de São Lourenço, which was built by the Dutch in 1711. Among the island's main attractions are some historic buildings, including the 1622 Nossa Senhora da Piedade (Chapel of Our Lady of Piety) and the 1610 Igreja de São Lourenço.

The island is connected to the mainland by a bridge at its narrow southern tip. The **Praia da Penha**, 10 miles (6 km) south, is a lovely beach with views of Salvador. The region's biggest resort, **Club Med**, lies on the Praia da Conceição, 12 miles (19 km) south of town.

❸ Santo Amaro

📍 60,000. 🚌 from Salvador. 🎭 Bembé do Mercado (May 13–18).

The laid-back town of Santo Amaro lies in the Recôncavo, the fertile zone at the top end of the Baía de Todos os Santos, which has formed the backbone of Salvador's colonial economy for almost 300 years. The region's high humidity, abundant rainfall, and rich soils were conducive to growing

tobacco and, more significantly, sugar cane. Until the crash of the sugar economy in the 19th century, Santo Amaro remained the focus of Recôncavo's sugar industry. Dilapidated mansions of the erstwhile sugar barons can still be seen along the old streets. Nowadays, this unpretentious town is known for its paper industry. It is also famous as the hometown of Caetano Veloso and Maria Bethânia, two of Brazil's most popular singers.

Many of the slaves, who were brought from Africa to work on plantations, remained in the Recôncavo after slavery was abolished in 1888. The region still has a very high percentage of Afro-Brazilian residents, and Santo Amaro plays a key role in preserving their distinct traditions. Every year, the city commemorates the abolition of slavery with a five-day festival

Lush hillsides in the Recôncavo, covered with sugar cane

of the Bembé do Mercado. During this time, offerings are made to Yemanjá, Goddess of the Sea, to celebrate freedom of religion. In the main square in front of the town market, local groups put on capoeira performances. Theater performances of pieces, such as Nego Fugido (Runaway Slave), recount the story of slaves fleeing their masters to join quilombos, independent communities set up by runaway slaves.

In an effort to keep folkloric traditions alive, the Afro-Brazilian community also organizes presentations of the lesser-known maculelê sword dance, an African fight-dance, and samba de roda dances performed by women.

❹ Cachoeira

📍 30,000. 🚌 ℹ Praça da Aclamação 4. 🎭 Festa da Boa Morte (mid-Aug, dates vary).

Historically more powerful than the other two main towns in the Recôncavo – Santo Amaro and São Félix – Cachoeira was also the most prominent. Its strategic location, between the Baía de Todos os Santos and the roads leading inland, made it an important crossroads between Salvador and the rest of the state.

The city once had a busy river port on the Paraguaçu. Boats sailed upstream from Salvador to load up with sugar and tobacco produced in the Recôncavo region. The town's

Cobblestoned streets lined with colorful houses in Cachoeira

privileged position as a commercial center is reflected in its imposing colonial architecture. However, with the creation of road access to Salvador, Cachoeira lost its key position and its port gradually faded away.

In the old city center, many of the city's churches and wealthy merchants' houses are still standing, although in a dilapidated condition. The city has, however, begun to renovate and preserve its historic center. As a cultural hub of the Recôncavo region Cachoeira celebrates the Festa da Boa Morte, one of the most important features of the Candomblé religion. Today, the city is as much celebrated for its robust wood-sculpting tradition as for its production of the best tobacco in Brazil.

Coronas cigar box, São Félix

❺ São Félix

🚌 from Cachoeira.

Regarded as the twin of Cachoeira, São Félix lies just across the Rio Paraguaçu, on a hillside overlooking the river. The railway bridge connecting the two towns was commissioned by Dom Pedro II, and built by British engineers in 1895. Cars, trains, and foot traffic all share the rickety railway bridge.

Several times a day, São Félix comes to a standstill as freight trains roll right through the town center.

Larger in size, though not as impressive as Cachoeira, São Félix used to earn a living in its own right as a producer of fine *charutos* (cigars). The heart of this industry was the Dannemann cigar factory, founded in 1873 by German cigar-maker Gerhard Dannemann. Blessed by optimum conditions for growing and processing tobacco, the Dannemann factory quickly became one of the region's finest cigar producers. The region still produces Dannemann cigars, but the original factory has now been converted into a cultural center, known as the **Centro Cultural Dannemann**. A small exhibit of old machinery tells the story of the early factory days. On weekdays, it is possible to watch the factory workers rolling cigars.

🏛 **Centro Cultural Dannemann**
Av Salvador Pinto 29. **Tel** (75) 3438 3716.
Open 8am–noon & 1–5pm Tue–Sat.

Market scene in São Félix, with a vendor selling fruit

Members of the Sisterhood of the Good Death in festive regalia

Festa da Boa Morte

Celebrated in mid August, the Festa da Boa Morte (Festival of the Good Death) is one of the most important events of Candomblé (see p39), a blend of African spirituality and Catholicism. The ceremonies are held by members of the Sisterhood of the Good Death, a religious and self-help organization composed entirely of women of African descent. The festival honors both the *iyás* (female spirits of the dead) and the Assumption of the Virgin Mary. A Catholic mass is followed by a large procession through the historic streets of Cachoeira. The women come dressed in multilayered lace skirts and blouses, white turbans, and traditional accessories in honor of various *orixás* (deities). At the head of the procession, they carry a statue of the Virgin Mary. At the end, the women prepare an all-white meal of rice, fish, potatoes, onions, and other white-colored foods. *Samba de roda*, a dance based on the African circle dances, marks the end of the ceremonies. Women take turns dancing in the circle to the pounding rhythm of the drums. Onlookers may also be called on to dance.

The ruins of Fortaleza do Tapirando in Morro de São Paulo

❻ Morro de São Paulo

🏠 50,000. ✈ from Salvador. ⛴ from Salvador. 🛈 (75) 3652 1104. 🅆 **morrodesaopaulo.com.br**

Although within easy reach of Salvador, the coast immediately south of the state capital does not have many large, developed tourist areas, apart from Morro de São Paulo. Now a picturesque beach destination, Morro de São Paulo, on the northern tip of Ilha da Tinharé, once played a key role in the coastal defences of Bahia. In 1630, Governor General Diego Luiz de Oliveira ordered **Fortaleza do Tapirando** to be strategically built here where it could control the Itaparica channel, one of the main approaches to Salvador. The ruins of the fort have been designated a National Heritage Site. The view of the sunset from the fort's crumbling walls is spectacular, and dolphin sightings are quite common.

Still accessible only by boat or plane, Morro maintains much of its original charm. No cars are allowed in the village. Lined with *pousadas*, boutiques, and restaurants, the "streets" are made of sand, and wheelbarrows and bicycles are the primary means of transportation. In the evenings, the village square transforms into a craft market, the small stands often lit only by candlelight, making for a very cozy atmosphere. Morro's beaches are famous in Brazil for their parties. During high

season, there are parties every night and the beaches are packed. Most nights start around midnight, when **Primeira** beach fills with locals and visitors, who dance *axé* and drink fruity cocktails. As you move away from the village, the beaches get wider and less developed. **Segunda** and **Terceira** beaches feature progressively more scattered *pousadas*. From **Quarta** beach onwards, the coast remains blissfully unspoilt, offering long stretches of white sand backed by waving groves of coconut palms.

Environs

Just south of Morro, **Ilha de Boipeba** offers a quiet, idyllic island getaway, with pristine, deserted beaches. Ponta de Castelhanos is especially known for diving. Travelers can get here via boat from Morro de São Paulo. Visitors coming from Salvador can drive to Valença, then take a boat (see www.ilhaboipeba.org.br).

❼ Peninsula de Maraú

⛴ from Itacaré or Camamu to Barra Grande. 🛈 Barra Grande, (75) 3258 9051. 🅆 **barragrande.net**

The main destination at the northern tip of the Peninsula de Maraú is **Barra Grande**, a delightful, remote fishing village. Beautiful beaches are scattered along the entire length of the peninsula, but it is difficult to get around without a car. Four-wheel drives ferry passengers from *pousadas* to various beaches around the peninsula. Alternatively, the 31-mile (50-km) walk across various palm-fringed beaches along the coastline is spectacular.

Most of the peninsula is covered in native Mata Atlântica rainforest, which has been relatively well preserved. The Baía de Camamu, one of Brazil's largest bays, separates the peninsula from the mainland. The long dirt road heading down the peninsula (often impassable after rains) leads to some of the best beaches facing the open ocean. **Praia Taipús de Fora**, 4 miles (7 km) south of Barra Grande, is considered one of Brazil's most beautiful beaches. At low tide, the coral reefs form a clear, natural pool, perfect for snorkeling and swimming.

There are also a handful of small fishing villages scattered along the coast. Local fishermen offer excursions to **Lagoa Azul** (Blue Lagoon), scenic view points, bay islands, and down the Rio Maraú.

Peninsula de Maraú, overlooking the Baía de Camamu

Capoeira

Bahia, the birthplace of *capoeira*, offers visitors plenty of opportunities to see this dazzling and mesmerizing mixture of dance, gymnastics, and martial arts. *Capoeira* was developed by African slaves within Brazil as a form of self-defense against their brutal slave masters. The music was added as a disguise. Many slaves successfully escaped and formed communities in the interior called *quilombos (see p219)*. Outlawed in 1890 and forced underground, the sport made a slow comeback over the next few decades as white Brazilians began to accept and celebrate the African aspects of Brazil's culture. *Capoeira* was fully rehabilitated in the 1930s, when President Vargas, calling it "the only true Brazilian sport," invited one of the most renowned *capoeiristas* of the day, Mestre Bimba, to perform in the presidential palace. Today, Mestre Bimba's school in Pelourinho is run by his son, Mestre Nenel.

Berimbau, a single-string instrument that produces a metallic droning sound, sets the *capoeira* beat.

African drums are the additional instruments used in *capoeira*.

The *roda*, or the circle in which *capoeira* is always performed, is created by participants who sit or stand and clap to the beat of a single-stringed *berimbau*. The people who form the *roda* will take turns, usually with no predefined order, to go inside the circle and participate.

Capoeira Moves

Capoeiristas exhibit incredible muscle control, strength, and flexibility as they carry out acrobatic moves, while keeping their opponent at bay. The capoeira *moves are carried out at lightning speed, but with a dance-like fluidity, where each move is a combination of skill, balance, and beauty.*

Escorpião, or the scorpion move, is a combination of back flips and cartwheels. Both participants try to create a beautiful performance.

Au malandro starts like a cartwheel, but only one hand goes down while the opposite leg kicks up in the air in a swift, fluid move.

The esquiva (escape), a low ducking move, is a very common one since *capoeiristas* primarily attack with kicks and sweeps.

The beautiful and unspoiled Prainha beach in Itacaré

❽ Itacaré

🏠 24,000. ✈ Ilhéus. 🚌 ℹ Rua João de Souza, Centro, (73) 3251 3922. 🌐 **itacare.com**

The small fishing town of Itacaré is part of Brazil's famous Discovery Coast. Portuguese explorer Pedro Álvares Cabral (*see p52*), who was the first European to officially "discover" Brazil, landed in Porto Seguro, close to Itacaré, in 1500.

Large areas of protected Atlantic rainforest, which were given World Heritage status by UNESCO in 1999, meet the sea along the coast of Itacaré. Relatively isolated, the town is favored by nature lovers. Itacaré is also known for its relaxed lifestyle and typical Afro-Brazilian culture.

The beaches have enormous waves, making it a popular surfing destination. Most are surrounded by lush forest and can only be accessed on foot. **Prainha**, Itacaré's main attraction, is considered to be one of Brazil's most beautiful beaches, and is accessible only by a trail through the rainforest from Ribeira beach, just south of town.

Environs
Known as the **Estrada Parque** (the Park Drive), the road that connects Itacaré to Ilhéus traverses a well-preserved strand of Atlantic rainforest. Care has been taken not to disrupt the ecosystem and to protect animals crossing the highway. In places, nets have been strung from tree to tree to provide safe passage for monkeys crossing the road. The 49-mile (80-km) drive

follows the coastline and allows access to a string of beautiful, secluded beaches, many of which have little or no facilities.

❾ Ilhéus

🏠 220,000. ✈ 🚌 ℹ Setur, (73) 3634 6008. 🌐 **brasilheus.com.br**

When farmers began growing cocoa trees imported from the upper Amazon basin in the early 20th century, Ilhéus, the largest city on Bahia's southern coast, established itself as a major cocoa-growing region. A disaster of epic proportions struck in 1989, when a parasite infected most of the plantations and destroyed the entire crop. The industry has yet to recover, but several of the old plantations have been converted into museums.

Ilhéus is best known as the setting for several novels by Bahia's most beloved author, Jorge Amado. One of his best

books, *Gabriela, Clove and Cinnamon*, takes place in the city's historic core at the height of the 1920s cocoa boom. Today, visitors can stroll along the promenades and see the famous Bar Vesúvio and Bataclã Cabaret that feature in his novel. The author's childhood home has been opened to visitors as the **Casa de Cultura Jorge Amado**.

Among the city's other sights is the 16th-century **Igreja de São Jorge**. There are several fine beaches to the north and south of town and **Cururupe**, near the village of Olivença, is a favorite.

🏛 **Casa de Cultura Jorge Amado**
Rua Jorge Amado 21. **Tel** (73) 3231 7531. **Open** 9am–noon, 2–6pm Mon–Fri, 9am–1pm Sat. 📷

🏛 **Igreja de São Jorge**
Praça Rui Barbosa. **Open** irregular hrs.

Casa de Cultura Jorge Amado, childhood home of the famed author

---

Jorge Amado (1912–2001)

The son of a cocoa plantation owner, Jorge Amado was born near Ilhéus in 1912. In 1931, Amado moved to Rio to study law, but his heart was already given to literature. That very year, he published his first novel, *O País do Carnaval*. He based his 1958 novel, *Gabriela, Clove and Cinnamon*, on the warring cocoa barons of his native Ilhéus, but infused it with a sense of humor that won him acclaim in Brazil and around the world. *Dona Flor and her Two Husbands* (1966), *Tieta do Agreste* (1977), and *Gabriela, Clove and Cinnamon* were later turned into popular and successful films. Armado published 21 novels, which were translated into 49 languages. He died in 2001.

Life-like statue of Jorge Amado, Ilhéus

Main square and the Matriz Nossa Senhora da Pena, Porto Seguro

⑩ Porto Seguro

🚗 140,000. ✈ 🚌 ℹ Av Portugal, Passarela do Alcool, Centro, (73) 3288 3708. 🌐 **portosegurotur.com**

Porto Seguro (Safe Port) is officially recognized as the site of the first Portuguese landing in 1500, where Pedro Cabral and his fleet arrived and said mass on Brazilian soil. The city's small historic center (Cidade Histórica) has several stately old buildings, including the **Matriz Nossa Senhora da Pena**, built in 1535. Its altar has an image of Saint Francis of Assisi, the first religious statue to be brought to Brazil in 1503. On the same square, the former jail built in 1772 is home to the **Museu de Porto Seguro**, which holds a collection describing the early colonization of the region.

Today, Porto Seguro is best known for its buzzing nightlife, beach parties, music festivals, and the notorious "Passarela do Alcool" (alcohol boardwalk), the nickname for the city's main street where vendors set up kiosks selling fresh fruit cocktails with a heavy alcoholic kick. Visitors looking for a more tranquil holiday experience usually head farther south to the lovely neighboring villages of Arraial d'Ajuda and Trancoso.

South of town are a few beaches that mainly attract backpackers. Less developed, but serene, these beaches can be accessed from Porto Seguro airport, which receives daily flights from all over Brazil. Road access can often be challenging, as distances are long and the coastal highways are in a state of disrepair.

🏛 **Museu de Porto Seguro**
Praça Pero Campos Tourinho s/n.
Tel (73) 3288 5182.
Open 9am–5pm daily.

⑪ Trancoso

🚐 Porto Seguro, then bus. 🚌
🌐 **trancosobahia.com.br**

Though just a short drive from Porto Seguro, Trancoso has a sense of tranquility that sets it apart from the nearby party town. Set on a high bluff overlooking the ocean, the town center, or *quadrado*, is a long, grassy space, anchored by a small church and framed by houses, many of which have turned their gardens into tasteful little cafés. Trancoso offers sophisticated services focusing on high-end travelers – upscale B&Bs, fine dining, and music. The beaches are backed by red sandstone cliffs, and remain largely secluded and unspoiled.

⑫ Parque Nacional Marinho de Abrolhos

🚐 ℹ Ibama, Praia do Kitongo, Caravelas, (73) 3297 1111.
🌐 **abrolhos.net**

Remote and uninhabited, the archipelago of Abrolhos, discovered by Amerigo Vespucci in 1503, offers excellent opportunities for viewing wildlife. The five islands are located off the coast of southern Bahia. In 1983, the islands, together with 351 sq miles (909 sq km) of surrounding ocean, were declared a National Marine Park, the first such park in Brazil. Known for its rare formations of south Atlantic coral, the park teems with sea turtles, squid, and a rich assortment of fish. A variety of bird species come to feed and lay eggs on the islands, which are otherwise dry and covered in grasslands. The best time for spotting humpback whales is between July and November, when the archipelago becomes a calving ground for them.

Only one of the five islands, Siriba, can actually be visited. Guided tours to the marine park should only be made with an operator accredited by Brazil's environmental agency, IBAMA. Visitors can also book a day or overnight excursion to the islands and surrounding coral reefs from the town of **Caravelas** on the mainland. For snorkeling and diving enthusiasts, underwater visibility is best between January and March.

Birds nesting on Siriba island, Parque Nacional Marinho de Abrolhos

Vacationers and locals relaxing at Praia do Forte, Bahia ▶

A view of the old diamond-mining town of Lençóis

⓭ Lençóis

🏠 9,000. ✈ 16 miles (25 km) E of town. 🚌 ℹ Sectur, (75) 3334 1380. 🎭 Festa de Senhor dos Passos (Jan), Festa de São João (Jun).
🌐 **guialencois.com**

Located in the foothills of the Chapada Diamantina mountains in central Bahia, the town of Lençóis sprang up almost overnight, as diamond fever struck in these interior highlands in the late 19th century. The name of the town, meaning "sheets," derives from the camp that grew up here during the diamond strike. The miners, too poor to afford tents, made do with sheets draped over branches.

Unlike many other mining boomtowns, however, Lençóis has a colonial air, with small Baroque churches, and tiny houses and shops painted in pastel colors. The town's distinguished main square, Praça Horácio de Matos, consists of 19th-century houses, characterized by high, arched windows. Another town landmark, Praça Otaviano Alves, lined with gracious colonial homes, is farther south of the main square.

Lençóis has reinvented itself as the base camp for ecotourists venturing out to explore the caves, waterfalls, and isolated mountaintops of the surrounding highlands. The town's pretty colonial homes now house trekking equipment stores, cafés, and tasteful photo galleries.

⓮ Parque Nacional de Chapada Diamantina

Towering red rock formations, interspersed with lush vegetation, characterize this 587-sq-mile (1,520-sq-km) park in the hinterland of Salvador, established in 1985. Numerous small rivers crisscross the highlands, cascading over waterfalls, carving through canyons, and tumbling down waterslides. Countless trails lead to caves and caverns. These undefined paths are best navigated with a guide.

Rio Santo António
Morro do Pai Inácio 3,675 ft (1,120 m) 🔺 242 *Salvad*
Rio Mucugêzinho
🔺 **Gruta do Lapão**
Rio Lençóis
Lençóis
Cachoeira da Fumaça
Caeté-Açú *Rio Copivora*
Rio C
Ri
SERRA DA GARAPA **Vale do Pa**
Rio Preto
Rio Capãozinho

★ **Morro do Pai Inácio**
The striking mesa is the park's signature mountain formation. The 3,675-ft (1,120-m) plateau offers breathtaking views of the northern half of the park.

Cachoeira da Fumaça, or the Waterfall of Smoke, wears a veil of mist as the water plunges down the 1,150-ft (340-m) precipice.

★ **Vale do Paty**
The multiday hike up this scenic valley offers extraordinary views of the highlands from Morro do Castelo. Other attractions include abandoned miners' settlements and waterfalls with natural swimming pools at Cachoeira dos Funis, as well as the sound of Barbado monkeys that inhabit this vast wilderness.

Rappeling in the Chapada Diamantina
The Chapada's main adventure sport is rappeling down a cliff face or into a cavern. Tour companies in Lençóis offer thrilling rappeling alongside amazing waterfalls.

VISITORS' CHECKLIST

Practical Information
Bahia. 🛈 Fundação Chapada Diamantina, Rua Pe de Ladeira 212, (75) 3334 1305. 🎫 Nas Alturas, (75) 3334 1054. 🆆 **nasalturas.net**; Chapada Adventure, (75) 3334 1054. 🆆 **chapadaadventure.com** 🔺 in Chapada Diamantina (free, no permit required for camping and sleeping in the park's caves; a local guide is recommended).

Transport
✈ 🚌

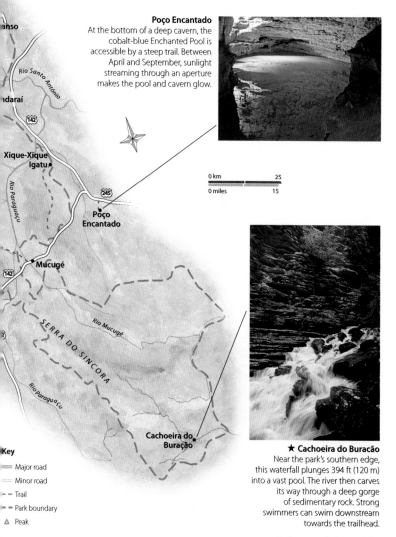

Poço Encantado
At the bottom of a deep cavern, the cobalt-blue Enchanted Pool is accessible by a steep trail. Between April and September, sunlight streaming through an aperture makes the pool and cavern glow.

0 km   25
0 miles   15

★ **Cachoeira do Buracão**
Near the park's southern edge, this waterfall plunges 394 ft (120 m) into a vast pool. The river then carves its way through a deep gorge of sedimentary rock. Strong swimmers can swim downstream towards the trailhead.

Key

━ Major road

┈ Minor road

╌ ╌ Trail

▬ ▬ Park boundary

△ Peak

For keys to symbols *see back flap*

Church and colorful houses in the small town of Canudos

⓯ Canudos

🗺 59,000. 🚌

Traveling through the sleepy town of Canudos, it is hard to imagine that this was once the staging ground for a year-long rebellion in 1897. Led by Antônio Conselheiro, the war wound up costing the lives of more than 20,000 people and almost destroyed the future of the Brazilian Republic.

An eyewitness account at the end of the Canudos War was written by journalist Euclides da Cunha, who was on the scene to cover the events for a São Paulo newspaper. He went on to write a book based on his coverage of the war. Published in 1902, *Os Sertões* (*Rebellion in the Backlands*) is one of the most important works of Brazilian literature. In 1997, the University of Bahia turned the

site of the 19th-century Canudos War into a state park, **Parque Estadual de Canudos**. To access the park, visitors should get permission from the Memorial de Canudos.

The original settlement of Canudos now lies at the bottom of the Lagoa Cocorobó, which flooded the area in 1970. However, many of the original battlefields escaped the deluge and have been made into an open-air museum which is part of the park, just on the outskirts of the town. The principal museum sites include Morro do Conselheiro (Counsellor Hill), Vale da Morte (Valley of Death), the Estrada Sagrada (Holy Road), and the Vale da Degola (Valley of Beheadings). The dry *sertão* landscape is quite striking – vegetation consists of *caatinga* bushes, cacti, bromeliads, *umbu* trees, and *favelas*, a small

thorn-covered shrub very common in the dry interior in Bahia. After the April rains, the landscape briefly turns lush and animals such as deer, hyacinth macaws, and armadillos can be spotted frequently.

In the Canudos region during the war, Republican soldiers were camped in the hills that were covered by *favela* trees. Upon their return to Rio, the soldiers never received the land which they had been promised. They ended up squatting on the hills, naming their new-found community *favela* after the trees in the *sertão*. Hence the name *favela* (*see p89*), now used to refer to the urban ghettos, traces its origins to the Canudos War.

🏛 **Parque Estadual de Canudos**
Tel (75) 3494 2000. 🎟 🗓 tours arranged by Memorial de Canudos.

Statue of Antônio Conselheiro

Antônio Conselheiro

Part Robin Hood, part religious fanatic, Antônio Conselheiro, the leader of Brazil's 1897 Canudos War, was born Antônio Vicente Mendes Maciel in 1830 in Ceará. Conselheiro traveled the dry *sertão* for decades, first as a salesman and legal *conselheiro* (counselor), then as a preacher and reformer, raging against the plight of the peasants. In 1893, Conselheiro, outraged at the newly imposed taxes on an already starving population, settled in the tiny upland town of Canudos and began creating what was, in effect, an independent state. Conselheiro began implementing an early form of socialism, heavily tinged with religious values. The poor of the region flocked to Conselheiro and Canudos quickly grew to a community of more than 8,000 people. With the prestige of the new Republican government at stake, the army sent three large forces against Canudos. All were destroyed. Finally, in November of 1897, the army mounted a full-scale invasion. Conselheiro died during the battle and all the residents of Canudos were slaughtered.

⑯ Linha Verde

The Linha Verde (Green Line) is the 152-mile (252-km) stretch of coast that runs north from Salvador all the way to Mangue Seco on the Sergipe border. It is often referred to as the Estrada do Côco, or Coconut Highway, because of the thick stands of palm trees that line the beaches. This part of the coast offers several popular holiday destinations and well-developed resorts. The most favored destinations are Praia do Forte and Costa do Sauípe. Farther north, the beaches are pristine and beautiful.

VISITORS' CHECKLIST

Practical Information
Bahia. 🅰 Odara, Av ACM s/n, Praia do Forte. **Tel** (71) 3676 1080.
Ⓦ praiadoforte.org.br
Ⓦ odaratours.com.br;
Centrotour, Av ACM s/n, Praia do Forte. **Tel** (71) 3676 1091.
Projeto Tamar: Av ACM s/n, Praia do Forte. **Tel** (71) 3676 1045.
Open 9am–6pm daily. 🅰 🅰
Ⓦ tamar.org.br

Transport
🚌 from Salvador.

Praia Sítio do Conde, a popular beach, is visited by locals on weekends. Small reefs form natural pools at low tide.

Barra do Itariri
In a lovely setting with green palm trees, white sand dunes, and mangroves, Barra do Itariri is an ideal beach destination.

Sapiranga Reserve
This eco-preserve protects some of the last remaining Atlantic rainforest in Brazil.

0 km 15
0 miles 15

Costa do Sauípe
The custom-built village at Costa do Sauípe offers high-end recreation including spas, sailing, and golf.

Key

— Main Road
--- Minor Road

Projeto Tamar
As part of a conservation plan, five turtle species are reared at Praia do Forte.

Praia do Forte
Natural pools at the north end of Praia do Forte provide snorkeling and swimming areas.

Map labels

SERGIPE
Mangue Seco
Praia do Coquiro
Praia Costa Azul
Praia Barra do Itapicuru
Barra do Itapicuru
Praia de Poças
Sítio do Conde
Conde
Praia Sítio do Conde
Barra do Itariri
BAHIA
Praia Baixio
Cardeal da Silva
Baixio
Subaúma
Praia Massarandupió
Porto do Sauípe
Costa do Sauípe
Itanagra
Imbassaí
Açu da Torre
Praia do Forte
Itacimirim
Pajuca
Guarajuba
Praia da Barra do Jacúpe
Mata da São João
Arembepe
Dias d'Avila
Praia do Arembepe
Camaçari
Lauro de Freitas
SALVADOR

ESTRADA DO COCO

SERGIPE, ALAGOAS & PERNAMBUCO

Long stretches of white beach bathed by a warm, blue-green ocean comprise the magnificent coastline of Sergipe, Alagoas, and Pernambuco. In contrast, much of the interior of this region is dry *sertão*, where the landscape is barren and harsh. Despite, or perhaps because of their material poverty, these northeastern states are culturally rich in music and folklore.

The states of Sergipe, Alagoas, and Pernambuco in the Northeast were among the first parts of Brazil to be colonized by Portugal, and for centuries afterward they were the richest region of colonial Brazil. The wealth of the region came from sugar. With slave labor, sugar cane could be cultivated in abundance, and sugar sold in the burgeoning markets of Europe. In 1654, the Portuguese reclaimed Pernambuco after a brief Dutch takeover, but opted to keep the new city, Recife, as the capital instead of Olinda.

Sugar still dominates the economy, but the beaches make this region one of Brazil's hottest tourist destinations. These states have also developed a rich culture and a penchant for lively festivals. Popular musical styles such as *forró* and *frevo* began or culminated in the Northeast.

All three states have pretty, historic towns, stunning coastlines, and picture-perfect beaches. Reefs of stone and coral provide natural habitats for fish, sea turtles, sharks, and other tropical marine life. The island archipelago of Fernando de Noronha, a municipality of Pernambuco, is one of Brazil's prime marine habitats and a preferred destination of scuba divers. The Rio São Francisco, the longest river in Brazil, passes through the beautiful scenery of Sergipe and Alagoas in the last leg of its journey before finally meeting the Atlantic Ocean.

Dois Irmãos (Mount of the Two Brothers), Parque Nacional Marinho de Fernando de Noronha

◀ View from Igreja de São Salvador do Mundo over the rooftops of Olinda

Exploring Sergipe, Alagoas & Pernambuco

Year-round warm weather makes this region a popular sunshine destination. The island archipelago of Fernando de Noronha in Pernambuco is Brazil's top scuba-diving destination, and it also offers a fascinating ecosystem rich in marine life. Recife and Olinda provide a captivating impression of 17th- and 18th-century Brazil, a legacy of Dutch and Portuguese colonization. São Cristóvão and Penedo, located on the border between the two states, are both charming Baroque colonial towns. Penedo has the added advantage of offering a spectacular view of the Rio São Francisco.

Rio São Francisco, the largest river in Northeast Brazil

Stunning blue sky and pastel-colored colonial houses in the picturesque town of Olinda

Sights at a Glance

Towns & Cities

1 Aracaju
2 São Cristóvão
3 Penedo
6 Marechal Deodoro
7 Maceió
9 *Recife pp220–23*
10 *Olinda pp224–6*
12 Caruaru

Beaches, Islands & Areas of Natural Beauty

4 Rio São Francisco
5 Cânion Xingó
8 Porto de Galinhas
11 Ilha de Itamaracá
13 *Fernando de Noronha pp228–9*

For hotels and restaurants in this region see pp375–6 and p392

Getting Around

Recife, Aracaju, Maceió, and Fernando de Noronha have good flight connections to the rest of Brazil. However, only Recife has an international airport. Cities on the coast are easily accessible by bus or car. Bus connections are fast and convenient throughout the region. Highway BR-101 connects Aracaju, Maceió, and Recife, while smaller coastal destinations are only a short drive east on secondary roads off the main highway. However, roads in the interior require a bit more patience as they are often in poor condition, making night driving hazardous. Gas stations and services become scarce in the sparsely populated interior; drivers should be prepared with a full tank of gas, snacks, and plenty of water.

Key

━━━ Highway
━━━ Major road
═══ Minor road
━━━ Railroad
━━━ State border

Sailboats near Fernando de Noronha with Morro do Pico at a distance

For keys to symbols *see back flap*

The wide boulevards of Sergipe's capital, Aracaju

❶ Aracaju

Sergipe. 570,000. ✈ ⓘ Centro de Turismo, (79) 3179 1932. 🎭 Festa de São João (Jan), Forró Caju Music Festival (Jun), Festa de Yemanjá (Dec). 🅦 aracaju.se.gov.br

Sergipe's original capital was São Cristóvão, located inland from the Atlantic Ocean. A burgeoning trade in sugar, however, made a sizable port necessary, and in 1855, the capital transferred to Aracaju, situated at the mouth of the Rio Sergipe. By 1901, the sleepy fishing village soon transformed into a stately capital, with a horse-drawn streetcar and a movie theater.

Today, Aracaju is a small city with a commercial downtown area along the south riverbank. Sea-life enthusiasts should visit **Oceanário**, which has models of various marine habitats. The main highlights here include the sea turtles and the shark tank. Another of the city's top attractions is the **Museu da Gente Sergipana**, a state-of-the-art museum exploring the history, culture, and traditions of the Sergipe region with interactive exhibits.

🏛 Museu da Gente Sergipana
Av Ivo do Prado 398. **Tel** (79) 3218 1551. **Open** Tue–Sun. 🎫

🐟 Oceanário
Av Santos Dumont. **Tel** (79) 3214 3243. **Open** 9am–9pm daily. 🎫

Environs
Aracaju's lively beach neighborhoods lie 6 to 12 miles (10 to 20 km) south of the city center. The most popular suburban beach is **Atalaia**, with its sports and recreation facilities, stages for cultural events, and good seafood joints. The other favorite is **Praia Atalaia Nova**, on the Ilha de Santa Luzia, an island just off the coast, accessible by boat from the ferry station in the city center.

❷ São Cristóvão

Sergipe. 73,000. 🚌 from Aracaju. ⓘ Centro de Turismo, (79) 3214 8848. 🎭 Festival de Arte de São Cristóvão (Oct). 🅦 recifecvb.com.br/pernambuco

A designated National Historic Heritage Site, São Cristóvão was founded in 1590, and is considered one of the oldest cities in Brazil. It served as the capital of Sergipe in the 17th and 18th centuries, but when the capital shifted to Aracaju it soon dwindled to the sleepy interior town it is today.

The town's charming historic center is a panoply of colonial squares and buildings, and is also a hub of commerce. The most beautifully preserved square, **Praça de São Francisco**, is easily identified by the large Franciscan cross at its center. Flanking the square are the Santa Casa Hospital, the former Governor's Palace, and the Convento de São Francisco, which now houses the **Museu de Arte Sacra** (Museum of Sacred Art). The museum has a fine collection of silver chalices and crosses, and a few beautifully sculpted statues of saints. The ceiling of the convent chapel was painted by the Bahian artist, José Teófilo de Jesus (1758–1847). In October, the annual Festival de Arte de São Cristóvão hosts popular art and music.

🏛 Museu de Arte Sacra
Praça de São Francisco. **Tel** (79) 3261 1385. **Open** 10am–4pm Tue–Sun. 🎫

Franciscan cross in front of Convento de São Francisco in São Cristóvão

…treets and historic buildings by the Penedo waterfront

❸ Penedo

Alagoas. 🗺 60,000. 🚌 from Maceió.
ℹ Teatro 7 de Setembro, Centro
Historico, (82) 3551 2727. 🎭 Bom
Jesus dos Navegantes (2nd Sun in
Jan). 🌐 turismoalagoas.com

The oldest settlement in
Alagoas, Penedo was founded
in 1565 by Duarte Coelho
Pereira on a strategic bluff
overlooking the Rio São
Francisco, about 19 miles
(30 km) upstream of the delta.
Invading Dutch forces
conquered the town in 1637,
and after eight years, the
Portuguese managed to regain
control. Today, Penedo's historic
center has been designated a
National Historic Monument.
Particularly noteworthy is the
complex housing the **Convento
de São Francisco** and **Igreja de
Santa Maria dos Anjos**, built
over a period of 100 years.

The **Igreja Nossa Senhora da
Corrente** (Church of Our Lady
of Chains), built in 1765 by the
Lemos de Gonzaga family, was
used as a refuge for runaway
slaves, who the family often
provided with forged certificates of freedom. It has a fine
Rococo-style main altar.

🏛 **Convento de São Francisco &
Igreja de Santa Maria dos Anjos**
Rua 7 de Setembro 218. **Open**
8–11:30am, 2–5pm Tue–Fri,
8am–11pm Sat & Sun.

🏛 **Igreja Nossa Senhora da
Corrente**
Praça 12 de Abril. **Open** 8am–4pm
Tue–Sun. 📷

Environs
The **Rio São Francisco Delta** is
easily accessed from the town of
Piaçabuçu, 9 miles (15 km) east
of Penedo. The delta, situated on
the Sergipe side of the river, is
rich in lagoons and mangrove
forests, and is home to turtles
and migrating seabirds. The
riverbank in Alagoas features
low-rolling sand dunes.

❹ Rio São Francisco

Sergipe, Alagoas, Pernambuco &
Minas Gerais.

The largest and most important
river in the region, the Rio São
Francisco has long served as
the main transport and
irrigation lifeline for the people
in the small towns of the arid
northeastern interior to the
bigger cities along the coast.
Considered a symbol of
national unity, Brazilians revere
the São Francisco, and it is the
subject of many myths and
fables. Nicknamed Velho Chico
(Old Chico), the 1,963-mile
(3,160-km) river meanders
through five states. Originating
in the Serra da Canastra
mountains in Minas Gerais,
it flows north through Bahia,
and crosses briefly into
Pernambuco before continuing
east, toward the Atlantic,
marking the border between
Sergipe and Alagoas in its final
run to the sea.

Lampião & Maria Bonita

In the 1920s and 1930s, bandit leader Lampião and his
wife Maria Bonita led a band of 40 outlaws, nicknamed
cangaceiros (*cangaço* means badlands), on a 15-year
spree of robberies, hold-ups, rapes, and
shoot-outs across the Northeast. As
their raids continued, Lampião and
Maria Bonita became notorious figures
throughout Brazil.
The duo even introduced their own
style of clothing, with the round leather
cangaceiro hat, the front brim turned
upward and decorated with stars or
coins. The police and militia searched
for them endlessly but were unable to
capture them. Finally, in 1938, Lampião,
Maria Bonita, and nine *cangaceiros* were
ambushed and killed by the police in
Sergipe. Their story has inspired
numerous songs, plays, and different
versions on film and TV.

Lampião and Maria Bonita
clay statues

❺ Cânion Xingó

Sergipe. 🚌 from Aracaju.
ℹ️ Reservatório de Xingó, (79) 9972 1320. 📷 trips to the dam at 11:30am Tue–Sun, call (79) 3346 1184 for further departure details. 🎣

Standing on the Rio São Francisco, the Xingó Dam in Sergipe is one of the largest in Brazil. When it was completed in 1994, the dam blocked off the São Francisco canyon at a point about 155 miles (250 km) from the ocean, causing the river to rise and create the Xingó Reservoir. This artificial lake is now a popular destination.

Catamarans and schooners depart from the dam and travel upstream, crossing the reservoir and re-entering the main part of the river. Several rock passageways that previously lay at the top of the canyon are now open to exploration by boat.

Situated 2 miles (3 km) from the dam, the **Museu de Arqueológia de Xingó** displays numerous archaeological objects from nearby sites that were flooded when the dam was created. Artifacts from the earliest sites, dating from around 5000 BC, include arrows, rock paintings, primitive stone mortars, and fish-cleaning tools. Later sites reveal a variety of items including bone jewelry, decorative ceramics, and clay containers.

🏛 Museu de Arqueológia de Xingó

2 miles (3 km) from Xingó dam at Rodoviaria Canindé-Piranhas. **Open** 8am–5pm Tue–Sun. 🎣 📷 ♿

Igreja de Santa Maria Madalena in Marechal Deodoro's historic center

❻ Marechal Deodoro

Alagoas. 🔼 30,000. 🚌 from Maceió.
ℹ️ (82) 8856 9091

The capital of Alagoas until 1839, Marechal Deodoro was founded in 1611 as Vila Madalena. The city was renamed in honor of its native son, Marshall Manuel Deodoro da Fonseca (1827–92), elected as Brazil's first president in 1891. Fonseca's childhood home is now a small museum, displaying much of the original furniture and family memorabilia.

The city's small, 18th-century colonial center features the Rococo **Igreja de Santa Maria Madalena**. Adjoining the church, the **Convento do São Francisco** houses a museum.

Just a 15-minute bus ride from the city is the **Praia do Francês**, with powdery sand and deep-blue water. It has enormous waves for surfing at one end, while the other end is protected by a large reef.

The authorities are working toward removing the restaurants that have been built right on the sand.

⛪ Convento do São Francisco

Praça Pedro Paulinho. **Tel** (82) 3551 2279. **Open** 8–11:30am, 2–5pm Mon–Fri, 8–11am Sat & Sun.

⛪ Igreja de Santa Maria Madalena

Praça João 23. **Tel** (82) 3263 1623. **Open** 9am–5pm Mon–Sun.

❼ Maceió

Alagoas. 🔼 930,000. ✈️ 🚌 (82) 221 4615. ℹ️ Rua Boa Vista 453, Centro, (82) 3315 5700. 🎭 Maceió Fest (Nov).
🌐 maceioconvention.com.br

The capital of Alagoas, Maceió is known for its many beautiful urban beaches. The best known from north to south, are **Jatiúca**, **Ponta Verde**, **Sete Coqueiros**, and **Pajuçara**. Protected by reefs, the beaches have little or no surf, warm water, and a Caribbean turquoise-green color. The shores are lined with thick groves of coconut palms, especially dense at Ponta Verde.

About 1 mile (2 km) offshore from Pajuçara, a series of large coral reefs are partially exposed at low tide, forming sizable natural pools that can be explored with a mask and snorkel. Small single-sail rafts known as *jangadas* depart daily at low tide from Ponta Verde and take about 20 minutes to reach the pools.

In addition to the beaches, Maceió has a small historic core. The neighborhoods of Jaraguá and Centro, just inland from the port, have a large number of well-preserved historic buildings which convey some of the atmosphere of the city's 19th-century sugar boom. One of the loveliest mansions on the waterfront has been beautifully restored and now houses the **Museu Théo Brandão**. Named after a local writer who wrote about Alagoan folk art and anthropology, the small museum has a good collection of native art. It also has some wonderfully creative displays

View of Praia de Francês, one of the popular beaches of Marechal Deodoro

For hotels and restaurants in this region see pp375–6 and p392

Jangadas, small sailboats, on the beach at Ponta Verde in Maceió

that use local crafts to depict the region's religious festivals, typical foods, the sugar-cane industry, and folklore.

The southern end of the city borders the **Lagoa Mundaú**, one of the many lagoons that have given Alagoas its name. The lagoon encompasses several mangrove islands teeming with crustaceans and other marine life. Boats make excursions into the lagoon's channels.

The **Pontal da Barra** neighborhood on the lagoon's shore is a small fishing village. There are several rustic restaurants overlooking the water, which serve the catch of the day. Dishes with *sururu* (a small type of clam) and crab are especially popular. In Pontal da Barra, visitors will find highly skilled *rendeiras*, or lace-makers, working on a variety of laces. The one most typical of the neighborhood is known as *filé*, a loose weave that is often brightly colored.

🏛 Museu Théo Brandão

Av da Paz 1490, Centro. **Tel** (82) 3214 1713. **Open** 9am–5pm Tue–Fri, 2–5pm Sat. 🗗 📷

Environs

Praia do Gunga is a pretty, palm-fringed beach located 9 miles (15 km) south of Maceió. Access to the beach is gained via a private road cutting across one of the region's largest coconut plantations. Permission to enter must be obtained at the gate, but beaches in Brazil are public property and access cannot be denied. One side of the beach faces the lagoon, while the other side looks toward the ocean, offering the option of fresh- or salt-water swimming, as well as kayaking.

❽ Porto de Galinhas

Pernambuco. 🗠 10,000. ✈ Recife Guararapes International Airport, 38 miles (60 km) N of town, then bus. 🛈 (81) 3552 1728.

Porto de Galinhas is one of the most popular tourist destinations in Northeast Brazil, and deservedly so. There are no high-rises dwarfing the beach here, just low-scale *pousadas* and bungalows. The star attraction of the area, in additions to the beach, are the natural tide pools that form in the reefs just a short distance offshore. Colorful *jangada* rafts take swimmers and snorkelers out to swim in the clear shallow waters that teems with tropical fish.

Porto de Galinhas also offers a lively atmosphere with excellent restaurants and shopping, and, better still, it does not take much effort to get away from the bustle. The main mode of transportation is the dune buggy, which allows for easy transit along the dirt and sand roads that lead to local beaches. A short distance south along the beach leads to **Ponta de Maracaípe**, a beautiful spot with a large white sandbar, where the Rio Maracaípe runs into the ocean. The mangroves in the estuary are home to several species of seahorse that live amid the roots of the tree.

Quilombos

Portrait of Zumbi

In the African Yorubá language, *quilombo* means dwelling place. In Brazil, the term was used to describe a community of runaway slaves. Brazil's most famous *quilombo*, Quilombo dos Palmares in Alagoas, grew to the size of a small city, with 30,000 residents. In the late 1600s, Zumbi, the *quilombo*'s second leader, successfully defended it from repeated Portuguese attacks. However, the Portuguese were relentless, and finally, in 1694, Palmares fell. Zumbi was beheaded and the community destroyed. A number of such places escaped Palmares' fate and survive even today. There are now 1,000 *quilombos* registered in Brazil. Zumbi's legacy is remembered every year on November 20, when Zumbi dos Palmares Day, or Black Awareness Day, is celebrated.

Clear-water rock pools offshore from Porto de Galinhas

❷ Recife

The Portuguese, who had built Olinda on a hillside, ignored the swampy islands below. The site of present-day Recife was only a fishing village when the Dutch took over Pernambuco in 1630. Count Maurice of Nassau commanded the draining and dyking of the flat islands at the mouth of the Rio Capibaribe. The islands of Santo Antônio, Boa Vista, and Recife Antigo (Old Recife) were connected to each other and the mainland with an ingenious system of bridges. Boa Viagem, south of Recife, has a popular beach, many hotels, and excellent nightlife.

Exploring Recife Antigo

In the heart of downtown Old Recife is the **Marco Zero** and the surrounding square, which marks the official point where the city was founded. The site of the original pier, it controlled all arrivals and departures taking place in the bay. This bustling district of the city makes for a pleasant walk during the day. It is possible to take a boat from the square across to the **Parque das Esculturas**, which features an imposing collection of tall, exotic sculptures made by one of Brazil's leading ceramic artists Francisco Brennand *(see p223)*.

The most interesting street in the historic quarter is **Rua do Bom Jesus**. During the brief period of Dutch rule the street was known as Rua dos Judeus (Street of the Jews). The Jewish community thrived under Dutch rule, but once the Catholic Portuguese re-established their control, most fled, converted, or went underground. A large number of the buildings on this street have been restored to their original 17th-century condition. Every Sunday, the street comes alive, as an art and crafts fair, live music, and outdoor festivities take place.

🏛 Paço da Alfândega
Rua da Alfândega 35. **Tel** (81) 3194 2100. **Open** 10am–10pm Mon–Sat, noon–8pm Sun & public hols. ♿
Ⓦ pacoalfandega.com.br

Just on the edge of the historical quarter, the Paço da Alfândega brings together the old and the new elements

of the city. Overlooking the Rio Capibaribe, the former customs building dates back to 1826, when Recife was one of Brazil's major ports. The renovated building houses restaurants, an art gallery, and a shopping and entertainment center.

Recife City Center
① Paço da Alfândega
② Kahal Zur Israel Synagogue
③ Paço do Frevo
④ Torre de Malakoff
⑤ Museu Cais do Sertão
⑥ Forte do Brum
⑦ Forte das Cinco Pontas
⑧ Praça da Republic
⑨ Igreja São Francisco & Capela Dourada
⑩ Catedral de São Pedro dos Clérigos
⑪ Casa da Cultura
⑫ Instituto Ricardo Brennand
⑬ Oficina Brennard

🏛 Kahal Zur Israel Synagogue
Rua do Bom Jesus 197. **Tel** (81) 3224 8351. **Open** 9am–5pm Tue–Fri, 2–5:30pm Sun. 🖼

Built in 1637, during the city's brief period of Dutch rule, this synagogue recounts the history of the Jewish community in Recife. It was the first synagogue anywhere in the Americas. Many of the Jews who immigrated to Dutch-

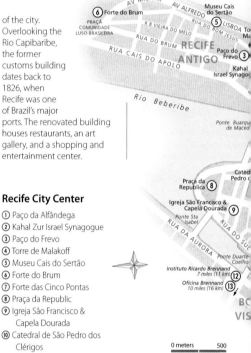

The well-preserved old buildings on Rua do Bom Jesus

For hotels and restaurants in this region see p376 and p392

controlled Recife, had originally come from Portugal, fleeing the Inquisition. At the height of Dutch rule, about half of Recife's white population was Jewish. Unfortunately, the period of religious tolerance was short-lived, and when the Dutch surrendered to the Portuguese in 1654 the Jews were given three months to liquidate their assets and leave. Many members of the Recife community set sail to New Amsterdam and helped found New York.

The synagogue was dismantled, and its role as a temple and meeting place of the Jewish community was completely forgotten.

The building was eventually torn down at the beginning of the 20th century.

Archaeologists have confirmed the exact location of the original synagogue after digging up part of a *mikveh* (ritual bath). The current synagogue has been rebuilt from the ground up, based on these findings, historical data, and other sources. The museum presents an excellent docu-mentary and display on the history of the Jews in Recife.

🏛 Paço do Frevo
Praça do Arsenal da Marinha s/n.
Tel (81) 3355 9500. **Open** 9am–5pm Tue–Fri, 2–6pm Sat & Sun. 🖼 🎫
W pacodofrevo.org.br

Come to this culture center to learn and experience all about Recife's unique musical rhythm. It includes a Documentation Center, Music School, School of Dance, and various temporary and permanent exhibitions.

🏛 Torre de Malakoff
Praça do Arsenal da Marinha, Rua do Bom Jesus. **Tel** (81) 3184 3180.
Open 10am–6pm Tue–Fri, 3–6pm Sat, 3–7pm Sun.

A relative newcomer to the Rua do Bom Jesus, the Malakoff Tower was built in 1845 as South America's first astronomical observatory, and is still functional today. Visitors can climb to the top terrace for a splendid view of the city courtesy of the LX 200 telescopes.

🏛 Museu Cais do Sertão
Av Alfredo Lisboa. **Tel** (81) 3089 2974. **Open** 9am–5pm Tue–Fri. 🖼

This well-designed, interactive museum explores the history and culture of the Sertão region and pays tribute to the Recife carnival, giving a taste of the lifestyle here. In one section, kids over seven may even play with musical instruments.

VISITORS' CHECKLIST

Practical Information
Pernambuco. 🗺 1,500,000.
ℹ Empetur, (81) 3182 8300.
🎭 Carnaval (Feb/Mar).
W www2.recife.pe.gov.br

Transport
✈ Aeroporto dos Guararapes, 7 miles (11 km) S of city center. 🚌 9 miles (14 km) SW of city center.

🏛 Forte do Brum
Praça Comunidade Luso-Brasileira.
Tel (81) 3224 4620. **Open** 9am–4pm Tue–Fri, 2–5pm Sat & Sun.

One of the few constructions to pre-date the Dutch, Forte Brum is located at the far end of Avenida Militar. Built by the Portuguese in 1629, it was taken over by the Dutch in 1630, and strengthened and expanded. Today it is a military museum.

🏛 Forte das Cinco Pontas
Praça das Cinco Pontas. **Tel** (81) 3355 3107. **Open** 9am–5pm Tue–Fri, 1–5pm Sat & Sun. 🖼 🎫

Somewhat deceptively, the Forte das Cinco Pontas (Five-Pointed Fort) actually only has four points. The original Dutch fort, built in 1630 to protect the new Dutch-Brazilian capital of Mauritsstad, had five. When the Dutch with-drew in 1654, the Portuguese leveled the unique shape and put up a more traditional four-pointer. Wonderfully restored, the fort now houses the city museum and contains an impressive collection of maps, paintings, and artifacts that tell the history of Dutch rule.

Frevo

Recife's signature beat is *frevo*. Fast, upbeat, almost polka-like, the rhythm is particularly popular during Carnaval (see p45). This distinct musical genre is reputed to have derived its name from the verb *ferver* (to boil), which refers to the frenetic beat of the brass bands. One of the accessories of a *frevo* dancer is the brightly colored hand-held parasol that is used in the choreography. First recorded in the 1930s, the rhythm made its way into the repertoire of mainstream Brazilian musicians by the 1950s and 1960s.

A dancer performing *frevo* with a colorful parasol

Exploring Modern Recife

Though modern Recife stretches onto the mainland, its center comprises the islands of Santo Antônio, Boa Vista, and Recife Antigo. Skyscrapers exist alongside a handful of old colonial buildings and crowded markets, lending the city a striking character. The area north of the center is as appealing, with leafy suburbs and a few museums and parks. The squares, dotted with impressive churches, retain much of their old-world charm.

The courtyard of Igreja São Francisco, with a graceful, colonnaded arcade

▦ Praça da República

Palácio do Campo das Princesas:
Tel (81) 3425 2124. **Open** 9–11am &
2–6pm Fri & Sat, 2–6pm Sun. Teatro
Princesa Isabel: **Tel** (81) 3355 3323.
Open check for performance timings.
Palácio da Justiça: **Tel** (81) 3182 0100.

Modern Recife's main civic square, Praça da República, is located at the tip of Santo Antônio island. Some of the city's finest public buildings can be found here.

The **Palácio do Campo das Princesas** (Governors' Palace) building was built in the 1840s. Over the years, renovations and additions have somewhat altered the original Neo-Classical design and made the building more eclectic. The lovely interior garden was designed by Brazil's premier landscape artist, Roberto Burle Marx. Unfortunately, the only view available to the public is the one through the wrought-iron fence posts.

The **Teatro Princesa Isabel**, a renovated pink theater, hosts many of Recife's prime cultural productions. The building is an elegant example of classic imperial architecture, marked by its symmetric forms and French and Italian decorative styles.

The **Palácio da Justiça,** with its dome-shaped cupola, was constructed in 1930 to mark the presidency of Getúlio Vargas (*see pp60–61*).

⛪ Igreja São Francisco & Capela Dourada

Rua do Imperador, Santo Antônio. **Tel** (81) 3224 0530. **Open** 8–11:30am, 2–5pm Mon–Fri, 8–11am Sat. ▨

One of the major attractions in Recife, Igreja São Francisco served as the convent of the Third Franciscan Order. It was built in 1606, when the island of Santo Antônio only had 200 inhabitants. The initial convent was small and rather plain. During the Dutch occupation of Recife (1630–54) it was used as army barracks. Renovations began after the return of the Franciscans. The courtyard was added with a surrounding arcade of delicate and ornate Tuscan columns. Blue-and-white Portuguese tiles (*azulejos*) were used to decorate the main altar and the walls of the small, charming cloister.

However, the *pièce de résistance* is the **Capela Dourada** (Golden Chapel), added in 1695, in an annex of the main church. All of the wood in the chapel is jacaranda and cedar and is covered in gold leaf or paint. The intricately carved altars, arches, and beams showcase some outstanding Portuguese Baroque art. Each altar consists of various arches, adding a depth of field to the statues on display. One of the walls in the church is adorned with a painting that depicts the Crucifixion of a group of Franciscan saints.

⛪ Catedral de São Pedro dos Clérigos

Rua São Pedro s/n, Santo Antônio. **Tel** (81) 3224 2954. **Open** 8am–noon, 2–4pm Mon–Fri.

Dating back to 1728, Catedral de São Pedro dos Clérigos is one of the most impressive churches in Pernambuco. Its striking façade is dominated by a statue of St. Peter, which was added in 1980. While from the outside the walls of the church look perfectly square and straight, on the inside the church nave is octagonal. The best features of the church are its stunning wood carving and the illusionistic ceiling. The main altar, balconies, and most of the remaining interior elements were renovated in the 19th century in the Rococo style. The only original pieces that remain are the two gold-painted wooden pulpits.

The square in front of the church, **Pátio de São Pedro**, is one of Recife's most popular public squares. The beautifully restored area hosts a number of cultural events. The most important, **Terça Negra** (Black Tuesday), takes place every Tuesday night. It is widely known for showcasing typical regional Afro-Brazilian musical styles, such as *afoxé*, *maculelê*, and *coco*. The area also has many fine restaurants.

ye-catching ceramic figures and souvenirs
n sale, Casa da Cultura

🏛 Casa da Cultura

Rua Floriano Peixoto s/n, São José.
Tel (81) 3224 0557. **Open** 9am–7pm
Mon–Fri, 9am–6pm Sat, 9am–2pm Sun.

Used as a jail until 1973, the
former penitentiary now
houses the Casa da Cultura,
the city's largest arts and craft
market. Each of the old jail
cells holds a shop showcasing
some of the finest leather,
lace, and ceramic crafts of this
region. Built in 1850, the jail
was modeled after US prisons
in New Jersey and Pennsylvania.
The four wings are in a cross
shape, allowing a view of
all four corridors from one
vantage position in the center
of the cross. The center brings
out the monthly *Agenda
Cultural*, an excellent listing
of cultural events.

🏛 Instituto Ricardo Brennand

Av Antônio Brennand, Várzea. **Tel** (81)
2121 0352. **Open** 1–5pm Tue–Sun. 🚻

Founded by the cousin of
ceramic artist Francisco
Brennand, the Instituto Ricardo
Brennand includes a small
castle, the Castelo São João,
which houses a large collection
of European art, an
impressive collection
of medieval armory
and weapons, and an
extensive archive of
paintings and
documents from the
years of the Dutch
conquest of Brazil.

Also worth seeing
is the Pinacoteca
gallery that features
a large collection of
17th-century paint-
ings and drawings
by landscape artists
Frans Post and Albert
Eckhout, both of
whom were hired by Dutch
count Maurice of Nassau to
portray Brazil's fauna and flora,
as well as scenes from everyday
life. Over the years, Brennand
has amassed the world's largest
collection of Post's work. The
exhibit also includes antique
maps and documents that
recount the brief, but eventful,
history of the Dutch in Brazil.

Ceramic tiles by
Francisco Brennand

🏛 Oficina Brennand

Access via Av Caxangá, Várzea.
Tel (81) 3271 2466. **Open** 8am–5pm
Mon–Thu, 8am–4pm Fri, 10am–4pm
Sat & Sun.

Acclaimed as the most unusual
cultural attraction in Recife,
the Oficina Brennand is the
famed artist's personal gallery.
Brennand (b.1927) is best
known for his large
collection of phallic-
shaped ceramic
sculptures, nearly all
of which are striking,
potent, and larger
than life. His collection
is creatively displayed
inside a ceramic-
covered brick factory
and its surrounding
gardens, beautifully
landscaped by Burle
Marx, a renowned
landscape architect
of the 20th century.

In addition to
Brennand's superb
ceramic art, the collection
also showcases thousands
of playfully designed ceramic
tiles, as well as some of his
paintings and drawings. The
bold mix of stylized imagery,
embellishment, and erotic
motifs, visible in all his works,
led one critic to define
Brennand's art as "tropical
sensual Baroque."

Gardens in Oficina Brennand, adorned with ceramic sculptures

⑩ Olinda

One of the best-preserved colonial cities in Brazil, Olinda was founded in 1535 by the Portuguese. Much of it was burned down during the Dutch occupation in 1631, and later beautifully restored to its former glory. Magnificent colonial buildings, gardens, Baroque churches, and numerous small chapels mark Olinda, which was designated a UNESCO World Heritage Site in 1982. Although much of this historic city lies on a steep hillside, it is only a short walk up, and the views of the Atlantic Ocean are splendid. Its narrow cobblestone streets are perfect for exploring on foot. The highlight of the walk suggested here is the Praça da Sé, which features historic churches and sweeping views of Recife (see pp220–23), only 6 miles (10 km) to the south.

The view of Olinda from Alto da Sé, with the sea in the background

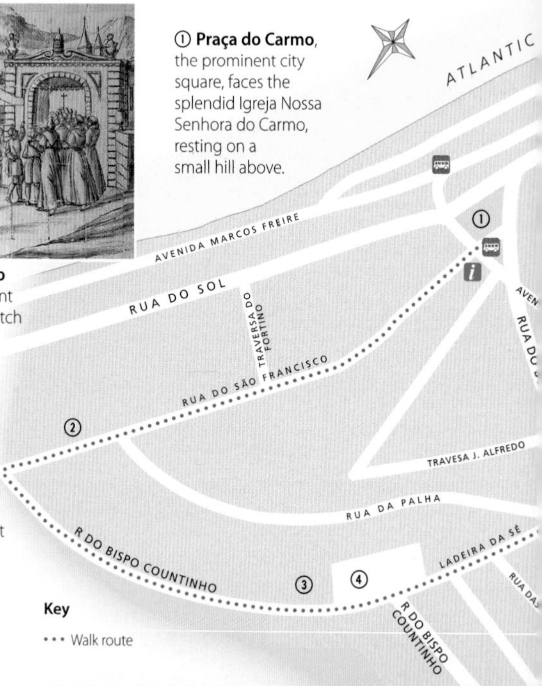

② Convento de São Francisco
Brazil's oldest Franciscan convent was built in 1585. When the Dutch invaded Olinda in 1630 the convent was abandoned, and rebuilt in the 18th century. The cloister walls, decorated with Portuguese tiles, depict the life of St. Francis.

① Praça do Carmo, the prominent city square, faces the splendid Igreja Nossa Senhora do Carmo, resting on a small hill above.

ATLANTIC

AVENIDA MARCOS FREIRE

RUA DO SOL

TRAVESSA DO FORTINHO

RUA DO SÃO FRANCISCO

AVEN

RUA DO

TRAVESA J. ALFREDO

RUA DA PALHA

LADEIRA DA SÉ

RUA DA

③ Igreja da Sé which was built in 1535, is the oldest parish church in Northeast Brazil. The church has undergone many renovations over the centuries. The last, in 1984, restored the building almost to its original 16th-century state.

R DO BISPO COUNTINHO

R DO BISPO COUNTINHO

③ ④

Key
••• Walk route

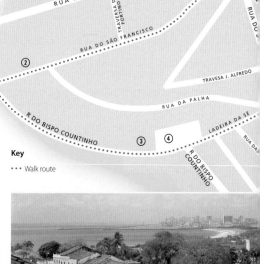

Tips for Walkers

Starting point: Secretaria de Turismo, Praça do Carmo.
Walking time: 2–3 hours. Flat, non-slippery footwear is best.
Best days: Tue–Sat. Museums are only open in the morning.
Places to eat: Oficina do Sabor, Rua do Amparo 335; Olinda Sorvetes e Sucos, Rua São Bento 358.

④ Alto da Sé
The Alto da Sé is one of the highest points in Olinda and offers a magnificent view of Recife in the distance. In the evenings, locals gather here to browse the crafts market, and eat tapioca and pancakes made from manioc.

⑤ Mercado da Ribeira

Originally the building where slaves were bought and sold, this 18th-century structure is now one of Olinda's busiest crafts markets. Especially popular are naive art ceramics, carnival masks, and *frevo* umbrellas *(see p221)*.

⑥ Igreja e Mosteiro São Bento

Founded in 1582, this church holds a magnificient gold altar. It took more than a year and 30 professionals to fully restore the altar in 2001. Gregorian chanters add a special touch to the Sunday morning mass.

⑦ Museu de Arte Contemporânea is

a fine 18th-century building and a former jail. This building now houses an interesting collection of artwork by contemporary Pernambucan artists.

⑧ Museu do Mamulengo displays

a large collection of puppets from all over the Northeast. Unique to Olinda's Carnaval, the giant puppets, carried by revelers along the parade route, are true works of art.

⑨ Rua do Amparo

More than a dozen artists have set up their studios in the historic buildings along Rua do Amparo. The street also boasts several excellent restaurants, cafés, and B&Bs.

For key to symbols *see back flap*

Exploring Olinda

A calm, colonial city, Olinda grew to be the capital of the rich sugar-growing region of Pernambuco. Reconstruction started in earnest only after Dutch forces were expelled in 1654. The city has maintained its 17th-century architectural fabric intact. Olinda is also home to a vibrant community of artists, musicians, and liberal professionals. The scenic city, though, is most renowned for its lively Carnaval.

The exterior of Igreja e Mosteiro de São Bento in Olinda

🏛 Museu de Arte Contemporânea

Rua 13 de Maio 149, Carmo. **Tel** (81) 3184 3153. **Open** 9am–5pm Tue–Sun.

Housed in a fine 18th-century building that originally served as an *ajube*, or jail working in conjunction with the Catholic church, the Museum of Contemporary Art displays both permanent and temporary exhibits. During the Inquisition, religious prisoners were brought here to pray and confess their sins. Today, the place holds some interest for those looking for serious modern art. Works by local contemporary artists are regularly displayed in front of the stairs.

🏛 Museu do Mamulengo

Rua do Sao Bento 344. **Tel** (81) 3493 2753. **Open** 10am–5pm Tue–Sat.

One of the region's unique gifts to the cultural scene in Brazil, *mamulengo*, or puppetry, is showcased in this fascinating museum. Nearly 1,000 puppets are featured here, with a portion of the collection dating from the 1800s. Having performed before political figures, royalty, and luminaries through the ages, these puppets are today used as popular entertainment. During folk festivals, the puppets can be seen enacting comedies, skits, and Pernambucan folk legends. For those interested in the puppets' historical background, there is a curator who can explain it by asking the puppets themselves.

🏛 Convento de São Francisco

Rua de São Francisco 280. **Tel** (81) 3429 0517. **Open** 8am–noon & 2–5pm Mon–Fri, 9am–noon & 2–4:30pm Sat.

The Convento de São Francisco was the first convent built by the Franciscan order in Brazil. The complex includes a 1585 church, Nossa Senhora das Neves (Our Lady of the Snow), and the adjacent chapels of St. Anne and St. Roque, built in 1754 and 1811, respectively. The highlight of the convent is the beautiful arcade surrounding the cloister. The tiled walls tell the story of St. Francis of Assisi. The sacristy's beautiful Baroque furniture, carved from dark jacaranda wood, is as impressive.

🏛 Igreja e Mosteiro de São Bento

Rua São Bento. **Tel** (81) 3316 3290. **Open** 8am–noon & 2–5pm daily. 🏛 6:30am Mon–Sat, 10am Sun (with Gregorian chants).

Built in 1582, this monastery was destroyed by the Dutch along with most of the city, and rebuilt in the late 18th century. It is acclaimed for its Baroque altar in the chapel and intricate wood carving, which features the image of São Bento (St. Benedict) himself. In 2001, the original wood altar was repainted with gold leaf. The sacristy's three large paintings, by 18th-century artist José Eloy da Conceição, portray scenes from the life of the saint.

The Olinda Carnaval

Every year during Carnaval, the cobblestoned streets of Olinda become the stage for a week-long street party. The meeting place is the square, known as *quarto cantos* (four corners), on the corner of Rua do Amparo and Rua Prudente de Moraes. Here, *blocos* (neighborhood groups) begin their parades through the streets, playing music, singing, and dancing as they go. The *blocos* often have themes or names such as "Virgins," "Elephant," or "Midnight Man." Dominating the festivities are enormous papier-mâché puppets that *bloco* members proudly carry along the parade route. The music varies from *frevo*, an upbeat, almost frenetic beat unique to Pernambuco, to *maracatu*, a much more African beat.

Revelers filling a street in Olinda, with larger-than-life papier-mâché puppets

⓫ Ilha de Itamaracá

Pernambuco. 🏠 16,000. 🚌 from Recife.

The island of Itamaracá played an important strategic role during the Dutch interregnum in Brazil. In 1631, the Dutch built the **Forte Orange** here, to protect their new domain from invading forces. The Portuguese destroyed the Dutch-built adobe when they took over in 1654. However, the location was so unique that the Portuguese created a new fort in stone on the site. During past renovations, artifacts dating back to the Dutch period were found. Just across from the fort is a small island, Coroa do Avião, which has natural reef pools. Boat tours to the island leave from the beach in front of the fort.

Itamaracá is also home to the **Projeto Peixe Boi**, a manatee research and rehabilitation center. Manatees live along the Brazilian coast from Alagoas to Amapá, but are threatened by loss of habitat, as well as by speedboats and their often-ethal outboard propellers. Scientists estimate that there are only around 400 animals in the wild along this coast. The center works to rehabilitate injured manatees, and to study those that cannot be released. A natural history exhibit on the manatee is offered along with a host of interactive learning activities for children. Visitors are only allowed to observe those animals that cannot be released into the wild. Projeto Peixe Boi is currently closed to visitors.

Pottery on display at a craft shop in Caruaru

The eastern part of Itamaracá, with its lovely ocean beaches, is also a popular weekend destination.

🏛 Forte Orange
Estrada do Forte. **Open** 9am–5pm Mon–Sat, 8am–5pm Sun. 🚫

🗺 Projeto Peixe Boi
Estrada do Forte Orange. **Tel** (81) 3544 1056. **Open** 10am–4pm Tue–Sun. ♿

⓬ Caruaru

Pernambuco. 🏠 300,000. 🚌 from Recife. 🎭 Festa do Forró (Jun–Jul).
W caruaru.pe.gov.br

Located 100 miles (160 km) on the mainland southwest of Itamaracá, Caruaru is a market town whose fame rests on its marvelous ceramic *figurinhas* (figurines). Artist Vitalino Perreira dos Santos (1909–63) made many of these brightly painted sculptures, and his hometown, Alto de Moura, a community of potters located 4 miles (6 km)

west of Caruaru, still specializes in producing figurines. **Casa Museu Mestre Vitalino** in Alto do Moura is dedicated to this great artist, and displays his tools and some personal possessions.

Caruaru's open market is the largest in the Northeast, and is a very popular tourist attraction. Besides figurines, leather bags, straw baskets, and ceramic pots are also sold at some of the best prices in Brazil. Apart from a bustling market scene, Caruaru, known as the capital of *forró (see p240)*, hosts Brazil's largest month-long *forró* festival. The **Museu do Barro** pays tribute to Luis Gonzaga, the father of *forró* music.

Figurine, Casa Museu Mestre Vitalino

Environs
Situated 17 miles (30 km) northwest of Caruaru, **Nova Jerusalém** is an intriguing re-creation of Jerusalem. In the week before Easter, thousands of people flock to watch an epic performance of the Paixão de Cristo (Passion of Christ). Local tour operators offer all-inclusive packages to the town and its annual play.

🏛 Casa Museu Mestre Vitalino
Rua Mestre Vitalino 281. **Tel** (81) 3725 0805. **Open** 8am–5pm Tue–Sat, 9am–5pm Sun.

🏛 Museu do Barro
Praça José de Vasconcelos. **Tel** (81) 3721 2545. **Open** 9am–5pm Tue–Sat, 9am–1pm Sun.

Rehabilitated manatees at the Projeto Peixe Boi, Ilha de Itamaracá

⑲ Fernando de Noronha

Discovered in 1503 by Amerigo Vespucci, the 21-island archipelago of Fernando de Noronha was fought over for the next two centuries by the French, Dutch, and Portuguese, who built forts on strategic lookout points. The island, located 220 miles (354 km) off the coast, was used in a variety of ways, including as a political prison during World War II. In 1988, the Parque Nacional Marinho de Fernando de Noronha was created in order to protect the fragile marine and island ecology of the archipelago. Today, a combination of crystal-clear water, fascinating wildlife, diverse marine life which includes multicolored fish, turtles, sharks, and whales, and stunning beaches make Fernando de Noronha one of the most beautiful destinations in Brazil. One of the best ways to explore the island is to rent a buggy.

ATLANTIC OCEAN

Key
--- Park boundary

Surfing on Praia do Boldró
Fernando de Noronha offers some of Brazil's best surfing, but only between December and March.

★ **Baía do Sancho**
The most beautiful and isolated beach on Noronha, Baía do Sancho is also a snorkelers' paradise with its clear, turquoise waters and myriad tropical fish.

Praia do Boldró

Praia Cacimba do Padre

Praia da Baía do Porcos

Praia da Baía do Sancho

BAÍA DOS GOLFINHOS

FERNA

MORRO BRANCO

Praia do Leão

MORRO DA QUIXABINHA

ILHA MORRO DO LEÃO

Ponta Capim Açu

★ **Spinner Dolphins**
Hundreds of dolphins gather at sunrise to leap and spin at Dolphin Cove in the Baía dos Golfinhos.

KEY

① **Praia do Meio** is located close to the ruins of Forte Nossa Senhora Conceição.

② **Baía do Sueste** is the site for the Projecto Tamar (see p211), and it is possible to swim with the turtles.

★ **Turtle Hatchlings**
Ilha Morro do Leão is a prime hatchery for green sea turtles. Between December and May, around sunset, scores of tiny turtle hatchlings break out of their shells and make a dash for the sea. The beach is closed to the public during hatching season from 6am to 6pm.

Morro do Pico
The sharp basalt finger of Morro do Pico, a testament to the island's volcanic heritage, stands 1,053 ft (321 m) above sea level.

ILHA DO RATA

ILHA DO MEIO

ILHA RASA

Ponta de Santo Antônio
Praia de Santo Antônio
Forte dos Remédios
Buraco da Raquel
Praia do Meio
Vila dos Remédios
Vila do Trinta
MORRO DO FRANCES
DE NORONHA
ORRO DO AO VISTA
Praia da Atalaia

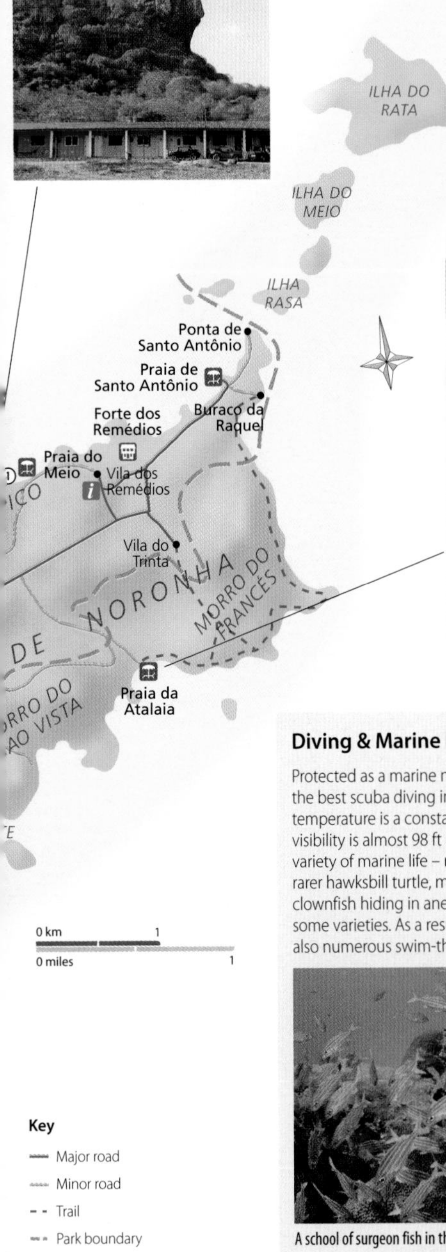

★ Praia da Atalaia
A shelf of volcanic rock extends out into the surf line. At low tide, tropical fish take refuge in the natural pools.

0 km   1
0 miles   1

Diving & Marine Life

Protected as a marine national park, Fernando de Noronha offers the best scuba diving in Brazil. Greatly suited for diving, its water temperature is a constant 28° C (82° F), and the depth of underwater visibility is almost 98 ft (30 m). Underwater there is an astounding variety of marine life – rays of all types, green sea turtles, and the even rarer hawksbill turtle, monkfish, lemon sharks and reef sharks, clownfish hiding in anemones, surgeon fish, and parrotfish are just some varieties. As a result of the island's volcanic heritage there are also numerous swim-throughs.

A school of surgeon fish in the coral reefs of Fernando de Noronha

Key
— Major road
⋯⋯ Minor road
- - Trail
— ⋅ Park boundary

For keys to symbols see back flap

PARAÍBA, RIO GRANDE DO NORTE & CEARÁ

Pristine beaches, lively beach towns, and massive shifting sand dunes are the main attractions of these three states. Natal, the capital of Rio Grande do Norte, and João Pessoa are pleasant, historic cities with good urban beaches. However, this part of Northeast Brazil is best experienced along its coast, and in its quiet, relaxed fishing villages and beautiful, isolated beaches.

In 1532, Paraíba, Rio Grande do Norte, and Ceará were among the first states in the Northeast to be colonized by the Portuguese. These states never grew as rich or settled as their more southerly neighbors because sugar cane did not thrive here. However, the three states have taken advantage of the constant sunshine and beautiful beaches and have developed tourism as the mainstay of the economy.

Ceará is famous for its beaches, with their warm, turquoise waters, set against a backdrop of red sandstone cliffs. The most popular include Morro Branco and the lively beach town of Canoa Quebrada, both located to the southeast of Fortaleza, and the isolated beach of Jericoacoara, north

and west of Fortaleza. Parque Nacional de Ubajara lies in western Ceará and comprises caves, eco trails, and magnificent waterfalls.

Rio Grande do Norte lies in the extreme northeast corner of Brazil. The real growth industry here is tourism. Natal, the capital city, has become one the Northeast's main points of entry for tourists from Western Europe. Nearly all come here for the sunshine and beaches.

Wedged in between Pernambuco and Rio Grande do Norte, Paraíba boasts some of Brazil's least spoilt beaches. Agriculture plays an important role in the state economy. The capital, João Pessoa, is a pleasant city with a small historic center. The city of Campina Grande is famous for its June festival, the Festas Juninas.

Pedra Furada rock formation, Jericoacoara beach

◀ Traditional wickerwork for sale at Mercado Central, Fortaleza

Exploring Paraíba, Rio Grande do Norte & Ceará

Most visitors to the states of Paraíba, Rio Grande do Norte, and Ceará focus on the natural beauty of the beaches and the coastline. The most popular gateway destinations are Natal in Rio Grande and Fortaleza in Ceará, which offer easy access to most of the region's attractions. Paraíba's capital, João Pessoa, with its colonial buildings, parks, and beaches, is a pleasant place to visit. In the interior of Paraíba, the monster rock formations in Cariri offer an almost other-worldly experience. Dinosaur fossils, discovered in Souza, have made the place archaeologically important. The harsh, arid interior landscape of these states has a unique, stark beauty.

Sights at a Glance

Towns & Cities

1. *João Pessoa pp234–5*
2. Campina Grande
4. Souza
5. Natal
7. Genipabu
10. Mossoró
12. *Fortaleza pp246–7*

National Parks

14. Parque Nacional de Ubajara

Areas of Natural Beauty

3. Cariri
8. Maracajaú
9. Costa Branca
11. Canoa Quebrada
13. Jericoacoara

Beaches & Resort

6. *Rota do Sol Beaches p241*

Downtown João Pessoa from across the lagoon

For hotels and restaurants in this region see pp376–7 and p393

Key

- ▬ Highway
- ▬ Major road
- ⋯ Minor road
- ⋯ Railroad
- ▬ State border

Colorful old buildings in the historic center of Fortaleza

Getting Around

All major cities and some smaller destinations, such as Campina Grande in Paraíba, can be reached by domestic flights. There are regular buses between all towns and cities. However, roads in this part of Brazil are in poor condition and are very badly maintained. The BR-101 connects João Pessoa to Natal. From Natal, travelers continuing north to Fortaleza take the BR-304, which veers west and cuts inland across Rio Grande do Norte to Ceará. The stretch of the BR-230 towards Souza is in rough shape. Ensure that the vehicle, preferably a 4WD, is in good condition. Be sure to carry extra gas, water, and supplies.

❶ João Pessoa

Founded in 1585 as Nossa Senhora das Neves, the city derives its present name from a former governor of Paraíba. Brazil's third-oldest city, João Pessoa maintains an air of old-world charm, with a host of well-restored colonial churches, convents, and monasteries. Local visitors, however, flock here mainly for the easy atmosphere of its great white sandy beaches along the coastline. The dense tropical forest that once covered the coastal strip of Paraíba now thrives only in patches, one of which lies within João Pessoa, forming one of the largest areas of natural wilderness in any city in the world.

Rococo-style painting on Igreja de São Francisco's ceiling

Majestic colonial buildings, Centro Histórico

Exploring João Pessoa

One of the oldest and less developed cities in Brazil, João Pessoa has a small historic core, which remains little changed despite the modernization drive. It is located a bit inland, on a small hill overlooking the Rio Sanhauá and Rio Paraíba. Modern João Pessoa, with fast emerging skyscrapers, gravitates towards the beaches. Due to a state law restricting the height of buildings within 490 ft (150 m) of the shoreline to four stories or less, the waterfront is free of the curtain wall of concrete high-rises that afflict some other Brazilian beachfronts.

🏠 Catedral Basílica de Nossa Senhora das Neves

Rua General Osório, Centro. **Tel** (83) 3221 2503. **Open** 2–5pm Mon–Fri, 5–7pm Sat. 🕊 5pm Mon–Fri, 7:30pm Sat, 6am, 9am, 7:30pm Sun. 🎫

After four major renovations little remains of the original cathedral built in 1586. The interior maintains a striking harmony, unlike many of the elaborate Rococo-style churches in Brazil.

🏠 Igreja de São Francisco

Praça São Francisco, Centro Histórico. **Tel** (83) 3218 4505. **Open** 9am–5pm Mon–Fri, 9am–2pm Sat & Sun. 🎫 🎫

One of the most spectacular churches in the city sits majestically atop a hill that bears the same name. The most striking feature of this impressive 18th-century church is the tower topped with an oriental dome. The altar contains an 18th-century statue of St. Benedict, one of the few black saints. The beautiful Rococo-style painting on

Façade of Igreja de São Francisco, João Pessoa's celebrated church

the ceiling of the church depicts various images of St. Francis. Even older than the church by a few decades is a stone cross across the courtyard. The church is part of the larger Centro Cultural de Sao Francisco complex, which also includes the Convento de Santo Antônio, chapels, and a museum of popular and sacred art, the result of grand-scale reforms carried out in 1718 and 1788.

🏛 Mosteiro de São Bento

Rua General Osório, Centro Histórico. **Tel** (83) 3241 1093. **Open** 8:30am–4pm Mon–Fri. 🕊 7am.

Built in the 17th century, this working monastery is a shining example of simplicity. Its unembellished, well-restored interior features a curved wooden ceiling.

🏖 Praia de Tambaú

4 miles (7 km) E of city center.
João Pessoa's most popular urban beach is Praia de Tambaú, a 4-mile- (7-km-) long stretch of sand lined with restaurants, cafés, and interesting food and craft stalls. In the evenings, locals stroll the seawall, enjoying the cool breeze.

🏖 Praia do Cabo Branco

S of Praia do Tambaú.
Better suited for swimming than Tambaú, Cabo Branco is a residential beach area looking out over the easternmost point in the Americas, **Ponta do Seixas** (Seixas Point). The point juts out into the ocean, and is topped by a small lighthouse, with a monument marking the spot.

Ilha de Picãozinho

N of Praia de Tambaú.

Actually a large coral reef, Ilha de Picãozinho is a popular spot. At low tide, boats depart from Praia do Tambaú, and take visitors over to swim and snorkel in the natural tide pools. Fish and starfish can be easily observed in the crystal-clear water. Check the tide table for specific times daily before taking a dip. For a few days every month, the tide is too high for the reef to be visited.

Ilha de Areia Vermelha

12 miles (20 km) N of town.

Another low-tide attraction is Ilha de Areia Vermelha (Island of Red Sand). For approximately 25 days every month, low tide exposes a beautiful beach of striking red-orange sand, a short distance off the coast of João Pessoa. With a choice of floating bars, it makes a perfect spot for swimming, snorkeling, or sunbathing. The temporary island is accessible from Praia da Camboinhas, 8 miles (13 km)

north of Tambaú. Trips to this island can be arranged by travel agencies.

Praia Tambaba

19 miles (30 km) S of town.

Tambaba is a beautiful, secluded nudist beach with lush vegetation, small reefs, and tide pools. Two coves make up this splendid beach. Clothing is optional on one of the coves. The other cove, which is exclusively a nudist beach, is closed off by a gate

VISITORS' CHECKLIST

Practical Information
Paraíba. 723,000. Sectur, Parque Solonde Lucena 216, (83) 3218 9852.
joaopessoa.pb.gov.br

Transport
7 miles (11 km) W of city center. Rodoviária at Rua Francisco Londres, Varadouro.

and allows men only if accompanied by women.

Praia Tambaba, located south of João Pessoa

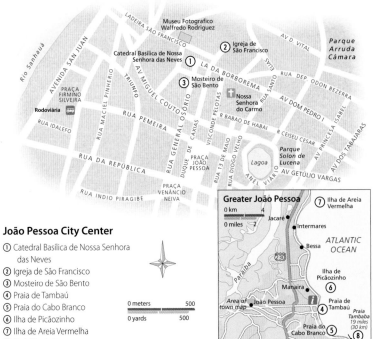

João Pessoa City Center

① Catedral Basílica de Nossa Senhora das Neves
② Igreja de São Francisco
③ Mosteiro de São Bento
④ Praia de Tambaú
⑤ Praia do Cabo Branco
⑥ Ilha de Picãozinho
⑦ Ilha de Areia Vermelha
⑧ Praia Tambaba

❷ Campina Grande

Paraíba. 400,000. from João Pessoa. Rua 13 de Maio 329, (83) 3310 6100. Micarande (late Apr), Festas Juninas (Jun).

Ideal for experiencing the unique *sertão* culture, Campina Grande is a large market town with some degree of industrial growth.

The autumn harvest festival, Festas Juninas, although celebrated everywhere in the Northeast, is biggest in Campina Grande. The vast, purpose-built fairground, **Parque do Povo**, includes several smaller theme parks such as the Sítio São João, a reproduction of a traditional ranch where visitors can observe the rural *nordeste* lifestyle, and the Arraial Hilton Motta, a replica of a small interior town.

The **Museu de Arte Assis Chateaubriand** has a striking collection of modern works, with a focus on the work of artists from the Northeast.

Museu de Arte Assis Chateaubriand
Rua João Lélis 581, Catolé. **Tel** (83) 3337 3637. **Open** 1:30–6:30pm Mon–Fri.

Parque do Povo
Tel (83) 3310 6100. **Open** only during Festas Juninas.

The Lajedo do Pai Mateus rock formation, Cariri

❸ Cariri

Paraíba. from Campina Grande. Cariri Ecotours, (84) 9660 1818. **caririecotours.com.br**

Situated in the Cariri Paraíbano, a large plateau in the Serra da Borborema, Cariri is the point at which the *sertão* proper begins. Tours in this area of aboriginal rock carvings and huge rock formations can be organized by Cariri Ecotours, based in Ponta Negra, Natal.

One of the formations, the **Lajedo do Pai Mateus**, sits on the private grounds of a *fazenda*. A vast slab of bare granite, it is littered with boulders bigger than houses, as if a giant had scattered his collection of pebbles – hence the local epithet, "Devil's Marbles." The most remarkable of these granite monsters is the Pedra do Capacete (Helmet Stone), a 20-ft- (6-m-) high boulder that is open in the front and hollow underneath, resembling a huge war helmet.

From the plateau, there are breathtaking views of the Borborema valley. The diverse landscape consists of small trees, bushes, cacti, and bromeliads. Sightings of emu birds, an ostrich-like avian, are common in this area.

❹ Souza

Paraíba. 60,000. from Campina Grande. Cariri Ecotours, (84) 9660 1818. **caririecotours.com.br**

Brazil's most important prehistoric site, Souza is located deep in the Paraíba interior, almost on the border with Ceará. It was a large shallow lake where hundreds of dinosaur species roamed, 130 million years ago. Today, the dry riverbed of the Rio de Peixe, also known as the **Vale dos Dinossauros**, contains one of the world's best collections of dinosaur tracks. The largest and best track forms a perfect 164-ft- (50-m-) long trail across the meandering riverbed.

Scattered throughout the valley are numerous other tracks, most of which have not yet been catalogued or protected. Some, indeed, have yet to be discovered. Cariri Ecotours can combine trips in this area with visits to Cariri.

A night scene of Campina Grande, lit up during the Festas Juninas

Festas Juninas

One of the most popular folklore traditions of the Northeast, the Festas Juninas began as a peasant celebration of the corn harvest and the June solstice, the longest night of the year in the Southern Hemisphere. June also coincided with the feasts of St. Anthony, St. John, and St. Peter. Over the years, the pagan rituals and Catholic events were melded together. The atmosphere is burlesque, as partygoers dress up in peasant outfits and perform square dances to the sounds of *forró (see p240)*. Bonfires are lit and fireworks sent aloft to safeguard the harvest and ward off evil spirits, as well as to bring light to the long night.

The Sertão

The *sertão* is a geographic region that encompasses almost half the territory of the Northeast. Aridity is its single most important characteristic. Rainfall is sparse, and the vegetation is primarily *caatinga,* which consists of small trees and bushes. Agriculture is difficult in the *sertão*, which makes it one of Brazil's poorest regions.

Traditionally, *sertanejos* have made a living herding goats or cattle. One of the country's original cowboy regions, the *sertão* has also seen the largest outflow of people in Brazil. Hard climatic conditions forced *en masse* migrations either to the coast, or to the big cities such as São Paulo and Rio de Janeiro. Not just the dislocated northeasterners, or *nordestinos,* but all Brazilians have an affinity for the *sertão* way of life: *forró* music is loved throughout the country, and Brazil's popular culture abounds with *sertanejo* stories and images.

After a sudden rain, the dry land will turn green and lush for a short period.

Palma cactus is often the only food available to livestock. The tough, chewy leaves are ground into a paste and used as cattle feed.

Caatinga, the vegetation growing in this arid landscape, consists of cacti, bromeliads, and scrubby trees and bushes. These plant species are suitable to the challenging conditions of the *sertão*.

Goats are the most important livestock in the *sertão*. More adaptable than other animals, the goat thrives in the dry and hot conditions. It is an important source of meat, milk, and leather.

Rio São Francisco is one of the main water sources in the *sertão*. Large irrigation projects are using the water to make agriculture possible. Many areas in Pernambuco grow fruits and vegetables.

Nordestino markets are where homesick communities of migrants from the Northeast meet, listen to *forró*, and eat some of their favorite foods. São Paulo and Rio de Janeiro have the largest *sertanejo* immigrant communities.

Luiz Gonzaga (1912–89), Brazil's most famous "Son of the *Sertão*," was a *forró* musician. Most of his songs celebrated or lamented the life of those living in the *sertão*.

A palm-lined beach in Fortaleza ▶

The small chapel in the central courtyard of the Forte dos Reis Magos

⑤ Natal

Rio Grande do Norte. 🖼 800,000. ✈
🚌 ℹ Centro de Turismo, Rua
Aderbal de Figueiredo 980, (84) 3211
6149. 🎭 Carnatal (Dec).

Natal is a pleasant, modern, and
safe city, increasingly sought out
as a sunshine destination by
winter-weary Europeans. It has
several attractions, including
beautiful beaches, sand hills,
lagoons, dune buggy rides,
unusual sand art, and an
incredible nightlife.

The city and its most famous
landmark, **Forte dos Reis
Magos** (Fort of the Magi),
date back to December 25,
1598, when the Portuguese
established a fort and settlement at the mouth of the Rio
Potengi. In honor of the season,
the city was named Natal, the
Portuguese word for Christmas.
The fort was named after the
three wise kings of the east

who had traveled to Bethlehem
bearing gifts. The Dutch
occupied the fort in 1633,
upgrading it into its current
five-pointed formation before
turning it back over to the
Portuguese in 1654. Access
to the fort is via a narrow
pedestrian walkway. At high
tide, the fort is cut off from land
by the waves. Visitors have the
full run of the fort, from the
garrisons and the mess hall to
the high ramparts, which offer
terrific views of the city skyline.

Natal was never a large
trading center, and there are
few historic buildings. The
city's 19th-century penitentiary
has been converted into the
Centro de Turismo, a showcase
for regional arts and crafts. All
of the dozens of prison cells
along four corridors have been
transformed into shops selling
leatherwork, lace, ceramics,
hammocks, and figurines from

northeastern folk festivals. A
restaurant and a cafeteria offer
some regional dishes. On
Thursday evenings, the
courtyard of the old prison
becomes an outdoor dance hall
as the center plays host to *forró
com o turista*, an evening of *forró*
dancing, with live music and
instructors on hand to help shy
and left-footed foreigners with
the dance steps.

Most visitors to Natal stay in
Ponta Negra, a waterfront
neighborhood in a modern
part of the city featuring a
lovely long beach with good
waves for surfing. At the far
end of the beach the Morro do
Careca, a towering 390-ft
(120-m) sand dune, is off-limits
to climbers because of the
danger of erosion.

On the coast between
the old downtown and the
modern parts of Natal there
stands the **Parque das Dunas**, a
12-sq-mile (6-sq-km) reserve
of coastal dunes and native
vegetation. The park has several
trails, but can only be visited
with a guide.

🏛 **Centro de Turismo**
Rua Aderbal de Figueiredo 980.
Tel (84) 3211 6149. **Open** 9am–7pm
daily. ♿

🏰 **Forte dos Reis Magos**
Praia do Forte. **Tel** (84) 3211 3820.
Open 8am–4:30pm daily. 🎫

🌳 **Parque das Dunas**
Av Alexandrino de Alencar s/n.
Tel (84) 3201 3985. **Open** 8am–6pm
Tue–Sun. 🎫 🎫

Couples dancing to the lively music
of *forró*

Forró

According to local legend, the
musical style known as *forró* is said
to have been inspired by visiting
foreigners. In the early days of
World War II, the Americans
created a massive air base near the
city. Locals invited the American
airmen to their parties, and to
make sure they felt welcome they
put up signs proclaiming that
simplified dances with a two-step
rhythm, were "for all." The label
stuck to the musical style, though
in common speech "for all"
became *forró*.

❻ Rota do Sol Beaches

Head south from Natal on the Rota do Sol (Route of the Sun), for beaches and more beaches, stretching from the edge of the city to the far southern border of the state. Variety is the key feature of this golden stretch of coast. There are beaches with small reefs and little surf, and others with strong and steady waves, much loved by avid surfers. There are deserted beaches surrounded by tall dunes, accessible only by dune buggy or 4WD, far from the hustle and bustle of even the smallest fishing village. Other beaches, particularly Pipa, are full to bursting with energetic young Brazilians.

Mãe Luiza lighthouse north of Ponta Negra

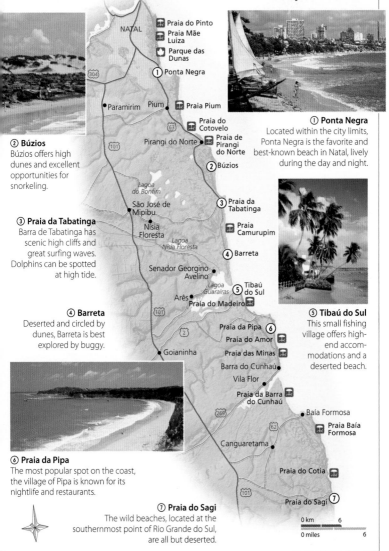

① Ponta Negra
Located within the city limits, Ponta Negra is the favorite and best-known beach in Natal, lively during the day and night.

② Búzios
Búzios offers high dunes and excellent opportunities for snorkeling.

③ Praia da Tabatinga
Barra de Tabatinga has scenic high cliffs and great surfing waves. Dolphins can be spotted at high tide.

④ Barreta
Deserted and circled by dunes, Barreta is best explored by buggy.

⑤ Tibaú do Sul
This small fishing village offers high-end accommodations and a deserted beach.

⑥ Praia da Pipa
The most popular spot on the coast, the village of Pipa is known for its nightlife and restaurants.

⑦ Praia do Sagi
The wild beaches, located at the southernmost point of Rio Grande do Sul, are all but deserted.

0 km   6
0 miles   6

For keys to symbols *see back flap*

Snorkeling in the coral reefs, Maracajaú

❼ Genipabu

Rio Grande do Norte. 🚶 5,000. ✈ Natal Airport. 🚌 ℹ Associação dos Bugueiros do Rio Grande do Norte, (84) 3225 2077.

The main reason to visit Genipabu is to experience the magnificent dunes. This small town is located north of Natal, close to the edge of an impressive landscape of shifting sands that pile up into high dunes and plunge down to the edge of the Atlantic Ocean. Though it is possible to ride a camel through the dunes or sandboard down them, the best way to enjoy these enormous ridges of sand is behind the roll bar of a dune buggy with an experienced driver at the wheel. The **Parque Dunas de Genipabu** is the perfect place to start. This area of 164-ft (50-m) tall shifting dunes is off-limits to all but licensed buggy drivers who know their way around every hump and dip. Passengers have the option of requesting a ride *"com ou sem emoção"* (with or without the thrills and heart palpitations). Well worth requesting, the thrill-ride is an amazing roller coaster of maneuvers up and down along the slippery front faces of the dunes, descending at almost 90-degree angles before zooming straight up another dune on the far side.

The best time of day to visit the Parque das Dunas is in the afternoon, to enjoy the lovely golden sunset over the dunes after the ride.

❽ Maracajaú

Rio Grande do Norte. 🚌 **Open** at low tide only.

Maracajaú's coral reefs offer one of the best spots for snorkeling along the whole of Brazil's north coast. The reefs lie approximately 4 miles (7 km) offshore. At low tide, the receding ocean leaves the reefs from just 3 to 9 ft (1 to 3 m) underwater, and forms natural pools, called *parrachos*, which combine the beauty of the tranquil water with a spectacular array of marine life. They are shallow enough for snorkelers and swimmers to observe dozens of species of colorful, tropical fish trapped inside the reefs. The water is crystal clear and warm round the year, making it a popular destination for scuba divers and swimmers alike. Tour operators offer scuba-diving trips, but the water is so shallow, it is hardly worth the effort or expense.

The best way to reach Maracajaú is by a dune buggy, departing from Natal (or Genipabu) and traveling north along the white, sandy beaches. Check the tide tables to time the journey in order to arrive in Maracajaú at, or a few hours before, low tide. The large **Mo-Noa Park**, replete with slides and swimming pools, en route to the coral reefs in Maracajaú, is an enjoyable stop for children.

Tourists enjoying a buggy ride on the white sand dunes in Genipabu

For hotels and restaurants in this region see pp376–7 and p393

Sailboats, known as *jangadas*, on Tibaú beach, one of the beach-villages along Costa Branca

9 Costa Branca

Rio Grande do Norte. 🚌
ℹ️ Catavento Turismo Fortaleza,
(85) 3433 6999.

The Costa Branca lies in the extreme northwest of Rio Grande do Norte. Starting at **Porto do Mangue**, it stretches across the villages of **Areia Branca** and **Grossos** and ends at **Tibaú**. The name "Costa Branca" refers to both the white dunes and the salt works found along this coast. The region has not yet been discovered by mass tourism, and its beaches, mangroves, dunes, and lagoons are blissfully devoid of crowds. **Praia do Rosado**, just west of Porto do Mangue, is famous for its pinkish sand dunes. The red soil underneath the shifting dunes mixes with the white sand of the beach giving the dunes an unusual and distinctly soft, pink hue.

The largest village on this coast, Areia Branca has around 20,000 residents and offers the best tourist facilities for those wanting to spend a few days exploring the region. Tibaú is the last village in Rio Grande do Norte, right on the border with Ceará. Its beach is mostly used by residents of the inland city of Mossoró. Local artisans use sand from the colored dunes to make artistic and pretty designs inside small glass bottles.

Sand design in glass bottle

10 Mossoró

Rio Grande do Norte. 🚗 225,000.
✈️ 🚌 ℹ️ Rua Ruy Barbosa 282
(84) 3315 4814. 📅 Batalha do
Mossoró (Jun).

Located 34 miles (55 km) inland from the coast, Mossoró is, in many ways, the archetypal *sertão* town of the northeastern interior. The main places of interest in Mossoró are connected to a glorious moment in history in 1924, when the townspeople fought off an attack by the legendary bandit leader Lampião and his gang of outlaws. The event is still commemorated every June 13 with great ceremony.

Mossoró is an ideal jumping-off point for visiting the **Lajedo de Soledade**, an archaeological site. Its limestone rocks were formed more than 90 million years ago. Tours begin at the visitors' center, at the Museu de Soledade. From here, visitors can depart on a guided walk featuring 10,000-year-old rock paintings, and impressive fossils containing the remains of extinct animals, including saber-toothed tigers.

🏛️ **Lajedo de Soledade**
Tel (84) 3333 1017. **Open** 8am–5pm
Tue–Sun. 🎫 📷
🌐 lajedodesoledade.org.br

Repentistas

Repentista is a popular form of entertainment in the interior of the Northeast. Its singers engage in a two-man musical duel, making their rhymes up on the spot, trying to score points off their opponent. Singers sometimes accompany themselves with a tambourine or the melodious *viola nordestina*, developed from the Portuguese seven-string guitar. The singing duelists take turns singing out a stanza, trying to win the favor of the audience by making fun of their opponent, preferably with a clever bit of rhyme. The adversary's manhood, sexual prowess, and ancestry are common topics, but politics and day-to-day events also play into the mix. In big cities with significant *nordestino* populations, such as São Paulo and Rio de Janeiro, *repentistas* make money on the downtown streets by creating impromptu songs to entertain homesick migrants.

Repentistas performing

⓫ Canoa Quebrada

Ceará. 🖾 65,300. 🚌 from Fortaleza.
🛈 Secretaría de Turismo, (88) 3446
2451. 🅦 canoaviagens.com.br

In just over four decades, Canoa Quebrada has transformed from a sleepy fishing village to a popular hippy hangout in the 1970s, and now a mainstream beach resort. According to a legend, the name Canoa Quebrada, meaning "Broken Canoe," originated with a Portuguese skipper who wrecked his ship close to shore and donated the useless craft to local fishermen. Never having seen such a craft before, locals named it a broken canoe.

The beaches of Canoa Quebrada, featuring red cliffs, fine sand, and offshore reefs, attract many visitors today. The village itself is a bustling place, known for its cafés and restaurants, and for the bars and clubs lining the main cobblestone street. It is also famous for its lacework. Even at the busiest times, however, it is not difficult to get away from the crowds and find a spot on one of the more deserted beaches or high sand dunes surrounding Canoa Quebrada. Buggy tours are a popular way to get out of town. The tour to Ponta Grossa, 18 miles (30 km) southeast, travels along miles of empty beaches framed by high red sandstone cliffs. Other activities include kite-surfing, riding, and sailing on a *jangada* (sailboat).

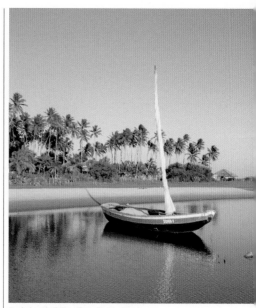

Beach along the fishing village of Jericoacoara

About 6 miles (10 km) northwest is the small town of **Aracati**. It is one of the few historic towns in this part of Northeast Brazil. An important center for the 18th-century cattle industry, Aracati has several buildings dating back to this time. Most noteworthy is the Mercado Central (Central Market), dating back to the 1700s, still used as the town's daily open-air market on Rua Pompeu.

⓬ Fortaleza

See pp246–7.

⓭ Jericoacoara

Ceará. 🖾 2,000. 🚌 from Fortaleza.
🅦 jericoacoara.com

The isolated village of Jericoacoara is a beach lover's paradise. Although no longer the sleepy fishing community it once was, it preserves much of its original charm. The village consists of five streets made of sand, and houses and apartments are simple, even rustic. In 2002, the entire region was declared a national park, putting a complete halt to the construction of new buildings.

Red sandstone cliffs in and around the beaches of Canoa Quebrada

For hotels and restaurants in this region see pp376–7 and p393

The spectacular Ubajara Cave in Parque Nacional de Ubajara

Surrounded by dunes and lagoons, Jeri (as locals call it) is a place for those who like water, waves, and wind. From June to January, the winds pick up and kitesurfers, windsurfers, and sailors from around the world flock to Jeri.

Dune buggies are used to explore the surrounding beaches and dunes and visit the various lagoons. The most beautiful are **Lagoa Azul** and **Lagoa do Paraíso**, located about 12 miles (20 km) east of the village. Jeri's postcard view is that of **Pedra Furada**, a basalt outcrop, on the edge of the sea with a 13-ft (4-m) hole in the middle. It sits on the beach at Praia Malhada, about 2 miles (3 km) east, a 15-minute walk from the village. The red rock glows in the late afternoon light and from June to September, the aperture lines up perfectly with the tropical setting sun. Another beautiful spot is **Duna do Pôr do Sol** (Sunset Dune).

➍ Parque Nacional de Ubajara

Ceará. 🚌 from Fortaleza. 🛈 Secretaría de Turismo, (88) 3634 2365; Park Headquarters, (88) 3634 1388. **Open** 8am–5pm Tue–Sun. 🅿️ ♿

Located almost exactly halfway between Fortaleza and Teresina, the Parque Nacional de Ubajara is the smallest national park in Brazil. Situated close to the small town of Ubajara, the park

features the **Ubajara Cave**. The entrance to the cave can be reached either by cable car (9am–2:30pm Tue–Sun) or via a steep, marked trail through the forest. The 3,937-ft- (1,200-m-) long cave is filled with stalactites and stalagmites, the work of several patient centuries of erosion and calcium deposition.

Fifteen chambers totaling 3,674 ft (1,120 m) have been mapped, of which 1,377 ft (420 m) are open to visitors. Eight galleries are lit up to display some of the amazing formations that have taken shape inside the cave. The main formations seen inside are Pedra do Sino (Bell Stone), Salas da Rosa (Rose Rooms), Sala do Cavalo (Horse Room), and Sala dos Retratos (Portrait Room). The cave is also home to 14 different types of bat.

The elevation gain is just over 1,640 ft (500 m), and the trail leading up to the cave, though rather strenuous, offers some spectacular views of the Serra da Ipiapaba and several waterfalls and beautiful natural pools. The hike takes about two hours, one-way. There are also many local guides available here to show visitors around the park's eco trails, caves, and waterfalls.

Buggies

Dune buggies are found everywhere on Brazil's northeastern coast. Essentially a Volkswagen Beetle chassis with a fiberglass body and soft, fat tires, the Brazilian dune buggy is the perfect vehicle for exploring the endless beaches and towering sand dunes that characterize Northeast Brazil.

Popular places to buggy here are Genipabu (see p242), just north of Natal, and Cumbuco and Canoa Quebrada, respectively north and south of Fortaleza. They all feature towering mountains of sand, and dune-buggy drivers are trained to make the most of them.

High-speed runs up, down, and along the sheer, steep face of sand dunes are among the most hair-raising maneuvers one can expect from such a tour.

Multiday buggy expeditions include tours from Natal to Fortaleza – nearly 311 miles (500 km) of untouched sand.

Dune buggy in Canoa Quebrada

⑫ Fortaleza

With pretty urban beaches, a pleasant year-round climate, and a constant cooling breeze coming off the ocean, Fortaleza has an appealing resort-like atmosphere. Founded in the early 1500s, Fortaleza remained a small town until after Brazilian independence in 1822, then rapidly developed into one of Brazil's largest ports, exporting vast amounts of cotton to England in particular. There is a small historic section with a 17th-century fort near the old port, now renovated as a nightlife area called Praia de Iracema, but beyond that Fortaleza has a modern feel, with apartment high-rises, beach boulevards, and outdoor cafés.

Brightly painted colonial buildings lining the streets

🎭 Teatro José de Alencar

Praça José de Alencar s/n. **Tel** (85) 3101 2566. **Open** 9am–noon, 2–5pm Tue–Sun 🎭 📷 hourly. ♿

Named after one of Brazil's famous novelists, the Teatro José de Alencar was built in 1908. The theater's high-Victorian cast-iron structure was imported straight from Glasgow. Additional elements, such as the stained-glass windows and interior furnishings, were done in the Art Nouveau style.

Ironwork, Teatro José de Alencar

🏛 Centro de Turismo

Rua Senador Pompeu 350. **Tel** (85) 3101 5508. **Open** 8am–6pm Mon–Fri, 8am–4pm Sat, 8am–noon Sun. ♿

This formerly grim 19th-century prison has been transformed into a bustling market, with a different shop in each of the old jail cells. The market specializes in local handicrafts, including fine lace, leather, and figurines. The market is a good place to stock up on top-quality cashew nuts.

🏛 Museu do Ceará

Rua São Paulo 51. **Tel** (85) 3101 2609. **Open** 9am–5pm Tue–Sat. 🎭 📷

The museum possesses a vast archive of things relating to the history of Ceará – coins, medals paintings, furniture, indigenous artifacts, folk art, and more. Its most prized exhibit is the dagger belonging to notorious outlaw Lampião *(see p217)*.

🏛 Centro Cultural Dragão do Mar

Rua Dragão do Mar 81, Iracema. **Tel** (85) 3488 8600. **Open** 8am–10pm Mon–Fri 8am–11pm Sat & Sun. 🎭 for movies & plays. 🌐 **dragaodomar.org.br**

Fortaleza's cultural center is a striking white building with a circular design. It houses the Museum of Contemporary Art, a history and anthropology museum, a planetarium, and a cinema and theater venue.

🏪 Mercado Central

Rua Maestro Alberto Nepomuceno 199 **Tel** (85) 3454 8586. **Open** 8am–6pm Mon–Fri, 8am–4pm Sat, 8am–1pm Sun ♿ 🌐 **mercadocentraldefortaleza** **com.br**

Fortaleza's central market is the cheapest place in town for fine leatherwork, lace, or textiles. The market is also an excellent place to sample local ice cream made from regional fruits.

Fortaleza

① Teatro José de Alencar
② Centro de Turismo
③ Museu do Ceará
④ Centro Cultural Dragão do Mar
⑤ Mercado Central
⑥ Praia de Iracema
⑦ Praia de Meireles
⑧ Praia do Futuro
⑨ Praia de Cumbuco

The Story of Iracema

Written by José de Alencar in 1865, the story of Iracema tells of the love that a Tabajara princess bore for Martim, a white Portuguese settler. Iracema uses magic to make Martim fall in love with her, and is ostracized by her community. Away from her people, she loses her magical powers and her lover. A statue of Iracema on Meireles beach is located where, according to legend, she stood awaiting the return of her beloved.

Statue of Iracema waiting for her lover

VISITORS' CHECKLIST

Practical Information
Ceará. 🚊 2,400,000. 🛈 Casa do Turista, Av Beira Mar at Rua Frei Mansueto, (85) 3105 2670. 🏺 daily craft market at Meireles beach. 🎉 Fortal (Jul), Regata de Jangadas (Jul), Semana do Folclore (Aug).
🌐 fortaleza.ce.gov.br/turismo

Transport
✈ 4 miles (6 km) S of town.
🚌 (85) 3235 0688.

Praia de Iracema

Just east of the city center lies the Praia de Iracema. Though called a beach, it is actually the very urban former port, now renovated and transformed into the city's most popular nightlife and restaurant area. The centerpiece of the area is a long ocean pier called Ponte Ios Ingleses (Englishman's Pier), first built in 1920, and modeled on the piers of Brighton. Many restaurants occupy other original turn-of-the-19th-century buildings in the area. Locally famous nightlife spots include Piratas (open Mondays), and Lupus Bier, known for its Wednesday evening folklore and variety show.

Praia de Meireles

The city's prettiest urban beach is lined with thick groves of coconut palms and waterside cafés, although the water is not considered good for swimming. Meireles is a great place for strolling, shopping, sunbathing, or people-watching while

Visitors at a waterside café, Praia de Meireles

sipping on fresh cashew juice. Home to what has become the city's prime residential and hotel nightlife in Fortaleza, Meireles' pedestrian boulevard, running beside the beach, becomes a night market every evening.

Praia do Futuro

Praia do Futuro is one of the best beaches in the city for swimming, and a bustling nightlife destination in its own right. The 7-mile- (11-km-) long beach southeast of the center is lined with restaurants and beach shacks that serve local cuisine. There are several discos on the beach that are popular on weekends. On Thursday nights, Fortalezans head to Barraca Chico do Caranguejo to feast on fresh crab and listen to popular live *forró (see p240)* music.

Praia de Cumbuco

21 miles (33 km) W of town. Cumbuco is the city's favorite beach playground. The Lagoa da Banana offers a wide variety of watersports, including jet-skiing, boating, banana boating, and kayaking, and has become a major kitesurfing destination. Lagoa do Parnamirim, just south of Cumbuco, is surrounded by tall dunes, making it perfect for "ski-bunda" (bum-skiing), where skiers slide on wooden boards down a dune into the lagoon. Other activities on offer include horseback riding and sailing on *jangadas*, or single-sail rafts.

meters | 500
yards | 500

MUCURIPE

⑧ Praia do Futuro

For keys to symbols *see back flap*

PIAUÍ & MARANHÃO

Although part of the Northeast, Piauí and Maranhão are different from the rest of the region culturally and geographically. Both states have violent histories. Piauí was the site of many skirmishes between the indigenous population and cattle herders, and Maranhão was forcibly settled in 1612 by the French. Today, the area is abundant in natural and cultural riches.

Unlike its southern neighbors, Piauí was settled by ranchers on horseback pushing northwards from the sugar plantations of Bahia in the late 1700s.

Largely visited in transit, Piauí is sparsely populated and possibly the poorest state in Brazil. The economy here is greatly dependent on agriculture and livestock. The only significant industry revolves around the *carnaúba* palm, which yields a wax that is an important ingredient of shellac. However, Piauí boasts a few fascinating natural attractions. The state capital, Teresina, located more than 186 miles (300 km) inland, is the only capital in Northeast Brazil which is not on the ocean, and has some interesting sights.

For many years after they first came to Brazil, the Portuguese showed little interest in the area that now forms Maranhão. Taking advantage of the Portuguese neglect of the Maranhão coast, the French, in 1612, landed a sizable force and founded São Luís, named in honor of King Louis XIII. Portuguese forces laid siege for four years to drive the new French colony out.

Maranhão's golden age came in the 19th century, with a rich agricultural export economy based on cotton and sugar. Ports such as São Luís and Alcântara grew wealthy. When slavery was abolished in 1888, Maranhão's sugar and cotton industries collapsed, causing an economic slump that lasted for most of the 20th century.

Maranhão is today an exciting destination, both in terms of natural and cultural treasures. The state's main festival, Bumba-meu-boi, celebrates the indigenous, Portuguese, and African cultures.

Mesmerizing sand dunes of Lençóis Maranhenses in Maranhão

◀ Beautifully decorated ceiling of the Igreja da Sé, São Luis

Exploring Piauí & Maranhão

Most of Piauí's attractions are a long way from the coast. The Serra da Capivara is one of the largest archaeological sites in the world, containing more than 30,000 prehistoric rock paintings. The only important destination on Piauí's tiny 41-mile (66-km) coastline is the town of Parnaíba. It sits at the edge of the Delta do Parnaíba, one of the largest deep-water river deltas in the world, and now an ecotourism destination. Most of the delta itself lies in Maranhão. Its capital, São Luís, rivals Salvador for its collection of restored colonial homes and heritage buildings. Outside of São Luís, the biggest draw is a spectacular region of stark beauty in the form of coastal sand dunes known as Lençóis Maranhenses.

Sights at a Glance

Towns & Cities

1. Teresina
5. *São Luís pp256–8*
6. Alcântara

National Parks & Areas of Natural Beauty

2. Parque Nacional de Sete Cidades
3. *Parque Nacional de Serra da Capivara pp252–3*
4. *Delta do Parnaíba & Parque Nacional dos Lençóis Maranhenses pp254–5*
7. Reentrâncias Maranhenses

Key

- Major road
- Minor road
- Railroad
- State border

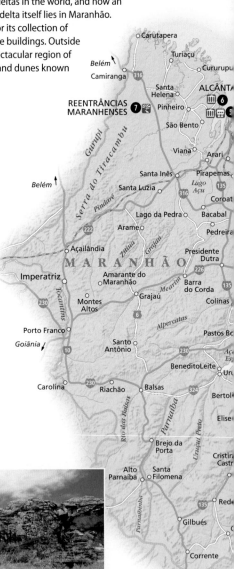

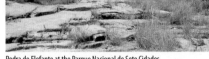

Pedra do Elefante at the Parque Nacional de Sete Cidades

For hotels and restaurants in this region see p377 and pp393–4

Pristine Caburé beach at Lençóis Maranhenses

④ DELTA DO PARNAÍBA & PARQUE NACIONAL DOS LENÇÓIS MARANHENSES

irinhas
Araiosos   Parnaíba

Parnaíba
nardo   Luzilândia   Cocal   343
222   *Fortaleza*
inha   Piracuruca
Batalha   **🅱② PARQUE NACIONAL DE SETE CIDADES**

Miguel   Piripiri
Alves   José de   343   Pedroll
Freitas
Campo Maior
① TERESINA   115   Castelo
do Piauí

narama   São Miguel
do Tapuio
almeirais   120
343   316   *Sambito*

de   *Fortaleza*
Valença
do Piauí
loriano
aha   Oeiras   230   Picos   Fronteiras
São José
do Peixe   *Itaim*   Jaicós   *Recife*
Costa   20   407
Simplício
Mendes   Paulistana
São João
do Piauí
③ PARQUE NACIONAL DE SERRA DA CAPIVARA

Raimundo
Nonato

Brasília

0 kilometers   100
0 miles   100

Getting Around

The São Luís airport in Maranhão has international flights, and Piauí's capital city Teresina can be reached by flights en route to São Luís. There are buses linking almost every town in this region, but roads are in very poor condition. It is also possible to rent a car. The inland attractions of Piauí are far from Teresina, and from each other, so travel well equipped with plenty of gas, water, and supplies.

Most of Maranhão's highlights are on the coast. The Lençóis Maranhenses are best accessed from Barreirinhas, located just on the edge of the Lençóis Maranhenses National Park. From São Luís, it is a 45-minute flight in a single-engine plane, or a four-hour drive. Once there, most excursions are by boat or in a 4WD, as there are no paved roads in the region.

Colonial-style houses and Ponte José Sarney, São Luís

For keys to symbols *see back flap*

Church exterior, Nossa Senhora do Amparo

❶ Teresina

Piauí. 🏙 815,000. ✈️ 🚌
ℹ️ Piemtur, (86) 3215 9426 or 3215 7476. 🌐 **teresina.pi.gov.br**

Founded in 1852, Teresina was named in honor of the Empress Teresa Cristina, wife of Brazilian Emperor Dom Pedro II. Teresina has the dubious honor of being one of Brazil's hottest cities, although Rio Parnaíba and Rio Poty, as well as several large, tree-shaded squares scattered throughout Teresina, moderate the worst of the city's scorching heat.

Most historic buildings date back only to the end of the 19th century. One of the oldest buildings is the cathedral, **Nossa Senhora do Amparo**. Construction was started in 1851 but completed only in 1952. More modern, but also interesting, is the Palácio Karnak, Piauí's new state legislature. Built in 1926, the palace's façade was modeled on an ancient Egyptian temple. The former state legislature is now home to the **Museu do Piauí**. Its small collection provides a good overview of regional history, including both pre-historic artifacts and folk art.

🏛 **Museu do Piauí**
Praça Marechal Deodoro da Fonseca, Centro. **Tel** (86) 3221 6027. **Open** 8am–5pm Tue–Fri, 8am–noon Sat & Sun.

🏛 **Nossa Senhora do Amparo**
Praça Marechal Deodoro da Fonseca s/n, Centro. **Open** daily.

Environs
Easily reached by bus, the **Parque Ambiental Encontro dos Rios** is located just north of Teresina, where the Poty and Parnaíba rivers join up. This pleasant park offers walking trails, fishing spots, gardens, two lookouts, a floating restaurant, a store with regionally made crafts and a statue of Crispim, the Bowl Head.

❷ Parque Nacional de Serra da Capivara

Piauí's most compelling park is the Serra da Capivara, located in the far south of the state. The park's impressive canyons, plateaux, and rock formations also form one of Brazil's most important prehistoric sites, one that was designated a UNESCO World Heritage Site in 1991. Over 30,000 rock paintings have been discovered within the park. The paintings portray aspects of prehistoric life such as the hunt, dances, and other rituals.

Andorinhas
Every evening, thousands of swifts (andorinhas) perform amazing aerial acrobatics before retiring to a nearby cave to spend the night.

Rock Painting
Scientists estimate that many of these rock paintings were created between 6,000 and 12,000 years ago. The oldest drawings may date as far back as 29,000 years.

Key
▬ Major road
▭ Other road
▬ Minor road
– – Trail
▬▬ Park boundary

For hotels and restaurants in this region see p377 and pp393–4

Trails leading up to rock formations at Parque Nacional de Sete Cidades

heat, and erosion, the rocks resemble animals, people, mythological beings, and even man-made structures. Among the shapes are **Mapa do Brasil**, a backward-facing map of Brazil, and **Biblioteca** (Library), both in Quarta Cidade (Fourth City). Segundo Cidade, the second of the seven "cities", has a 147-ft- (45-m-) tall look-out with views out over five of the cities of stone. There are also more than 2,000 prehistoric rock paintings,

some 6,000 years old. The most impressive painting, **Pedra de Inscrição** (Inscribed Rock), said to be marked with cryptic Indian runes, can be seen at Quinta Cidade (Fifth City). Other formations include **Pedra do Elefante** (Elephant Rock) at Sexta Cidade (Sixth City), and lookout points such as the **Arco de Triunfo** (Triumphal Arch), a 59-ft- (18-m-) tall arch-shaped rock, lying between Quarta Cidade and Quinta Cidade.

❷ Parque Nacional de Sete Cidades

Maranhão. 🚌 from Teresina.
ℹ️ Ibama Office, Centro de Visitantes, (86) 3343 1342. **Open** 8am–5pm daily.
🅿️ 🅿️ Parque Hotel Sete Cidades, (86) 3276 2222.

The name Sete Cidades (Seven Cities) refers to seven distinct and unusual rock formations, spread out in the park along 7 miles (12 km) of trails. Only the first six are accessible to the public. Sculpted by rain, wind,

Crispim, the Bowl Head

A popular Piauí legend tells the story of Crispim, a fisherman who lived by the banks of the Rio Parnaíba. He came home one day frustrated after not having caught any fish. Outraged with the meager lunch of beef-bone soup, Crispim took up a large bone and beat his mother. As she lay dying, she cursed him, condemning him to live in the river as a bowl-headed monster.

Rio Parnaíba, reputedly haunted by Crispim

The curse would be lifted when he devoured seven virgins named Maria. Locals still tell of spotting Crispim in the river, looking for virgins to eat.

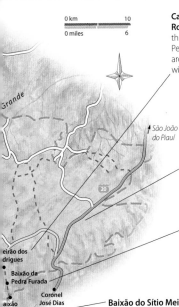

Caldeirão dos Rodrigues, a walk through Baixão da Pedra Furada, leads to archaeological sites with rock paintings.

Desfiladeiro da Capivara is a 2-mile- (4-km-) long trail, leading to many rock-painting sites.

Baixão do Sítio Meio is the site where a pottery shard nearly 9,000 years old was found. It is the oldest in the Americas.

VISITORS' CHECKLIST

Practical Information
Coronel José Dias, Piauí.
ℹ️ Museu de Homem Americano, Bairro Campestre, São Raimundo Nonato, (89) 3582 1612. **Open** 9am–5pm Tue–Sun. Best time to visit is Mar–Jun. 🎟️ valid for three days. 📷 tour groups up to a maximum of 10 people.
🏨 Hotel Serra da Capivara, Santa Luiza, (89) 3582 1389.
🌐 fumdham.org.br

Transport
🚌 from Teresina to São Raimundo Nonato, then taxi.

Baixão da Pedra Furada
The trail leading to the large unusual-shaped rock, known as Pedra Furada (Pierced Rock), leads to 10 different archaeological sites.

Delta do Parnaíba & Parque Nacional dos Lençóis Maranhenses

The Delta do Parnaíba stretches roughly from the Piauí border some 56 miles (90 km) farther up the coast in Maranhão, where the Rio Parnaíba runs into the sea. Shaped like a hand, the river breaks into five fingers, meandering through some 83 islands. Small villages thrive on sea salt, cashews, and crabs. Tourism is still in its infancy. Straddling Piauí and Maranhão, the Parque Nacional Lençóis Maranhenses offers over 600 sq miles (1,555 sq km) of spectacular white sand dunes created by strong coastal winds. From May to August, rain collects in the basins between dunes, forming countless crystal-clear freshwater lagoons. In June, when the water levels are at their highest, the Lençóis dunes look like an array of white stripes, interspersed with sparkling ribbons of blue, turquoise, and green.

★ **Queimada dos Britos**
Deep inside the park is an oasis, surrounded by sand dunes. It can be visited by 4WD from Sucuruju.

Atlantic Ocean

Lagoa Travosa

Lagoa de Santo Amaro

Queimada dos Britos

Santo Amaro do Maranhão

Provoado de Sucuruju

Primeira Cruz

Alegre

★ **Scarlet Ibis**
Born gray, these birds obtain their distinct red color from eating tiny crustaceans found in tide flats in the estuary of the Rio Preguiças.

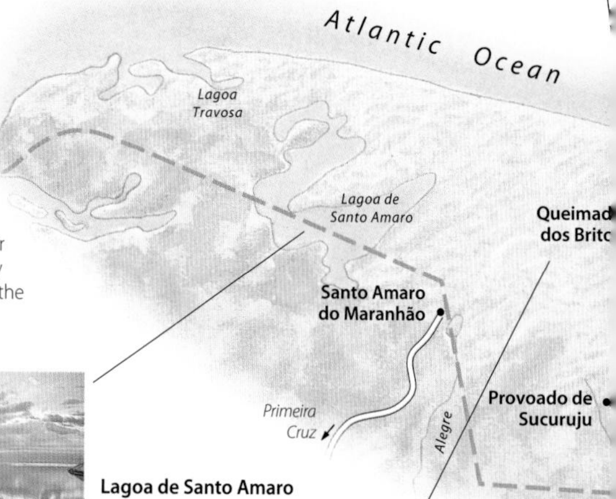

Lagoa de Santo Amaro
This beautiful clear-water lake near the tiny village of Santa Amaro do Maranhão sits isolated amid sand dunes.

Key

▭▭▭ Major road
▭▭▭ Minor road
▬ ▬ Trail
▬▬▬ Park boundary

KEY

① **Baixa Grande** oasis can be reached by hiking across the dunes.

② **Barreirinhas** is a small town, and the main access point to the park.

★ **Lençóis**
On foot, visitors can only access a small portion of the park. To appreciate the size and scale of the dunes, it is worth taking a sightseeing flight from São Luís. The views of the large dunes and lagoons are breathtaking.

The Versatile Buriti Palm Tree

The delta area's dense vegetation is dominated by the multipurpose buriti palm tree. The fruit can be eaten or used for wine, the trunk is used for house poles, while the fronds make thatch roofs and baskets. Buriti fiber is crucial for the strong but limber pouch used to squeeze the poison from manioc root. The twigs make good placemats, the seeds can be fashioned into jewelry, and the bark can be spun into twine.

Buriti palm tree with its hanging fruit

Atins

Sitting on a sandpit a short distance from the Atlantic Ocean, this tiny settlement is a good starting point for reaching the northeastern part of the Lençóis Maranhenses by ferry.

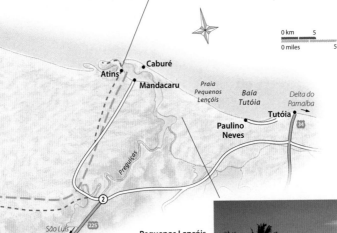

Atins • Caburé
Mandacaru

Praia Pequenos Lençóis

Baía Tutóia

Delta do Parnaíba

Tutóia

Paulino Neves

Preguiças

São Luís

Pequenos Lençóis

This small desert of dunes rises out of Rio Preguiças. Ropes assist in hiking to the Boi hill.

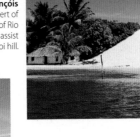

Delta do Parnaíba

Formed where the Rio Parnaíba meets the Atlantic Ocean, the Parnaíba delta, comprising 83 islands with immense beaches, is one of the richest habitats for birdlife in the Northeast.

❺ Street-by-Street: São Luís

One of Brazil's finest examples of Portuguese colonial architecture, São Luís was, ironically, founded by the French in 1612, and later taken over by Dutch invaders. In 1644, the city was finally settled under Portuguese rule, serving as the export point for sugar and cotton. Expensive houses and buildings covered with brightly colored Portuguese tiles were built in the city's urban center. By the late 1800s, with slavery at an end, São Luís went into a decline. At the end of the 1970s, the state government began to invest in preserving the city's historic center, and in 1997, the historical core of São Luís was designated a UNESCO World Heritage Site.

A row of colorful houses along one of the streets in São Luís

★ Palácio dos Leões
Built in 1766 on the site of the original French Fort St. Louis, the Palácio dos Leões is now home to the Maranhão state government.

Beco Catarina Mina
This picturesque 18th-century alley connects the lower-lying streets of the historic center with Avenida Dom Pedro II.

Museu de Arte Visuais is covered in elaborate Portuguese tiles.

Casa do Maranhão
The former 19th-century customs building now houses a fine collection of Bumba-meu-boi folklore. Guides walk visitors through the colorful exhibits.

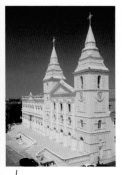

Igreja da Sé
The cathedral little resembles the original 1699 structure. Extensive renovations were carried out in 1922, including the addition of a Neo-Classical façade, giving the cathedral its imposing look.

VISITORS' CHECKLIST

Practical Information
Maranhão. SETUR, Rua da Palma 53, São Luís. **Tel** (98) 3212 6210. **Open** 8am–6pm daily.
saoluis.ma.gov.br/setur
Casa das Tulhas: Rua da Estrela 401. Palácio dos Leões: Av Dom Pedro II. **Open** 2–5:30pm Wed–Fri, 3–5:30pm Sat & Sun

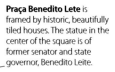

0 meters 100
0 yards 100
RUA 28 DE JULHO
RUA DE ESTRELA
RUA 14 DE JULHO
TRAV. M. ALMEIDA
TRAV. BOAVENTURA
RUA DA ESTRELA
BECO DA PRENSA
Key
Suggested route

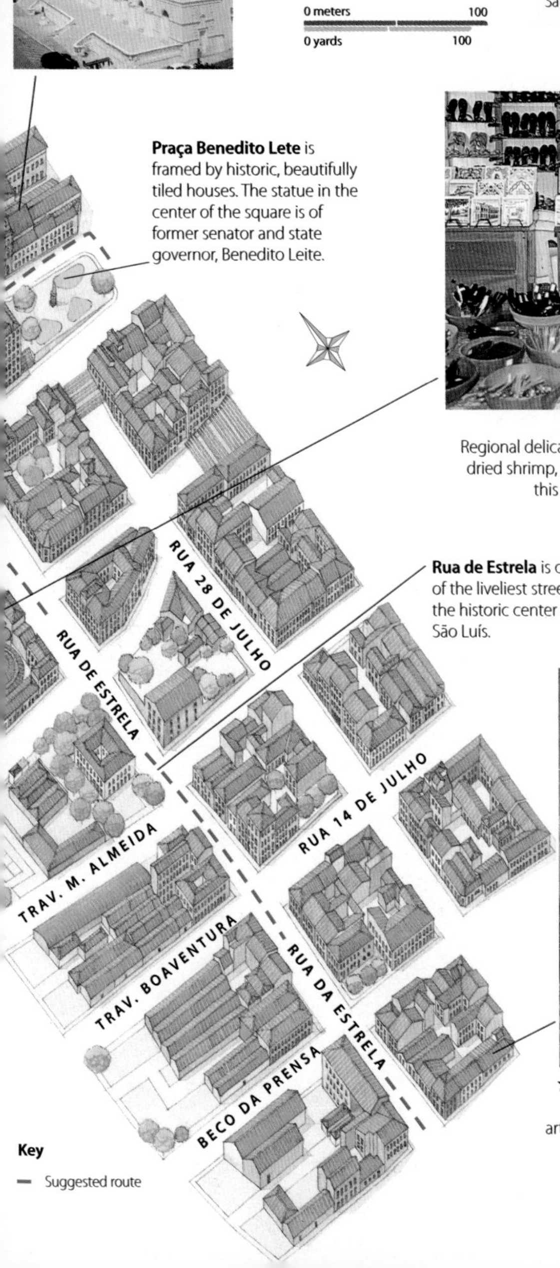

Praça Benedito Lete is framed by historic, beautifully tiled houses. The statue in the center of the square is of former senator and state governor, Benedito Leite.

Rua de Estrela is one of the liveliest streets in the historic center of São Luís.

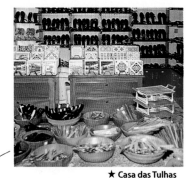

★ **Casa das Tulhas**
Regional delicacies, such as cashew nuts and dried shrimp, are on sale in the food stalls of this 19th-century market building.

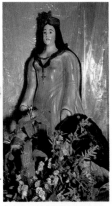

★ **Centro de Cultura Popular**
This center exhibits costumes, artifacts, and photographs of the Festa do Divino, one of Maranhão's most popular religious festivals.

José Sarney Bridge connecting the historic district to São Francisco, São Luís

Exploring São Luís

The rich and diverse historical center of São Luís makes it ideal for touring on foot. This is the oldest part of the city, known interchangeably as the Praia Grande, the Reviver, and the **Centro Histórico**. All the city's museums and beautifully preserved historic sites are located here.

The **Casa do Maranhão** is one of the city's most interesting museums, offering two floors of colorful exhibits that elaborately explain the Festa do Bumba-meu-boi.

Cazumba figure, Casa do Maranhão

The **Centro de Cultura Popular** (also known as the Casa da Festa) is dedicated to showcasing the traditions and customs of the Festa do Divino Espírito Santo. The highlights of the museum are the poster-size photographs of the actual celebrations, including some compelling black-and-white images of the elderly women who once served as festival queens.

The building that once housed the city slave market is now home to the **Cafua das Mercês**, also known as the Museu do Negro. This small museum contains numerous artifacts from the slave era, including musical instruments and tribal artwork, and sinister tools of the slave trade, such as shackles and instruments of torture. One of the more poignant monuments is the Pelourinho, or the whipping post, on display in the museum's central courtyard.

The **José Sarney** Bridge leads from the Centro Histórico into the newer parts of the city. Across the bridge lies São Francisco, the city's small central business district. Just beyond São Francisco, there is a large freshwater lake, the Lagoa de Jansen, circled by a boardwalk with a number of bars and restaurants. Much calmer than the Centro Histórico, it is a very popular place to stroll in the evenings. São Luís is blessed with a string of excellent beaches, all of which can be easily accessed by bus from the Terminal de Integração in the city center.

Farther south, beyond the Lagoa de Jansen, the popular beaches are Ponta d'Areia, São Marcos, Praia do Calhau, **Calhau**, and Olho d'Agua. Calhau, located 6 miles (10 km) from São Luís, is considered by many to be one of the nicest beaches around the city. Many busy kiosks and restaurants line the beachside boulevard. The quiet far end of the beach, where the water is calm and restaurants fewer, is known as Caolho.

🏛 **Cafua das Mercês**
Jacinto Maia 54. **Open** 9am–6pm Mon–Fri.

🏛 **Casa do Maranhão**
Rua do Trapiche s/n. **Tel** (98) 3218 9954. **Open** 9am–6pm Tue–Sat, 9am–1pm Sun. 📷

🏛 **Centro de Cultura Popular**
Rua do Giz 221. **Tel** (98) 3218 9926. **Open** 9am–6pm Tue–Sat, 9am–1pm Sun. 📷

❻ Alcântara

Maranhão. 🚗 21,000. ⛴ from São Luís. ℹ Casa Municipal de Turismo, (98) 3337 1140. 🎭 Festa do Divino Espírito Santo (May).

Just across from São Luís, Alcântara lies on the other side of the Baía de São Marcos. The city was founded by the Portuguese in the 1640s, and used as a temporary capital and base during the campaign to drive the Dutch away from São Luís. Alcântara reached its zenith in the 19th century as the

Bumba-meu-boi

A unique folklore event endemic to Northeast Brazil, the Festa do Bumba-meu-boi revolves around a legendary folktale about the life, death, and resurrection of a magical Brazilian bull. Over the centuries, the celebration has grown into a huge carnivalesque festival, with different neighborhood groups competing to put on the best re-enactment of the story. In São Luís alone, more than 100 groups take to the streets. A papier-mâché bull is created each year and displayed in raucous parades, where participants take on the roles of medicine men, Indians, peasants, and cowboys. The largest celebrations take place in the second half of June. The music is upbeat and lively, with different groups using different rhythms and instruments.

A colorful celebration of the Bumba-meu-boi festival

For hotels and restaurants in this region see p377 and p394

Pillory, restored mansions, and ruin of a church in Alcântara

regional center for the surrounding sugar and cotton plantations. It was the place where wealthy slave-owning aristocrats built their splendid city mansions. When slavery was abolished in 1888, the local economy crashed, the white upper class departed, and many of the fine mansions stood abandoned.

Appreciation of Alcântara's heritage value began as early as the 1950s, but restoration has been slow and quite a few of its churches and mansions remain as ruins, giving the city its own charm. These ruins are now the town's main tourist attractions. Day-trippers from São Luís come here to stroll the quiet cobblestoned streets, peer among the ruins, and admire the often brightly tiled mansions of this former colonial capital.

The Brazilian Heritage Institute, Iphan, has restored several of the old mansions as museums. The best is the **Casa Histórica do Iphan**, featuring period furniture and glassware. Informative wall plaques and well-trained guides make getting around easy in the museum.

Another attraction to Alcântara is the Festa do Divino Espírito Santo, a vibrant religious festival held in May every year.

🏛 **Casa Histórica do Iphan**
Praça de Matríz s/n. **Open** 9am–5pm Tue–Sun. 📷

❼ Reentrâncias Maranhenses

Maranhão. 🚌 from São Luís to Cururupu. ⛴ from Cururupu. ℹ Setur, Rua da Palma 53, São Luís, (98) 3212 6210. 📷 Maramazon, (98) 3235 3994. 🅦 **maramazon.com**

One of the world's largest wetlands, the Reentrâncias Maranhenses is also one of Maranhão's more off-the-beaten-track natural attractions. The small town of **Cururupu** to the north of São Luís offers the best access to the Reentrâncias Maranhenses, with boats departing regularly.

Spread over an area of 10,350 sq miles (26,800 sq km), the Reentrâncias Maranhenses forms an important habitat for shorebirds such as scarlet ibis, spoonbills, whimbrels, egrets, willets, ruddy turnstones, and black-bellied plovers, as well as an array of marine life, including

Scarlet ibis, one of the shorebirds found in Reentrâncias Maranhenses

sea turtles and manatees. Many species of fish and crustaceans are also found in the Reentrâncias. The region is geographically diverse and consists of a complex riverine system of extensive bays, coves, and rugged coastline covered mainly by mangrove forest. Many low-lying islands are also found here.

In order to protect the flora and fauna of this region, the Reentrâncias Maranhenses was designated an Area de Proteção Ambiental (Area of Environmental Protection) and was also made a Ramsar site (a wetland site listed under the Convention on Wetlands of International Importance) in 1993.

One of the more popular destinations here is the **Ilha dos Lençóis**, to the northeast of Cururupu. The island's geography somewhat resembles the Lençóis Maranhenses (see pp254–5), with its endless landscapes of dunes and lagoons.

A small community of about 300 people live on Ilha dos Lençóis and still practice subsistence fishing. Some of them are descendants of the Filhos da Lua (Sons of the Moon), an albino community that settled here at the beginning of the 20th century. The isolation and flooding was harsh on the residents and not many survived. Some of the fishermen work as local tour guides for a small fee.

NORTHERN BRAZIL

Introducing Northern Brazil   **262–267**

Pará & Amapá   **268–279**

Amazonas, Roraima,
    Acre & Rondônia   **280–293**

Introducing Northern Brazil

The six states of Pará, Amapá, Amazonas, Roraima, Acre, and Rondônia cover almost half of Brazil. Northern Brazil was relatively quiet until the rubber boom in the late 19th century. With expansive savannas to the north, and a rich diversity of flora and fauna in the east, today the region's economy is sustained by traditional forest products. Belém, Manaus, Santarém, Rio Branco, and Porto Velho, cities created by the rubber industry, are growing fast, connecting Amazônia to the outside world.

Boa Vista's Monte Roraima *(see p292)*, with its massive uplifted plateau, inspired Sir Arthur Conan Doyle's book *The Lost World*.

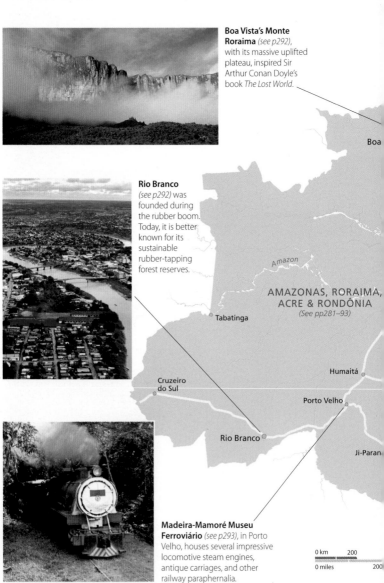

Rio Branco *(see p292)* was founded during the rubber boom. Today, it is better known for its sustainable rubber-tapping forest reserves.

AMAZONAS, RORAIMA, ACRE & RONDÔNIA *(See pp281–93)*

Tabatinga

Cruzeiro do Sul

Humaitá

Porto Velho

Rio Branco

Ji-Paran

Boa

Amazon

Madeira-Mamoré Museu Ferroviário *(see p293)*, in Porto Velho, houses several impressive locomotive steam engines, antique carriages, and other railway paraphernalia.

0 km   200
0 miles   200

◄ *Ribeirinhos* ("river people") boating down the Picanco River, Amazonian Estuary

The river scenery of Santarém *(see p278)*, known for its serene beauty, is the primary reason for visiting this popular Amazon port town.

Ilha de Marajó *(see p274)* is the world's largest inland river island. Its eastern half is savanna dotted with small woodland copses.

The old port of Belém
(see pp272–3) possesses more character than any other sector of the city. Attractive fishing boats bob up and down in the harbor, with the large old white fort on one side and the colorful Ver o Peso market on the other.

Macapá

Salinópolis

Óbidos

Amazon

Belém

Santarém

us

PARÁ & AMAPÁ
(See pp268–79)

Marabá

São Martinho

The Amazon river
(see pp288–91), known as Rio Solimões in its upper reaches, was first identified by Vicente Yáñez Pinzón. Its lower reaches are called Rio Negro.

Teatro Amazonas *(see pp286–7)*, in Manaus, exudes the opulence of its rubber-boom architects. It took the finest of materials and the most skilled of craftsmen to re-create an Italian Renaissance-style edifice, with a steel structure from Scotland and marble imported from Italy.

The Amazon Ecosystem

Brazil has over 1.3 million sq miles (3.5 million sq km) of rainforest, the largest in the world. This massive river system contains a fifth of the world's fresh running water at any moment. The Amazon is home to an incredible variety of plant, bird, fish and insect species. From the air, its magnificent canopy hides a variety of ecosystems, many with dramatic seasonal changes. Between December and April, visitors explore the flooded forest swamps and creeks that offer access to the fascinating flora and fauna.

Ecological Concern

An estimated 20 percent of the Amazon rainforest has been cut down since the 1970s and an additional 20 percent may be lost in the next two decades. Stringent measures being taken to save this ecological treasure include expansion of protected areas and sustainable use of forest resources.

Rubber trees (*Hevea brasiliensis*) growing on riverbanks are the source of valuable latex, which is later transformed into rubber.

The ceiba tree (*Ceiba pentandra*), with elegant buttress roots that surround the trunk's base, is the biggest tree in the Amazon, with an average height of 120 ft (37 m).

Walking palms appear to migrate across the forest floor due to their characteristic stilt roots loosely attached to the ground.

Flowering Bromeliads are epiphytes that gather water and nutrients from raindrops on leaves as well as from dew.

Amazon river winding through dense rainforest

The upper canopy, about 131 ft (40 m) above the ground, is active with reptiles, mammals, tropical birds, and other wildlife.

Buriti Palm

The guamo tree, found all across the Amazon, grows very fast to an average height of 30 ft (10 m).

Pau-d'arco-amarelo bears bright yellow flowers from August to November, while shedding all its leaves.

The black water owes its color to its source in low-lying forests where rotting vegetation is absorbed into the river system.

Fauna

One of the world's most diverse ecosystems, the Amazon harbors an infinite variety of animal life. There are plenty of remote areas that provide habitats for jaguars, tapirs, and wild pigs. However, spotting these elusive creatures is difficult. Monkeys, sloths, and alligators are more commonly sighted.

The emerald tree boa is not venomous, but feeds on rodents and small animals of the forest.

Hoatzins, one of the most primitive of birds, live in flocks and build their nests in low canopy trees.

The three-toed sloth inhabits the forest canopy, moving incredibly slowly in search of its vegetarian diet of fruits, leaves, and sprouting plants.

Tapirs, the largest of all Amazon mammals, can weigh up to 661 lb (300 kg). These herbivores take refuge in water to escape danger.

Freshwater river dolphins, both gray and pink, live in the main rivers and lakes of the Amazon basin.

Piranhas are known for their razor-sharp teeth. Only a few species pose a threat to larger animals.

The People of Amazônia

Approximately 900,000 indigenous people, distributed among 240 groups, live in Brazil. Each group has its own unique dialect, mythology, arts, and culture. A majority of them are semi-nomadic, and live by hunting, gathering, fishing, and migratory farming. These indigenous people live in close harmony with the rhythms of the rainforest, and conservation and sustainability are an integral part of their life. The degree of exposure to western society varies greatly. Some people, such as the nomadic Maku, are incredibly isolated, while others, such as the literate Ticuna (*see p30*), are heavily reliant on modern Brazilian society.

Man peering through a *cokar* (headgear) of blue macaw feathers

Yanomami people

The Yanomami live in the rainforests of southern Venezuela and Northern Brazil. One of the most recently contacted tribes in Amazônia, they number around 20,000 today. Considered fierce warriors, the tribe consists of four subdivisions, each with its distinct language.

The patterns painted on a Yanomami adult have an aesthetic, as well as magical and religious significance.

During Rehao, a yearly ceremony of paying obeisance to the dead, the Yanomami decorate their arms and shoulders with colorful feathers.

Hammocks, slung under palm leaf roofs along the inside perimeter of the circular hut, are commonly used by old and young alike.

Tukano People

The name Tukano is used for a number of ethnolinguistic subgroups living in northwestern Brazil along the Rio Uapés. The individual groups live in communal houses, which are spaced out along the river at a distance of several hours by canoe. The Tukano grow bitter manioc and cultivate sweet potato, peanut, and plantain.

Tukano handicrafts are sold in local markets, or used as trade items favored by non-indigenous people in the area.

The traditional flute, played by male initiates, is characterized by a piercing echo. The flute is believed to be the earthly manifestation of spirits which dominate the magical and religious world of the Tukano.

The maloca, a hut made from wood and palm leaves, provides shelter to the whole village.

Impact of Globalization

The need for national development, fueled by globalization, is prompting the government of Brazil to enforce economic policies that are inimical to the tribal way of life. Pipelines to expand fuel production, and highway projects for transporting goods for global enterprises, are opening up indigenous lands to loggers, miners, ranchers, and colonists. The positive impact of globalization may involve easier access to the modern world, including medicines, education, and tools.

Women gaining access to modern tools

Kayapó People

Around 12,000 Kayapós live in the Amazon River Basin in an area the size of Austria, with villages along the Rio Xingú. Circles are one of the tribe's main symbols, representing the course of the sun and moon. Body paint, which is worn at all times, is equally symbolic. The Kayapó also wear ear plugs and lip discs, according to which their social status can be determined, particularly their right to speak and be heard.

A large lip disc is worn by older Kayapó men. Its size increases with the age and importance of the person within the community. Children and women usually wear ear discs.

Ritual communal dancing constitutes a crucial part of the Kayapó celebration of important events in the year. This is the time when Kayapó men and women show off their interesting headdresses – usually made from macaw and parrot feathers – and other ritual adornments.

Beautiful Bead Bracelets, created by Kayapó women, bear geometric designs with symbolic meanings. These are similar to the brightly colored patterns painted on their bodies with vegetable dyes.

Ashaninka People

Originally from Peru, the Ashaninka fled to parts of Brazil to escape the rubber boom from 1839 to 1913. Still possessing a fairly traditional material culture, the Ashaninka wear long *cushmas* that the women weave from cotton grown in small forest gardens. They make a living from hunting, fishing, and small-scale gardening. Rice, coffee, and chocolate supplement their way of life with bought-in goods including metal tools and soaps.

Red face paint is traditionally applied by most of the Ashaninka people. The strong color comes from seeds of the garden-grown annatto bush.

Small dugout canoes or balsawood rafts are regularly used by the riverine Ashaninka for traveling on the rivers along with their families.

Ashaninka women weave cotton cloth on primitive back-strap looms, almost every day, to make the men's pretty robes.

PARÁ & AMAPÁ

The states of Pará and Amapá in the eastern Amazon are the gateway to the world's largest river basin. In many ways, they are different from one another. Pará covers an enormous area, and has benefited from the natural wealth of the Amazon rainforest. Much smaller than Pará, Amapá is relatively poor. Both states rely on the mineral extraction industry.

It is the Amazon river itself that brings most visitors to this part of Brazil. Pará stretches west as far as the straits of Óbidos, where the river suddenly becomes narrow. This happens due to a geological meeting of the Guyana Shield from the north and the Brazilian Shield from the south. North of the Amazon, Amapá occupies an isolated region, stretching from the Amazon delta all the way to the borders of French Guyana and Suriname.

Pará has many places of cultural and ecological interest. The capital city, Belém, has been a vital Atlantic port since the colonial era, and still boasts many extravagant period buildings. Santarém, another sizable city, is a busy and attractive river port replete with fascinating beaches. The massive island, Ilha de Marajó, which has vast areas of

mangrove swamps, some splendid beaches, and a scattering of resorts, is located in the heart of the Amazon river delta.

Pará is also known for large modern iron ore mines, such as Grande Carajás and the older gold mine of Serra Pelada, once infamous for the vast scale of human labor used for extraction. In southern Pará, the rainforest transforms into *caatinga*, a scrubby savanna landscape.

Once exploited for its natural resources, Amapá is now making concerted efforts towards sustainable development. More than half of the state is under environmental protection. Macapá, the state capital of Amapá, lies on the equator. The English, Dutch, and French clamored for a base in this part of Amazon, before the Portuguese settled at Macapá in 1738.

Fishing boats moored at the old harbor near Ver o Peso market, Belém

◄ Aerial view over the city of Belém, with the Basílica de Nossa Senhora do Nazaré in the foreground

Exploring Pará & Amapá

Even with their widespread rainforest canopy, which can
only be seen clearly from the air, it is ocean and river travel
that have long been the hallmark of Pará and Amapá states.
Their highlights include the tasteful, restored historic
buildings of Belém in Pará, along with the Amazon river
itself, as well as splendid riverine beaches such as Alter do
Chão, close to Santarém, and those found on the Ilha de
Marajó. Macapá, the capital of Amapá, with its refreshing
sea breeze, was founded around the Forte de São José. It
lies on the equator in a strategic position on the north side
of the Amazon river estuary. More than half of the state is
under environmental protection.

Corner tower, Fortaleza de São José de
Macapá, Macapá

Sights at a Glance

Towns & Cities

1 Belém pp272–3
2 Salinópolis
4 Macapá
5 Santarém
6 Óbidos
7 Monte Alegre

Areas of Natural Beauty

3 Ilha de Marajó

0 km   100

0 miles   100

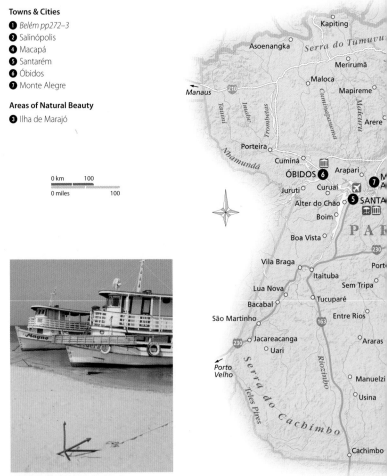

Ferries moored on the shore of Rio Tapajós,
Santarém, Pará

For hotels and restaurants in this region see p378 and p394

Mountains of fresh fruit at Ver o Peso market, Belém

Getting Around

Rivers are the transport arteries of Pará, where virtually every village has some form of riverboat service. There are regular riverboat services connecting Belém, Macapá, and Santarém. While there are very few bus routes in Pará, most access is by road in Amapá. However, the roads are mainly unsurfaced, and bus travel during the rainy season can be treacherous in both states. Air services are widespread. Belém and Macapá can be reached from most cities in Brazil by air, and there are daily flights from Belém to most larger towns in the Amazon.

Key

—— Major road

···· Minor road

Railroad

▨▨▨ International border

—— State border

A creek near Araruna beach, Ilha de Marajó

For keys to symbols *see back flap*

❶ Belém

The attractive city of Belém was founded by the Portuguese in 1616 to guard the mouth of the Amazon river against other European powers. As the Amazon region's resources, mainly spices, were exploited, the city soon became a major trading port. It was ravaged during the 1835 Cabanagem Rebellion, when poor settlers attacked the wealthy local elite. By the end of the 19th century, Belém had more than recovered its economic position, largely due to the rubber boom. It is still the most important port in Northern Brazil, and a fascinating place in which to explore the wealth of colonial and republican architecture.

Cannon on display at the 17th-century Forte do Castelo

Ships docked on the waterfront at the Ver o Peso market

🏠 Estação das Docas
Blvd Castilho França, Campina.
Tel (91) 3212 5525.
Open 10am–midnight daily.
w estacaodasdocas.com.br

Three former warehouses overlooking the river have been converted into a stylish, air-conditioned shopping, dining, and entertainment space. Visitors enjoy the lively atmosphere until late at night.

🏠 Ver o Peso
Av Castilhos França. **Open** 6am–2pm daily.

Incredibly hectic early in the morning, Ver o Peso, or "See the Weight," was originally a colonial customs point (Posto Fiscal), where goods were assessed for taxation purposes. These days, its most obvious feature is the iron-built fish market, the Mercado de Ferro, which was designed and made in England and assembled here in the late 19th century. The variety of seafood inside is staggering. Outside, the main market expands into stalls that sell everything from jungle fruits

and *farinha* (manioc, or cassava-root, flour) to medicinal herbs and aromatic oils. The market extends along the promenade where there are further stalls and kiosks selling craft goods and local food specialties.

🏛 Forte do Presépio
Praça Frei Caetano Brandão 117, Cidade Velha. **Tel** (91) 4009 8828.
Open 10am–4pm Tue–Sun.

Sitting at the confluence of Rio Guamá and the Baía do Guajará, this fort was first built of

wood and mud plaster by the Portuguese colonists in 1616. It was rebuilt six years later, and again in 1878. It now houses the Museu do Encontro, a small historical museum presenting the city's history and the early conquest of the Amazon.

🏛 Palácio Antônio Lemos
Praça Dom Pedro II. **Tel** (91) 3114 1028. **Open** 10am–6pm Tue–Fri, 9am–1pm Sat & Sun.

This splendid palace housed the municipal authorities between 1868 and 1883. It still has offices for the Prefeitura, but much of the building is open to the public, with some furnished period rooms upstairs. The palace is home to the Museu de Arte de Belém, which houses a fine collection of Brazilian 20th-century paintings.

🏛 Teatro da Paz
Praça da República. **Tel** (91) 4009 8750.
Open 9am–5pm Tue–Fri, 9am–noon Sat, 10–11am Sun. on the hour.

This grand Neo-Classical opera house was built in 1878, along

Transamazônica

Until the middle of the 20th century, riverboat or mule trail were the only viable forms of travel across Amazônia and Northern Brazil. With the ambitious construction of Highway BR-230 during the late 1960s, the Atlantic port of Belém was effectively connected all the way to the Peruvian border. Known as the Transamazônica, this road is in a poor state of repair along much of its length. In 2005, a river bridge to Peru was opened in the remote jungle state of Acre, completing the Brazilian end of the Transamazônica.

Unpaved section of the Transamazônica

Elegant interior of the Neo-Classical Teatro da Paz

on 16 major arches, each ornately covered in stone mosaics and supporting a breathtaking red cedar roof. It was completed in 1909, to house the miraculous Virgin image of Nossa Senhora de Nazaré, which is traced back to early Christian Nazareth.

Linked to the icon, the Círio de Nazaré, or the Festival of Candles, attracts over a million visitors to the city every October. In one of the main symbolic acts, hundreds of local people work together, dragging an enormous rope from the mud and water of the port, through the streets of the city to the Basílica de Nossa Senhora de Nazaré. For those who participate, their sins are purged, and their hopes and wishes for

the very Parisian Avenida Presidente Vargas. Inspired by La Scala in Milan, the furnishings are still largely original. Legendary Russian ballerina Anna Pavlova was one of the great artists to have performed here.

⬆ Basílica de Nossa Senhora de Nazaré

Praça Justo Chermont. **Tel** (91) 4009 8400. **Open** 7am–6pm Mon–Sat, 6:30am–noon, 4:30–8pm Sun. Museu Círio de Nazaré: **Open** 9am–6pm Tue–Fri.

The basilica's spectacular interior makes it one of the most stunning churches in Brazil. Partially modeled on St. Peter's in Rome, it stands

VISITORS' CHECKLIST

Practical Information
Pará. 🚇 1,385,000. 🛈 Belémtur, Av Presidente Vargas 158, (91) 3073 9802; Paratur, Praça Waldemar Henrique, (91) 3110 5000. 🎉 Círio de Nazaré (Oct, 2nd Sun).

Transport
✈ 7 miles (12 km) N of town. 🚌 Av G. José Malcher, (91) 3266 2625. 🚢 from Macapá, Manaus & Santarém. Taxi: Radiotaxi Aguia, (91) 3276 4000

the year are granted. The basilica also houses the **Museu Círio de Nazaré**, which is devoted to the cult of the Círio and exhibits over 500 pieces relating to the religious festival.

Nave of the Basílica de Nossa Senhora de Nazaré

Belém City Center

① Estaçāo das Docas
② Ver o Peso
③ Forte do Presépio
④ Palácio Antônio Lemos
⑤ Teatro da Paz
⑥ Basílica de Nossa Senhora de Nazaré

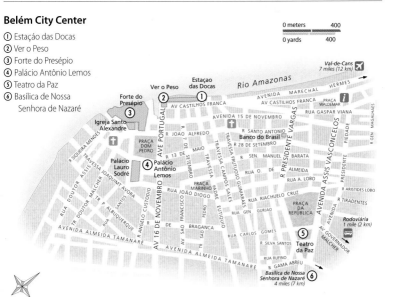

❷ Salinópolis

Pará. 🏙 40,000. ✈ Belém Val de Caes Airport, 110 miles (180 km) SE of town, then bus. 🚌 Av Miguel Santa Brigada. *i* Paratur (91) 3423 2203.

The town of Salinópolis, locally known as Salinas, is just about as far east as the Amazon river delta reaches. Very much the traditional summer resort for city folk, Salinas has plenty of beaches fringed with beach huts and second homes. The busiest beach is the central **Praia do Maçarico**, which has several bars and restaurants. More pleasant still, there is the **Praia do Atalaia**, not far from the center of town, backed by sand dunes and well provided with *barracas* (tents) for food and drink. A continuation of this beach, the **Praia do Farol Velho**, is thickly lined with beach houses, and is most popular during July, when it can often get rather crowded.

Environs
About 19 miles (30 km) west of Salinópolis is the relatively sleepy fishing settlement and beach resort of **Algodoal**. The resort lies on the western edge of Ilha de Maiandeua, just a 40-minute boat ride away. There are no motorized vehicles in the

A secluded beach near Souré, Ilha de Marajó

village or on Maiandeua island, adding to the remote and idyllic feel. Electricity only reached the island in 2004, so facilities are improving.

The main beach for the village is the **Praia da Vila do Algodoal**. More popular, however, is the palm-fringed **Praia da Princesa do Farol**, a superb stretch of sand secluded from the main beach by a short walk at low tide or a canoe ride. There are trails on the island, offering the opportunity to spot wildlife and explore the area around an inland freshwater lake. It is advisable to carry adequate cash to visit the island, since there are no banks or ATMs.

❸ Ilha de Marajó

Pará. 🏙 250,000. 🚢 from Belém to Porto Camará. *i* Trapiche Municipal, Rua 1, Souré, (91) 8769 8756.

The world's largest river island, Ilha de Marajó covers over 18,533 sq miles (48,000 sq km), mostly dedicated to cattle ranches, or *fazendas*. The island is famous for having the biggest and finest buffaloes in Brazil. Their meat, leather, and dairy products are widely available to purchase. Ilha de Marajó was also the ancient home to the indigenous culture of the Marajoaras, notable for their exquisite ceramic burial and ceremonial urns.

The unofficial capital of the island is **Souré**, which has the most shops, restaurants, and other facilities, but the ferry port is **Porto Camará**, some 16 miles (27 km) south of Souré. Located between Porto Camará and Souré, the best and most secluded beach is at the small town of **Joanes**, some 3 miles (5 km) off the main road. There are good beaches at the other town on the island, **Salvaterra**, where there are also several hotels and *pousadas*. The Praia Grande beach in Salvaterra is well served with beach chairs, snack *barracas*, and refreshment stands.

During the peak rainy season (February–May) many of the roads are inaccessible for long periods; this includes the road to Joanes and Salvaterra at times. Boats for moving around the island can be found easily at Souré, Salvaterra, and Porto Camará.

Pottery on Ilha De Marajó

Marajó pottery displayed in Museu Goeldi, Belém

In 1948, anthropologists Betty Meggers and Clifford Evans discovered a large, painted anthropomorphic vessel on Ilha de Marajó. The ancient inhabitants, the Marajoaras, left behind not only burial mounds, some almost 3,000 years old, but also some very fine ceramics, leading archaeologists to believe that between the 5th and 13th centuries, there were sophisticated societies living along the banks of the Amazon river. Excavations reveal that the dead were buried in line according to their social ranking, with larger urns indicating higher status. Most of these ceramics, representing abstract feminine figures, demonstrate the matrilineal nature of this early Amazonian society. As well as funerary ceramics, there were also bowls, vases, spindle whorls, and stools. The larger urns generally took three main forms: humanoid, cyclindrical, and round; and around 15 different finishing techniques are known to have been utilized. Some excellent examples of the urns can be found in the Museu Goeldi in Belém.

❹ Macapá

Amapá. 🌄 395,000. ✈ 🚢 from Belém. 🚌 Bairro São Lázaro, (96) 3251 2009. ℹ Setur, Rua Independência 29, Centro, (96) 3212 5335. 🎭 O Marabaixo (May).

A replica of a typical indigenous home, Museu SACACA, Macapá

Split in two by the equator, Macapá is hot and humid all year round. The city occupies its position as Amapá's capital sitting on the northern bank of the Amazon river, very close to the giant river's mouth. It is rather isolated, with mostly air and boat transportation, rather than road connections.

The history of the city is rich and varied. Several European countries, including England and France, attempted to take it over from the Portuguese, but the Portuguese established their hold here by completing the grand **Fortaleza de São José de Macapá** in 1782, after almost 20 years of construction by black and Indian slave labor. The bricks used were brought over from Portugal as ballast on the ships.

Just to the north of the fort there is an attractive pier, the Trapiche Eliezer Levy, which dates back to the 1930s. The pier stretches far out into the water and it is an enjoyable stroll to the end of it, especially on a breezy evening. The charming Trapiche Restaurante, also located at the end of the pier, has a breathtaking view overlooking the river.

These days, Macapá is the capital of a progressive state. Following the election of the environmentalist João Capiberibe as state governor in 1995, successive governors have kept the spirit of environmentalism alive. One present project is to connect all the state's protected areas with wildlife or biodiversity corridors. The **Museu SACACA**, or the Museum of Sustainable Development, just a short distance south of the town center, offers fascinating guided tours of replica *ribeirinho* (river-dweller) houses.

The **Mercado dos Produtos da Floresta** offers a wide range of local art and craft goods, ranging from *balata* (ceramics) dusted with manganese ore to indigenous crafts, leather goods, carved wooden statues, and all-natural medicines.

The Marco Zero monument, a large obelisk-cum-sundial, 4 miles (6 km) southwest of the city center, marks the equatorial line on Avenida Equatorial. A sports stadium and *sambódromo* also form part of the same complex.

Wooden artifact, Museu SACACA

🏯 **Fortaleza de São José de Macapá**
Av Candido Mendes. **Tel** (96) 3212 5118. **Open** 9am–6pm Tue–Sun. 🎫

🛍 **Mercado dos Produtos da Floresta**
Rua São José 1500. **Tel** (96) 9 9961 0913. **Open** 8am–6pm Mon–Fri.

🏛 **Museu SACACA**
Av Feliciano Coelho, 1509. **Tel** (96) 3212 5361. **Open** 9am–6pm Tue–Sun. 🎫

Buildings inside the Fortaleza de São José de Macapá

Wooden house on stilts on the Amazon River, with the rainforest behind ▶

❺ Santarém

Pará. 🏛 295,000. ✈ ⛴ 🚌 from Docas do Pará (W of center). 🛈 Santarém Tour, Rua Adriano Pimentel 44. (93) 3522 4847. 🌐 **santaremtur.com.br**

Amazônia's fourth-largest city, Santarém sits at the mouth of the Rio Tapajós, surrounded by brilliant white sandy beaches. Modern Santarém began in 1661 as a Jesuit mission, following 30 years of military action in the area to subdue the fierce, indigenous Tapuiçu Indians.

In 1867, there was an influx of ex-Confederates from the USA, a handful of whose descendants still survive. However, it was the rubber boom and Santarem's strategic position as a pit stop en route along the Amazon river that turned the town into a buzzing commercial center.

In the late 19th century, Henry Wickam, an English settler in Santarém, smuggled rubber tree seeds out to establish rubber plantations in Asia. Within 40 years, and just in time for World War I, Asian rubber plantations greatly outproduced the Brazilian Amazon.

The local economy is today based on rubber, logging, soya, brazil nuts, and tourism. Colorful boats and frantic movement of produce at the port and along the attractive riverfront are typical today.

Ferries moored on the shore of the Amazon river at Santarém

An ancient center for the production of fine ceramics, the town showcases its distinct Santarém Phase Pottery in a striking museum, the **Museu de Santarém**. The exhibits prominently feature burial urns, reputed to be among the oldest in South America. Also known as Centro Cultural João Fona, the museum has a striking interior, painted by João Fona, an artist from Pará.

Burial urn, Museu de Santarém

Another attraction is the **Museu de Arte Sacra de Santarém**, which has a decent collection of religious art.

Environs

Located 20 miles (33 km) west of Santarém, the river-beach town of **Alter do Chão** has fine sandy beaches set against a calm bay on the Rio Tapajós. Canoes ferry visitors across the bay in order to climb the low-lying hills that offer breathtaking views. Closer to the main beach is another prominently shaped hill that resembles a church altar.

Fordlândia, 62 miles (100 km) south of town, was Henry Ford's first rubber plantation, founded

Belterra, a rubber plantation set up by John Ford in the 1930s

The Rubber Story in Brazil

In the mid-1700s, Charles-Marie de la Condamine was presented with latex syringes from the *Hevea brasiliensis* tree by the Omagua people living in Amazônia. He returned to France with samples, and rubber became known to the world. Soon it was being used for everything from insulation to tyres, and *Hevea brasiliensis* had become the oil of its day. In Amazônia, where the rubber tree grew in abundance, foreign banks and companies began to set up plantations. The rubber boom ushered Manaus and Belém into the *belle époque* era, with electric lights, lavish opera houses, and mansions for the rubber barons. Brazil emerged as the world's largest producer of natural rubber. The euphoria lasted until 1910, when the British colonies in Asia – Malaya, Ceylon, and Singapore – outproduced the Brazilian rubber. Unprepared for competition, Brazil was elbowed out of the rubber market by 1914. The indigenous Brazilians, who had been rounded up and forcibly settled to work on the plantations, returned to relative freedom. Today, much of Brazil's rubber is imported from Asia.

in the 1920s to produce rubber for the Ford Motor Company. In the 1930s, he also established **Belterra**, 12 miles (20 km) south. Both ventures failed, and Ford had to sell them to the Brazilian government in 1945. These towns are accessible by boat from Alter do Chão.

🏛 Museu de Arte Sacra de Santarém
Rua Siqueira Campos 439, Centro. **Tel** (93) 3523 0658. **Open** 10am–1pm, 2–6pm Mon–Fri; 10am–1pm, 2–7pm Sat & Sun.

🏛 Museu de Santarém
Rua do Imperador, Praça de Santarém. **Tel** (93) 2101 5100. **Open** 8am–5pm Mon–Fri. 🏛 donation expected.

❻ Óbidos
Pará. 🔼 47,000. 🚢 from Santarém. 🔼 Rua Idelfonso Guimarães, Praça da Cultura, (93) 3547 1134.

The real gateway to the deeper Amazon, Óbidos marks the narrowest section of the Amazon river valley. It was created 40 million years ago, when a massive inland lake burst through to the Atlantic at this point, where the Guyanan Shield meets the Brazilian Shield.

The pretty waterfront has some beautifully tiled buildings and the 17th-century Forte Pauxias. There is also a free museum featuring, among other exhibits, luxury items from the rubber-boom days. The museum opens on request.

A surfer catching the "Pororoca" tidal wave

Pororoca Wave
Revered by surfers, the Pororoca is a legendary wave, over 16 ft (5 m) tall, that regularly rolls up the Amazon river. The name Pororoca comes from a local Tupi Indian phrase which means "great destructive noise." Predicted to happen twice daily during full moons between January and April every year, the wave comes in from the Atlantic causing some devastation along the riverbanks. Following a low tide in the rainy season, the force of the mighty river against the turning tide creates the large and powerful wave that rolls, literally unstoppable, up the Amazon. The surfing record so far is 37 minutes in time and 7 miles (12 km) in distance, while the tidal waves are known to travel over 12 miles (20 km) per hour at times.

❼ Monte Alegre
Pará. 🔼 23,500. 🚢 🚗 Rua do Jaquara 320.

Located impressively on top of a small hill beside the Amazon river, the town of Monte Alegre was one of the first places on the river to be colonized by Europeans. A band of English and Irish sailors were the earliest to settle here in the 1570s, soon to be expelled by the Portuguese. Over the last 200 years, Monte Alegre has benefited from ranching and the rubber industry. It is best known for the rock paintings of **Serra Paytuna** and **Serra Ererê**, located 19 miles (30 km) out of town. Estimated to be 10,000 years old, the paintings feature abstract patterns, mostly geometric in form, and some stylized representations of human and animal figures. It is obligatory to hire a guide and a vehicle to visit them. Monte Alegre is also renowned for scenic waterfalls and its wealth of birdlife, for which a local guide and a canoe will be required.

Boats moored along the waterfront in Óbidos, with rows of houses in the background

AMAZONAS, RORAIMA, ACRE & RONDÔNIA

The states of Amazonas, Roraima, Acre, and Rondônia form the heartland of the vast Amazon rainforest region, which is drained by the world's largest network of freshwater lakes and rivers. Despite hundreds of years of European presence and the ravages of 20th and 21st century deforestation, the region is still home to some of the world's most isolated indigenous peoples.

Amazonas is larger than the other three states put together. Manaus, its capital, is the most popular place from which to explore the jungle. The city sits at the confluence of two of the world's largest rivers – the Solimões (as the Amazon river is called in this section) and the Rio Negro. The vast Rio Madeira lies downstream of Manaus.

Roraima, which literally juts up into Venezuela and Guyana, is best known for its superb plateau-topped mountains, lakes, and substantial rainforest. A host of indigenous groups live here, tenaciously holding on to their land and culture. Roraima also boasts open savannas that have been transformed into cattle ranches. The state capital, Boa Vista, is a well-planned city on the banks of the Rio Branco.

Acre and Rondônia, in the very southwest corner of the Brazilian Amazon, possess some fantastic protected areas of biodiversity, home to many indigenous communities. Acre, the rubber-tapping center of the Amazon, is known for its lush beauty. Environmental destruction has been met with equally forceful conservation movements here. The state capital, Rio Branco, was where activist Chico Mendes fought to defend the forest in the late 1980s.

Rondônia, an area which has developed beyond recognition, still retains some of Brazil's best flora and fauna. It also offers fascinating gems in terms of heritage, such as the Madeira-Mamoré railway museum in the state capital, Porto Velho.

Village huts surrounded by tall palm tree plantations in Acre

◀ A wooden canopy walkway through Brazilian nut trees, Rio Branco, Acre

Exploring Amazonas, Roraima, Acre & Rondônia

This region offers the ultimate rainforest experience. Most people travel here to explore the dense forests, picturesque river islands, and tranquil waterways. The sights include Manaus, the legendary capital city of Amazonas, which offers much architectural and cultural interest. Also located in Amazonas is the Mamirauá Reserve, Brazil's first sustainable development reserve. The secluded and beautiful mountains of Roraima are worth a visit, as is Acre, with its natural beauty, history, and *seringueiros* (rubber-tappers) culture. Porto Velho, the capital of Rondônia, overlooking the Amazon's longest tributary, the mighty Rio Madeira, is a lively place to visit. Riverboat excursions on the Rio Madeira are a good way to idle away a few hours and spot a few pink dolphins.

Spectacled caimans can be found near Manaus

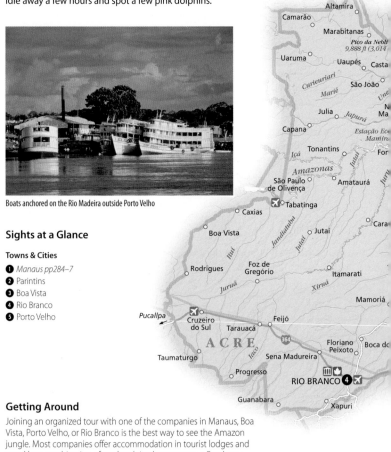

Boats anchored on the Rio Madeira outside Porto Velho

Sights at a Glance

Towns & Cities

1 *Manaus pp284–7*
2 Parintins
3 Boa Vista
4 Rio Branco
5 Porto Velho

Getting Around

Joining an organized tour with one of the companies in Manaus, Boa Vista, Porto Velho, or Rio Branco is the best way to see the Amazon jungle. Most companies offer accommodation in tourist lodges and travel by a combination of road and riverboat or canoe. For those who want to travel independently, it is possible to move around the jungle on local riverboats. Road travel is also possible from all cities. Manaus, for instance, is only 6 hours by bus from Novo Airão, on the Rio Negro, where it is possible to bathe in jungle rivers and swim with pink dolphins.

For hotels and restaurants in this region see pp378–9 and p394

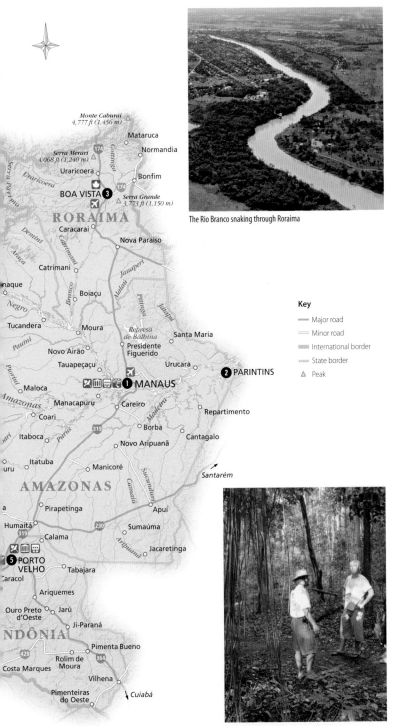

The Rio Branco snaking through Roraima

Key

— Major road

··· Minor road

▬ International border

▭ State border

△ Peak

Visitors exploring the forest near Manaus

For keys to symbols *see back flap*

❶ Manaus

Manaus is a legendary city, located at the heart of the Amazon forest on the banks of the Rio Negro, close to where this massive river blends with the even larger Amazon river, or Rio Solimões as it is known along this section of its course. Manaus is a busy city bringing together the hectic pace of a modern port with the hot, laid-back feel of a jungle town. The brief period of economic boom between 1888 and 1912, due to the export of rubber, catapulted Manaus into wealthy city status. The only signs that remain of this time are the fancy European buildings of the port and the even more splendid Teatro Amazonas.

🏛 Mercado Municipal Adolfo Lisboa

Rua dos Barés 46. **Open** 6am–6pm Mon–Sat, 6am–noon Sun.

The municipal market was built in 1902, very close to the port, and is an amazing building. Looking up to its elegant ceiling and Art Nouveau ironwork structure, it is not difficult to see that Gustave Eiffel himself had a hand in its design. The cultural evening held here on the last Friday of every month offers a chance to experience regional music, food, and entertainment.

🏛 Alfândega

Rua Marquês de Santa Cruz. **Tel** (92) 3622 3025. **Open** 8am–noon Mon–Sat.

Constructed in 1906 at the height of the rubber boom, the Alfândega (Customs House), like many of the well-engineered features of Manaus from this period, was entirely pre-fabricated in England. The stone used for the building was brought from Scotland. The tower used to be a lighthouse. Much of this refined building's glory can be seen from the Praça Adalberto Valle opposite.

🏛 Teatro Amazonas

See pp286–7.

🏛 Palacete Provincial

Praça da Policia, Centro. **Tel** (92) 3631 6047. **Open** 9am–7pm Tue–Thu (to 8pm Fri & Sat.

Built in 1874 originally to house the police headquarters, the Palacete Provincial is now a cultural center, which is home to several interesting small museums and collections, including the Museum of Image and Sound, the Military Police Museum, and the Numismatic Museum. The Palacete's highlight is the art gallery, which features modern and contemporary art by regional painters, photographers, and installation artists. The exuberant paintings of local flora and fauna by Manaus painter Rita Loureiro are especially noteworthy.

🏛 Homem do Norte

Centro Cultural dos Povos da Amazônia, Praça Francisco Pereira da Silva. **Tel** (92) 2125 5300. **Open** 8:30–11:30am, 2–4:30pm Mon–Fri.

An anthropology and ethnology museum, the fascinating Museu do Homem do Norte (Museum of Northern Man) has exhibits on the way of life of the people of Northern Brazil. It is particularly dedicated to the *caboclos* (copper-colored) mixed descendants of the indigenous people and Portuguese who live along the riverbanks. Cultural, social, and economic aspects of life in Northern Brazil are detailed with photographs, documents, artifacts, and everyday objects, such as historic cooking utensils, costumes, and an interesting collection of indigenous weapons, including the infamous *furador de olhos* (eye piercer). There are also exhibitions on *guaraná* and rubber production.

🏛 Palácio Rio Negro

Av 7 de Setembro 1546. **Tel** (92) 3232 4450. **Open** 9am–3pm Mon–Fri.

A remarkably well-preserved colonial-period mansion, the almost garish Palácio Rio Negro

The Rio Negro with the Porto Flutante (Floating Port) and the Catedral Metropolitana in the background

For hotels and restaurants in this region see pp378–9 and p394

was built in 1913 during the rubber boom. It was originally home to an eccentric German rubber baron, Waldermar Scholz. In later years, it housed the local government. These days, much of it has been opened to the public as a cultural center. The palace hosts art exhibitions and events, as well as film screenings.

🏛 Museu do Índio

Rua Duque de Caxias 296. **Tel** (92) 3635 1922. **Open** 8:30am–4:30pm Mon–Fri (to 11:30am Sat). 🐾

An excellent ethnographic museum, the Museu do Índio was established by Salesian nuns and is based on their work as missionaries in the Rio Negro area. There are many feather-work exhibits and some weapons and tools, as well as household and sacred objects on display, along with musical instruments and artworks. The Tukano people *(see p266)* are particularly well represented here. Explanations of the displays are in Portuguese, English, and German. The museum has a good craft shop, with a wide range of handicrafts on sale.

VISITORS' CHECKLIST

Practical Information
Amazonas. 🏠 1,800,000.
ℹ️ AmazonasTur, Manaus Airport, (92) 3652 1120.
🎭 Manaus Opera Festival (Apr/May), Festival Folclórico do Amazonas (Jun).
🌐 **manausonline.com**

Transport
✈️ 🚁 🚌 Rua Recife 2784, (92) 642 5805. ⛴ Porto Flutuante.

🗺 Zoológico do CIGS

Estrada Ponta Negra 750.
Tel (92) 2125 6402. **Open** 8am–5pm Tue–Sun. 🐾

One of the few places around Manaus where you might see a jaguar at close quarters, the Zoológico do CIGS is a great place to take children. Located 8 miles (13 km) from Manaus toward Ponta Negra in the army jungle training center, this small zoo is home to over 300 animals including many caimans, monkeys, exotic birds, and an unforgettable large pit full of anacondas.

Traditional indigenous longhouse at the Museu do Índio

Manaus City Center

① Mercado Municipal Adolfo Lisboa
② Alfândega
③ Teatro Amazonas
④ Palacete Provincial
⑤ Homem do Norte
⑥ Palácio Rio Negro
⑦ Museu do Índio
⑧ Zoológico do CIGS

0 meters 200
0 yards 200

For keys to symbols *see back flap*

Manaus: Teatro Amazonas

Built at the end of the 19th century during the *belle époque*, when fortunes were made from the extraction of rubber in Manaus, the Teatro Amazonas remains one of the jewels of the Amazon region. This grand Renaissance-style opera house was designed by Gabinete Português de Engenharia de Lisbon (Portuguese Engineering Academy of Lisbon). Inaugurated on December 31, 1896, it was two more years before construction was completed and the prominent landmark with a glistening dome appeared above the port. Major restoration was carried out in 2016.

The Teatro façade, restored to pink at the close of the 20th century

★ The Painted Curtain
The main stage curtain was created by Manaus-based artist Crispim do Amaral (1845–1911) to depict the Meeting of the Waters *(see p289)*, and also a local river goddess, Iara. The curtain is pulled up into the specially designed cupola at the start of each performance.

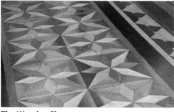

The Wooden Floor
The opera-house floor, laid with thousands of pieces of Amazon timber, is a masterpiece of craftsmanship. The light and dark patterns represent the meeting of the Negro and Amazon rivers *(see p289)*.

KEY

① **The roof** is made of red tiles that were imported from Alsace in France.

② **The columns** are made from Italian Carrara marble.

③ **Outside balconies** are built in finely cut Portuguese stone.

Events
Regular musical events and operas include those of the Companhia de Dança and the resident Orquestra Filarmônica do Amazonas.

★ The Cupola
The impressive cupola was created using 36,000 colorful ceramic tiles, imported from Alsace on the Franco-German border.

VISITORS' CHECKLIST

Practical Information
Av Eduardo Ribeira 659, Manaus.
Tel (92) 3622 1880.
Open 9am–2pm Tue–Sat. 🌿 🎭
Shows: opera, theater & dance performances through the year.

★ The Four Painted Pillars
A key feature of the main auditorium is a ceiling rosette whose four pillars were painted in Paris and reassembled in Manaus. The pillars create the impression of gazing up from underneath the Eiffel Tower.

Lobby
The lobby is furnished with *Murano* chandeliers made with Venetian glass and French bronzework.

Main Auditorium
Designed in the shape of a harp, the theater can seat almost 700 people. Like the main columns and the three curving balconies, the seats are made from English cast iron. The polished wooden armchairs are made from local jacaranda. The lower columns bear the names of many classical composers.

Amazon Excursions from Manaus

Manaus is well located as a base from which to explore the rainforest. The main destinations include the Rio Negro, Lago Mamori, Rio Juma, Lago Manaquiri, Presidente Figueiredo, and, farther west, the splendid reserve at Mamirauá. Operators run tours, offering everything from basic accommodation to four- or five-star luxury lodges and boats. It is good to have at least half a day out of Manaus in order to have a reasonable chance of seeing a wide range of tropical birds and mammal wildlife such as agoutis, monkeys, deer, or wild boar.

The Rio Urubuí and Cachoeira Iracema near Presidente Figueireido

Presidente Figueiredo
62 miles (100 km) N of Manaus. 🚌
ℹ️ Centro Turistico, (92) 3324 1308.

Presidente Figueiredo is a small town linked to Manaus by a relatively good road. There are more than 100 waterfalls dotted around the town, as well as some caves. Tours in and around the area can be booked from Manaus or directly with local guides through the tourist information office located at the bus stop. One of the best waterfalls is the **Pedra Furada**, where the water gushes out of a hole in the rocks. The waterfalls **Cachoeira Iracema**, **Pedra da Lua Branca**, and **Natal** are on the **Rio Urubuí** and only accessible by boat. The **Caverna Araras** is on a trail bordering the Rio Urubuí. Another attractive cave is **Caverna Maruaga**, which has shallow river running over its floor. Permission to visit the caves has to be obtained from the tourist information office in Manaus.

📷 Rio Negro & Ilhas de Anavilhanas
60 miles (90 km) NW of Manaus. 🚌
ℹ️ Amazonastur, Av Ajuricaba s/n, Novo Airão, (92) 3365 1391.

One of the least visited regions of South America, the Rio Negro area possesses distinctive flora created by its acidic waters and soil type. There is a lower density of wildlife here than any other area along the Rio Negro. There are few towns and even fewer tourist facilities along the river, which stretches right up to the Colombian and Venezuelan borders.

Ilhas de Anavilhanas is a biological reserve and the largest group of freshwater islands in the world. Tours to visit these islands are offered from Manaus or from Novo Airão. There are over 250

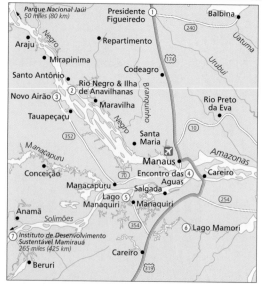

Sights at a Glance

① Presidente Figueiredo
② Rio Negro & Ilhas de Anavilhanas
③ Novo Airão
④ Encontro das Aguas
⑤ Lago Manaquiri
⑥ Lago Mamori
⑦ Instituto de Desenvolvimento Sustentável Mamirauá

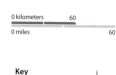

0 kilometers   60

0 miles   60

Key
▬▬ Main road
═══ Other road

For keys to symbols *see back flap*

The Rio Negro winding through the rainforest

uninhabited islands stretching for more than 187 miles (300 km). Depending on the season and time of day, it is possible to see caimans, sloths, snakes, frogs, and a wide range of bird species. Sprawled across an area of 1,350 sq miles (3,500 sq km) of protected rainforest on the left bank of the Rio Negro, the Estação Ecológica de Anavilhanas (Ecological Station of Anavilhanas) is part of the Anavilhanas islands. Created in 1998 and named after the Archipelago dos Anavilhanas, it boasts several species in great danger of extinction, including jaguars and night monkeys.

A day-and-a-half's journey from Ilhas de Anavilhanas, Barcelos, the only town of any size along the river, is an interesting place to start a jungle expedition. Another two days upriver is the town of São Gabriel Da Cachoeira, a beautiful place deep in the Amazon with stunning jungle scenery and wildlife.

Visitor feeding fish to pink dolphins in Novo Airão

Novo Airão

71 miles (115 km) W of Manaus. 🚌 from Manaus. 🚐 from Manaus. Ibama: Rua Ministro João Gonçalves de Souza s/n, Manaus. **Tel** (92) 3878 7102. Parque Nacional Jaú: **Tel** (92) 3365 1345.

The small town of Novo Airão is located on the western side of the Rio Negro, opposite the Archipelago dos Anavilhanas. Pleasant, yet laid-back, with only a handful of attractions, the town draws tourists mainly for the pink dolphins that come to a floating platform at Novo Airão's small port. They are fed fish every hour and visitors get the opportunity to stroke them while they are fed, coming into close contact with these friendly creatures. Some, however, may prefer to see the dolphins out in the wild by taking a boat tour.

Toco toucan in Amazonas

The area neighboring Novo Airão is home to a number of interesting sights, such as **Airão Velho**, the overgrown ruins of the old town center, with prehistoric spiral and figure-like petroglyphs. The beautiful and peaceful **Igarapé do Mato Grosso**, a forested section of a tributary river nearby, makes a great place for a walk or a swim in fresh water. The **Parque Nacional Jaú** is a two-day trip from Novo Airão, and is a wonderful opportunity to visit virgin Amazon rainforest. A permit is required to enter the park from the **Ibama** office in Manaus and the trip is best done with a tour operator.

🐟 Encontro das Aguas

🚐 from Manaus.

One of the main tours offered from Manaus, the Encontro das Aguas (Meeting of the Waters) is where the Rio Solimões joins the Rio Negro. The relatively creamy and alkaline light brown or "white" water of the Solimões (Amazon) river takes several miles to absorb the dark, acid water coming in from the Rio Negro. The Solimões is light because it starts mainly in the Andes and brings plenty of silt with it. The Rio Negro wells up primarily in the swamplands and smaller hills of the northeastern Amazon and contains much more decomposed plant life than it does soil or silt.

Small boats go out from Manaus allowing tourists to take photographs and see the clear line between light brown and black running down the middle of the river. It is a two-hour return trip from Manaus, and the best time to visit is between 7 and 10am.

Meeting of the Rio Solimões and Rio Negro at Encontro das Aguas

For hotels and restaurants in this region see pp378–9 and p394

Limpid blue sky mirrored in the clear waters of Lago Mamori

🦜 Lago Manaquiri
40 miles (64 km) SW of Manaus.
🌐 amazonas.am.gov.br/
o-amazonas/turismo

A 5-hour boat ride from Manaus, the backwater lake of Manaquiri is best entered first via the Rio Solimões, then upstream to a tributary that leads to the lake. Its waters rise and fall with the seasons. Relatively isolated, the Lago Manaquiri is usually a good spot for seeing waterbirds, including the great egret (*Casmerodius albus*) and fish eagles. It is not unusual to see caimans and large Amazonian alligators on the sandy shore.

The lake provides sustenance to the small fishing town of Manaquiri. Local economy depends more on fishing than on tourism. In 1995 and 2005, however, both were hit by the worst drought in over 40 years, when the lagoons evaporated, and thousands of dead fish lay on the bed of the dried-up lake. The changed climatic conditions continue to deplete fish in the area. Nonetheless, fishing remains the main activity, and there are many tour operators based in Manaus, offering budget fishing packages.

It is always best to book your trip through a travel company registered with the Brazilian Tourism Bureau (Embratur) *(see p409)*. Some of the tour agencies provide typical Amazon riverboats, which may come fully equipped with kitchen, dining area, canopied sundeck, bathroom, and shower. Fishing is best in the dry season, which usually lasts from August to December or January.

🦜 Lago Mamori
60 miles (96 km) SE of Manaus.
Gero's Tours: Rua 10 de Julho 695,
Manaus. **Tel** (92) 3232 4755.
🌐 amazongero.com Nature Safaris:
Amazon Green Tours, Rua 10 de Julho
718, Manaus. **Tel** (092) 99106 5650.
🌐 amazongreentours.com.br

Easily accessible by road and boat from Manaus, the elongated and breathtaking Lago Mamori is located in a lush rainforest setting. Much of it is surrounded by narrow creeks, hidden among forests full of sloths, monkeys, and colorful, noisy tropical birds. The river and lake offer the opportunity to see both pink and gray river dolphins, as well as to go piranha fishing. Nearby, the Lago Arara is great for fishing, and home to a pink dolphin feeding ground. The local people, known as *caboclos*, have been here for generations and live in scattered riverside communities, occasionally coming together for celebrations. They earn their living by making *farinha* (manioc flour), rearing cattle, and fishing. Visits to the *caboclo* homes can be organized by **Gero's Tours**. Run independently by English-speaking Gero Mesquita, it can book hotels, arrange transport, and meticulously plan tours.

Farther upstream and deeper into the forest from here, the Rio Juma region offers better access to wildlife, but requires expedition-type preparation and several days.

Amazon Green Tours, a tour company based in Manaus, can arrange expeditions in Amazônia, offering short package tours, as well as longer safaris. It is possible to stay either in a floating lodge, or one of the many jungle lodges along the Rio Juma. Most of them offer jungle hikes, piranha fishing, and caiman spotting at night.

Caimans luxuriating on the sandy riverbank of Manaquiri, with a great egret in the foreground

Cormorants and great egrets in the Mamirauá Reserve

Instituto de Desenvolvimento Sustentável Mamirauá

280 miles (450 km) W of Manaus. uakarilodge.com.br Programa de ecoturismo: **Tel** (97) 3343 4160.

Located at the confluence of two rivers, the Rio Solimões and Rio Japurá, the Mamirauá Sustainable Development Reserve covers an area of 5703 sq miles (14,770 sq km). Since 1990, when it was declared an ecological station, the Mamirauá Reserve has been one of Brazil's most prized ecotourism spots.

Splendid and luxuriant, its várzea (seasonally flooded) vegetation offers plenty of opportunity for spotting abundant wildlife, including endemic species such as the white uakari monkey and black-headed squirrel monkey. The annual flood transforms the life of the whole region. During the high-water season, fish invade the flooded forest and disperse seeds as they move about. More than 300 species of fish have already been catalogued in the reserve. Mamirauá is also home to pink river dolphin, great egret, and the rare scarlet macaw. The Neotropic cormorant, whose diet consists mainly of fish, can be spotted swimming and feeding in large, noisy flocks.

In the dry season, which lasts from September to December, one can walk on trails, or paddle almost silently through them on canoes. The preserve's eco-tourism program features a range of activities, which includes guided nature expeditions in the lakes and trails in the forest.

The preserve also offers comfortable and ecologically sound accommodation at the floating Uakari Lodge (see p378) close to forest trails, pretty jungle lakes, and caboclo communities. Book through a Manaus tour company, or directly with the **Programa de Ecoturismo** in Tefé, 16 miles (25 km) south.

❷ Parintins

Amazonas. 🖾 105,000.
🚤 from Manaus. 🎭 Festa do Boi Bumbá (Jun); Festa das Pastorinhas (Dec–Jan).

A large jungle town, Parintins was originally the refuge of a community of indigenous riverine people, known as caboclos, who were escaping Portuguese slave traders. Today, Parintins is best known for its popular Festa do Boi Bumbá. The festival is celebrated in June, when the town gets so packed that visitors often stay on boats.

Though there is little else to see, besides the well-preserved colonial architecture, Parintins is known for its rich indigenous culture, and the local handicrafts make unique souvenirs. The flea markets sell everything from trinkets, lace, and bead-work to masks and mahogany carvings. During the dry season, boat trips can be taken to nearby lakes and river beaches.

Festa do Boi Bumbá

The vibrant festival, Festa do Boi Bumbá, is centered around a ritualistic dance recounting the death and rebirth of a legendary boi (ox). Originating on the 18th-century Northeast plantations, the festival arrived in Parintins almost 100 years ago with the Cid brothers from Maranhão. They brought with them the Bumba-meu-boi (see p47) musical influence, steeped in the vibrant rhythms of the Northeast. The last few decades saw the festival gaining in prominence. Every June, at least 35,000 people crowd into Bumbódromo, a purpose-built stadium in the town center, to join in the revelries. The fantastic procession incorporates dazzlingly dressed participants, including mythological beasts. The rivalry between the two competing camps, the red Garantido and the blue Caprichoso groups, is expressed in traditional songs. Over the years, this competitive spirit, which goes right down to who wears the most outlandish costume, has brought forth some radical and electrifying spectacles.

Garantido in bright red headgear, gearing up for the contest

Tranquil waters of the Rio Branco, flowing past Roraima's capital Boa Vista

❸ Boa Vista

Roraima. 🗺 285,000. ✈ 🚆 🚌
ℹ Centro Turismo, (95) 3623 2365.
ⓦ **turismo.rr.gov.br** 📋 Roraima
Adventures, (95) 3624 9611.
ⓦ **roraima-brasil.com.br**

Created in 1991, Roraima is one of Brazil's newest states, and Boa Vista is its capital city. While the savannas surrounding it are an important cattle-ranching territory, the gold rush of the 1980s still drives development in the region.

The Praça Cívica forms the heart of the town's arch-shaped street layout. The modern Palácio Municipal is here beside the Monumento ao Garimpeiro, a local monument honoring the gold miners who have brought significant wealth to this state.

There are good swimming beaches on the Rio Branco, only 15 minutes by bus from Boa Vista. The sandy beaches right in the town center, opposite the Orla Taumanam, offer excellent swimming when the river is low.

Environs
Boa Vista is blessed with lush tropical rainforest, endless stretches of savanna plains, and pretty river beaches, which make the surrounding region well worth exploring. Though ecotourism is still in its initial stages, organized tours are fairly developed.

A significant staging port en route south to Manaus or north to Guyana and Venezuela, Boa Vista is easily connected by bus to the Venezuelan town of **Santa Elena de Uairén**, located 147 miles (237 km) north. The route from Boa Vista to Santa Elena is dotted with some interesting sights. The ecological island preserve of **Ilha do Maracá**, 62 miles (100 km) north of Boa Vista, is known for its species preservation and biodiversity. Fringed with groves of cashew trees, the enchanting **Lago Caracaranã** is located 112 miles (180 km) north.

Santa Elena de Uairén offers the best access to the **Parque Nacional de Monte Roraima**. The park is ideal for trekking through a variety of eco-niches with changing vegetation to climb **Monte Roraima**, a point where Brazil, Guyana, and Venezuela meet. At 8,970 ft (2,734 m) above sea level, good camping equipment, guides, and preparation is essential.

Several Boa Vista-based companies offer excellent week-long packages. International visitors require a Venezuelan tourist card, which can be obtained at the Venezuelan consulate in Boa Vista.

❹ Rio Branco

Acre. 🗺 335,000. ✈ 🚆 🚌 ℹ Via
Chico Mendes s/n, Arena da Floresta,
(68) 3901 3024.

Another relatively new state, Acre was annexed from Bolivia in the early 20th century by a pioneering army of Brazilian rubber-tappers. It was founded in 1904, under the name of a rubber company, Seringal Empressa, by Newtel Maia from Ceará.

The Parque de Maternidade has magically transformed a small town water canal into a long, green city walk. In the town center, just a couple of blocks north from the Rio Acre, which cuts the town in half, stands the **Palácio Rio Branco**. Though restored, the building maintains its original Neo-Classical façade with four columns at the entrance. It was built in the 1930s as headquarters for the state government, and retains a good collection of period furniture

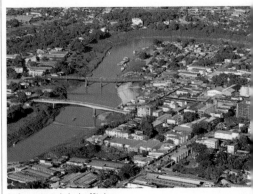

Rio Branco city on the banks of Rio Acre

from the 1940s and 1950s. A main feature of the palace, the largest painting in Brazil, depicts a scene in homage to the revolutionary heroes who liberated Acre from Bolivia. The palace also contains several large rooms dedicated to the prehistory and history of the region. The main focus is on the 20th-century history of Acre, and there is a superb room dedicated to indigenous culture, displaying some stupendous feather headdresses. Artifacts relating to local history and tribes are also displayed in the palace.

A few blocks north, the **Museu da Borrachá** (Rubber Museum) focuses on the fascinating local ethnic culture, rubber-tappers, and *ayahuasca* churches, known for their ceremonial use of hallucinogenic herbs.

Rio Branco is transforming the city's south bank of the Rio Acre, which was the focal point during the rubber boom and until the new north-based commercial center emerged in the mid-20th century. The municipality is restoring many of the buildings, which once served the river port as hotels, bars, and a splendid movie theater, as well as merchants' stores, making for a lively atmosphere. The promenade, La Gameleira, makes a perfect location for a riverside walk.

The **Parque Ambiental Chico Mendes** (Chico Mendes Environmental Park) is located in the former rubber plantation at Itucumã near Vila Acre, 6 miles (10 km) south of Rio Branco. It contains virgin forest areas, some replica *malocas* (indigenous longhouses) and rubber-tapper dwellings, as well as a zoo and the Chico Mendes memorial.

🏛 **Museu da Borrachá**
Av Ceará 1441. **Tel** (68) 3223 1202. **Open** 8am–6pm Tue–Fri, 4–9pm Sat & Sun.

🏛 **Palácio Rio Branco**
Praça E. Gaspar Dutra s/n. **Tel** (68) 3223 9241. **Open** 8am–6pm Tue–Fri, 4–9pm Sat & Sun. 📷 ♿ ✉

🗺 **Parque Ambiental Chico Mendes**
Rodovia AC-40 Km 7, Vila Acre. **Tel** (68) 3221 1933. **Open** 7am–5pm Tue–Sun.

Visitors walking through the ruined Forte Príncipe da Beira, Guajará-Mirim

❺ Porto Velho

Rondônia. 🏙 425,000. ✈ 🚌 ⛴
🛈 Departamento do Turismo, (69) 3216 5973.

A very fast growing jungle city, Rondônia's capital, Porto Velho, has grown out of a few streets beside the giant Rio Madeira in the last 100 years. River trips to the nearby beach of Santo Antônio are popular for freshly cooked fish at a waterside restaurant.

The star attraction, however, is the **Madeira-Mamoré Museu Ferroviário**, where several steam locomotives, some under cover, still defiantly symbolize a rusting industrial vision in the middle of the Amazon jungle. In the main museum shed, there are interesting exhibits from the turn of the 19th century, when the railway was being built. Unfortunately, its inauguration

in 1912 was just in time to witness the collapse of Brazil's rubber industry.

Environs
Guajará-Mirim is on the Bolivian border. From here, it is possible to visit the lonely jungle fort, the **Forte Príncipe da Beira**, built by the Portuguese in 1773.

The **Reserva Biologica do Guaporé** near Costa Marques town, which is located 12 miles (20 km) east of Principe de Beira town, is known for its diverse bird species. The Ibama in Porto Velho arranges trips for researchers.

🏛 **Madeira-Mamoré Museu Ferroviário**
Praça Madeira-Mamoré. **Open** 8am–noon, 2–6pm Mon–Fri. 📷 ♿ **Tel** (69) 3901 3651.

🗺 **Reserva Biologica do Guaporé**
Av Cabixi com Limoeiro 1942. **Tel** (69) 3651 3782.

Chico Mendes (1944–88)

Environmentalist Chico Mendes

A rubber-tapper union leader and environmental activist, Chico Mendes helped establish the National Council of Rubber Tappers. His design for extractive rainforest preserves won him recognition by the UN in 1987, with a Global 500 award. He received another award from the Better World Society, before his assassination by hired men employed by the ranchers on December 22, 1988. His untimely death brought international attention, for the first time, both to the plight of the rainforest and the positive solution offered simply by harvesting the rainforest's fruits and sustainable products. Many leading Brazilian human rights activists, environmental campaigners, and church organizations came together to establish the Chico Mendes Committee, which successfully dedicated itself to seeing his murderers brought to justice.

CENTRAL WEST BRAZIL

Introducing Central
  West Brazil   296–301

Brasília, Goiás &
  Tocantins   302–317

Mato Grosso &
  Mato Grosso do Sul   318–327

Introducing Central West Brazil

The Federal District of Brasília and four other states make up Brazil's Central West. Goiás and Tocantins in the east of the region and Mato Grosso and Mato Grosso do Sul in the west, are areas where the expansive wilderness of craggy *cerrado*-covered plateaus, vast wetlands, rainforests, and deserts are beginning to give way to industrialization. The slow pace of life in colonial mining towns such as Cidade de Goiás and Pirenópolis is being eclipsed by the urban attractions of cities such as Campo Grande and Brasília. However, the Central West remains one of the best regions in which to savor Brazil's traditional rural way of life as well as spot amazing wildlife.

BRAZIL

CENTRAL
WEST
BRAZIL

Cristalino Jungle Lodge *(see p323)* is situated on the banks of the Rio Cristalino, in Alta Floresta. This region is rich in the Amazon flora and fauna, and has a number of splendid birding trails. Guided hiking tours are also on offer.

Sinop

Comodoro

MATO GROSSO &
MATO GROSSO DO
(See pp318–27)

Cuiabá

Rondonópolis

Corumbá

Campo
Grande

Bonito

Dou

Bonito *(see p327)*, a small, quiet town located at the southern edge of the Pantanal, offers visitors light adventure activities such as snorkeling in clear-water rivers, visiting caves, and hiking along short wildlife trails.

◀ Pantanal landscape

Ilha do Bananal *(see p315)*, one of the world's largest river islands, contains rivers that extend up to 155 miles (250 km), and is home to several indigenous peoples. A bird-watcher's paradise, the island's wild interior is not easily accessible.

Paraíso do
Norte

Gurupi

**BRASÍLIA, GOIÁS
& TOCANTINS**
(See pp302–17)

Uruaçu

Pirenópolis
Brasília

Goiânia

Rio Verde

Brasília *(see pp306–9)*, the country's capital, is renowned for its Modernist buildings, many of which were designed by the noted architect Oscar Niemeyer.

0 km   150
0 miles   150

Pirenópolis *(see pp312–13)*, a picturesque former mining town with colonial buildings and impressive restaurants, is a popular weekend retreat. It is also a base for exploring the *cerrado* and the region's numerous waterfalls.

Creation of a Capital

President Juscelino Kubitschek and his team of designers, planners, and architects, led by Oscar Niemeyer, envisaged Brasília not only as a city, but also as a monument to the national motto – Order and Progress. In creating this, they turned to European Modernism, following the doctrine of Charles-Edouard Jeanneret (1887–1965), or "Le Corbusier," for their inspiration. The concept stated that modern cities should be zoned functionally with separate areas for housing (in high-rise blocks), recreation, and administration, broken by green belts and roads.

Juscelino Kubitschek was the president of Brazil between 1956 and 1961. He was responsible for the creation of Brasília as the new, modern capital of the country.

The Missão Cruls was commissioned by President Floriano Peixoto in 1892 and led by the Belgian scientist Luiz Cruls. It sought to find a possible site for a new capital in the Brazilian interior to make a more regionally neutral federal capital where resources could be equally divided.

Eixo Rodoviária Sul is one of the main roads in the "wings" connecting Brasília from one end to the other.

The *candangos* were workers from the Northeast brought to Brasília in vast numbers to build the city. Homes for their descendants were not included in the grand plan and today Brasília is ringed with the slum cities of their children.

Brasília

Located at the heart of the country, Brazil's capital city is today on UNESCO's list of World Heritage Sites, and is famous for its innovative urban planning and daring architecture.

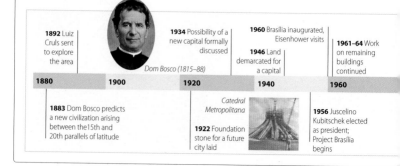

1892 Luiz Cruls sent to explore the area

Dom Bosco (1815–88)

1934 Possibility of a new capital formally discussed

1946 Land demarcated for a capital

1960 Brasília inaugurated, Eisenhower visits

1961–64 Work on remaining buildings continued

1880　　**1900**　　**1920**　　**1940**　　**1960**

1883 Dom Bosco predicts a new civilization arising between the 15th and 20th parallels of latitude

Catedral Metropolitana

1922 Foundation stone for a future city laid

1956 Juscelino Kubitschek elected as president; Project Brasília begins

Lúcio Costa and Roberto Burle Marx, the urban planner and the landscape designer behind Brasília, intended that every element, from the layout of the residential and administrative districts to the symmetry of the buildings, should be in harmony with the city's overall design.

Ministerial buildings were built to flank Praça dos Três Poderes and Eixo Monumental *(see pp306–7)*.

Oscar Niemeyer

Born in Rio de Janeiro in 1907, Niemeyer went on to become one of the most important names in modern architecture. His first job was with Le Corbusier and Lúcio Costa on Rio's Ministry of Education in 1936. After this he went on to design a series of landmark buildings such as the Contemporary Museum of Art in Niterói *(see p93)*. Niemeyer's socialist beliefs led to his exile under the coup of 1964. He returned to Rio in the 1980s and continued to work. He died in 2012.

Oscar Niemeyer at his office in Rio de Janeiro

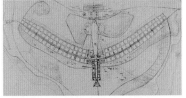

Original pen and ink drawings submitted by Lúcio Costa in 1956 in the competition for a new capital city show Brasília's distinctive shape, which has been variously interpreted as an airplane, a bird in flight, and a bow and arrow.

Superquadra 309, a residential neighborhood, was built in one of the "wings" of Brasília.

The **Juscelino Kubitscheck Bridge**, designed by architect Alexandre Chan, opened in 2002. The striking steel and concrete bridge links the eastern shore of Lake Paranoá to the center of the city and has become a landmark.

The inauguration of Brasília by President Juscelino Kubitschek on 21 April 1960 was attended by thousands of people. The new capital saw the installation of the three powers of the republic – parliament, judiciary, and presidency.

Flora & Fauna in the Cerrado

The Brazilian *cerrado* (meaning impenetrable in Portuguese) is a biome unique to South America and is the tropical world's largest woodland savanna. The *cerrado* landscape is made up of scattered woods and vast swathes of grassland along riverbanks and in small valleys. One of the richest ecosystems in the world, the *cerrado* is home to almost every species of large mammal found in South America, together with an enormously prolific birdlife. The *cerrado* landscape is home to some 10,000 plant species, of which 4,400 are endemic to the region.

B R A Z I L

Key
■ The *cerrado*
■ The Pantanal

Hyacinth macaws are an endangered species due to overcollection for the caged-bird trade. They are also hunted by the Kayapó people *(see p266)*, who use their bright blue feathers in their headdresses.

The *cerrado*, a sprawling 1.2-million-sq-mile (3-million-sq-km) mix of forest and savanna, covers 75 percent of Brazil.

Capybaras, abundant in the *cerrado*, are semi-aquatic, herbivorous rodents. They live in herds and spend most of their time feeding on river-banks, where they are easily spotted during mornings and evenings.

The marsh deer is generally a solitary animal, or lives in herds of fewer than six. It has webbed feet which help it walk on flooded land.

The rhea is a large, flightless bird native to South America. Because rheas will eat almost any crop plant, farmers sometimes kill the birds. This, along with egg gathering and habitat loss, has led to a significant drop in their numbers. The species is listed among the wildlife of "special concern."

The maned wolf is the only large canid in the world that does not form packs. The animal, now endangered, was hunted by poachers for its body parts, notably the eyes, which were believed to be good-luck charms.

Buriti Palms often grow over subterranean water. They are an important source of food for many large parrots and primates.

Savanna formations in the *cerrado* are not homogenous. Hilly areas have denser, more varied flora than the grasslands.

Tractors paving the way for a new farm in the *cerrado*

Conservation of the Cerrado

Central Brazil's ancient *cerrado* forests are rapidly being cleared for soya plantations and cattle ranches. Since the late 1990s, steps have been taken to identify conservation-priority areas and better manage protected areas. Recently, private reserves, established under the Private Natural Heritage Reserve system, have become an important component of biodiversity protection in the *cerrado*. There have also been more intensive faunal and floral surveys of the region. In 2016, an agreement between the state authorities, landowners, and conservation groups set out an urgent action plan to protect designated reserves.

Ipê Tree is a large canopy tree. Its vibrant trumpet-shaped flowers bloom in spectacular yellow, pink, and mauve throughout the *cerrado*.

Flora in the Cerrado

The cerrado *is characterized by its vast expanses of grassland, scattered forests, and palm groves. The landscape varies between the "open* cerrado*," predominantly grassland, without trees and shrubs, and "closed* cerrado*," the more forested areas.*

Flora & Fauna of Pantanal

Although the world's largest wetland forms part of the southern extreme of the cerrado*, the Pantanal (see pp324–5) comprises habitats most associated with the Amazon. Many* cerrado *species live here, as well as marsh deer, capybara, caimans, waterbirds, and monkeys.*

The white-necked heron *is a common sight in the Pantanal, especially along riverbanks, where it feeds. This graceful bird builds its nest on a platform on trees close to the river.*

Caiman *numbers in the Pantanal have increased after a ban on hunting them for their skin and teeth (considered charms against witchcraft) took effect.*

Guira cuckoos are slightly scruffy-looking birds that nest, roost, and feed in groups, eating insects, frogs, and eggs off the ground.

BRASÍLIA, GOIÁS & TOCANTINS

The capital of Brazil since 1960, Brasília is the region's only metropolis. Its striking city plan and futuristic architecture make it vastly different from any other city in the country. Goiás and Tocantins make up Brazil's heartland. Northern Goiás and Tocantins are mainly wilderness areas of mountains and dry savanna, while in the south lie the colonial towns of Pirenópolis and Goiás Velho.

Until the mid-20th century, only *bandeirante* slavers and gold hunters had ventured into the wilderness of central Brazil, a land of *cerrado* (savanna) woodland, *mesetas* (tabletop mountains), and giant winding rivers, peopled by indigenous groups such as the Xavante. Some gold prospectors stayed on, building a handful of colonial towns near their mines. Cidade Goiás and Pirenópolis in central Goiás are very well preserved, so much so that the former is now a UNESCO World Heritage Site. Pirenópolis is famous for its festivals, the liveliest of which, the Festa do Divino Espírito Santo, re-enacts the battles between the Christians and the Moors. The city is also a center for ecotourism,

and a favorite watering hole for nearby Brasília's middle class. The Utopian, but impersonal, capital city sits on an exposed plain under an expansive sky. Its brave new domes, churches, and steel-reinforced monoliths, now ringed with *favelas*, should not be missed.

Northern Goiás and Tocantins remain frontier lands, where fields of soya are fast encroaching upon the foothills of the *mesetas* in Chapada dos Veadeiros National Park, the dune-filled expanses of the Jalapão *cerrado*, and indigenous lands on the world's largest river island, Ilha do Bananal. The scenery here is spectacular, and adventure activities, such as canyoning and rappeling, are well developed.

The Palácio do Itamaraty (Palace of Arches), one of the most impressive modern buildings in Brasília

◀ Tribute to Northeast Brazil's migrant workers, Bruno Giorgio's sculpture *Os Candangos*, in Brasília, the city they helped build

Exploring Brasília, Goiás & Tocantins

Cidade de Goiás and Pirenópolis in Goiás remain pleasant colonial towns, while the spectacular Chapada dos Veadeiros National Park in northern Goiás showcases the unique flora and fauna of high-altitude *cerrado*. Brasília, the capital city of Brazil from 1960 onward, was built from the dust and scrub of the central western *cerrado*, and is a Modernist marvel. In Tocantins state, the Ilha do Bananal, one of the largest islands in Brazil, is also the point at which three ecosystems converge – rainforest, *cerrado*, and wetland. The dune deserts of Jalapão in Tocantins are fringed by dry *sertão*, vast horizons of soya farms, waterfalls, crystalline rivers, and forests inhabited by the Xavante and Xingú indigenous groups.

Rio Preto waterfall at Chapada dos Veadeiros

Sights at a Glance

Towns & Cities

1 Brasília pp306–9
2 Pirenópolis pp312–13
3 Cidade de Goiás
5 Palmas

National Parks & Areas of Natural Beauty

4 Parque Nacional Chapada dos Veadeiros pp316–17
6 Jalapão
7 Ilha do Bananal
8 Parque Nacional das Emas

For hotels and restaurants in this region see p379 and p395

Araguatins

o Novo O
cantins   *Teresina*

oa   O Tocantinópolis

na
    O
erlândia

aguaína
         O Piaca

Craolândia O

   Itacajá
      O

dos Parecis

edro Afonso O

Perdida

acema do   Lizarda
ntins   O

OCANTINS

Sono

ALMAS
     JALAPÃO
     🏞️6

al   Ponte Alta   *La Três*
            do Norte   *Ríos*

  Natividade   Dianópolis
      O   O

uel Alves   40

                   Salvador

                  Tagu
                  atinga
                     O
Paraná
  O   118

te Alegre   Campos Belos
de Goiás O   O
                        São
                       O Domingos

RQUE NACIONAL
DA DOS VEADEIROS
🏞️4

araíso O   Iaciara
Goiás   O
         118
ndia
      O São João   O Mambai
        da Aliança

           O Formosa

🏛️🏨
BRASÍLIA

  O Gama

Luziânia
        50
       O Cristalina
olis   O
        40

o   *Belo*
    Horizonte

     50

O Catalão

presa de
mborcação

o Paulo

Ministry buildings, Catedral Metropolitana, and Museu Nacional, in Brasília

Getting Around

Travel inevitably begins in Brasília. There is an international airport, and flights connecting with most larger Brazilian cities, including frequent flights to Goiânia in Goiás and Palmas in Tocantins. Roads radiate out from these cities to other towns and states cutting through the harvest land and the stunning scenery. Pirenópolis, a weekend getaway from Goiânia, is reached from Brasília via a filigree of small roads and regular buses. There are daily buses to Cidade de Goiás from Goiânia via the BR-070. The Chapada dos Veadeiros, which, together with Pirenópolis, boasts the best ecotourism infrastructure, is reached from the little towns of São Jorge or Alto Paraíso in northern Goiás. These are connected to Brasília via the GO-118. Apart from the main north–south artery, the BR-153, transportation in Tocantins is difficult. Ilha do Bananal in the west and Jalapão in the east are remote and best visited on tours.

0 km   100

0 miles   100

Key

— Major road

∷∷∷ Minor road

— State border

Sweeping sand dunes in Jalapão

For keys to symbols *see back flap*

❶ Brasília

Brasília is the embodiment in concrete of President Juscelino Kubitschek's promise of "fifty years of economic and social development in five," and of the national motto – Order and Progress. The city was built by vast teams of *candangos*, workers from the Northeast, who carved it from the *cerrado* at breakneck speed. They were led by urban planner Lúcio Costa, architect Oscar Niemeyer, and landscape engineer Roberto Burle Marx *(see p299)*. The capital of Brazil shifted from Rio de Janeiro to Brasília on April 21, 1960. Brasília was added to UNESCO's list of World Heritage Sites in 1987 as an example of daring urban planning and modern architecture. Today, Brasília is a stately, organized city, albeit a little quiet.

Aerial view of the Eixo Monumental

Quartel General do Exército

Memorial dos Povos Indígenas is fashioned like a *maloca*, a traditional longhouse. It is a tribute to Brazil's indigenous peoples.

TV Tower is the best place to get a bird's-eye view of the city. The observation deck is on top of the 426-ft- (75-m-) high building.

VIA N-1 OESTE

VIA S-1 OESTE

0 meters 250
0 yards 250

VIA S-1 OESTE

PARQUE SARA KUBITSCHEK

VIA S-2

VIA W3 SUL

Eixo Monumental

The Eixo Monumental, Brasília's main thoroughfare, forms the centerpiece of the city. Kubitschek stands at one end of the Eixo, waving from his towering Modernist column to the seat of government, the Congresso Nacional and Palácio do Planalto, which sit around the Praça dos Três Poderes. Many of Brazil's most famous architects and sculptors were involved in its construction.

Memorial Juscelino Kubitschek
Built in honor of the president responsible for the construction of Brasília, this monument contains his mausoleum, with photographs of, and documents about, the construction of the city.

Quartel General do Exército
This fusion of curves, straight lines, and jagged waves echoes the Congress complex and is the headquarters of the Brazilian army – at times the key player in affairs of state.

For hotels and restaurants in this region see p379 and p395

Esplanada dos Ministérios
Tall ministry buildings, 19 in all, are lined up in rows along Esplanada dos Ministérios, with the Juscelino Kubitscheck bridge in the background.

VISITORS' CHECKLIST

Practical Information
Brasília Distrito Federal.
2,200,000. Tourist Office, Presidente Juscelino Kubitschek International Airport, (61) 3364 9102. **wbrasilia.com/cat.htm**

Transport
Presidente Juscelino Kubitschek International Airport, (61) 3033 9000.

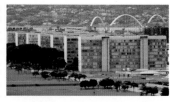

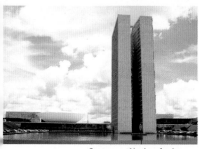

Congresso Nacional e Anexos
Oscar Niemeyer's most famous and celebrated group of Modernist buildings at the heart of Brasília is also Brazil's seat of government.

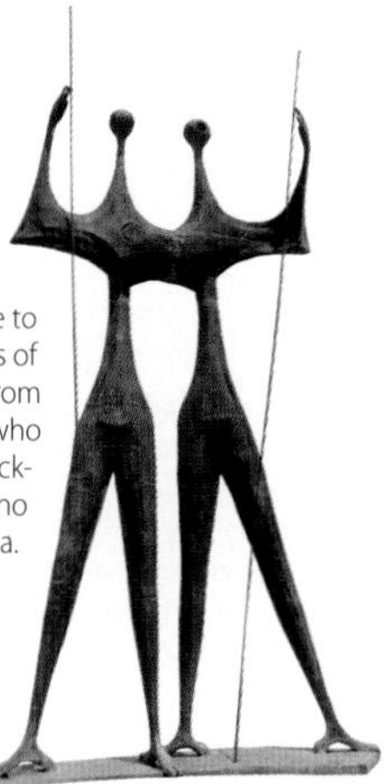

Os Candangos
Artist Bruno Giorgio's *Os Candangos* was built in homage to the thousands of migrant workers from Northeast Brazil who went by this nickname and who helped build Brasília.

Esplanada dos Ministérios
VIA L2 NORTE
Rodoviária
VIA N-1 OESTE
VIA N-2
EIXINHO L
ESPLANADA DOS MINISTÉRIOS
VIA S-1 OESTE
VIA L2 SUL
VIA S-2
Fundaçãs Biblioteca Nacional

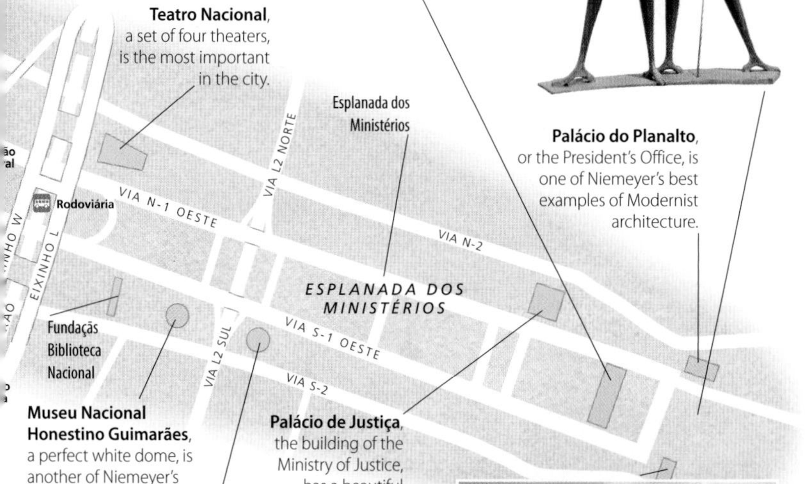

Teatro Nacional, a set of four theaters, is the most important in the city.

Palácio do Planalto, or the President's Office, is one of Niemeyer's best examples of Modernist architecture.

Museu Nacional Honestino Guimarães, a perfect white dome, is another of Niemeyer's buildings.

Palácio de Justiça, the building of the Ministry of Justice, has a beautiful internal garden.

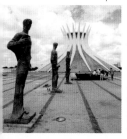

Catedral Metropolitana Nossa Senhora Aparecida
Niemeyer's iconic cathedral with its curved columns and stained-glass interior is flanked by haunting sculptures of the four apostles.

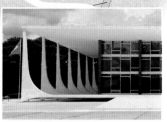

Supremo Tribunal Federal
The highest court in the country, the Supremo Tribunal Federal is the seat of Brazil's judicial power.

Exploring Brasília

The capital of Brazil, Brasília, is shaped like an airplane in homage to what was then the incipient jet age. While to its north and south lie the residential wings, the Eixo Monumental *(see pp306–7)* forms the body of the jet, with the city's major attractions.

Praça dos Três Poderes

Eixo Monumental.
Congresso Nacional e Anexos:
Tel (61) 3303 4671. **Open** 8:30am–5:30pm daily. 🔊 Palácio do Planalto:
Tel (61) 3411 2042. **Open** 9:30am–2:30pm Sun. Palácio Itamaraty:
Tel (61) 3411 6155. 📷 9am, 10am, 11am, 2pm, 3pm, 4pm, 5pm Mon–Fri; 9am, 11am, 2pm, 3pm, 5pm Sat & Sun.
Palácio da Justiça:**Tel** (61) 2025 3216.
Open 9–11am, 3–5pm Mon–Fri.

This vast square is flanked by buildings that form the locus of the Brazilian government. The axis of the federal state, the **Congresso Nacional e Anexos** is a harmonious fusion of lines and curves, creating the most monumental and timeless architecture in the city. On the other side of the square are the seats of two other branches of power – the **Palácio do Planalto**, the executive office of the presidency, and opposite it, the **Supremo Tribunal Federal**, the Supreme Court headquarters, which is closed to the public.

Immediately below this group of buildings are the **Palácio Itamaraty** and the **Palácio da Justiça**, two of Brasília's few buildings that are more aesthetic than monumental.

Palácio da Justiça with lily pond in the foreground

The interior of Santuário Dom Bosco, bathed in blue light

The latter's Modernist columns seem to rise gently from the lily pond lying at its feet to form smooth arches. Inside is a vast hall decorated with fine sculpture and paintings. The highlight is 19th-century artist Pedro Américo's *O Grito de Ipiranga*, depicting the moment when Dom Pedro I proclaimed Brazilian Independence *(see p56)*.

🔒 Catedral Militar de Nossa Senhora da Paz

Canteiro Central do Eixo Monumental Oeste. **Tel** (61) 3323 3858.
Open 7am–8pm daily.
This brilliant white triangular church, with its jagged windows and vast gable, echoes the French Notre Dame du Haut, designed by Niemeyer's mentor, Le Corbusier. It was completed in 1991, and was built to house the papal altar used by John Paul II on his visit to Brasília in 1980.

Quartel General do Exército

Setor Militar Urbano.
At the northeastern end of the Eixo Monumental, this vast complex of imposing buildings is set in a sea of lawns and watched over by a towering obelisk. It was built during the military dictatorship and was intended to show the presence of military power in the government, which was notably absent from the Praça dos Três Poderes. The intimidating stature of the buildings conveys Niemeyer's objective of constructing something grand for the generals. He was determined that the monumentalism of these generals should not be eclipsed by that of President Juscelino Kubitschek *(see p62)*.

🔒 Santuário Dom Bosco

Av W3 Sul, Quadra 702. **Tel** (61) 3223 6542. **Open** 7am–7pm daily. ✉
The city's finest church honors the 19th-century Italian visionary saint and founder of the Salesian order. His proclamation that a new civilization would arise in the third millennium between the 15th and 16th parallels of latitudes, inspired Kubitschek to build Brasília on the edge of an artificial lake. The stunning interior features an almost seemless panoply of glass, which ranges from light to dark blue and indigo, as it ascends. In the late afternoon, shafts of light penetrate the building, illuminating the marble statue of the Virgin and the vast cross whose vertical was carved from a single piece of tropical cedar. The church was blessed by John Paul II on his 1980 visit.

Templo da Boa Vontade

Setor Garagem Sul 915. **Tel** (61) 3114 1070. **Open** 24 hrs daily.
Many religions, some orthodox, some decidedly alternative, thrive in and around Brasília. This marble pyramid with seven open sides was built to reflect the ecumenical attitude towards spirituality which characterizes the city. The building's geometry is based on multiples of seven in accordance with sacred numerology. The sides rise to 69 ft (21 m), the cavernous nave spans 92 ft (28 m), and spiral steps wind around the interior. The central portion of the temple is illuminated by light, filtering through an enormous and priceless rock crystal found at Cristalino in Goiás.

Catedral Metropolitana Nossa Senhora Aparecida

Designed by Oscar Niemeyer to resemble a crown of thorns, this cathedral features 16 soaring curved pillars spread like an open hand. Between them, a filigree of glass windows is united by a fluid series of colors. The main altar and the altarpiece was given by Pope Paul VI in 1967, who also blessed the metal cross sitting atop the building. The statues of the evangelists outside the cathedral are by the Mineiro sculptor Alfredo Ceschiatti, who also sculpted the archangels suspended from the ceiling inside.

VISITORS' CHECKLIST

Practical Information
Esplanada dos Ministérios.
Tel (61) 3224 4073.
Open 8am–6pm Tue–Sun.
Closed during masses: 12:15pm, 6:15pm Tue–Fri, 5pm Sat, 8:30am, 10:30am, 6pm Sun
w catedral.org.br

The Catedral Metropolitana, etched against a cloudy Brasília sky

Subterranean Entrance
The remarkable entrance was intended to recall the catacombs where Christ was interred, with visitors emerging out of darkness into the cathedral's light.

Curved Concrete Pillars, all 16 of them, are held together at their apex by a high-tensile steel ring.

São Mateus
Designed by sculptor Alfredo Ceschiatti (1918–89), this 10-ft-(3-m-) high bronze figure of St. Matthew is one of the four sculptures that stand in front of the cathedral.

Stunning Interior
Archangels hover over the central altar, while the light marble and ample daylight infuse the entire building with a transcendent glow. The glass panels in the interior reflect sunlight from the rippling water outside.

The breathtaking *cachoeira* (waterfall) that crashes into the Cânion do Rio Preto in the Parque Nacional Chapada dos Veadeiros, Goiás ▶

❷ Pirenópolis

The picturesque town of Pirenópolis is gathered around the Rio das Almas, surrounded by verdant *cerrado* woodlands, and tucked away at the feet of low ragged hills. Pirenópolis skillfully balances the old and the new, the traditional and the contemporary. Crowned by Portuguese Baroque churches, the cobbled streets clatter to the sound of cowboys on horseback. The streets are lined with chic little restaurants, housed in rustic 18th-century bungalows, or designed in low-key 20th-century Art Deco style. The entire historical center can be walked around in less than two hours. There are only a few streets – the principal ones being Rua Direita, Rua da Aurora, Rua do Bonfim, and Rua do Rosário, which has the bulk of the restaurants. At weekends, a bustling crowd from Brasília fills up the streets.

Display of costumes from the Festa do Divino, Museu das Cavalhadas

Souvenir shops selling traditional handicrafts on Rua Rui Barbosa

🏠 Igreja Nosso Senhor do Bonfim

Praça do Bonfim. **Open** during mass: 10:30am Sun.

This simple but elegant little church on Rua do Bonfim was built between 1750 and 1754. One of the best-preserved churches in Goiás, this modest Baroque building is architecturally similar to Matriz de

The well-maintained Igreja Nosso Senhor do Bonfim

Nossa Senhora do Rosário and has a plain white façade. The image of Nosso Senhor do Bonfim, in the main altarpiece, was brought here from Salvador by a convoy of 250 slaves.

🏠 Igreja Matriz de Nossa Senhora do Rosário

Praça da Matriz. **Open** check with tourist office before visiting.

This parish church, founded in 1728, is the largest and the oldest ecclesiastical building in Goiás. Until 2002, when the entire attractive colonial edifice was gutted in a fierce fire, it also had one of the finest Baroque interiors in the state. The church boasted an altarpiece decorated with motifs taken from the flora of the surrounding *cerrado*, and an impressive ceiling painted by the Brazilian artist, Inácio Pereira Leal, in 1864. The church was restored and opened anew in 2006, but a shortage of funds has left it with a plain interior.

🏛 Museu das Cavalhadas

Rua Direita 39. **Tel** (62) 3331 1166. **Open** 8am–8pm daily. 📷

This small museum contains an incredible display of Carnaval masks, ornate metal armor costumes, photographs, and folklore relating to the hugely popular Festa do Divino Espírito Santo. The festival was originally Spanish but the court costumes and the animal masks are uniquely Brazilian, originating from Afro-Brazilian and indigenous customs. The collection occupies the ground floor of a home belonging to a family which has for generations played a central role in performances at the festival.

🎭 Teatro de Pirenópolis

Praça da Matriz s/n. **Tel** (62) 3331 2029 (box office). **Open** 8–11am & 1–5pm Mon–Fri, 9am–8pm Sat, 9am–3pm Sun.

This delightful, restored miniature 19th-century theater is one of the town's hidden treasures and commemorated the centenary of its foundation in 2001. The Teatro de Pirenópolis is best visited during one of the regular plays, performances, and shows. One of the most interesting small acts in the past has featured the popular Mato Grosso do Sul-born guitarist Almir Sater. The Goiás singer-songwriter, Maria Eugenia, and the Tocantins *forró* singer, Dorivã, regularly play here. Just around the corner, on the Rua do Direita, is the little Art Deco **Cine Teatro Pireneus**, whose eclectic program includes films, plays, concerts, and art exhibitions.

Festa do Divino Espírito Santo

This festival is based on Iberian lore dating from the Crusades and Catholic Whitsuntide celebrations, with the Cavalhadas horse parades as a central feature. The festival begins 15 days before Pentecost Sunday, at the Matriz, where a gathering of riders known as the Folia do Divino proceed out of Pirenópolis into the surrounding countryside. Masked dancers, parades of horsemen dressed as Crusaders, Moors, or Cavalhadas, and many cultural and musical events follow. The festival culminates on Pentecost Sunday in the stadium, the Cavalhadodrómo.

Cavalhadas parade costume

🌿 Santuário de Vida Silvestre Fazenda Vagafogo

4 miles (6 km) NW of Pirenópolis. **Tel** (62) 3335 8515. **Open** 9am–5pm daily. 🚶

A beautifully preserved patch of forest lined with streams and exquisite trails, Santuário Vagafogo makes for a good excursion. This stunning nature preserve of *cerrado* and gallery forests (forests along a river or stream) is home to a number of bird and animal species such as brown capuchins and armadillos. The sanctuary offers activities, such as tree climbing and rappelling. On weekends and on holidays, a small restaurant at the visitors' center serves fantastic fare. Visitors can hire a motorbike taxi from

pick-up points in town – an inexpensive way to get to the sanctuary – or hire a cab.

A canopy walkway in the Santuário de Vida Silvestre Fazenda Vagafogo

🏛 Fazenda Babilonia

GO 431, Km3, Pirenópolis. **Tel** (62) 9294 1805. **Open** 9am–3:30pm Sat & Sun, weekdays for groups of 10+ by appt. 🚶 🌐 **fazendababilonia.com.br**

This late 18th-century *fazenda* used to be the largest sugar-cane refinery in Goiás. Founded by Joaquim Alves de Oliveira, the *fazenda* also produced manioc flour and cotton.

Today, the well preserved farm is still a working ranch. Visitors can take guided tours of the grounds, with its colonial wooden and terracotta-tiled buildings and the chapel of Nossa Senhora da Conceição, which retains its glorious original interior. The restaurant serves local food made from the *fazenda's* own produce.

Pirenópolis

1. Igreja Nosso Senhor do Bonfim
2. Igreja Matriz de Nossa Senhora do Rosário
3. Museu das Cavalhadas
4. Teatro de Pirenópolis
5. Santuário de Vida Silvestre Fazenda Vagafogo
6. Fazenda Babilonia

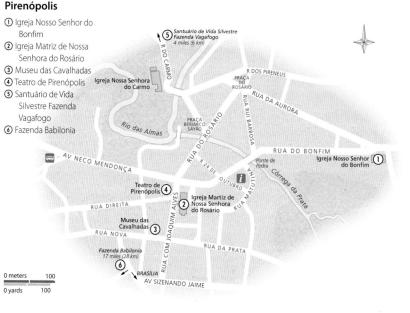

A cobbled street lined with town houses in Cidade de Goías

❸ Cidade de Goiás

Goiás. 🗻 29,000. ✈ 🚌 ℹ
Secretaría de Turismo, (62) 3201
8100. 🎭 Semana Santa (Apr),
Festival Internacional de Cinema
Ambiental (Jun). 🖥 **goiasturismo.
go.gov.br**

Like most colonial towns in Brazil's interior, Cidade de Goiás grew rich on gold. Until the middle of the 20th century, it was the capital of what was once the largest Brazilian state apart from Amazonas. Also known as Goiás Velho, or just Goiás, Cidade de Goiás is a magical little city nestled at the foot of the rugged Serra Dourado hills. Winding cobbled streets lined with 18th-century town houses lead to hills capped with churches, leafy squares and little markets. Life here seems to trot along as it has done for centuries.

While historic, Goiás is far from being lost in a bygone age. The city's busy social calendar is a testament to its successful fusion of the old with the new. There is something happening almost every weekend through the year in Goiás, from thoroughly traditional hooded parades in Semana Santa (Holy Week) to some of the best world-cinema festivals and classical music concerts in Brazil.

Many buildings and museums testify to the city's illustrious past, and Goiás is small enough to see them all leisurely on foot. The best place to begin a tour is at **Praça Brasil Caiado**, the large square which graces the town's southern end. There are a number of museums and

monuments here. These include the **Museu das Bandeiras**, the former seat of government, which preserves a forbidding dungeon and a set of rooms with period furniture, a magnificent Baroque public fountain, Chafariz de Cauda, and the Quartel do Vinte, an 18th-century barracks, which now houses the tourist office.

Immediately north of Praça Brasil Caiado and capped with an attractive, though modest, Baroque church is another square, **Praça do Coreto**. The most interesting of all the city's museums, **Museu de Arte Sacra** in the Igreja de Boa Morte, is located here, preserving a series of hauntingly lifelike religious effigies by José Joaquim da Veiga Valle (1806–74), a self-taught sculptor. Opposite this museum is the **Palácio Conde dos Arcos**, complete with 18th-century furniture and still used by the governor on city visits.

🏛 Museu de Arte Sacra
Praça do Coreto. **Tel** (62) 3371 1207.
Open 9am–5pm Tue–Sat, 9am–1pm Sun. 🈲

🏛 Museu das Bandeiras
Praça Brasil Caiado. **Tel** (62) 3371 1087.
Open 9am–5pm Tue–Sat, 9am–1pm Sun. 🈲

🏛 Palácio Conde dos Arcos
Praça Dr. Tasso de Camargo. **Tel** (62) 3371 1200. **Open** 8am–5pm Tue–Sat, 8am–noon Sun. 🈲

❹ Chapada dos Veadeiros

See pp316–17.

❺ Palmas

Tocantins. 🗻 265,000. ✈ 🚌 (63)
3228 5600. ℹ CATUR (Centro de
Atendimento ao Turista), (63) 2111
0213. 🎭 Carnaval (Feb/Mar).

Built in 1989, Brazil's newest state capital sits at the base of a range of forested low hills. It is a pleasant, but sprawling, modern city. Most visitors come to Palmas as it is a good jumping-off point for the numerous attractions that lie within the interior of Tocantins state, most notably Jalapão and the Ilha do Bananal.

Aside from the vast Palmas lake formed by the dam on the Rio Tocantins, Palmas' most interesting area is its vast, grassy main square, Praça Giróssois, which is lined by grandiose public buildings and various monuments to its founder, José Wilson Siqueira Campos, and his legacy.

The sparkling Rio Tocantins in Palmas at sunset

❻ Jalapão

Tocantins. 🚗 Korubo, (11) 9 8222
5028, 🖥 **jalapao.com**; or Bananal
Ecotour (63) 3028 4200.

A journey through Brazil's interior would be incomplete without a visit to Jalapão. Located deep within eastern Tocantins, this breathtaking area is one of South America's great wilderness destinations. Jalapão, stretching across 13,130 sq miles (34,000 sq km), is made up of a state park, three private protected areas, and an ecological station, Estação

Ecológica. The best time to visit is the dry season between June and September.

Beyond the inaccessible reaches of southern Piauí, the arid *cerrado* forests and incipient *caatinga* thornlands are more pristine here than anywhere else. Many fast-flowing rivers cut through spectacular canyons and thunder over myriad waterfalls throughout Jalapão. A number of rivers are born in limpid glassy springs that bubble forth from the sands of Jalapão. Others wind their way through groves of buriti palms called *veredas*. These are visited by Spix's macaws and Brazilian Merganser ducks, two of the extremely rare birds lost to the rest of the continent but still found in Jalapão.

Towering over Jalapão's seemingly interminable plains and striding out to the endless horizons are stands of monolithic tabletop mountains, winding yellow sand dunes, and craggy rock pinnacles. The air is so clear that even when these are far in the distance, they appear close enough to touch. Trails running across the mountain summits range from moderate to difficult, depending on the experience of the hiker.

The views from the top of the mountains and dunes are mesmerizing. But for the whistling breeze, it is so silent that the infrequent pick-ups running across the very few dirt roads can be heard clearly even when they are quite a long distance away.

Dark waters of the Rio Javaés, one of Ilha do Bananal's rivers

❼ Ilha do Bananal

Tocantins. 🗺 3,500. 📞 Bananal Ecotour Quadra 103-S, Loja 28, Palmas, (63) 3028 4200.

The Rio Araguaia runs from southern Goiás across Tocantins state to join the Rio Tocantins before draining into the Amazon. In the middle of this river sits the Ilha do Bananal, an island so vast that it has its own rivers running through it and contends with Ilha de Marajó *(see p274)* for the title of the world's largest river island. Access to the island's wild interior is not easy. Visits here are only possible with a licensed tour operator.

Three ecosystems converge on the island – rainforest, wetland, and *cerrado*. Bananal's southern extremes are mostly Terras Indígenas (indigenous territories), where tourists are not welcome. Its center and north are impenetrable without a guide. Indigenous communities, including the Javaés and the Karajás, inhabit the island, some of whom produce carved wooden animals and pottery figurines. The southern part of the island also comprises seasonally flooded forests, lakes, and swamps filled with wildlife. This is a wonderful area for bird-watching, particularly waterbirds. There are also black caimans, which grow to an immense size in the dark, fish-filled waters.

❽ Parque Nacional das Emas

Goiás. ℹ Rua do Bonfim, Centro Historico, (62) 3331 2633. 📞 Drena, Rua Aurora 21, Centro Histórico Pirenópolis, (62) 9291 3017 . 🏨 Fazenda Santa Amélia, (64) 3634 1380.

Tucked far away in the southwest corner of Goiás and surrounded by a sea of soya, Emas National Park is a 500-sq-mile (1,300-sq-km) island of grassland and sparse *cerrado*, dotted with millions of termite hills and cut by blackwater rivers. The park is considered the best preserved *cerrado* in the country. In 2001, it was designated a UNESCO World Heritage Site.

Populations of larger mammals, particularly the armadillo, maned wolf, and puma, are so healthy here that the park is a favorite location for film crews from the BBC Natural History Unit. It is also an important destination for bird-watchers, with the greatest concentration of blue-and-yellow macaws outside Amazônia.

Although there is no compulsion to go on a guided tour, it is a good idea to organize a trip through a tour operator in Pirenópolis, or through the tourist office in the nearby town of Chapadão do Céu, east of the park. Facilities at the park are minimal. Accommodation is limited to very rustic, simply appointed **Fazenda Santa Amélia** in Chapadão do Céu.

A breathtaking view of Tocantins landscape from a dune, Jalapão

❹ Parque Nacional Chapada dos Veadeiros

Named for the marsh deer that inhabit the area, this national park sits on the edge of the *cerrado*, one of the largest areas of wild country in the interior of Brazil. Most easily accessed from the small town of Alto Paraíso, the park is set in a stunning landscape. The surrounding area is just as magical; sprawling forest is broken up by rushing waterfalls and meadows, and dotted with stands of buriti palms. This remarkably isolated destination offers truly spectacular walks and pretty trails for nature lovers as well as exciting outdoor adventure activities, such as rappeling and canyoning.

Buriti palm groves, widely scattered in the Chapada

★ **Cânion Rio Preto**
The narrow gorges of the Rio Preto, which runs through the middle of the park, cut into the sandstone cliffs. The most stunning precipice has waterfalls gushing down the cliffs.

Giant Anteater
One of the larger mammals in the Chapada, the giant anteater is a common sight.

Colinas

Morro da Chapéu
3,300 ft (1,000 m)

SERRA DE SANTANA

Rio Preto

SERRA RIO PR

Rio Ron

239

Cachoeira Cariocas   Cânion I

Cachoeira do Rio Preto   Cânion II

Salto do Rio Preto

Rio São Miguel

São Jorge

VALE DA LUA

| 0 km | | 10 |
| 0 miles | | 6 |

Vale da Lua The light in this shallow canyon is particularly beautiful at sunset. The rocks have been sculpted into strange Daliesque shapes by the Rio São Miguel.

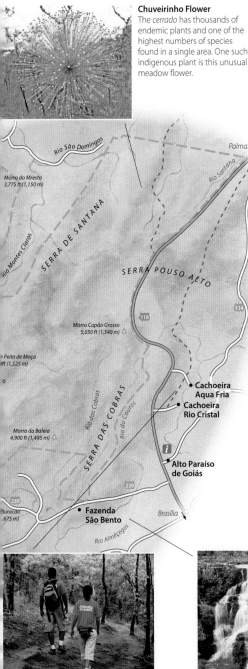

Chuveirinho Flower
The *cerrado* has thousands of endemic plants and one of the highest numbers of species found in a single area. One such indigenous plant is this unusual meadow flower.

Key

━━━ Highway
═══ Minor road
– – Trail
– • Park boundary
△ Peak

Adventure Sports
The Chapada is one of the most popular places in Brazil for outdoor adventure sports such as abseiling and canyoning.

Trekking
The Chapada is home to several forest trails, which are perfect for avid hikers and nature lovers.

★ Cachoeira Almeçegas
A picturesque many-tiered waterfall drops over 260 ft (80 m) into deep pools, which are good for swimming. Access is along a rather tortuous trail.

For keys to symbols *see back flap*

MATO GROSSO & MATO GROSSO DO SUL

Once a destination for explorers and gold hunters, today Mato Grosso and Mato Grosso do Sul attract avid nature lovers. The world's largest wetland and a vital ecosystem, the Pantanal straddles both states. Blessed with crystalline rivers and spectacular national parks, and dotted with ranches and farms, this vast region is still home to a large population of indigenous groups.

Explorations of Mato Grosso were limited to nature expeditions and Jesuit missionaries until the discovery of gold in the 18th century. The gold rush led to clashes between Europeans and indigenous groups. Many of these groups, such as the Bororo and Kayapó, still live in this state. The building of Brasília as the new capital of Brazil brought waves of migrant workers to the Central West in the mid-20th century. In 1979, the state was split into Mato Grosso and Mato Grosso do Sul, divided by the star attraction of the region, the wetlands of the Pantanal.

Very few places in the world can boast such enormous numbers of large birds as the Pantanal. While wildlife can be difficult to see in the closed forests of the Amazon, it is visible in abundance here. From July to October, storks, ibis, herons, and huge, colorful parrots swarm the Pantanal, and can even be seen while driving along dirt roads. The wetlands are home to a diverse range of wildlife, including the anaconda, the elusive jaguar, and giant otter.

Outside the Pantanal, large tracts of farmland are broken by low mountains and giant, sluggish rivers. Amazon forests cling on in places such as Alta Floresta, Chapada dos Guimarães, and Bonito despite the expansion of the soya industry. The entire region offers prime opportunities for bird-watching, angling, and snorkeling.

Capybara, the largest rodent in the world, frequently spotted in water ponds of the Pantanal

◀ Snorkelers in the Lagoa Misteriosa, Mato Grosso do Sul

Exploring Mato Grosso & Mato Grosso do Sul

Both Mato Grosso and Mato Grosso do Sul are regions of enormous plains with a handful of mountain ranges. The main attraction of this region is the Pantanal, the world's largest wetland. This harbors an important ecosystem with varied fauna such as caimans, jaguars, and a profuse variety of birds. Cuiabá, Corumbá, and Campo Grande are good springboards for ecotourists who wish to travel into or through the Pantanal. Alta Floresta, in the extreme north of Mato Grosso, is considered one of the best places for spotting rare birds and mammals. Bonito, in Mato Grosso do Sul, is an area of plunging waterfalls, caves, and crystal-clear rivers – ideal for walks through mountains and forests, and rafting and snorkeling. Flowing from central Mato Grosso, the Rio Xingú has indigenous peoples from nine distinct ethnic groups living along its banks.

Sights at a Glance

Towns & Cities

- ❶ Cuiabá
- ❻ Corumbá
- ❼ Miranda
- ❽ Campo Grande
- ❾ Bonito

National Parks & Areas of Natural Beauty

- ❷ Chapada dos Guimarães
- ❸ Xingú
- ❹ Alta Floresta
- ❺ Pantanal pp324–5

Jabiru storks, also known as *tuiuiú*, gather to feed in the Pantanal

For hotels and restaurants in this region see pp379–80 and p395

Clear water of the Rio Sucuri at Bonito

↑ *Santarém*

Peixoto de Azevedo

Xingu

Liberdade

Villa Rica

de Azevedo

S. José do Xingu

Tapirapé

nissauá Missu

XINGÚ ❸

322

Porto Alegre do Norte

Suiá Missur

Arraias

Culhene

Querência

atobá

Gaúcha do Norte

Garapu

Rio das Mortes

Manitsauá

Araguaia

Planalto do

Canarana

Mato Grosso

158

argão

Paranatinga

Areões

Cocalinho

Nova Xavantino

PADA DOS MARÃES

General Carneiro

70

Goiânia

Poxoréu

Guiratinga

Barra do Garças

donópolis

364

Correntes

163

Goiânia

ão

Pedro Gomes

n

Paraíso

Cassilândia

Camapuã

MATO

hedo

GROSSO

Inocência

Coxim

DO SUL

Aparecida do Tabuado

✈ **CAMPO** ❽ **GRANDE**

Água Clara

262

Sidrolândia

Três Lagoas

São Paulo

257

Bataguaçu

aju

Rio Brilhante

São Paulo

Dourados

Ivinheima

Paraná

Porã

Naviraí

mambaí

163

Iguatemi

0 km   100

0 miles   100

Getting Around

Distances are huge in these states and there are few paved roads. However, the capital cities – Campo Grande in Mato Grosso do Sul and Cuiabá in Mato Grosso have airports with good connections to the rest of Brazil. Alta Floresta also has an airport. Corumbá, Bonito, and Miranda in Mato Grosso do Sul are connected to Campo Grande by fast, comfortable buses. Tour operators are based in the capital cities and in Corumbá and Bonito. Most can organize bookings through their websites. Tours to the Pantanal are also organized, and usually enter the Pantanal by road and spend a couple of days exploring in canoes, motorboats, or on horseback from a land base. Rented 4WD are also a possibility, though visitors would be limited to only a few tracks along the fringes that is suitable for such vehicles.

Key

▬▬ Highway

▬▬ Major road

::::: Minor road

⌁⌁⌁ Railroad

▬▬ International border

▬▬ State border

For keys to symbols *see back flap*

The spectacular vista of the Chapada dos Guimarães plateau, Mato Grosso

❶ Cuiabá

Mato Grosso. 485,000.
 Sedtur, (65) 3613 9300.
 Festa de São Benedito (Jul).

Mato Grosso's capital and the warmest city in Brazil sits on a low, languid plain at the foot of the Chapada dos Guimarães hills. Situated on the banks of the Rio Cuiabá, a tributary of the Rio Paraguai, the city has some leafy squares and is known as the Cidade Verde or the Green City. Cuiabá is also a good starting point for excursions into the Pantanal, a vast wetland area *(see pp324–5)*.

Kadiwéu pottery, Museu Rondon

Like Cidade de Goiás *(see p314)* and Ouro Preto *(see pp130–31)*, Cuiabá was originally a flourishing gold-mining town, full of handsome buildings and fine churches. Almost all were demolished in a spate of hasty modernization in the late 1960s. The town has lost most of the splendid works of José Joaquim da Veiga Valle (1806–74), one of the country's great geniuses of the Baroque. Fortunately, some of his exquisite crafts-manship can still be seen in the well-preserved, vast, rectangular interiors of the modern concrete Catedral do Bom Jesus, which has an unusual square, Moorish façade.

The most interesting of the city's sights is the small university-run **Museu do Índio Marechal Rondon**, in which some exquisite and priceless pieces of indigenous art are kept. These include exhibits of the Xavante, Bororo, and Karajá peoples. The museum houses some beautiful Bororo and Rikbaktsa headdresses and superb pieces of Kadiwéu ceramics from Mato Grosso do Sul.

🏛 **Museu do Índio Marechal Rondon**
Av Fernando Correia da Costa.
Tel (65) 3615 8489. **Open** 8–11:30am, 1:30–5:30pm Tue–Fri; 1–5pm Sat, Sun & hols.

❷ Chapada dos Guimarães

Mato Grosso. 13,500. from Cuiabá. Eco Turismo, Av Cipriano Curvo 655, Centro, (65) 3301 1393.
 Festival de Inverno (Jul–Aug).
 chapadadosguimaraes.com.br

The town of Chapada dos Guimarães is set on a plateau of the same name. Said to be up to 500 million years old, the majestic honey-colored tablelands and escarpments of the plateau are among the oldest rock formations in the world. As the continent's

geodesic center, the tablelands of the Chapada dos Guimarães are reputedly imbued with energizing powers strong enough to reduce the speed of a car and said to be attractive to UFOs. While the residents of the Chapada claim that this effect has been documented, skeptics believe otherwise.

The little town has numerous shops and cafés, and a daily fair selling local arts and crafts. There are also several spiritual centers devoted to the New Age movement, which is growing in Brazil. Nature lovers come here to admire the scenery. The edge of the Chapada offers sweeping vistas out over the patchy, remnant

Véu de Noiva, the highest waterfall in Chapada dos Guimarães

cerrado forests of the Mato Grosso plains. There are several waterfalls in the area, the most famous and tallest of which is the **Véu de Noiva**, or the Bridal Veil Falls.

Although the Chapada has seen far more aggressive agricultural development than its counterparts in Goiás and Tocantins, many upland bird species that are not found either in the Pantanal or the Amazonian forests can be seen here. The high *cerrado* forests, savannas, and pasturelands of the Chapada hold a special attraction for bird-watchers, who come here in droves to catalog the variety of birds, and perhaps to catch a lucky glimpse of mammals, such as maned wolves, ocelots, and black-tailed marmosets.

Red-capped cardinal, Alta Floresta

❸ Xingú

Mato Grosso. 🚌 ℹ️ Fundação Nacional do Índio (Funai), Rua 8, Qd. 15, (65) 3644 1839, Cuiabá. 🌐 **funai.gov.br**

By the end of the 19th century all of the great Amazon tributaries had been explored and colonized, and their indigenous peoples enslaved or completely wiped out. The remote region of Xingú, in the extreme northeast of Mato Grosso, was the only indigenous settlement to survive the onslaught and be established as a preserve.

Home to one of the largest areas of tribal lands in the country, it sits as a huge island of forest in a vast ocean of soya plantations. These tracts of land are concentrated around the beautiful clear-water Rio Xingú. Known to be sophisticated, the indigenous peoples flourishing in the Xingú specialize in furniture-making and basket-weaving, among other things.

Tourism is extremely limited here and visits to indigenous villages can only be undertaken with prior permission from Fundação Nacional do Índio (Funai).

❹ Alta Floresta

Mato Grosso. 🏘️ 43,000.
✈️ to Cuiabá, then bus.
ℹ️ Anaconda Pantanal Operators, (65) 3028 5990. 🛏️ Cristalino Jungle Lodge, (66) 3512 7100.
🌐 **cristalinolodge.com.br**

Situated in the extreme north of Mato Grosso, Alta Floresta sits on the edge of the pristine southern Amazon rainforest, and is a rapidly growing frontier town. This remote town is also a thriving agricultural settlement. Its surrounding areas are considered some of the best in the Brazilian Amazon for spotting rare birds and mammals. One of the highlights of Alta Floresta is the four-star hotel, Floresta Amazônica, which serves as a base for the **Cristalino Jungle Lodge** *(see p379).*

The Cristalino Jungle Lodge sits in the Cristalino Forest Reserve deep in the forest, north of Alta Floresta. The lodge is situated on the banks of the Rio Cristalino, which is the blackwater tributary of the Rio Tapajós, whose blue waters flow into the Amazon at Santarém *(see p278).* The lodge is most famous for the profuse birdlife surrounding it, as well as an enormous variety of butterflies and other insects, reptiles, and mammals. All the

A view out over the forests of the Rio Cristalino preserve

large Neotropical rainforest mammals, including the endangered white-nosed bearded saki monkey, brown titi monkey, giant river otter, and three-toed sloth, as well as jaguar, puma, and tapir are present and can often be spotted here. Facilities for jungle walks and viewing wildlife are excellent and include English-speaking, specialist guides, two 164-ft- (50-m-) high canopy towers, and a very good library of decent field guides.

Other more challenging outdoor adventure activities, such as camping in the forest, trekking, survival techniques, rappeling, canyoning, and canoeing, can also be arranged through the Cristalino Jungle Lodge.

Cristalino Jungle Lodge, in the Rio Cristalino Forest Reserve, Alta Floresta

❺ Pantanal

The world's largest wetland, the Pantanal provides a habitat for the greatest concentration of animals in the Western Hemisphere. Innumerable waterbirds gather toward the end of the dry season. There are plenty of reptiles and large mammals, including caimans, tapirs, giant anteaters, and all of Brazil's eight feline species. The secret to the vast numbers of animals lies in the diversity of vegetation and the geography of the Pantanal, a gently sloping bowl which floods when nutrient-rich tributaries drain from the ancient sedimentary rocks of the Brazilian Shield and get trapped. Aquatic plants breed profusely and these provide ample food for fish and birds, who, in turn, feed the rest of the food chain.

Green Kingfisher
The green kingfisher is one of five types of kingfisher to inhabit the Pantanal. It is seen on the banks of small, undisturbed rivers and makes its nest in a tunnel.

Anhinga
The anhinga is a relative of the cormorant and is a common sight in the Pantanal. As it has no wax in its feathers, it must dry its wings in the sun after diving for fish.

0 km   50
0 miles   50

Brahmin Cattle
The most common animals in the Pantanal are Brahmin cattle who are herded by local cowboys, or *pantaneiros*.

KEY

① **The Estrada Parque** dirt road cuts through the southern Pantanal and leads to the wildlife-rich region of Nhecolândia. Like the Transpantaneira, it is lined with *fazendas* (farms).

② **The Parque Nacional do Pantanal Matogrossense** formally protects a small percentage of the Pantanal UNESCO World Heritage Site.

Key

▬ Major road
═ Minor road
— Railroad
– – International border

Map labels: Barra do Bugres, Santa Bárbara, Barbado, Sepotuba, Paraguai, Porto Esperidião, Jauru, Cáceres, Aguapeí, San Matías, Bento Go, Corixa Grande, Paraguai, PN do Pantanal Matogrossense, Amo, Palag, Corumbá, Urucu, Piraputangas, Puga, Carandaz, Bod, São Simão, Porto Murtinho, San Lázaro

For hotels and restaurants in this region see pp379–80 and p395

★ Estrada Transpantaneira
The dirt road of Estrada Transpantaneira is lined with *fazendas*, many of which have accommodation for tourists. Wildlife viewing is excellent and the road is navigable in a normal car.

VISITORS' CHECKLIST

Practical Information
Mato Grosso & Mato Grosso do Sul. 🛈 Av Afonso Pena 4909, Campo Grande.
Tel (67) 3314 3142.
🔲 organized tours available in Campo Grande & Cuiabá. The dry season (Apr–May & Sep–Oct) is the best time to visit. Bird-watching ideal in Jul–Sep. Fishing best in Apr, but requires a permit from Ibama, (67) 3317 2966.

Transport
✈ Campo Grande & Corumbá.
✈ Caceres & Cuiabá.

★ Fazendas
Originally built as cattle ranches, many *fazendas* have been converted into ranch-style hotels. The *fazendas* are connected by excellent bird-watching walkways throughout the Pantanal.

Igapó Forest
Among the most diverse of the Pantanal's eco-systems, the *igapó* is a seasonally flooded forest on blackwater rivers. It is a wonderful place for wildlife-viewing by canoe.

River Excursions
Fazendas near Miranda (*see p326*) offer boat trips on the various Pantanal rivers. Binoculars are essential for bird and caiman spotting.

For keys to symbols *see back flap*

Boats moored on the Rio Paraguai, Corumbá

❻ Corumbá

Mato Grosso do Sul. ![] 95,000.
✈ 🚌 🚐 🚢 along Rio Paraguai.
ℹ Secretaría de Turismo, (67) 3231
2886. 🎭 Festa de Nossa Senhora de
Candelária (Jan–Feb).

Corumbá , on the banks of the
Rio Paraguai, is a small town
surrounded by the Pantanal
region's unspoilt beauty. Boat
rides along the river as well
as wetland excursions form
Corumbá's major attractions.
Sportfishing, one of the main
highlights, is provided at the
nature lodges, floating hotels,
and charming *fazendas* in
this area.

Corumbá was first explored
by Portuguese and Spanish
adventurers in search of gold. By
the 18th century, the growing
strategic importance of the Rio
Paraguai led to the construction
of forts. The **Forte Junqueira**,
built during the Paraguayan War
(see p57), is the only fort still
standing intact.

Another place worth a visit is
the **Casa do Artesão**, a former
prison housing an interesting
museum of indigenous and
local *objets d'art*. The **Museu do
Pantanal** also has a small
collection of indigenous art.

🏛 **Casa do Artesão**
Rua Dom Aquino 205. **Open** 8–11am
& 2–5pm Mon–Fr, 8–11am Sat.

🏯 **Forte Junqueira**
Rua Cáceres 425. **Tel** (67) 3231 5828.
Open 8am–5pm daily.

🏛 **Museu do Pantanal**
Rua Manoel Cavassa, 275. **Tel** (67)
3231 0303. **Open** 1–6pm Tue–Sat.

❼ Miranda

Mato Grosso do Sul. ![] 23,000.
🚌 🚐 ℹ Setur, (67) 3242 3051.
🎭 Festa do Homem Pantaneiro (Nov).

The tiny town of Miranda, in the
heart of the Pantanal, hosts the
region's liveliest festival, the
Festa do Homem Pantaneiro.
This grand celebration of the
ranching and cowboy way of
life features lasso contests (in
the mornings for women, at
night for men), and rodeos. Live
sertanejo bands and dancing
carry on all night.

Miranda is an ideal base for
visiting the southern Pantanal's
various *fazenda* ranches *(see
pp379–80)*, many of which lie
on the outskirts of town. The
Fazenda San Francisco is one
of the best locations in inland
Brazil for big cats, especially
ocelot and jaguar. The **Fazenda
Baía Grande** preserves a diverse
range of Pantanal habitats,
including a large caiman-filled
lake and extensive forest. The

Fazenda Meia Lua lies just on
the edge of town and is an
ideal soft adventure option.

Environs
Known for their distinctive
painted terra-cotta ceramics,
the Terena indigenous villages
surround Miranda. Tour operators in Miranda can arrange
trips to a Terena village, as well
as to the **Rio Salobrinho**, a
beautiful clear-water river lined
with gallery forest. Expect to
find rare bird species, including
kingfishers and black-crowned
night herons.

❽ Campo Grande

Mato Grosso do Sul. ![] 665,000. ✈
✈ 🚌 🚐 ℹ Centro Informação
Turistica e Cultural, (67) 3314 3142.

Mato Grosso do Sul's capital,
Campo Grande is also known as
Cidade Morena because of its
red earth. It is a prosperous,
modern city devoted far more
to agro-business than tourism.
Yet most visitors to the southern
Pantanal arrive here because
the tourist infrastructure is
excellent. Commerce,
education, and tourism are
fast-growing industries here.
The city itself has few major
attractions, though there are
many good restaurants, hotels,
and bars, particularly along and
around Rua Barão do Rio
Branco. For those who do not
want to rough it out with a
Pantanal camping tour, travel
agencies sell packages to
comfortable farm hotels.

Rodeo at the Festa de Homem Pantaneiro

Rio Sucuri flowing near Bonito, reflecting the lush greenery around

❾ Bonito

Mato Grosso do Sul. 🏠 17,000. 🚌
🛈 Comtur. 🚗 Taika Tour, R. Coronel
Pilad Rebuá 2111, (67) 3255 1354;
Ygarapé Tours, Pilad Rebuá 1853, (67)
3255 1733.

A one-street town, Bonito is
lined with *pousadas*,
restaurants, shops, and
tour operators whose
lifeline is tourism. It lies
just beyond the
Pantanal's southern
extremities, in the Serra
do Bodoquena, a low,
cerrado-covered range
of rugged hills busy
with primates and birds,
including the black-collared
hawk. There are numerous sights
around Bonito, all protected by
regulations. Only Bonito-based
tour agencies can organize trips
and arrange permits.

Black-collared hawk

🌿 Aquário Natural Baía Bonita

4 miles (7 km) SE of Bonito. **Tel** (67)
3255 1193. **Open** 7:30am–3:30pm
daily. 🚫 🌐 **aquarionatural.com.br**

One of the natural springs in
the area, the Baía Bonita features
a pristine aquarium, which
contains 30 different varieties of
fish. Facilities within the complex
include a warm swimming pool
and relaxation cabin. Snorkeling
trips to the Rio Sucuri and Rio
da Prata are offered by tour
companies. Wetsuits and
snorkels are also provided.

🌿 Rio Sucuri

12 miles (20 km) SW of Bonito.

This glassy river is broken by
waterfalls and large pools filled
with 3-ft- (1-m-) long *piraputanga*
(ray-finned fish, typical of the
Rio Paraguai basin) and silver
dourado fish. Many pools are set
in woodland cut with
wildlife trails. The gentle
flow of the Rio Sucuri
and the excellent
facilities draws a plethora
of snorkelers and rafters,
from morning to
afternoon, mainly in
the high season.
Particularly popular are
the flotation points
where visitors begin a pleasant
1-mile (1.6-km) float downstream.
Tour agencies provide meals
and equipment.

🌿 Gruta do Lago Azul

12 miles (20 km) W of Bonito.
Open 7am–2pm daily. 🚫

The Serra do Bodoquena is
dotted with caves, the most
spectacular of which is the
Gruta do Lago Azul. The main
highlight is a radiant underground lake that shines as
blue as a sapphire in the
morning light. From the
cave's spectacular mouth, a
narrow path leads deep down
through striking stalactite
formations. At the bottom lies
the lake, illuminated by ambient
light that streams through the
cave's opening.

🌿 Estância Mimosa

15 miles (24 km) NW of Bonito.
Tel (67) 8403 5213. **Open** 8am–3pm
daily. 🚫 🌐 **www.estanciamimosa.
com.br**

Some of the best hiking
opportunities are offered in the
Estância Mimosa trail, which
features rivers, natural pools,
and as many as eight waterfalls.
There are various bathing spots
located in and around these
natural features. The trail goes
past the gorgeous riverside
forest of the Rio Mimoso, with
caves and a rich array of wildlife.
The fauna includes a variety of
birds and mammals, while
various kinds of fern, orchid,
and bromeliad are part of the
lush vegetation found in this
area. An optional horseback
excursion is also available.

Lake and stalactites at the Abismo
Anhumas cavern

🌿 Abismo Anhumas

16 miles (25 km) W of Bonito.
Open 7:30am–noon daily. 🚫
Training Center, Bonito: **Tel** (67) 3255-
3313. 🌐 **abismoanhumas.com.br**

A pothole that descends a
vertical 240-ft (73-m) deep, the
Abismo Anhumas is a cavern
filled with a large, clear, blue
lake featuring vast stalagmites,
stalactites, and many other cave
deposits. The entrance to the
cave is by rappel. Once visitors
have descended to the lake,
they can float in it, snorkel, and
take a boat tour. A maximum of
20 people are permitted in the
cave on any given day. Book with
the Training Center in advance
as preparation is required.

SOUTHERN BRAZIL

Introducing Southern
  Brazil   330–335

Santa Catarina & Paraná   336–351

Rio Grande do Sul   352–363

Introducing Southern Brazil

The states of Paraná, Santa Catarina, and Rio Grande do Sul form Southern Brazil – the only Brazilian region that lies entirely outside the tropics. Often dismissed as somehow not being truly Brazilian, this region is distinctive due to more than its temperate climate. Although there are vital indigenous, African, and Portuguese elements to the population, the region is largely associated with descendants of European immigrants. The landscape features tremendous contrasts – the pampas grasslands, mountains, and the highland plateau. The distinctive cultures that have emerged there, as along the equally varied coast, are a reflection of Brazil's diversity.

BRAZIL

SOUTHERN BRAZIL

Foz do Iguaçu *(see pp344–7)* is one of South America's most impressive natural features. These spectacular waterfalls are shared by Brazil and Argentina, with each side offering unique perspectives. From Brazil, visitors enjoy a complete panorama, while the trails in Argentina allow visitors to see the falls close-up.

Cascavel

Foz do Iguaçu

Chapecó

Ijuí

0 km 150
0 miles 150

Santa Maria

Uruguaiana

Rosário
do Sul

RIO GRAN
DO SUL
(See pp352–

Bagé

São Miguel das Missões *(see p363)* is Rio Grande do Sul's best-preserved Jesuit ruin. This haunting place offers ample evidence of the sophistication of native Guaraní Baroque architecture that emerged in this remote region in the mid-17th century.

◀ Foz do Iguaçu (Iguaçu Falls), Paraná

Curitiba *(see p340)*, the capital of Paraná, is a pretty, well-planned town. Built during the city's cattle and coffee boom, today Curitiba has well-preserved historic buildings, less pollution and traffic than other Brazilian cities, plenty of green spaces, a great music scene, and several interesting sights.

drina

ringá

Ponta Grossa

Curitiba

Paranaguá

TA CATARINA
& PARANÁ
(see pp336–51)

Joinville

Itajaí

Lajes

Florianópolis

Caxias do Sul

Novo Hamburgo

to
e

Grande

Florianópolis *(see pp350–51)*, the vibrant capital city of Santa Catarina on Ilha de Santa Catarina, is surrounded by quiet fishing communities and excellent beaches. The sheltered north shore has the most developed beaches, while the east coast lures surfers attracted by giant Atlantic rollers.

Porto Alegre *(see pp356–7)*, the capital of Rio Grande do Sul, has a host of Neo-Classical buildings dating from the 19th and early 20th centuries. The Palácio Municipal is one such expression of civic pride, built in 1898, when Porto Alegre was developing into a significant city.

Multicultural Southern Brazil

More than anywhere else in the country, Southern Brazil has been shaped culturally and economically by immigrants. Unlike tropical Brazil to the north, this part was considered unsuitable for plantation agriculture, and instead immigrants were recruited for land colonization schemes. The legacy of its physical isolation from "mainstream" Brazilian society is reflected in the languages and cultures of the immigrants. The architectural heritage is highly valued, festivals showcase traditional music and dance, while handicrafts and local products are sold in villages and on farms.

An illustration of European immigrants aboard a ship bound for Brazil

Azoreans

In the 18th century, Azoreans settled along the coast of Southern Brazil, bringing with them fishing, farming, and lace-making skills. Villages were created, in particular on the island of Santa Catarina, whose white-and-blue buildings resemble those of the Portuguese mid-Atlantic islands.

Azorean lace-making is one of the important traditions that have been maintained by women in villages on the island of Santa Catarina.

Fishing, the main economic activity of the Azorean community in Santa Catarina

Germans

Germans were the first non-Portuguese immigrants to settle in Southern Brazil, in the 1850s. They were drawn to the highlands of Rio Grande do Sul and the river valleys of north-eastern Santa Catarina. Their dialects and traditions continue in many rural areas, while German architectural styles are apparent in cities such as Blumenau and Nova Hamburgo.

Old-world architecture still dominates in the areas of Southern Brazil settled by German immigrants. Many buildings are exact replicas of ones found in towns in southern Germany. In the countryside, distinctive half-timbered farmhouses, built by pioneer immigrants, remain a common sight.

German-Brazilian celebration of Oktoberfest

Italians

The first Italian immigrants settled in Rio Grande do Sul in 1875, with tens of thousands arriving there, and in Santa Catarina and Paraná, over the next 50 years. The vast majority came from the northern Italian provinces of Veneto and Trento, introducing rich culinary traditions and the ability to cultivate lucrative grape vines on the steepest of hillsides.

Vineyards in the Serra Gaúcha *(see p359)* have become as much a part of the landscape as they are in Italy. These endless stretches of lush greenery form the center stage for the region's wine production, known both in and outside Brazil.

Slavs

Paraná is the state most closely associated with Slavic immigrants from Central and Eastern Europe, with Poles settling in and around Curitiba from 1869, Ukrainians in the south-center of the state from 1895, and Russians around Ponta Grossa in the early 1960s. The Ukrainians have been especially successful in maintaining their ethnic identity.

São Josafat, a typical Byzantine-style church in Prudentópolis, is easily recognizable by its onion dome features. The Ukrainian Catholic church is pivotal in maintaining Ukrainian identity in Brazil.

A log cabin, housed in the Museu da Imigração Polonesa in Curitiba, is one of the structures that were built by Polish immigrants in the 19th and 20th centuries.

Other Communities

At the beginning of the 20th century, Jews from Eastern Europe founded agricultural communities in Rio Grande do Sul. They later moved to Porto Alegre, establishing Brazil's third-largest Jewish community. In the 1920s and 1930s, many Japanese immigrants relocated to Paraná from São Paulo, setting up coffee and soya farms. Immigrants from other ethnic backgrounds were too few to leave legacies. Some exceptions are the Austrians who settled in central Santa Catarina in the 1930s, and the Dutch who came to Paraná after World War II.

Praça Ministro Andreas Thaler, in Treze Tílias, is named for the then Austrian Minister of Agriculture, who founded the city in 1933 for Austrian immigrants.

Castrolanda, a Dutch settlement thriving on dairy and agricultural products, mainly soya, continues to celebrate its past in the traditional folk dances of the Netherlands.

The Gaúcho Life

The *gaúcho* culture developed in colonial times in what is now northeastern Argentina, Uruguay, and Southern Brazil. In Rio Grande do Sul, the natives of the state – whether urban or rural, and regardless of their ethnic origin – are called *gaúchos*. Traditionally, *gaúchos* were semi-nomadic people who lived by hunting wild cattle. With the introduction of fencing and border agreements, they were reduced to being ranch hands. Nonetheless, their legacy continues to be strongly visible in the distinct *gaúcho* culture of today. In the interior of the state, in the grasslands of both the pampas and *serra*, the heirs of the traditional *gaúcho* employ their skills as tough horsemen on cattle *estancias* (ranches).

Old *estancia* Sobrado, a traditional ranch, Rio Grande do Sul

Clothing

Traditional gaúcho *attire remains commonplace among the rural population of the pampas and highlands of Southern Brazil. On special occasions, city dwellers also don* gaúcho *clothing, an outward sign of the distinctiveness of Rio Grande do Sul society.*

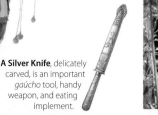

Gaúcho Dress is worn with immense pride. "Gaúcho pants" (*bombachas*), a linen shirt, kerchief, poncho, rimmed felt-hat, and pleated boots with fancy spurs are essential components of traditional *gaúcho* clothing.

A Silver Knife, delicately carved, is an important *gaúcho* tool, handy weapon, and eating implement.

Parade celebrating *gaúcho* culture in Argentina

Centro de Tradições Gaúchas

The worldwide Brazilian-*gaúcho* organization, Centro de Tradições Gaúchas, (Center for Gaúcho Traditions) was founded by eight Porto Alegre students in 1948, to preserve and promote *gaúcho* traditions. Today, it has more than 4,500 affiliate clubs that stage rodeos, *gaúcho* dances, parades, barbecues, and other social events. A *centro* can now be found wherever *gaúchos* live, both within Rio Grande do Sul and as far afield as Bolivia, Japan, and Portugal. The *centros* are perhaps the most convenient way for an outsider to observe *gaúcho* traditions, which are emerging as a part of popular culture even in non-*gaúcho* areas. Local tourist offices and hotels will be able to provide information on upcoming events.

Way of Life

The *gaúcho* way of life was originally a nomadic one, with the horsemen wandering the pampas, hunting wild cattle for their hides. Working as cattle hands today, *gaúchos* still cling to many of the traditions.

Rodeos, often lasting several days, test the skills of cattlemen, serve as social events for local townsfolk, and help break the isolation of rural inhabitants.

Cattle drives by *gaúchos* on horseback are common sights en route to Rio Grande do Sul's extensive grassland regions.

Dance & Music

Dance performances are integral to social gatherings. The music originates from a mixing of Portuguese, Spanish, Basque, African, German, and Italian cultures, with lyrics typically about local tales. Polkas and marches form the basis of traditional gaúcho dance.

A colorful kerchief is part of a *gaúcho's* typical dress.

Bombachas, or loose-fitting trousers belted with a *tirador* (sash), are traditionally worn by the *gaúchos*.

Accordion music first came to Southern Brazil with Portuguese colonists, but was transformed by exposure to other influences. The accordion and acoustic guitar are the most common folk instruments.

Food & Drink

Meat, especially beef, is central to the traditional gaúcho *diet. While the* gaúcho *grill is legendary, rice, usually cooked with* charque *(jerked beef), is also a staple. Pumpkin and other varieties of squash are often incorporated into stews.*

Chimarrão, a sugarless *chá mate* tea, is the characteristic and most popular drink of Rio Grande do Sul. The caffeinated herbal tea is sipped through a *bomba* (a silver straw) from a *cuia* (gourd). The same *cuia* is generally used by a group of *chimarrão* drinkers.

Churrasco, barbecued beef popular throughout Brazil, is cooked on metal or wood skewers rested on a support or stuck into the ground, and roasted over a charcoal or firewood flame.

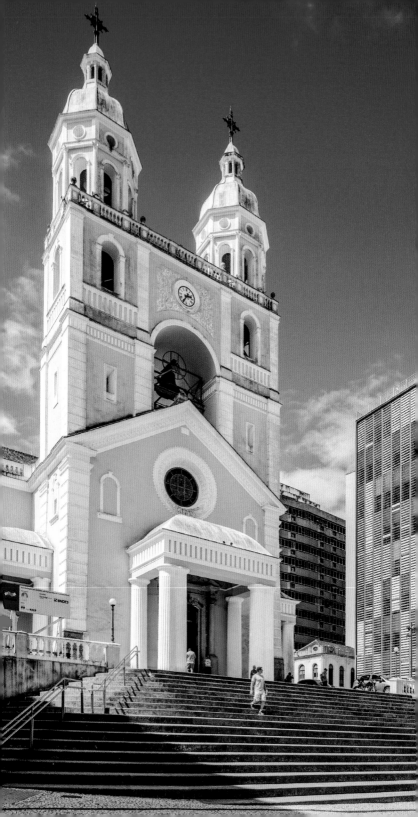

SANTA CATARINA & PARANÁ

Brazil's southern states are a delight for nature lovers, with Paraná's spectacular Iguaçu Falls surrounded by lush rainforest and lovely beaches fringing the coast of tiny Santa Catarina. The region's long history of immigration from Europe has created a unique, multi-layered cultural identity.

During the 17th and 18th centuries, military garrisons were established all along the coast of Southern Brazil to guard against possible Spanish encroachment, and immigrants from the Portuguese mid-Atlantic islands of the Azores were brought in to establish farming and fishing settlements. Over time, these settlements grew into important towns, and Curitiba – on the trade route between Rio Grande do Sul and Minas Gerais – transformed into one of Brazil's most dynamic cities.

From 1840 to the mid-1900s, the interiors of Paraná and Santa Catarina were opened to immigration, with waves of European and other settlers staking out small farms. The newcomers settled along ethnic lines, with the Polish concentrated around Curitiba, Ukrainians in southern Paraná, Germans in Santa Catarina's Itajaí Valley, and Italians in the southern part of the state. The physical and cultural isolation of ethnic groups has resulted in distinct identities being maintained in rural areas to this day. The towns of Paranaguá, Antonina, and Morretes in Paraná, and Laguna, Florianópolis, and São Francisco do Sul in Santa Catarina also retain visible characteristics of their European origins.

The main destinations for visitors to Paraná are the Iguaçu Falls and the surrounding rainforest. The state's coast has escaped the excesses of development despite the natural beauty of Ilha do Mel, Guaraqueçaba, and Superaguï Island. Visitors to Santa Catarina make straight for the beaches of Florianópolis. The mountainous interior around São Joaquim and Lages is worth visiting for its spectacular scenery.

Turquoise waves hitting Florianópolis beach, Santa Catarina

◄ Catedral Metropolitana de Florianópolis, on the Ilha de Santa Catarina

Exploring Santa Catarina & Paraná

Although the uncontested highlights of this region are Paraná's magnificent Iguaçu Falls and Santa Catarina's island resort of Florianópolis, these two states have much more to offer. Santa Catarina's 310-mile (500-km) coast features sheltered coves and long expanses of beach, where it is possible to observe right whales reproducing from July to September. In Paraná, the Atlantic forest preserves of the Parque Nacional Ilha de Superagüi encompass dense virgin forest. Ilha do Mel, at the mouth of Paranaguá Bay, is a popular beach resort, and just across the bay on the mainland is the scenic port of Paranaguá. Inland, both states have a robust agricultural industry. Vast soya farms dominate large parts of Paraná, while small family holdings are characteristic of Santa Catarina. Descendants of European immigrants continue their traditions in these states, such as the Austrians in Treze Tílias.

Sights at a Glance

Towns & Cities

❶ Curitiba
❸ Paranaguá
❼ Florianópolis & Ilha de Santa Catarina pp350–51

National Parks, Islands & Areas of Natural Beauty

❷ Serra da Graciosa p341
❹ Ilha do Mel
❺ Ilha de Superagüi
❻ Foz do Iguaçu pp344–7

Façade of the Mercado Público in Florianópolis, Santa Catarina

Low-lying islands covered with thick vegetation, Paraná

Bandeirantes

Represa
Capivara

Cornélio
Procópio

Jacarezinho

aponga
carana

Represa de
Xavantes

Marlândia
do Sul

Ibaiti

Venceslau
Bráz

jueira

Telêmaco
Borba

Ventania

Jaguariaíva

Reserva

Piraí do Sul

Ribeira

São Paulo

P A R A N Á

Iváí

Castro

Cerro Azul

116

Ponta Grossa

373

Palmeira

SERRA DA
GRACIOSA

ILHA DE
SUPERAGÜI

Irati

277

CURITIBA

①

②

④ ⑤

③

ILHA DO MEL

puava

Lapa

Iguaçu

PARANAGUÁ

São Mateus
do Sul

116

Guaratuba

Baía de
Guaratuba

Mallét

476

Rio
Negro

101

São Francisco
do Sul

da
ia

Porto União

Canoinhas

Joinville

Caçador

Itaiópolis

Jaraguá
do Sul

Bara Velha

C A T A R I N A

Serra do Mar

Blumenau

Itajaí

Curitibanos

Rio
do Sul

Brusque

470

Porto Belo

mpos
vos

Ituporanga

Tijucas

Baía de Tijucas

Lajes

Serra Geral

São José

⑦ FLORIANÓPOLIS &
ILHA DE SANTA CATARINA

Bocaíno
do Sul

Palhoça

101

438

São
Joaquim

Imbituba

Lagoa do
Mirim

Orleaes

Laguna

Criciúma

Tubarão

Araranguá

Lagoa do
Sombrio

Porto
Alegre

Torres

Key

━━━ Highway

━━━ Major road

- - - Minor road

∼∼∼ Railroad

▥▥▥ International border

━━━ State border

0 km   50

0 miles   50

Getting Around

Both Paraná and Santa Catarina have excellent
transportation facilities. Curitiba and Florianópolis have
international airports. Foz do Iguaçu's international
airport also serves many regional destinations. The road
network is good, with only a few towns connected with
gravel or dirt roads. The main north–south highway (BR-
101) that hugs the coast of Santa Catarina is well
maintained but is often extremely congested in the
summer. Bus travel is excellent between the region's
main centers as well as the smaller towns. There is only
one passenger railroad network – the spectacular
68-mile (110-km) route linking Curitiba with Paranaguá.

For keys to symbols *see back flap*

The main greenhouse in Jardim Botânico, Curitiba

❶ Curitiba

Paraná. 🚲 1,750,000. ✈
🚉 from Morretes. 🛈 Rua da
Glória 362, (41) 3350 6456.
🌐 turismo.curitiba.pr.gov.br

Founded in 1693 as a gold-mining encampment, Curitiba developed to become the largest city in Southern Brazil. It emerged from being a minor administrative, commercial, and agro-processing center to grow into one of Brazil's most dynamic cities. Since the early 1990s, Curitiba has rivalled São Paulo as a location for corporate investment, in large measure attracted by the city's quality of life, accessibility, and public services, which are an example to the rest of the country.

The Largo da Ordem marks the heart of Curitiba's oldest quarter and features many well-preserved historic buildings. Dating from 1737, the Igreja da Ordem is the city's oldest church and the finest example of Portuguese ecclesiastical architecture in the state. The plain, whitewashed structure is decorated inside with typically Portuguese blue-and-white tiles and Baroque altars. Alongside the church is the **Museu de Arte Sacra** with its small but well-presented collection of relics gathered from churches in Curitiba. On the same side of the square is the **Igreja do Rosário**, originally serving Curitiba's slave population. First built in 1737, the church was completely reconstructed in the 1930s but retains its original Portuguese colonial style.

Across the square is the early 18th-century Casa Romário Martins, Curitiba's oldest surviving house and now a cultural center featuring exhibitions on the history of the city.

Up the hill from here, virtually adjoining the Largo da Ordem, are Garibaldi and João Cândido squares. The squares are surrounded by brightly painted late 19th- and early 20th-century houses, now used as art galleries, antiques shops, and restaurants. The grandest building, however, is the Palácio São Francisco, built in 1929 and later serving as the state governor's official residence. Renovated and extended, the building now houses the **Museu Paranaense**,

Façade of Igreja do Rosário on Largo do Ordem

its displays concentrating on Paraná's archaeology, anthropology, and history.

The city's commercial center extends along Rua XV de Novembro. Rua das Flores is the pedestrianized section lined with early 20th-century pastel-colored shops. The distinctive Art Nouveau former city hall at Praça Generoso Marques, in front of the flower market, is now a cultural center. The most visited sight in this area is **Jardim Botânico**, a French-style botanic garden with greenhouses, fountains, waterfalls, and lakes.

To celebrate the contributions of European immigrants to the city, parks have been built in their honor. The best example is the **Bosque Papa João Paulo II Memorial Polonês**, where log cabins built by Polish immigrants in the 1880s have been re-erected. The buildings, including a farmhouse, chapel, and barns, are set amid a small araucaria preserve, pine trees that originally dominated the landscape. Bordering the Bosque Papa João Paulo II and representing modern Curitiba is the **Museu Oscar Niemeyer**. Popularly referred to as "The Eye" after the construction's central feature, the building is considered one of Oscar Niemeyer's greatest architectural achievements.

Detail outside Museu Paranaense

🏛 **Bosque Papa João Paulo II Memorial Polonês**
Av Mateus Leme/ Rua Euclides Bandeira 1200 (Portal Polonês). **Tel** (41) 3350 9891. **Open** 24 hours daily. Memorial: 9am–6pm Tue–Sun. 🚻

🌿 **Jardim Botânico**
Rua Eng. Ostoja Roguski. **Tel** (41) 3264 6994. **Open** 6am–8pm daily.

🏛 **Museu de Arte Sacra**
Largo da Ordem s/n. **Tel** (41) 3321 3265. **Open** 9am–noon, 1–6pm Tue–Fri, 1–6pm Sat, 9am–3pm Sun. 🚻 📧

🏛 **Museu Oscar Niemeyer**
Rua Marechal Hermes 999 (Centro Cívico). **Tel** (41) 3350 4400. **Open** 10am–6pm Tue–Sun. 🚻 🚻

🏛 **Museu Paranaense**
Rua Kellers 289. **Tel** (41) 3304 3300. **Open** 9am–6pm Tue–Fri, 10am–4pm Sat & Sun. 🚻

For hotels and restaurants in this region see pp380–81 and pp396–7

❷ Serra da Graciosa

The mountain range that separates Paraná state's coast from its interior is known as the Serra do Mar. Its southern extension, Serra da Graciosa, is one of the largest remaining areas of Mata Atlântica (Atlantic forest) in Southern Brazil. The Serra is rich in flora and fauna, ranging from lowland subtropical to cloud forest varieties. The road and railroad linking Morretes and Curitiba are amazing feats of 19th-century engineering, zigzagging through some of the most spectacular terrain in the country. The area is often shrouded with mist or fog, the result of cool air from the highlands colliding with the warm air of the subtropical coast. The forest thrives on such precipitation.

VISITORS' CHECKLIST

Practical Information
Paraná. 🛈 Casa Rocha Pombo:
Largo José Pereira S. Andrade, s/n,
(41) 3414 1104. 📧 in Morretes.
Parque Estadual Pico do Marumbi:
Tel (41) 3462 3598. **Open** 24 hours
daily. Litorina: **Tel** (41) 3888 3488;
advance booking required.
🆆 serraverdeexpress.com.br

Transport
🚉 Litorina 🚌 Viação Graciosa.

Parque Estadual Pico do Morumbi
Usually shrouded with mist, trails with stunning vistas crisscross this vast expanse of Mata Atlântica.

The Estrada Graciosa
Completed in 1873, the Estrada Graciosa winds its way through the forbidding terrain of the Serra do Mar.

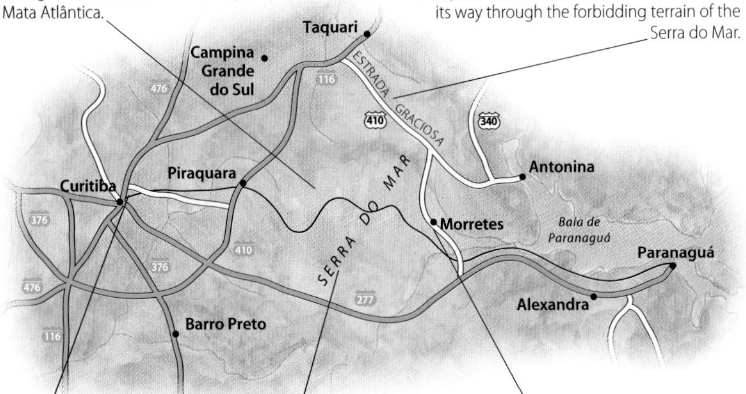

Taquari

Campina
Grande
do Sul

ESTRADA GRACIOSA

116

410

340

Piraquara

Antonina

Curitiba

376

410

Morretes

Baía de
Paranaguá

Paranaguá

476

SERRA DO MAR

277

Barro Preto

Alexandra

Serra do Mar, with its forest-
covered mountain range,
separates Paraná's coastal plain
and highland plateau.

Morretes makes an
excellent base to explore
the surrounding region.

The Litorina
The remarkable Curitiba–Paranaguá
railroad line passes through 13 tunnels and
across 30 bridges. For much of the route,
the line clings to a seemingly sheer
mountainside from which, on clear days,
there are wonderful views across
untouched forest toward the coast.

Key

▬▬ Major road

═══ Minor road

─── Railroad

0 km   10

0 miles   10

Colonial buildings along the waterfront in Paranaguá

❸ Paranaguá

Paraná. 🏠 151,000. 🚉 from Curitiba.
🚌 ℹ Av Arthur de Abreu 44, (41)
3420 2785. 🌐 **paranagua.pr.gov.br**

Founded in 1585, Paranaguá is the oldest city in Paraná and is one of Brazil's most important ports today. Paranaguá's historic center is small enough to explore on foot. The oldest buildings are located in the compact historic core on the shore of Paranaguá Bay. Most of these dilapidated, but distinguished-looking, 19th-century merchants' houses now serve as shops or inexpensive hotels. Also along the shore is the former Colégio dos Jesuítas, an imposing building that now houses the **Museu de Arqueologia e Etnologia**, whose rich collection relates to the region's indigenous inhabitants and popular culture.

Two churches in the historic center are worth seeking out. The **Igreja de Nossa Senhora do Rosário**, built between 1571 and 1575, has suffered considerable changes over the centuries but the main structure retains a Portuguese colonial appearance. Built between 1600 and 1650 by slaves, the **Igreja de São Benedito** is an excellent example of popular colonial architecture. The simple, whitewashed building has undergone renovation and contains a small collection of sacred art.

🏛 Museu de Arqueologia e Etnologia
Rua 15 de Novembro 575.
Tel (41) 3423 2511. **Open** 9am–noon, 1–6pm Tue–Fri, noon–6pm Sat, Sun & public hols. 🅿

❹ Ilha do Mel

Paraná. 🏠 1,200. 🚢 from Paranaguá.
🌐 **ilhadomelonline.com.br**

The most beautiful of Paraná's islands, Ilha do Mel offers a combination of almost entirely undeveloped beaches, isolated coves, and sandy trails. The island guards the entrance to Paranaguá Bay and there are well-preserved ruins of the mid-18th-century fort, **Fortaleza de Nossa Senhora dos Prazeres**, that was constructed to ward off English, French, and Spanish attacks. The **Farol das Conchas** (Conchas Lighthouse), imported from Glasgow and placed on the island's most easterly point in 1872, is the best place for a stunning panoramic view of the island, bay, and mountains.

Tourist development is low-key. Visitor numbers are controlled, and there are no roads or motor vehicles on the island. Building work is also strictly regulated. *Pousadas* are all small and very simple, but most are all the more charming for this. The Ilha do Mel attracts predominantly young visitors and in the

Farol das Conchas lighthouse on the eastern tip of Ilha do Mel

A flock of migratory birds in the Parque Nacional de Superagüi, Ilha de Superagüi

summer it transforms into a party island, with beachside bars open through the night. In spite of this, there can be few more peaceful spots on the southern Brazilian coast than on this island. The beaches, some with waves suitable for skilled surfers, others with warm, calm water ideal for swimming, are never overcrowded. Some of the best beaches, such as **Praia Grande** and **Praia de Fora**, are located on the eastern part of the island.

❺ Ilha de Superagüi

Paraná. 🚤 from Paranaguá. 🚤 Pousada Superagui, (41) 3482 7149. **W pousadasuperagui.com.br**

Just a few dozen people who make a living from fishing and tourism inhabit the island of Superagüi. The island is part of the **Parque Nacional de Superagüi**, a large stretch of intact Atlantic rainforest, or Mata Atlântica *(see p113)*. The park is home to jaguars and parrots, and is known for its mangroves and salt marshes, where an amazing variety of orchids grow. The park is also part of the Atlantic forest reserves that were given UNESCO World Heritage listing in 1999. The island is reached by boat, most easily from Paranaguá, although arrangements can also be made

from Ilha do Mel. Most of the low-lying island is covered with shrub forest and mangrove. Very basic accommodation is available at **Barra de Superagüi**, a village located on the southeast of the island. The only other part of the island that is accessible to visitors is **Praia Deserta**, a glorious 24-mile- (38-km-) long expanse of white

sand. The island attracts various migrating birds, but the flocks of rare, red-faced parrot (*Amazona brasiliensis*) are endemic. Visitors can observe them during the early hours of the evening.

🗺 **Parque Nacional de Superagüi** Barra de Superagüi. **Open** 24 hrs. 🏛 arranged at Pousada Superagüi.

Barreado, a regional specialty of Paraná

Barreado

In Paraná's coastal towns, *barreado* is listed on the menu of most restaurants. Now available throughout the year, *barreado*, considered a poor man's meal, used to be eaten during Carnaval. *Barreado* is a dish that can provide food for several days and requires little attention while cooking. The dish is made of beef, bacon, tomatoes, onion, cumin, and other spices. Traditionally these ingredients are placed in layers in a large clay urn, covered, and then sealed with a paste of ash and *farinha* (manioc flour), before being cooked in a wood-fired oven for up to 15 hours. Today, pressure cookers are sometimes used, and gas or electric ovens are substituted for wood-fired ones. *Barreado* is served with *farinha*, which is spread on a plate; the meat and gravy is placed on top, and the dish is eaten with banana and orange slices.

❻ Foz do Iguaçu

Iguaçu Falls rate as one of South America's great natural sights. The falls are formed by a succession of 275 interlinking cataracts up to 246 ft (75 m) in height cascading over a 1.8-mile- (3-km-) wide precipice. The falls owe their origins to several successive volcanic layers of rock built up over 110 million years. Shared between Brazil and Argentina, the falls are completely surrounded by nature preserves. The two preserves of Brazil's Parque Nacional do Iguaçu and Argentina's Parque Nacional Iguazú contain one of the largest surviving tracts of Atlantic forest in South America.

★ **Garganta do Diabo**
At the Garganta do Diabo (Devil's Throat), the river falls into the depths below with immense power, producing a thick cloud of misty spray.

Walkway
The walkway snaking along one tier of the falls is where visitors can peer into the depths of the magnificent, multiple cascading cataracts.

KEY

① **Estrada Velha de Guarapuava**

② **Porto Canoas Restaurant,** with its outdoor deck, has a wonderful view of the upper falls.

③ **Estación Cataratas** is the starting point of most of the trails. The station also has a rest area and a food court.

④ **The railroad track** runs through vast expanses of lush forest where wildlife and bird sightings are common.

⑤ **Pasarelas de la Isla San Martín**

★ **Hotel das Cataratas**
This majestic 1958 hotel *(see p381)* is the only one that lies in the Brazilian national park.

Tren Ecológico
Access to the trails leading to the falls in the Argentinian park is by a miniature train which runs on natural gas. The train stops at three stations along the way.

Isla San Martín Surroundings
Walkways lead up to views of seven cascading waterfalls, including the powerful Salto San Martín.

Powerboat Trips
The falls can be experienced from close up in hired powerboats that skim the rapids to the very foot of the falls.

★ **Wildlife**
The forests around Foz do Iguaçu host many rare wildlife species, including jaguar, ocelot, and harpy eagle.

The Argentina Falls

Although the Brazilian side is the best place for panoramic views of the falls, it is easier to get closer to both the main cataracts as well as a series of smaller ones from the network of trails on the Argentinian side. The Argentinian forest preserve is larger than the Brazilian one, with good walkable trails, requiring more time to explore. There is also a greater likelihood of being able to spot wildlife on the Argentinian side.

The Sheraton Internacional Iguazú, close to the falls

Exploring Iguaçu

The spectacular falls are located near the Brazilian city of Foz do Iguaçu and the sleepy Argentinian town of Puerto Iguazú. Thanks to excellent roads and tourist facilities, the huge numbers of visitors do little to detract from this majestic sight. Both sides are flanked by lush national parks, abundant with wildlife, and offering sweeping views of the falls, as well as options to go closer to the cascades by boat. The region of Iguaçu, meaning "Great Waters" in Tupi-Guaraní *(see p51)*, was declared a UNESCO World Heritage Site in 1986.

The ground-dwelling red-winged tinamou at Parque das Aves

Key

━━━ Major road
━━━ Minor road
▪▪▪ International border
- - - Park boundary

Foz do Iguaçu

400 miles (639 km) W of Curitiba.
🚌 📧 ℹ️ Av das Cataratas, Km 2.5, (45) 2105 8128. Itaipu Binacional: Av Tancredo Neves 6731. **Tel** (45) 3520 6999. **Open** 8am–4pm daily. 🅿️ 🅲 mandatory. 🅳 🔲 itaipu.gov.br

Foz do Iguaçu, also referred to just as Foz, was a sleepy little border town until the 1970s, when construction work began on the nearby **Itaipu Binacional**, the world's largest hydroelectricity plant. Today, Foz is a base from which visit the city's main attraction, the

Jungle Explorer trucks transporting visitors to the falls

For hotels and restaurants in this region see pp380–81 and p396

spectacular waterfalls located to the east. Foz also boasts a wide range of accommodations, as well as reasonably good bars and restaurants.

🐦 Parque das Aves

Rodovia das Cataratas Km 17. **Tel** (45) 3529 8282. **Open** 8:30am–5:30pm daily. 🅿️ 🅳 🔲 parquedasaves. com.br

Located close to the main entrance to the **Parque Nacional do Iguaçu**, the Parque das Aves serves as an excellent intro-duction to Brazilian birdlife. The park has large aviaries housing some 180 species of birds from different Brazilian and other ecosystems and include macaws, parrots, toucans, red-winged tinamous, and flamingos. Apart from a butterfly habitat and a reptile exhibit, the park also has a successful breeding program that concentrates on Brazilian endangered species.

🏞️ Parque Nacional do Iguaçu

Tel (45) 3521 4400. **Open** 9am–5pm daily. 🅿️ 🅲 🅳

🔲 cataratasdoiguacu.com.br

Created in 1939, Brazil's second oldest national park is today one of the most visited sights in the country. Public and tour buses leave visitors at the visitors' center near the park's entrance where they transfer onto electric-powered, open-topped buses for the falls, located 6 miles (10 km) into the park. The bus stops at the Estação Macuco Safari, where visitors can (for an additional charge) transfer onto a smaller electric-powered vehicle that takes them along a forest trail to the Rio Iguaçu. There, inflatable powerboats carry visitors across rapids toward the Garganta do Diabo (Devil's Throat) and to virtually the foot of the falls.

Along the way are various rest points from where there are spectacular panoramic views of the main series of falls. At the trail's lowest point there is a secure walkway that leads to a platform where one can peer into the stunning Garganta do Diabo, a deep gorge into which the fierce, cascading waters of the falls plummet.

Exploring the Argentinian Side

The Argentinian side of Iguaçu has a larger share of the waterfalls, and offers an intimate experience with a greater variety of perspectives. The quiet little town of Puerto Iguazú is a good place to make a base.

🏛 Parque Nacional Iguazú

Tel (54) 3757 491469.
Open 8am–6pm daily. 🅿 🄲 ♿
W iguazuargentina.com

Whereas the Brazilian park's great attractions are the spectacular panoramic views of the falls, the Argentinian park has an extensive network of forest and waterside trails, which offer visitors close-up views of the smaller falls. As well as the Passeio Garganta do Diablo, there are trails to the Passeio Inferiores and the Passeio Superiores.

From the park's excellent visitors' center, a miniature railroad leads to the Estación Central where the Passeio Inferiores and Passeio Superiores circuits begin. From the Passeio Superiores, visitors can look down onto and across dozens of cataracts. This circuit has concrete catwalks going behind the falls, which used to lead to the Garganta do Diablo until the floods swept them away.

A rainbow arcs above the Río Iguazú, Parque Nacional Iguazú, Argentina

The Passeio Inferiores is a short circuit offering even more spectacular views of the falls from below. This circuit takes a little over an hour and involves climbing up and down stairs. Especially remarkable are the parts of the trail across catwalks allowing amazing views over cascading water. At the lowest point, boats make the short crossing to the **Isla San Martín**, an island located in the heart of the falls. Walking on the island also requires a high level of fitness, as it involves clambering up steep slopes and across some jagged rock formations. The Passeio Garganta do Diablo catwalk begins at a quiet point upstream, passing several small islands before reaching its final, majestic destination.

Puerto Iguazú

6 miles (10 km) S of Foz do Iguaçu. ✈
🚌 ℹ Av Victoria Aguirre 66, (37) 5742 0722. W iguazuturismo.gov.ar

Traveling between Foz and the Argentinian park by public transport involves changing buses in the Argentinian town of Puerto Iguazú. Although Puerto Iguazú boasts few sights, its quiet, tree-lined streets make for attractive wandering, with wooden, rather than concrete, buildings predominating.

A short walk along Puerto Iguazú's main artery, Avenida Victoria Aguirre, leads to the Hito Tres Fronteras (Triple Borders Landmark). From here there are superb views of the Rio Iguaçu and Rio Paraná rivers and across the rivers to Brazil and Paraguay.

Wildlife in the Iguaçu Region

Capucin monkey, Parque Nacional Iguazú

Coati, one of the most commonly spotted mammals in the park

The extent of native flora and fauna that the parks offer is varied. Over 2,000 species of flora have been identified, including ferns, bromeliads, orchids, and many large species of trees that serve as support for an equally large variety of climbing plants. In turn, this serves as a habitat for a similarly varied range of wildlife, lured by fruit, nesting spots, and dens. Although there are 450 varieties of bird amid this forested area, by far the most likely place to spot many of these is the Parque das Aves. With a practiced eye, birds can also be spotted within the forests and clearings of the national parks; the best time for bird-watching is early in the morning and at dusk when toucans, parrots, and hummingbirds abound. Some 80 kinds of mammals, with five varieties of feline, including jaguars and pumas, also rove the forest. Early morning and evening are the best time to see animals, with monkeys sometimes seen drinking from pools in the Argentinian park, or swinging overhead through the forest's canopy. The most commonly sighted mammal is the coati. One of the great joys of Iguaçu during the warm summer months is the immense quantity and variety of colorful butterflies that flutter about.

The bright colors of the historic downtown area of Curitiba, Paraná ▶

❼ Florianópolis & Ilha de Santa Catarina

Santa Catarina's capital, Florianópolis, is one of South America's hippest destinations. A gateway to the Ilha de Santa Catarina, the sprawling urban center of Florianópolis is also the main transport hub for the island. The industrial zone occupies the mainland, while the colonial center sits across the bay on the island. The island's north shore has pretty beaches and warm, tranquil waters that are popular with families. The Atlantic rollers of the east coast have made the island one of the world's great surfing centers. In the daytime, Praia Mole and Praia Joaquina are crowded, while the bars of Lagoa bustle until early morning.

Colorful fishing boats moored in the village of Riberão da Ilha

Canasvieras
During the summer (Dec–Feb), the warm water and safe swimming of the resort of Canasvieras especially attract families from São Paulo and Argentina.

Ingleses do Rio Vermelho

Praia dos Ingleses

Cachoeira do Bom Jesus

Praia Grande/ Moçambique

Ponta das Canas

São João do Rio Vermelho

Praia de Canasvieras

Canasvieras

Vargem Grande

Praia da Barra da Lagoa

Rio Ratones

Praia de Jurerê

Praia de Daniela

Forte de São José

Santo Antônio de Lisboa

Cos Le

Praia do Forte

Sambaqui

Cacupé

BAÍA NORTE

★ **Santo Antônio de Lisboa**
This charming little village, with the church as its focal point, is the best preserved of the island's 18th-century Azorean settlements. Fishing provides the community's basic livelihood, along with tourism.

KEY

① **Centro da Lagoa**, an important fishing center, is primarily known for its lively nightlife, stylish bars, and restaurants.

② **Campeche** is renowned for one of the finest beaches on the island.

③ **Ribeirão da Ilha** is mainly visited for its excellent seafood restaurants, the prime attraction being oysters, farmed just offshore.

FLORIANÓP

Biguaçu

★ **Florianópolis**
The attractions of Florianópolis include Mercado Público, which features upbeat bars, as well as some 120 stands with fruits, vegetables, seafood, and handicrafts.

Angelina

Barra da Lagoa

This pleasant fishing village and beach sits at the mouth of the Canal da Barra da Lagoa. Lined with a choice of accommodations and restaurants, it is particularly lively in the summer season (Dec–Feb). The clear river water is perfect for swimming.

VISITORS' CHECKLIST

Practical Information
Santa Catarina. **i** Terminal Rodo-viário Santa Maria: Av Paulo Fontes 1101, (48) 3228 1095. Mercado Público: R Jerônimo Coelho 60, (48) 3240 4407. 🎭 🏳️‍🌈 Pop Gay Carnaval (Feb); Festa do Divino (May, Jun or Jul); National Oyster and Azorean Culture Festival (Oct) **W** vivendofloripa.com.br

Transport
✈ 7 miles (12 km) S of Florianópolis, then bus or taxi. 🚌 for all beaches: Av Paulo Fontes, Centro, Florianópolis. Taxi: (48) 3240 6009.

★ Praia Mole
Surfers and hang-gliding enthusiasts favor the laid-back Praia Mole to showcase their talents. A number of pleasant beach bars and eateries line the relaxed beach.

Praia Joaquina
Brazil's famous surfing center is backed by huge dunes. The cold water and the rough sea suggest caution.

Key
— Major road
   Minor road

0 km   5
0 miles   3

ILHA DE SANTA CATARINA

For keys to symbols *see back flap*

RIO GRANDE DO SUL

The vast rolling pampas, rugged landscape, and fertile valleys of the Serra Gaúcha range are the dominant physical features of Rio Grande do Sul. A distinctive regional identity emerged with the semi-nomadic *gaúcho*, whose culture is still most apparent here. Although arable farming is important, the area is dominated by large, sprawling cattle *estancias* or ranches.

In 1494, even before Brazil was officially "discovered," the Treaty of Tordesillas divided South America between Portugal and Spain. An imaginary line was drawn through the continent with land to its west awarded to Spain and that to its east to Portugal. Although Brazil was Portuguese, the area that is now Rio Grande do Sul was Spanish. Neither power, however, controlled this frontier region.

Even after Brazil's independence in 1822, only a few military garrisons and small coastal settlements existed here until the mid-1800s. Apart from its obvious strategic significance, the economic potential of this sparsely populated province was gradually being recognized. Until the mid-19th century, indigenous Guaraní people and *gaúchos* inhabited the pampas, largely the preserve of wild cattle.

The forested highlands had an even smaller population. European immigrants settled here on small farms in the mid-18th century. These agricultural, wine-producing colonies grew rapidly and soon transformed the Serra's landscape and economy. By the early 19th century, Rio Grande do Sul had become synonymous with beef. The *charque* (dried beef) industry developed around the southern town of Pelotas. The introduction of railroads and refrigeration gave a further boost to the industry.

Beautiful mountain resorts and extraordinary hiking can be found around the canyons of Parque Nacional dos Aparados da Serra. Both *gaúcho* and European influences have instilled a distinct cultural identity in this state, offering a unique Brazilian experience.

Pastoral scene of cows grazing in Rio Grande do Sul

◀ A tourist steam train readying for departure in Caxias do Sul

Exploring Rio Grande Do Sul

The pampas that characterize the interior of southern and western Rio Grande do Sul are the state's economic heartlands. Porto Alegre, the state's capital, is a bustling city which is culturally rich and ethnically diverse. The windswept coast is for the most part unrelentingly bleak, and is fringed by lagoons and sandbars, making it one of the world's longest beaches. The araucaria pine forests, immense canyons, and terraced vineyards of Bento Gonçalves and Flores da Cunha in the northeast make perfect backdrops for charming country hotels, wineries, and mountain resorts. In the far west, the ruins of São Miguel das Missões are a haunting reminder of the Jesuit legacy in Brazil.

RIO GRANDE
DO SUL

Key

Area illustrated

Sights at a Glance

Towns & Cities

1. *Porto Alegre pp356–7*
2. Nova Petrópolis
3. Gramado
4. Canela
6. Bento Gonçalves
7. Caxias do Sul
8. Flores da Cunha
9. Antônio Prado

National Parks & Beach Resorts

10. Parque Nacional dos Aparados da Serra
11. Torres

Churches

12. *São Miguel das Missões p363*

Tour

5. *Vale dos Vinhedos p359*

Forested hill, Parque Nacional dos Aparados da Serra

For hotels and restaurants in this region see p381 and p397

Key

▬▬▬ Highway
▬▬▬ Major road
▭▭▭ Minor road
▭▬▭ Railroad
▬▬▬ State border

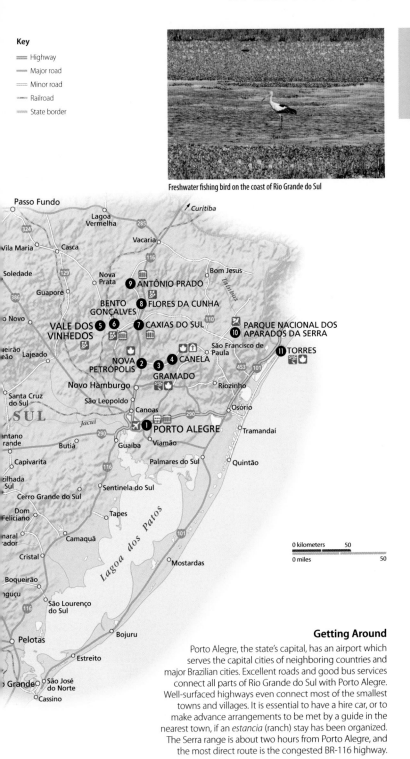

Freshwater fishing bird on the coast of Rio Grande do Sul

Getting Around

Porto Alegre, the state's capital, has an airport which serves the capital cities of neighboring countries and major Brazilian cities. Excellent roads and good bus services connect all parts of Rio Grande do Sul with Porto Alegre. Well-surfaced highways even connect most of the smallest towns and villages. It is essential to have a hire car, or to make advance arrangements to be met by a guide in the nearest town, if an *estancia* (ranch) stay has been organized. The Serra range is about two hours from Porto Alegre, and the most direct route is the congested BR-116 highway.

For keys to symbols *see back flap*

➊ Porto Alegre

Founded in 1772 on the right bank of the Rio Guaiba, Porto Alegre served as a Portuguese military garrison that guarded against Spanish encroachment into southern Brazil. Today, it is Rio Grande do Sul's capital and an important hub for culture, business, and events. The city has some impressive public buildings and a lively street life. Most sights are located in the Centro Histórico, Cidade Baixa, Moinhos de Vento, and Rio Guaiba's waterfront, where the best accommodations, restaurants, and entertainment are also to be found.

🏢 Mercado Público
Praça XV de Novembro.
Open 7:30am–7:30pm Mon–Fri,
7:30am–6:30pm Sat. 🛗

Dating back to 1869, the Neo-Classical-influenced Mercado Público has a vast collection of stalls selling household goods, fruit, vegetables, herbs, wine, meat, and fish. Characteristic of the region are the herb stalls selling *chá mate* (herbal tea) as well as *bombas* and *cuias* (silver straws and drinking gourds). Also of interest are the stalls devoted to African-Brazilian religions, a reminder of the importance of those traditions in a part of the country associated primarily with European culture.

Façade of the Mercado Público, an excellent market for regional items

🏛 Praça da Matriz
Catedral Metropolitana: **Tel** (51) 3225 4980. **Open** 7:30am–7:30pm daily.
🛗 Museu Júlio de Castilhos: **Tel** (51) 3221 3959. **Open** 8am–7pm Mon–Fri. Palácio Piratini: **Tel** (51) 3210 4100. **Open** 8am–7pm Mon–Fri. Teatro São Pedro: **Tel** (51) 3227 5100. **Open** noon–6pm Tue–Fri, 4–6pm Sat & Sun (subject to change – phone ahead). 📷 📱

Designed by Italian architect Giovanni Giovenale, the 1773 **Catedral Metropolitana** features graceful classical columns, geometric designs, and a large hemispherical dome. The present structure dates from 1921.

Just off Praça da Matriz is the **Museu Júlio de Castilhos**, with artifacts relating to the region's history. The imposing **Palácio Piratini**, just west of the cathedral, houses the state government and the governor's residence. It was built in 1909 in a mix of Neo-Classical, Baroque, and Rococo styles. To the square's north, the grand Neo-Classical **Teatro São Pedro** is the city's prestigious concert hall and cultural complex that includes educational facilities and a popular restaurant.

Porto Alegre City Center

① Mercado Público
② Catedral Metropolitana
③ Museu Júlio de Castilhos
④ Palácio Piratini
⑤ Teatro São Pedro
⑥ Museu de Arte do Rio Grande do Sul
⑦ Santander Cultural
⑧ Memorial do Rio Grande do Sul
⑨ Casa de Cultura Mário Quintana
⑩ Usina do Gasômetro
⑪ Museu de Ciência e Tecnologia
⑫ Brique de Redenção
⑬ Caminhos Rurais

Ornate foyer of the Neo-Classical Teatro São Pedro

🏛 Museu de Arte do Rio Grande do Sul

Praça da Alfândega. **Tel** (51) 3227 2311. **Open** 10am–7pm Tue–Sun. 🎫 📷 💻 ♿ **W** margs.rs.gov.br

Late 20th-century works by local artists are prominently displayed in this museum. More absorbing, however, is the small section devoted to 19th-century art. The museum also hosts a number of interesting traveling exhibitions.

🏛 Santander Cultural

Rua 7 de Setembro 1028. **Tel** (51) 3287 5500. **Open** 10am–7pm Mon–Sat, 1pm–7pm Sun. ♿

This vibrant arts complex features an impressive repertoire of music, cinema, and art exhibitions. The Neo-Classical building originally served as a bank between 1927 and 1932. Despite extensive renovations, it retains many of its original features including stained-glass windows.

🏛 Memorial do Rio Grande do Sul

Praça da Alfândega. **Tel** (51) 3224 7210. **Open** 10am–7pm Tue–Fri, 2–6pm Sat. ♿ **W** memorial.rs.gov.br

The memorial houses exhibits relating to the state's social and political history, the state archives and an oral history center.

🏛 Casa de Cultura Mário Quintana

Rua dos Andrades 736. **Tel** (51) 3221 7147. **Open** 9am–9pm Tue–Fri, noon–9pm Sun & hols. ♿ **W** ccmq.rs.gov.br

This Neo-Classical building was designed as a hotel in

VISITORS' CHECKLIST

Practical Information
🗺 1,409,000. ℹ️ Mercado do Bonfim, Loja 12, Parque Farroupilha, (0800) 517 686. 🎭 Semana Farroupilha (Sep). **W** portoalegre.travel

Transport
✈ 4 miles (6 km) N of city. 🚌

1923 by German architect Theo Wiedersphan. For many years, it was also the home of Mário Quintana, one of the state's foremost poets. Today, it hosts a range of attractions including cinema, theatre, and exhibitions relating to art and literature.

🏛 Usina do Gasômetro

Av Presidente João Goulart 551. **Tel** (51) 3289 8112. **Open** 9am–9pm Tue–Fri, 10am–9pm Sat & Sun.

Built in 1928 as a thermo-electrical power station, the Usina opened in 1991 as a cultural center hosting theater and art exhibitions. It also houses a wine museum and an art-house cinema. The west-facing terrace offers spectacular views of the sunset over the lake. A tourism stand offers information on boat trips from the adjacent pier.

🏛 Museu de Ciência e Tecnologia

Av Ipiranga 6681. **Tel** (51) 3320 3521. **Open** 9am–5pm Tue–Thu (to 9pm Fri), 10am–6pm Sat & Sun. ♿ 📷

At one of Latin America's largest science museums visitors can interact with more than 800 experiments and observe marine life in 30 aquariums.

🏛 Brique da Redenção

Parque Farroupilha, Av José Bonifácio. **Open** 9am–6pm Sun.

This weekly cultural fair in the city's popular park has 300 stalls selling food, crafts, jewelry, and antiques, and features performances by musicians, actors, and capoeira artists.

🏛 Caminhos Rurais

Southern Porto Alegre. **W** caminhosrurais.com.br

In the rural area, which covers a large part of Porto Alegre, Caminhos Rurais, or Rural Paths,

is a collection of small properties offering rural and ecotourism experiences ranging from agroecological practices to horseriding and organic wine tasting.

❷ Nova Petrópolis

66 miles (106 km) N of Porto Alegre. 🗺 20,000. 🚌 ℹ️ Torre Turística: Av XV de Novembro 100, (54) 3281 1398. 🎭 Festa do Folclore (Jul), Frühlingsfest (Oct). **W** novapetropolis.rs.gov.br

German immigrants arriving in the 1820s were the first to settle in the hills north of Porto Alegre. Nova Petrópolis, founded in 1858, remained relatively isolated until the mid-20th century and retains a strong German character.

Stretching along Avenida 15 de Novembro, the town's commercial center features a number of German-style buildings. Midway along the avenue is the **Parque Aldeia do Imigrante**, which pays tribute to the region's early settlers. Set within an araucaria forest, the park houses beautifully reconstructed, half-timbered buildings dating between 1870 and 1910, which re-create the atmosphere of a 19th-century German hamlet. The park also hosts festivals and concerts and features a large bandstand as well as a beer hall.

The hamlets and farmsteads surrounding Nova Petrópolis also have a German flavor, and German is still the dominant language.

🔷 Parque Aldeia do Imigrante

Av 15 de Novembro 1966. **Tel** (54) 3281 1254. **Open** 8am–5:30pm daily. 📷 ♿

A turreted German-style building in Nova Petrópolis

Swiss-style chalet, a common sight in Gramado

❸ Gramado

🏠 32,000. 🚌 from Porto Alegre.
ℹ️ Av Borges de Medeiros 1647, (54)
3286 1475. 🎭 Festival de Gramado
(Aug), Natal Luz (Nov 3–Jan 15).
🌐 gramado.rs.gov.br

Brazil's best-known mountain resort, Gramado mimics a central European village. The hilly landscape, reaching just 2,706 ft (825 m) around Gramado, is quite dramatic and the views are fantastic. The flower-filled **Parque Knorr** and the **Lago Negro**, an artificial lake bordered by pine trees imported from Germany's Black Forest, allow for pleasant strolls.

"Swiss chalet" is the dominant architectural style and the profusion of geranium-filled window boxes, chocolate shops, and restaurants specializing in cheese fondues, gives a feeling of being in Switzerland. However, only a very tiny minority of the population is actually of Swiss origin.

Gramado survives almost entirely on tourism. During the first two weeks in August, the city hosts the Festival de Gramado, one of Brazil's most prestigious film festivals, which also attracts an international crowd.

Environs

Just 4 miles (6 km) north from Gramado's main avenue is the **Vale do Quilombo**. Approached by a steep dirt road, much of the valley's original dense Mata Atlântica (Atlantic rainforest) remains and the climate is warmer and more humid. The **Ecoparque Sperry** supports an abundance of fauna including coati, toucans, and howler and capuchin monkeys. Forest trails pass magnificent waterfalls that enhance the valley's scenic splendor.

The valley floor is cultivated and picturesque. Half-timbered farm buildings, which were built by German immigrants in the 19th century, are to be seen alongside the road.

🏕 Ecoparque Sperry

Vale do Quilombo.
Tel (54) 99629 8765.
Open 9am–5pm Tue–Sun.
🅿️ 🚻 ♿

❹ Canela

🏠 38,000. 🚌 from Porto Alegre.
ℹ️ Central de Informações, Praça
João Corrêa, (54) 3282 2200.
🌐 canela.rs.gov.br

Chilly winters, refreshing summers, and unspoilt nature attract visitors to Canela, once a stop-off point for cattle being herded across Rio Grande do Sul's grasslands. The town is dominated by the Igreja Matriz Nossa Senhora de Lourdes, an imposing stone church built in 1953 in English Neo-Gothic style, with other buildings in an eclectic mix of local and European styles. The presence of students from local tourism colleges gives the town a vibrant feel.

Environs

Most of the forests of the Serra were devastated in the 19th century in the quest for araucaria pine. Today, some of this forested area is being preserved. Approximately 5 miles (8 km) north of Canela is the **Parque do Caracol**, a forest reserve with a 429-ft (131-m) waterfall. A highlight here is the 927-step stairway leading to the base of the cascade from where visitors can best appreciate its force and the surrounding forests. A farther 3 miles (5 km) north along the road from Caracol is the **Parque da Ferradura**, a forest reserve notable for the dramatic views of the horseshoe-shaped Rio Caí and of the Arroio Caçador canyon and waterfall.

The area is a popular destination for adventure tourism, with rafting along the fast-flowing Rio Paranhana. Rapeling down its gorge allows for clos-up views of the terrain.

🏕 Parque da Ferradura

Estrada do Caracol.
Tel (54) 3278 9000.
Open 9am–5pm Tue–Sun. ♿

🏕 Parque do Caracol

Estrada do Caracol.
Tel (54) 3278 3035.
Open 9am–5:30pm daily. ♿

Majestic waterfall, Parque do Caracol, near Canela

❾ Tour of Vale dos Vinhedos

Some of the best wine in Brazil is produced in Vale dos Vinhedos. The majority of inhabitants here are descendants of immigrants from Veneto, Italy, and life in the Vale dos Vinhedos follows a pattern very similar to that in the corner of northeast Italy. In an area of virtual monoculture, grape is central to the year's activity, while the Catholic chapels are cornerstones for the maintenance of Italian traditions.

⑥ Casa Valduga
Comfortable guest rooms and excellent food is offered by this pioneer of the production of high-quality Brazilian wines and agritourism.

Picturesque vineyard in the Vale dos Vinhedos

⑦ Capela das Neves
Built in 1907, this is the earliest surviving chapel in Vale dos Vinhedos.

⑤ Vinícola Pizzato
Still small-scale producers, the Pizzato family offers tastings and sell an extensive range of wines.

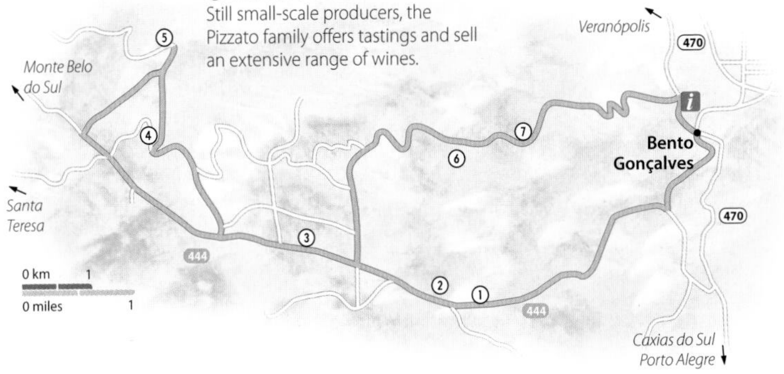

Veranópolis `470`

Monte Belo do Sul

Bento Gonçalves

Santa Teresa

`470`

`444`

0 km   1
0 miles   1

`444`

*Caxias do Sul
Porto Alegre*

④ Famiglia Tasca
These typical stone and wood farm buildings are among the oldest wineries in the valley.

② Memorial do Vinho
This small, fascinating exhibition charts the development of the local wine production from 1875 to present.

① Capela das Graças
Honoring Our Lady of Grace, this *capela* is one of the many Catholic chapels that are central to the valley's Italian immigrants.

Key

═══ Tour route

═══ Other road

Tips for Drivers

Starting point: Bento Gonçalves *(see p360)*.
Length: Allow a full day to visit several wineries and a stop for lunch.
Driving conditions: The main road is paved while the side roads have good-quality gravel surfaces.

③ Vinícola Miolo
The largest vineyard in the valley, Vinícola Miolo produces some of Brazil's best wine. The visitors' center tells the story of Miolo's development and allows tastings.

For keys to symbols *see back flap*

Vinhos Salton, one of the many wineries in Bento Gonçalves

❻ Bento Gonçalves

115,000. 🚍 ℹ️ Rua Mal Deodoro 70, (54) 3055 7160/7163.
🌐 **turismobento.com.br**

Examine a bottle of Brazilian wine and, in all likelihood, the label will indicate Bento Gonçalves as its place of origin. Bento, as the city is usually called, is one of the largest producers of wine in Brazil, with virtually every patch of land outside the city growing vines. The city's economy relies mainly on grapes and wine production, as a result of which Bento's vintners dominate the Brazilian market.

Bento was one of the earliest Italian communities established in the Serra Gaúcha in 1875. However, the rapid growth of the city's urban center in recent decades has left few traces of Italian influence during the early years of immigration. The **Museu do Imigrante** has a rich collection of artifacts relating to Bento's pioneer settlers, with rooms focusing on the arrival of the immigrants and the central role of the Catholic church in the community and farming, in particular viticulture.

The **Cooperativa Vinícola Aurora** is the best known cooperative, and Aurora is the most prominent wine producer in Brazil, with a membership of some 1,300 families, most of whom farm in the valley. Visitors to the cooperative are shown the entire production process from the crushing of grapes

Wine produced in Bento Gonçalves

to bottling. Tours culminate with a tasting. Fine wines are also produced by some smaller wineries. Visitors can find these a short distance away from town, around the beautiful Vale dos Vinhedos (see p359).

Adventure lovers can try extreme sports such as bungee-jumping, climbing, and rapeling at the **Parque de Aventuras Gasper**, located 5.5 miles (9 km) outside town.

Parque de Aventuras Gasper
Linha Eulália. **Tel** (54) 3454 1072, (54) 99109 4824.
Open 8:15–11:30am, 1–6pm Mon–Fri.

Cooperativa Vinícola Aurora
Rua Olavo Bilac 500, Cidade Alta.
Tel (54) 3455 2000.
Open 8:15am–5:15pm Mon–Sat, 8:30–11:30am Sun. 📷 ♿

🏛️ **Museu do Imigrante**
Rua Erny Hugo Dreher 127, (Planalto). **Tel** (54) 3451 1773.
Open noon–6pm Tue–Sat.

Environs

Garibaldi, a small town just 12 miles (20 km) south of Bento Gonçalves, is known for its surprisingly good champagne-style sparkling wines. Part of the attraction of getting to this little town is the ride on the steam engine known as Maria Fumaça, or "Smoking Mary," a name commonly given to tourist steam trains (see p424).

Passing through the landscape's patchwork of vineyards, the 15-mile (23-km) route is covered in an hour and a half. The high point of the journey is the stop at an observatory overlooking the Rio das Antas at the point where the route curves in a horseshoe shape.

❼ Caxias do Sul

395,000. ✈️ 🚍 ℹ️ Praça Dante Alighieri, 0800 541 1875.
🌐 **caxias.tur.br**

Founded in 1875, Caxias do Sul – or simply Caxias, as it is usually called – along with Bento Gonçalves, was one of the earliest Italian *colonias* to be established in the Serra. Like its neighboring settlements, commercial activity at first revolved entirely around wine production, but over the next century other agro-processing industries, as well as textiles and metalworking, developed. Today, Caxias is Rio Grande do Sul's second-largest city after Porto Alegre.

Although tower blocks and other concrete buildings have overtaken much of Caxias, some visible traces of the city's heritage survive. The **Museu Municipal**,

Maria Fumaça, plying between Bento Gonçalves and Garibaldi

Artifacts displayed in Museu Casa de Pedra in Caxias do Sul

built in 1880 as a private residence, documents the history of Caxias, starting with the arrival of the first immigrants from Veneto. The museum's permanent collection includes objects, documents, and photographs charting the development of the city.

The **Museu Casa de Pedra**, housed in a carefully preserved stone farmhouse built in 1878, sheds light on the lives of the pioneer settlers with displays of tools, furniture, and photographs.

🏛 **Museu Casa de Pedra**
Rua Matteo Gianella 531, Bairro Santa Catarina. **Tel** (54) 3901 1463. **Open** 9am–5pm Tue–Sat, 11am–5pm Sun. 🖼

🏛 **Museu Municipal**
Rua Visconde de Pelotas, 586.
Tel (54) 3221 2423. **Open** 9am–5pm Tue–Sat. 🖼 🎴

❽ Flores da Cunha

🏠 30,000. 🚌 from Caxias do Sul.
Tel (54) 3292 1722. Museu Municipal: Av Vinte e Cinco de Julho 1608, (54) 3292 2777. 🖥 **floresdacunha. rs.gov.br**

The fact that Flores da Cunha boasts the title of the largest wine-producing city in Brazil will come as no surprise. Just about every available patch of land in the municipality is given to grape vines and *cantinas*, ranging from small artisan wine producers to huge cooperatives.

The town of Flores da Cunha itself is remarkable for its beautiful setting and friendly people, also to be found in the surrounding villages, which could be mistaken for Italian farming communities. The people maintain the Venetian dialect of their immigrant

forbears, making Flores da Cunha the most Italian of Brazilian towns. Visit **Museu Municipal** to learn more about its history.

Environs

Located in a fertile and picturesque valley, **Otávio Rocha**, 8 miles (13 km) southwest of Flores da Cunha, is especially striking, with vines extending down to the main streets. The village has become a popular place to eat and there is a good choice of restaurants specializing in simple, but tasty, northern Italian country fare.

Another 4 miles (7 km) west of Otávio Rocha is **Nova Pádua**, another wine-producing *município*, whose inhabitants are descended from Venetian immigrants. The village's focal point is the church, characteristically Italian in style with a bell tower set slightly to the side of the main structure. A little farther west, there are breathtaking views below onto the fast-flowing Rio das Antas and a landscape of the Antas Valley, a mix of vineyards and primary forest.

❾ Antônio Prado

🏠 14,000. 🚌 from Caxias do Sul.
ℹ Rua Luiza Bocchese 68, (54) 3293 1500. 🖥 **antonioprado.com.br**

The last of the major settlements, Antônio Prado was established in the Italian colonial zone in 1886. Located in the zone's northern extreme and, until fairly recently, with poor links to other centers, Antônio Prado failed to make the transition from farming community to industrial town.

The lack of development is one of the reasons why the town was declared a National Heritage Site in 1989. Its particular attraction is its concentration of wooden, stone-base buildings erected by Italian immigrants.

Clustered around the town's central square, **Praça Garibaldi**, and the roads that extend immediately off it, some 48 historic buildings are protected and perfectly maintained. Most of the brightly painted clapboard structures with their unchanged interiors have been turned into shops or small government offices.

One of these buildings is now the town hall on Praça Garibaldi. Also located on Praça Garibaldi, the **Museu de Antônio Prado** offers a useful historical overview of the development of the town.

🏛 **Museu de Antônio Prado**
Rua Luisa Bochese 34.
Tel (54) 3293 5656. **Open** 8:30–11:45am Tue–Fri, 1:30–5pm Sat & Sun.

Colorful stone-base wooden houses in Antônio Prado

Araucaria pine trees above the Cânion do Itaimbezinho, Aparados da Serra

❿ Parque Nacional dos Aparados da Serra

🚌 from Canela to Cambará do Sul, then taxi, or from Caxias do Sul or Criciúma. 🛈 RS-427, km18, (54) 3251 1277. **Open** 8am–6pm Tue–Sun. 🅿
🌐 **icmbio.gov.br/parnaaparados daserra**

The highland plateau of Southern Brazil emerged from the accumulation of layers of ocean sediment, with the resulting rock formations lifted up to form the Brazilian Shield. Some 150 million years ago, lava poured onto the shield to create a thick layer of basalt rock. Cracks emerged at the edge of the plateau, taking the form of narrow, but deep, canyons. It is around one of the largest of these canyons – **Canion do Itaimbezinho** – that the Parque Nacional dos Aparados da Serra, one of Brazil's first national parks, was created in 1959.

Canion do Itaimbezinho is a 2,360-ft- (720-m-) deep, 4-mile- (6-km-) long canyon featuring several ecosystems merging into one another with transition zones between them. The plateau around Itaimbezinho is mainly given over to cattle pasture, while dense Mata Atlântica *(see p113)* covers Itaimbezinho's lower reaches. The abundant flora ranges from lichens and mosses to orchids and other flowering plants and giant araucaria pines. Trails around the edge of the canyon are well marked, varying in length between 1 mile (2 km) and 4 miles (6 km), with observatories offering views of the canyon. The longest trail,

Trilha do Rio do Boi, can be challenging for unseasoned hikers. Due to the risk of flooding, the river is monitored regularly around the trail. Nearby, is the Parque Nacional da Serra Geral, with trails and the beautiful Canyon Fortaleza.

The best season to visit the park is in winter (May to August), when visibility stretches to the base of the canyon and toward the coast. September is the worst time to come here, with low cloud and heavy rainfall. During the rest of the year, fog often obscures views, though it can lift very quickly.

⓫ Torres

🏙 35,000. 🚌 from Porto Alegre or Santa Catarina. 🛈 Rua José Antonio Picoral 79, Centro, (51) 3626 9150.
🌐 **torres.rs.gov.br**

The main highlight of the long coastline of Rio Grande do Sul is Torres, located near the border with the neighboring state of Santa Catarina. Torres is named for a series of huge basalt rocks, or "towers," that jut into the ocean and break the otherwise seemingly unending beach. The towers are located in the **Parque da Guarita**, on the southern perimeter of town. Between the sea-cliff towers are sandy coves offering protection from fierce Atlantic rollers. Stairs lead to caves on the cliffs facing the open sea, which were formed over the course of millions of years by the force of the ocean. From a hill at the southern edge of the park, visitors can enjoy tremendous views of the beautifully rugged coastline or trek through the dunes of 2-mile- (4-km-) long Praia de Itapeva. The water at Itapeva is tranquil and favorable for swimming. Off Torres's coast is Ilha dos Lobos, a small island and wildlife refuge.

Waves lapping against the cliffs, Parque da Guarita

The Rise and Collapse of Jesuit Missions

Santa Cecilia, wood sculpture

For much of the 17th and 18th centuries, the Guaraní Indians of what is now northwestern Rio Grande do Sul, as well as parts of Argentina and Paraguay, were controlled by the Jesuits. The first *redução* (community) was established in 1610; 30 others followed, including Brazil's São Miguel, which was founded in 1632. Over time, Guaraní-influenced Baroque music, architecture, painting, and sculpture began to flourish. The Spanish and Portuguese authorities became increasingly concerned about the power of the Jesuits, while Rome was worried that the order was too independent of papal authority. In 1756, Spanish and Portuguese forces expelled the Jesuits. The missions were razed to the ground or abandoned to nature.

⑫ São Miguel das Missões

Surviving through centuries of neglect, the São Miguel Mission presents a fine example of the Guaraní-Baroque style, a blend of Iberian and indigenous architectural elements. These influences are visible in architectural details, particularly in the carved stonework and in the wooden sculptures housed in the museum. The mission was designated a UNESCO World Heritage Site in 1984. Although the area around São Miguel has been given over to farmland, the mission retains an air of isolation.

VISITORS' CHECKLIST

Practical Information
São Miguel. 🛈 (55) 3381 1294.
🎫 📷 Semana Farroupilha (Sep).
🌐 **saomiguel-rs.com.br**
Museu das Missões: Rua São Nicolau s/n. **Open** 9am–noon, 2–6pm daily (winter); 9am–noon, 2–8pm daily (summer). ♿ 📷
🏛 Sound & Light Show: 8pm (winter), 9:30pm (summer) daily. 📷

Transport
🚌 from Porto Alegre to Santo, then bus.

The Bell
The mission's bell was not only rung as a call to prayers, but also to warn of attacks by roving gangs hunting for slaves.

Inner Corridors
A network of corridors gives a sense of the extent of the original mission site, which at its height housed 4,000 people.

The façade is a replica of Il Gesù, the Jesuits' mother church in Rome. Only one of the two original towers remains intact.

Brick and stonework, made from local materials, was mainly used in the mission's construction.

Entrance

Museu das Missões
Designed in 1937 by Lúcio Costa, this early Modernist building was inspired by Jesuit-Baroque architecture. The museum houses statues and other relics excavated locally.

Ruins of Jesuit Buildings
Little remains of the workshops, school rooms, cloisters, and living quarters of the Jesuit mission. However, it is still possible to make out their distinct areas in the ruins.

TRAVELERS' NEEDS

Where to Stay **366–381**

Where to Eat & Drink **382–397**

Shopping in Brazil **398–399**

Entertainment in Brazil **400–401**

Specialized Holidays &
Outdoor Activities **402–405**

WHERE TO STAY

Given the size and diversity of Brazil, it is no surprise that the country offers an excellent selection of accommodations to suit every taste and pocket. Large cities have a wide range of business hotels that comprise everything from budget brands and deluxe international properties such as Grand Hyatt, Sofitel, and Belmond (the latter formerly known as Orient-Express), to privately owned, cutting-edge boutique hotels such as the Fasano and Unique in São Paulo. In tourist areas, the options include large, fancy, all-inclusive, internationally known resort properties, as well as Brazilian-owned chain and individual hotels. There are also small, privately owned establishments, or *pousadas*, that may only have two or three rooms and are either very simple and basic or very sophisticated and, depending on size, border on being boutique hotels. There has also been a growth in good-quality hostels. Some of the best places to stay are listed on pages 370–81. Prices are quoted in US dollars.

Booking

Brazil is one of the most active Internet countries in the world, and the majority of accommodations have their own websites. Many larger properties also appear on international booking engines and travel sites such as **Expedia**, **Last Minute** and **Booking.com**, which may offer large discounts, sometimes up to 50%, on the room rates quoted by the hotel.

In the age of the Internet, it is important for the traveler to check how financially protected they are if they do book directly and the property they choose goes out of business.

During the high season (during Carnaval, the Christmas-to-New Year period, and in July and August), many hotels and *pousadas* in Brazil will expect guests to stay for a minimum number of nights. This will need to be taken into consideration if you want to move around, since one- or two-night stays may be difficult to find. Book in advance during high season, as good rooms are not easy to come by at the last minute. Weekends can also get quite crowded.

Prices & Payments

If booking online or by phone, some properties will require either a deposit or payment in advance to cover the cost of the entire duration of the stay, especially in high season or for weekend specials.

Hotels that do not require a deposit or full payment in advance usually ask the client to provide their credit card details to secure the reservation. Be careful to check the cancellation policy.

Credit cards are accepted as payment at most properties, especially in cities. Only the larger hotels in bigger cities will handle traveler's checks. Many places accept payment in US dollars, but they will set the exchange rate, which will often be high.

When booking, it is important to check what taxes are included in the price. These may include a 10 percent service tax, a 5 percent sales tax, and, in some areas of Brazil, a nightly tourist tax.

Prices throughout Brazil vary greatly, and it is rare that any traveler should ever need to pay the rack rate as advertised by the hotels. Like airlines, hotels often make special offers available even through their own websites. Some hotels – normally smaller, privately owned properties – still think they can charge different prices

The famous Copacabana Palace Hotel in Rio de Janeiro *(see p370)*

◀ Street cafés in the World Heritage Site of Paraty, Rio de Janeiro

Bungalow accommodation at Txai Hotel, a deluxe boutique hotel in Itacaré *(see p374)*

for Brazilian travelers and foreign visitors, so it is worth checking the rates on the Portuguese-language version of the website. Prices also vary due to exchange rates. The price often reflects not only the quality of the accommodation, but also the location. Hotels in popular cities such as Rio de Janeiro tend of course to be more expensive than those in smaller towns in the countryside. There will also be notably different rates for rooms at the front of a beachfront property and those at the side or behind.

Prices are likely to be higher in high season or on the weekend except at some business and chain hotels, which have cheaper rates on weekends.

Tipping

It is customary and much appreciated for guests to leave a tip for the staff who have served them well during their stay. This could be the chambermaid, the bellboy, or bar staff. Many of the people who serve visitors will be earning the minimum wage of around US$300 per month, so any tips can make a real difference.

Children

Children are always welcome at most hotels, with only a very few smaller, normally romantic *pousadas* having any restrictions, which will be clearly stated on their websites or at the time of booking. The vast majority of hotels and *pousadas* in Brazil are child-friendly. Larger properties will have high chairs and possibly cots, and many

resorts also have special child-friendly areas, playrooms, and even separate kitchens for mothers needing to prepare food for babies and smaller children. Many large hotels can also organize babysitters.

Advise the hotel of the age of your children and any special requirements you may need for them in advance. If the hotel does not already have what you need, it may be willing to obtain it by the time you arrive.

Travelers with Special Needs

The situation for disabled travelers in Brazil has greatly improved in the 21st century, but not all accommodation options, especially the smaller properties with narrow lifts or those in the remoter areas of the country, can offer wheelchair access or the facilities that disabled travelers may require. Brazilians by nature, however, will do everything they can to assist, so do not hesitate to ask.

Chain Hotels

Brazil's hotel chains include a number of long-established Brazilian groups, such as **Othon** and **Tropical**. There are also several hundreds of modern hotels throughout the country that operate under different international brands, such as the **Accor** and **Marriott** groups.

Brazilian hoteliers have not been left behind, with the introduction of **Blue Tree**, **Bristol**, the **Atlântica Hotels** group (which operates as Radisson, Clarion, Quality, Comfort Suites, Four Points, Sleep Inn, and Go Inn), **Transamérica**, and in Rio de Janeiro, **Windsor Hoteis**.

The majority of chain hotels, which vary greatly in terms of price, infrastructure and quality, tend to be targeted at Brazilian and South American business travelers unless they are in obvious tourist destinations. Only the properties in the tourist areas are likely to consider adding a Brazilian or tropical flavor to the surroundings or decorations.

Apart-Hotels

Though not strictly for budget travelers, apart-hotels, in most of the main Brazilian cities, offer good value for money. These come with one, two, or more bedrooms, a living area, and a kitchen. Some will have restaurants and cafés, as well as swimming pools and gyms.

One of the main chains with properties throughout Brazil is Accor's Parthenon group, while in São Paulo, Transamérica Flats is a very prominent brand.

Children's playroom, a feature in many Brazilian hotels

A brightly decorated room in Sandi, a *pousada* in Paraty *(see p372)*

Pousadas

Outside of the main city and town centers, the majority of accommodations on offer are smaller, privately owned properties, many in historic, colonial-era villas and mansions. *Pousadas* vary dramatically in terms of cost, quality, and facilities offered. Some will be very basic but certainly clean, while others can be considered world-class boutique hotels set in lovely locations. *Pousadas* are usually charming, offer good value, and give a real flavor of Brazil.

It is a good idea to visit the website of an individual *pousada* to see the pictures of the property and what it has to offer. Most good tour operators know the best *pousadas* in each category and area. **Roteiros de Charme**, a network of outstanding *pousadas*, is also very useful, as is the **Hidden Pousadas** website. In the **Vale do Café** region in Rio de Janairo State, a network of *pousadas* offer stays in some of the country's grandest old coffee *fazendas*.

If staying in Rio de Janeiro, check out **Cama a Café**, an organization that looks after many bed-and-breakfast options across the city, the majority in Santa Teresa. These offer the chance to stay in a room in a local resident's house.

Boutique Hotels

Luxuriously appointed hotels, these usually have only about a dozen rooms or fewer. Some are housed in beautiful historic buildings in stunning natural settings, such as in Brazil's many national parks. Most boutique hotels are expensive, but offer a personalised experience. They are particularly popular for honeymoons and for other special occasions.

Resorts

World-class resorts, many all-inclusive, can be found across Brazil. One of the largest is the Costa do Sauípe, just north of Salvador, and close by in Praia do Forte, Tivoli Ecoresort, Iberostar Praia do Forte, and Iberostar Bahia. Among the best are Transamérica on Ilha de Comandatuba in Bahia, Ponta dos Ganchos in Santa Catarina, Nannai in Porto de Galinhas, and Sofitel Jequitimar in Guarujá, to name but a few.

Budget Options

In the main areas visited by tourists, there are many *pousadas* that can be considered budget accommodation. There is also a good and growing network of modern and comfortable hostels in Brazil for those on a really tight budget. New independent hostels can be found right across Brazil, from the tourist areas of Rio de Janeiro, to the business heart of São Paulo. The website of the **Federação Brasileira de Albergues da Juventude** has a full list of hostels in Brazil that are approved by the organization.

Couchsurfing

This worldwide trend, where visitors can get a free bed for the night in private houses, has been taking off in Brazil. More common in larger towns and cities, couchsurfing gives travelers the opportunity to meet local families and to experience the domestic lives of Brazilians firsthand. Visit **couchsurfing.org** for places on offer, along with details of the host families.

Similarly, **Homestays** and **AirBnB** are good budget options, with listings of rooms available throughout Brazil.

Private Rentals

Ideal for families and groups of friends, houses and apartments can be rented through various agencies, such as **Aluguel Temporada**, **Brazilian Beach House**, and **Brazil Rent My Home**. The huge variety of accommodations on offer

The Costa do Sauípe Golf & Spa, Bahia *(see p374)*

ranges from simple options to luxuriously appointed places with even chauffeur, cook and maid services.

Motels

Motels in Brazil have nothing in common with the ones to be found in North America or in Europe. In Brazil, these tend to be "love hotels," renting rooms out to couples by the hour. Guests are not normally encouraged to spend more than one night at these establishments.

Camping

Brazil offers a massive number of places where it is possible to camp. However, campers should make sure they have not wandered on to private property or into a restricted area. Security, too, is an issue, and not just from miscreants, but also from Brazilian wildlife. If you are not an experienced camper, you should stick to official campsites, the majority of which are run and organized by the **Camping Clube do Brasil**. If using one of the national parks, check first with the park authorities where camping is permitted. Having your own tent, or hiring

Camping in the Serra dos Órgãos National Park

one, is useful in ecotourist regions, such as the Amazon and the Pantanal.

Lodges

The majority of wildlife lodges that will help visitors to see and enjoy some of the remoter parts of Brazil are located in the Amazon (see p378) and the Pantanal (see pp379–80). While there are some outstanding exceptions, the facilities and home comforts of many of these lodges may be quite basic, since visitors are more keen on exploring the surrounding countryside, flora, and fauna. It is recommended for travelers to consider traveling light, leaving the bulk of their belongings back in their main

hotel, an airport locker, or at the city office of the lodge prior to making the transfer.

Recommended Hotels

The many different hotels, resorts, pousadas, and lodges in this book have been carefully selected for their facilities, good location, and value. A wide variety of accommodations is covered, from lodges in remote rainforest locations, to stylish boutique hotels in Brazil's towns and cities.

Entries labeled as DK Choice highlight establishments that are exceptional or notable in some way – for their stunning location, outstanding rooms, superb restaurant, excellent service, or a combination of these.

DIRECTORY

Booking

Expedia
W expedia.com

Last Minute
W lastminute.com

Chain Hotels

Accor
Tel (0800) 703 7000.
W accor.com.br

Atlântica Hotels
Tel (0800) 55 5855.
W atlanticahotels.com.br

Blue Tree
Tel (0300) 150 5000.
W bluetree.com.br

Bristol
Tel (0800) 645 1816.
W bristolhoteis.com.br

Marriott
W marriott.co.uk

Othon
Tel (0800) 725 0505.
W othon.com.br

Transamérica
Tel (0800) 012 4400.
W transamericagroup.com.br

Tropical
Tel (0800) 70 12670.
W tropicalhotel.com.br

Windsor Hoteis
Tel (11) 3259 5323.
W windsorhoteis.com

Pousadas

Cama a Café
Tel (21) 2225 4366.
W camacafe.com.br

Hidden Pousadas
Tel (21) 98122 2000.
W hiddenpousadas brazil.com

Roteiros de Charme
Tel (21) 2287 1592.
W roteirosdecharme.com.br

Vale do Café
Tel (24) 2471 7462.
W portalvaledo cafe.com.br

Budget Options

Federação Brasileira de Albergues da Juventude
W hihostelbrazil.com.br

Couchsurfing

AirBnB
W airbnb.com

Homestays
W homestay.com/brazil
W couchsurfing.org

Private Rentals

Aluguel Temporada
Tel (21) 3956 9709.
W aluguetemporada.com.br

Brazil Rent My House
W brazilrentmyhouse.com

Brazilian Beach House
Tel (598) 2605 6913.
W brazilianbeach house.com

Camping

Camping Clube do Brasil
W campingclube. com.br

Where to Stay

Rio de Janeiro City

AIRPORT: Linx $$
Business
Av Vinte de Janeiro s/n
Tel (21) 2468 3400
Ⓦ linxriodejaneiro.com.br
This is the best choice if you
need suitable accommodation
near the international airport for
connecting flights.

BARRA DA TIJUCA:
Royal Tulip São Conrado $$
Resort
Rua Aquarela do Brasil 75
Tel (21) 3323 2200
Ⓦ royaltulipriodejaneiro.com
The England soccer team stayed
here during the 2014 World Cup.
It offers great views and the pool
area is one of the best in Rio.

BARRA DA TIJUCA:
Windsor Barra $$$
Business
Av Lucio Costa 2630
Tel (21) 2195 5000
Ⓦ windsorhoteis.com
With extensive event facilities, this
large modern beachfront property
is popular for conferences. There
are good beach and sea views
from most rooms.

CENTRO: Manga $
Hostel **Map** 5 D5
Rua do Lavradio 186
Tel (21) 3852 5742
Ⓦ mangahostelrio.com
Close to Rio's street party scene
in Lapa, this hostel is also well
located for sightseeing and
the metro for the Ipanema,
and Copacabana beaches.
Dormitories have bright
colours and basic amenities.

The façade and entrance of the Porto Bay
Rio Internacional, Copacabana

CENTRO: Novotel Santos
Dumont $$
Business **Map** 5 F4
Rua Marechal Câmara 300
Tel (21) 3506 8500
Ⓦ novotel.com
A modern, well-equipped, no-
frills Novotel, the Santos Dumont
is well positioned for those
working downtown or taking
domestic flights from Santos
Dumont airfield.

CENTRO: Vila Galé Rio de
Janeiro $$
Historical **Map** 5 D5
Rua Riachuelo 124
Tel (21) 2460 4500
Ⓦ vilagale.com/en/hotels/rio-de-
janeiro/vila-gale-rio-de-janeiro
Located close to Lapa and
downtown Rio, this renovated
colonial-era mansion has a
pleasant mix of new and old. The
rooms are tasteful and elegant.
Good base for sightseeing.

CENTRO: Windsor Asturias $$
Business **Map** 5 E5
Rua Senador Dantas 14
Tel (21) 2195 1500
Ⓦ windsorhoteis.com
This good, standard business
hotel, housed in a 1930s building,
has a rooftop terrace with
lovely views.

COPACABANA & LEME:
Rio Lancaster $$
Business **Map** 3 F2
Av Atlântica 1470
Tel (21) 2169 8300
Ⓦ hotelriolancaster.com.br
The front rooms of this Art
Deco building on Copacabana
beachfront have balconies and
beautiful views.

COPACABANA & LEME:
Sofitel Rio $$
Luxury **Map** 3 D5
Av Atlântica 4240
Tel (21) 2525 1232
Ⓦ sofitel.com
There are stunning views along
the beach from the large pool
area at this hotel located at the
Ipanema end of Copacabana
beach. All rooms have a balcony.

COPACABANA & LEME:
Windsor Excelsior $$
Business **Map** 3 E2
Av Atlântica 1800
Tel (21) 2195 5800
Ⓦ windsorhoteis.com
This is a solid choice for a beach-
front business hotel near to but
cheaper than the Copacabana
Palace. It has a rooftop pool.

COPACABANA & LEME:
Windsor Leme $$
Boutique **Map** 3 D4
Av Atlântica 656
Tel (21) 2195 7800
Ⓦ windsorhoteis.com
This is a luxury, stylish, top-of-the-
line hotel on the beachfront, with
chic rooms. The rooftop pool area
offers glorious views of the beach.

DK Choice

COPACABANA & LEME:
Copacabana Palace $$$
Historic **Map** 3 E2
Av Atlântica 1702
Tel (21) 2548 7070
Ⓦ belmond.com/copacabana
palace
Famous in Rio and around the
world, with a guest list of
celebrities to match, this top-end
luxury grand beachfront hotel
from Belmond, first opened in
1923. It features Rio's best and
most glamorous hotel pool.

COPACABANA & LEME:
JW Marriott $$$
Luxury **Map** 3 D3
Av Atlântica 2600
Tel (21) 2545 6500
Ⓦ marriott.com
This boutique hotel is one of Rio's
best choices for staying on the
Copacabana beachfront. The
rooftop terrace offers amazing
views of Sugar Loaf Mountain.

COPACABANA & LEME:
Porto Bay Rio Internacional $$$
Business **Map** 3 F2
Av Atlântica 1500
Tel (21) 2546 8000
Ⓦ portobay.com
The roof terrace at this beachfront
hotel has sweeping views of
Copacabana. Corner rooms have
floor-to-ceiling windows.

COPACABANA & LEME: Rio
Othon Palace $$$
Business **Map** 3 D3
Av Atlântica 3264
Tel (21) 2106 1500
Ⓦ othon.com.br
Towering, landmark hotel on
the beachfront. The rooms and
facilities are a bit dated, but
many have spectacular views.

The opulent lobby at the Windsor Atlântica

**COPACABANA & LEME:
Windsor Atlântica** $$$
Luxury Map 3 F1
Av Atlântica 1020
Tel (21) 2195 7800
W windsorhoteis.com
This stylish flagship property
from the Windsor Group has
wonderful views and excellent
facilities including a rooftop
pool and terrace, a spa, and
two restaurants. The staff are
friendly and helpful.

**FLAMENGO & BOTAFOGO:
Discovery** $
Hostel
Benjamin Constant 26
Tel (21) 3449 0672
W discoveryhostel.com
Located in Glória, a short
distance from the metro, this
terrific small hostel has private
rooms and a studio apartment,
as well as shared dorms. There's
a bar, lounge, and small patio.

**FLAMENGO & BOTAFOGO:
El Misti** $
Hostel
Praia de Botafogo 462, Casa 9
Tel (21) 2226 0991
W elmistibota.com
Close to Botafogo metro station,
beach, and Sugar Loaf Mountain,
this excellent hostel has shared
dorms and private rooms. There
is a large shared kitchen, chill out
area with games, and a library

**IPANEMA & LEBLON:
Ipanema B&B** $
Hostel Map 2 C5
Rua Canning 18, Casa 1
Tel (21) 2287 2928
W ipanemabb.com
Conveniently located within
walking distance of both
Copacabana and Ipanema
beaches, this hostel offers dorms
and suites. The pleasant rooftop
terrace has hammocks to relax in.

DK Choice

**IPANEMA & LEBLON:
Mango Tree** $
Hostel
Rua Prudente de Moraes 594
Tel (21) 2287 9255
W mangotreehostel.com
This 1930s colonial-style house
located a block away from
Ipanema beach became a local
hotspot after hosting Norway's
sailing team during the 2016
Olympics. It offers high comfort,
a friendly, laidback atmosphere,
and a sumptuous Brazilian
breakfast. Try the *caipirinhas*.

**IPANEMA & LEBLON:
Hotel Arpoador** $$
Business Map 2 C5
Rua Francisco Otaviano 177
Tel (21) 2523 0060
W hotelarpoador.com
At this little gem, rooms are simple
but slightly dated. It does not have
a pool, but there's a short path
between the hotel and beach.
Book a high-up oceanfront room.

**IPANEMA & LEBLON: Ipanema
Plaza** $$
Business Map 2 B5
Rua Farme de Amoedo 34
Tel (21) 3687 2000
W ipanemaplaza.com.br
This popular Ipanema hotel with
a rooftop terrace is located one
block back from the beach, close
to many restaurants and bars.

**IPANEMA & LEBLON:
Mar Ipanema** $$
Business Map 1 C4
Rua Visconde de Pirajá 539
Tel (21) 3875 9191
W maripanema.com
Located on the main shopping
street and just two blocks from
the beach, the Mar Ipanema has
elegant, tasteful rooms.

**IPANEMA & LEBLON: Praia
Ipanema** $$
Business Map 1 C5
Av Vieira Souto 706
Tel (21) 2141 4949
W praiaipanema.com
This pleasant hotel on Ipanema
beachfront has a small rooftop
pool, bar, and restaurant. The
light and airy rooms have tiled
floors and balconies.

**IPANEMA & LEBLON: Sol
Ipanema** $$
Business Map 2 A5
Av Vieira Souto 320
Tel (21) 2525 2020
W solipanema.com.br
Book a seafront room for the
view at this hotel in an excellent
beachfront location in the very
heart of Ipanema close to
restaurants, bars, and stores. It
has a small rooftop pool.

**IPANEMA & LEBLON:
Caesar Park** $$$
Luxury Map 2 A5
Av Vieira Souto 460
Tel (21) 2525 2525
W sofitel.com
Under Sofitel management, the
stylish Caesar Park has been a
popular choice for business and
leisure travelers for decades. It has
a small pool and rooftop terrace.
One of Ipanema's very best.

**IPANEMA & LEBLON:
Fasano** $$$
Luxury Map 2 B5
Av Vieira Souto 80
Tel (21) 3202 4000
W fasano.com.br
There are lovely sea views from
all the rooms at this chic, stylish,
boutique hotel with a gorgeous
rooftop pool deck, a great
restaurant, and fashionable bar.

**IPANEMA & LEBLON:
Sheraton Grand Rio** $$$
Resort
Av Niemeyer 121
Tel (21) 2529 1122
W sheraton-rio.com.br
Rio's largest resort property
is located almost on its own
beach just a short hop along
the coast from Leblon. A great
choice for families.

**SANTA TERESA: Santa
Teresa** $$$
Luxury
Av Alm Alexandrino 660
Tel (21) 3380 0200
W santateresahotelrio.com
This boutique hotel is tucked away
in bohemian Santa Teresa. Far
from the beach and Copacabana,
it is an oasis of calm. Stylish
rooms overlook the gardens.

For more information on types of hotels *see pages 366–9*

Rio de Janeiro State & Espírito Santo

Rio de Janeiro State

ANGRA DOS REIS: Vila Galé Eco Resort $$$
Resort
Estrada Vereador Benedito Adelino 8413, Fazenda Tanguá
Tel (24) 3379 2800
W vilagale.com.br
This well-structured, comfortable resort property is located on its own beach and is excellent for families. This is one of the major resorts that is closest to Rio.

BÚZIOS: Abracadabra $$$
Pousada
Alto do Humaitá 13
Tel (22) 2623 1217
W abracadabrapousada.com.br
Just 5 minutes from the center of the action in Rua das Pedras, this small, well-appointed *pousada* offers a stunning swimming pool with great views over the Atlantic.

BÚZIOS: Casas Brancas Boutique Hotel & Spa $$$
Boutique
Rua Alto do Humaitá 10
Tel (21) 2623 1458
W casasbrancas.com.br
Slightly larger than the *pousadas* but with many extra facilities, this hotel has individually decorated rooms, some with a balcony and a private pool.

DK Choice

BÚZIOS: Insolito Boutique Hotel $$$
Boutique
Rua E1, Lotes 3 and 4, Praia da Ferradura
Tel (22) 2623 2172/5210
W insolitohotel.com
In a beautiful location on the edge of Praia da Ferradura, one of the region's very best beaches, this stylish French-owned hotel offers the highest comfort and relaxation. It has individually styled suites, a wellness center, lovely pool areas, and a good restaurant.

BÚZIOS: Vila d'Este $$$
Pousada
Alto do Humaitá 11
Tel (22) 2623 1546
W viladeste.eco.br
A cross between a *pousada* and boutique hotel, within walking distance of town, this establishment has a good restaurant and a pool deck.

The sun deck at Vila d'Este, Búzios, offering beautiful views of sea and sky

ILHA GRANDE: Ancoradouro $$
Pousada
Rua da Praia 121 A1, Abraão
Tel (24) 3361 5153
W pousadancoradouro.com.br
This cute *pousada*, typical of those to be found in and around the main town of Ilha Grande, offers spacious and clean rooms.

ILHA GRANDE: Naturalia $$
Pousada
Rua da Praia 149
Tel (24) 3361 9583
W pousadanaturalia.net
A short walk from where the boats dock and from the center of town, this comfortable *pousada* is well positioned for exploring the island.

DK Choice

ILHA GRANDE: Pousada do Preto $$
Pousada
Praia do Bananal
Tel (24) 9 9968 9310
W pousadadopreto.com.br
Tucked away on a small beach, this cozy Japanese-Brazilian *pousada* brings guests by boat from Angra dos Reis to a homely building next to a brook. This is an ideal hideaway for those looking to forget urban life while enjoying boat trips to Ilha Grande's beaches. All meals are served in high season; breakfast and dinner only in low season.

PARATY: Sandi $$
Pousada
Largo do Rosário 1
Tel (11) 2503 0195/01956
W pousadadosandi.com.br
Set in a colonial building in Paraty's historic center, the Sandi is full of character, which captures the spirit of the town. Comfortable rooms have stylish furnishings.

PARATY: Casa Turquesa $$$
Pousada
Rua Doutor Pereira 50
Tel (24) 3371 1037
W casaturquesa.com.br
Understated class is the mark of this stylish and romantic *pousada* in the historic center, a perfect base from which to explore the town.

PARATY: Literária $$$
Pousada
Rua do Comércio 362
Tel (24) 3371 1460/1568
W pousadaliteraria.com.br
This *pousada* has a literary theme, reflecting the fact that the town holds South America's leading literary festival. The rooms are spacious and have tasteful decor.

PETRÓPOLIS: Grande Hotel $$
Historic
Rua do Imperador 545
Tel (24) 2244 6500
W grandehotelpetropolis.com.br
In a perfect location for sightseeing, this hotel balances the modern with the historic.

PETRÓPOLIS: Solar do Império $$
Historic
Av Koeller 376
Tel (24) 2103 3000
W solardoimperio.com.br
Set in two large houses that date from 1875 and 1983, this small classic hotel is well positioned for sightseeing.

Espírito Santo

VITORIA: Golden Tulip Porto Vitoria $
Business
Av Nossa Senhora dos Navegantes 635
Tel (27) 3533 1300
W goldentulipportovitoria.com
Providing good value, this modern, well-appointed hotel has good facilities and enjoys a central location.

VITORIA: Senac Ilha do Boi $$
Business
Rua Bráulio Macedo 417
Tel (27) 3345 0111
 hotelilhadoboi.com.br
As a part of Brazil's national hotel
and catering school, this hotel
offers great value and excellent
food. The setting is lovely, in one
of Vitoria's nicest neighborhoods,
and offers great views.

Minas Gerais

**BELO HORIZONTE: Holiday Inn
Belo Horizonte** $$
Business
Rua Professor Moraes 600
Tel (31) 3064 6555
 ihg.com
This convenient and modern
Holiday Inn offers all you would
expect from the chain.

**BELO HORIZONTE: Ouro
Minas Palace** $$
Business
Av Cristiano Machado 4001
Tel (31) 3429 4001
 ourominas.com.br
Considered by many to be
the top business hotel in Belo
Horizonte, this is a fashionable
venue for events and conferences.

**OURO PRETO: Grande Hotel
Ouro Preto** $
Pousada
Rua Senador Rocha Lagoa 164
Tel (31) 3551 1488
 grandehotelouropreto.com.br
Designed by Oscar Niemeyer in
1938, this historic hotel has
gardens created by Burle Marx.
The panoramic restaurant offers
views over Ouro Preto, as do
the duplex suites.

The pool at Belo Horizonte's top business
hotel, Ouro Minas Palace

OURO PRETO: Mondego $$
Pousada
Largo do Coimbra 38
Tel (31) 3552 7700
 mondego.com.br
Set in a colonial building, this
comfortable *pousada* is located
close to the main square and is a
perfect base for exploring Ouro
Preto. The pleasant bistro offers
light meals.

DK Choice

**OURO PRETO: Solar do
Rosário** $$
Pousada
Rua Getúlio Vagas 270
Tel (31) 3551 5200/5040
 hotelsolardorosario.com.br
This small hotel has traditional
charm, coupled with modern
comforts. It includes lovely
gardens and pools, a gym, and
an excellent restaurant. Close to
the historic center, it is handy
for sightseeing around Ouro
Preto on foot.

**PARQUE NACIONAL DA SERRA
DO CIPÓ: Cipó Veraneio** $$
Pousada
Rodovia MG-010, Km 94
Tel (31) 3718 7000
 cipoveraneiohotel.com.br
With a lovely garden and pool on
the edge of the River Cipo, this
pleasant hotel has simple rooms.

**TIRADENTES: Pequena
Tiradentes** $$
Historical
Av Governador Israel Pinheiro 670
Tel (32) 3355 1262
 pequenatiradentes.com.br
Inspired by the history and
architecture of old Tiradentes, the
rooms at this small hotel look like
typical houses, and the corridors
are like streets with plants and
streetlights. A fun spot for families.

TIRADENTES: Solar da Ponte $$
Pousada
Praça das Mercês s/n
Tel (32) 3355 1255
 solardaponte.com.br
Old-style hospitality and modern
comforts are found at this well-
maintained *pousada* in the historic
center of Tiradentes, set up in 1974
by a British engineer and his wife.

TIRADENTES: Três Portas $$
Pousada
Rua Direita 280A
Tel (32) 3355 1444
 pousadatresportas.com.br
This delightful rustic *pousada*
with cozy rooms is located in the
city's main square and offers
significant discounts on weekdays.

São Paulo City

**AIRPORT (GUARULHOS):
Pullman São Paulo** $$
Business
Rodovia Hélio Smidt s/n
Tel (11) 2124 5800
 pullmanhotels.com
Close to the airport, this is a good
option if you have flight connections to make. The shuttle takes
10 minutes to reach the terminals.

**JARDINS & AVENIDA PAULISTA:
Viva Hostel Design** $
Hostel
Rua Girassol 1262
Tel (11) 3812 9142
 vivahostel.com.br
This colorful, popular, well-
located hostel has clean, modern,
spacious rooms or small dorms.

**JARDINS & AVENIDA PAULISTA:
Porto Bay L'Hotel** $$
Boutique   **Map** 4 F3
*Alameda Campinas 266,
Jardim Paulista*
Tel (11) 2183 0500
 portobay.com
Well-located for Avenida Paulista,
this popular, small and friendly
hotel offers European-style
elegance and service.

**JARDINS & AVENIDA PAULISTA:
Emiliano** $$$
Luxury   **Map** 4 D3
Rua Oscar Freire 384
Tel (11) 3069 4369
 emiliano.com.br
A stylish boutique hotel that is
considered one of the city's best,
Emiliano is well located for both
business and leisure.

DK Choice

**JARDINS & AVENIDA
PAULISTA: Fasano** $$$
Luxury   **Map** 4 D3
Rua Vittorio Fasano 88
Tel (11) 3896 4000
 fasano.com.br
Offering exclusive style, charm,
and five-star comfort, Fasano
boasts the Fasano Italian
restaurant and the bar Baretto,
both considered among the
best in their class, as well as a
lovely pool and spa.

**JARDINS & AVENIDA PAULISTA:
Unique** $$$
Luxury   **Map** 4 E5
Av Brigadeiro Luís Antônio 4700
Tel (11) 3055 4710
 hotelunique.com.br
This trendy boutique hotel has a
beautiful pool area, superb
restaurant, and superb city views.

For more information on types of hotels *see pages 366–9*

The upstairs lounge area with views of the city at the Grand Hyatt, São Paulo City

**MORUMBI & BROOKLIN:
Hilton Morumbi** $$
Business
Av das Nações Unidas 12901
Tel (11) 2845 0000
w hiltonmorumbi.com.br
Handy for the business district
of Brooklyn and Morumbi, this
large Hilton is in demand for
conferences and events. Rooms
have mountain or sea views.

**MORUMBI & BROOKLIN:
Grand Hyatt** $$$
Luxury
Av das Nações Unidas 13301
Tel (11) 2838 1234
w saopaulo.grand.hyatt.com.br
Top of the line and elegant, the
Grand Hyatt Hotel has stylish and
spacious rooms. Great facilities
include a highly rated spa and a
gourmet center.

São Paulo State

**GUARUJÁ: Casa Grande Hotel
Resort & Spa** $$$
Resort
Av Miguel Stefano 1100
Tel (13) 3389 4000
w casagrandehotel.com.br
This comfortable, colonial-style
resort set in large grounds and
situated directly on one of the
beaches closest to São Paulo has
five restaurants and four bars.
Wonderful for children.

**GUARUJÁ: Sofitel Jequitimar
Guarujá** $$$
Resort
Av Marjori da Silva Prado 1100
Tel (13) 2104 2000
w accorhotels.com
In a lovely spot, this exceptional
Sofitel is also a well-regarded spa,
resort, and convention center. The
hotel's outstanding restaurant
serves up amazing seafood while
offering views of the ocean.

DK Choice

**ILHABELA: DPNY Beach
Hotel** $$
Boutique
*Av José Pacheco do
Nascimento 7668*
Tel (12) 3894 3000
w dpnybeach.com.br
One of Brazil's trendiest and
most fashionable beach hotels,
DPNY is popular with some of
São Paulo's most demanding
jet-setters looking to relax in
style. It has three charming
restaurants, a huge outdoor
pool in a great beach setting,
and a popular spa. Day
passports are offered for those
not staying at the hotel or for
those arriving by boat.

ILHABELA: Maison Joly $$
Pousada
Rua Antônio Lisboa Alves 278
Tel (12) 3896 2364
w maisonjoly.com.br
Situated close to the historic
center of the island's main town,
this charming *pousada* offers
amazing ocean views from
public areas and rooms.

MARESIAS: Maresias Beach $$
Pousada
Rua Francisco Loup 1109
Tel (12) 3891 7500
w maresiasbeachhotel.com.br
The great beach location, pool,
and grounds make up for the
average standard of the rooms at
this *pousada*. Good for families.

SANTOS: Mendes Plaza $
Business
Av Floriano Peixoto 42
Tel (13) 3208 6400
w mendeshoteis.com.br
This friendly, comfortable hotel is
conveniently located for the
beach and some of the city's
shopping malls.

UBATUBA: Picinguaba $$
Pousada
Rua G 130, Vila Picinguaba
Tel (11) 2495 1586
w picinguaba.com
In an exceptional coastal setting,
this charming *pousada* is an oasis
of understated style and comfort
and within easy reach of Paraty.

Bahia

**COSTA DA SAUIPE: Costa do
Sauipe Golf & Spa** $$
Resort
Rodovia BA 099, Km 76, s/n
Tel (71) 2104 7020
w costadosauipe.com.br
Accommodations range from
luxury to simple *pousadas* at this
massive resort with several
properties set on a beach close
to a rainforest and dunes.

**ILHEUS: Transamérica Ilha de
Comandatuba** $$$
Resort
Estrada P/Canavieiras, Km 77, Una
Tel (73) 3686 1122
w transamerica.com.br
Since opening in 1989, this place,
located one hour from Ilheus on
Ilha de Comandatuba, has been
regarded as one of Brazil's best
and most consistent resort
properties. It is great for families.
There is an excellent golf course.

ITACARÉ: Itacaré Eco Resort $$$
Resort
*Rodovia Ilhéus, Km 65, Condomínio
Vila São José*
Tel (73) 3251 3133
w ier.com.br
This eco resort is located in an
old coffee plantation. You can
stay in the main hotel or chalets
in the rainforest. Lovely beach.

ITACARÉ: Txai $$$
Boutique
BA-001, Itacaré
Tel (73) 2101 5000
w txairesorts.com.br
One of Brazil's most fashionable
and in-demand boutique hotels
offers bungalow accommodations
with understated luxury in a
wonderful setting. There is a
good spa and restaurant.

LENÇOIS: Canto das Aguas $$
Pousada
Av Senhor dos Passos 01
Tel (75) 3334 1154
w lencois.com.br
The best hotel in Lençois from
which to explore the town and
national park offers lovely
grounds and views, as well as
a superb restaurant.

MORRO DE SÃO PAULO:
Vila dos Orixas $$
Boutique
Praia do Encanto s/n
Tel (75) 3652 2055
🌐 hotelviladosorixas.com
This intimate haven on a quiet
beach is one of the most stylish
options in Morro de São Paulo. It
has pretty rooms and bungalows.

PRAIA DO FORTE: Iberostar
Bahia & Praia do Forte $$$
Resort
*Rodovia BA 099, Km 56, Praia do
Forte, 48280 000*
Tel (71) 3676 4300
🌐 iberostar.com.br
Two neighboring resort
properties have over 1,000 rooms
between them and the necessary
infrastructure to handle that
number of guests. Great choice
for families. Closed Jun 7–Jul 1.

PRAIA DO FORTE: Tivoli
Ecoresort $$$
Resort
Av do Farol
Tel (71) 3676 4000
🌐 tivolihotels.com
In a pleasant setting, this family-
friendly eco resort has spacious
rooms – all with a balcony with
sea views. There are aso some
lovely restaurants.

SALVADOR: F Design Hostel $
Hostel
Travessa Prudente de Moraes 65
Tel (71) 3035 9700
🌐 fdesignsalvador.com.br
Facilities at this trendy hostel
include a small pool, restaurant,
and bar. It has private rooms and
small dorms.

SALVADOR: Casa Amarelindo $$
Historical
Rua das Portas do Carmo 6
Tel (71) 3266 8550
🌐 casadoamarelindo.com
Attractive and popular *pousada*
in a 19th-century house in the
historic Pelourinho area. There is
a pool, a restaurant, two bars, and
a roof terrace with lovely views.

DK Choice

SALVADOR: Convento do
Carmo $$
Historic
Rua do Carmo 1
Tel (71) 3327 8400
🌐 pestana.com
Set in a convent building dating
from 1586 in the historic heart
of the city, this small hotel is
elegant and refined and has
a lovely pool area and
courtyard. Good service.

SALVADOR: Sheraton da
Bahia $$
Business
Av 7 de Setembro 1537
Tel (71) 3021 6700
🌐 sheratondabahia.com
Located close to Castro Alves
square and theater, this property
offers minimalist rooms with
warm decor, two outdoor
pools, a spa, a poolside bar,
and a good breakfast.

SALVADOR: Solar dos
Deuses – Suites de Charme $$
Boutique
Largo do Cruzeiro do São Francisco 12
Tel (71) 3322 1911
🌐 solardosdeuses.com.br
In a 17th-century building, this
enchanting hotel located in the
historic heart of Salvador has just
six individually themed suites
based on the Candomblé gods.
Closed in June.

SALVADOR: Zank by Toque $$
Boutique
Rua Almirante Barroso 161
Tel (71) 3083 4000
🌐 zankhotel.com.br
This stylish and good-value
hotel is located out of the city
center in Rio Vermelho, close
to Farol da Barra. All rooms
have sea views.

SALVADOR: Villa Bahia $$$
Historical
Largo do Cruzeiro do São Francisco 16
Tel (71) 3322 4271
🌐 lavillabahia.com
Set in the Pelourinho area in
two magnificent colonial
mansions, the rooms here have
been renovated but preserve
their original character. There are
two garden courtyards and a
panoramic terrace.

TRANCOSO: Etnia Pousada $$$
Pousada
Trancoso
Tel (73) 3668 1137
🌐 etniabrasil.com.br
This stylish and fashionable
pousada offers eight themed
rustic-chic bungalows tucked
away in the woodland greenery.
Closed in June.

TRANCOSO:
Uxua Casa Hotel $$$
Boutique
Trancoso
Tel (73) 3668 2277
🌐 uxua.com
Located in a tropical garden off
the main square, this has become
one of the places to see and be
seen in Trancoso. The ten rustic-
style houses include four
fishermen's cottages.

TRANCOSO: Villas de
Trancoso $$$
Pousada
Trancoso
Tel (73) 3668 1151
🌐 villasdetrancoso.com
In a lovely setting, this luxury
beachfront *pousada* is great for
a romantic hideaway or for
families. This is one of the best
places for a special Brazilian and
Bahian experience.

Sergipe, Alagoas & Pernambuco

Sergipe

ARACAJU: Radisson Aracaju $$
Business
Rua Dr. Bezerra De Menezes, Atalia 40
Tel (79) 3711 3300
🌐 atlanticahotels.com.br
This modern, comfortable
Radisson hotel off Atalaia beach
is close to the beachfront, bars,
and restaurants.

Alagoas

MACEIÓ: Jatiúca $$
Resort
*Dr. Mario Nunes Vieira 220,
Mangabeiras*
Tel (82) 2122 2000
🌐 hoteljatiuca.com.br
Well located in front of Jatiúca
Beach, this urban resort property
is good for families.

MACEIÓ: Radisson Maceió $$
Business
Av Doutor Antônio Gouveia 925
Tel (82) 3202 4900
🌐 atlanticahotels.com.br
Good-sized rooms are offered at
this hotel, close to the town's best
urban beach and other attractions.

Tasty breakfast options at Solar dos
Deuses – Suites de Charme, Salvador

For more information on types of hotels *see pages 366–9*

Pernambuco

DK Choice

FERNANDO DE NORONHA: Maravilha **$$$**
Pousada
BR-363 s/n, Vila do Vai quem Sabe
Tel (81) 3325 5302
W pousadamaravilha.com.br
One of the more luxurious *pousadas* on the island. The rooms have spectacular sea views, and there is a gorgeous pool area and a spa. Choose between romantic bungalows or more family-friendly rooms. Tours of the island, by land and sea, are organized, plus diving and fishing. Lovely restaurant.

FERNANDO DE NORONHA: Solar dos Ventos **$$$**
Pousada
Rod BR-363, Vila Do Sueste
Tel (81) 3619 1347
W pousadasolardosventos.com.br
This place has a stunning setting and is a perfect base for exploring the island. Rooms are set in bungalows and have their own verandas with astonishing views. Close to the beach. No pool.

FERNANDO DE NORONHA: Vale **$$$**
Pousada
Rua Pescador Sérgio Lino 18
Tel (81) 3619 1293
W pousadadovale.com
One of the nicest places to stay on the island, this comfortable *pousada* is located in Jardim Elizabeth. It is just a short walk to the sea, bars, and restaurants.

OLINDA: Quatro Cantos **$**
Pousada
Rua Prudente de Moraes Carmo 441
Tel (81) 3429 0220
W pousada4cantos.com.br
A popular and charming *pousada* in the heart of Olinda, Quatro Cantos is set on the carnival route in an old family home.

DK Choice

OLINDA: Amparo **$$**
Pousada
Rua do Amparo 199
Tel (81) 3439 1749
W pousadadoamparo.com.br
The best known of the *pousadas* located in the historic center of Olinda. Charming and quirky, with a great colonial atmosphere, Amparo is a good base for visiting and exploring both Olinda and Recife. It also has a very good restaurant.

A king-size bed in one of the bungalows at Solar dos Ventos, Fernando de Noronha

OLINDA: Sete Colinas **$$**
Historical
Rua São Francisco 307
Tel (81) 3493 7766
W hotel7colinas.com.br
With more facilities and larger grounds than the *pousadas*, this small hotel's beautiful gardens have tropical vegetation and a pool. The setting is simple and tranquil. Good choice for families.

PORTO DE GALINHAS: Tabajuba **$**
Pousada
Lot. Merepe II, Quadra I, Lotes 5/6
Tel (81) 3552 1651
W tabajuba.com
A gorgeous, beachfront *pousada*, this charming and intimate place is within walking distance of the village. It has an outdoor pool and a good restaurants. No children under 12 are allowed.

PORTO DE GALINHAS: Armação **$$**
Resort
Lot. Merepe II, Quadra G1, Lote 1A
Tel (81) 2126 2160
W hotelarmacao.com.br
This unpretentious, good-value property is on one of the best stretches of beach in Brazil. It offers simple, tasteful rooms and a beachfront pool area. There is easy access to the village just a little over 1 mile (2 km) away.

PORTO DE GALINHAS: Nannai Beach **$$$**
Resort
Praia de Muro Alto
Tel (81) 3552 0101
W nannai.com.br
At this stylishly decorated resort property with Polynesian influences the bungalows have their own dip pools. Good spa.

RECIFE: Atlante Plaza **$**
Business
Av Boa Viagem 5426, Boa Viagem
Tel (81) 3302 3333
W atlanteplaza.com.br
One of the most popular high-rise beach hotels on Boa Viagem, Atlante Plaza has comfortable, large rooms, a rooftop pool, and lovely views.

RECIFE: Courtyard Recife Boa Viagem **$**
Business
Av Eng Domingos Ferreira 4661
Tel (81) 3256 7700
W marriott.com
With well-equipped rooms, this modern hotel near the beach is part of the Marriott chain. It has an outdoor pool.

RECIFE: Beach Class Suites **$$**
Business
Av Boa Viagem 1906, Boa Viagem
Tel (81) 2121 2626
W beachclasssuites.com
All rooms have sea views at this excellent beachfront hotel, centrally located on Boa Viagem. Good amenities.

Paraíba, Rio Grande do Norte & Ceará

Paraíba

JOÃO PESSOA: Verdegreen **$**
Business
Av João Maurício, Manaíra 255
Tel (83) 3044 0000
W verdegreen.com.br
There are not a great deal of accommodation options in João Pessoa, but this beachfront hotel will tick most boxes. It has clean, modern rooms.

Rio Grande do Norte

NATAL: Manary Praia Hotel **$$**
Boutique
Rua Francisco Gurgel 9067
Tel (84) 3204 2900
W manary.com.br
A gorgeous and charming hotel on Ponte Negra, Manary Praia consistently delivers high standards and comfort. It has a wonderful restaurant.

NATAL: Serhs Natal Grand **$$**
Resort
Av Senador Dinarte Medeiros Mariz 6045
Tel (84) 4005 2000
W serhsnatalgrandhotel.com
This large, sophisticated beachfront resort has good restaurants, a lovely beach, and sea views.

For key to prices *see page 370*

PRAIA DE PIPA: Sombra e Água Fresca $$
Resort
Rua Praia do Amor 1000
Tel (84) 3246 2376
W sombraeaguafresca.com.br
This property is divided into a resort, hotel, and spa and is 165 yards (150 m) from Praia do Amor. The decor has an Asian vibe. Popular with couples.

PRAIA DE PIPA: Toca da Coruja $$
Pousada
Av Baia dos Golfinhos
Tel (84) 3246 2226
W tocadacoruja.com.br
In a wonderful garden setting close to the centre of Pipa, this place has a perfect mix of rustic charm and understated luxury. There is a free transfer to the beach, where the hotel has its own excellent bar/restaurant.

TIBAU DO SUL: Ponta do Madeiro $$
Pousada
Av Antônio Florêncio 2695
Tel (84) 3246 4220
W pontadomadeiro.com.br
The ocean views are breathtaking from this *pousada's* clifftop location. Take the staircase (over 200 steps) down to the beach, where the hotel has its own beach bar and facilities. Transfers to Pipa.

Ceará

CANOA QUEBRADA: Azul Marinho $
Pousada
Rua Leandro Bezerra s/n
Tel (88) 3421 7003
W azul-marinho.com
This charming clifftop *pousada* is one of the town's best, with great ocean and beach views. Closed in May.

CANOA QUEBRADA: Long Beach $
Boutique
Rua Quatro Ventos
Tel (88) 3421 7404
W longbeachcanoa.com
Gorgeous, unpretentious hotel with rustic charm. The pool area has sea views. It is a short walk to the beach and 15 minutes to the town center. Good for families.

FORTALEZA: Ibis Fortaleza $
Business
Rua Doutor Atualpa Barbosa Lima 660
Tel (85) 3052 2450
W ibis.com
A short walk from the main beach area of Iracema, this modern hotel has a small pool and sun deck.

FORTALEZA: Luzeiros $
Boutique
Av Beira Mar 2600
Tel (85) 4006 8585
W luzeirosfortaleza.com.br
On the Meireles beachfront, this impressive hotel is close to many amenities and attractions. Most rooms have verandas.

FORTALEZA: Gran Marquise $$
Business
Av Beira Mar 3980, Meirelles
Tel (85) 4006 5000
W granmarquise.com.br
This standard beachfront hotel with good facilities is suitable for both business and leisure trips. Try to book an oceanfront room.

JERICOACOARA: Recanto do Barão $
Pousada
Rua do Forró 433
Tel (85) 9989 2469
W recantodobarao.com
A typical example of the charming *pousadas* that make up the bulk of the accommodation options at Jericoacoara.

DK Choice

JERICOACOARA: My Blue Hotel $$
Boutique
Rua Ismael s/n
Tel (88) 3669 2203
W mybluehotel.net
On the beachfront, with two pool areas, My Blue Hotel has set the standard for other hotels in Jericoacoara. The colorful rooms and suites are stylish and sophisticated and have sea, pool, or garden views. Some also have a terrace. There is a spa, a gym, a restaurant, and a wine bar directly on the beach with panoramic views.

Piauí & Maranhão

Piauí

BARREIRINHAS: Encantes do Nordeste $$
Pousada
Rua Boa Vista s/n
Tel (98) 3349 0288
W encantesdonordeste.com.br
This simple *pousada* located by a river a couple of miles from Barreirinhas town is a good base from which to visit the Lençois park and dunes. It offers organized tours and activities.

TERESINA: Metropolitan $$
Business
Av Frei Serafim 1696
Tel (86) 3216 8000
W metropolitanhotel.com.br
Teresina does not have many hotels, but the centrally located Metropolitan has consistently been the best on offer.

Maranhão

SÃO LUIS: Luzeiros $
Business
Rua João Pereira Damasceno 02
Tel (98) 3311 4949
W luzeirossaoluis.com.br
In a lovely setting on the beachfront at Ponta do Farol, this modern design hotel offers large, airy rooms all with sea views.

SÃO LUIS: Pestana São Luis $
Business
Av Avicênia 1, Praia do Calhau
Tel (98) 2106 0505
W pestana.com
Well located for both business and leisure, this hotel is within walking distance of Calhau Beach and a short cab ride to the historic center. It has an excellent pool area.

The beautifully kept, tranquil gardens at Toca da Coruja, Praia de Pipa

For more information on types of hotels *see pages 366–9*

Pará & Amapá

Pará

BELEM: Grand Mercure $$
Business
Av Nazaré 375
Tel (91) 3202 2000
Ⓦ grandmercure.com.br
Consistently one of Belém's best, this hotel is close to tourist attractions, restaurants, bars, and the financial district, making it great for both business and sightseeing.

BELEM: Radisson Belem $$
Business
Av Comandante Bras do Aguir 321
Tel (91) 3205 1399
Ⓦ atlanticahotels.com.br
This central Radisson property delivers the standards expected of the brand. It has comfortable and functional rooms, great for business and leisure travelers.

ILHA DE MARAJO: Fazenda Sanjo $
Fazenda
Margens do Igarapé São Sebastião
Tel (91) 3228 1385
Ⓦ sanjo.tur.br
There are limited accommodation options on Ilha de Marajo, but this lodge is the best base for exploring, since it is located in the heart of the island. It offers one-, two-, and three-night stays.

SANTAREM: Barrudada Tropical Hotel $
Business
Av Mendonça Furtado 4120
Tel (93) 3222 2200
Ⓦ barrudadatropicalhotel.com.br
This is probably the best hotel in Santarem, and offers three different kinds of rooms with modern decor, two outdoor pools, and a terrace bar.

The comfort of Amazon Ecopark, perfectly located for Manaus

For key to prices *see page 370*

Amapá

MACAPÁ: Ekinox $
Pousada
Rua Jovino Dinoá 1693
Tel (96) 3223 0086
Ⓦ ekinoxpousada.yahoostore.com
This friendly, well-located little *pousada* is ideal if you want to avoid staying in the mediocre hotels on offer in Macapá.

MACAPÁ: Ibis Macapá Hotel $
Business
Rua Tiradentes Centro 303
Tel (96) 2101 9050
Ⓦ accorhotels.com
Comfortable, modern, and well-located, this Ibis hotel is simple but does the job.

Amazonas, Roraima, Acre & Rondônia

Amazonas

MANAUS: Caesar Business $
Business
Av Darcy Vargas 654, Bairro do Chapada
Tel (92) 3306 4700
Ⓦ accorhotels.com
Run by Accor, this good-quality, attractive hotel is close to the huge Amazonas Shopping Center and convention center.

MANAUS: Holiday Inn Manaus $
Business
Av General Rodrigo Otávio 3775
Tel (92) 3182 0100
Ⓦ holidayinn.com
Although basic, this modern and comfortable Holiday Inn hotel offers a good base from which to explore Manaus and the region.

MANAUS: Amazon Ecopark $$
Rainforest Lodge
Tel (92) 9146 0594; (21) 3005 5536
Ⓦ amazonecopark.com.br
The pleasant, comfortable Amazon Ecopark is in a lovely river setting and is one of the closest to Manaus.

DK Choice

MANAUS: Tropical $$
Historical/Resort
Av Coronel Teixeira 1320, Praia da Ponta Negra
Tel (92) 2123 5000
Ⓦ tropicalmanaus.com.br
Almost an attraction in its own right, this luxurious ecoresort in a secluded riverside location has been a popular choice for decades. The large, colonial-style resort is an excellent base from which to head into the Amazon.

MANAUS: Amazon Jungle Palace $$$
Rainforest Lodge
Tel (92) 3211 3955
Ⓦ amazonjunglepalace.com.br
An unusual option, this modern floating lodge is an easy, comfortable, slightly sanitized way to be introduced to the rainforest. There are panoramic river views from all the rooms.

MANAUS: Anavilhanas $$$
Rainforest Lodge
Tel (92) 3622 8996
Ⓦ anavilhanaslodge.com
This family-friendly lodge is one of the region's best. There is a viewing platform to see across the rainforest. Stay in beautiful wooden bungalows or chalets.

MANAUS: Dolphin Lodge $$$
Rainforest Lodge
Tel (92) 3663 0392
Ⓦ dolphinlodge.tur.br
This rustic lodge located 78 miles (126 km) southeast of Manaus is popular with international tour operators. Transfer is by van and boats, which is an adventure in itself. Rooms are wooden buildings with thatched roofs.

DK Choice

MANAUS: Juma Lodge $$$
Rainforest Lodge
Tel (92) 3232 2707
Ⓦ jumalodge.com
A popular lodge for travelers looking to immerse and integrate themselves in the full Amazon experience. The lovely rooms are on stilts. Tasty food is on offer in the restaurant, and there are lots of organized activities. It is three hours from Manaus by boat, or 30 minutes by hydroplane, but the transfer is part of the adventure.

MANAUS: Uakari Lodge $$$
Rainforest Lodge
Tel (97) 3343 4160
Ⓦ uakarilodge.com.br
Set in pristine jungle surroundings, this well-regarded floating lodge can host just 24 guests at any one time. Special packages are also offered.

Roraima

BOA VISTA: Aipana Plaza $
Business
Praça Centro Cívico 974
Tel (95) 3212 0800
Ⓦ aipanaplaza.com.br
If you need a place to stay in Boa Vista, you cannot go far wrong with the Aipana Plaza, in a good

Cristalino Jungle Lodge, one of the best ecolodges in the world, Alta Floresta

downtown central location with cozy rooms and all the necessary facilities and perks.

Acre

RIO BRANCO (ACRE): Holiday inn Express Rio Branco $
Business
Rua Rio Grande do Sul 332
Tel (68) 3302 2300
W hiexpress.com
This centrally located Holiday Inn Express has a rooftop pool and fitness center.

Rondônia

PORTO VELHO: Oscar Hotel Executive $
Business
Av 7 de Setembro, 934
Tel (69) 2182 0600
W oscarhotelexecutive.com.br
This hotel is located in the city center and is close to restaurants and bars. There's a small rooftop pool and bar with city views.

Brasília, Goiás & Tocantins

Brasília

BRASÍLIA: Kubitschek Plaza $
Business
HN Quadra 2, Bloco E, Asa Norte
Tel (61) 3319 3543
W kubitschek.com.br
Reliable, centrally situated hotel that is popular for events and small conferences.

BRASÍLIA: Quality Hotel $
Business
SMAS Trecho 3, Conjunto 2, Bloco A
Tel (61) 2196 6090
W atlanticahotels.com.br
This popular, modern, low-rise hotel is situated about 15 minutes' drive from the city center. It offers

good-value spacious, comfortable rooms, a pool, and a large outdoor area.

BRASÍLIA: Meliá Brasíl 21 $$
Business
Setor Hoteleiro Sul, Quadra 6 Bloco D
Tel (61) 3218 4700
W solmelia.com
This towering hotel, located in the heart of the city, is close to the TV Tower and National Stadium. It offers a "Women Traveling Alone" program. Rooms and suites are elegant and have ample facilities.

DK Choice

BRASÍLIA: Royal Tulip Brasília $$
Business
Setor Hoteleiro Norte, Trecho 01, Conjunto 1B, Bloco C
Tel (61) 3424 7000
W royaltulipbrasiliaalvorada.com
In a city full of fairly nondescript hotels, the stylish Royal Tulip is more of a resort property than just a business hotel. Situated on the edge of Lake Paranoá close to the residence of the Brazilian president, the hotel's front rooms have lake views and there is an excellent large pool area. The city center is a ten-minute taxi ride.

Goiás

CHAPADA DOS VEADEIROS: Casa Rosa $
Pousada
Rua Gumercindo Barbosa 233
Tel (62) 3446 1319
W pousadacasarosa.com.br
With a pleasant garden and pool, this simple *pousada* is close to the entrance to the national park and is ideal for those who appreciate nature. Accommodation is in the main house and a number of chalets.

Mato Grosso & Mato Grosso do Sul

Mato Grosso

DK Choice

ALTA FLORESTA: Cristalino Jungle Lodge $$$
Rainforest Lodge
Av Teles Pires 2001
Tel (66) 3521 1396
W cristalinolodge.com.br
This highly regarded establishment is considered one of the world's best ecolodges. Located within a private forest reserve, it has 16 stylish and comfortable guest quarters offering every convenience. There's a floating deck, a restaurant with views, and two 165-ft (50-m) observation towers to look over the canopy of trees. It offers a full program of activities.

CUIABÁ: Deville Cuíabá $$
Business
Av Isaac Póvoas 1000
Tel (63) 3319 3000
W deville.com.br
Situated in the city center, this modern hotel is close to bars, restaurants, and nightlife. It is a good base for heading in and out of the Pantanal.

CUIABÁ: Gran Odara Hotel $$
Business
Av Miguel Sutil 8344, Ribeirão da Ponte
Tel (65) 3616 2014
W en.hotelgranodara.com.br/hotel
This comfortable, well-run hotel is ideal when having to stay overnight in Cuiabá before or after transfers to and from the Pantanal.

POCONÉ: Araras Lodge $$$
Rainforest Lodge
Est Parque Transpantaneira Zona Rural
Tel (65) 3682 2800
W araraslodge.com.br
This ecolodge is particularly popular with birders but offers a full range of Pantanal activities for which it is well sited and equipped.

Mato Grosso do Sul

BONITO: Zagaia Eco-Resort $$
Resort
Rod Bonito–Três Morros, Km 0
Tel (0800) 979 4400
W zagaia.com.br
Close to Bontio, this family-friendly ecolodge is a good base from which to explore the surrounding area and the crystal-clear waters.

For more information on types of hotels *see pages 366–9*

The lush greenery of the grounds at Meia Lua, which also has a pool for guests

CAMPO GRANDE: Grand Park Hotel $$
Business
Av Afonso Pena 5282
Tel (67) 3044 4444
W grandparkhotel.com.br
The modern, centrally located Grand Park Hotel is close to bars and restaurants and in front of the city's main shopping center. It is a good choice if staying overnight before or after a visit to a Pantanal lodge.

CAMPO GRANDE: Jandaia $$
Business
Rua Barão do Rio Branco 1271
Tel (67) 3316 7700
W jandaia.com.br
Slightly dated, this is still a good hotel option for overnight stays before or after visiting the Pantanal. It is also conveniently located for the airport.

MIRANDA: Meia Lua $
Rainforest Lodge
BR 262, Km 547, Zona Rural
Tel (67) 9686 9064
W pantanalranchmeialua.com
This ranch set in lovely grounds a few miles outside of Miranda makes a simple, unfussy base from which to explore parts of the Pantanal. It offers organized activities such as fishing and horseback riding.

MIRANDA: Refúgio Ecológico Caiman $$$
Rainforest Lodge
Estância Caiman s/n, Zona Rural
Tel (67) 3242 1450
W caiman.com.br
One of the best-equipped Pantanal lodges, in the heart of the region, this comprises two comfortable pousadas and private villas and is still a working farm. Rates include guided tours and transfers.

Santa Catarina & Paraná

Santa Catarina

FLORIANÓPOLIS: Blue Tree Towers Florianópolis $$
Business
Rua Bocaiuva 2304
Tel (48) 3251 5555
W bluetree.com.br
Better for business than leisure, as it is away from the island's main beaches, this modern, centrally situated hotel is close to restaurants, bars, and a shopping center.

FLORIANÓPOLIS: Quinta do Bucanero $$
Resort
Estrada Geral do Rosa s/n
Tel (48) 3355 6056
W bucanero.com.br
An oasis of calm at the end of a dirt track, this charming, romantic pousada, located about 53 miles (85 km) south of Florianópolis, is in a glorious setting overlooking Praia do Rosa. No children under 14.

FLORIANÓPOLIS: Vila Tamarindo $$
Business
Av Campeche 1836
Tel (48) 3237 3464
W tamarindo.com.br
This popular pousada on Praia do Campeche is a 10-minute stroll from the activities at Riozinho. It has lovely grounds.

FLORIANÓPOLIS: Costão do Santinho Resort Golf & Spa $$$
Resort
Rodovia Vereador Onildo Lemos 2505
Tel (48) 3261 1000, 0800 645 0928
W costao.com.br
Rooms vary at this large resort; some are more modern than others. There is a golf course.

DK Choice

FLORIANÓPOLIS: Ponta dos Ganchos $$$
Resort
Rua Eupídeo Alves do Nascimento 104
Tel (48) 3262 5000
W pontadosganchos.com.br
This stylish, romantic boutique resort is one of the best in Brazil, and truly world-class. In a stunning beachfront setting on a private peninsula north of Florianópolis, it has breathtaking views. Stay in deluxe bungalows. No children under 18. Book well in advance.

FLORIANÓPOLIS: Quinta das Videiras $$$
Boutique
Rua Afonso Luiz Borba 113
Tel (48) 3232 3005
W quintadasvideiras.com
This elegant 19th-century Portuguese style residence is very exclusive, with only 11 suites. Period furnishings are combined with modern amenities. It is close to Lagoa's bars and restaurants.

Paraná

CURITIBA: Four Points by Sheraton $$
Business
Av Sete de Setembro 4211
Tel (41) 3340 4000
W starwoodhotels.com
Good standard Four Point hotel that is located in the Batel residential area, close to restaurants, bars, malls, and the historic center. There is a floor exclusively for women.

CURITIBA: Mercure Curitiba Golden $$
Business
Rua Desembargador Motta 2044
Tel (41) 3322 7666
W mercure.com
This well-located hotel in the Batel area offers all the facilities you expect from the Mercure group.

CURITIBA: Slaviero Conceptual Full Jazz Hotel $$
Business
Rua Silveira Peixoto 1297
Tel (41) 3312 7000
W slavierohoteis.com.br
With jazz as its theme, this Slaviero property makes a welcome change from the town's more standard business hotels. Large rooms with city views. Live jazz twice a week in the bar.

FOZ DO IGUAÇU: Che Lagarto $
Hostel
Av Juscelino Kubitschek 874
Tel (45) 3027 8300
W chelagarto.com
Centrally located in Foz and close to public transport, this popular hostel offers dorms or private rooms. It has a nice roof terrace with a pool, a Jacuzzi, a bar, and beautiful sunset views.

FOZ DO IGUAÇU: Nadai Confort Hotel & Spa $
Business
Av República Argentina 1332
Tel (45) 3521 5050
W nadaiconforthotel.com.br
Centrally located and very well appointed, Nadai offers modern accomodations in a pleasant and comfortable ambience.

FOZ DO IGUAÇU: Bourbon Resort

Resort **$$**

Rodovia das Cataratas, Km 2
Tel (45) 3521 3900
W bourbon.com.br

This large, self-contained resort is frequented by both Brazilian and foreign visitors. It is located between the town and the falls and is good for families.

DK Choice

FOZ DO IGUAÇU: Hotel das Cataratas Belmond $$$

Historical / Resort

Iguaçu National Park
Tel (45) 2102 7000, (21) 2545 8878
W belmond.com/
hoteldascataratas

This grand hotel is the place to stay when visiting the falls, as it is the only property located in the park itself. Standards are everything you would expect from Belmond: lovely rooms, pool area, and so on. The park closes at night, so early in the morning and during the night, guests have the Brazilian side of the falls to themselves, which is worth paying a bit more for.

MORRETES: Santuário Nhundiaquara $$

Lodge

*Est das Prainhas, Km 02,
Porto de Cima*
Tel (41) 9972 5543, (41) 3462 1938
W nhundiaquara.com.br

This is a good base when exploring Morretes and the Serra do Mar and provides rustic charm at a reasonable price.

PARANAGUÁ: San Rafael $$

Business

Rua Julia da Costa 185
Tel (41) 3721 9000
W sanrafaelhotel.com.br

There is not a lot of choice if you need to stay in Paranaguá, but San Rafael is well located and comfortable, if unremarkable.

Rio Grande do Sul

BENTO GONÇALVES: Don Giovanni $$

Pousada

Linha Amadeu 28, Km 12
Tel (54) 3455 6293
W dongiovanni.com.br

This 20th-century Italian-style farmhouse surrounded by the Don Giovanni vineyards is 8 miles (12 km) outside of Bento Gonçalves. It combines rustic charm with contemporary style.

BENTO GONÇALVES: Pousada Casa Valduga $$

Pousada

*Via Trento 2355, Linha Leopoldina,
Vale dos Vinhedos*
Tel (54) 2105 3154
W villavalduga.com.br

Five charming, modern *pousadas* are offered at the Villa Valduga winery, close to Bento Gonçalves. Breakfast and a wine course and tasting are included. No children under eight.

CANELA: Cravo & Canela $$

Pousada

Rua Ten Manoel Correa 144
Tel (54) 3282 1120
W pousadacravoecanela.com.br

Ideal for exploring Canela, this delightful little *pousada* has lovely rooms and grounds. It is close to the town center in a quiet residential road.

GRAMADO: Saint Andrews $$$

Boutique

Rua das Flores 171
Tel (54) 3295 7700
W saintandrews.com.br

This elegant, well-kept intimate hotel has lovely mountain views. The restaurant is excellent and the service impeccable.

GRAMADO: St Hubertus $$$

Boutique

Rua da Carrieri 974
Tel (54) 3286 1273
W sthubertus.com

Set in lovely grounds 1 mile (2 km) from the city center, this welcoming, romantic hotel overlooks Lago Negro. It is a good base for exploring Gramado and the surrounding countryside.

PORTO ALEGRE: Solar 63 $

Hostel

Rua Octávio Corrêa 63
Tel (51) 3092 0063
W solar63hostel.com.br

Close to the historic center, bars, and restaurants, this clean, friendly hostel has five small dorms and one double room.

PORTO ALEGRE: Laghetto Viverone Moinhos $$

Business

Rua Doutor Vale 579
Tel (51) 2102 7272
W laghettohoteis.com.br

The reception area here is in a restored historic building at the front of the modern hotel. The hotel is centrally located and close to restaurants and bars.

PORTO ALEGRE: Sheraton Porto Alegre $$

Business

Rua Olavo Barreto Viana 18
Tel (51) 2121 6000
W sheraton-poa.com.br

This smart hotel is in a central location, next to the elegant Moinhos Shopping Mall. It has spacious rooms and offers everything you would expect of a Sheraton.

SÃO MIGUEL DAS MISSÕES: Pousada das Missões $

Pousada

Rua São Nicolau 601
Tel (55) 3381 1202
W pousadadasmissoes.com.br

With private rooms and dorms, this simple, well-located property near the Jesuit ruins is a good choice when visiting the missions. It has lovely grounds and a pool.

A choice of pools at the popular, large Bourbon Resort, Foz do Iguaçu

For more information on types of hotels *see pages 366–9*

WHERE TO EAT & DRINK

As a melting pot of races and influences, Brazil has a rich diversity of regional culinary styles *(see pp182–3 and pp384–5)*.

Although the term "haute cuisine" does not strictly apply to Brazilian fare, the art of eating well, or *arte do comer bem*, is known to all Brazilians. A light breakfast, a hearty lunch that can last from noon to 3pm, and a late afternoon snack are followed by an even later dinner that may go on beyond midnight. Saturday and Sunday lunches are an elaborate, extended family affair,

possibly a *feijoada* (meat and bean stew). Everywhere in Brazil it is easy to get well-cooked, filling meals. For light snacks, there are umpteen *lanchonetes*, or corner snack bars. For lunch, a *botequim*, or simple gastro pub, can be fun, while dining at a formal *rodízio* all-you-can-eat barbecue is a must. Famous for offering the widest varieties of cuisine, São Paulo is seen as the best place for an authentic culinary experience. A wide variety of places to eat are listed on pages 386–97. Prices are quoted in US dollars.

Restaurants & Bars

In Brazil, restaurants and bars come in every shape and size. From the corner *botecos* (pubs) and beach bars to elegant world-class restaurants, Brazil has it all. Even dining in top-notch restaurants, especially away from Rio de Janeiro and São Paulo, offers value for money in comparison to anywhere in Europe or North America.

Most Brazilian restaurants have a website, so check the photos to get a clearer idea of whether or not a place is to your taste.

Local Eating Habits

Visitors will recognize that many Brazilian eating habits have been influenced by European countries. Eating is a leisurely affair. Those who want to snatch a quick bite will not be disappointed. Several restaurants are open all through the day, so the lunch hour is spread over many hours.

Brazilians generally eat dinner late, many of them preferring to start at 10pm or later. At the weekend, numerous restaurants in the bigger cities take orders well after midnight. It is not unusual to see Brazilians retreating to the bar if they have to wait for a table. Most restaurants take reservations, and this is often necessary at the more fashionable venues, especially those in the larger cities.

Due to the many different culinary styles, it is virtually impossible to say what a typical Brazilian meal will be, although rice and beans will probably make an appearance at some point. Many of the dishes are

specific to a region. Breakfast can be a meal in itself, and in most cases it will be a hearty spread of fruits, cold meats, cheeses, breads, and pastries. Often this is included in your hotel room rate.

Dress Code

The easygoing Brazilian nature is also reflected in the dress code. In corner bars, one can walk in wearing casual attire. In Rio and other coastal areas, it is not unusual to see women in bikinis at beach bars. Dress codes, usually more relaxed and tropical in the north, tend to become more formal in the south.

A collar and tie for men may be the norm only in restaurants in the business quarter of cities, or in Brasília, where the politicians and civil servants prefer formal dressing. It's also worth carrying an extra layer of clothing when dining at more upscale restaurants as they tend to be cold due to air-conditioning.

Paying & Tipping

The majority of restaurants take credit cards. By far the most widely accepted credit cards are MasterCard and Visa. Amex and Diners Club cards are also useful. However, it is recommended to check first, especially at the more expensive restaurants, where you might not have the cash to cover the bill. If you do get stuck in a "no credit card" situation, do remember that you can probably get cash out of the local ATM machine on your credit card.

Technically, restaurants are not meant to add a service charge to the bill; however, in many places, it will be expected as a tip for the staff. If the service charge has not been added, the waiter will normally let you know. It is ideal to leave 10 to 12 percent or, if the service charge has been included, simply round up the bill to the next suitable number. Given the average wage of the staff, tips, however small, are always welcome.

Outdoor tables at Aprazível, a fine-dining restaurant in Santa Teresa *(see p388)*

Food Hygiene

As most of Brazil is hot and tropical, every Brazilian knows the importance of keeping food fresh and well refrigerated. Food poisoning, even among visitors, is rare.

The majority of restaurants use ice cubes made from filtered water. However, in small back-street bars, it is best to avoid ice.

Alcohol & Drinks

On the whole, Brazilians are not great alcohol drinkers. Beer, however, is extremely popular. The majority of Brazilian beer is a refreshingly cold light lager that comes in bottles (*cerveja*) or on tap (*chopp*). Also common, and much stronger, is a wide variety of drinks containing *cachaça*, a sugarcane-based spirit. The most notable and well known of these is the *caipirinha* with fresh lime.

Though Scotch is regarded as a status symbol, wine is rapidly growing in popularity, but it is still expensive, particularly imported wine from beyond South America. Brazil already produces some excellent table wines, as do neighboring Argentina and Chile. Brazilians also like soft drinks, especially *guaraná*, which is as omnipresent as Coca-Cola. Most bars and restaurants will have bottled water *com* (with) and *sem* (without) gas. *Casas de sucos* (fresh-juice bars), offering juices made from a huge range of Brazil's native exotic fruits, are very popular. Some of these also serve light snacks.

Smoking

There are strict regulations about smoking in Brazil. Visitors should be aware that smoking inside enclosed public spaces, including bars and restaurants, is absolutely forbidden. It is also not permitted in the outside areas of restaurants that are partially covered.

Children

Brazil is a child-friendly country and most restaurants will welcome children. Staff will normally go out of their way to entertain them. If they don't have

Drinks kiosk on the beach in Morro de São Paulo

a suitable chair, they will almost certainly try to improvise something. It is not uncommon for young children to be eating out late with their parents.

Vegetarians

Vegetarian options are limited in Brazil. However, there are a few specialized restaurants offering vegetarian dishes, ranging from basic to highly innovative. *Por quilo* restaurants *(see below)* can be a good option, since they offer large salads and a range of vegetable-based dishes.

Churrascaria Rodízio/ Por Quilo

There are two styles of eating out in Brazil that can take visitors by surprise. The first is the *churrascaria rodízio*, or large barbecue houses, found throughout the country. Here, one fixed price covers the starter and main course. Go to a *churrascaria rodízio* when you are really hungry, as they will keep bringing you succulent pieces of grilled meat. Many offer a "traffic-light system" where each diner will have a card. Leave the green side up if you want more food; red, if not.

The *por quilo* type are self-service restaurants with a buffet of varying degrees of sophistication, common in larger towns and cities. What you pay for at the check-out, as far as the food is concerned, will be based on exactly what your plate weighs – hence the name *por quilo*, or "by-the-kilo."

Recommended Restaurants

The restaurants featured on the following pages have been carefully selected to give a cross-section of options in every region: you will find everything from the equivalent of Michelin-starred fine dining and traditional restaurants, to contemporary Brazilian, international cuisine, and bistro fare. The entries are divided into geographical areas corresponding to the chapters in this guide; the entries are then organized by town.

The fine-dining options include some of the best restaurants in Brazil, often in atmospheric and scenic locations. Given the size of the country, Brazilian cuisine varies dramatically from region to region. For example, a typical Bahian dish will be very different from that served in the rest of the Northeast or in the south. The barbecue house is probably the only constant. The international options serve mostly global favorites, while bistros generally offer a range of cuisine alongside Brazilian fare. All will reflect Brazilian influences and ingredients.

The DK Choice entries highlight exceptional establishments that offer more than just excellent food. Most of these are popular with local residents and visitors, so be sure to inquire regarding reservations in advance, or you may face a lengthy wait for a table.

Por kilo self-service buffet at the Mangai restaurant *(see p392)*

The Flavors of Brazil

Brazil offers a vast range of regional cuisines. Climate and geography influence ingredients, from the exotic tropical fruits and spices in Northern Brazil to Bahian seafood *(see p183)* and the heavy meat dishes of the southern states. Cultural heritage plays a part as well. In Amazônia, the diet is based on fruits and fish native to the forest and the rivers, with many dishes adapted from indigenous recipes. Farther south, settlement by Portuguese and, later, Italian and German immigrants put a distinctly European stamp on the cooking.

Brazilian Coffee

Freshly caught Bonito tuna on sale at a coastal fish market

Meat

Brazil is a nation that truly enjoys its meat and the wide variety of ways in which beef, chicken, and pork are prepared. The ability to devour large quantities of succulent Brazilian beef is considered a mark of manliness. The family barbecue (*churrasco*) is a Sunday tradition, but for visitors the best way to enjoy

Brazil's superb beef is at a *churrascaria rodízio* (barbecue house). Waiters bring large skewers of freshly barbecued beef and other meats, and slice off cuts directly onto the plate. You can state your preference for *mal passado* (rare), *ao ponto* (medium), or *bem passado* (well done), or you can just point to the part that looks good. Cuts include *filet mignon* (tenderloin), *fraldinha* (bottom sirloin), *picanha* (sirloin), *alcatra* (top sirloin), and *maminha* (sirloin tip). *Cupim* is the soft floppy hump on a cow's shoulders. This tender beef, mixed heavily with fat, is an acquired taste and may not necessarily be liked by all.

Fish & Seafood

Brazilians inherited a love of fish from their Portuguese

Papaya   Limes   Pineapple   Mangoes   Coconuts   Bananas
Part of Brazil's lush harvest of ripe tropical fruits

Brazilian Dishes & Specialties

Now considered Brazil's national dish, *feijoada* was not always the chic cuisine it is today. The rich black-bean stew traces its humble origins to the kitchens of the country's slave quarters. To make a meal with the leftovers from their masters' tables, the slaves improvised by combining the cast-off bits of meat into a hearty stew with black beans, flavored with garlic, onion, and bay leaves. Nowadays, a full *feijoada completa* spread is typically eaten for lunch on Saturdays, and in some places, such as São Paulo, on Wednesdays. In addition to the black beans, the stew contains several kinds of meat, including sausage, bacon, and sun-dried beef. Side dishes include rice, roasted cassava flour (*farofa*), sautéed kale, and slices of orange. A *batida de limão* (*cachaça* with ice shavings and lime) is served before the *feijoada*.

Black beans

Salgados, such as deep-fried pastries stuffed with cheese or meat, are popular Brazilian snacks.

Table laid out with all the elements that make up a *feijoada completa*

forebears. Cod, a Portuguese staple, is sold dried and heavily salted in grocery stores, while cod balls (*bolinhos de bacalhau*) or cod fillets are found on many menus. For fresher fare, Brazil's long coastline offers a bounty of excellent fish and seafood. The colder waters off Santa Catarina offer the country's best oysters. Ilhabela, off São Paulo's Costa Verde, is known for its cold-water jumbo shrimp (*camarão*). Farther north are mollusks, squid, octopus, crab, lobster, shrimp, and, of course, fish. Some of Brazil's best fish come not from the ocean but from the fresh waters of the Pantanal

The celebrated Brazilian *caipirinha*

and the Amazon rainforest. The Pantanal's prize fish is the *dourado*, a fish with firm flesh that is delicious when grilled. Other popular and tasty fish include the *pacú* and *pintado*. In the Amazon, the astounding variety of freshwater fish includes the *tambaqui, aruanã*, and *tucanaré*. They are often served grilled, or in soups with local herbs. Another Amazon freshwater favorite is *caldo de piranha* (piranha broth).

Brazilian Fruits

Along with tropical staples, there are regional fruits, most of which have no English name. In Rio and parts of Southern Brazil, one finds small, tart *jaboticaba*, and red *acerola* berries, often mixed in juices with other fruits. Farther north are vast orchards of cashew (*caju*) – not the nut, but the large fruit that grows above. In the Amazon, there are *taperaba, cupuaçu*, and the queen of Amazon berries, *açaí*. These are often puréed with *guaraná* berry powder or syrup and can be mixed with banana for a high-nutrition smoothie.

WHAT TO DRINK

Brazil's best-known drink is almost certainly the *caipirinha*, made with lime, sugar, ice, and *cachaça* (sugar-cane liquor). A better choice for quenching thirst, however, are the wide variety of tropical fruit juices. Brazil's most popular soft drink is the domestically produced *guaraná*. This fizzy drink is prepared with wild *guaraná* berries from Amazônia. Also enormously popular is *chopp*, or draft lager, served ice-cold after a hot day on the beach. *Chá mate*, herbal tea, is usually consumed hot in Southern Brazil, but in the rest of Brazil, it is served cold as iced tea. Although Brazil is very much a cold beverage country, the exception is the ubiquitous *cafézinho*, strong filter coffee, served in small cups. Most Brazilians drink it very sweet and at almost any time of the day.

Camarão na Moranga is a stew of large, juicy prawns cooked in coconut milk and served in a pumpkin.

Picanha steak is a sirloin steak and usually comes served with only a dusting of coarse salt.

Pudim de Leite, a traditional Portuguese dessert, is made from eggs, condensed milk, and caramelized sugar.

Where to Eat & Drink

Rio de Janerio City

BARRA DA TIJUCA: Fratelli $$
Italian
Av Sernambetiba 2916
Tel (21) 2494 6644
This popular eatery close to Barra beachfront opened in 1988 and serves rustic, traditional Italian, including pizza. Good wine list.

BARRA DA TIJUCA: Gero $$
Italian
Av Érico Veríssimo, 190
Tel (21) 2484 9455   **Closed** *Mon*
Part of the exclusive Fasano chain, Gero serves sophisticated cuisine in a fashionable setting. A less expensive executive menu is offered at lunch on Fridays.

BARRA DA TIJUCA: Ráscal $$
Mediterranean
Av. Ayrton Senna 2150
Tel (21) 3325 0894
Italian chef Nadia Pizzo offers a wide variety of delicious Mediterranean dishes as a buffet or à la carte at this restaurant inside the Casa Shopping mall.

DK Choice

CENTRO: Nova Capela $
Brazilian   **Map** 5 D5
Av Mem de Sá, 96
Tel (21) 2252 6228
Much loved in Rio's bohemian nightlife scene, this authentic and unpretentious institution dates back to 1903 and serves consistently good food until 3am or later. The signature dish is roast goat with broccoli rice, but other highlights include Brazilian cod balls. Expect large portions. Superb *chopp* on tap.

CENTRO: Ancoramar $$
Seafood   **Map** 5 E3
Praça Marechal Âncora, 184
Tel (21) 2240 8378   **Closed** *dinner*
Opened in1933, this traditional seafood restaurant is set in the last surviving tower of the old Municipal Market, close to Praça XV. Ask for a window seat, and enjoy views over Guanabara Bay.

CENTRO: Atrium del Rey $$
International   **Map** 5 E3
Praça XV de Novembro, 48
Tel (21) 2220 0193
Pleasant café in what was a palace for the Imperial family from 1808. This is a good choice if looking for a place for lunch during a tour of downtown.

CENTRO: Cais do Oriente $$
Brazilian   **Map** 5 E3
Rua Visconde de Itaboraí, 8 Centro
Tel (21) 2203 0178/ 2253 7855
Set in a warehouse dating from 1878, this attractive and eclectic restaurant is popular for lunch and dinner with those working downtown or visiting historic sights. The menu focuses on contemporary Brazilian dishes.

CENTRO: Confeitaria Colombo $$
International   **Map** 5 D3
Rua Goncalves Dias, 32
Tel (21) 2505 1500   **Closed** *Sun*
A tourist attraction in its own right, this place has changed little since opening in 1894. It is a coffee shop, tearoom, and restaurant. Many famous people have visited, including King Albert of Belgium and Britain's Queen Elizabeth II.

COPACABANA & LEME: Cervantes $
Botequim   **Map** 3 F1
Av Prado Junior 335
Tel (21) 2275 6147   **Closed** *Mon*
A mix of small bar, *botequim*, and restaurant. Famous for sandwiches, late-night snacks, and "one for the road" as night turns to day. Always buzzing and fun.

COPACABANA & LEME: Don Camillo $$
Italian   **Map** 3 D3
Av Atlântica, 3056
Tel (21) 2549 9958
Most of Copacabana's beachfront bars are not up to much when it comes to food. Don Camillo is one of the exceptions, serving excellent Italian cuisine. Choose to sit either on the outside terrace or inside in a more formal dining area.

COPACABANA & LEME: La Fabrique $$
French   **Map** 3 F1
Av. Atlântica 994
Tel (21) 2541 2416
Run by French and Tunisian chefs, this bistro offers traditional French cuisine with Brazilian coastal influences in a relaxed atmosphere. Try the fried mussels, a customers' favorite.

COPACABANA & LEME: Cipriani $$$
Italian   **Map** 3 E2
Av Atlântica, 1702
Tel (21) 2548 7070 **Closed** *Sun dinner*
This is an outstanding restaurant offering top northern Italian cuisine. The setting, overlooking the pool of the Copacabana

Palace, makes it even more special. Not surprisingly, it is popular with visiting celebrities.

FLAMENGO & BOTAFOGO: Esterla do Sul $$
Brazilian
Rua General Severiano 97
Tel (21) 2275 6280
This chain, also present in other neighborhoods, brings the traditional barbecue from the gauchos of Rio Grande do Sul all the way to Rio. It also offers a buffet of salads and warm dishes.

FLAMENGO & BOTAFOGO: Fogo de Chão $$
Brazilian
Av Repórter Nestor Moreira, s/n
Tel (21) 2542 1545
One of Brazil's best-known *rodízio* all-you-can-eat barbecue houses serving tender, tasty meats. Beef is the specialty, but chicken, pork, and lamb are also available. Enjoy views over Sugar Loaf Mountain and Guanabara Bay as you eat.

FLAMENGO & BOTAFOGO: Irajá $$
Brazilian
Rua Conde de Irajá 109
Tel (21) 2246 1395
This restaurant has helped build Botafogo's growing reputation as a hub for interesting, inventive,

Cais do Oriente, set in a 19th-century building, Centro

and contemporary dishes in fun surroundings. Special tasting menu of eight courses.

FLAMENGO & BOTAFOGO:
Majoríca $$
Steakhouse
Rua Senador Vergueiro, 15
Tel (21) 2205 6820
At this traditional and reliable barbecue house, you order from an extensive menu. It is a favorite with residents and visitors alike for some of the best meat in town.

FLAMENGO & BOTAFOGO:
Miam Miam $$
French/Brazilian
Rua General Goes Monteiro, 34
Tel (21) 2244 0125 **Closed** *Sun*
Contemporary and creative comfort food and a relaxed retro vibe have made Miam Miam a popular option. Try the oxtail in crispy-crust pastry, or shrimp with spaghetti, peach palm, and garlic couscous. If you can't decide, go for the tasting menu.

FLAMENGO & BOTAFOGO:
Lasai $$$
Spanish/Brazilian
Rua Conde de Irajá 191
Tel (21) 3449 1834 **Closed** *Sun & Mon*
Chef Rafa Costa e Silva has worked at Spain's two-Michelin-starred Mugaritz. On offer are two daily-changing contemporary set menus of innovative and inventive dishes.

IPANEMA & LEBLON:
Capricciosa $$
Pizzeria **Map** 2 B5
Rua Vinícius de Moraes, 134
Tel (21) 2523 3394
This popular and family-friendly pizzeria is considered by many to offer the best pizza in Rio, but it isn't the cheapest.

IPANEMA & LEBLON:
Casa da Feijoada $$
Brazilian **Map** 2 B5
Rua Prudente de Moraes 10
Tel (21) 2247 2776
Feijoada is one of Brazil and Rio's most traditional dishes, but is often only to be found on a Saturday. Casa das Feijoada solves this problem by serving this and other Brazilian dishes every day.

IPANEMA & LEBLON:
Sawasdee $$
Asian **Map** 1 A4
Rua Dias Ferreira 571
Tel (21) 2511 0057
This Leblon branch is the flagship of a well-dressed group that consistently serves some of the city's best and most interesting Asian cuisine, with a focus on Thai. The curries are excellent.

Modern meets rustic at the innovative Lasai, Botafogo

IPANEMA & LEBLON:
Le Vin Bistro $$
French **Map** 2 A4
Rua Barão da Torre, 490
Tel (21) 3502 1002
Comfortable and relaxing French bistro in the heart of Ipanema. Instantly recognizable dishes, such as duck confit with sautéed potatoes.

IPANEMA & LEBLON:
Antiquarius $$$
Portuguese **Map** 1 A5
Rua Aristides Espínola 19
Tel (21) 2294 1049
An elegant, old-school institution serving quality Portuguese fare, international favorites, and a highly regarded *feijoada*. For four decades, this has been one of Rio's better restaurants.

IPANEMA & LEBLON:
Esplanada Grill $$$
Steakhouse **Map** 1 C4
Rua Barão da Torre, 600
Tel (21) 2512 2970
Cozy steakhouse in the middle of Ipanema that delivers consistently high standards. There are more than 30 cuts of meat to choose from.

IPANEMA & LEBLON:
Fasano al Mare $$$
Italian **Map** 2 B5
Av Vieira Souto 80
Tel (21) 3202 4030
Italian, Mediterranean, and seafood are on offer at this elegant flagship restaurant of the Fasano chain. Designed by Philippe Starck, this hotel is also home to Baretto-Londra, one of Rio's top bars. Book ahead.

IPANEMA & LEBLON:
Satyricon $$$
Seafood **Map** 2 B4
Rua Barão Da Torre, 192
Tel (21) 2521 0627
Smart, elegant, reliable seafood restaurant, of which there is a

surprisingly limited choice in Rio. It made a name for itself after Madonna dropped in, quickly followed by Diana Ross and other celebrities.

LAGOA & JARDIM BOTÂNICO:
Bar Lagoa $
German/Botequim **Map** 2 A4
Av Epitacio Pessoa, 1674
Tel (21) 2523 1135 **Closed** *lunch Mon–Fri*
Art Deco bar overlooking the Lagoa that serves a menu of snacks and main meals with a German touch. Great draft beer. Built in 1934 as Bar Berlin, this has become a Rio institution.

LAGOA & JARDIM BOTÂNICO:
Lagoon $$
International **Map** 1 B3
Av Borges Medeiros 1424
Tel (21) 2529 5300
Lagoon is an entertainment complex, so it has several restaurants, including Giuseppe Grill Mar, Gula Gula, Quadrifoglio, Pax Delícia, and Sushi Lagoa.

DK Choice

LAGOA & JARDIM BOTÂNICO:
Olympe $$$
French **Map** 2 A2
Rua Custódio Serrão 62
Tel (21) 2539 4542 **Closed** *Sun dinner, Sat & Mon lunch*
Claude Troisgros, Rio's most famous and respected chef, has perfected the art of combining Brazilian ingredients such as baroa potato and açaí with the best he can bring from France. Small, elegant Olympe is the flagship of the Troisgros empire, and Claude is now joined by his brother Thomas, a partnership that has garnered the restaurant several awards.

For more information on types of restaurants *see pages 382–3*

LAGOA & JARDIM BOTÂNICO:
Roberta Sudbrack $$$
Brazilian
Av Lineu de Paula Machado, 916
Tel (21) 3874 0139   **Closed** *Sun &*
Mon
Close to the Botanical Gardens,
Roberta Sudbrack offers modern
Brazilian dishes with a twist.
There is a "gastronomic discount"
every Tuesday.

LAGOA & JARDIM BOTÂNICO:
Rubaiyat $$$
Steakhouse   **Map** 1 A2
Rua Jardim Botânico 971
Tel (21) 3204 9999   **Closed** *Sun*
dinner
In 2014, Rio finally got a branch
of São Paulo's upmarket
steakhouse. The views of Christ
the Redeemer and the Jockey
Club are a bonus. Ask for a table
on the balcony.

DK Choice

SANTA TERESA: Aprazível $$$
Brazilian
Rua Aprazível 62
Tel (21) 2508 9174   **Closed** *Sun*
dinner, Mon
This is one of those places to
which locals take visitors for
long lunches. Hidden in Santa
Teresa, and with superb views,
it offers tropical dining and
interesting dishes in a rustic,
yet classy setting. Try the grilled
salt-water fish with orange
sauce, coconut rice, cashew
nuts, and baked plantain.

Rio de Janeiro State & Espírito Santo

Rio de Janeiro State

BÚZIOS: Estância Don Juan $$
Steakhouse
Rua das Pedras, 178
Tel (22) 2623 2169   **Closed** *Tue &*
Wed in low season
Seafood rules in Búzios, but if
you want a good Argentinian
steak in relaxed surroundings,
head for Don Juan.

DK Choice

BÚZIOS: Parvati $$
Italian
Rua das Pedras 144
Tel (22) 2623 1375
The decor at this trattoria is
Venice meets Búzios – an
attraction in its own right. Try
the seafood risotto or one of
several homemade fresh pastas.

The rustic and charming Aprazível in
Santa Teresa

BÚZIOS: Cigalon $$$
French
Av José Bento Ribeiro Dantas 199
Tel (22) 2623 1249
One of the prettiest restaurants
in Búzios with views across the
bay, Cigalon is located in the
house where Brigitte Bardot
stayed in 1964. French-inspired
dishes and seafood take pride
of place.

BÚZIOS: Satyricon $$$
Seafood
Av José Bento Ribeiro Dantas 500
Tel (22) 2623 2691
Satyricon is considered one of
Rio's best seafood restaurants,
and the produce is as fresh as
can be. Consistently good.

PARATY: Banana da Terra $$
Seafood
Rua Doutor Samuel Costa, 198
Tel (24) 3371 1725   **Closed** *Tue;*
lunch Mon, Wed, Thu
Located in the historic center in
a 17th-century house, this
charming, innovative seafood
restaurant is under the command
of chef Ana Bueno.

PARATY: Bartholomeu $$
French
Rua Doutor Samuel Costa, 176
Tel (24) 3371 5032
Delightful contemporary French
restaurant that captures the
historic spirit of Paraty in its
setting. It also offers the more
informal garden setting of Bartô
in the city square.

PARATY: Punto Divino $$
Italian
Rua Marechal Deodoro, 129
Tel (24) 3371 1348
Seafood and pizza – and even a
seafood pizza – take pride of place
on the menu in this romantic little

restaurant just off the main
square. There is often live music.

PETRÓPOLIS: Imperatriz
Leopoldina – Solar do
Império $$
Portuguese
Av Koeller, 376
Tel (24) 2103 3000
Elegant setting within Petrópolis's
centrally located hotel, which is
situated within two grand 19th-
century houses. It is well known
for its tea served on Friday and
Saturday at 5pm.

PETRÓPOLIS: Lago Sul $$
Steakhouse
Rua República da Argentina 259
Tel (24) 2237 1947
This offers the best value for a
diverse barbecue *rodízio* in town,
and includes Japanese food.

Espírito Santo

VITÓRIA: Lareira Portuguesa $$
Portuguese
Av Saturnino de Brito, 260
Tel (27) 3345 0331
This attractive, modern restaurant
is famous for its *bacalhau* (cod)
and *moquecas* (fish stews).

Minas Gerais

DK Choice

BELO HORIZONTE:
Glouton $$
Brazilian
Rua Bárbara Heliodora, 59
Tel (31) 3292 4237   **Closed** *Mon*
Innovative, high-quality,
contemporary Brazilian and
international fare is part of
an ever-changing menu at this
simple yet elegant restaurant
with a small garden.

BELO HORIZONTE:
Hermengarda $$
Brazilian
Rua Outono, 314
Tel (31) 3225 3268   **Closed** *Mon,*
Tue–Fri lunch, Sun dinner
Come here for excellent contem-
porary dishes with a strong
infusion of Minas Gerais recipes,
in a house that pays homage to
the chef's grandmother.

BELO HORIZONTE: Trindade $$
Regional
Rua Alvarenga Peixoto 388
Tel (31) 2512 4479   **Closed** *Mon,*
Tue–Thu lunch, Sun dinner
Delicious, fresh Mineiro cooking
is given a contemporary and
creative touch in this modern

and comfortable restaurant. Choose to sit either on the veranda or in the main room.

BELO HORIZONTE: Vecchio Sogno $$
Italian
Rua Martim de Carvalho, 75
Tel (31) 3292 5251 **Closed** *Sat lunch & Sun dinner*
Classic Italian dining with local touches that keep the menu fresh, besides offering a daily set menu with traditional desserts. For over 20 years, this central restaurant has been considered one of Belo Horizonte's best and most consistent.

OURO PRETO: O Passo Pizza Jazz $
Italian
Rua São José 56
Tel (31) 3552 5089
Known for its international-style pizza and live jazz, O Passo also offers a fuller menu of a surprisingly high standard. Try to get a table on the terrace, with views over the historic town.

OURO PRETO: Senhora do Rosário $
Regional
Rua Getúlio Vargas 270
Tel (31) 3551 4200
In an elegant setting in one of Ouro Preto's most charming and well-structured *pousadas*, here you will find a menu of local favorites and international dishes.

OURO PRETO: Bené da Flauta $$
Regional
Rua São Francisco de Assis, 32
Tel (31) 3551 1036
Located close to the church of São Francisco, this place serves traditional Mineiro fare and international classics in a beautiful colonial house. The upper floor has the best views.

OURO PRETO: Chafariz $$
Regional
Rua São José 167
Tel (31) 3551 2828 **Closed** *dinner, Mon*
Very popular for its large, well-priced buffet of Mineiro dishes – a great way to try many of the local specialties at one sitting.

TIRADENTES: Estalagem do Sabor $
Regional
Rua Ministro Gabriel Passos 280A
Tel (32) 3355 1144 **Closed** *dinner*
One of the oldest and most respected restaurants in Tiradentes serves typical Mineiro cuisine from the freshest local ingredients. Small and homely.

TIRADENTES: Angatu $$
Brazilian
Rua da Cadeia 38
Tel (32) 999 035 734 **Closed** *Mon & Tue; Wed–Sun lunch*
This restaurant's name means "well-being" in tupi-guarani, and those who taste its creative cuisine tend to agree. Romantic, cozy as well as sophisticated.

TIRADENTES: Tragaluz $$
Regional
Rua Direita, 52
Tel (32) 99968 4837 **Closed** *Tue*
Wonderful romantic setting in a small colonial town house. The menu features dishes that have a modern take on Mineiro cuisine, as well as international favorites.

TIRADENTES: Uaithai $$
Asian/Regional
Rua Direita 205A
Tel (32) 999 279 903 **Closed** *Wed; Sun dinner*
Blending Thai aromas with Minas Gerais' traditional ingredients, this exotic bistro also caters to vegetarians with authentic southeast Asian fare.

São Paulo City

CENTRO: La Casserole $$
French **Map** 1 B2
Largo do Arouche, 346
Tel (11) 3331 6283 **Closed** *Sun dinner, Mon*
This intimate, traditional French restaurant opened in 1954. The vibe is business at lunch and romantic in the evening.

CENTRO: Famiglia Mancini $$
Italian **Map** 1 B3
Rua Avanhandava, 81
Tel (11) 3256 4320
In a city with many fine Italian restaurants, this traditional *cantina* serving superb food is a favorite with the locals.

CENTRO: Terraço Itália $$
Italian **Map** 1 B2
Av Ipiranga, 344
Tel (11) 2189 2929
The main draw atTerraço Itália is the stunning views over the city center from the 42nd floor.

HIGIENÓPOLIS: Ici Bistro $$
French
Rua Pará, 36
Tel (11) 3259 6896
The steak is a highlight at this cozy and romantic French bistro, which is highly regarded. There's a good wine list, too.

JARDINS & AV PAULISTA: Amadeus $$
Seafood **Map** 4 E2
Rua Haddock Lobo, 807
Tel (11) 3061 2859
This elegant, traditional family restaurant serves high-quality modern and traditional seafood dishes. It's considered the place to go for seafood in São Paulo.

JARDINS & AV PAULISTA: Rodeio $$
Steakhouse **Map** 4 D3
Rua Haddock Lobo, 1498
Tel (11) 3474 1333
One of the city's oldest and most charming barbecue houses opened in 1958 and helped make the Jardins fashionable. It is within walking distance of some of the city's most exclusive boutiques.

JARDINS & AV PAULISTA: Tordesilhas $$
Brazilian **Map** 4 D2
Alameda Tietê, 489
Tel (11) 3107 7444 **Closed** *Mon; lunch Tue–Fri; dinner Sat & Sun*
The finest traditional dishes from all over Brazil are offered here. A good English-language menu helps visitors on this voyage of discovery.

Airy and spacious dining room at the Bené da Flauta, Ouro Preto

For more information on types of restaurants *see pages 382–3*

DK Choice

JARDINS & AV PAULISTA: D.O.M. $$$
Brazilian   Map 4 D3
Rua Barão de Capanema 549
Tel (11) 3088 0761   Closed *Sat lunch, Sun*
Alex Atala is globally recognized as one of the world's most creative chefs. His flagship restaurant regularly features in the list of the world's top ten. A meal at D.O.M. is not something you are going to forget, but that also means making a reservation at least a month in advance. This may be one of the highlights of your visit to São Paulo.

JARDINS & AV PAULISTA: Fasano $$$
Italian   Map 4 D3
Rua Vittorio Fasano, 88
Tel (11) 3062 4000   Closed *Sun, lunch daily*
Sophisticated, classy Italian with prices to match, but always with fine cuisine at its heart. This is the highly regarded eponymous flagship of the Fasano group.

JARDINS & AV PAULISTA: Figueira Rubaiyat $$$
Steakhouse   Map 4 D3
Rua Haddock Lobo, 1738
Tel (11) 3087 1399
Diners come here for some of the best beef in town in an informal, chic setting. Fish and vegetarian dishes are also available.

LIBERDADE: Sushi Yassu $$
Asian   Map 1 C4
Rua Tomas Gonzaga 98
Tel (11) 3209 6622   Closed *Mon*
São Paulo has one of the largest Japanese communities in the world, and they consider this the best traditional Japanese restaurant in town. Located in the heart of the Japanese quarter.

PINHEIROS: Arturito $$
Mediterraneanl
Rua Artur de Azevedo 542
Tel (11) 3063 4951
The food here is creative and tasty; the setting, modern and charming. Chef Paola Carosella hails from Argentina and is a judge on Brazilian TV's *MasterChef*.

PINHEIROS: Mani $$$
Brazilian   Map 3 B3
Rua Joaquim Antunes, 210
Tel (11) 3085 4148   Closed *Mon*
Mani is regularly on the list of the world's best restaurants, and Helena Rizzo is its award-winning chef. It is stylish and modern, yet homely – all of which is reflected in the menu.

PINHEIROS: Vecchio Torino $$$
Italian
Rua Tavares Cabral, 119
Tel (11) 3816 0592   Closed *Sun dinner, Mon*
Hidden away in a fairly nondescript house in a side road, this place offers sophisticated, traditional Italian cuisine. The *gnocchi* is highly rated, and there is an impressive wine list.

VILA MADALENA: Canto Madalena $$
Brazilian
Rua Medeiros de Albuquerque 471
Tel (11) 3813 6814   Closed *Mon; dinner Sat & Sun*
Traditional dishes, especially from Minas Gerais and Bahia, are prepared to a high standard in this charming, fresh, and welcoming restaurant.

VILA OLÍMPIA & ITAIM BIBI: Attimo $$
Italian
Rua Diogo Jácome, 341
Tel (11) 5054 9999   Closed *Mon, dinner Sun*
Modern, stylish, and cool, this restaurant has a creative and interesting menu with classic Italian influences.

DK Choice

VILA OLÍMPIA & ITAIM BIBI: Rascal $$
Buffet
Av Presidente Juscelino Kubitschek
Tel (11) 3152 6111
The flagship branch of Rascal has built a reputation for its high-quality, competitively priced all-you-can-eat buffet, to which other dishes may be added from the à la carte menu.

DK Choice

VILA OLÍMPIA & ITAIM BIBI: Fogo de Chão $$$
Barbecue (Churrascaria)
Av dos Bandeirantes, 538
Tel (11) 5505 0791
When it comes to upmarket *rodízio* all-you-can-eat barbecue houses that really deliver, then Fogo de Chão is often found at the top of the list. It may appear pricey at first glance, but the variety and quality of the food on offer is worth the cost.

VILA OLÍMPIA & ITAIM BIBI: Kinoshita $$$
Asian
Rua Jacques Félix, 405
Tel (11) 3849 6940   Closed *Sun*
Highly regarded authentic Japanese cuisine with a twist of fusion and Kappo cuisine. It is all delivered in a stylish, elegant, and tasteful atmosphere. In a city well renowned for its good Asian options, this is one of the best.

VILA OLÍMPIA & ITAIM BIBI: Skye $$$
International   Map 4 E5
Av Brigadeiro Luís Antônio, 4700
Tel (11) 3055 4702
This is the rooftop restaurant and bar that São Paulo's most stylish and fashionable boutique hotel deserves, with jaw-dropping views across São Paulo. It is the place to see and be seen, and the contemporary international menu does not disappoint.

São Paulo State

GUARUJÁ: Farol di Mare $
Italian
Av Miguel Stéfano, 4659
Tel (13) 3351 5559   Closed *Wed*
Opened in 1972, this popular beachfront eatery offers Italian- and Mediterranean-inspired dishes. Good selection of fresh seafood. Lovely views over the sea.

The modern interior of Mani in Pinheiros

Elegant, relaxed dining area at A Casa Vidal, Salvador

GUARUJÁ: Casa Grande $$
International
Av Miguel Stéfano, 1100
Tel (13) 3389 4000
Casa Grande is a sprawling colonial resort on the beachfront with five restaurants and four bars of varying levels of sophistication. Good choice if visiting for the day or touring in the area.

ILHABELA: Viana $$
Seafood
Av Leonardo Reale 2301
Tel (12) 3896 1089
Fresh and tasty seafood drive the menu here. Sit either in the main restaurant overlooking the beach or on the deck and tables on the sand. Dip in and out of the sea between courses.

DK Choice

SÃO SEBASTIÃO: Manacá $$
International
Rua Manacá, 102
Tel (12) 3865 2546 **Closed** *Mon–Wed (in low season)*
Tucked off the road and surrounded by luscious vegetation, this is one of those places you have to make the effort to visit, but it offers a special experience. It started out in 1988 to supply breakfast to surfers but is now known for its ambience and excellent fresh fish and seafood.

UBATUBA: Solar das Águas Cantantes $$
Seafood
Estrada do Saco da Ribeira 951
Tel (12) 3842 0178/0288
Seafood and traditional *moquecas* (fish stews) are served in this *pousada's* restaurant, which sits on one of the prettiest beaches in Ubatuba. Family-friendly.

Bahia

ITACARE: Boca de Forno $$
Pizzeria
Rua Lodonio Almeida 108
Tel (73) 3251 3121
The eclectic and cool decor here, including chandeliers and colorful artworks, help this hip eatery stand out from the crowd.

LENÇOIS: Cozinha Aberta $
International
Av Rui Barbosa, 42, Centro
Tel (75) 3334 1321
Just off the main square, this charming restaurant serves a varied international menu of "slow food." This covers everything from Hungarian goulash to Thai curry.

LENÇOIS: Os Artistas da Massa $
Italian
Rua da Baderna, 49
Tel (75) 3334 1886 **Closed** *Oct and Nov*
This is a simple Italian-owned restaurant that serves excellent well-priced pasta, as well as other Italian dishes.

MORRO DE SÃO PAULO: Pimenta Rosa $$
Seafood
Quarta Praia – Morro de São Paulo
Tel (75) 3652 1506
Located right on the fourth beach, this beach bar and restaurant has a good infrastructure, great views, and friendly staff. Try the Caipifruta, a version of a *caipirinha*.

SALVADOR: Solar Café $
International
Rua da Graça, 284
Tel (71) 3328 3444 **Closed** *Mon*
This small, unpretentious café/restaurant is located in the Palacete das Artes, which also houses a cultural center and a museum of modern art. Guests can also enjoy great views over the bay of Todos os Santos from the terrace.

DK Choice

SALVADOR: A Casa Vidal $$
Spanish
Rua Afonso Celso, 294
Tel (71) 3565 8008 **Closed** *lunch, Sun*
This small, contemporary Spanish restaurant, with a large infusion of Bahian and other Brazilian influences, has established itself high on the list of the best places to eat in Salvador. Don't miss the variety of tapas to start, and then try the mixed seafood platter.

SALVADOR: Al Carmo $$
Italian
Rua do Carmo, 42
Tel (71) 3242 0283 **Closed** *Sun*
Its location just off the Pelourinho (old city center) makes Al Carmo a good choice when sightseeing. It serves simple, classic Italian dishes in a beautifully restored colonial building. The back terrace has views over the bay of Todos os Santos and the lower city.

SALVADOR: Fogo de Chão $$
Barbecue (Churrascaria)
Praça Colombo, 4, Rio Vermelho
Tel (71) 3555 9292
If you are looking for a change from seafood and Bahian cuisine, try this branch of São Paulo's excellent upmarket all-you-can-eat barbecue chain housed in a large building that was formerly a theater. Meat lovers will not be disappointed.

SALVADOR: Quattro Amici $$
Pizzeria
Rua Dom Marcos Teixeira, 35
Tel (71) 3264 5999
Hidden away in a historic house down a side street, this popular and charming eatery serves delicious pizzas.

SALVADOR: Soho $$
Asian
Av Lafayete Coutinho (Av Contorno) 1010, Bahia Marina
Tel (71) 3322 4554
Part of a popular and fashionable chain of upmarket Japanese restaurants, this stunning flagship branch in the marina offers glorious views over the bay of Todos os Santos. The menu includes a wide variety of sushi, sashimi, and grilled dishes.

SALVADOR: Yemanjá $$
Brazilian
Av Otávio Mangabeira, 4661
Tel (71) 3461 9010
Sited on the coast, and with beach views, this is the place to come to for an introduction to and immersion into the local Bahian cuisine and customs – something of a gastronomic institution.

TRANSCOSO: O Cacau $$$
Brazilian
Praça São João Batista, 96
Tel (73) 3668 1266 **Closed** *Mon*
The entrance to this attractive restaurant is off the main square, with a candlelit path leading up to the wide deck. It serves delicious Bahian cuisine with an Oriental twist. Some dishes are made with cacao.

For more information on types of restaurants *see pages 382–3*

TRANSCOSO: Capim Santo $$$
Seafood
Rua do Beco, 55
Tel (73) 3668 1122   **Closed** *Sun*
There is a wonderful ambience
here in the colorful grounds of
the *pousada* of the same name.
Creative modern Brazilian menu.

Sergipe, Alagoas & Pernambuco

Sergipe

ARACAJU: Cariri $$
Brazilian
Av Santos Dumont
Tel (79) 3243 1379
This lively restaurant serves
large portions of meat and
seafood regional dishes. The
show house offers *forró* and
other entertainment.

ARACAJU: Muratto $$
Mediterranean
Rua Doutor Bezerra de Menezes, 102
Tel (79) 3255 2376   **Closed** *Mon*
Choose between contemporary
Mediterranean-inspired dishes
and Japanese sushi at this
elegant venue. There is
occasional live music.

Alagoas

MACEIO: Wanchako $
Peruvian
Rua São Francisco de Assis, 93
Tel (82) 3377 6024   **Closed** *Sun*
This is one of Maceio's most
popular eateries, serving Peruvian
recipes with Brazilian ingredients.

MACEIO: Sur $$
Regional
Rua Paulina Maria Mendonça 759
Tel (82) 9678 1687 **Closed** *lunch, Sun*
This critically acclaimed restaurant
serves exquisite contemporary
dishes with an Alagoan influence.

Pernambuco

**FERNANDO DE NORONHA:
Cacimba Bistro** $
International
*Praça Pres Eurico Dutra 9, Vila dos
Remedios*
Tel (81) 3619 1200
Romantic bistro that is beautifully
lit at night. Choose between the
pretty veranda or the cozy indoors.

**FERNANDO DE NORONHA:
Ecologikus** $$
Seafood
Estrada Velha do Sueste
Tel (81) 3619 1807   **Closed** *Sun*
This simple, cozy family-run
restaurant offers a nice selection

Atmospheric dining area at the Capim Santo, Transcosco, Bahia

of fresh seafood and other dishes.
It's not the easiest place to find
but is worth the effort.

OLINDA: Don Francesco $
Italian
Rua Prudente de Morais, 358
Tel (81) 3429 3852   **Closed** *Mon*
Tucked away in the cobbled
streets of Olinda, this simple
trattoria serves up tasty,
unpretentious Italian cooking.

DK Choice

OLINDA: Oficina do Sabor $$
Brazilian
Rua do Amparo, 335
Tel (81) 3429 3331 **Closed** *Mon*
This "workshop of flavors" is
the best known of Olinda's
restaurants and perfectly
captures the spirit and
atmosphere of the area. It
offers a creative menu of local
Pernambucan and Brazilian
dishes, many featuring fresh
fish and seafood.

**PORTO DE GALINHAS:
Domingos** $
Brazilian/French
Rua Beijupirá 116, Galeria Paraoby
Tel (81) 3552 1464
Along with Beijupira, this
charming and romantic
restaurant is the best in town.
A varied menu of French and
Brazilian influences offers
something for every taste.

**PORTO DE GALINHAS:
Peixe na Telha** $
Seafood
Av Beira Mar, 40-B
Tel (81) 3552 1323
Informal beachfront restaurant
that works in tandem with its
neighbor, the Encontro dos Mares
bistro, serving northeastern
specialties with fresh seafood.

DK Choice

**PORTO DE GALINHAS:
Beijupirá** $$
Seafood
*Rua Beijupirá s/n, Praia dos
Carneiros*
Tel (81) 3552 2354
Inventive contemporary
Brazilian dishes are served with
a variety of tropical sauces
at this colorful and atmospheric
spot. The restaurant is almost
as famous as the town itself –
a must-visit.

RECIFE: Chica Pitanga $
Buffet
Rua Petrolina, 19
Tel (81) 3465 2224
A pleasant "by the kilo" restaurant
offering a good-quality buffet at
reasonable prices, where you
only pay for what you take. It is
popular with locals and visitors,
and well located for hotels on
Boa Viagem.

RECIFE: Leite $$
Portuguese
Praça Joaquim Nabuco, 147
Tel (81) 3224 7977   **Closed** *Sat*
A piece of history, Leite has been
operating since 1882 and is still
going strong, one of the oldest
restaurants in Brazil. The menu
features regional and Portuguese
influences served in an elegant,
colonial setting.

RECIFE: Ponte Nova $$
French
Rua do Cupim, 172
Tel (81) 3327 7226   **Closed** *Mon*
The decor and menu here are
inspired by French Art Nouveau,
but with a distinctively contem-
porary Brazilian feel to both. The
restaurant is as charming by
candlelight as it is by the natural
light of day for Sunday lunch.

For key to prices *see page 386*

Paraíba, Rio Grande do Norte & Ceará

Paraíba

JOÃO PESSOA: Mangai $
Brazilian
Av General Édson Ramalho, 696
Tel (83) 3226 1615
The very large buffet here – there are more than 200 recipes – offers a great introduction to many northeastern specialties and delicacies. Look for branches in Natal and Brasília, too.

JOÃO PESSOA: Quintal Restô $$
Brazilian
Rua Eutiquiano Barreto, 863
Tel (83) 9179 3900 **Closed** *Sun–Tue*
Call to make a reservation, and wait to be charmed by the culinary skills on display in the place that serves the best food in the city. The menu changes almost daily.

Rio Grande do Norte

GENIPABU: Bar 21 $$
Brazilian
Praia de Genipabu
Tel (84) 3224 2484
The setting – on stilts above the sea at the bottom of a sand dune – is the main attraction of this thatched-roofed bar/restaurant. Order the catch of the day and you can't go wrong. Lunch only.

NATAL: Âncora Caipira $
Brazilian
Av Campos Sales 474
Tel (84) 3202 9364 **Closed** *Mon & Carnaval*
This friendly venue is a firm favorite with the locals for its authentic northeastern cuisine. It is also famed for its sun-dried meat (*carne do sol*).

Tasty prawn and shrimp dish at Potiguarias Camarão, Natal

NATAL: Manary Gastronomia & Arte $$
Seafood
Rua Francisco Gurgel, 9067
Tel (84) 3204 2900
In Natal's best boutique hotel, this is a glorious setting for lunch and dinner, with sea views and sounds.

NATAL: Potiguarias Camarão $$
Seafood
Rua Pedro Fonseca Filho, 8887
Tel (84) 3209 2425
If you like shrimp or prawns, you will be in heaven here, but there are many other dishes on offer. One of Natal's largest and most popular restaurants.

PRAIA DE PIPA: Pizzeria Dall'Italiano $
Italian
Av Baia dos Golfinhos 731
Tel (84) 9152 8651 **Closed** *Mon & Wed in low season*
Nicely decorated, cozy, informal pizzeria located just off the main street. The menu also includes seafood, pasta, and salads.

PRAIA DE PIPA: Camamo $$
Brazilian
Fazenda Pernambuquinho
Tel (84) 98813 8511
Here you will be treated to a set menu of six courses at a table on the candlelit veranda of the chef's lovely house. Numbers are very limited each night, so make a reservation for this exclusive dining experience.

Ceará

CANOA QUEBRADA: L'Atelier do Brasil $
International
Rua Nascer do Sol, 360
Tel (88) 8817 9964 **Closed** *Wed*
Track down this cozy, romantic, atmospheric restaurant, one block off the bustle of "Broadway," and sample its international favorites.

CANOA QUEBRADA: Pizza Nostra $
Pizzeria
Rua Dragão do Mar 2040
Tel (88) 9680 5863 **Closed** *Mon*
Grills, seafood, and vegetarian options are also all on offer at this pizzeria in the center of the village.

FORTALEZA: L'O $
Brazilian
Av Pessoa Anta 217
Tel (85) 3265 2288
A mixture of Art Deco and more modern touches has resulted in one of the city's most sophisticated and striking dining spots with a lovely garden bar.

DK Choice

FORTALEZA: Coco Bambu $$
Seafood
Av Beira Mar, 3698
Tel (85) 3198 6000
Founded in Fortaleza in 2001, this is a reliable chain of modern, informal seafood restaurants that won't disappoint. This branch is one of three in Fortaleza and is right on the seashore. The menu is very varied and includes a wide selection of salads and traditional dishes served in generous portions. Try the fish fillet with banana and white sauce, or with mango sauce and nuts.

FORTALEZA: Colher de Pau $$
Brazilian
Rua Ana Bilhar, 1178
Tel (85) 3267 6680
All the color and flavor of regional dishes of both the coast and interior of Ceará can be enjoyed at this lovely outdoor restaurant.

Piauí & Maranhão

Piauí

TERESINA: Coco Bambu $$
Seafood
Rua Professor Joca Vieira, 1227
Tel 86 3232 8100
This popular branch of the reliable Coco Bambu seafood chain is one of the best in town and a favorite meeting point. Outdoor and indoor seating.

TERESINA: Favorita Comida Típica $$
Brazilian
Rua Angélica, 1059
Tel (86) 3232 2020
Rustic yet comfortable, this spot is generally thought to serve the best regional fare in town. The Favorito group has five more restaurants in Teresina, including the pizzeria Favorito Forneira.

Maranhão

LENCOIS MARANHENSES: Luzía $
Seafood
Canto do Atins
Tel (98) 9 8709 7661
The only restaurant and *pousada* within the Parque dos Lençóis Maranhenses, on the edge of the sand dunes, Luzía serves delicious specialties of prawn, fresh fish, and goat.

For more information on types of restaurants *see pages 382–3*

SÃO LUIS: Antigamente $
Brazilian
Rua da Estrela, 220
Tel (98) 9 8876 7151
In the historic center, this pretty restaurant with a large patio is good for snacks and a beer, as well as full meals.

DK Choice

SÃO LUIS: Cabana do Sol $
Brazilian
Rua João Rereiro Damasceno 24, Km 5, Ponta do Farol
Tel (98) 3304 4235
Sun-dried beef (*carne de sol*), goat, chicken, and other local dishes are the specialties at this popular, well-regarded restaurant with locally inspired decor and a bar area.

SÃO LUIS: Senac $
Buffet
Rua de Nazaré, 242
Tel (98) 3198 1100
Part of the national hotel and catering school, this exceptional all-you-can-eat buffet provides a good introduction to local and other Brazilian dishes.

Pará & Amapá

Pará

BELEM: Lá em Casa $
Brazilian
Estação daws Docas – Av Boulevard Castilho França, Galpão 2
Tel (91) 3212 5588
Serving regional Amazonian dishes, Lá em Casa is located inside the dock area in the beautiful mall, offering views over the river. There is an open-air terrace, too.

Bright and lively dining area at Antigamente, São Luis

For key to prices *see page 386*

DK Choice

BELEM: Remanso do Bosque $$
Regional
Av Rômulo Maiorana, 2350
Tel (91) 3347 2829   **Closed** *Mon*
Innovative and creative use of local Amazonian ingredients makes this the most interesting choice for foodies who want a gourmet experience – Amazonian chic, if you like. It has the same owners as the less sophisticated Remanso de Peixe, considered Belém's best restaurant for seafood.

Amapá

MACAPA: Estaleiro $
Seafood
Av 1 Maio
Tel (96) 3222 8375
The nautically themed Estaleiro is considered one of the best and most reliable restaurants in Macapa.

Amazonas, Roraima, Acre & Rondõnia

Amazonas

MANAUS: Canto da Peixada $
Seafood
Av Ayrão, 1677
Tel (92) 3234 3021
One of Manaus' best-known fish restaurants, this is the ideal place to try many of the local Amazon river fish that you will not find anywhere else in the world.

MANAUS: Fiorentina $
Italian
Rua José Paranaguá, 44
Tel (92) 3215 2233
This pleasant, popular Italian restaurant in the center of Manaus serves a range of pasta, sushi, and other standard dishes. *Feijoada* is offered on Saturdays.

DK Choice

MANAUS: Banzeiro $$
Brazilian
Rua Libertador, 102
Tel (92) 3234 1621
Credited with breathing new life into Amazonian cuisine, this restaurant is considered the best option at which to try out Amazonian dishes that use a selection of exotic ingredients. If you have come all the way to Manaus and like to experiment, don't miss the experience.

MANAUS: Bufalo Churrascaria $$
Barbecue
Rua Pará 490
Tel (92) 9219 7243
Considered the best restaurant in town for meat, this is a popular *rodízio* all-you-can-eat barbecue house. It also serves sushi and has an American bar.

MANAUS: Himawari $$
Asian
Rua 10 de Julho, 618
Tel (92) 3233 4229   **Closed** *Mon*
The best and most traditional Japanese restaurant in Manaus is conveniently located right next to the famous Opera House. Great sushi and sashimi are served here.

Roraima

BOA VISTA: Tropical Peixada $
Seafood
Rua Ajuricaba, 1525
Tel (95) 3224 6040   **Closed** *Wed & 3rd Sun of month*
This street-corner restaurant with an airy outdoor seating area is popular for lunch and has a family-friendly kids' room. The menu favors seafood and Amazon fish.

Acre

RIO BRANCO: Point do Pato $
Regional
Praca Jose Bisteni
Tel (68) 9972 8112   **Closed** *Sun*
Trendy and popular with locals – young and old alike – this spot specializes in regional dishes such as alligator steaks, as well as international favorites, including pasta and pizza. Live music.

Rondõnia

PORTO VELHO: Caravela do Madeira $
Seafood
Rua José Camacho, 104
Tel (69) 3221 6641   **Closed** *Mon*
This rustic, cozy restaurant, with views of the Madeira river and rainforest, specializes in river fish, including grilled piranha. The shrimps and other seafood are great too.

PORTO VELHO: Miyoshi $
Asian
Av Amazonas 1280, Nossa Senhora das Graças
Tel (69) 3224 4600
Amazonian ingredients are used to create a large menu of traditional Chinese and Japanese dishes at this modern and pleasant restaurant that is part of a well-regarded chain.

A typcially large portion at Casa do João, Bonito

Brasília, Goiás & Tocantins

Brasília

BRASÍLIA: Corrientes 348 $$
Steakhouse
Setor de Clubes Esportivos Sul Trecho 2, Lote40
Tel (61) 3345 1348 **Closed** *Mon*
This is a branch of the excellent Argentine steakhouse chain that has restaurants in São Paulo and Rio de Janeiro. It has an informal, relaxed atmosphere and views over Lagoa Paranoá.

BRASÍLIA: Dalí Camões $$$
Portuguese/Spanish
Setor Hoteleiro Sul, Qd 6, Bl B (Brasil 21)
Tel (61) 3039 8156 **Closed** *Sun*
Located in Hotel Brasil 21, this smart, elegant restaurant serves a nice selection of Portuguese and Catalan specialties. Don't miss the seafood selection platter.

BRASÍLIA: Fogo de Chão $$$
Barbecue (Churrascaria)
SHS Quadra 5, Bloco E, Asa Sul
Tel (61) 3322 4666
This is a branch of the excellent Fogo de Chão barbecue house, recognized as one of the best all-you-can-eat barbecues in Brazil. Centrally located, it is, not surprisingly, one of the city's most popular, and it seats 600.

BRASÍLIA: Gero $$$
Italian
SHIN, CA 4, Lote A, loja 22
Tel (61) 3577 5520
Located in the Shopping Iguatemi mall, this is a branch of Fasano's fashionable and popular contemporary Italian eatery. Stylish, yet relaxed, it is one of the best restaurants in town.

DK Choice

BRASÍLIA: Taypá $$$
Peruvian
Setor de Habitações Individuais Sul, Quadra 17, Bl 9, Shopping Fashion Park
Tel (61) 3248 0403
Highly regarded by critics and considered one of the city's very best, this unpretentious Peruvian restaurant has an innovative, ever-changing menu. As well as superb ceviche, it also serves contemporary international dishes and has a *pisco* bar.

BRASÍLIA: Trattoria da Rosario $$$
Italian
Shopping Fashion Park – SHIS Qi 17, Bl H s/n
Tel (61) 3248 1672 **Closed** *Mon*
One of the most consistent Italian restaurants in town – although not the cheapest – is this smart spot in Fashion Park.

Goiás

**CHAPADA DOS VEADEIROS:
Massa da Mamma** $
Italian
Rua São José Operário, 305
Tel (62) 3446 1362
As its name suggests, this is a simple Italian *cantina*. Its specialty is pasta, but it also offers pizza.

Tocantins

PALMAS: Adelaide Bistro $
Brazilian
Quadra 110 Sul, Alameda 21 lotes 73/75
Tel (63) 9214 0792
In a residential area, this is the best place in Tocantins for a relaxing meal. It has a pretty veranda and pool area and offers reliable home-style cooking with attentive service.

Mato Grosso & Mato Grosso do Sul

Mato Grosso

CUIABÁ: Getúlio $$
Regional
Av Presidente Getúlio Vargas, 1147
Tel (65) 3624 9992 **Closed** *Mon*
Good steaks and other grills, including fish, are served here. Although this is a high-end restaurant, the atmosphere is casual, and there's always a lively buzz. A popular nightclub is located above the restaurant.

CUIABÁ: Mahalo Cozinha Criativa $$
Brazilianl
Rua Pres Castello Branco 359
Tel (65) 3028 7700 **Closed** *Sun*
This smart, charming and innovative restaurant is led by Paris-trained chef Ariani Malouf, offering a contemporary fusion of Brazilian and inter-national cuisine. It is also open Thursdays for afternoon tea from 4:30pm to 7pm.

Mato Grosso do Sul

BONITO: Casa do João $
Seafood
Rua Coronel Nelson Felício dos Santos 664A
Tel (67) 3255 1212
Casa do João should satisfy most diners, offering a good variety of tasty local dishes in large portions.

CAMPO GRANDE: Cantina Romana $$
Italian
Rua da Paz 237
Tel (67) 3324 9777
This is a popular, reliable Italian *cantina* that has built a name and local following since opening in 1978. The owner also operates the busy Pizzeria Romana in Campo Grande.

CAMPO GRANDE: Fogo Caipira $$
Brazilian
Rua José Antônio Pereira 145
Tel (67) 3324 1641 **Closed** *Mon*
Considered the best restaurant in Campo Grande for regional Pantanal fare, Fogo Caipira is very popular on weekends, so consider booking in advance. It also serves lighter meals and snacks in the late afternoon.

Santa Catarina & Paraná

Santa Catarina

FLORIANÓPOLIS: Restinga Recanto $
Seafood
Rodovia Rafael da Rocha Pires, 2759
Tel (48) 3235 2093   **Closed** *Sun dinner, Mon*
This popular rustic restaurant serves super-fresh Portuguese-style seafood. It has panoramic beach and sea views from the terrace and there is folk-dancing on weekends.

FLORIANÓPOLIS: Arante $$
Seafood
Rua Abelardo Otácilio Gomes 254, Pântano do Sul
Tel (48) 3237 7022
Something of a local fixture, this large beachside bar and restaurant gets crowded on weekends and on summer evenings, it serves reliable seafood dishes. The walls are covered in notes left by visitors since the 1970s.

FLORIANÓPOLIS: Ostradamus $$
Seafood
Rod Baldicero Filomeno, 7640
Tel (48) 3337 5711   **Closed** *Mon*
Oysters are a specialty here and are freshly harvested from the neighboring oyster beds, 18 miles (30 km) from the center of Florianópolis. Other seafood options are available, too, served with a wide variety of well-preserved wines.

FLORIANÓPOLIS: Villa Maggioni $$
Mediterranean
Rua Canto da Amizade 273, Canto da Lagoa
Tel (48) 3232 6859 **Closed** *Mon & Tue*
This intimate award-winning restaurant on the shores of Lagoa da Conceição has an international menu featuring Italian and Mediterranean dishes,

Paraná

CURITIBA: Madalosso $
Italian
Av Manoel Ribas, 5875
Tel *41 3372 2121*
A very large restaurant (it seats 4,500), Madalosso is an attraction in its own right, serving a good-quality, fixed-price Italian buffet in a number of salons. It is located in the Italian quarter of the city, in Santa Felicidade.

Notes written by diners adorning the walls of Arante, Florianópolis

CURITIBA: Barolo Trattoria $$
Italian
Av Silva Jardim, 2487
Tel (41) 3243 3430
Dishes at this excellent, charming *trattoria* have a few Brazilian influences. Nice, sophisticated atmosphere. Good wine list.

CURITIBA: Batel Grill $$
Brazilian
Av Nossa Senhora Aparecida, 78
Tel (41) 3342 8101
This large, modern, popular *rodizio* all-you-can-eat barbecue house is considered the best of its type in Curitiba.

DK Choice

CURITIBA: Durski $$
International
Av Jaime Reis 254
Tel (41) 3225 7893 **Closed** *Mon– Tue; lunch Wed–Fri; dinner Sun*
Named best restaurant in Curitba in 2016, Durski offers an international menu with Slavic specialties. Try the tasting menu for an intense experience. The wine list includes offerings from as early as 1780.

CURITIBA: L'Épicerie $$
French
Rua Fernando Simas, 340
Tel (41) 3079 1889   **Closed** *Sun & Mon*
Considered the city's best French restaurant, this is a charming, reliable, comfy bistro in one of Curitiba's best neighborhoods.

CURITIBA: Famiglia Caliceti – Ristorante Bologna $$
Italian
Alameda Doutor Carlos de Carvalho, 1367
Tel (41) 3076 9477   **Closed** *Tue*
A pretty and traditional Italian restaurant, this has been something of an institution since opening in 1972.

CURITIBA: Terra Madre $$$
Italian
Rua Desembargador Otávio do Amaral, 515
Tel (41) 3335 6070   **Closed** *Mon; lunch Tue–Fri; dinner Sun*
Modern Italian and international fare with Brazilian influences is offered here, on a well-balanced menu. Terra Madre also has a wine bar and store.

FOZ DO IGUAÇU: Bufalo Branco $
Brazilian
Rua Engenheiro Rebouças, 530
Tel (45) 3523 9744
Probably the best barbecue house in town, the casual and fun Bufalo Branco serves excellent quality meats. It is centrally located but offers free transfers from some of the out-of-town hotels.

FOZ DO IGUAÇU: Clube Maringá $
Seafood
Rua Dourado, 111
Tel (45) 3527 9683   **Closed** *Mon*
Part of the local fishing club, this is a good choice for lunch, with a great view across the river and on to Paraguay. The fixed-price buffet includes not only international dishes, but also the local delicacy, Pirá de Foz –fish fillet in white wine and ginger sauce.

FOZ DO IGUAÇU: La Mafia $
Italian
Alameda Watslaf Nieradka, 195
Tel (45) 3572 1015
This fun, quirky Mafia-themed Italian *trattoria* and wine bar is popular with visitors and serves tasty food at reasonable prices. Their pastas and bruschettas are not to be missed.

DK Choice

FOZ DO IGUAÇU: Itaipu $$$
Brazilian
Belmond Hotel das Cataratas, Iguaçu National Park
Tel (45) 2102 7000
Even if not staying at the Hotel Cataratas, you should head out for dinner either at the Itaipu, with its terrace overlooking the falls, or the more popular poolside Ipê Grill. Itaipu offers an interesting fusion of international and Brazilian dishes, while Ipê Grill serves an outstanding high-class buffet including barbecue, a wide choice of salads, and Brazilian desserts. Contact the hotel for reservations.

PARANAGUÁ: Danúbio Azul $$
Seafood
Rua XV de Novembro, 95
Tel (41) 3423 3255 **Closed** *Sun dinner*
On the water's edge, this restaurant, open since 1953, specializes in seafood and Paraná cuisine. Try for a table by the window. A buffet is served at lunch.

Rio Grande do Sul

DK Choice

BENTO GONÇALVES:
Casa di Paolo $
Brazilian
BR-470, Km 221.6
Tel (54) 3463 8505 **Closed** *Sun dinner*
A southern specialty is mouthwatering, slow-barbecued chicken (*galeto*), and the Casa di Paolo chain, which also serves other dishes, is often voted best in class. You will find branches across the south including Balneário Cambroiú, Porto Alegre, Caxias, and Gramado.

BENTO GONÇALVES:
Maria Valduga $$
Italian
Via Trento, 2355 – Vale dos Vinhedos
Tel (54) 2105 3122
Four charming dining areas make up Maria Valduga, located within the Valduga winery. A set meal is served at lunch, and it opens for dinner for groups of 20 or more.

GRAMADO: Belle du Valais $$
Swiss
Av das Hortências, 1432
Tel (54) 3286 1744 **Closed** *lunch*
This popular, cozy spot is great for fondue and *raclette* in the colder winter months, and is one of the best Swiss restaurants in Brazil.

GRAMADO: La Caceria $$$
Brazilian
Av Borges de Medeiros 3166
Tel (54) 3295 7575
The charming top restaurant of the Casa da Montanha hotel has a small but interesting menu with a focus on game and other by-products of the hunt. The hotel also houses the cozy Bistrô da Varanda.

GRAMADO: Saint Andrews Primrose $$$
French/Italian
Rua das Flores 171
Tel (54) 3295 7700
Housed in one of Gramado's best boutique hotels, the elegant Primrose restaurant offers high-quality fine dining.

PORTO ALEGRE: Via Veneto Galeteria $
Brazilian
Rua José de Alencar, 501
Tel (51) 3233 1400 **Closed** *Sun dinner*
Barbecued chicken is the specialty at this excellent restaurant, but there is also a full buffet of other dishes and accompaniments.

PORTO ALEGRE: Al Dente $$
Italian
Rua Mata Bacelar, 210
Tel 51 3343 1841 **Closed** *Sun; dinner Mon*
A small, cozy, intimate Italian restaurant. Classic, consistently well-prepared north Italian dishes are the main thrust here.

PORTO ALEGRE: Koh Pee Pee $$
Asian
Rua Schiller, 83
Tel (51) 3333 5150 **Closed** *Sun*
Since opening in 1997, this stylish, authentic Thai restaurant has kept its standards high. It is regarded as one of Porto Alegre's very best restaurants of any type.

PORTO ALEGRE: NB Steak $$
Barbecue (Churrascaria)
Av Nilo Peçanha, 2131
Tel (51) 3333 1413
This is part of a chain of smart, comfortable *rodízio* all-you-can-eat barbecue houses, with a more elegant presentation than many of its rivals.

PORTO ALEGRE: Paris 6 $$
French
Rua Padre Chagas 32
Tel (51) 3574 0265
Part of a chain based in São Paolo, this restaurant serves everything from fresh croissants to homemade pastas, many of which are named after celebrities who often show up here.

PORTO ALEGRE: Puppi Baggio $$
Italian
Rua Dinarte Ribeiro, 155
Tel (51) 3346 3630 **Closed** *Mon*
Some of the best and most reliable pasta dishes in town, as well as great pizzas, are served here, in a rustic, chic setting inside a lovely house. Puppi Baggio is well loved by the locals.

PORTO ALEGRE: Ratskeller Baumbach $$
German
Av Para 1324
Tel (51) 3346 4322 **Closed** *Mon; Sun dinner*
Popular ever since it first opened in 1967, Ratskeller Baumbach is considered by many to serve the best German food in Porto Alegre. It also serves some Central European dishes, including Hungarian delicacies. Reasonably priced, it offers buffet or á la carte options for lunch, as well as kids' set menus.

DK Choice

PORTO ALEGRE: Floriano Spiess Cozinha de autor $$$
International
Praça do Japão, 155
Tel (51) 3237 7601 **Closed** *Sun & Mon*
This is the city's most talked about and written about contemporary restaurant, yet still retains a culinary foot in the best of the past. Serious gourmands should indulge in the creative eight-course tasting menu prepared by the award-winning owner and chef, and served in an elegant but friendly setting. Make sure you save room for dessert. Book ahead.

The warm decor at Koh Pee Pee, Porto Alegre

For more information on types of restaurants *see pages 382–3*

SHOPPING IN BRAZIL

The most exciting aspect of shopping in Brazil is that it never fails to surprise visitors with its amazing variety. Major cities, such as Rio *(see pp94–5)* and São Paulo *(pp154–5)*, have expansive, world-class shopping centers that have everything from sophisticated boutiques to high-tech items. Craft centers, artisans' houses, and *ateliers* (workshops) showcase the unique, attractive products manufactured by the local people. Colorful street markets and *camelódromos* offer a truly exhilarating Brazilian shopping experience. The prices are, by and large, reasonable, and large items can be shipped home. In most state capitals and tourist areas the opening hours are extended for convenience.

Opening Hours

Business hours are normally 8am to 6pm on weekdays and 8am to 1pm on Saturdays. In large cities, tourist areas, and resorts, hours are more flexible. Stores in central areas stay open until 7 or 8pm on weekdays and 4pm on Saturdays. Shopping centers are open 10am to 10pm from Monday to Saturday. In resorts and tourist areas, even small stores are open daily until midnight in the high season.

How to Pay

Major credit cards are accepted in most stores in large cities and resorts, though there may be a minimum spend value (about R$50). International debit cards are commonly accepted even for small amounts. US dollars are sometimes accepted in tourist areas, but in small towns it is best to pay in cash using the *real (see p415)*.

Interior of an upmarket clothing store in Jardins, São Paulo

Shopping Centers & Hypermarkets

More convenient than street stores and offering much more than shopping alone, shopping centers have multiplied in the last few years. Fast-food chains and restaurants, department stores and boutiques, clothes repair, cobblers, and other services can all now be found within one complex. A combination of supermarket and department store, hypermarkets are often located on main roads and the outskirts of towns. Apart from the ubiquitous local chain, Extra, foreign names such as Wal-Mart and Carrefour also have a formidable presence in Brazil.

In resorts, smaller shopping centers sell souvenirs and fashionable items. Department stores such as C&A and Lojas Americanas have found their way into shopping centers, although they exist more prominently as street shops in the large city centers.

Markets & Camelódromos

Almost every medium-size city in Brazil has its own special market, some located in beautiful historical buildings. Lively and picturesque, these markets sell an array of fresh products from meat and fish

Ver o Peso, Belém's picturesque waterfront *mercado* (market)

to fruit and cheese. Authentic regional food, typical sweets, and crafts can also be found here. Ver o Peso market in Belém (see p272) and public markets in Olinda (Pernambuco), Manaus (Rua dos Bares), and Porto Alegre (Rio Grande do Sul) are good examples.

Everywhere in Brazil, street traders or *camelôs* sell goods on improvised stands, or at places called *camelódromos*. A wide range of items, from clothes to electronics of fairly decent quality, are sold at reasonably reduced prices.

It is possible for shoppers to bargain at open-air markets. Vendors will often start at double the price of products, but with a little skill and some charm on the part of the buyer, this can be reduced. Be on guard in crowded street markets, as pickpockets are not uncommon. Be discreet when taking out money to pay.

Traditional musical instruments and masks for sale in Bahia

Art & Crafts

Every region in Brazil has its own distinctive handicrafts. The use of specific raw materials makes every piece of work unique. The best way to buy these pieces is to go directly to the *ateliers*. Tourist information offices can provide the addresses. Craft centers, where artists can be seen at work, offer lower prices than the upmarket souvenir shops.

Typical Amazonian crafts include indigenous masks, jewelry, plume helmets, basketwork, and bows and arrows in Manaus, Belém, and Santarém. Attractive replicas of Marajoara pottery are sold

in Belém and the Ilha de Marajó. Delicate lacework is found in all northeastern states, while Pernambuco and Bahia are famed for their fine ceramics.

Woven items, hand-crafted furniture, and Arraiolo tapestry are popular in Minas Gerais. In the south, Santa Catarina's crystalware is exceptional. In the state of Rio Grande do Sul, it is worth looking for good-quality leather as well as woolen items in Gramado and Caxias do Sul.

Gems

Brazil is one of the leading countries in the world's gem reserves. It is the world's largest exporter of rough-cut gems and the sixth-largest exporter of worked gems. The variety and quantity of precious stones are spectacular. Amethyst, citrine, diamond, emerald, opal, and royal topaz are just a few of the gems that Brazil is famous for. Rough and worked pieces can be bought in the cities of Ouro Preto (Minas Gerais), Cuiabá (Mato Grosso), Salvador and Chapada Diamantina (Bahia), and Porto Alegre. Designed jewelry can also be found in these places, as well as in São Paulo and Rio de Janeiro.

Although gems are largely sold in open-air markets, it is best to buy them at stores offering origin warranty certificates, which gives the weight (in carats), quality, origin, and – in the case of ready-made jewelry – the characteristics of any precious metal used.

Salesman displaying gems, Howard Stern Jewelers, Ipanema

Food & Drink

Brazil is known for its rich variety of conserves, dried fruits, and cakes (see pp384–5). Another favorite is fruit – figs, citron ciders, pineapples, and oranges – crystallized in compôte. These delicacies can be bought at public markets, craft centers, and confectioners' shops, found everywhere in Brazil.

An immensely popular beverage, *cachaça* (sugar-cane liquor) is produced all over the country and locally distilled (see p385). The best *cachaça* comes from Minas Gerais, Rio de Janeiro, Bahia, Pernambuco, and Ceará. It can also be bought at craft centers, local bars, and in hypermarkets in the larger cities.

Excellent coffee and gourmet blends are easily available in all big cities in Brazil. Look out for the ABIC seal on the packets, as this certifies the coffee quality.

Cachaça emporium in Paraty, with a large array of different types for sale

ENTERTAINMENT IN BRAZIL

Entertainment in Brazil varies according to the region and the city, but one thing is certain – Brazilians love going to bars, cafés, or *botecos* (a kind of bar with snacks and an old-fashioned atmosphere) to meet with friends and drink cold beer. This usually happens before and after other activities such as watching movies, plays, and shows. Dancing is another popular activity with Brazilians. In a country known for the richness of its rhythms, there are venues catering to all kinds of music and dancing, from *forró*, *samba*, and *axé* to techno and hiphop. Outdoor activities, such as soccer and volleyball, are national pastimes. Water parks, beaches, and public gardens are also good places to enjoy the warm weather and outdoor activities.

Information & Booking

Most Brazilian shows, such as plays and operas, do not run for very long and tickets must be booked quickly. Rio and São Paulo have specific magazines with a good listing of events and entertainment *(see p99 & p157)*. In most other Brazilian cities, local newspapers are the best way to find out what's on. They usually come with special sections or supplements on Fridays or on weekends showing cinema, theater, and other entertainment listings.

Only the most active theaters and concert houses provide listings on the Internet. In some big cities, shows can also be booked via Ticketmaster using Visa, MasterCard, and American Express, for a small additional service fee. Hotel concierges can often be helpful and informative when it comes to finding out what shows are on and booking them as well.

Discount Tickets & Free Events

In general, students and seniors (over 60) get a 50 percent discount for most events. The conditions for students vary from state to state. Students must usually show their university identity card or proof of enrollment. There are many free events at museums and cultural centers, but as they become crowded quickly, arriving early is wise.

Almost every city has one or more cultural centers. Supported by the government or by private companies, they often offer cheap tickets or free access to a variety of events, such as plays, dance, and art exhibitions, performed by professional or amateur companies.

Performing Arts

Theater and dance shows are popular in bigger cities in Brazil, where the theaters feature regular shows. At some resorts, dance or musical performances take place during the high season, or during specific summer or winter festivals. Most plays run only for a season. There is a fair amount of traditional and experimental theater, many dance performances, and chamber and classical music recitals to attend. Some performances have become annual traditions, such as *The Passion of Christ* play staged during Passion Week at an open-air theater in Nova Jerusalém *(see p227)* in the state of Pernambuco. Another big performance takes place every January in São Vicente *(see p173)*, retelling the story of the foundation of the town.

Musical shows are as prolific in Brazil. They take place at venues ranging from bars and theaters to sophisticated cultural centers. During music festivals, concerts are held in open-air areas, such as squares, public parks, or beaches. The really big and famous acts, which can be costly, usually perform in the stadia and require advance booking of tickets.

Cinema

In larger cities, most of the modern multiplex cinemas are located in shopping centers.

A view of the private boxes in the Teatro Amazonas, Manaus *(see pp286–7)*

Inside Rio City's world-famous soccer stadium, Estádio Maracanã *(see p88)*

These cinemas mainly feature recent Hollywood and European movies, as well as Brazilian films. There are also a few good cineclubs, especially in Rio and São Paulo, that host feature- and short-film festivals, often screening films with English subtitles. There are four main cinema chains operating in Brazil – United Cinemas International (UCI), Cinemark, Brazilian Playarte, and Cinemais. They offer facilities for disabled people, and sell tickets in advance via the Internet, or at the box office.

Bars, Cafés & Botecos

Nightlife is always exciting in large cities, resorts, and tourist areas. Bars are open through the week, usually after 6pm until 1 or 2am (some continue until sunrise, especially those on the beaches); some are open 24 hours. Most cities offer a wide variety of bars to visit – dance bars, bars with live music, and in the bigger cities, gay and lesbian bars. *Botecos* – traditionally *carioca* bars known for their simplicity and good snacks – have now been adopted by many cities and have increased in popularity and sophistication.

Happy hour is an institution in many of the larger cities. It begins at 6pm and extends until 9 or 10pm, after which many people carry on at all-night bars. Bars and kiosks on and near the beaches are often crowded

and buzzing with activity through the week, and especially on weekends. Cities without beaches generally make do with tables and chairs spread over the sidewalks with impromptu cafés sprouting up outside restaurants.

Soccer Matches

Soccer is a national passion – across Brazil there are 800 soccer clubs, 13,000 amateur teams, and 300 stadia, including Rio City's Estádio Maracanã *(see p88)*, which hosted the 2014 World Cup final. There are many championships through the year, with matches on Wednesdays, Thursdays, and weekends.

It is not always easy to get a ticket for these games, and very often there are immense queues to purchase tickets. Clubs and stadia do not

sell tickets on the Internet. There are some websites that sell tickets online, provided this is done well in advance. Most travel agencies and hotel concierges are able to assist with the finding and buying of soccer tickets.

Gardens & Theme Parks

Public gardens and parks are always crowded on weekends. Many of them offer jogging tracks, roller-skating rinks, sports courts for playing soccer, volleyball, basketball, tennis, and other games.

Theme parks are becoming increasingly popular everywhere in Brazil. Nowadays, most of these parks include some form of outdoor activity, such as swimming pools, waterslides, water tobogganing, horse-riding, and roller coasters.

Live music in the popular Carioca da Gema, Lapa district, Rio de Janeiro

SPECIALIZED HOLIDAYS & OUTDOOR ACTIVITIES

The climate and great variety of beautiful landscapes – mountains, flatlands, waterfalls, and forests – make Brazil an outstanding outdoor destination. This ecological paradise offers great opportunities to observe its fascinating flora and fauna, or to indulge in adventure sports that allow close contact with the environment. Visitors can choose from a range of thrilling activities such as rappeling down cliffs, canyoning, or climbing peaks in spectacular settings. However, the infrastructure varies from region to region. It is best to get in touch with reputed tour operators licensed by the Brazil Ministry of Tourism *(see p409)*, a government tourism agency. Other interesting activities may involve learning to dance to the beautiful rhythms of *forró* and *samba*, performing the legendary *capoeira*, or even joining a game of soccer.

Ecotourism

Brazil's rich and varied ecosystem has much to offer, and ecotourism has become a popular way to experience the wildlife up close. Visitors can capture on film the splendor of the Amazon rainforest near Manaus or Belem, or enjoy excursions deeper into the forest organized by jungle lodges. The farther away the lodges are from cities, the better the chances of spotting wildlife. **Amazon Mystery Tours** and **Amazon Gero** are based in Manaus; in Belém contact **Amazon Star**. **Pantanal Explorer** offers tours and expeditions into the wilderness of Pantanal, Nobres, and Chapada dos Guimarães from Cuiabá.

Serra da Capivara *(see pp252–3)* and Sete Cidades parks (Piauí) *(see p253)* offer hikes to see rock formations, while Chapada Diamantina in Bahia *(see pp208–9)* and Chapada dos Veadeiros *(see pp316–17)* in Goiás have good trekking trails, forested areas, and scenic waterfalls. National parks such as Serra dos Órgãos *(see p119)*, Parque Nacional do Itatiaia *(see p115)*, and Aparados da Serra *(see p362)*, and natural reserves such as Ilha do Cardoso *(see p175)* offer a broad range of biodiversity. Look for **Fazenda Palomas** or contact **Fellini Turismo** for special rural tours in Rio Grande do Sul.

When booking a tour, check the size of the group, how long will be spent at each location, whether an expert nature guide will be leading the tour, and what exactly is included. A key feature of ecotourism is the active involvement of the local community, so it is worth asking whether the tour will be visiting any families for meals or other activities. If the tour is by boat, going during wetter months, May–June, will allow small craft to go up side-creeks, with better possibilities of spotting wildlife. On the other hand, if much walking is involved, going during the drier months (July–Nov), will mean paths will be easier going and skies will be clearer.

Bird-Watching & Safaris

Home to almost a fifth of the world's bird population, Brazil offers a surfeit of bird-watching excursions. **Birding Brasil Turismo** provides good deals. **Iara Turismo** conducts special programs. **Estação Ecológica Santa Lúcia** organizes regular bird-watching. Ornithologist **Edson Endrigo** runs tours to Parque Nacional Itatiaia *(see p115)* and Ubatuba. A typical safari can be experienced at Jalapão State Park *(see p314–15)*. The travel agency **Korubo Expedições** uses a truck with hatches for professional photo equipment.

Off-Road Driving

Many beautiful sites in Brazil are accessible only by off-road vehicles. The Transpantaneira road (Pantanal) and the Estrada Park road are attractions in themselves, allowing passengers to leisurely observe the flora and fauna. The Transpantaneira extends 93 miles (149 km) from Poconé to Porto Jofre in Mato Grosso and has 126 wooden bridges to cross. Many inns and farms receive visitors

The rare and striking scarlet ibises that inhabit the Ilha de Marajó *(see p274)*

along this road. Stretching 73 miles (117 km), the Estrada Park road links Corumbá to Buraco das Piranhas (Piranha's Hole) in the state of Mato Grosso do Sul. Another enjoyable road experience is to cross Jalapão State Park, a wonderful contrast of golden dunes and gushing waterfalls. **Korubo Expedições** offers week-long packages leaving from Palmas. The Northeast region's off-road adventure *Rota das Dunas* (Dunes Route) runs from Fortaleza (Ceará) to São Luís (Maranhão), passing through Jericoacoara Beach and Delta do Parnaíba (a group of 80 islands) and Parque Nacional dos Lençóis Maranhenses *(see pp254–5)*. For bookings contact **Jeri Off-Road**.

Ecotourism by bicycle, Parque Nacional dos Lençóis Maranhenses

Cycling & Biking

Cycling and mountain biking have been attracting increasing numbers of enthusiasts to Brazil. Many tour operators rent bikes, and provide necessary equipment, food, and accommodation. Trancoso (Bahia) is the starting point of the Discovery Route – a crossing that passes through wonderful beaches. Contact **Sampa Bikers** for details. Another popular mountain-biking destination in Bahia is the Chapada Diamantina. **Terra Chapada Expedições** organizes multiday tours through the park.

Mountain biking is an interesting way to discover the attractions of Florianópolis

(Santa Catarina). There are 30 trails that traverse its 42 beaches, lakes, and stunning landscape. These and other options in the state can be found at **Caminhos do Sertão**. Cycling tours near the Parque Nacional Aparados da Serra covering the cities of Gramado, Canela, and the Vale dos Vinhedos *(see p359)* are organized by **Casa da Montanha Adventures**. Accommodation can be found at the Parador Casa da Montanha, a kind of luxurious camping site.

Water Sports

Vast stretches of beach, and an abundance of rivers, lakes, and waterfalls make water sports widely available and accessible in Brazil. Fernando de Noronha (Pernambuco) and Itacaré (Bahia) are hot destinations for water sports such as snorkeling, surfing, and windsurfing. Búzios and Rio (Rio de Janeiro), and Ubatuba and Guarujá (São

Paulo) are easier, while Praia Joaquinas and other beaches in Florianópolis offer more challenging water-sports activities *(see pp350–51)*.

The country has many scuba-diving options. **PDIC Brasil** (Professional Diving Instructor's Corporation) is a good place to contact. Rio de Janeiro state, Cabo Frio, Angra dos Reis, Paraty, and Ilhabela in São Paulo are outstanding places for diving and exploring shipwrecks. Beaches in the Northeast are a snorkeler's paradise.

Among the sail sports, kite-surf reigns in Ceará's beaches and lakes near Jericoacoara. **Info Kite School** provides facilities, tours, and safaris for intermediate to advanced kiters in Preá, a small fishing village east of Jericoacoara.

Rafting and canoeing enthusiasts should head to Brotas and Socorro, in São Paulo; Três Rios, in Rio de Janeiro; Domingos Martins, in Espírito Santo; Jaguariaíva and Tibagi, in Paraná; Apiúna, in Santa Catarina; and Rio Cristlino, in the Amazon rainforest of Mato Grosso.

Cascading and canyoning can be challenging, but highly enjoyable, in the waterfalls of Chapada dos Veadeiros in Goiás, and in the Cipó mountains in Minas Gerais where visitors can get in touch with **ABETA (Brazilian Adventure Travel Trade Association)**.

For those who enjoy fishing, **Clube de Pesca Cananéia** helps organize expeditions. This club also makes arrangements for the obligatory fishing license.

Canoeing on the Rio Cristalino near Cristalino Jungle Lodge *(see p323)*

Language & Culture

Almost 70 universities in the country offer Portuguese classes to foreign students. Many of these courses are now open to visitors. Some language schools also offer flexible Portuguese courses, which can stretch from one week to many months. These lessons may include lectures on Brazilian culture and guided tours of museums and galleries. Some of them prepare for the Portuguese Proficiency Certificate (CELPE-Bras), the Portuguese-language qualification granted by the **Ministério da Educação**. **Excellence Idiomas**, **Idiomas to Go**, and **Diálogo Language School** are some of the better private-school options.

Music & Dance

The sensuous dance forms of Brazil have evoked a lot of interest worldwide. With their natural hospitality, Brazilians are easily motivated to teach dance steps at bars, dance houses, parties, and local performances. You can also arrange to take professional dancing classes in the cities. In Rio de Janeiro, it is possible to learn with the famous dancer Carlinhos de Jesus at **Casa de Dança**. Diálogo Language School conducts workshops on dancing and singing to Brazilian rhythms, which may be tied in with Portuguese-language classes. Also, keep your ears open for reggae beats on the streets throughout the Northeast.

Couples dancing the *forró* on a festive occasion

Samba Schools

The neighborhood *samba* schools in Rio de Janeiro and other major cities are at the heart of the annual Carnaval. They work year round on their music and dance preparations, including making costumes and extravagant creations for their parades. Whether attending the Carnaval or not, visitors can take part in dance rehearsals, which is a fun way of meeting the locals and learning some samba moves. Top samba schools in Rio de Janeiro include **Beija Flor**, **Grande Rio**, **Mangueira**, **Portela**, and **Mocidade**.

Soccer

Soccer was introduced into Brazil by a Scottish railway engineer in the 1890s and grew to become the nation's favorite sport. It is possible to arrange day and residential soccer camps, as well as team and individual training sessions or family packages. The coaching programs vary from a week to several months and may include friendly games and tournaments for players between 6 and 18 years of age. Good options are **Central de Intercambio** in São Paulo City and **Cruzeiro Esporte Clube** in Belo Horizonte (Minas Gerais).

Capoeira Classes

The amalgam of acrobatic movements, rhythm, music, and song make *capoeira* (see p203) a big draw. Almost every city has an academy. In Salvador, **Filhos de Bimba** is one of the best and most famous *capoeira* schools. With several branches outside Brazil, it strives to keep alive the regional spirit of *capoeira*.

Volunteer Programs

Volunteers can work in non-profit organizations contributing in the fields of education, child welfare, health, ecology, and the environment. This is a good way of getting to know local people, and at the same time making a social contribution. These programs are open to adults of any age, and may include homestay with a Brazilian family. The program duration commonly varies from two to ten months. To enroll contact **Diálogo Language School**, **World Study** or **AFS Intercultura Brasil**. For all such programs, a basic knowledge of Portuguese is required.

A rigorous soccer training session, Ipanema beach, Rio de Janeiro City

DIRECTORY

Ecotourism

Amazon Mystery Tours
Rua 2, Casa 23 Parque Tropical.
Tel (92) 9 8430 7763.
W amazon-outdoor.com

Amazon Gero
Rua 10 de Julho 695, Manaus.
Tel (92) 3232 4755.
W amazongero.com

Amazon Star
Rua Henrique Gurjão 236, Belem, Pará.
Tel (91) 3212 6244.
W amazonstar.com.br

Fazenda Palomas
BR-158 Santana do Livramento, Rio Grande do Sul.
Tel (55) 3505 6417.

Fellini Turismo
Rua Gen Bento Martins, 24 Conj. 401, Porto Alegre, Rio Grande do Sul.
Tel (51) 3216 6300.

Pantanal Explorer
Av Governador Ponce de Arruda 670, Varzea Grande, Mato Grosso.
Tel (65) 3682 2800.

Bird-Watching & Safaris

Birding Brasil Turismo
Conjunto Acariquara 214, Manaus, Amazonas.
W birdingbraziltours.com

Edson Endrigo
Rua Antonio Aggio 1296/11, São Paulo.
Tel (11) 3742 8374.
W avesfoto.com.br

Estação Ecológica Santa Lúcia
Av José Ruschi 4, Museu Mello Leitão, Santa Teresa, Espírito Santo.
Tel (27) 3259 1182.

Iara Turismo
Av Gov José Maicher 815, Belém, Pará.
Tel (91) 4006 3850.
W iaraturismo.com.br

Korubo Expedições
Rua Traipu 260, São Paulo.
Tel (11) 8222 5028.
W jalapao.com

Off-Road Driving

Jeri Off-Road
Rua Principal 208. Jericoacoara, Ceará.
Tel (88) 3669 2268.
W jeri.tur.br

Cycling & Biking

Caminhos do Sertão
Rua Caminho do Arvoredo 169, Rio Vermelho, Florianópolis, Santa Catarina.
Tel (48) 3234 7712.
W caminhosdosertao.com.br

Casa da Montanha Adventures
Av Borges Medeiros 3116, Gramado.
Tel (54) 3295 7525.
W paradorcasadamontanha.com.br

Sampa Bikers
Rua Baluarte 672, São Paulo.
Tel (11) 5517 7733.
W sampabikers.com.br

Terra Chapada Expedições
Tel (75) 3334 1428.
W terrachapada.com.br

Water Sports

ABETA (Brazilian Adventure Travel Trade Association)
Rua Minerva 156, Perdizes, São Paulo.
Tel (11) 2371 5336.
W abeta.tur.br

Clube de Pesca Cananéia
Rua João Maciel, Porto Cubatão, Cananéia, São Paulo.
Tel (13) 3851 6117.
W pescacananeia.com.br

Info Kite School
Rua Sao Francisco, Jeri Center, Jericoacoara.
Tel (88) 9922 0922.

PDIC Brasil (Professional Diving Instructors Corporation)
Av Presidente Vargas 446, Grupo 1006, Rio de Janeiro.
Tel (21) 2263 8068.
W pdic.com.br

Language & Culture

Diálogo Language School
Rua João Ponde 240, Barra, Salvador, Bahia.
Tel (71) 3264 0053.
W dialogo-brazilstudy.com

Excellence Idiomas
Rua Barata Ribeiro 391, Copacabana.
Tel (21) 2225 7430.
W excellenceidiomas.com.br

Idiomas to Go
Alameda Jauaperi 1020, São Paulo.
Tel (11) 5052 4802.
W idiomastogo. com.br

Ministério da Educação
Esplanada dos Ministérios, Bloco L, Sala 227, Brasília.
Tel (0800) 616161.
W sisu.mec.gov.br

Music & Dance

Casa de Dança
Rua Álvaro Ramos 11, Botafogo, Rio de Janeiro.
Tel (21) 2541 6186.
W carlinhosdejesus.com.br

Samba Schools

Beija Flor
Pracinha Wallace Paes Leme 1025, Nilópolis.
Tel (21) 2247 4800.
W beija-flor.com.br

Grande Rio
Colégio São José, Avenida Presidente Kennedy, Duque de Caxias.
Tel (21) 2671 3585.
W academicosdograndrio.com.br

Mangueira
Rua Visconde de Niterói 1072, Mangueira.
Tel (21) 2567 3419.
W mangueira.com.br

Mocidade
Avenida Brasil, 31.146, Padre Miguel.
Tel (21) 3291 8700.
W mocidadeindependente.com.br

Portela
Rua Clara Nunes 81, Madureira.
Tel (21) 2247 4800.
W gresportela.org.br

Soccer

Central de Intercambio
Av Paulista 726, Loja 7, São Paulo.
Tel (11) 3262 4012.

Cruzeiro Esporte Clube
Av Otacílio Negrão de Lima 7100, Bairro Bandeirante, Belo Horizonte.
W cruzeiro.com.br

Capoeira Classes

Filhos de Bimba
Rua Gregório de Mattos 51, Pelourinho, Salvador, Bahia.
Tel (71) 3322 5082.
W filhosdebimba.com.br

Volunteer Programs

AFS Intercultura Brasil
Rua Teófilo Otoni, 82 Centro.
Tel (21) 0800 291 0121.
W afs.org.br

World Study
Rua Piumí 987, Sion, Belo Horizonte, Minas Gerias.
Tel (31) 2535 0987.
W worldstudy.com.br

SURVIVAL GUIDE

Practical Information   408–417

Travel Information   418–427

PRACTICAL INFORMATION

Tourism is a major industry in Brazil, and the country has invested heavily in airports, hotels, and other facilities. Brazil offers a variety of travel experiences for all ages and tastes, from the cities of Rio de Janeiro and São Paulo to the Amazon jungle, rainforests, and beaches . Its sheer size makes air travel almost a necessity for those interested in exploring beyond just one region. All major tourist destinations are very well set up to receive international visitors. English and Spanish are generally spoken by those who work in the tourism industry. However, very few other Brazilians speak English. Fortunately, the friendliness and outgoing nature of the people more than makes up for these challenges and Brazilians overall are very helpful in assisting foreigners.

When to Go

High season in Brazil runs from Christmas to Carnaval (held in February or early March). Many musical and cultural events take place in these months. A second peak season is during July and August when schools and universities have their winter break and many Europeans and North Americans visit on their summer holidays. The best times of year for lower prices and fewer travelers are the low seasons from March to May and September to November.

What to Take

Dress standards in Brazil seem largely a matter of personal taste. A sarong or sheet sleeping bag is invaluable for use as a towel, a bedsheet, or beach towel. Bring a first-aid kit, raincoat, sun hat, penknife, flashlight, wax earplugs, insect repellent, eye mask, and a chain for securing luggage to bus seats. For a jungle trip, a hammock and mosquito net will be useful.

A local travel agency with Internet facilities, Morro de São Paulo

Visas & Passports

All travelers to Brazil except those from some South American countries must have a valid passport. Holders of European Union and of most European, New Zealand, Mexico, and South African passports do not require a visa. Those with US, Canadian, or Australian passports need to apply for a visa at the Brazilian embassy or consulate in their country of residence. Always check the latest entry requirements with the Brazilian embassy in your country before leaving.

Upon arrival, visitors receive a 90-day entry stamp, which can be extended for another 90 days by the **Polícia Federal**, up to a maximum of 180 days per year. (Some nationalities are unable to extend beyond 90 days.) Visitors must also fill out an entry card to be kept with their passport at all times. It must be surrendered on leaving Brazil. Failure to produce this entry card may lead to a fine and difficulties. The 90 days are added on the day of renewal, so request the extension close to the expiry date. An expired visa cannot be extended.

The Polícia Federal may ask to see an outbound ticket and proof of sufficient funds for the remainder of your stay. Those who outstay their visa term will be fined upon departure.

Polícia Federal badge

Travel Safety Advice

Visitors can get up-to-date travel safety information from the **State Department** in the US, the **Foreign and Commonwealth Office** in the UK and the **Department of Foreign Affairs and Trade** in Australia.

Tourist Information

All international and domestic airports in Brazil have tourist information booths that offer maps, brochures, and general information. These are usually run by either the state or city's tourist office. The **Brazilian Ministry of Tourism**'s website is a useful source of information. Brazil's embassies or larger consulates have tourist sections, where visitors can get information brochures and advice. Popular destinations such as Rio and Salvador have helpful tourist offices.

Language

The language of Brazil is Portuguese, but it is quite different in style and pronunciation from the Portuguese spoken in Portugal. The language has quite a few similarities with Spanish. In major tourist areas, the staff will speak some English and/or Spanish. However, in general, English is not widely spoken and often Brazilians will only have a basic intermediate knowledge of the language.

Religion

Brazil is often called "the largest Catholic country on earth," although, to be accurate, one should probably call it the "largest and least devout" of

◀ A small airplane flies over Parque Nacional dos Lençóis Maranhenses

Catholic nations. Many Brazilians consider themselves culturally Catholic, without being regular churchgoers. In recent years, the influence of the Church has greatly diminished. Traditional Afro-Brazilian religions are still followed, especially in the North and Northeast, with the religious ceremonies and practices gaining more acceptance over the years.

Time

Brazil has four time zones. Most of the country is three hours behind GMT (known as the Brasília Time Zone), including Rio de Janeiro and São Paulo, as well as all of Southern and Northeast Brazil and Pará and Amapá states. The island group of Fernando de Noronha is two hours behind GMT. The states of Mato Grosso, Mato Grosso do Sul, Amazônia, Rondônia, and Roraima are four hours behind GMT. The state of Acre, in the far western corner, is five hours behind GMT. During daylight saving hours it gets a little bit more complicated. The southern states set their clocks back an hour, but the states in the North and Northeast do not.

Electricity

There is no uniform voltage across Brazil. Some cities are 110 volts, others 220 volts. Rio de Janeiro and São Paulo are both 110 volts. Brasília is 220 volts. Hotels will often have plugs for both voltages and are good at labeling the outlets. Adaptors for laptops and cell phone chargers can normally handle the full range of voltage, but it is always better to check the specifications of your equipment to be sure.

Etiquette

Brazilians are very friendly and outgoing, even when meeting someone for the first time. When introduced, men will greet each other with a handshake and a friendly slap on the shoulder. Good friends usually

Local tour guide with a group of tourists in Cachoeira

embrace. When introduced to a woman, it is customary to greet her with a handshake and a kiss on the cheek (one kiss in São Paulo and the South, two kisses in Rio, the North, and Northeast). When introduced to a group of people, everybody has to kiss or shake hands with everybody else.

Women Travelers

A woman alone, especially at night, will attract some form of attention. It usually depends on where you are. Steer clear of the area around bus stations, since it is likely to be a red-light area at night. The transport terminals themselves, though, are usually policed and fairly safe at all hours.

Special Needs

Travelers with mobility problems will find Brazil a very challenging country. Although it is relatively easy to find wheelchair-accessible hotels and restaurants, very few public places are accessible or wheelchair-friendly. Older buildings may still lack elevators or ramps, and streets and sidewalks are often uneven or broken. The metro system in Rio has electronic wheelchair elevators, but these are not always operational. For short distances, buses are not the best option for disabled travelers to get around. Taxis are better, and plentiful in most cities. For long distances, however,

Wheelchair parking sign

buses are generally comfortable, with special services offering fully reclining seats. Wheelchairs are available at all main airports.

Traveling with Children

Those traveling with small children will find Brazilians very child-friendly and accommodating. There are virtually no places that do not welcome children. Brazilians themselves think nothing of bringing their children to restaurants, theaters, cafés, concerts, or other events.

Public Toilets

Public toilets are not that hard to find in Brazil, but vary greatly in cleanliness. Clean toilets can usually be found in hotel lobbies, shopping centers, and in public locations such as bus stations, parks, or beaches. A fee is sometimes charged. Note that toilet paper is sometimes dispensed from a central dispenser outside the stalls. It is a good idea to carry a roll of toilet paper.

Directory
Visas & Passports

Polícia Federal
Aeroporto Internacional Antônio Carlos Jobim, Terminal 1, Rio de Janeiro.
Tel (21) 3398 3182.
W dpf.gov.br

Travel Safety Advice

Australia
Department of Foreign Affairs and Trade. W dfat.gov.au
W smartraveller.gov.au

UK
Foreign and Commonwealth Office. W gov.uk/foreign-travel-advice

US
US Department of State.
W travel.state.gov

Tourist Information

Brazilian Ministry of Tourism
W visitbrazil.com

Health & Medical Matters

Brazil has a free national public health-care system. Even foreign tourists will receive medical attention in any of the public hospitals, should they require it. Unfortunately, the public health system is overloaded and inadequately funded, especially in the rural areas of Brazil. Queues can be long and tedious, and facilities are not always up to European or North American standards. However, Brazil's private hospitals and clinics, though not free, offer world-class medical facilities. A good travel insurance policy will give access to these private facilities in an emergency, but remember to check the fine print carefully. Overall, hygiene standards in Brazil are high. Normal care is required with food and drink, and with preventive vaccinations, particularly when visiting the most remote parts of the country.

A fire brigade ambulance parked outside a fire control office

Vaccinations

It is a good idea to consult a travel clinic or family doctor for an International Certificate of Vaccinations, an up-to-date list of the required vaccinations. The most commonly recommended are a DTP (diphtheria, tetanus, and polio) booster, as well as vaccinations for typhoid and hepatitis A.

Vaccination against yellow fever (endemic to many parts of South America) is highly recommended, especially if you are planning to visit rural areas in Minas Gerais, Espírito Santo, and Northern Rio de Janeiro State. It is advisable to take this vaccination 10 days prior to arriving in Brazil. Anti-malarial tablets may be advisable for those visiting some of the more remote parts of the Amazon.

Tropical Diseases

Visitors to Brazil's major tourist destinations rarely have to worry about tropical diseases.

However, a tropical disease that can occur anywhere in the country, but is most abundant in towns, cities, and surrounding areas, is dengue fever. It is a viral infection that prevails through-out South America. The disease is transmitted by mosquitoes, and there is no vaccine to prevent it. It is much more common in the summer months, from December to

March. Symptoms include high fever, joint pain, and headaches (especially behind the eyes). The illness usually runs its course in a week or 10 days, but a check-up is recommended to avoid any complications. Visitors to Brazil should take steps to avoid being bitten by mosquitoes by using mosquito repellent, especially between dusk and dawn.

Cholera occasionally occurs in remote areas, but is mostly preventable by taking proper hygiene precautions such as drinking filtered water and washing and peeling fruit and vegetables. The most important precaution is to wash hands frequently.

Pharmacies

For minor ailments, travelers can turn to Brazil's *farmácias*, or pharmacies. These can be found everywhere, are always well supplied, and are often open late. Every city will have at least one that is open 24 hours. Many medications that in other countries are available only by prescription can be bought over the counter in Brazil. Take care to remember the generic name of a medication taken regularly. A trained pharmacist is normally on hand to recommend the appropriate medication for common ailments such as diarrhea, allergies, rashes, or infections. It is possible to get injections and free medical advice in pharmacies all over Brazil.

A well-stocked pharmacy in São Paulo

Vacationers relaxing under umbrellas on the beach

Private Hospitals

Brazil does not offer the best medical facilities in its public hospitals. Foreign visitors, in particular, may find it difficult getting a bed, unless for an infectious disease. In most public hospitals, the level of health care will not match European or US standards.

Private hospitals, however, offer excellent facilities. Though good medical care may be rare to find in rural areas, in the larger cities you will never be far from a decent private hospital. In many big cities, local tourist offices and some good hotels can provide a list of doctors who can speak English, French, and German.

For medical emergencies in a remote area, an air ambulance service offers a pick-up within 24 hours of calling. However, it is advisable to contact the travel insurance company before requesting this service.

Though fairly affordable by international standards, private treatment in Brazil may turn out to be expensive. Many doctors and hospitals do not accept travel-health insurance, and insist on payment in cash.

Health Precautions

A visit to Brazil, by and large, does not require special health precautions. Impure water and contaminated food are usually the reasons for most diseases. Tap water in the main cities,

such as Rio de Janeiro and São Paulo, is generally safe to drink. In rural areas it is best avoided. Hygiene standards of food and drink are high in major tourist areas. Water is usually filtered or bottled and ice cubes are made from filtered water. Even in the most remote parts, mineral water can easily be bought.

A local drink seller on a Rio de Janeiro beach

Sun protection

Visitors from the Northern Hemisphere should take extra care with Brazil's intense tropical sun, especially for the first few days in the country. Brazil basks in almost year-round sunshine, making adequate sun protection absolutely crucial. Avoid exposure between 11am and 3pm and apply sunscreen to all exposed parts of the body. Wear sunblock (minimum SPF 30) and limit tanning to only a few hours. Pharmacies and grocery

stores sell a variety of national and international sunscreen brands. Those sold on the beach itself, or in street markets, are best avoided. The contents may either be fake, or have been kept in storage for a long time, which causes the active ingredients to deteriorate.

Directory

Emergency Numbers

Ambulance
Tel 192.

Private Hospitals

Rio de Janeiro
Hospital Samaritano, Rua Bambina 98, Botafogo.
Tel (21) 3444 1000.
W hsamaritano.com.br

Copa d'Or, Rua Figueiredo de Magalhães 875, Copacabana.
Map 3 D1.
Tel (21) 2545 3600.
W copador.com.br

Hospital Federal de Ipanema, Rua Antônio Parreiras 67, Ipanema.
Map 2 C4.
Tel (21) 3111 2303.

São Paulo
Hospital Albert Einstein, Av Albert Einstein 627–701, Morumbi.
Tel (11) 2151 1233. For ambulance: (11) 3747 0200.
W einstein.br

Hospital Sírio-Libânes, Rua Dona Adma Jafet 91, Bela Vista.
Map 4 F2.
Tel (11) 3394 0200.
W hospitalsiriolibanes.org.br

Safety for Travelers

Brazil is known to have a higher crime rate than anywhere in North America and Europe. However, in reality, the kind of violence that affects travelers is mostly limited to the bigger cities, and is usually restricted to thefts of valuables such as cameras, credit cards, cell phones, or cash. Such assaults are rare in the countryside and smaller towns. While some parts of Brazil can truly be regarded as violent and dangerous, travelers can be assured of personal security by using common sense and observing some very basic precautions.

A Guarda Municipal policewoman patrolling on a bicycle, Rio City

Local showing the way to visitors, Salvador

Personal Safety

The large cities, especially Rio de Janeiro, São Paulo, and Salvador, are generally considered more prone to violence than the rest of Brazil. Statistically, crime rates in these cities are significantly higher than in cities in Europe or the US. However, much of the violent crime is confined to poorer neighborhoods and *favelas* in parts of the city where travelers should not venture on their own without a tour guide. The crime that visitors are most likely to is susceptible to is theft or robbery. The most basic precaution is not to carry anything worth stealing and to avoid empty beaches and nearly empty streets after dark. Avoid ostentatious behavior such as walking around with expensive equipment; instead keep it in a plain bag.

When sightseeing, keep all belongings in a bag that can be placed in a money belt. Never carry large amounts of cash. Credit cards are widely accepted and can be used for purchases in most hotels and stores. Keep a few small bills handy in a pocket so that when making small purchases, the wallet doesn't have to be pulled out in a busy area. Public transport is safe in the daytime, but in the evenings taxis are a better option. If you get robbed, just hand over your valuables, as robbers are often armed with a gun or a knife. Streets and public places can be unsafe at times. A very common technique is to distract the victim by spraying something on their shoulder. An accomplice may then offer to clean the mess, while the thief will make off with your belongings. The best and safest way is to politely turn down any such offer.

It is always best to exercise caution when someone unknown offers a drink, or even cigarettes. Instances of drugging, or spiked drinks are not uncommon in Brazil.

Police

Brazil has several different types of police that travelers are likely to encounter. Known to be the most efficient by far, the **Polícia Federal** *(see p408)* are responsible for passport control at airports and border crossings. Dressed in plain clothes, they deal with visas and their extensions.

Dressed in gray uniforms and caps, the **Polícia Militar** are responsible for public safety and can be seen patrolling the streets, beaches, and highways. These policemen often carry out "blitzes" (traffic checks) along major streets or roads. These can appear a little intimidating as the Polícia Militar come out in full gear, carrying automatic weapons. If you are driving a car, slow down, turn on the interior light, and roll down the windows.

A brightly painted tourist police station in Olinda

A few cities with a strong tourist presence, such as Rio and Salvador, also have **Polícia de Turismo**, or tourist police, who offer assistance in case of any difficulty. Unfortunately, many of them do not speak English. A special Delegacia do Turista (tourist department) is available for those who require further help or wish to report a crime.

The state-controlled **Polícia Civil** handle local laws and investigate more serious crimes. When there is no tourist police post in the vicinity, thefts are reported to these policemen. Rio City has an unarmed guard force, **Guarda Municipal** (Municipal Civil Guards), to complement state police patrolling of parks and beaches. Polícia Federal car

Reporting a Crime

If you have been the victim of a crime, it can be reported at the nearest police station or tourist police office. This should be done within 24 hours of the crime. To obtain a report of the incident or theft for insurance purposes, insist that you receive a copy of the *boletim de ocorrência*. There may be nobody at the police station who speaks English, so it may be useful to request a hotel employee or tour guide to accompany you if you need

Polícia Militar booth in São Paulo, responsible for traffic checks

to file a report. Missing credit cards should be reported to the relevant company *(see p414)*. If you have lost or damaged your passport, it is recommended that you contact your nearest consulate or embassy.

Identification

It is mandatory in Brazil to carry some form of photo identification. Often you will be asked to show some form of ID when entering an office building or government agency, or sometimes even a museum or library. To avoid carrying around a passport, keep a photocopy, and carry some other form of less valuable ID such as a student card, or a health card that has your picture, name, and date of birth.

Directory

Police

Guarda Municipal
W rio.rj.gov.br/web/gmrio

Polícia Civil
Tel 197.

Polícia Militar
Tel 190.

Polícia de Turismo
RIO DE JANEIRO
Av Afrânio de Melo Franco 159,
Leblon. **Map** 1 B4.
Tel (21) 2332 2924.
SALVADOR
Praça São Francisco 14,
Pelourinho. **Tel** (71) 3322 1188.
SÃO PAULO
Rua Cantareira 390, Centro.
Map 2 D2. **Tel** (11) 3120 4417.

Consulates

Australia
Av Presidente Wilson 231, Centro,
Rio de Janeiro.
Map 5 E5. **Tel** (21) 3824 4624.
W brazil.embassy.gov.au
Alameda Santos 700,
Jardim Paulista, São Paulo.
Tel (11) 2112 6200

Canada
Av Atlântica 1130, 5th Floor,
Copacabana, Rio de Janeiro.
Map 3 F1. **Tel** (21) 2453 3004.
Av Nações Unidas 12901,
São Paulo. **Tel** (11) 5509 4321.
W brazil.gc.ca

Ireland
SHIS QL 12 Conjunto 5 Casa 9,
Lago Sul, Brasília.
Tel (61) 3248 8800.
Avenida Paulista 2421, Centro,
São Paulo. **Tel** (11) 3898 7400

New Zealand
SHIS QI 09, Conjunto 16,
Casa 01, Brasília.
Tel (61) 3248 9900.

UK
Praia do Flamengo 284, Rio de
Janeiro. **Tel** (21) 2292 7117.
Rua Ferreira de Araújo 741,
Pinheiros, São Paulo.
Tel (11) 3094 2700.

USA
Av Presidente Wilson 147, Rio de
Janeiro. **Map** 5 E5.
Tel (21) 3823 2000.
Rua Henri Dunant 500, São Paulo.
Tel (11) 3250 5000.

Guarda Municipal car in Rio de Janeiro

Banking & Local Currency

Brazil provides a range of banking facilities and money exchange services. Except for the US dollar and euro, foreign currencies are rarely accepted outside of major tourist regions. Exchange rates for cash transactions are usually not very good, and the best rates can be obtained on credit card or *caixa automática* (ATM) transactions. By far the most convenient are credit cards (particularly Visa and MasterCard), which are widely accepted in most establishments and can be used to withdraw local currency (*real*), giving a more favorable exchange rate. Traveler's checks are not widely accepted and can be difficult to cash.

Banking Hours

Bradesco has a number of banks that are open from 9am to 5pm on all weekdays. Most other banks, including **Banco do Brasil**, are also open on weekdays, but only from 10am to 4pm. Hours for changing money are even more limited, usually falling between 11am and 2pm. ATMs have more flexible hours but are not always open 24 hours.

ATMs

The easiest way of getting cash in big cities is by using ATMs (*caixa automática*), which are widely found and accept foreign cards. Check with your bank prior to traveling to Brazil whether your ATM card can be used internationally for cash withdrawals and that you have the appropriate PIN (*numero de identificao*). In addition to ATM cards, most bank machines will also give a cash advance on a credit card. Banco do Brasil,

ATM (*caixa automática*) at a branch of Banco do Brasil

HSBC, Citibank, Bradesco, and Banco 24 Horas have reliable networks that work with international cards.

Bank machines are often updated and adjusted so other banks may join the network. For safety reasons, bank machines are not always open 24 hours. ATMs may close at 8 or 10pm, or be programmed to dispense only a small amount of money.

Branch of Banco do Brasil

Directory

Credit Cards

AmEx
Tel 0800 761 1794.

Diners Club Citibank
Tel 0800 701 2484.

MasterCard
Tel 0800 891 3294.

Visa
Tel 0800 891 3680.

Banks

Banco do Brasil
Av Paulista 2163, São Paulo.
Map 4 E2. Tel (11) 4004 0001.

Rua Joana Angélica 124,
Ipanema, Rio de Janeiro.
Map 2 A4. Tel (21) 3554 9700.
W bb.com.br

Bradesco
Av Paulista 949, São Paulo.
Map 4 E2. Tel (11) 4004 4722.

Av Nossa Senhora de
Copacabana 583, Rio de Janeiro.
Map 3 E2. Tel (21) 3816 8100.
W bradesco.com.br

It is also good to plan ahead on weekends or statutory holidays when machines sometimes run out of cash. Keep in mind, too, that some small towns and islands do not have ATMs.

Credit Cards

Credit cards are widely accepted in Brazil. The most commonly used cards are **MasterCard**, **Visa**, and **AmEx**. **Diners Club** is less widely used. Credit cards can be used in almost all stores, hotels, and restaurants. Street markets and kiosks, usually only take cash. When you pay by credit card the cashier will usually ask "*débito ou credito*" (debit or credit). It is important to state "*credito*" as most international credit cards do not work as debit cards. Debit cards are also widely accepted. Credit cards with a PIN can also be used to make cash withdrawals from ATMs at banks. The service fee is higher for using a credit card instead of a regular ATM card. It is a good idea to instruct your bank that you will be using your card in Brazil, so as to avoid any transaction problems at a later stage.

Very few banks other than a handful in major cities, will cash traveler's checks, and at those that do, there is a high fee and a long wait. Some hotels and some tour operators will accept traveler's checks, but the exchange is always unfavorable. American Express will cash AmEx traveler's checks for free, but they only have offices in a few major cities in Brazil. It is more convenient to use a credit card for major expenses incurred at hotels and on excursions. Another option is to obtain a prepaid currency card and load it with Brazilian Reais before you travel. Use it in Brazil like a debit card to withdraw money from ATMs, or to pay for goods at most places.

Currency

The currency of Brazil is the *real* (R$, plural *reais*). All bank notes have a print of a Brazilian animal on them. The smallest R$2 note is blue, featuring a sea turtle. The purple R$5 and the red R$10 have pictures of a heron and a macaw respectively. The yellow R$20 notes feature the endangered *mico-leão dourado* (golden lion tamarin) monkey. The brown R$50 notes come with a picture of a jaguar. R$100 bills, featuring the endangered dusky grouper fish, are often impossible to break at small shops, so stock up on change at drugstores and grocery stores.

Banknotes

Brazilian reais bills come in denominations of 2, 5, 10, 20, 50, and 100. Brazilian bank notes are bright, with each denomination coming in a different color.

2 *reais*

5 *reais*

10 *reais*

20 *reais*

50 *reais*

100 *reais*

Coins

*Coins come in the following denomination:
5, 10, 25, 50 centavos and 1 real.
100 centavos make up 1 real.*

5 *centavos*   10 *centavos*   25 *centavos*   50 *centavos*   1 *real*

Communications & Media

Brazil has an efficient and well-developed communications system. Cell phones are widely used, making Brazil's one of the world's biggest networks, with more than 270 million registered phones. Postal services, including registered post and express mail, are quite reliable. Most hotels subscribe to a digital or satellite television service with international channels. Although there are no foreign-language Brazilian newspapers, foreign magazines and some newspapers are available in all major cities, mostly in the main airports, business districts, and tourist centers.

Public telephones, not as widespread in Brazil as they once were

Local & International Phone Calls

Most telephone numbers in Brazil (fixed or cell) are now eight or nine digits. If you do come across a seven-digit number (or eight-digit cell), it is best to confirm if it is still correct. All cell phone numbers begin with a 9.

Local calls do not require a two-digit area code, whereas long-distance calls do. All long-distance calls (within Brazil and international) also require the use of a long-distance service provider (*prestadora*). The two-digit code of the *prestadora* needs to be dialed before the area code or country code for international calls; there are different services for fixed and cell lines. In listings, long-distance numbers often look like this: 0-XX-11-3455-3288. The two-digit *prestadora* number is inserted in place of the "XX" and is known as the *código de seleção de prestadora* (CSP).

Customers have several options when choosing a service provider, depending on the region. **Embratel** is Brazil's largest telecommunications company. If using Embratel to call São Paulo, the number would look like this: 0-21-11-3455-3288. This can be confusing because some *prestadora* codes are the same as some area codes – Embratel and Rio, for example.

Cell Phones

Cell phones are common all over the country. Most tri-band GSM phones will work in Brazil. Coverage for 4G is available in major cities, but in many other places, and especially rural areas, there is 3G or 2G coverage. You can purchase a local SIM chip upon arrival and obtain a local number. Most local cell operators offer a very straightforward package for international visitors, including for data.

Check with your phone company whether your phone needs to be unlocked before leaving home. If your service provider has a roaming agreement with Brazil, you can use your regular number.

A woman on her cell phone in the Ipanema neighborhood of Rio de Janeiro

However, inquire about roaming fees to avoid nasty surprises on your phone bill. Due to the size of Brazil, most cell phone packages are relevant to the city or state it is issued in, so you may still be charged roaming fees when using a Brazilian cell number – for example, for using a Rio cell number in São Paulo. Brazilians who regularly visit different cities in Brazil often have cell numbers for each one.

The main cell operators in Brazil are **Claro** (21), **Oi** (31), **Tim** (41), and **Vivo** (15). It is always cheapest to use the *código de seleção de prestadora* (CSP) of the network you are linked to when calling.

Public Telephones

As in many countries, public telephones (*orelhões*, or "big ears") are diminishing in Brazil. Pay phones do not take coins. You must purchase a phone card (*cartão telefonico*), available at newsstands, drugstores, and post offices.

Internet

Internet service is widely available in Brazil and it is the world's fourth largest country of internet users. If traveling with a

---

Dialing Codes

- A local call requires only the eight- or nine-digit number of the land line or cell without the area code. Some key area codes are: Belo Horizonte, 31; Brasília, 61; Curitiba, 41; Fortaleza, 85; Manaus, 92; Natal, 84; Porto Alegre, 51; Recife, 81; Rio de Janeiro, 21; Salvador, 71; São Paulo, 11.
- To make a long-distance call, dial 0 or +, then the *prestadora* code (CSP), followed by the area code, and phone number.
- To call abroad from Brazil, dial 00, then the *prestadora* code, followed by the country code, area code, and phone number.
- Contact Embratel at 0800 703 2100 or 0800 703 2111 to ask for collect calls or international calls.

The distinct blue and yellow colors of a post office in Rio de Janeiro

laptop, ask about the hotel's Wi-Fi Internet access rates, although at more and more hotels it is free. Cyber cafés, such as **Cyber Copa Café** in Rio de Janeiro, are not as widespread as they once were.

There are free Wi-Fi hotspots in some public areas in big cities such as Rio de Janeiro and São Paulo, including squares, shopping malls, and beaches. Some cafés, restaurants, and bookstores, such as **FNAC Centro Cultural** and **Icone Espaço Cultural** in São Paulo and **Livraria da Travessa** in Rio de Janeiro, have free Wi-Fi.

Postal Services

The Brazilian postal service is quite efficient for registered mail. Post offices (*correios*) are open from 9am to 5pm Monday to Friday. Large shopping centers and airports will have branches with longer opening hours, including Saturdays. Regular delivery service within Brazil takes two to four days, and overseas six to 12 days. For guaranteed or registered delivery, the *correios* offer the excellent SEDEX (domestic Brazilian express mail) service, which functions like a courier service. For international mail, there is SEDEX Mundi and Express Mail Service (EMS). The *correios* has a good website, parts of which are in English, which allows you to check addresses, postal codes (known as CEP), locate post office branches, or track deliveries. In larger cities, there are also several international couriers for

express overseas delivery, such as **DHL**, **FedEx**, **Skynet**, and **World Courier**. Delivery from Brazil to the main cities and towns in the US or Europe normally takes 48 hours.

Addresses

Most addresses are fairly straight-forward, giving the street name first, followed by the number. Landmark buildings or houses in small towns may be listed as s/n (*sem número*, or without number). Other abbreviations in addresses include lj or *loja* (shop) and sl or *sobreloja* (first floor or mezzanine). You should add the zip or postal code (CEP), if you have it.

Newspapers & Magazines

Brazil does not have any English-language daily newspapers or magazines. The main Brazilian dailies are, like in the US, regional, the best known being *O Globo* (Rio de Janeiro) and the *Folha de São Paulo* (São Paulo). The Friday editions include a cultural and entertainment section with detailed information on concerts, plays, movies, and exhibitions. The bestselling weekly news magazines are *Época*, *Veja*, and *Isto É*. In Rio de Janeiro, São Paulo, and other large cities, the *Veja (see p156)* includes listings related to cultural events.

Newspapers and magazines are most commonly sold at a newsstand (*banca de jornal*). Newsstands in Ipanema in Rio and Praça de Republica in São Paulo have a good range of international magazines, as do the better bookstores, especially in major shopping centers.

Television & Radio

Brazil is well served when it comes to both television and radio, although most of the local programming will be in Portuguese, but this can add to the flavor of a local football match or sporting event. The media giant in Brazil is Globo. It is responsible for the country's most popular TV network, as

well as a large number of national and regional radio networks, newspapers, magazines, and websites. At hotels and in many houses, visitors will have access to hundreds of digital or satellite channels that include inter-national news services such as CNN and the BBC. On the Internet, you will be able to access radio stations from around the world.

Directory

Local & International Phone Calls

Embratel
W embratel.com.br

Cell Phones

Claro
W claro.com.br

Oi
W oi.com.br

Tim
W tim.com.br

Vivo
W vivo.com.br

Internet

Cyber Copa Café
Av Nossa Senhora de Copacabana 1077, Rio de Janeiro.
Map 2 C4. **Tel** (21) 2287 9403.

FNAC Centro Cultural
Praça do Omaguás 34, Pinheiros, São Paulo. **Tel** (11) 3579 2000.

Icone Espaço Cultural
Rua Augusta 1415, São Paulo.
Map 4 F1. **Tel** (11) 3288 9206.

Livraria da Travessa
Rua Visconde de Pirajá 572, Ipanema, Rio de Janeiro.
Map 2 4A **Tel** (21) 3205 9002

Postal Services

Correios
W correios.com.br

DHL
W dhl.com.br

FedEx
W fedex.com/br

Skynet
W skynetsao.com

World Courier
W worldcourier.com

TRAVEL INFORMATION

Most travelers arrive in Brazil by plane. There are regular scheduled flights from Europe, North and South America, and Africa. Travelers from Asia will most likely have to connect elsewhere before continuing to Brazil. Several airlines offer stopovers to or from Brazil at no extra cost. Almost all direct flights land at São Paulo's international airport or in Rio de Janeiro. There are a few regular flights to Salvador, Recife, Brasília, Belo Horizonte, and Fortaleza. However, most direct flights to these and other destinations in the Northeast, such as Natal, are European charter flights. Air travel within Brazil is efficient, and most remote locations are accessible by plane.

Arriving by Air

Most direct international flights land either in Rio de Janeiro or São Paulo, but there are also flights into other major cities, such as Brasília, Manaus, Belo Horizonte, Recife, and Salvador. Convenient connections are available for other domestic destinations. Travelers will clear customs at the airport where they first enter Brazil.

Modern, well-equipped Belém International Airport

International Airlines

Most major European and North and South American airlines operate regularly scheduled flights to Brazil. Delta, **American Airlines**, Continental Airlines, KLM, Lufthansa, Air France, British Airways, Alitalia, Iberia, Tap, and others offer nonstop flights to Rio de Janeiro and São Paulo. The largest Brazilian airline, **LATAM**, has regular flights to Europe and the USA. There are also nonstop flights to Salvador de Bahia from Madrid

with **Air Europa**, and from Miami with American Airlines. **Gol**, Brazil's second-largest airline, flies internationally to Latin American destinations only.

On Arrival

All tourists must fill out a *cartao de entrada/saida* (entry/exit card). Immigration officials will keep half and return the other to you. This card serves as proof of

stay in Brazil and will be checked on departure. Loss of the card may result in a major hassle and possibly a fine *(see p408)*. Officials will also stamp your passport, and in case they are not granting you the usual 90-day stay in Brazil, the number of days will be written beneath the word *Prazo* on the stamp in your passport. For an extension of the 90-day entry stamp, contact the Polícia Federal *(see p408)*.

A Gol aircraft at the Deputado Luíz E. Magalhães International Airport, Salvador

Taxis waiting outside Congonhas Airport, São Paulo City

Customs Requirements & Duty Free

All international travelers are allowed to purchase up to US$500 at the Brazilian duty-free shop in the arrival hall. Purchases must be made prior to exiting the customs area. Visitors may bring items for their personal use, including electronics. Gadgets, such as cameras or laptops, may need to be registered upon arrival to ensure that they will be taken out of the country again. Gifts up to a value of US$500 can be brought in without additional duties; Brazilian duty-free purchases are not included in this amount.

Getting from Airports

In Rio City, taxis can be a rip-off. Either take a set-price yellow cab from Rio airport or keep an eye on the taximeter. You could also take the **Real Auto Bus**, which runs an efficient half-hourly bus service. São Paulo City offers excellent air-conditioned shuttles known as the "Airport Service." These run every 30 minutes, and depart from the arrivals terminal.

Taxis, too, are easily available at a fixed price. Salvador's international airport is linked to the city center by an hourly shuttle express bus service.

Travel Agencies & Packages

European residents have access to attractive package deals to Northeast Brazil. Packages typically include hotel and airfare to a popular destination such as Fortaleza, Natal, or Recife. Though affordable, these package tours do not offer a lot of flexibility. Independent travelers who wish to visit several destinations, must book their own airfare and hotels. Confirm hotel prices with travel operators, as Brazilian hotels often reserve their best prices for agencies.

A number of travel agencies, such as **Brazil Nuts**, offer customized tours or programs, including activities for seniors, youths, gay travelers, or for those interested in cultural activities. **Journey Latin America**, a UK-based travel

agency, offers tailor-made tours across Brazil. Based in Miami, **Brol** (BR Online Travel) is the first American online travel company to specialize in Brazil. It sells air passes for multiple flights around Brazil or South America.

Airport	Information	Distance to City Center	Average Taxi Fare	Average Journey Time
Internacional de Guarulhos	(11) 2445 2945	São Paulo City 17 miles (28 km)	US$50	40–120 minutes (in rush hour)
International Airport Tom Jobim	(21) 3004 6050	Rio de Janeiro City 12 miles (20 km)	US$40	40–90 minutes (in rush hour)
Deputado Luíz E. Magalhães	(71) 3204 1010	Salvador 17 miles (28 km)	US$55	40 minutes
Internacional dos Guararapes	(81) 3322 4188	Recife 11 miles (18 km)	US$30	20 minutes
Eduardo Gomes	(92) 3652 1210	Manaus 10 miles (16 km)	US$40	25 minutes
Internacional Salgado Filho	(51) 3358 2000	Porto Alegre 4 miles (6 km)	US$15	15 minutes

Domestic Air Travel

The sheer size of Brazil makes air travel the preferred mode of transportation. The country has an excellent network of airlines and most airports have been modernized. Air travel is an important means of transportation to reach remote areas in Amazônia and the interior of Brazil. All towns in the country have at least an airstrip, and all cities have an airport, usually some distance from the city, or located fairly centrally, as in the case with São Paulo City and Rio City.

Gol Linhas Aereas Inteligentes aircraft taxi at Congonhas Airport, São Paulo

Domestic Airlines

Domestic air travel within Brazil is a well-organized and efficient form of transportation. There are currently two major airlines that fly both international and domestic routes – **LATAM** and **Gol**. Domestic bargain airlines include **Avianca Brazil**, **Azul**, **Gol**, and **Trip**. The nation's largest airline, LATAM, operates flights between São Paulo and Mato Grosso do Sul and has built up a wide and inexpensive network throughout the Amazon region. A useful website for comparing prices is decolar.com.

Checking In

Check-in for domestic flights is normally 60 minutes prior to departure. A valid ID is required, and foreigners are required to show their passport upon check-in. Make sure to keep the luggage claim tags handy upon arrival, as airport staff will check for those when exiting the baggage claim area.

Airpass

Nonresidents of Brazil who arrive on an international flight are entitled to buy an airpass with LATAM, making long-distance flights within Brazil quite affordable. A LATAM Pass is based on a frequent flyer system, which allocates reward kilometers for internal flights. Passengers can also earn kilometers by staying at hotels, renting cars and using a US Bank LATAM Pass card. Reward kilometers can also be accumulated on oneworld and associated airlines. Check the airline's website for more detailed information and the terms and conditions.

High Season

High season for domestic air travel corresponds with the major holidays and vacation periods in Brazil. The peak season is in the Brazilian summer, from the week of Christmas until Carnaval in mid-February or early March. The month of July is also peak season when schools and universities are off on their winter break. Other popular periods are Easter, Corpus Christi, and Independence Day (September 7).

LATAM offers significant discounts for those who take night flights or fly at off-peak hours. As unpleasant as departures and arrivals in the wee hours may be, the savings can be significant. It is also advisable to book well ahead of time when planning to take flights Friday evening or Monday morning between major cities.

Air Taxi

Many parts of Brazil, and particularly Amazônia, feature air taxi companies. Air taxis, known locally as *teco-tecos*, are not the most reliable form of transportation. Before taking one, be aware that the airstrips are often dangerous. These small planes routinely fly overloaded, and are very often in questionable condition. There are no checks made on the qualifications of pilots, so taking an air taxi is at the traveler's own risk.

Teco-teco (air taxi) in the Amazon region

An Avianca flight taking off at Curitiba Airport

Reservations & Cancellations

Flights tend to be booked in advance so book your tickets as far ahead as possible. The only exception to this is the Rio–São Paulo shuttle, where you can purchase tickets on the spot. Flights at the beginning and end of working days and on weekends are usually quite crowded.

Confirm onward flights a day or two in advance. This can be done over the phone, as most airlines have English-speaking staff.

If you have an airpass and you happen to change your flight, remember to cancel the original flight. If you don't do so, the computer will flag you as a no-show, and all your other airpass reservations will also be canceled. Similarly, if you miss a flight, reconfirm all onward flights on your airpass. If you don't, all your other flights will be canceled.

Domestic Airports

Along with domestic airports, such as **Aeroporto de Congonhas** in São Paulo, and **Aeroporto Santos Dumont** in Rio de Janeiro, there are small domestic airports all over Brazil, including Recife, Belo Horizonte, Cuiabá, Campo Grande, Curitiba, Fernando de Noronha, Florianópolis, and Fortaleza. Both Congonhas and Santos Dumont airports are close to the commercial areas. The shuttle service from Congonhas Airport to the city center takes 50 minutes.

DIRECTORY

Domestic Airlines

Avianca Brazil
Tel 0800 286 6543.
w avianca.com.br

Azul
Tel 0800 887 1118
w voeazul.com.br

Gol
Tel 0300 115 2121.
w voegol.com.br

LATAM
Tel 0300 570 5700.
w latam.com

Trip
Tel 0800 887 1118.
w voetrip.com.br

Domestic Airports

Aeroporto de Congonhas
Tel (11) 5090 9000.

Aeroporto Santos Dumont
Tel (21) 3814 7070.

Flight Duration Chart

1:15 = Duration in hours:minutes

Rio de Janeiro	São Paulo	Florianópolis	Brasília	Manaus	Belém	São Luís	Fortaleza	Recife	Salvador	Belo Horizonte
0:45										
2:30	1:00									
1:30	1:35	2:17								
3:00	2:55	6:00	2:45							
3:35	5:25	4:40	2:20	1:00						
4:00	5:45	5:25	2:27	4:20	1:00					
3:00	2:30	0:55	2:30	4:25	2:50	1:10				
2:45	3:00	6:18	2:20	7:30	4:20	2:45	1:10			
1:50	0:45	5:10	1:55	7:30	7:45	4:35	1:40	1:10		
0:50	1:00	3:00	1:10	7:00	5:00	4:45	4:00	3:55	1:35	

GETTING AROUND
Due to the size and distances across Brazil, the fastest and easiest way to travel around the country is by air. All big cities, smaller towns, and even more remote areas across the country have airports, or at least an airstrip of some sort. Domestic flights are available to and from just about any major city across Brazil.

Bus & Car Travel

Intercity bus travel is well organized and most routes offer efficient and comfortable express services. Driving a car can be a challenge in Brazil due to distances and the often poor quality of many public roads. Brazil possesses a total of 932,000 miles (1.5 million km) of federal, state, and local roads but only 49,000 miles (79,000 km) are paved and in decent condition. Though car rentals are widely available, given the distances and poor road quality, a car is not really advisable for longer trips, but it can be a convenient way to explore attractions close to the cities.

Busy *rodoviária* (central bus terminal) in São Paulo

Buses

Brazil has an excellent network of long-distance buses which makes traveling around the country easy and economical. Intercity buses leave from a central station, called a *rodoviária*, usually located on the outskirts of the city. Buses are operated by numerous private companies, but prices are standardized, and very reasonable.

Several categories of buses operate on longer routes. Regular buses (*ônibus comum*) sometimes do not have air-conditioning, so check beforehand. *Comum com ar* are regular buses with air-conditioning. The *executivo* bus is more comfortable, its chairs wider and equipped with footrests. The best buses for overnight trips are known as *semi-leito* or *leito*. *Semi-leito* have seats that recline almost horizontally and have large footrests. *Leito* buses offer a fully horizontal bed-like seat. Both normally offer onboard refreshments, blankets, and pillows. Nearly all buses have onboard bathrooms. Buy your tickets from the *rodoviária* ahead of time, especially on holidays.

Car Rentals

All major cities and most smaller cities and towns offer car rental services, such as **Avis** and **Localiza**. Car rental offices, known as *locadoras*, can be found at every airport and in most towns. Foreigners need to show a valid driver's license from their home country, state, or province, their passport, and a major credit card. It is also a good idea to carry an International Driver's Permit (IDP). A wide variety of cars are available in Brazil, from small economy models with no air conditioning, to large air-conditioned 4WDs. Rental agreements can be with full or partial insurance, with unlimited driving or with a per-kilometer charge. In terms of price, a four-door mid-size sedan with air conditioning, unlimited driving, and full insurance will cost about R$150 (US$83) per day in a larger city. In smaller towns and remote areas, prices go up by 50 to 100 percent. It is a good idea to check with locals about the condition of the roads you plan on taking.

Gas Stations

Cars in Brazil run on either gasoline or alcohol, but many new models run on both. Service stations selling gasoline are more common, especially in remote areas. On long-distance road trips, service stations may be few and far between, so ensure that the car is in good condition. Always be well prepared with some cash, water, enough car fluids, a good spare tire with tools, and a flashlight.

Driving in Towns

Driving in Brazilian towns and cities can sometimes be a frustrating experience. Any time after about 9pm, especially in Rio and São Paulo, drivers begin to treat red lights as strictly optional. Be especially alert at intersections at night (even as a pedestrian). Often the driver running the red light won't even slow down, because of the risk of robberies at isolated intersections. On highways and secondary roads,

Posto de Gasolina (gas station) in Rio de Janeiro

drivers tend to be fearless overtaking other vehicles, even when they can't see what's around the bend.

Parking, especially in cities, can be a bit tricky due to security and space constraints. It is worth paying extra for a hotel with a lock-up garage facility. Do not leave valuables in the car. It is also worth paying a few *reais* to self-appointed "guards" who may approach you to watch over your car. Consult a local regarding how much to tip.

Parking sign

Rules of the Road

Officially, the rules of the road are much the same as in Continental Europe or the United States. Drive on the right side of the road; unlike the USA, right turns on red lights are not allowed. Roundabouts are common only in Brasília. The right of way is always with the car already in the roundabout, or to the left. On highways, keep headlights on or risk being fined

However, it is the application of these rules – or lack thereof – that sets Brazil apart. Most Brazilians are aggressive and impatient drivers. They tend to drive fast, overtake often, either on the right or left, and when they cannot, they hang impatiently on your back bumper. Do not expect the large

bus driving next to you to stay in its lane. Drivers switch lanes constantly, for no apparent reason, normally without signaling.

However, the use of photo radar and regular alcohol checks have improved driving conditions. Seatbelt laws are also rigorously enforced. Note that in larger cities such as São Paulo, Rio, and Salvador, traffic is still very chaotic. In case of an emergency, it is best to call the Polícia Militar *(see pp412–13)* or **Highway Police** *(Polícia Rodoviária)*.

Road Network

Brazil's intercity road network is made up of state and federal highways. Federal highways are denoted by the initials BR followed by the number of the highway (BR-163). State roads are indicated by the state initials (RJ for Rio de Janeiro, PA for Pará, and so on) followed by the highway number (PA-150). Toll roads have become more common. Most are run by private companies. They are usually well maintained and offer roadside assistance.

Most other state and federal highways are undivided two-lane blacktops, with occasional passing lanes. Care is required when driving on these roads. Generally speaking, the roads

in southern states such as Rio and São Paulo are much better than in northeastern or Amazônian states such as Bahia or Rondônia. Even in the South, roads in bad condition are not uncommon.

Traveling by night is best avoided. With very few exceptions, highways in Brazil are poorly lit, and completely lacking in reflective paint, reflective signage, and the roadside reflectors that show the edge of the road.

The best source of national road maps can be found on the Viagem website (viajeaqui.abril. com.br), which gives detailed routes, distances, and traffic information for Brazil and the rest of South America, as well as other useful travel tips and features.

Directory

Car Rentals

Avis
Tel 0800 725 2847.
W avis.com.br

Localiza
Tel 0800 979 2000.
W localiza.com

Emergency

Highway Police
Tel 191 (Road Emergencies).

Road sign meaning "slow down" on a highway near Goiás

Train & Boat Travel in Brazil

Train travel is not a common mode of transportation in Brazil. While large parts of the country have never seen train tracks, in other areas, many routes have been deactivated in favor of roads. Today, the few remaining routes are of more interest to train aficionados, and are often of great scenic beauty. In some parts of Brazil, boat travel is still the only mode of transportation. With few roads connecting the major cities, particularly in the Amazon and along the northern coast, locals depend entirely on boats to get around. On the Rio Paraguay, on the western edge of the Pantanal, boats are used for multiday fishing charters.

Trains waiting at the Luz railroad station in São Paulo

Train Travel

Although Brazil does not have a large train network, there are a few specific routes that can be useful for travelers and are good for a scenic ride. The Minas–Vitória train journey is an excellent day trip, and perfect for those traveling between the cities of Belo Horizonte, in the heartland of Minas Gerais, and Vitória on the Espírito Santo coast.

The quickest and most comfortable way to travel between São Luís and the interior of Pará, in Northern Brazil, is the São Luís Carajás railroad. In the state of Amapá, also in Northern Brazil, a passenger and cargo train runs from the port of Santana, 124 miles (200 km) inland, to the former mining town of Serra de Navio. Its passenger cars, though old and in need of maintenance, are still functional. Brazil offers a few charming,

short historic routes. Steam locomotive trains, lovingly called Maria Fumaça, or "Smoking Mary," run on these routes. One of the journeys this unique steam engine makes is a regular 7-mile (12-km) run on weekends between São João del Rei and Tiradentes *(see p136)*, historic towns in Minas Gerais. An appealing short trip is offered along the route between the beautiful, historic mining town of Ouro Preto, one of Brazil's best-preserved colonial towns, and Mariana, also in Minas. Even though the towns are only 7 miles (12 km) apart, the route buzzes with history, as gold miners and gem hunters in the days of the gold rush used to travel through these hills. Contact the **Estação Ferroviária** for further details.

Another spectacular route is the Curitiba–Paranaguá train ride through the Atlantic rainforest of the Serra do Mar. The most unforgettable stretch is between Curitiba and Morretes *(see p341)*. For information, contact the **Curitiba Ticket Office**.

The interior of a Maria Fumaça steam locomotive train

Boat Travel

In many parts of Brazil, boats are a vital form of transport. The network is extensive, and services are regular, although the facilities largely depend on the type of boat chosen for traveling.

In the Amazon, rivers are still the major highways, and old-style wooden riverboats are an important part of the transportation system. The most common and popular route runs between Manaus and Belém. The journey takes four days downstream and five days upstream. On this route, there are also several larger and more modern boats, which feature air-conditioned cabins and even enclosed air-conditioned hammock spaces. Continuing right up to Tefé, **AJATO** runs a speedboat service every Wednesday and Saturday, with airplane-style seating.

On most other routes, the boats are the older, smaller traditional type, with small wooden cabins, and two open

A picturesque view of one of the Maria Fumaça steam trains

Cruise ship Iberostar moored on the Manaus harbor

decks – upper and lower – where passengers sling their hammocks. Meals and water are provided.

Boats of the old style ply dozens of routes throughout the Amazon basin. The most common routes run between Manaus and Porto Velho, Manaus, Tabatinga, and São Gabriel de Cachoeira, near the borders of Peru and Columbia, respectively, and Manaus and Santarem, halfway to Belém. The Manaus–Santarem route also has a high-speed catamaran which makes the journey in a single day. Those more keen on tours than transportation can go for one of the comfortable boats for charter in Manaus, such as **Viverde**, that take passengers on a personal exploration of the Amazon River. For information on buying tickets in advance, contact **Amazonastur**, the state tourism agency.

The Rio Paraguay on the western edge of the Pantanal has a large fleet of boats, most of which are outfitted for multi-day sportfishing cruises. These boats depart from both Corumbá in Mato Grosso do Sul and Caceres in Mato Grosso.

On the Northeast coast, an absence of roads connecting the Maranhão and Piauí coast makes boat travel the only alternative to long detours inland. The most scenic option is to travel from Parnaíba in Piauí through the islands and inlets of the Delta da Parnaíba to Tutóia, one of the gateways to the Lençóis Maranhenses.

Cruise Travel

A very leisurely way to travel the Brazilian coast is on board a cruise ship. Several companies offer three- to five-day cruises, most typically between Santos, Rio de Janeiro as far as Salvador, or other northeastern cities. Another route starts in Recife and travels to Fernando de Noronha. There is now also a regular cruise ship, the **Iberostar Grand Amazon**, that departs from Manaus on three- and four-day cruises on the Amazon. The old-style **Amazon Clipper Cruises** can be excellent for a tour of the Rio Negro.

Directory

Train Travel

Curitiba Ticket Office
Tel (41) 3888 3488.
🆆 serraverdeexpress.com.br

Estação Ferroviária
Praça Cesário Alvim 102, barra, Ouro Preto. Tel (31) 3551 7310.
🆆 tremdavale.org

Boat Travel

AJATO
Av. Lourenço Braga, Centro, Manaus
Tel (92) 3622 6047.

Amazonastur
Tel (92) 3182 6250.
🆆 amazonastur.am.gov.br

Viverde
Rua das Guariúbas 47, Manaus
Tel (92) 3248 9988.
🆆 viverde.com.br

Cruise Travel

Amazon Clipper Cruises
Tel (92) 3656 1246.
🆆 amazonclipper.com.br

Iberostar Grand Amazon
Tel (92) 2126 9927.
🆆 iberostar.com.br

Yachts at anchor near Ubatuba beach, São Paulo state

Getting around Brazilian Towns

Public transportation in Brazil varies greatly from city to city and region to region. Large cities such as São Paulo and Rio de Janeiro have modern metro systems that offer quick access to many parts of the city and decent bus systems. However, in most cities and towns, the main mode of transportation is the bus and its variations, such as minivans and minibuses. Taxis are plentiful and quite affordable. In very small communities where there is little in the way of regular public transportation, people often use motorcycle taxis (moto-taxis). It is a cheap and fast one-person ride.

Moto-taxi stand, and drivers, in Camamu town, Bahia

Visitors exploring the town of Búzios on foot

On Foot

Visitors to Brazil often seem preoccupied with street crime. What they should really worry about is traffic. Pedestrians get little or no respect. It is safest to assume that cars have the absolute right of way everywhere at all times. Even when the pedestrian has the right of way, such as when crossing with a green light, extreme care should be exercised at all times.

After dark, or when traffic is light, or when police are absent, cars tend to run red lights. Also, when making a right turn, cars rarely give preference to pedestrians trying to cross. Pedestrians should also be aware of bikes or motorcycles that may go down the wrong way on a one-way street. Always look both left and right.

Motorcyclists often weave in and out between the cars at high speeds. Be very careful when walking in between stationary or slow-moving traffic.

Taxis & Moto-Taxis

Taxis are affordable and a quick mode of transportation. Prices generally run 50 to 70 percent lower than in Europe or North America. Most taxis work on the meter. When starting the ride, make sure that the meter is cleared and shows "tariff 1" except from 11pm to 6am, Sundays, and in December when "2" is permitted. Drivers sometimes "forget" to start the meter and end up charging a flat rate.

The only taxis allowed to charge a flat rate are radio taxis or cooperatives at airports, bus stations, or other specific locations. The price will be set before the passenger gets in. Rates are typically 30 to 40 percent higher than regular metered taxis, but you know what the final price will be. Although these prepaid taxis are not a bargain, they may be good value when taking a taxi from the international airports in Rio de Janeiro and São Paulo *(see p419)*, where taxi drivers have developed the unfortunate habit of taking advantage of tourists who don't speak Portuguese and aren't familiar with Brazil.

In most cities, taxis can be hailed on the street, at numerous taxi stands, or booked via mobile apps. Renting a taxi for the day is an inexpensive alternative to renting a car. The price is negotiated with the driver. Taxis in small towns do not have meters, so it is best to agree upon a price in advance.

Another option in smaller towns is the moto-taxi, or motorcycle-taxi. The driver carries an extra helmet, and the passenger just hops on the back and rides pillion after fixing a price.

Metro

The metro is the safest form of public transport in Rio and São Paulo. Both cities have metro systems that are very convenient for visitors, as they offer reliable transportation to a number of interesting sites. It is much easier and faster to take the metro to

Yellow Rio taxis, plentiful and relatively inexpensive

Passengers waiting to board the bus at a city bus stand in Paraná

the stop closest to your destination and then take a taxi, rather than figure out a complicated and often slow bus system.

In Rio de Janeiro, the metro runs from 5am to midnight Monday through Saturday, and from 7am to 11pm on Sundays and holidays. During Carnaval, it runs nonstop for the five days of the festival. Special return tickets are required from Copacabana on New Year's Eve. The metro has two main lines, both of which are clean and safe, even in the evenings. Line 1 from Gal Osório to Uruguai has 20 stops. The line splits at Central, with one line continuing west, while Line 2 goes north to São Cristóvão and beyond. Line 4, inaugurated in 2015, runs along the coastline from Gal Osório to Barra through Ipanema, Leblon, and São Conrado. The stops of most interest to visitors are downtown and along the southern beach neighborhoods, as well as the first few stops along the northern line to the Maracanã Stadium and Quinta da Boã Vista. Rio's metro now also offers a series of integrated metro-bus routes, which offer connections on air-conditioned buses to many of the city's attractions that are off the metro system, such as Santa Teresa, Sugar Loaf, and Ipanema. Passengers must ask for a special integrated ticket (*integração*) at the time of purchase.

São Paulo's metro system covers quite a large part of the city. It runs from 4:40am to midnight every day, and is clean, efficient, and safer than the buses.

For both systems, one-way (*unitário*), round-trip (*duplo*), or ten-ride (*múltiplo*) tickets are available. However, no discounts are offered for multiple-ride tickets. Transfers between lines are allowed. Free metro maps are available at most ticket booths of both metro systems.

Buses

Buses are plentiful in the big cities. Most buses list their destination in large letters on their front window, while another sign with smaller lettering lists key landmarks along the route. Most lines in Rio and São Paulo run 24 hours a day, but with fewer circulating in the middle of the night. In Rio, most buses going from the south to the center will go to Copacabana. Keep in mind that buses are often crowded, and get stuck in terrible time-consuming traffic snarls. They are also often the sites of many of the city's robberies. To avoid pickpockets, try to sit at the front of the bus and to stay away from windows.

In São Paulo, a couple of the main bus transfer points are at Praça da Republica and the busy Terminal Bandeira, where it is also possible to catch different buses to far-off destinations within the city.

Tickets are sold on the bus by a ticket-seller, who sits at a turnstile, or by the driver. Keep small change handy. Brazilian bus drivers can drive fast, so hold on at all times, especially when standing. It is safer to take buses in the daytime. In the evenings, it is advisable to take taxis.

São Paulo metro arriving in the Barra Funda station

General Index

Page numbers in **bold** type refer to main entries

90 Mile Beach 448
505 (Sydney) 146, 147

A

A Batalha do Avaí (Américo) 78
A Cruz Caída (Cravo) 187
Abismo Anhumas **327**
Abraão 107
Acre *see* Amazonas, Roraima, Acre and Rondônia
Addresses **417**
Afonso de Sousa, Martim 165, 173
Afro-Brazilian culture **180–81**
  Museu Afro-Brasileiro (Salvador) 190, **192**
  religions 39
Agostinho de Piedade, Frei 34, 146
Air travel **418–21**
  air taxis 420
  airpass 420
  domestic air travel **420–21**
  international travel **418–19**
Akihito, Emperor of Japan 149
Alagoas *see* Sergipe, Alagoas and Pernambuco
Alcântara 249, **258–9**
  festivals 46
Alcohol 383
Aleijadinho 32, 34, 76, **135**
  Basílica do Senhor Bom Jesus de Matosinhos 134
  Igreja da São Francisco de Assis (Ouro Preto) 132
  Mariana 133
  Matriz de Santo Antônio (Tiradentes) 136
  Museu de Arte Sacra (São Paulo) 146
  Ouro Preto 130
  portrait of 131
Alencar, José de 246, 247
Alfândega (Manaus) **284**
Algodoal 274
All Souls' Day 47
Almeida, José Ferraz de Júnior 34
Alta Floresta **323**
  hotels 379
Alter do Chão 278
Amado, Jorge 25, 35, **204**
  Fundação Casa de Jorge Amado (Salvador) 191, **192**
  Ilhéus 204

Amapá *see* Pará and Amapá
Amaral, Cláudio Gurgel do 79
Amaral, Crispim do 286
Amaral, Tarsila do 34, 35
  Estação Pinacoteca (São Paulo) 146
  Estrada de Ferro Central do Brasil 152
  Museu de Arte Contemporânea (São Paulo) 152

Amaralina 199
Amazon river 263, 269, 281
  Encontro das Aguas **289**
  Pororoca wave **279**
Amazonas, Roraima, Acre and Rondônia **281–93**
  hotels 378–9
  Manaus **284–9**
  map 282–3
  restaurants 394–5
Amazônia 15, 26, 276–7
  The Amazon ecosystem **264–5**
  boat travel 424–5
  excursions from Manaus **288–91**
  history 51
  The people of Amazônia **266–7**
  The rubber story in Brazil **278**
  Transamazônica 62, 63, **272**
  wildlife **28**
Ambulances 411
Américo, Pedro 152, 308
  A Batalha do Avaí 78
Anavilhanas, Ilhas de **288–9**
Anchieta, José 35, 139
Anchieta, Padre 142, 146
Andrade, Mário de 35
Andrade, Oswald de 35
Angra dos Reis 14, **114**
  festivals 45
  hotels 372
Antônio Prado **361**
Antropofagismo movement 34, 35
Aparados da Serra, Parque Nacional dos 353, 354, **362**
Apart-hotels 367
Aquariums
  Aquário de Santos 173
  Aquário de Ubatuba 168
  Aquário Natural Baia Bonita (Bonito) 327
  Oceanário (Aracaju) 216
Aracaju **216**
  festivals 45
  hotels 375
  restaurants 392
Aracati 244
Araguaia, Rio 315
Araruama, Lake 121
Araujo, José Soares de 128
Architecture **32–3**
Arco de Telles (Rio de Janeiro) Street-by-Street map 74
Arcos da Lapa (Rio de Janeiro) 78
Areia Branca 243
Areia Vermelha, Ilha de (João Pessoa) **235**
Argentina
  Foz do Iguaçu 344, 345, **347**
Arraial do Cabo 121
Art *see* Museums and galleries
Artists 35
Arts and crafts *see* Crafts
Ashaninka people 267
Atalaia 216

Athayde, Mestre (Manuel da Costa) 34
  Igreja da São Francisco de Assis (Ouro Preto) 131, 132
  Mariana 133
  Museu de Arte Sacra (São Paulo) 146
  Ouro Preto 130
Atlantic coastal forest *see* Mata Atlântica
ATMs **414**
Autumn in Brazil **46**
Avenida Paulista (São Paulo) 13, **148**
Azoreans **332**
Azul, Lagoa 202, 245
Azulejos (tiles)
  Igreja de São Francisco de Assis (Belo Horizonte) 129
  Salvador 188, 195

B

Bahia **185–211**
  capoeira **203**
  hotels 374–5
  Linha Verde **211**
  map 186–7
  Parque Nacional de Chapada Diamantina **208–9**
  Salvador **188–99**
  restaurants 391–2
Baía de Castelhanos 169
Baía de Guanabara **92**
Baía do Sueste 228
Baianas 31
Balaiada Rebellion (1838–41) 56
Bananal, Ilha do 297, 303, **315**
Bandeira, Manuel 35
Banking **414–15**
Banknotes 415
Barbosa de Oliveira, Rui 76
  Museu Casa de Rui Barbosa (Rio de Janeiro) **85**
Bardot, Brigitte 107, 120
Baroque architecture 32
Barra do Itariri 211
Barra Grande 202
Barra da Lagoa 351
Barra Shopping Center 14, **90**
Barra de Superagui 343
Barra da Tijuca (Rio de Janeiro) 14, 90–91
  hotels 370
  map 90
  restaurants 386
Barreado **343**
Barreirinhas
  hotels 377
Barreta 241
Barreto, Afonso Lima 35
Barretos
  festivals 47
Bars 382, **401**
  Rio de Janeiro **97**, 99
Basílica de Nossa Senhora da Assunção (Mariana) 133

Basílica de Nossa Senhora de Nazaré (Belém) **273**
Basílica de São Pedro dos Clérigos (Mariana) 133
Basílica do Senhor Bom Jesus de Matosinhos (Congonhas) **134–5**
Batuque 39
Beaches
  Aracaju 216
  Brazilian beach culture **42–3**
  Búzios 120–21
  Cananéia 175
  Copacabana 12, 71, **82**
  Costa do Sol **120–21**
  Fortaleza 247
  Grumari **91**
  Guarapari 122
  Guarujá 169
  Ilha do Mel 343
  Ipanema 12, 83
  Itacaré 204
  João Pessoa 234–5
  Leblon 12, 83
  Maceió 218, 219
  Maresias **169**
  Morro de São Paulo 202
  Niterói 93
  Paraty **112**
  Peninsula de Maraú 202
  Porto de Galinhas 219
  Porto Seguro 205
  Praia da Barra da Tijuca **90**
  Praia Prainha **91**
  Rota do Sol **241**
  Salinópolis 274
  Salvador's Atlantic coast 13, **198–9**
  São Paulo State 165
  Sergipe, Alagoas and Pernambuco 213
  Ubatuba 168
Beça, Aníbal 35
Beer 383
Belém 263, 268, 269, 271, **272–3**
  climate 49
  festivals 44
  flight duration chart 421
  hotels 378
  map 273
  restaurants 394
Bell, Alexander Graham 119
Bellini, Giovanni 147
Belo Horizonte 125, **129**
  climate 49
  festivals 44
  flight duration chart 421
  history 58
  hotels 373
  restaurants 388–9
Belterra 279
Benedictine order 142–3
Bento Gonçalves 22, **360**
  hotels 381
  restaurants 397
Bernl, Richard 142
Bethânia, Maria 200
Beuque, Jacques van de 91
Biggs, Ronald 81

Biking **403**, 405
Bill, Max 33
Birds **28–9, 402**, 405
  Chapada dos Guimarães 323
  Mata Atlântica **113**
  Pantanal 319
  Parque das Aves (Iguaçu) 15, **346**
  see also Wildlife
Biribiri 128
Blumenau
  festivals 44
Boa Vista 262, 281, **292**
  hotels 379
  restaurants 394
Boats **424–5**
  cruises **425**
  Ilhabela Sailing Week 47
Boff, Leonardo 38
Bolpeba, Ilha de 202
Bond, James 81
Bonete 169
Bonito 296, **327**
  hotels 379
  restaurants 395
Bookshops
  São Paulo 155
Boqueirão Norte 175
Borrifos 169
Bosch, Hieronymus 147
Bosco, Dom 298, 308
Bossa nova 36
  Rio de Janeiro **97**, 99
Bosten, Mathias 119
Botafogo (Rio de Janeiro) 25
  hotels 371
  restaurants 386–7
Botecos **401**
Botocudos 53
Botofogo Bay 70
Branco, Rio 281, 283
Brandão, Théo 218–19
Braque, Georges 146, 147
Brasil, Vital 152
Brasília 15, 21, 297, **306–9**
  architecture 33
  Catedral Metropolitana Nossa Senhora Aparecida (Brasília) 307, **309**
  climate 49
  creation of a capital **298–9**
  flight duration chart 421
  history 62
  hotels 379
  map 306–7
  restaurants 395
Brasília, Goiás and Tocantins **303–17**
  hotels 379
  map 304–5
  Parque Nacional Chapada dos Veadeiros **316–17**
  Pirenópolis **312–13**
  restaurants 395
Brazil, naming of **53**
Brazilian Formula 1 Grand Prix 44

Brecheret, Victor 34
  Monumento às Bandeiras 150
  Museu de Arte Contemporânea (São Paulo) 152
  Museu de Arte de São Paulo 147
Brendan, St 53
Brennand, Francisco 223
Breu, Ilha do 112
Brito, Francisco Xavier de 34
  Basílica de Nossa Senhora da Assunção (Mariana) 133
  Igreja de São Francisco da Penitência (Rio de Janeiro) 76
  Matriz de Nossa Senhora do Pilar (Ouro Preto) 132
  Museu de Arte Sacra (São Paulo) 146
Brown, Carlinhos 37, 180
Bry, Theodor de 50
Buarque, Chico 35, 37
Buddhism **39**
Bueno, Maria Esther 25
Buggies **245**
Bumba-meu-boi **258**
Buriti palm trees **255**
Burle Marx, Roberto
  Belo Horizonte 129
  Brasília 299, 306
  Parque Burle Marx (São Paulo) 153
  Recife 222, 223
  Sitio Roberto Burle Marx (Barra da Tijuca) 14, **91**
Buses **422**
  in cities **427**
  from airport 419
Búzios 12, 107, **120–21**, 241
  hotels 372
  restaurants 388

C
Cabanagem Rebellion (1835) 272
Cable cars
  Sugar Loaf Mountain (Rio de Janeiro) 80–81
Cabo Frio 107, 121
Cabral, Pedro Álvares 51, **52–3**
  Itacaré 204
  monument 150
  Porto Seguro 205
Caburé 251, 255
Cáceres
  festivals 44
Cachaça (alcohol) 383, 399
Cachoeira **200–201**
Cachoeira da Água Branca 169
Cachoeira Almeçegas 317
Cachoeira d'Anta 137
Cachoeira do Buraçao 209
Cachoeira da Toca 169
"Café com leite" Republic 58
Cafés **401**
Cafua das Mercês (São Luís), 258
Caipira Picando Fumo (Júnior) 145
Calhau 258
Calixto, Benedito 34
  Fundação Pinacoteca Benedito Calixto (Santos) 172

Calixto, Benedito (cont.)
  Igreja da Consolação (São Paulo)
    143
  Mãe Douro 172
  Museu de Arte Sacra (São Paulo)
    146
Calliari, Ivo 77
Câmara, Hélder 38
Camélodromos (street traders) 398–
  9
Campeche 350
Campina Grande 231, **236**
  festivals 47
Camping 369
Campo Grande **326**
  hotels 380
  restaurants 395
Cananéia **175**
Canasvieiras 350
Candomblé 24, 39, 181, 185
  Festa da Boa Morte **201**
  Lavagem do Bonfim **199**
Canela **358**
  festivals 47
  hotels 381
Canion do Itaimbezinho 362
Cânion Xingó **218**
Canoa Quebrada 231, **244**
  hotels 377
  restaurants 393
Canoeing 403
Canudos **210**
Canudos War (1897) 210
Canyoning 403
Capela Dourada (Recife) **222**
Capela das Graças
  Vale dos Vinhedos tour 359
Capela das Neves
  Vale dos Vinhedos tour 359
Capiberibe, João 275
Capoeira 13, **180**, 185, **203**
  classes **404**, 405
Caracaranã, Lago 292
Caravelas 205
Cardoso, Fernando Henrique 22, 63
Cardoso, Ilha do 165, **175**
Caribé 84
Cariocas **31**, 71
Cariri **236**
Carnatal (Natal) 45
Carnaval 25, 45, 47
  Museu das Cavalhadas
    (Pirenópolis) **312**
  Olinda **226**
  Rio de Janeiro **68–9**
  Salvador **197**
  São Paulo 139
Cars **422–3**
  driving in São Paulo 159
  driving in towns 422–3
  gas stations 422
  off-road driving **402–3**, 405
  parking 423
  Rally dos Sertões 47
  rental 422, 423
  rules of the road 423
  see also Motor racing; Tours by car
Carstairs, Henrietta 80
Caruaru **227**
  festivals 47

Carvalho, João Antunes de 134
Carybé 190, 192
Casa do Artesão (Corumbá) 326
Casa de Cadeia (Paraty) **110**
Casa de Chica da Silva (Diamantina)
    128
Casa dos Contos (Ouro Preto) 130
Casa da Cultura (Recife) **223**
Casa de Cultura Jorge Amado
    (Ilhéus) 204
Casa de Cultura Mário Quintana
    (Porto Alegre) **357**
Casa Daros (Rio de Janeiro) **85**
Casa Esperança (São Sebastião) 169
Casa França-Brasil (Rio de Janeiro)
    75
Casa Histórica do Iphan (Alcântara)
    259
Casa do Maranhão (São Luís) 258
Casa Martim Afonso (São Vicente)
    173
Casa Museu Mestre Vitalino
    (Caruaru) 227
Casa do Pontal (Barra da Tijuca) 14,
    91
Casa das Rosas (São Paulo) 148
Casa de Santos Dumont (Petrópolis)
    117
Casa Valduga
  Vale dos Vinhedos tour 359
Casaldaliga, Pedro 38
Cascading 403
Cascatinha do Taunay 92
Cash machines **414**
Castelo Branco, Marshal Humberto
    62
Castles and fortifications
  Fortaleza de Nossa Senhora dos
    Prazeres (Ilha do Mel) 342
  Fortaleza de Santa Cruz (Niterói)
    93
  Fortaleza de São José de Macapá
    275
  Forte do Brum (Recife) **221**
  Forte das Cinco Pontas (Recife) **221**
  Forte de Copacabana 82
  Forte Defensor Perpétuo (Paraty)
    111
  Forte Junqueira (Corumbá) 326
  Forte Orange (Ilha de Itamaracá)
    227
  Forte do Presépio (Belém) **272**
  Forte Príncipe da Beira 293
  Forte dos Reis Magos (Natal) 240
  Forte de Santo Antônio (Salvador)
    13, **197**
  Forte de São Felipe (Salvador)
    198–9
Castro Maya, Raymundo Ottoni de
    92
Castrolanda 333
Cathedrals
  Catedral Basílica (Salvador) 190,
    192–3
  Catedral Basílica de Nossa Senhora
    das Neves (João Pessoa) **234**
  Catedral de São Pedro de
    Alcântara (Petrópolis) **116**
  Catedral de São Pedro dos
    Clérigos (Recife) **222**

Cathedrals (cont.)
  Catedral Metropolitana (Porto
    Alegre) 356
  Catedral Metropolitana (Rio de
    Janeiro) **77**
  Catedral Metropolitana (São
    Paulo) 12, 138, **142**
  Catedral Metropolitana de
    Florianópolis 336
  Catedral Metropolitana Nossa
    Senhora Aparecida (Brasília) 307,
    309
  Catedral Militar de Nossa Senhora
    da Paz (Brasília) **308**
  Igreja da Sé (São Luís) 249, 257
  Nossa Senhora do Amparo
    (Teresina) 252
  see also Churches
Catholic Church 24, **38**
Cattle
  gaúchos 335
  Rio Grande do Sul 353
Caves
  Abismo Anhumas **327**
  Gruta do Lago Azul **327**
  Presidente Figueiredo 288
  Ubajara 245
Caxias do Sul 353, **360–61**
  festivals 45
Ceará *see* Paraíba, Rio Grande do
  Norte and Ceará
Cell phones **416**
Central West Brazil **295–327**
  Brasília, Goiás and Tocantins
    303–17
  creation of a capital **298–9**
  flora and fauna in the cerrado
    300–301
  map 296–7
  Mato Grosso and Mato Grosso do
    Sul **319–27**
  Pantanal **324–5**
  Parque Nacional Chapada dos
    Veadeiros 303, 304, **316–17**
Centro de Conveções Riocentro
    (Barra da Tijuca) **91**
Centro de Cultura Popular (São Luís)
    257, 258
Centro Cultural do Banco do Brasil
    (Rio de Janeiro) **89**
Centro Cultural Banco do Brasil (São
    Paulo) **143**
Centro Cultural Dannemann (São
    Félix) 201
Centro Cultural Dragão do Mar
    (Fortaleza) **246**
Centro Cultural FIESP (São Paulo)
    148
Centro Cultural Yves Alves
    (Tiradentes) 136
Centro da Lagoa 350
Centro de Tradições Gaúchas **334**
Centro de Turismo (Fortaleza) **246**
Centro de Turismo (Natal) 240
Cerrado 27
  flora and fauna in the cerrado
    300–301
  wildlife **29**
Ceschiatti, Alfredo
  São Mateus 309

Céu 37
Cézanne, Paul 147
Chafariz da Piramide (Rio de Janeiro) 74
Chagall, Marc 146, 147
Chain hotels 368, 369
Chapada Diamantina, Parque Nacional de 13, **208–9**
Chapada dos Guimarães **322–3**
Chapada dos Veadeiros, Parque Nacional 303, 304, **316–17**
hotels 379
restaurants 395
Children 409
in hotels 367
in restaurants 383
in São Paulo 157
Cholera 410
Churches
art **34**
Basílica de Nossa Senhora da Asunção (Mariana) 133
Basílica de Nossa Senhora de Nazaré (Belém) **273**
Basílica de São Pedro dos Clérigos (Mariana) 133
Basílica do Senhor Bom Jesus de Matosinhos (Congonhas) **134–5**
Capela Dourada (Recife) 222
Capela das Graças (Vale dos Vinhedos) 359
Capela das Neves (Vale dos Vinhedos) 359
Igreja da Consolação (São Paulo) **143**
Igreja e Convento de São Francisco (Salvador) 13, 32, 190, **194–5**
Igreja Matriz (São Sebastião) 168, 169
Igreja Matriz de Nossa Senhora do Rosário (Pirenópolis) **312**
Igreja Matriz de São Vicente Mártir (São Vicente) 173
Igreja e Mosteiro São Bento (Olinda) 225, **226**
Igreja Nossa Senhor do Bonfim (Pirenópolis) **312**
Igreja da Nossa Senhora do Carmo (Ouro Preto) 131
Igreja Nossa Senhora da Corrente (Penedo) 217
Igreja Nossa Senhora da Glória do Outeiro (Rio de Janeiro) **79**
Igreja Nossa Senhora do Rosário dos Pretos (Salvador) 191
Igreja da Ordem Terceira de São Francisco (Salvador) 191
Igreja de Santa Maria dos Anjos (Penedo) 217
Igreja de Santa Maria Madalena (Marechal Deodoro) 218
Igreja de São Francisco (João Pessoa) **234**
Igreja São Francisco (Recife) **222**
Igreja de São Francisco de Assis (Belo Horizonte) 129
Igreja da São Francisco de Assis (Ouro Preto) 124, 131, **132**

Churches (cont.)
Igreja de São Francisco de Assis (São João del Rei) 137
Igreja de São Francisco de Assis (São Paulo) **142**
Igreja de São Francisco da Penitência (Rio de Janeiro) **76**
Igreja de São Jorge (Ilhéus) 204
Igreja da Sé (Olinda) 224
Igreja da Sé (São Luís) 249
Igreja Terceira Ordem de São Francisco (Salvador) 195
Matriz de Nossa Senhora da Conceição (Ouro Preto) 131, **132**
Matriz de Nossa Senhora do Pilar (Ouro Preto) 130, **132**
Matriz Nossa Senhora dos Remédios (Paraty) **111**
Matriz de Santo Antônio (Tiradentes) 136
Nosso Senhor do Bonfim (Salvador) **198–9**
Nossa Senhora de Candelária (Rio de Janeiro) 75
Nossa Senhora do Carmo (Diamantina) 128
Nossa Senhora das Dores (Paraty) **111**
Nossa Senhora do Rosário (Diamantina) 128
Nossa Senhora do Rosário e São Benedito (Paraty) **110**
Santa Rita dos Pardos Libertos (Paraty) **110**
Santuário Dom Bosco (Brasília) **308**
Santuário Santo Antônio do Valongo (Santos) 172, 173
São Josafat (Prudentópolis) 333
São Miguel das Missões 330, **363**
see also Cathedrals
Churrascaria rodízio (barbecue houses) 383
Cid brothers 291
Cidade das Artes (Barra da Tijuca) **90**
Cidade de Goiás 303, **314**
festivals 46
Cidade do Samba (Rio de Janeiro) **88–9**
Cigars
São Félix 201
Cinelândia (Rio de Janeiro) **77**
Cinema 25, 62, **400–401**
Cinelândia (Rio de Janeiro) **77**
festivals 44, 47
James Bond's *Moonraker* 81
Rio de Janeiro **98**, 99
São Paulo 157
shopping in São Paulo 154, 155
Circo Voador (Rio de Janeiro) 12, 78
Círio de Nazaré (Belém) 44
Climate **48–9**
wet and dry seasons 26
Climbing
Sugar Loaf Mountain (Rio de Janeiro) 80

Clothes
Afro-Brazilian culture 181
Brazilian beach culture 43
festivals 46
gaúcho 334
in restaurants 382
São Paulo Fashion Week **149**
shopping in Rio de Janeiro 95
shopping in São Paulo 154, 155
what to take 408
Clubs
Rio de Janeiro **97**, 99
São Paulo 156–7
Coelho, Paulo 25, 35
Coelho Pereira, Duarte 217
Coffee **56–7**, 399
Cog train (Rio de Janeiro) 12, 87
Coins 415
Collor de Mello, Fernando 63
Colonial literature **35**
Communications **416–17**
Communists 59
Composição (Volpi) 144
Comprida, Ilha 175
Conceição, Frei Domingos da 34, 76
Conceição, José Eloy da 226
Condamine, Charles-Marie de la 278
Confeitaria Colombo (Rio de Janeiro) 12, **76–7**
Congonhas
Basílica do Senhor Bom Jesus de Matosinhos **134–5**
Congresso Nacional e Anexos (Brasília) 24, 307
Conselheiro, Antônio 35, **210**
Constable, John 147
Consulates 413
Conti, Júlio 193
Convento de São Francisco (Olinda) 224, **226**
Convento de São Francisco (Penedo) 217
Convento do São Francisco (Marechal Deodoro) 218
Cooperativa Vinícola Aurora (Bento Gonçalves) 360
Copacabana 12, 71, **82**
festivals 45
hotels 370–71
map 82–3
restaurants 386
Coral reefs
Maracajaú 242
Corpus Christi 47
Corumbá **326**
Costa, Cláudio Manuel da 35
Costa, Lúcio 153
Brasília 299, 306
Museu das Missões (São Miguel das Missões) 363
Costa, Manuel da *see* Athayde, Mestre
Costa, Manuel Inácio da 194
Costa Branca **243**
Costa Coelho, Caetano da 76
Costa do Sauípe 211
hotels 374
Costa e Silva, Artur da 62
Costa do Sol
beaches **120–21**

Costa Verde (Green Coast) **114**
  A week on the Costa Verde 14
Crafts
  Afro-Brazilian culture **181**
Crafts shops **399**
  Mercado Modelo (Salvador)
  196
  Rio de Janeiro 95
  São Paulo 155
Cravo, Mario
  A Cruz Caída 187
Credit cards 412, **414–15**
  in hotels 366
  in restaurants 382
  in shops 398
Crime 412–13
  São Paulo **159**
Crispim **253**
Cristalino Jungle Lodge 296, 323
Cristo de Rapadura (Dias) 151
Cristo Redentor (Rio de Janeiro) 12,
  21, **86–7**
Cruises **425**
Cruls, Luiz 298
Cuiabá 15, **322**
  hotels 379
  restaurants 395
Cunha, Euclides da 34, 35, 58, 210
Curitiba 331, 337, **340**, 348–9
  hotels 380
  restaurants 396
Currency **414–15**
Curucirarí people
  architecture 32
Cururupe 204
Cururupu 259
Customs and duty free 419
Cycling **403**, 405

D

Dams
  Italpu Binacional 15, 346
  Xingó 218
Dance 400
  classes **404**, 405
  festivals 47
  frevo **221**
  gaúcho 335
  Rio de Janeiro **98**, 99
  São Paulo 156, 157
Dance bars
  São Paulo 156–7
Dannemann, Gerhard 201
Darwin, Charles 84
David, Jacques-Louis 147
Debret, Jean-Baptiste 34, 78
Dedo de Deus 119
Delta do Parnaíba **254–5**
Dengue fever 410
Deodoro da Fonseca, Marechal
  Manuel 58, 218
Di Cavalcanti, Emiliano 34, 147
Dialing codes 416
Diamantina 67, 125, 126, **128**
Diamonds
  Lençóis 208
Dias, Caetano
  Cristo de Rapadura 151
Dinosaur tracks
  Souza 236

Disabled travelers 409
  in hotels 367
Discounts
  air travel 420
  entertainment 400
Diving 403
  Fernando de Noronha **229**
Docks & Waterfront (Rio de Janeiro)
  76
Doctors 411
Dois Irmãos 213
Domingas Dias 168
Dorivã 313
Doyle, Sir Arthur Conan 262
Drape, Dorothy 117
Drinks
  shopping in São Paulo 154, 155
  see also Food and drink
Drummond, Carlos 35
Dry season 26
Dunes
  buggies **245**
  Costa Branca 243
  Genipabu **242**
  Natal 240
Dutch immigrants 333
Dutra, General Eurico 59, 117
Duty-free allowances 419

E

Eckhout, Albert 223
Eclectic architecture 33
Economy 22–3
Ecoparque Sperry 358
Ecosystems 22, **28–9**
Ecotourism **402**, 405
Edifício Altino Arantes (São Paulo)
  12, 138, **143**
Edifício Itália (São Paulo) 12, **143**
Eiffel, Gustave 284
Einstein, Albert 84, 86
Eisenhower, Dwight D 298
Eixo Monumental (Brasília) 306
Electricity 409
Elevador Lacerda (Salvador) 13,
  193
Elizabeth II, Queen of England 93
Emas, Parque Nacional das **315**
Emergencies 411, 423
Encontro das Águas **289**
Enseada de Botafogo 25
Entertainment **400–401**
  bars, cafés and botecos **401**
  cinema **400–401**
  discount tickets and free events
  400
  gardens and theme parks **401**
  information and booking 400
  performing arts **400**
  Rio de Janeiro **96–9**
  São Paulo **156–7**
  soccer matches **401**
Ernst, Max 152
Espaço Cultural da Marinha (Rio de
  Janeiro) 75, **92**, 93
Espírito Santo *see* Rio de Janeiro
  and Espírito Santo
Esplanada dos Ministérios (Brasília)
  307
Estação das Docas (Belém) **272**

Estação da Luz (São Paulo) 13, **146**
Estação Pinacoteca (São Paulo)
  146
Estádio do Maracanã (Rio de
  Janeiro) **88**
Estado Nôvo 59, 60, 151
Estância Mimosa **327**
Estrada de Ferro Central do Brasil
  (Amaral) 152
Estrada Graciosa 341
Estrada Parque 204
Estrada Real 125
Etiquette 409
Eu, Count d' 116
  tomb 116
European immigrants 30
Evangelical Protestantism **38–9**
Evans, Cliford 274
Events **44–7**
Expoflora (Holambra) 44

F

Famiglia Tasca
  Vale dos Vinhedos tour 359
Faria, Captain Rodrigues de 198
Fascism 59, 60
Fashion *see* Clothes
Favelas
  Rio de Janeiro **89**
  safety 412
Fazenda Babilonia (Pirenópolis) 313
Fernando de Noronha 179, **228–9**
  hotels 376
  map 215, 228–9
  restaurants 392
Fernando de Noronha, Parque
  Nacional Marinho de 213, 228
Ferradurinha 121
Fest Verão Paraíba (João Pessoa)
  45
Festa do Bembé do Mercado
  (Santo Amaro) 46
Festa da Boa Morte **201**
Festa do Boi Bumbá (Parintins) 47,
  291
Festa do Bumba-meu-boi (São Luís)
  47, **258**
Festa do Divino Espírito Santo 46,
  313
Festa Literária Internacional de
  Paraty 47
Festa Nacional da Maçã (São
  Joaquim) 46
Festa Nacional da Uva (Caxias do
  Sul) 45
Festa da Nossa Senhora das Neves
  (João Pessoa) 47
Festa do Peão de Boiadeiro
  (Barretos) 47
Festa do Pinhão (Lages) 47
Festa Santa Bárbara (Salvador) 45
Festa de São Lázaro (Salvador) 45
Festas Juninas 46–7, **236**
Festas dos Ticumbi & Alardo
  (Itaúnas) 45
Festival de Gramado 47
Festival de Inverno (São Paulo)
  47
Festival Internacional da Dança
  (Joinville) 47

Festivals **44–7**
  Carnaval in Rio de Janeiro **68–9**
  Lavagem do Bonfim **199**
Figueiredo, General João 62, 63
Film see Cinema
First Republic **58**
Fiscal, Ilha 92–3
Fish and seafood
  The flavors of Brazil **384–5**
Fishing 403
  festivals 44
Fittipaldi, Emerson 25
Flamengo (Rio de Janeiro)
  hotels 371
  restaurants 386–7
Flora and fauna **28–9**
  in the cerrado **300–301**
  Pantanal **301**
  see also Wildlife
Flores da Cunha 361
Florianópolis 331, 337, 338, **350–51**
  flight duration chart 421
  hotels 380
  restaurants 396
Flowers
  Brazil's Flora and fauna **28–9**
  Expoflora (Holambra) 44
Food and drink
  barreado **343**
  Brazilian beach culture 42
  festivals 47
  The flavors of Brazil **384–5**
  The flavors of Northeast Brazil
    182–3
  gaúcho 335
  safety 411
  shopping 399
  shopping in São Paulo 154, 155
  see also Restaurants; Wines
Football see Soccer
Ford, Henry 278–9
Fordlândia 278–9
Forró **240**
Fortal (Fortaleza) 47
Fortaleza 233, 238–9, **246–7**
  festivals 47
  flight duration chart 421
  hotels 377
  map 246–7
  restaurants 393
Fortaleza de Nossa Senhora dos
  Prazeres (Ilha do Mel) 342
Fortaleza de Santa Cruz (Niterói) 93
Fortaleza de São José de Macapá
  275
Forte do Brum (Recife) **221**
Forte das Cinco Pontas (Recife) **221**
Forte de Copacabana 82
Forte Defensor Perpétuo (Paraty)
  111
Forte Junqueira (Corumbá) 326
Forte Orange (Ilha de Itamaracá)
  227
Forte do Presépio (Belém) **272**
Forte Príncipe da Beira 293
Forte dos Reis Magos (Natal) 240
Forte de Santo Antônio (Salvador)
  13, **197**
Forte de São Felipe (Salvador) 198–9
Foua, João 278

Foz do Iguaçu 15, 330, 337, **344–7**
Foz do Iguaçu (town) **346**
  hotels 380–81
  restaurants 396
France 54–5
Franco, Siron 34
Frevo **221**
Freyre, Gilberto 35
Friedenreich, Artur 40
Fruit
  The flavors of Brazil **385**
Fundação Casa de Jorge Amado
  (Salvador) 191, **192**
Fundação Eva Klabin (Lagoa
  Rodrigo de Freitas) 84
Fundação Pinacoteca Benedito
  Calixto (Santos) 172, 173

G

Gafieira
  Rio de Janeiro **97**, 99
Gainsborough, Thomas 147
Galleries see Museums and galleries
Gama, José Basilio da 35
Gardens see Parks and gardens
Garibaldi 360
Garrincha 40
Gas stations 422
Gaúchos **334–5**
  Rio Grande do Sul 353
Gay and lesbian travelers
  Rio de Janeiro **98**, 99
Geisel, Ernesto 62, 63
Gems, shopping 399
Génio do Repouso Eterno (Rodin) 145
Genipabu **242**
  restaurants 393
German immigrants **332**
Getz, Stan 36, 83
Gil, Gilberto 36, 37
Gilberto, Astrud 83
Gilberto, João 83
Giorgi, Bruno 84
  Os Candangos 302, 307
Gipóia, Ilha 114
"The Girl from Ipanema" **83**
Glaziou, Auguste 88
GLBT Parade (São Paulo) 47
Goiás see Brasília, Goiás and
  Tocantins
Gold 55
Golden Law (1888) 57
Gonçalves, Andre 92
Gonzaga, Luiz 227, 237
Gonzaga, Tomás Antônio 35
Goulart, João 62
Governador, Ilha do 92
Goya y Lucientes, Francisco José
  147
Gramado **358**
  festivals 47
  hotels 381
  restaurants 397
Grande, Ilha 14, 107, **114**
  hotels 372
Grande Carajás 269
El Greco 147
Green Coast see Costa Verde
Green Line see Linha Verde
Gresnicht, Adelbert 34

Grumari (Rio de Janeiro) **91**
Gruta do Lago Azul **327**
Guanabara Bay 71, 80, **92**
Guaraní people 353, 362
Guarapari **122**
Guarujá 165, **169**
  hotels 374
  restaurants 391
Guimarães Rosa, João 35

H

Hals, Franz 147
Hatoum, Milton 35
Health **410–11**
Helicopter tours
  Rio de Janeiro **98**, 99
Hell, Maximiliano 142, 143
Higienópolis (São Paulo City)
  restaurants 389
History **51–63**
Holambra
  festivals 44
Holanda, Sérgio Buarque de 35
Holbein, Hans 147
Holidays, public 47
Homem do Norte (Manaus) **284**
Horse racing
  Jóquei Clube Brasileiro (Rio de
    Janeiro) **84**
  Rio de Janeiro **98**, 99
Horses
  gaúchos 335
Hospitals 411
Hot-Air Balloon Festival (Torres)
  46
Hotel das Cataratas Belmond 15
Hotel Unique (São Paulo) 33, 150
Hotels **366–81**
  Amazonas, Roraima, Acre and
    Rondônia 378–9
  apart-hotels 367
  Bahia 374–5
  booking 366, 369
  Brasília, Goiás and Tocantins 379
  budget options 369
  chain hotels 368, 369
  children in 367
  disabled travelers 367
  Mato Grosso and Mato Grosso do
    Sul 379–80
  Minas Gerais 373
  Pará and Amapá 378
  Piauí and Maranhão 377
  pousadas 366, **368**, 369
  prices and payments 366–7
  resorts 368
  Rio de Janeiro City 370–71
  Rio de Janeiro State and Espírito
    Santo 372–3
  Rio Grande do Sul 381
  Santa Catarina and Paraná 380–81
  São Paulo City 373–4
  São Paulo State 374
  Sergipe, Alagoas and Pernambuco
    375–6
  tipping 367
Hydroelectricity
  Italpu Binacional 15, 346
Hygiene 411
Hypermarkets 398

I

Identification 413
Igapó forest 325
Igreja da Consolação (São Paulo) **143**
Igreja e Convento de São Francisco (Salvador) 13, 32, 190, **194–5**
Igreja Matriz (São Sebastião) 168, 169
Igreja Matriz de Nossa Senhora do Rosário (Pirenópolis) **312**
Igreja Matriz de São Vicente Mártir (São Vicente) 173
Igreja e Mosteiro São Bento (Olinda) 225, **226**
Igreja Nossa Senhor do Bonfim (Pirenópolis) **312**
Igreja da Nossa Senhora do Carmo (Ouro Preto) 131
Igreja Nossa Senhora da Corrente (Penedo) 217
Igreja Nossa Senhora da Glória do Outeiro (Rio de Janeiro) **79**
Igreja Nossa Senhora do Rosário dos Pretos (Salvador) 191
Igreja da Ordem Terceira de São Francisco (Salvador) 191
Igreja de Santa Maria dos Anjos (Penedo) 217
Igreja de Santa Maria Madalena (Marechal Deodoro) 218
Igreja de São Francisco (João Pessoa) **234**
Igreja São Francisco (Recife) **222**
Igreja de São Francisco de Assis (Belo Horizonte) 129
Igreja da São Francisco de Assis (Ouro Preto) 124, 131, **132**
Igreja de São Francisco de Assis (São João del Rei) 137
Igreja de São Francisco de Assis (São Paulo) **142**
Igreja de São Francisco da Penitência (Rio de Janeiro) **76**
Igreja de São Jorge (Ilhéus) 204
Igreja da Sé (Olinda) 224
Igreja da Sé (São Luís) 249, 257
Igreja Terceira Ordem de São Francisco (Salvador) 195
Iguaçu, Foz de 15, 330, 337, **344–7**
Iguaçu, Parque Nacional do 344, **346**
Iguape **174–5**
Iguazú, Parque Nacional 15, **347**
Ilha *see islands by name*
Ilhabela 14, 165, **169**
  hotels 374
  restaurants 391
Ilhabela Sailing Week 47
Ilhéus **204**
  hotels 374
Immigration 24, 30–31
  Japanese **173**
  multicultural Southern Brazil **332–3**
  regulations 418
Imperial Museum (Petrópolis) **118–19**
Inconfidência Mineira rebellion (1789) 55, 130, 131

Independence Day 47
Indigenous peoples 30
  architecture **32**
  history 51, 52
  Museu do Índio (Manaus) 15, **285**
  Museu do Índio (Rio de Janeiro) 12, **85**
  Museu do Índio Marechal Rondon (Cuiabá) 322
  The people of Amazônia **266–7**
  religion **39**
  slavery 54
  see also individual tribes
Instituto Butantã (São Paulo) 13, **152–3**
Instituto de Desenvolvimento Sustentável Mamirauá **291**
Instituto Itaú Cultural (São Paulo) 148
Instituto Ricardo Brennand (Recife) **223**
Integralistas 59, 60
International Book Biennial (São Paulo) 46
International Festival of Culture and Gastronomy (Tiradentes) 47
International Fishing Festival (Cáceres) 44
International Puppet Theater Festival 47
Internet **417**
Ipanema 12, **83**
  hotels 371
  map 82–3
  restaurants 387
Iracema **247**
Isabel, Princess
  abolition of slavery 77, 78
  Petrópolis 116
  tomb 116
Islam **39**
Itacaré **204**
  hotels 374
  restaurants 391
Italian immigrants **333**
Italpu Binacional 15, 346
Itamaracá, Ilha de **227**
Itaparica, Ilha de 13, **200**
Itapuã 199
Itatiaia, Parque Nacional 107, 108, **115**
Itaúnas 107, **123**
  festivals 45

J

Jalapão 305, **314–15**
Japanese immigrants 31, **173**, 333
  Liberdade (São Paulo) **149**
  religion 39
Jardim de Alá 199
Jardim Botânico (Rio de Janeiro) 12, **84**
  restaurants 387–8
Jardim Botânico (São Paulo) **153**
Jardim Zoológico (Rio de Janeiro) 88
Jardins and Avenida Paulista (São Paulo)
  hotels 373
  restaurants 389–90

Jaú, Parque Nacional 289
Jericoacoara 231, **244–5**
  hotels 377
Jesuits 38
  colonization of Brazil 53
  literature 35
  The rise and collapse of Jesuit missions **362**
  São Miguel das Missões 330, **363**
  São Paulo City 139, 142
Jesus, José Teófilo de 216
Jewelry
  Afro-Brazilian culture 181
  buying gems 399
  shopping in Rio de Janeiro 94, 95
Jews **39**, 333
  Kahal Zur Israel Synagogue (Recife) **220–21**
Joanes 274
João III, Dom 52, 53, 54
João VI, Dom 56, 74
  Igreja Nossa Senhora da Glória do Outeiro (Rio de Janeiro) 79
  Jardim Botânico (Rio de Janeiro) 84
  Museu Nacional de Belas Artes (Rio de Janeiro) 78
  Museu Nacional (Rio de Janeiro) 88
João Pessoa 231, 232, **234–5**
  festivals 45, 47
  hotels 376
  map 235
  restaurants 393
Jobim, Antônio Carlos ("Tom") 36, 83, 97
John XXIII, Pope 38
John Paul II, Pope 79, 86, 88, 308
Joinville
  festivals 47
Jóquei Clube Brasileiro (Rio de Janeiro) **84**
Jorge, Seu 78
Juazeiro do Norte
  festivals 44
Judaism **39**
Júnior, Almeida 147
  Caipira Picando Fumo 145
Junta, military 62

K

Kahal Zur Israel Synagogue (Recife) **220–21**
Kardec, Allan 39
Kayapó malocas (longhouses) 32
Kayapó people 267
Kitesurfing 403
Klabin, Eva 84
Kubitschek, Juscelino 62, 79
  Belo Horizonte 125, 129
  Brasília 298, 299, 306, 308
  bust of 304
  Museu de Juscelino Kubitschek (Diamantina) 128
  Palácio Rio Negro (Petrópolis) 116
Kuerten, Gustavo 25

L

Labor Day 47
Lacerda, Antônio Francisco de 193
Lages
  festivals 47
Lagoa *see lakes by name*
Lajedo de Soledade 243
Lampião **217**
Landowski, Paul 86
Landscape **26–7**
  The Amazon ecosystem **264–5**
  sertão **237**
Languages 21, 408
  classes **404**, 405
Lapa (Rio de Janeiro) 12, **78**
Laranjeiras 112
Latifundia 58
Lavagem do Bonfim (Salvador) 45, 181, **199**
Lázaro 168
Le Corbusier 33, 153, 299
  and Brasília 298, 308
Leblon 12, **83**
  hotels 371
  map 82–3
  restaurants 387
Leme
  hotels 370–71
  restaurants 386
Lemos de Gonzaga family 217
Lempião 243
Lençóis 13, 178, **208**
  hotels 374
  restaurants 391
Lençóis, Ilha dos 259
Lençóis Maranhenses, Parque Nacional do 249, 251, **254–5**
  restaurants 394
Leo III, Pope 77
Leopoldina, Empress 88
  tomb 152
Liberation Theology 34, **38**
Liberdade (São Paulo) 13, **149**
  restaurants 390
Lima, Joaquin Eugenio de 148
Linha Verde (Green Line) 13, **211**
Linnaeus, Carl 153
Lisboa, Manuel Francisco 132
Lispector, Clarice 35
Literature 25, **35**
The Litorina 341
Lodges 366, 369
Lopes Mendes 114
Louis XIII, King of France 249
Loureiro, Rita 284
Luis, Washington 60
Lula da Silva, Luiz Inácio 22, 23, 63, 139

M

Macapá 269, 270, **275**
  hotels 378
  restaurants 394
Maceió **218–19**
  hotels 375
  restaurants 392
Machado de Assis, Joaquim Maria 34, 35
Madeira, Rio 281, 282

Madeira-Mamoré Museu Ferroviário (Porto Velho) 262, 281, **293**
Mãe Douro (Calixto) 172
Magazines **417**
  shopping in São Paulo 155
Mail services **417**
Malfatti, Anita 34, 146, 152
  Tropical 145
Mamori, Lago **290**
Manaquiri, Lago **290**
Manatees
  Projeto Peixe Bot (Ilha de Itamaracá) 227
Manaus 15, 281, **284–91**
  airport 419
  Amazon excursions from **288–91**
  climate 48
  flight duration chart 421
  hotels 378
  map 285
  restaurants 394
  Teatro Amazonas **286–7**
Manet, Edouard 147
Manguezal de Vitória 122
Mantegna, Andrea 147
Manuel I, Emperor of Portugal 52
Maps
  Amazon excursions from Manaus 288
  Amazonas, Roraima, Acre and Rondônia 282–3
  Bahia 186–7
  Barra 90
  Belém 273
  Brasília 306–7
  Brasília, Goiás and Tocantins 304–5
  Brasília: Greater Brasília 16
  Brazil 16–17
  Central and South America 17
  Central West Brazil 296–7
  Climate of Brazil 48–9
  Copacabana, Ipanema and Leblon 82–3
  Costa do Sol: beaches 120–21
  Delta do Parnaíba 254–5
  Fernando de Noronha 215, 228–9
  Florianópolis and Ilha de Santa Catarina 350–51
  Fortaleza 246–7
  Foz do Iguaçu 346
  João Pessoa 235
  The landscapes of Brazil 26–7
  Linha Verde 211
  Manaus 285
  Mato Grosso and Mato Grosso do Sul 320–21
  Minas Gerais 126–7
  Northeast Brazil 178–9
  Northern Brazil 262–3
  Olinda 224–5
  Ouro Preto 130–31
  Pantanal 324–5
  Pará and Amapá 270–71
  Paraíba, Rio Grande do Norte and Ceará 232–3
  Paraty 111
  Paraty: beaches and islands around 112
  Parque Nacional de Chapada Diamantina 208–9

Maps (cont.)
  Parque Nacional Chapada dos Veadeiros 316–17
  Parque Nacional do Lençóis Maranhenses **254–5**
  Parque Nacional de Serra do Capivara 252–3
  Petrópolis 116–17
  Piauí and Maranhão 250–51
  Pirenópolis 313
  Porto Alegre 356
  Recife 220–21
  Rio de Janeiro 72–3
  Rio de Janeiro: Greater Rio de Janeiro City 73
  Rio de Janeiro: Street Finder 100–105
  Rio de Janeiro and Espírito Santo 108–9
  Rio Grande do Sul 354–5
  Rota do Sol beaches 241
  Salvador 188–9
  Salvador: Greater Salvador 189
  Salvador: Pelourinho 190–91
  Salvador's Atlantic coast 198–9
  Santa Catarina and Paraná 338–9
  São Luís 256–7
  São Paulo 140–41
  São Paulo: Street finder 158–63
  São Paulo State 167
  Sergipe, Alagoas and Pernambuco 214–15
  Serra da Graciosa 341
  Southeast Brazil 18–19, 66–7
  Southern Brazil 330–31
  Vale dos Vinhedos tour 359
Maracá, Ilha do 292
Maracajaú **242**
Marajó, Ilha de 263, 269, 271, **274**
  hotels 378
Maranhão *see* Piauí and Maranhão
Marcelino, Antônio 192
Marechal Deodoro **218**
Maresias 14, **169**
  hotels 374
Maria Bonita **217**
Maria Eugenia 313
Mariana **133**
Maricá 120
Marina da Glória 92, 93
Marinho de Abrolhos, Parque Nacional 185, **205**
Markets **398–9**
  Casa da Cultura (Recife) **223**
  Macapá 275
  Mercado Central (Fortaleza) **246**
  Mercado Modelo (Salvador) **196**
  Mercado Municipal Adolfo Lisboa (Manaus) **284**
  Mercado Público (Porto Alegre) **356**
  Mercado Ribeira (Olinda) 225
Marumbi, Parque Estadual de 341
Mata Atlântica (Atlantic forest) 27, 63, 107, 108, **113**, 125, 165, 167
  Salvador 13, **198–9**
  Parque Nacional de Superagui 343
  Pedra Azul 123
  Serra da Graciosa 341
  wildlife **29**

Matisse, Henri 152
Mato Grosso and Mato Grosso do
    Sul **319–27**
    hotels 379–80
    map 320–21
    Pantanal **324–5**
    restaurants 395
Matos, Gregório de 35
Matriz de Nossa Senhora da
    Conceição (Ouro Preto) 131, **132**
Matriz de Nossa Senhora do Pilar
    (Ouro Preto) 130, **132**
Matriz Nossa Senhora dos Remédios
    (Paraty) **111**
Matriz de Santo Antônio
    (Tiradentes) 136
Mauá, Visconde de 146
Maurice of Nassau 223
Mayrink Chapel (Tijuca) 92
Meat
    The flavors of Brazil **384**
Media **416–17**
Medical care **410–11**
Médici, General 62–3
Meggers, Betty 274
Meireles, Vitor 78
Meirelles, Fernando 89
Mel, Ilha do **342–3**
Mello, Francisco de 57
Memling, Hans 147
Memorial das Conquistas (Santos)
    173
Memorial do Rio Grande do Sul
    (Porto Alegre) **357**
Memorial do Vinho
    Vale dos Vinhedos tour 359
Memorial dos Povos Indígenas
    (Brasília) 306
Mendes, Chico 281, **293**
Mendes, Feliciano 134
Mendes, Sergio 36
Mercado Central (Fortaleza) **246**
Mercado Modelo (Salvador) 13, **196**
Mercado Municipal Adolfo Lisboa
    (Manaus) **284**
Mercado Público (Porto Alegre)
    356
Mercado Ribeira (Olinda) 225
Mercury, Daniela 37
Meros, Ilha dos 112
Metro **426–7**
Mileage chart 19
Miller, Charles 40
Millet, Jean François 147
Minas Gerais 12, 15, 21, **125–37**
    Basílica do Nossa Senhor Bom
        Jesus de Matosinhos (Congonhas)
        134–5
    festivals 46
    hotels 373
    map 126–7
    restaurants 388–9
Mines 269
Ministry of Education (Rio de
    Janeiro) 33, 61
Miranda **326**
    hotels 380
Miranda, Carmen 25, 61, 75, 82
Mirante do Morro do Espio (Iguape)
    174

Mireilles, Fernando 25
Missão Cruls 298
Misteriosa, Lagoa 318
Modernism
    architecture 33
    literature **35**
Modigliani, Amadeo 152
Monasteries and convents
    Convento da Nossa Senhora da
        Penha (Vitória) 122
    Convento de São Francisco
        (Olinda) 224, **226**
    Convento de São Francisco
        (Penedo) 217
    Convento do São Francisco
        (Marechal Deodoro) 218
    Convento de São Francisco
        (Salvador) 32, 190, **194–5**
    Mosteiro de São Bento (João
        Pessoa) **234**
    Mosteiro de São Bento (Rio de
        Janeiro) **76**
    Mosteiro São Bento (São Paulo)
        142–3
Money **414–15**
Monte Alegre **279**
Monte Roraima 262, 292
Monte Roraima, Parque Nacional de
    292
Monumento às Bandeiras (São
    Paulo) 150
Moonraker (film) 81
Moore, Roger 81
Moraes, Vinícius de 35, 36, 83, 97
Moriconi, Roberto 84
Morretes 341
    hotels 381
Morro Branco 231
Morro do Corcovado (Rio de
    Janeiro) 12, **86–7**
Morro do Pai Inácio 208
Morro do Pico 215, 229
Morro de São Paulo 13,
    202
    hotels 375
    restaurants 391
Morro da Urca (Rio de Janeiro) 12,
    80
Mosaico Juréia-Itatins **174**
Mossoró **243**
Mosteiro de São Bento (João
    Pessoa) **234**
Mosteiro de São Bento (Rio de
    Janeiro) **76**
Mosteiro de São Bento (São Paulo)
    142–3
Motels 369
Moto-taxis 426
Motor racing 25, 44
Mountain biking **403**, 405
Mulattoes 31
Mundaú, Lagoa 219
Museums and galleries
    Bolsa e Museu do Café (Santos)
        172, 173
    Cafua das Mercês (São Luís)
        258
    Casa de Cultura Jorge Amado
        (Ilhéus) 204
    Casa Daros (Rio de Janeiro) **85**

Museums and galleries (cont.)
    Casa Histórica do Iphan
        (Alcântara) 259
    Casa do Maranhão (São Luís) 258
    Casa Martim Afonso (São Vicente)
        173
    Casa Museu Mestre Vitalino
        (Caruaru) 227
    Casa do Pontal (Barra da Tijuca) **91**
    Centro de Cultura Popular (São
        Luís) 257, 258
    Centro Cultural do Banco do Brasil
        (Rio de Janeiro) **89**
    Centro Cultural Banco do Brasil
        (São Paulo) **143**
    Centro Cultural Dannemann (São
        Félix) 201
    Centro Cultural Dragão do Mar
        (Fortaleza) **246**
    Centro Cultural Yves Alves
        (Tiradentes) 136
    Espaço Cultural da Marinha (Rio
        de Janeiro) 75, **92**, 93
    Estação Pinacoteca (São Paulo) **146**
    Fundação Casa de Jorge Amado
        (Salvador) 191, **192**
    Fundação Eva Klabin (Lagoa
        Rodrigo de Freitas) 84
    Fundação Pinacoteca Benedito
        Calixto (Santos) 172, 173
    Homem do Norte (Manaus) **284**
    Imperial Museum (Petrópolis)
        118–19
    Instituto Itaú Cultural (São Paulo)
        148
    Instituto Ricardo Brennand (Recife)
        223
    Madeira-Mamoré Museu
        Ferroviário (Porto Velho) 262, 281,
        293
    Museu Abelardo Rodrigues Solar
        do Ferrão (Salvador) 191
    Museu do Açude (Tijuca) 92
    Museu Afro Brasil (São Paulo) 150
    Museu Afro-Brasileiro (Salvador)
        190, **192**
    Museu do Antônio Prado 361
    Museu de Arqueologia e
        Etnologia (Paranaguá) 342
    Museu de Arqueológia de Xingó
        (Cânion Xingó) 218
    Museu Arquidiocesano de Arte
        Sacra (Rio de Janeiro) 77
    Museu de Arte Assis
        Chateaubriand (Campina Grande)
        236
    Museu de Arte da Bahia (Salvador)
        197
    Museu de Arte Contemporânea
        (Niterói) 93
    Museu de Arte Contemporânea
        (Olinda) 225, **226**
    Museu de Arte Contemporânea
        (São Paulo) **152**
    Museu de Arte Moderna (MAM,
        Rio de Janeiro) **78–9**
    Museu de Arte Moderna (MAM,
        São Paulo) 13, 151
    Museu de Arte Moderna
        (Salvador) 13, 196

Museums and galleries (cont.)
Museu de Arte do Rio (Rio de Janeiro) 76
Museu de Arte do Rio Grande do Sul (Porto Alegre) **357**
Museu de Arte Sacra (Cidade de Goiás) 314
Museu de Arte Sacra (Curitiba) 340
Museu de Arte Sacra (Iguape) 175
Museu de Arte Sacra (Mariana) 133
Museu de Arte Sacra (Salvador) 13, **196**
Museu de Arte Sacra (São Cristóvão) 216
Museu de Arte Sacra (São Paulo) 13, **146**
Museu de Arte Sacra (São Sebastião) 168, 169
Museu de Arte Sacra de Santarém 278, 279
Museu de Arte de São Paulo (MASP) 11, 13, **147**
Museu das Bandeiras (Cidade de Goiás) 314
Museu do Amanhã (Rio de Janeiro) 76
Museu do Barro (Caruaru) 227
Museu da Borrachá (Rio Branco) 293
Museu Cais do Sertão (Recife) **221**
Museu Casa do Diamante (Diamantina) 128
Museu Casa de Pedra (Caxias do Sul) 361
Museu Casa de Rui Barbosa (Rio de Janeiro) **85**
Museu das Cavalhadas (Pirenópolis) **312**
Museu do Ceará (Fortaleza) **246**
Museu Ferroviário (São João del Rei) 137
Museu do Futbol (São Paulo) 13, **148–9**
Museu da Gentre Sergipana (Aracaju) 216
Museu Histórico e Arqueológico (Iguape) 174–5
Museu Histórico Nacional (Rio de Janeiro) **78**
Museu da Imagem e do Som (Copacabana) 82
Museu da Imigração Japonesa (São Paulo) 149
Museu da Imigração Polonesa (Curitiba) 333
Museu do Imigrante (Bento Gonçalves) 360
Museu Imperial (Petrópolis) 32
Museu do Índio (Manaus) 15, **285**
Museu do Índio (Rio de Janeiro) 12, **85**
Museu do Índio Marechal Rondon (Cuiabá) 322
Museu da Inconfidência (Ouro Preto) 131
Museu Internacional de Arte Naïf (Rio de Janeiro) 12, 87
Museu Júlio de Castilhos (Porto Alegre) 356
Museu de Juscelino Kubitschek (Diamantina) 128

Museums and galleries (cont.)
Museu do Mamulengo (Olinda) 225, **226**
Museu de Microbiologia (São Paulo) 153
Museu Mineiro (Belo Horizonte) 129
Museu das Missões (São Miguel das Missões) 363
Museu Municipal (Cananéia) 175
Museu Municipal (Caxias do Sul) 361
Museu Nacional (Rio de Janeiro) 88
Museu Nacional de Belas Artes (Rio de Janeiro) **78**
Museu Nacional Honestino Guimarães (Brasília) 307
Museu Oscar Niemeyer (Curitiba) 340
Museu Padre Anchieta (São Paulo) 142
Museu do Pantanal (Corumbá) 326
Museu Paranaense (Curitiba) 340
Museu Paulista do Ipiranga (São Paulo) 152
Museu do Piauí (Teresina) 252
Museu de Porto Seguro 205
Museu Regional de São João del Rei 137
Museu da República (Rio de Janeiro) **79**
Museu Rodin-Bahia (Salvador) **197**
Museu SACACA (Macapá) 275
Museu de Santarém 278, 279
Museu Seleção Brasileira (Barra da Tijuca) **90–91**
Museu Tem포stal (Salvador) **192**
Museu Théo Brandão (Maceió) 218–19
Museu Villa-Lobos (Rio de Janeiro) **85**
Oficina de Cerâmica Francisco Brennand (Recife) **223**
Oi Futuro Ipanema (Rio de Janeiro) **79**
Palacete Provincial (Manaus) **284**
Palácio Rio Branco 292–3
Pinacoteca de São Paulo 13, **144–5**
Solar do Unhão (Salvador) 13
Usina do Gasômetro (Porto Alegre) **357**
Music 25, **36–7**, **404**, 405
Afro-Brazilian culture **180**
capoeira **203**, **404**, 405
forró **240**
frevo **221**
gaúcho 335
"The Girl from Ipanema" **83**
Museu da Imagem e do Som (Copacabana) 82
Museu Villa-Lobos (Rio de Janeiro) **85**
repentistas **243**
Rio de Janeiro **98**, 99
São Paulo 156, 157
shopping in Rio de Janeiro 95
shopping in São Paulo 154, 155
Música popular Brasileira 37
Muslims **39**
Mussolini, Benito 60

N

Naming of Brazil **53**
Napoleon I, Emperor 56, 74
Natal 179, 231, **240**
festivals 45
hotels 376
restaurants 393
National Handicraft Fair (Belo Horizonte) 44
National parks
Aparados da Serra 353, 354, **362**
Chapada Diamantina 13, **208–9**
Chapada dos Veadeiros 303, 304, **316–17**
Emas **315**
Fernando de Noronha 213, 228
Iguaçu 344, **346**
Iguazú 15, **347**
Itatiaia 107, 108, **115**
Jaú 289
Lençóis Maranhenses **254–5**
Marinho de Abrolhos 185, **205**
Monte Roraima 292
Pantanal Matogrossense 324
Serra da Canastra 66, 125, 127, **137**
Serra da Capivara **252–3**
Serra do Cipó 125, **129**
Serra dos Órgãos 107, **119**
Sete Cidades 250, **253**
Superagui 343
Tijuca 12, 87, **92**
Ubajara 231, **245**
Negro, Rio 281, 284, **288**, 289
Neo-Classical architecture 32
Nestrovski, Arthur 146
Netherlands 54–5
Neves, Tancredo 62, 63
Newspapers **417**
Niemeyer, Oscar 33, **299**
Belo Horizonte 125, 129
Brasília 297, 298, 306
Catedral Metropolitana Nossa Senhora Aparecida (Brasília) 307, 309
Catedral Militar de Nossa Senhora da Paz (Brasília) 308
Congreso Nacional e Anexos (Brasília) 307
Museu de Art Contemporânea (Niterói) 93
Museu Oscar Niemeyer (Curitiba) 340
Palácio do Planalto (Brasília) 307
Parque Burle Marx (São Paulo) 153
Parque do Ibirapuera (São Paulo) 150, 151
Sambódromo (Rio de Janeiro) 69, 88–9
São Paulo 143
Niterói **93**
Nóbrega, Manuel da 139
Northeast Brazil **177–259**
Afro-Brazilian culture **180–81**
Bahia **185–211**
The flavors of Northeast Brazil **182–3**
map 178–9
Paraíba, Rio Grande do Norte and Ceará **231–47**

Northeast Brazil (cont.)
Piauí and Maranhão **249–59**
Rota do Sol beaches 241
Sergipe, Alagoas and Pernambuco **213–29**
sertão **237**
Northern Brazil **261–93**
The Amazon ecosystem **264–5**
Amazonas, Roraima, Acre and Rondônia **281–93**
map 262–3
Pará and Amapá **269–79**
The people of Amazônia **266–7**
Northern Highlands 26
Nosso Senhor do Bonfim (Salvador) **198–9**
Nossa Senhora do Amparo (Teresina) 252
Nossa Senhora de Candelária (Rio de Janeiro)
Street-by-Street map 75
Nossa Senhora do Carmo (Diamantina) 128
Nossa Senhora das Dores (Paraty) **111**
Nossa Senhora do Monte do Carmo (Rio de Janeiro) 74
Nossa Senhora dos Navegantes (Porto Alegre) 45
Nossa Senhora do Rosário (Diamantina) 128
Nossa Senhora do Rosário e São Benedito (Paraty) **110**
Nova Jerusalém 227
Nova Pádua 361
Nova Petrópolis **357**
Novo Airão **289**
Nunes, Clara 36

O
O Obelisco aos Heroís de 32 (São Paulo) 151
Óbidos **279**
Oca do Ibirapuera (São Paulo) 151
Oceanário (Aracaju) 216
Off-road driving **402–3**, 405
Oficina de Cerâmica Francisco Brennand (Recife) **223**
Ohtake, Ruy 33, 145
Hotel Unique (São Paulo) 150
Ohtake, Tomie 34, 147
Pintura 145
Oi Futuro Ipanema (Rio de Janeiro) **79**
Oktoberfest (Blumenau) 44
Olho de Boi 121
Olinda 212, 214, **224–6**
Carnaval **226**
hotels 376
map 224–5
restaurants 392
Oliveira, General Diego Luiz de 202
Ondina 198
Opening hours
banks 414
shops 94, 154, 398
Opera
Rio de Janeiro **98**, 99
Orellana, Francisco de 32
Orixás 181

Orquidário Aranda (Teresópolis) 119
Os Candangos (Giorgio) 302, 307
Osório, General Manuel Luis
statue of 74
Otávio Rocha 361
Our Lady of Aparecida Day 47
Ouro Preto 125, 126, **130–32**
hotels 373
restaurants 389
Street-by-Street map 130–31
Outdoor activities **402–5**

P
Paço da Alfândega (Recife) **220**
Paço do Frevo (Recife) **221**
Paço Imperial (Rio de Janeiro)
Street-by-Street map 74
Padre Cícero Pilgrimage (Juazeiro do Norte) 44
Pagodinho, Zeca 36
Palace of Justice (São Paulo) 138
Palacete Provincial (Manaus) **284**
Palácio Antônio Lemos (Belém) **272**
Palácio Conde dos Arcos (Cidade de Goiás) 314
Palácio do Itamaraty (Brasília) 303, 308
Palácio de Justiça (Brasília) 307, 308
Palácio do Planalto (Brasília) 307, 308
Palácio Rio Branco (Rio Branco) **292–5**
Palácio Rio Branco (Salvador) **193**
Palácio Rio Negro (Manaus) **284–5**
Palácio Rio Negro (Petrópolis) **116**
Palm trees **255**
Palmares, Quilombo dos 219
Palmas 114, **314**
restaurants 395
Pancetti, José
Serie Bahia Musa da Paz 144
Pantanal 15, 26, 319, **324–5**
flora and fauna **301**
map 324–5
wildlife **29**
Pantanal Matogrossense, Parque Nacional do 324
Pão de Açúcar (Rio de Janeiro) 80
Paquetá, Ilha 93
Pará and Amapá **269–79**
Belém **272–3**
hotels 378
map 270–71
restaurants 394
Paraguayan War (1864–70) **57**
Paraíba, Rio Grande do Norte and Ceará **231–47**
Fortaleza **246–7**
hotels 376–7
João Pessoa **234–5**
map 232–3
restaurants 393
Rota do Sol beaches 241
sertão 237
Paraiso, Lagoa do 245
Paraná *see* Santa Catarina and Paraná
Paranaguá **342**
hotels 381
restaurants 396

Paraty 14, 107, 109, **110–12**
beaches **112**
festivals 47
hotels 372
map 111
restaurants 388
Paraty-Mirim 112
Parintins **291**
festivals 47
Parking 423
Parks and gardens **401**
Bosque Papa João Paulo II Memorial Polonês (Curitiba) 340
Jardim Botânico (Rio de Janeiro) 12, **84**
Jardim Botânico (São Paulo) **153**
Museu Nacional (Rio de Janeiro) 88
Oficina de Cerâmica Francisco Brennand (Recife) 223
Orquidário Aranda (Teresópolis) 119
Parque Aldeia do Imigrante (Nova Petrópolis) 357
Parque Burle Marx (São Paulo) **153**
Parque da Catacumba (Lagoa Rodrigo de Freitas) 84
Parque do Ibirapuera (São Paulo) **150–51**
Parque Trianon (São Paulo) 148
Quinta da Boa Vista (Rio de Janeiro) **88**
Sítio Roberto Burle Marx (Barra da Tijuca) 14, **91**
see also National parks
Parliament buildings (Brasília) 33
Parnaíba, Rio 255
Parque Ambiental Chico Mendes 293
Parque Ambiental Encontro dos Rios 252
Parque dos Atletas **91**
Parque das Aves (Iguaçu) 15, **346**
Parque Burle Marx (São Paulo) **153**
Parque do Caracol 358
Parque das Dunas (Natal) 240
Parque Estadual de Canudos 210
Parque Estadual de Marumbi 341
Parque da Ferradura 358
Parque do Ibirapuera (São Paulo) 13
Parque da Independência (São Paulo) **152**
Parque Nacional dos Aparados da Serra 353, 354, **362**
Parque Nacional de Chapada Diamantina 13, **208–9**
Parque Nacional Chapada dos Veadeiros 303, 304, **316–17**
Parque Nacional das Emas **315**
Parque Nacional do Iguaçu 344, **346**
Parque Nacional Iguazú 15, **347**
Parque Nacional do Itatiaia 107, 108, **115**
Parque Nacional Jaú 289
Parque Nacional do Lençóis Maranhenses **254–5**
Parque Nacional Marinho de Abrolhos 185, **205**
Parque Nacional Marinho de Fernando de Noronha 213, 228
Parque Nacional de Monte Roraima 292

Parque Nacional do Pantanal Matogrossense 324
Parque Nacional Serra da Canastra 66, 125, 127, **137**
Parque Nacional de Serra do Capivara **252–3**
Parque Nacional Serra do Cipó 125, **129**
Parque Nacional da Serra dos Órgãos 107, **119**
Parque Nacional de Sete Cidades 250, **253**
Parque Nacional de Superagui 343
Parque Nacional da Tijuca 12, 87, **92**
Parque Nacional de Ubajara 231, **245**
Parque Trianon (São Paulo) 148
Passports 408, 409
Pátio do Colégio (São Paulo) 12, **142**
Paul VI, Pope 38, 309
Paulistanos **31**, 151
Pavilhão Japonès (São Paulo) 150
Pavlova, Anna 77, 273
Pedra Azul 107, **123**
Pedra Furada 245
Pedro I, Dom 56
    Brasília 308
    Jardim Zoológico (Rio de Janeiro) 88
    Museu Paulista do Ipiranga (São Paulo) 152
    Petrópolis 116
    portrait of 118
    tomb 152
Pedro II, Dom 56, 58
    Cog train (Rio de Janeiro) 87
    Ilha Fiscal 92
    Museu Nacional (Rio de Janeiro) 88
    Palácio Imperial (Petrópolis) 118–19
    Petrópolis 116
    São Félix 201
    statue of 108
    throne 77
    tomb 116
    trains 137
Peixoto, Floriano 298
Pelé 25, 40, 41, **172**, 173
Pelourinho (Salvador) 13, 184, 185
    Street-by-Street map 190–91
Penedo **217**
Peninsula de Maraú **202**
Peninsula da Ponta da Fortaleza 168
Peoples of Brazil **30–31**
Pequenos Lençóis 255
Pereira Leal, Inácio 312
Pereira dos Santos, Vitalino 227
Perequê 169
Pernambuco *see* Sergipe, Alagoas and Pernambuco
Pescadores do Rio Vermelho (Salvador) 45
Petrobras 22, 23, 61
Petrópolis 12, 67, **116–19**
    hotels 372
    map 116–17
    Palácio Imperial **118–19**
    restaurants 388
Pharmacies 410

Phones **416**, 417
Photo identification 413
Piauí and Maranhão **249–59**
    Delta do Parnaíba and Parque Nacional dos Lençóis Maranhenses **254–5**
    hotels 377
    map 250–51
    Parque Nacional de Serra da Capivara **252–3**
    restaurants 393–4
    São Luís **256–8**
Picãozinho, Ilha de (João Pessoa) 235
Picasso, Pablo 146, 147, 152
Pignatari, "Baby" 153
Pinacoteca de São Paulo 13, **144–5**
Pinga Festival (Paraty) 47
Pinheiros (São Paulo)
    restaurants 390
Pintura (Ohtake) 145
Piquet, Nelson 25
Pirenópolis 297, 303, **312–13**
    festivals 46
    map 313
Pius XII, Pope 86
Planetarium
    São Paulo City 150
Poço das Andorinhas 112
Poço Encantado 209
Poconé
    hotels 379
Police 412–13, 423
Politics 23–4
Ponta Negra 241
Population 24, **30–31**
    The gaúcho life **334–5**
    multicultural Southern Brazil **332–3**
    The people of Amazônia **266–7**
Por quilo restaurants 383
Pororoca wave **279**
Portinari, Candido 34
    Estação Pinacoteca (São Paulo) 146
    Igreja de São Francisco de Assis (Belo Horizonte) 129
    Mayrink Chapel 92
    Museu de Arte Contemporânea (São Paulo) 152
    Museu de Arte de São Paulo 147
Porto Alegre 331, **356–7**
    airport 419
    climate 48
    festivals 45
    hotels 381
    map 356
    restaurants 397
Porto da Barra 198
Porto Camará 274
Porto de Galinhas **219**
    hotels 376
    restaurants 392
Porto Maravilha (Rio) 76
Porto Seguro **205**
Porto Velho **293**
    hotels 379
    restaurants 394–5
Portuguese colonists 21, 24, 30, **52–3**, 54
    history 51
    religion 38

Portuguese language 408
    classes **404**, 405
Post, Frans 34, 78, 147, 223
Postal services **417**
Pottery on Ilha de Marajó **274**
Pousadas 366, **368**, 369
Praça da Matriz (Porto Alegre) **356–7**
Praça da República (Recife) **222**
Praça da Sé (Salvador) **193**
Praça dos Três Poderes (Brasília) **308**
Praça XV de Novembro (Rio de Janeiro)
    Street-by-Street map 74–5
Praia da Atalaia 229
Praia Atalaia Nova 216
Praia Azeda 121
Praia Azedinha 121
Praia da Barra da Tijuca **90**
Praia de Boa Viagem 199
Praia Brava 121
Praia do Cabo Branco **234**
Praia do Camburí 122
Praia do Cepilho 112
Praia da Costa 122
Praia de Cumbuco **247**
Praia Deserta 343
Praia da Ferradura 121
Praia de Fora 112
Praia do Forte 206–7, 211
    hotels 375
Praia do Francês 218
Praia do Futuro **247**
Praia do Gunga 219
Praia de Iracema **247**
Praia do Jabaquara 112
Praia João Fernandes 121
Praia João Fernandinho 121
Praia Joaquina 351
Praia de Maresias 169
Praia do Meio (Fernando de Noronha) 228
Praia do Meio (Guarapari) 122
Praia do Meio (Paraty) 112
Praia de Meireles (Fortaleza) **247**
Praia Mole 351
Praia do Morro 122
Praia das Pedrinhas 175
Praia da Penha 200
Praia da Pipa 241
    hotels 377
    restaurants 393
Praia do Pontal 112
Praia Prainha (Rio de Janeiro) **91**
Praia do Rosado 243
Praia do Sagi 241
Praia Sítio do Conde 211
Praia da Tabatinga 241
Praia Taipús de Fora 202
Praia Tambaba **235**
Praia de Tambaú **234**
Praia Vermelha do Norte 168
Praia Vermelha do Sul 168
Praia do Viareggio 175
Prainha 204
Pré Cajú (Aracaju) 45

Prehistoric sites
 Cariri 236
 pottery on Ilha de Marajó **274**
 Monte Alegre 279
 Parque Nacional de Serra do
  Capivara 252–3
 Parque Nacional de Sete Cidades
  253
 Souza 236
Presidente Figueiredo **288**
Preto, Rio 316
Processão do Bom Jesus dos
 Navegantes (Salvador) 45
Processão dos Navegantes (Angra
 dos Reis) 45
Procissão do Fogaréu (Cidade de
 Goiás) 46
Projac-TV Globo (Barra da Tijuca) **91**
Projeto Tamar 168, 211
Protestantism, Evangelical **38–9**
Prudentópolis 333
Public holidays 47
Public toilets 409
Puerto Iguazú (Argentina) **347**
Puppets
 Carnaval in Rio de Janeiro 68
 International Puppet Theater
  Festival 47
 Museu do Mamulengo (Olinda)
  225, **226**

Q

Quadros, Janio 62
Quartel General do Exército (Brasília)
 306, **308**
Queimada dos Britos 254
Quilombos **219**
Quinta da Boa Vista (Rio de Janeiro)
 88
Quintana, Mário 357
Quitandinha (Petrópolis) **117**

R

Racing *see* Horse racing; Motor
 racing
Radio **417**
Rafting 403
Railway stations
 Estação da Luz (São Paulo) **146**
Railways *see* Trains
Rainforest *see* Amazônia; Mata
 Atlântica
Rally dos Sertões 47
Raphael
 Resurrection of Christ 147
Rappeling
 Chapada Diamantina 209
Recife 213, **220–23**
 airport 419
 climate 49
 festivals 44
 flight duration chart 421
 hotels 376
 map 220–21
 restaurants 392–3
Recifolia (Recife) 44
Reentrâncias Maranhenses **259**
Religion 24, **38–9**, 409
 Afro-Brazilian culture **181**
 see also Candomblé

Rembrandt 147
Renting cars 422, 423
Repentistas **243**
Republic Proclamation Day 47
Reserva Biologica do Guaporé 293
Restaurants **382–97**
 alcohol and drinks 383
 Amazonas, Roraima, Acre and
  Rondônia 394–5
 Bahia 391–2
 Brasília, Goiás and Tocantins 395
 children in 383
 churrascaria rodízio (barbecue
  houses) 383
 dress code 382
 The flavors of Brazil **384–5**
 The flavors of Northeast Brazil
  182–3
 food hygiene 383
 local eating habits 382
 Mato Grosso and Mato Grosso do
  Sul 395
 Minas Gerais 388–9
 Pará and Amapá 394
 Paraíba, Rio Grande do Norte and
  Ceará 393
 paying and tipping 382
 Piauí and Maranhão 393–4
 por quilo 383
 Rio de Janeiro 386–8
 Rio de Janeiro State and Espírito
  Santo 388
 Rio Grande do Norte and Ceará
  393
 Rio Grande do Sul 397
 Santa Catarina and Paraná 396
 São Paulo 389–90
 São Paulo State 391
 Sergipe, Alagoas and Pernambuco
  392–3
 smoking 383
 vegetarian meals 383
 see also Food and drink
Resurrection of Christ (Raphael) 147
Reveillon at Copacabana (Rio de
 Janeiro) 45
Reynolds, Joshua 147
Ribeiro, Darcy 35
Riberão da Ilha 350
Rio Branco 262, 281, **292–3**
 climate 48
 hotels 379
 restaurants 394
Rio Grande do Norte *see* Paraíba, Rio
 Grande do Norte and Ceará
Rio Grande do Sul **353–63**
 hotels 381
 map 354–5
 Porto Alegre **356–7**
 restaurants 397
 São Miguel das Missões **363**
 Vale dos Vinhedos tour **359**
Rio de Janeiro 11, 14, 15, 21, 67,
 71–105
 airport 419
 Barra **90–91**
 Cariocas **31**, 71
 Carnaval **68–9**
 climate 49
 entertainment **96–9**

Rio de Janeiro (cont.)
 favelas **89**
 festivals 45
 flight duration chart 421
 history 54, 55
 hotels 370–71
 map 72–3
 Morro do Corcovado and Cristo
  Redentor **86–7**
 Praça XV de Novembro and
  Centro: Street-by-Street map 74–5
 restaurants 386–8
 shopping **94–5**
 Street Finder 100–105
 Sugar Loaf Mountain **80–81**
 travel in **426–7**
 two days in Rio de Janeiro 12
Rio de Janeiro and Espírito Santo
 107–23
 Beaches of Costa do Sol **120–21**
 Costa Verde **114**
 hotels 372–3
 map 108–9
 Mata Atlântica **113**
 Paraty **110–12**
 Petrópolis **116–19**
 restaurants 388
Rio Preto waterfall 304, 310–11
Rivaldo 40
Roads **423**
 Transamazônica 62, 63, **272**
Rocha, José Joaquim da 34, 197
Rocha, Paulo Mendes de 144
Rock art
 Cariri 236
 Monte Alegre 279
 Parque Nacional de Serra do
  Capivara 252–3
 Parque Nacional de Sete Cidades
  253
Rodeos 335
Rodin, Auguste
 Génio do Repouso Eterno 145
 Museu Rodin-Bahia (Salvador) **197**
Rodrigo de Freitas, Lagoa 12, **84**
Rolla, Joaquim 117
Romário 40, 41
Ronaldinho 40
Ronaldo 40, 41
Rondónia *see* Amazonas, Roraima,
 Acre and Rondônia
Roraima *see* Amazonas, Roraima,
 Acre and Rondônia
Roraima, Monte 262, 292
Rota do Sol beaches **241**
Rousseff, Dilma 23, 63
Rubber trees 264, **278**
Rubens, Peter Paul 147
Rules of the road 423

S

Sabinada Rebellion (1837–38) 56
Saco de Mamanguá 112
Safaris **402**, 405
Safety **412–13**
 beaches 43
 food hygiene 383
 pedestrians 426
 São Paulo **159**
 women travelers 409

Sailing 403
Ilhabela Sailing Week 47
Sala São Paulo **146**
Salgado, Sebastião 34
Salinópolis **274**
Salles, Walter 25
Salobrinho, Rio 326
Salvador 15, 179, 185, **188–99**
airport 419
Atlantic coast **198–9**
Carnaval **197**
climate 49
festivals 45
flight duration chart 421
hotels 375
Igreja e Convento de São
Francisco **194–5**
map 188–9
Pelourinho: Street-by-Street map
190–91
restaurants 391
two days in Salvador 13
Salvaterra 274
Samba 36
Rio de Janeiro 68, **97**, 99
Sambódromo and Cidade do
Samba (Rio de Janeiro) **88–9**
Samba Schools 404
Sambódromo (Rio de Janeiro) 69,
88–9
Santa Catarina, Ilha de **350–51**
map 350–51
Santa Catarina and Paraná **337–51**
Florianópolis and Ilha de Santa
Catarina **350–51**
Foz do Iguaçu **344–7**
hotels 380–81
map 338–9
restaurants 396
Serra da Graciosa **341**
Santa Elena de Uairén 292
Santa Rita dos Pardos Libertos
(Paraty) **110**
Santa Teresa (Rio de Janeiro) **78**
hotels 371
restaurants 388
Santander Cultural (Porto Alegre)
357
Santarém 263, 269, 270, **278–9**
hotels 378
Santo Amaro **200**
festivals 46
Santo Amaro, Lagoa de 254
Santo Antônio de Lisboa 350
Santo Daime 39
Santos **172–3**
hotels 374
Santos Dumont, Alberto
Casa de Santos Dumont
(Petrópolis) **117**
Santos-São Paulo Railroad 57
Santuário Dom Bosco (Brasília) **308**
Santuário Santo Antônio do
Valongo (Santos) 172, 173
Santuário de Vida Silvestre Fazenda
Vagafogo (Pirenópolis) **313**
São Cristóvão **216**
São Félix **201**
São Francisco, Rio 213, 214, **217**,
218, 237

São João (Caruaru and Campina
Grande) 47
São João del Rei **136–7**
São Joaquim
festivals 46
São Josafat (Prudentópolis) 333
São Luís 178, 249, 251, **256–8**
festivals 47
flight duration chart 421
hotels 377
restaurants 394
Street-by-Street map 256–7
São Mateus (Ceschiatti) 309
São Miguel das Missões 330, **363**
hotels 381
São Paulo 14, 21, 66, **139–63**
airport 419
climate 49
crime **159**
entertainment **156–7**
Fashion Week **149**
festivals 44–7
flight duration chart 421
hotels 373–4
map 140–41
Museu de Arte de São Paulo
(MASP) **147**
music 37
Parque do Ibirapuera **150–51**
Paulistanos **31**
Pinacoteca de São Paulo **144–5**
restaurants 389–90
shopping **154–5**
Street finder 158–63
travel in **426–7**
two days in São Paulo 12–13
São Paulo Art Biennial 44
São Paulo Fashion Week 46
São Paulo International Film Festival
44
São Paulo State **165–75**
coast 66
hotels 374
map 166–7
restaurants 391
São Pedro 169
São Pedro dos Clérigos (Recife)
32
São Sebastião 14, **168–9**
restaurants 391
São Silvestre Race (São Paulo) 45
São Vicente **173**
Sapiranga Reserve 211
Saquarema 120
Sater, Almir 313
Sattamini, João 93
Scholz, Waldemar 285
The Schoolboy (Van Gogh) 147
Scliar, Moacyr 35, 39
Scuba diving 403
Security **412–13**
Segall, Lasar 34, 146
Semana Santa 46
Senna, Ayrton 25
Sergipe, Alagoas and Pernambuco
213–29
Fernando de Noronha **228–9**
festivals 46
hotels 375–6
map 214–15

Sergipe, Alagoas and Pernambuco
(cont.)
Olinda **224–6**
Recife **220–23**
restaurants 392–3
Serie Bahia Musa da Paz (Pancetti)
144
Serra da Canastra, Parque Nacional
66, 125, 127, **137**
Serra da Capivara, Parque Nacional
de **252–3**
Serra do Cipó, Parque Nacional 125,
129
hotels 373
Serra Gaúcha 22, 333, 353
Serra da Graciosa **341**
Serra do Mar (Angra dos Reis) 114
Serra do Mar (Serra da Graciosa) 341
Serra dos Órgãos, Parque Nacional
107, **119**
Serra Pelada 269
Sertão 27, **237**
wildlife **28**
Sete Cidades, Parque Nacional de
250, **253**
Seurat, Georges 147
Shoe shops
Rio de Janeiro 95
Shopping **398–9**
arts and crafts 399
food and drink 399
gems 399
how to pay 398
markets and *camélodromos* 398–9
opening hours 94, 154, 398
Rio de Janeiro **94–5**
São Paulo **154–5**
shopping centers and
hypermarkets 398
Silva, Benedita da 62
Silva, Bernardo Pires da 134
Silva, Francisca (Chica) da 128
Silva, Francisco Joaquim
Béthencourt da 85
Silva, Leônidas 40
Siqueira Campos, José Wilson 314
Sitio Roberto Burle Marx (Barra da
Tijuca) 14, **91**
Slav immigrants **333**
Slaves 24, 54
abolition of slavery **57**
Afro-Brazilian culture 180–81
capoeira **203**
Salvador 185
Santo Amaro 200
Smoking
in restaurants 383
Snorkeling 403
Soccer 25, **40–41**, **401**
Estádio do Maracanã (Rio de
Janeiro) 88
Memorial das Conquistas (Santos)
173
Museu do Futbol (São Paulo) 13,
148–9
Museu Seleção Brasileira (Barra da
Tijuca) **90–91**
Pelé **172**, 173
Rio de Janeiro **98**, 99
São Paulo 157

Soccer (cont.)
training sessions **404**, 405
World Cup 40, 59, 61, 62, 63
Sociedade Hípica Brasileira (Lagoa
Rodrigo de Freitas) 84
Sócrates 41
Solano Lopez, Francisco 57
Solar do Unhão (Salvador) 13, **196**
Solimões, Rio 281, 289
see also Amazon river
Souré 274
Sousa, Manuel Rabello de 133
Sousa, Martim Alfonso da 52
Sousa, Tomé de 54, 193
Southeast Brazil **65–175**
map 66–7
Minas Gerais **125–37**
Rio de Janeiro **71–105**
Rio de Janeiro and Espírito Santo
107–23
São Paulo **139–63**
São Paulo State **165–75**
Southern Brazil **329–63**
Foz do Iguaçu **344–7**
The gaúcho life **334–5**
map 330–31
multicultural Southern Brazil **332–
3**
Rio Grande do Sul **353–63**
Santa Catarina and Paraná **337–
51**
Serra da Graciosa **341**
Vale dos Vinhedos tour **359**
Souza **236**
Souza, Tome de 190
Specialized holidays **402–5**
Spiritism **39**
Sport 25
Brazilian beach culture 43
see also Soccer
Spring in Brazil **44**
Statues
Cristo Redentor (Rio de Janeiro)
12, 21, **86–7**
Steckel, Frederico 93
Stockler, Cristiano 146
Sucuri, Rio 321, **327**
Sugar 54, 58
Sergipe, Alagoas and Pernambuco
213
Sugar Loaf Mountain (Rio de
Janeiro) 12, 70, **80–81**
Summer in Brazil **45**
Sun protection 411
Superagui, Ilha da **343**
Superagui, Parque Nacional de 343
Supremo Tribunal Federal (Brasília)
307, 308
Surfing 403
Pororoca wave **279**
The Surrender of Uruguaiana 57
Synagogues
Kahal Zur Israel Synagogue
(Recife) **220–21**

T

Tamoio Indians 165
Taunay, Nicolau 92
Taxes
in hotels 367

Taxis **426**
air taxis 420
airport 419
Teatro Amazonas (Manaus) 10, 15,
33, 263, **286–7**
Teatro José de Alencar (Fortaleza)
246
Teatro da Paz (Belém) **272–3**
Teatro de Pirenópolis **313**
Telephones **416**, 417
Television **417**
Telles, Lygia Fagundes 35
Templo da Boa Vontade (Brasília)
308
Templo Busshinji (São Paulo) 149
Tennis 25
Terena villages 326
Teresa Cristina, Empress 88, 252
tomb 116
Teresina 249, **252–3**
hotels 377
restaurants 393
Teresópolis **119**
Terreiro de Jesus (Salvador) 190
Thaler, Andreas 333
Theater **400**
Rio de Janeiro **98**, 99
Theatro Municipal (Rio de Janeiro)
12, **77**
Theatro Municipal (São Paulo) **143**
Theft 412
São Paulo **159**
Theme parks **401**
Tibaú do Sul 241
hotels 377
restaurants 393
Ticuna community 30
Tijuca, Parque Nacional da 12, 87, **92**
Time zones 409
Tintoretto 147
Tipping
in hotels 367
in restaurants 382
Tiradentes **136**
festivals 47
hotels 373
restaurants 389
Tiradentes (rebel) 55, 130
statue of 130
Tiradentes Day 47
Titian 147
Tocantins *see* Brasília, Goiás and
Tocantins
Toilets, public 409
Toque Toque Grande 169
Toque Toque Pequeno 169
Tordesillas, Treaty of (1494) 51, 353
Torre de Malakoff (Recife) **221**
Torres **362**
festivals 46
Toulouse-Lautrec, Henri de 147
Tourist information 408, 409
Tours by car
Vale dos Vinhedos **359**
Trains **424**, 425
Cog train (Rio de Janeiro) 12, 87
The Litorina 341
Madeira-Mamoré Museu
Ferroviário (Porto Velho) 262, 281,
293

Trains (cont.)
Museu Ferroviário (São João del
Rei) 137
Tren Ecológico (Foz do Iguaçu)
345
Trancoso **205**
hotels 375
Transamazônica (Trans-Amazon
Highway) 62, 63, **272**
Transcoso
restaurants 392
Travel **418–27**
air **418–21**
Amazonas, Roraima, Acre and
Rondônia 282
Bahia 187
boats **424–5**
Brasília, Goiás and Tocantins 305
buses **422, 427**
cars **422–3**
in cities **426–7**
Mato Grosso and Mato Grosso do
Sul 321
metro **426–7**
Ouro Preto 126
Pará and Amapá 271
Paraíba, Rio Grande do Norte and
Ceará 233
Piauí and Maranhão 251
Rio de Janeiro 73
Rio de Janeiro and Espírito Santo
109
Rio Grande do Sul 355
Salvador 189
Santa Catarina and Paraná 339
São Paulo City 141
Sergipe, Alagoas and Pernambuco
215
taxis **426**
trains **424**, 425
Travel agencies 419
Traveler's checks **415**
in hotels 366
Travessa do Comércio (Rio de
Janeiro) 75
Trees
Buriti palm trees **255**
Tren Ecológico (Foz do Iguaçu)
345
Treze Tilias 333
Trindade 112
Tropical (Malfatti) 145
Tropical diseases 410
Tropicalismo 37
Tukano people 266
Tupi-Guaraní people 51
Tupinambá people 51, 53
Turner, JMW 147
TV Tower (Brasília) 15, 306

U

Ubajara, Parque Nacional de 231,
245
Ubatuba 14, 165, 167, **168–9**
hotels 374
restaurants 391
Umbanda 39
UNESCO World Heritage Sites
Brasília 298, 306
Cidade Goiás 303

UNESCO World Heritage Sites (cont.)
Diamantina 67, 128
Foz do Iguaçu 346
Itacaré 204
Mata Atlântica 63, 343
Olinda 224–6
Paraty 110
Parque Nacional das Emas 315
Parque Nacional de Serra do Capivara 252
Pelourinho (Salvador) 13, 190
Salvador 179
São Luís 178, 256–7
São Miguel das Missões 363
Urubuqueçaba, Ilha 164
Usina do Gasômetro (Porto Alegre) **357**

V
Vaccinations 410
Vale do Paty 208
Vale do Quilombo 358
Vale dos Vinhedos **359**
Valentim, Mestre 34, 146
Van Gogh, Vincent
  The Schoolboy 147
Vargas, Getúlio Dornelles 59, **60–61**
  capoeira 203
  death 59, 79
  Confeitaria Colombo (Rio de Janeiro) 77
  Igreja Nossa Senhora da Glória do Outeiro (Rio de Janeiro) 79
  Palácio Imperial (Petrópolis) 118
  Palácio Rio Negro (Petrópolis) 116
  Paulistano rebellion 151
  Recife 222
Veen, Otto van 195
Vegetarian meals 383
Veiga Valle, José Joaquim da 34, 314, 322
Velázquez, Diego de Silva y 147
Veloso, Caetano 37, 200
Ver o Peso (Belém) **272**
Vespucci, Amerigo 52
  Abrolhos 205
  Baía de Guanabara 92
  Fernando de Noronha 228
Véu de Noiva 322, 323

Vieira, Father Antônio 35, 192
Vila do Abraão 114
Vila Ilhabela 169
Villa-Lobos, Heitor 25, 36, 77
  Museu Villa-Lobos (Rio de Janeiro) **85**
Vila Olímpia and Itaim Bibi (São Paulo)
  restaurants 390
Vinícola Miolo
  Vale dos Vinhedos tour 359
Vinícola Pizzato
  Vale dos Vinhedos tour 359
Visas 408, 409
Vitória **122**
  hotels 372–3
  restaurants 388
Volpi, Alfredo 34
  Composição 144
Volunteer programs **404**, 405

W
Walking, in cities 426
War of the Triple Alliance (1864–70) 57
Water, drinking 411
Water sports 43, **403**, 405
Waterfalls
  Cachoeira da Água Branca 169
  Cachoeira Almeçegas 317
  Cachoeira d'Anta 137
  Cachoeira do Buraçao 209
  Cachoeira da Toca 169
  cascading and canyoning 403
  Cascatinha do Taunay 92
  Foz do Iguaçu 15, 330, 337, **344–7**
  Parque do Caracol 358
  Presidente Figueiredo 288
  Rio Preto 304, 310–11
  Véu de Noiva 322, 323
Weather see Climate
Wet season 26
Wetlands
  Pantanal 15, 26, **29**, **301**, 319, **324–5**
Wheelchair access see Disabled travelers
When to go 408
Wickam, Henry 278
Wiederspahn, Theo 357
Wildlife
  Alta Floresta 323
  Amazon ecosystem **265**

Wildlife (cont.)
  Amazon excursions from Manaus **288–91**
  Brazil's flora and fauna **28–9**
  Ecoparque Sperry 358
  ecotourism **402**, 405
  flora and fauna in the cerrado **300–301**
  flora and fauna of Pantanal **301**
  Iguaçu region 345, **347**
  Ilha do Cardoso 175
  Mata Atlântica **113**
  Mosaico Juréia-Itatins **174**
  Pantanal 15, **29**, 319, **324–5**
  Reentrâncias Maranhenses **259**
  Rio de Janeiro and Espírito Santo 107
  see also Aquariums; Birds; National parks; Zoos
Wind surfing 403
Wines 383
  Bento Gonçalves 360
  Flores da Cunha 361
  Vale dos Vinhedos tour **359**
Winter in Brazil **46–7**
Women travelers 409
Workers' Party (PT, Partido dos Trabalhadores) 23, 63
World Cup (soccer) 40, 59, 61, 62, 63
World Heritage Sites see UNESCO World Heritage Sites
World War I 58–9
World War II 79
Writers 34, **35**

X
Xavier, José da Silva 136
Ximenes, Ettore 152
Xingú **323**

Y
Yánez Pinzón, Vicente 51
Yanomami people 266

Z
Zagury, Bob 120
Zoos
  Jardim Zoológico (Rio de Janeiro) 88
  Zoológico do CIGS (Manaus) **285**
  see also Aquariums; Wildlife
Zumbi 219

Acknowledgments

Dorling Kindersley would like to thank the many people whose help and assistance contributed to the preparation of this book.

Main Contributors
Shawn Blore, a Rio de Janeiro-based journalist, publishes travel and investigative articles in magazines and newspapers in Canada, the USA, the UK, and elsewhere.

Dilwyn Jenkins (1957–2014) began travelling in South America in 1976. Anthropologist, sustainable development expert, and travel writer, he made documentaries for television for 30 years.

Oliver Marshall has been visiting Brazil regularly since 1982. Specializing in travel and history, he has written extensively on Latin America.

Christopher Pickard lived in Brazil for nearly 20 years and has written widely about the country. He is vice-chairman of the Latin American Travel Association.

Alex Robinson is a travel writer and photographer with a client list that includes *Conde Nast Traveller*, *Wanderlust*, *Footprint*, BBC, and Channel 4.

Neiva Augusta Silva writes for Brazilian travel guides and magazines, as well as on adventure sports and rural tourism.

Fact Checkers
Alexandra de Vries, Fernanda Drummond, Stephen Wingrove

Proofreader
Susanne Hillen

Indexer
Hilary Bird

Design and Editorial
Publisher Douglas Amrine
Publishing Managers Jane Ewart, Scarlett O'Hara, Anna Streiffert
Senior Designer Paul Jackson
Senior Cartographic Editor Casper Morris
Editorial Assistance Alexandra Farrell, Fay Franklin
DTP Designer Natasha Lu
Picture Researcher Ellen Root
Production Controller Shane Higgins
XML Coordinator Bulent Yusuf

Additional Photography
Geoff Brightling, Geoff Dann, Barnabus Kindersley, Cyril Laubscher, Ian O'Leary, Jose Olimpio.

Additional Illustrations
Chapel Design and Marketing Ltd.

Additional Picture Research
Julia Harris-Voss, Phoebe Lowndes, Susie Peachey, Ellen Root, Lucy Sienkowska

Cartography Credits
Base mapping for São Paulo derived from Netmaps, and assistance from Ed Merrit.

Special Assistance
Dorling Kindersley would like to thank José Mayrink, Sônia Lúcia da Costa Conrado, Leonardo A. P. Silva, and Adriana Teixeira for their assistance.

Revisions Team
Hansa Babra, Neha Chander, Rachel Fox, Rhiannon Furbear, Lydia Halliday, Kaberi Hazarika, Huw Hennessy, Bharti Karakoti, Sumita Khatwani, Priya Kukadia, Jude Ledger, Phoebe Lowndes, Alison McGill, Rada Radojicic, Alex Robinson, Jun Shimada, Sands Publishing Solutions, Beverly Smart.

Picture Credits
The publisher would like to thank the following for their kind permission to reproduce their photographs:

Key: a-above; b-below/bottom; c-center; f-far; l-left; r-right; t-top.

Alta Floresta: Cristalino Jungle Lodge; Belém: Basílica de Nossa Senhora de Nazaré, Teatro da Paz; Brasília: Catedral Metropolitana Nossa Senhora Aparecida, Santuário Dom Bosco; Caxias do Sul: Museu da Casa de Pedra; Congonhas: Basílica do Senhor Bom Jesus de Matosinhos; Curitiba: Hotel Burbon; Diamantina: Igreja Nossa Senhora do Carmo; Itamaracá Island: Projeto Peixe Boi; João Pessoa: Igreja de São Francisco; Manaus: Teatro Amazonas; Olinda: Convento de São Francisco, Mosteiro de São Bento; Ouro Preto: Casa dos Contos, Igreja de São Francisco de Assis, Matriz de Nossa Senhora da Conceição de Antônio Dias, Museu do Aleijadinho; Paraty: Casa de Cadeia, Igreja de Nossa Senhora do Rosário e São Benedito; Petrópolis: Museu das Cavalhadas, Palácio de Cristal; Piauí & Maranhão: Maranhão State Government Tourist Board, Sea and Air Maranhão; Porto Alegre: Museu de arte de Rio Grande do Sul, Teatro São Pedro; Recife: Casa da Cultura, Oficina Cerâmica Francisco Brennand, Kahal Zur Israel Synagogue; Rio de Janeiro: Barra Shopping, Blue Man, Confeitaria Colombo, H. Stern, Museu do Índio, Museu Nacional de Belas Artes, Nossa Senhora da Candelária, Rio Scenarium Bar; Salvador: Catedral Basílica, Fundação Casa de Jorge Amado, Igreja e Convento de São Francisco, Memorial das Conquistas do; Santos: Museu Afro-Brasileiro, Museu Tempostal; Santos: Bolsa e Museu do Café; São Paulo City: Igreja São Francisco de Assis, Jacaré do Brasil, Mosteiro de São Bento de São Paulo, Museu de Arte Contemporânea, Museu de Arte de São Paulo, Museu de Arte Sacra de São Paulo, Museu de Arte Moderna de São Paulo, Vila Madalena; Tiradentes: Igreja Matriz de Santo Antônio.

Works of art have been reproduced with the kind permission of the following copyright holders:

Alfredo Volpi, *Composição* (1976) 144tr; José Pancetti, *Serie Bahia Musa da Paz* 144cl; Anita Malfatti, *Tropical* 145tc, Almeida Júnior, *Caipira Picando Fumo* 145cra; Tomie Ohtake, *Pintura* (1969) 145crb.

4Corners: Antonino Bartuccio 336; Giordano Cipriani 406–7; Guido Cozzi 328–9; Schapowalow/Chris Seba 348–9; SIME/Antonino Bartuccio 184, 206–7.
A Casa Vidal: 391tl.
Alamy Stock Photo: 1Apix 404t; age fotostock/P&R Fotos 280; AM Corporation 149tr; Arco Images GmbH 22tl, 24br, 325tl, /Therin-Weise 248, 258tc, 403tr; Aurora Photos/ Matthew Wakem 394bl; Ricardo Beliel 30tr; ARDUOPRESS / Andre M Chang 152t, BrazilPhotos /Ricardo Beliel 31tl, 43br, /Nando Neves 293cb, /Marco A. Rezende 37tr, /Ricardo Siqueira 107b; George Brewin 242b; Cristiano Burmester 253cr; Gary Calton 260–61; Cephas Picture Library 359cla, 359br; Gary Cook 181br, 287cr; David Crausby 62bc; David Davis Photo Productions 384cla, 89br; Danita Delimont 324tr; Nigel Dickinson 266cr; Didi 230; dpa picture alliance 44b; Redmond Durrell 265bc; Dynamic Graphics Group/ Creatas 182cl; Chad Ehlers 81cla; Julio Etchart 41cb; Eye Ubiquitous 28cl; Robert Fried 115br, 265cla, 347tr; Mike Goldwater 267crb, 267bl; Hemis 235cr; Andrew Holt 60tr; ImageState 159br; IML Image Group Ltd 401br; Jacques Jangoux 113cla; Jon Arnold Images 265tl; Brian Kelly 262cla; Y levy 368t; Alex Maddox 181cra; Mediacolor's 42–3c, 237bl, 420br; John Michaels 313c, 367tl; David Muscroft 81tl; Network Photographers 286cla; niceartphoto 106; David Parker 212; Beren Patterson 197bl; Natalie Pecht 30–31c; Pictorial Press Ltd 61tl, 81crb; Fabio Pili 350br, 351tl; Popperfoto 40br, 41bl, 41bc, 59bc, 61tr, 172bl; Pulsar Imagens 304cl; Ricardo Ribas 396tc; Richard Wareham Fotografie 345crb; robertharding 137tl; Robert Harding World Imagery/Michael Runkel 15tr; Robert Harding World Imagery/Yadid Levy 20; Marcelo Rudini 352; Kevin Schafer 29bl; Sdbphoto Brasil 335cr; Andre Seale 179b, 199br, 228br, 301cb; David South 178bl; richard sowersby 413bl; StockBrazil 121c, 208br, 209cl, 365tr; Sue Cunningham Photographic 30cl; Angel Terry 87cr; Travelstock44 31bl, 96b; Peter Treanor 25t, 68bl, 82tl; Genevieve Vallee 252c, 297tr, 301cra, 315tc; Mireille Vautier 8–9, 180br; Visual Arts Library (London) 56bc; Andrew Woodley 83tl; Worldwide Picture Library 137tr, 267cr, /Sue Cunningham 183c; Noel Yates 83tr.
Amazon Ecopark: Fabio Colombini 378bl.
Aprazível: 388tc.
AWL Images: Christian Heeb 364–5; Alex Robinson 138, 151bl, 268, 310–11, 318.
Bené da Flauta: 389bl.
Bourbon Resort: 381bl.
Bridgeman Images: Archives Charmet/Bibliothéque de L'Arsenal, Paris – *Cross-section of a model of a slave ship, late 18th century* (wood) by French School 54br; Archives Charmet/Bibliothéque National, Paris *The Dinner, a white couple being served and fanned by black slaves,* from Voyages Pictoresque et Historique au Brésil 1839 Jean Baptiste Debret 57bc; Giraudon/Museu de Arte, Sao Paulo *The Slave Hunter* (oil on canvas) Jean Baptiste Debret 54tl; Giraudon/Private Collection *The Funeral of the Emperor of Brazil: The Carriage* from 'Le Petit Journal December 1891 Henri Meyer 58tc. Index/Museu Historico Nacional, Buenos Aires *The Surrender of Uruguaiana,* Candido Lopez 1865 57tr, 57bc; Index/Museu Historico Nacional, Rio de Janeiro *'Independence or Death', the Shout of Ipiranga on the 7th September 1822* Dome Pedro di Figueredo 56tl; Stapleton Collection *Botocudos family,* Rio Grande, from *Le Costume Ancien et Moderne, Volume II plate 37,* Jules Ferrario, published c. 1820s–30s 53tr;
Marcio Cabral: 208c.
Cais do Oriente: 386br.
Camarões Potiguar: 393bl.
Capim Santo: 392tr.
Casa do João: 395tl.
Sonia Conrado: 191crb.
Corbis: Alinari Archives 58bc; Theo Allofs 265crb, 319b; Archivo Iconografico, S.A. 54crb, 56crb; Ricardo Azoury 97tr, 120clb, 253br; Yann Arthus Bertrand 26bc, 26br, 41cra, 345br; Bettmann 36tr, 58cl, 59tc, 59c, 60br, 60–61c, 62c; Tom Brakefield 265cr, 300cl, 316bl; Joao Luiz Bulcao 404bl; Pierre Colombel 51bc; Andrea Comas 180cl; Corbis Sygma 266cra, 266cl, 266br, /Bernard Bisson 38bl, /Collart Herver 266bl, /Le Segretain Pascal 25cl, /Manchete 86clb; /Whitemore Hank 267cla; Ecoscene/Joel Creed 345cra; EPA/Caetano Barreira 47br; Eye Ubiquitous/James Davis 195br, 344br, Paulo Fridman 63bl, 299cra, Gallo/Martin Harvey 300br; Farrell Grehan 299tc; Darrell Gulin 113br; Martin Harvey 28cb, 264bl; Collart Herve 226bl; Eric and David Hosking 113clb; Wolfgang Kaehler 264clb, 287tl; Kuba 399bc; Lawrence Manning 52tr; Stephanie Maze 399tr; Joe McDonald 265fcra; Wilson Melo 267cra; Diego Lezama Orezzoli 257tl; Fabio Polenghi 40tr; Jose Fuste Raga 71b; Reuters/Paulo Whitaker 420cla, /Sergio Moraes 279tr; Kevin Schafer 113bl, 300bl, 301br; Staffan Widstrand 26cl, 265ca; Paulo Whitaker 157tr, 267tr.
Cristalino Jungle Lodge: Katia Kuwabara 379tl.
Dorling Kindersley Ltd: Andy Crawford/Courtesy of the Football Museum, Preston 40clb.
Dreamstime.com: Marcos Casiano 299crb; Dabldy 11crb, 63crb, 78tl; Ekaterinabelova 366b; Alexandre Fagundes De Fagundes 10cl, 357br; Filipe Frazao 159tr, 195tl; Eric Gevaert 4cr; Pedro Gomes 37br; Jakazvan 303b; Katoton 167br; Keystone-France 40cl, 40bc; Lazyllama 12bl, 13br; Giancarlo Liguori 11tl; Marchello74 70; Megumi 4tc; Antonio De Azevedo Negrão 231b; Sergey Mostovoy 108cl, 136tl; Pixattitude 124, 302; Kseniya Ragozina 255cl; Luis Ribeiro 155tr; Rodrigolab 76br; Celso Pupo Rodrigues 63tc; Luca Roggero 176–7; Sjors737 43bl; Samystclair 5cr; Marcio Silva 340tl; Thiagogleite 13tl; Tupungato 14br, 421tl.
Getty Images: AFP/Mauricio Lima 35tr; AFP/Stringer 390bl; Bloomberg 416bc; EACC 64–5; FotoArena 156br; FotoArena/CON 41bc; Lonely Planet Images/John Maier Jr 350tr; Rebeca Mello 170–71; Popperfoto 40ca; SambaPhoto/Eduardo Barcellos 183tl; Stone/Will & Deni McIntyre 181bl; Stringer/Atsushi Tomura 37tl; Time Life Pictures 62tl; Priscila Zambotto 164.

The Granger Collection, New York: 35cl, 50, 52cla, 52bl, 52–9c, 53tl, 53cl, 55t, 57cb, 332tr.

Hyatt Hotels: 374tl.

Imagem Brasil: Gentil Barreira 27tl, 44cr, 254clb; Alex Uchôa 255bl; Flávio Veloso 38cl.

Imperial Palace: 118tr, 118cl, 118c, 119tl, 119ca, 119cb.

iphotostock.com: dabldy 306tr; filipefrazao 294–295; Phototreat 298–299c; Yuri de Mesquita Bar 2–3.

Koh Pee Pee Restaurant: 397br.

Lasai: 387tl.

Latin Photo: Biosfera 267tl, 267br; Carlos Ortiz Fragalá 334bl.

Marriott Resort & Spa: 368b.

Mary Evans Picture Library: 53bl, 60bl.

Masterfile: Mark Leibowitz 32tr; F Lukasseck 29crb; David Mendelsohn 21b, 23t; Brian Sytnyk 43tr; Jeremy Woodhouse 24tl, 29cr.

Meia Lua: 380tl.

Museu de Arte de São Paulo: Eduardo Ortega 147b.

Paul Mowatt: 290tl.

Octavio Campos Salles: 289bl.

Olhar Imagem: Aristides Alves 201bl, 208tl; Daniel Augusto Jr. 37c, 198cr; Ricardo Azoury 32clb, 69br, 74clb, 113crb, 181tr, 262cl, 262bl, 283tr; Flávio Bacellar 291br; Cynthia Brito 199tr; Maristela Colucci 228clb; Salomon Cytrynowicz 46tl; Adri Felden 357cr; Iolanda Huzak 332cr; Marcos Issa 210bl, 237cla, 337b; Zig Koch 27cr, 300–1c, 317cr; Stefan Kolumban 180–81c; Delfim Martins 29tc, 174b; Juca Martins 31tr, 31cr, 34bc, 38crb, 39tr, 42cl, 110cl, 115t, 123b, 148tl, 178cl, 199cl, 237cr, 237br, 272br, 290b, 292t, 325cra; Renata Mello 27br; Sonia Oddi 343t; Saulo Petean 39br; Rogério Reis 36bl, 180bl, 258br, 331cr; Zaida Siqueira 264cla; Monica Vendramini 279b; Luciana Whitaker 121bl, 293tr.

Ouro Minas Palace: 373bl.

PA Photos: Peter Robinson 41tl.

Photographers Direct: David Davis Photoproductions 43c; Chris Fairclough Worldwide 254br;Jahan Images 285c; Marcelo Krause Photography 121br.

Photolibrary: JTB Photo 334–5c, 385tl.

Porto Bay Hotels & Resorts: 370bl.

Peter Price: 300cb.

Private Collection: 35br, 55b, 298cl.

Pulsar Imagens: Ricardo Azoury 45tl, 68–9c, 213b, 256tr, 256br, 324clb; J. L. Bulcão 185b; Armando Catunda 113c; Daniel Cymbalista 145bl, 423b; Adriano Gambarini 28crb, 245t; Artur Keunecke 29bc, 322br; Marcio Lourenço 28bl; Delfim Martins 33br, 46b, 122t, 122bl, 234cla, 241cla, 241cr, 251br, 301tcl, 418b, 422cl; Juca Martins 30bl, 33cl, 200t, 289t, 427br; Manoel Novaes 28cr, 29cb; Rogério Reis 28bc,

47tl, 120tr; André Seale 28tr, 205br, 229br, 265br; Paula Simas 23br; Mauricio Simonetti 29tl, 29cr, 66ca, 127tr, 137b, 240bl, 322t, 404tr; Luciana Whitaker 93bl; Palê Zuppani 325cr.

Reuters: Alexandra Beier 41fbr; Andrea Comas 37cb; Alex Grimm 40–41c; Lucas Jackson 36bc; Jose Patricio 30br; Claudio Pedroso 139b; Paulo Whitaker 36–7c, 149br.

Robert Harding Picture Library: Holger Leue 276–7; Sakis Papadopoulos 238–9.

Sofitel Hotels & Resort: Christian Knepper 188cl, 190clb, 191tc, 367bc, 399cl.

Solar dos Deuses: Alessandro Iglesias 375bl.

Solar dos Ventos: José Henrique Moura 376tc.

Lori Stilger: 300cla.

SuperStock: age footstock/Haroldo Palo Jr. 169clb.

Toca da Coruja: 377br.

Tyba Photographic Agency: J.R. Couto 80cl, 88bl, 90bl; Alberto Ferreira 298clb, 298bc, 299bl; Antonio Gusmão 36clb; Paulo Jares 36ca, 299tl; Marcello Lourenço 281b, 292br; Ciro Mariano 210t; L.C. Marigo 291tl; Claus Meyer 135cr, 299cr, 335tr; OBrito News 298tr; Rogério Reis 68cb, 91tl, 98tr, 236clb, 243br, 249b; Ricardo Ribas 333br; David Santos Júnior 209tl; André Valentim 282cl; Flávio Vidigal 351cl.

Alex Sandro do Amaral Uchôa: 209br, 229cr, 244tr.

Viana Photography: Sergio Viana 252tl.

Vila d'Este: 372tr.

Visage Media Services: Hulton Archives/Evans 61cr, 61bl, 61br; Iconica/Wild Pics 351cr; Photographer's Choice/Fernando Bueno 86cla; Time & Life Pictures/ Leonard Mccombe 60cl.

Wikipedia: 53clb, 86tr, 298bl.

Windsor Hotels: 371tl.

Front Endpaper:
4Corners: SIME/Antonino Bartuccio Lbc, Rcra; Alamy Images: age fotostock/P&R Fotos Lcl; Arco Images GmbH/Therin-Weise Rtl; Didi Rtc; niceartphoto Rcrb; David Parker Rtr; Marcelo Rudini Lbl; AWL Images: Alex Robinson Ltl, Lc, Rbc; Dreamstime.com: Marchello74 Rfcb; Pixattitude Lbr, Rbr; Getty Images: Priscila Zambotto Rbl.

Cover:
Front and spine – Getty Images: Flavio Veloso.
Back – Dreamstime.com: Attila Jandi

All other images © Dorling Kindersley
For further information see: www.dkimages.com

Phrase Book

The Portuguese spoken in Brazil differs in various ways from the Portuguese spoken in Portugal. In general, Brazilian pronunciation tends to omit far fewer sounds, especially the sounds at the end of words, and rarely runs two words together, both of which are common practice in Portugal. One feature of Brazilian Portuguese, particularly in the Rio de Janeiro area, is that an "r" sound can be spoken like an "h." So *carro* (car) may sound like "ka-hoo." Another difference lies in the ways of saying "you." The Portuguese form of placing the definite article in front of a person's name (o João, a Cristina), as a way of saying "you," does not exist in Brazil, where *você* and *vocês* are the most common words for "you." The Portuguese *tu* is not used much in Brazil. A huge number of other vocabulary differences exist, many at the level of everyday speech: train is *trem* in Brazil, *comboio* in Portugal; breakfast is *café da manhã* in Brazil, *pequeno almoço* in Portugal; bathroom is *banheiro* in Brazil, *casa de banho* in Portugal; goalkeeper is *goleiro* in Brazil, *guarda-redes* in Portugal; to drive is *dirigir* in Brazil, *conduzir* in Portugal. The sound indicated by "i" in the phrase book is like the "i" in English word "hi." "J" sounds like the "s" in the word "pleasure."

In an Emergency

Help!	**Socorro!**	sookoorroo
Stop!	**Pare!**	pahree
Call a doctor!	**Chame um médico!**	shamih oong mehjikoo
Call an ambulance!	**Chame uma ambulância!**	shamih ooma amboolans-ya
Where is the hospital?	**Onde é o hospital?**	ohnd-yeh oo oshpital
Police!	**Polícia!**	poolees-ya
Fire!	**Fogo!**	fohgoo
I've been robbed	**Fui assaltado**	fwee asaltadoo

Communication Essentials

Yes	**Sim**	seeng
No	**Não**	nowng
Hello	**Olá**	ohla
How are you?	**Como vai?**	kohmoo vĩ
How is it going?	**Tudo bem/ tudo bom?**	toodoo bayng/ toodoo bong
Goodbye	**Tchau**	tshow
See you later	**Até logo**	ateh logoo
Excuse me	**Com licença**	kong lisaynsa
I'm sorry	**Desculpe**	dishkoolp
Thank you	**Obrigado (if a man is speaking)/ obrigada (if a woman is speaking)**	obrigadoo/obrigada
Good morning	**Bom dia**	bong jeea
Good afternoon	**Boa tarde**	boh-a tarj
Good evening/ night	**Boa noite**	boh-a noh-itsh
Pleased to meet you	**Muito prazer**	mweengtoo prazayr
I'm fine	**Estou bem/ tudo bem**	shtoh bayng/ toodoo bayng
Today	**Hoje**	ohJ
Yesterday	**Ontem**	ohntayng
Tomorrow	**Amanhã**	aman-yang
What?	**O que?**	oo kay
When?	**Quando?**	kwandoo
How?	**Como?**	kohmoo
Why?	**Por que?**	poorkay

Useful Phrases

On the left/right	**À esquerda/direita**	a-shkayrda/jirayta
I don't understand	**Não entendo**	nowng ayntayndoo
Please speak slowly	**Fale devagar por favor**	falee jivagar poor favohr
What's your name?	**Qual é seu nome?**	kwal eh say-oo nohm
My name is...	**Meu nome é...**	may-oo nohm eh
Go away!	**Vá embora!**	va aymbora
That's fine	**Está bem**	shtah bayng
Where is...?	**Onde está/fica...?**	ohnj shtah/feeka
When does the bus leave/arrive?	**A que horas sai/ chega o ônibus?**	a kih orash sĩ/ shayga oo ohniboosh
Is this the way to the...?	**Este é o caminho para...?**	aysht-yeh oo kameen-yoo pra

Useful Words

big	**grande**	granj
small	**pequeno**	pikaynoo
hot	**quente**	kayntsh
cold	**frio**	free-oo
bad	**mau**	mow
good	**bom**	bong
enough	**suficiente**	soofis-yayntsh
open	**aberto**	abehrtoo
closed	**fechado**	fishadoo
dangerous	**perigoso**	pirigohzoo
safe	**seguro**	sigooroo
full	**cheio**	shay-oo
empty	**vazio**	vazee-oo
straight on	**reto**	rehtoo
under	**debaixo**	dibishoo
over	**em cima**	ayng seema
in front of	**em frente de**	ayng frayntsh ji
behind	**atrás de**	atraJ jih
first floor	**primeiro andar**	primayroo andar
ground floor	**térreo**	tehrryoo
lift	**elevador**	elevadohr
toilet	**banheiro**	ban-yayroo
men's	**dos homens**	dooz ohmaynsh
women's	**das mulheres**	dash mool-yehrish
quick	**rápido**	rapidoo
soon	**cedo**	saydoo
late	**tarde**	tarj
now	**agora**	agora
more	**mais**	mĩsh
less	**menos**	maynoosh
a little	**um pouco**	oong pohkoo
a lot	**muito**	mweengtoo
too much	**demais**	dimĩsh
entrance	**entrada**	ayntrada
exit	**saída**	sa-eeda
passport	**passaporte**	pasaportsh

Post Offices & Banks

bank	**banco**	bankoo
bureau de change	**(casa de) câmbio**	(kaza jih) kamb-yoo
exchange rate	**taxa de câmbio**	tasha jih kamb-yoo
post office	**correio**	koorray-oo
postcard	**cartão postal**	kartowng pooshtal
postbox	**caixa de correio**	kisha jih koorray-oo
ATM	**caixa automática**	kisha owtoomatshika
stamp	**selo**	sayloo
cash	**dinheiro**	jeen-yayroo
withdraw money	**tirar dinheiro**	tshirar jeen-yayroo

Shopping

How much is it?	**Quanto é?**	kwantweh
I would like...	**Eu quero...**	ay-oo kehroo
clothes	**roupa**	rohpa
This one	**Esta**	ehshta
That one	**Essa**	ehsa
market	**mercado**	merkadoo
supermarket	**Supermercado**	soopermerkadoo
Do you accept credit cards?	**Aceitam cartão de crédito?**	asaytowng kartowng jih krehditoo
expensive	**caro**	karoo
baker's	**padaria**	padaree-a
butcher's	**açougue**	asohgee
chemist's	**farmácia**	farmas-ya

Sightseeing

museum	**museu**	moozay-oo
art gallery	**galeria de arte**	galiree-a jih artsh
national park	**parque nacional**	parkee nas-yoonal
beach	**praia**	prī-a
park	**parque**	parkee
river	**rio**	ree-oo
church	**igreja**	igray-Ja
cathedral	**catedral**	katidrow
district	**bairro**	birroo
garden	**jardim**	Jardeeng
tourist office	**informações turísticas**	infoormasoayngsh tooreeshtsheekash
guide	**guia**	gee-a
guided tour	**excursão com guia**	shkoorsowng kong gee-a
ticket	**bilhete/ingresso**	bil-yaytsh/ingrehsoo
map	**mapa**	mapa

Transport

bus	**ônibus**	*ohniboosh*
boat	**barco**	*barkoo*
train	**trem**	*trayng*
airport	**aeroporto**	*a-ayroopohrtoo*
airplane	**avião**	*av-yowng*
flight	**vôo**	*voh-oo*
bus station	**rodoviária**	*roodohvyar-ya*
bus stop	**ponto de ônibus**	*pohntoo j-yohniboosh*
train station	**estação de trem**	*stasowng jih trayng*
ticket	**passagem**	*pasajayng*
taxi	**táxi**	*taxee*
subway	**metrô**	*metroh*

Health

I feel bad/ill	**Sinto-me mal/doente**	*seentoomih mow/dwayntsh*
I need to rest	**Preciso descansar**	*priseezoo jishkansar*
diarrhoea	**diarréia**	*j-yarreh-ya*
pharmacy	**farmácia**	*farmas-ya*
headache	**dor de cabeça**	*dohr jih kabaysa*
medicine	**remédio**	*rimehd-yoo*
sanitary towels/ tampons	**absorventes/ tampões**	*absoorvayntsh/ tampoyngsh*
mosquito	**mosquito**	*mooshkeetoo*
repellent	**repelente de**	*ripelayntsh dih*
doctor	**médico**	*mehjikoo*
condom	**camisinha**	*kamizeen-ya*

Staying in a Hotel

hotel	**hotel**	*ohteh-oo*
boutique hotel	**pousada**	*pohzada*
guesthouse	**pensão**	*paynsowng*
hostel	**albergue**	*owbehrgee*
Do you have a room?	**Tem um quarto?**	*tayng oong kwartoo*
I have a reservation	**Tenho uma reserva**	*tayn-yoo ooma risehrva*
single/double (room)	**(quarto de) solteiro/casal**	*(kwartoo jih) sooltayroo/kazow*
shower	**chuveiro**	*shoovayroo*
sheet	**lençol**	*laynsoh*
bed	**cama**	*kama*
pillow	**travesseiro**	*travisayroo*
towel	**toalha**	*twal-ya*
toilet paper	**papel higiênico**	*papeh-oo iJ-yehnikoo*

Eating Out

I want to reserve…	**Quero reservar…**	*kehroo rizirvar*
Do you have…?	**Tem…?**	*tayng*
The bill, please	**A conta, por favor**	*a kohnta, poor favohr*
menu	**cardápio/menu**	*kardap-yoo/maynoo*
wine list	**lista de vinhos**	*leeshta de veen-yoosh*
glass	**copo**	*kopoo*
bottle	**garrafa**	*garrafa*
fork	**garfo**	*garfoo*
knife	**faca**	*faka*
spoon	**colher**	*kool-yehr*
restaurant	**restaurante**	*rishtowrantsh*
breakfast	**café da manhã**	*kafeh da man-yang*
lunch	**almoço**	*owmohsoo*
dinner/supper	**jantar**	*Jantar*
(mineral) water	**água (mineral)**	*agwa (minerow)*
vegetarian	**vegetariano**	*vigitar-yanoo*
Is service included?	**O serviço está incluído?**	*oo sirveesoo shtah inklweedoo*

Menu Decoder

açúcar	*asookar*	sugar
alho	*al-yoo*	garlic
arroz	*arrohsh*	rice
azeite	*azaytsh*	olive oil
batatas fritas	*batatash freetash*	chips
bebida	*bibeeda*	drink
bem passado	*bayng pasadoo*	well done
bife	*beefee*	steak
café	*kafeh*	coffee
carne	*karnee*	beef
cerveja	*sirvayJa*	beer
chá	*sha*	tea
churrasco	*shoorrashkoo*	barbecue
feijão (preto)	*fayJowng (praytoo)*	(black) beans
feijoada	*fayJwada*	bean and meat stew
farofa	*farofa*	dish based on manioc/cassava meal
frango	*frangoo*	chicken
fruta	*froota*	fruit
grelhado	*gril-yadoo*	grilled
lanche	*lanshee*	snack
leite	*laytsh*	milk
manteiga	*mantayga*	butter
muqueca de peixe	*mookehka jih payshee*	fish stew with coconut milk
ovo cozido	*ohvo koozeedoo*	hard-boiled egg
pão	*powng*	bread
pão de queijo	*powng jih kay-Joo*	cheese cookie
pastel de carne	*pashteh-oo jih karnee*	puff-pastry patty filled with mince
pastel de queijo	*pashteh-oo jih kay-Joo*	puff-pastry patty filled with cheese
peixe	*payshee*	fish
pimenta	*pimaynta*	pepper
mal passado	*mow pasadoo*	rare
ao ponto	*ow pohntoo*	medium
quindim	*keenjeeng*	coconut and egg sweet
refrigerante	*rifrigirantsh*	soft drink
sal	*sow*	salt
sorvete	*sohrvaytsh*	ice cream
suco	*sookoo*	fruit juice
vinho	*veen-yoo*	wine

Time

minute	**minuto**	*minootoo*
hour	**hora**	*ora*
half an hour	**meia hora**	*may-a ora*
next week	**na próxima semana**	*na prosima simana*
last month	**no mês passado**	*noo maysh pasadoo*
Monday	**segunda-feira**	*sigoonda fayra*
Tuesday	**terça-feira**	*tayrsa fayra*
Wednesday	**quarta-feira**	*kwarta fayra*
Thursday	**quinta-feira**	*keenta fayra*
Friday	**sexta-feira**	*sayshta fayra*
Saturday	**sábado**	*sabadoo*
Sunday	**domingo**	*doomeengoo*
January	**janeiro**	*Janayroo*
February	**fevereiro**	*feverayroo*
March	**março**	*marsoo*
April	**abril**	*abree-oo*
May	**maio**	*mi-oo*
June	**junho**	*Joon-yoo*
July	**julho**	*Jool-yoo*
August	**agosto**	*agohshtoo*
September	**setembro**	*sitaymbroo*
October	**outubro**	*ohtoobroo*
November	**novembro**	*noovaymbroo*
December	**dezembro**	*dizaymbroo*

Numbers

1	**um/uma**	*oong/ooma*
2	**dois/duas**	*doh-ish/doo-ash*
3	**três**	*traysh*
4	**quatro**	*kwatroo*
5	**cinco**	*seenkoo*
6	**seis**	*saysh*
7	**sete**	*seht*
8	**oito**	*oh-itoo*
9	**nove**	*novee*
10	**dez**	*dehsh*
11	**onze**	*ohnzee*
12	**doze**	*dohzee*
13	**treze**	*trayzee*
14	**catorze**	*katohrzee*
15	**quinze**	*keenzee*
16	**dezesseis**	*dizesaysh*
17	**dezessete**	*dizesehtee*
18	**dezoito**	*dizoh-itoo*
19	**dezenove**	*dizenovee*
20	**vinte**	*veentee*
21	**vinte e um**	*veentih-oong*
30	**trinta**	*treenta*
40	**quarenta**	*kwaraynta*
50	**cinqüenta**	*sinkwaynta*
60	**sessenta**	*sesaynta*
70	**setenta**	*setaynta*
80	**oitenta**	*oh-itaynta*
90	**noventa**	*nohvaynta*
100	**cem, cento**	*sayng/sayntoo*
1000	**mil**	*mee-oo*

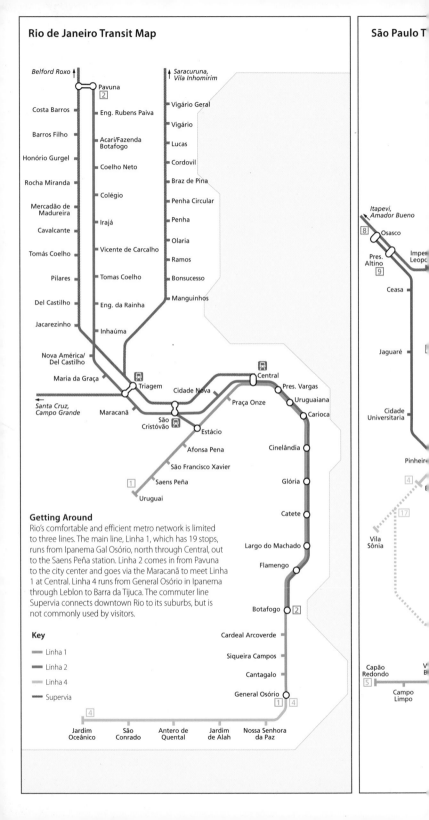

Rio de Janeiro Transit Map

São Paulo T

Belford Roxo

Pavuna
2

*Saracuruna,
Vila Inhomirim*

Costa Barros — Eng. Rubens Paiva — Vigário Geral

Barros Filho — Acari/Fazenda Botafogo — Vigário

Honório Gurgel — Coelho Neto — Lucas

Rocha Miranda — Colégio — Cordovil

Mercadão de Madureira — Irajá — Braz de Pina

Cavalcante — Penha Circular

Tomás Coelho — Vicente de Carcalho — Penha

Pilares — Tomas Coelho — Olaria

Del Castilho — Eng. da Rainha — Ramos

Jacarezinho — Inhaúma — Bonsucesso

— Manguinhos

Nova América/ Del Castilho

Maria da Graça — Triagem — Central

Santa Cruz, Campo Grande — Cidade Nova — Pres. Vargas

Maracanã — Praça Onze — Uruguaiana

São Cristóvão — Carioca

Estácio — Cinelândia

Afonsa Pena

São Francisco Xavier — Glória

Saens Peña — Catete

Uruguai

Largo do Machado

Flamengo

Getting Around
Rio's comfortable and efficient metro network is limited to three lines. The main line, Linha 1, which has 19 stops, runs from Ipanema Gal Osório, north through Central, out to the Saens Peña station. Linha 2 comes in from Pavuna to the city center and goes via the Maracanã to meet Linha 1 at Central. Linha 4 runs from General Osório in Ipanema through Leblon to Barra da Tijuca. The commuter line Supervia connects downtown Rio to its suburbs, but is not commonly used by visitors.

Botafogo 2

Cardeal Arcoverde

Siqueira Campos

Cantagalo

General Osório
1 4

Key
Linha 1
Linha 2
Linha 4
Supervia

4
Jardim Oceânico — São Conrado — Antero de Quental — Jardim de Alah — Nossa Senhora da Paz

Itapevi, Amador Bueno

8 Osasco — Imper Leopo

Pres. Altino
9

Ceasa

Jaguaré

Cidade Universitaria

Pinheir

4

17

Vila Sônia

Capão Redondo
5

Campo Limpo